On the Borders of Love and Power

On the Borders of Love and Power

Families and Kinship in the Intercultural American Southwest

Edited by

David Wallace Adams and
Crista DeLuzio

UNIVERSITY OF CALIFORNIA PRESS
Berkeley   Los Angeles   London

University of California Press, one of the most distinguished university presses in the United States, enriches lives around the world by advancing scholarship in the humanities, social sciences, and natural sciences. Its activities are supported by the UC Press Foundation and by philanthropic contributions from individuals and institutions. For more information, visit www.ucpress.edu.

University of California Press

Berkeley and Los Angeles, California

University of California Press, Ltd.

London, England

© 2012 by The Regents of the University of California

Library of Congress Cataloging-in-Publication Data

On the borders of love and power : families and kinship in the intercultural American Southwest / edited by David Wallace Adams and Crista DeLuzio.
    p.   cm.
  Includes bibliographical references and index.
  ISBN 978-0-520-27238-5 (cloth, alk. paper) — ISBN 978-0-520-27239-2 (pbk., alk. paper)
  1. Indians of North America—Kinship—West (U.S.) 2. Indians of North America—Cultural assimilation—West (U.S.) 3. Hispanic Americans—Kinship—West (U.S.) 4. Hispanic Americans—Cultural assimilation—West (U.S.) 5. Frontier and pioneer life—West (U.S)—History. 6. Family—West (U.S.)—History. 7. Kinship—West (U.S.)—History. 8. West (U.S.)—Ethnic relations. 9. West (U.S.)—History. I. Adams, David Wallace. II. DeLuzio, Crista.
E78.W5O54   2012
305.800978—dc23   2011044243

Manufactured in the United States of America

21 20 19 18 17 16 15 14 13 12

10 9 8 7 6 5 4 3 2 1

In keeping with its commitment to support environmentally responsible and sustainable printing practices, UC Press has printed this book on 50# Enterprise, a 30% post consumer waste, recycled, de- inked fiber and processed chlorine free. It is acid-free, and meets all ANSI/NISO (z 39.48) requirements.

For David and Carol Weber

CONTENTS

List of Illustrations ix
Acknowledgments xi

    Introduction 1
    David Wallace Adams and Crista DeLuzio

PART ONE. DIVERSE FAMILIES AND RACIAL HIERARCHY

1. Breaking and Remaking Families: The Fostering and Adoption of Native American Children in Non-Native Families in the American West, 1880–1940   19
 Margaret Jacobs

2. Becoming Comanches: Patterns of Captive Incorporation into Comanche Kinship Networks, 1820–1875   47
 Joaquín Rivaya-Martínez

3. "Seeking the Incalculable Benefit of a Faithful, Patient Man and Wife": Families in the Federal Indian Service, 1880–1925   71
 Cathleen D. Cahill

4. Hard Choices: Mixed-Race Families and Strategies of Acculturation in the U.S. West after 1848   93
 Anne F. Hyde

PART TWO. LAW, ORDER, AND THE REGULATION OF FAMILY LIFE

5. Family and Kinship in the Spanish and Mexican Borderlands: A Cultural Account — 119
   Ramón A. Gutiérrez

6. Love, Honor, and the Power of Law: Probating the Ávila Estate in Frontier California — 141
   Donna C. Schuele

7. "Who has a greater job than a mother?" Defining Mexican Motherhood on the U.S.-Mexico Border in the Early Twentieth Century — 163
   Monica Perales

8. Borderlands/*La Familia*: Mexicans, Homes, and Colonialism in the Early Twentieth-Century Southwest — 185
   Pablo Mitchell

PART THREE. BORDERLAND CULTURES AND FAMILY RELATIONSHIPS

9. Intimate Ties: Marriage, Families, and Kinship in Eighteenth-Century Pueblo Communities — 209
   Tracy Brown

10. The Paradox of Kinship: Native-Catholic Communities in Alta California, 1769–1840s — 231
    Erika Pérez

11. Territorial Bonds: Indenture and Affection in Intercultural Arizona, 1864–1894 — 255
    Katrina Jagodinsky

12. Writing Kit Carson in the Cold War: "The Family," "The West," and Their Chroniclers — 278
    Susan Lee Johnson

Selected Bibliography — 319
List of Contributors — 327
Index — 331

ILLUSTRATIONS

MAP

6.1 Land grants in Mexican California   *144*

FIGURES

1.1 Zinka Nuni, ca. 1891   *23*
1.2 Fanny and Betty Wetherill, early to mid-1920s   *33*
1.3 Bonita Wa Wa Calachaw with husband Manuel Nuñez, ca. 1920   *38*
2.1 Captives' sex and age at capture   *53*
2.2 Captives' ethnic extraction by decade   *63*
2.3 Semeno's tombstone in Highland Cemetery, Lawton, Oklahoma   *64*
3.1 Faculty of the Albuquerque Indian School, 1883   *81*
3.2 Yakima Indian employees and schoolchildren, Fort Simcoe, Washington, ca. 1888   *82*
4.1 Donald McKay, Dr. William McKay, and son   *99*
4.2 Jane Johnston Schoolcraft, 1800–1842   *102*
4.3 John Bernardo Wilson, 1848–1870   *108*
6.1 Painting of Antonio Ygnacio Ávila by Henri Penelon   *142*
10.1 Photograph of baptismal font from the mission San Luís Obispo   *236*
11.1 Jack Swilling with Guillermo Swilling, ca. 1875   *265*
11.2 Portrait of Jack Swilling with Guillermo Swilling removed, ca. 1890   *266*
12.1 Kit Carson, 1840s   *281*
12.2 Josefa Jaramillo, 1840s   *282*
12.3 Bernice Blackwelder and Harold Blackwelder, 1970s   *300*
12.4 Quantrille McClung, 1970s   *301*

ACKNOWLEDGMENTS

This book's journey began when David Weber and Sherry Smith suggested that the role and significance of the family in the history of the American West offered a potentially illuminating perspective on the region's past and asked the editors of this volume if they would be interested in organizing a symposium on the subject. The background we knew well. The William P. Clements Center for Southwest Studies at Southern Methodist University (David was the founding director) annually sponsored two symposia on some topic in southwestern history, a two-step process designed to produce historical studies of the highest quality. So, of course, we accepted. And so we begin by thanking David and Sherry, both important voices in the field of western history and the source of invaluable advice and support for this book at critical junctures.

Ben Johnson's sound practical and intellectual suggestions were always helpful. To Andrea Boardman, whose dedication to both the Clements Center and southwestern history in general were in sharp focus during her expert planning of the 2010 Dallas symposium, we are immensely grateful. It is impossible to sufficiently sing the praises of Ruth Ann Elmore, whose ability to negotiate the day-to-day challenges of making things happen while maintaining her wonderful sense of humor must be without comparison.

It is difficult to imagine the success of this project without considering the support of Virginia Scharff, director of the Center for the Southwest at the University of New Mexico, and Stephen Aron, director of the Institute for the Study of the American West at the Autry National Center, Los Angeles. All the contributors will long remember Gingy's role in orchestrating the Albuquerque symposium, her gracious hospitality, and how she reminded us of the magic of

New Mexico. We are also indebted to Gingy and Steve for providing generous financial support from their respective centers, as well as their many insights that helped shape this collection.

Niels Hooper, at the University of California Press, took an immediate interest in this project and urged us to press forward with it at every step along the way (including at the Dallas meeting, which he attended). We feel exceptionally fortunate to have had the benefit of his thoughtful guidance and of the skill of other talented people at the University of California Press. A special thanks to Kim Hogeland, who answered in a most timely manner many questions about the acquisition and reproduction of the images used in the volume, and to Sharron Wood for her meticulous copyediting of the manuscript. We also wish to acknowledge the encouragement and discerning comments of James Brooks and one anonymous reviewer of the manuscript. Most of the suggestions were taken to heart and, we believe, considerably strengthened the final product of our labors.

This volume was from the beginning a collaborative enterprise. We wish to thank all the contributors for conscientiously responding to our seemingly endless requests and deadlines along the way. And, not incidentally, we want to thank them for teaching us new things about the meaning of family and kinship in the American West.

Introduction

David Wallace Adams and Crista DeLuzio

The year is 1840. The location, Bent's Fort, a mammoth adobe-walled trading firm built at a strategic point just north of the Mexican border on the Santa Fe Trail, a dangerous but highly traveled highway stretching from St. Louis to Chihuahua. William Bent, the fort's manager, is mostly interested in bison hides, with the Southern Plains tribes being his principal source. Bent is a shrewd bargainer, but on this particular day, with his warehouse already stocked with robes, he is perhaps wondering how the bargaining is going for a different sort of prize. Alexander Barclay, his bookkeeper and supervisor of stores, is out in the Cheyenne camp hoping to secure a budding Cheyenne beauty for a wife. Bent is able to imagine the delicate negotiations. He is married to a Cheyenne, Owl Woman (the two would eventually have four children), and knows something about cross-cultural courting. Was Barclay having any luck?

Actually, it was not going well at all. As Barclay would later describe the scene in a letter to his brother, "I had conceived the liaison for the prettiest girl among the Cheyenne tribe, and would have bought her at any price." The problem was that the girl's father was conducting a bidding war. One Cheyenne, whom the father seemed to favor from the start, offered eight horses. Barclay was too embarrassed to admit the amount of his final bid. "I offered more than on calm reflection I can own without a blush." Even then, however, the father was still not satisfied, and in a breach of "fair trade" he demanded that Barclay throw in an American horse worth two hundred dollars. What the girl who was the object of these negotiations thought about them, we do not know, but at this point the exasperated Barclay informed the patriarch that the negotiations were over, declaring in the Indian's language that "I loved his daughter, but he could keep her and I could keep my presents."[1]

Barclay's futile efforts at purchasing a wife remind us that the desire to construct intimate connections through marriage, kinship, and other relationships is one of the most basic of human longings. For our purposes, two aspects of the story are particularly noteworthy: the intercultural nature of the deliberations, and the fact that they took place on the edge of the American empire. Indeed, it is Barclay's efforts at constructing a family within a specific place and historical moment that make this uniquely a "western" story, something reaffirmed when considering Barclay's later adventures in quest of a mate. In late 1845, Barclay, now an independent trader in Pueblo, Colorado, entered into a common-law marriage with María Teresa Sandoval of Taos, New Mexico. In "marrying" this reputedly beautiful Hispana, Barclay acquired not only a wife but a full-fledged family as well, for María brought to the relationship several children, the offspring of two previous marriages, the first sanctified by the church, the second of the common-law variety. Within a few years, however, the Barclay-Sandoval union was on the rocks and Barclay was once again in search of a mate. In 1854 he wrote his brother that he had "taken another rib as helpmate." More than the biblical suggestion prompted him to go wife hunting: in a letter to his brother, he wrote, "A house without one [a wife] is a body without a soul, a prison denied one cheering ray of sunshine." The ethnoracial background of his new wife is unknown.[2]

Just as we can imagine William Bent peering down on the Cheyenne camp from one of the fort's two bastions pondering his storekeeper's fortunes bargaining for a Cheyenne wife, so readers might ponder: why a volume on the history of the family in the American West—in this instance, one with particular but not exclusive focus on the region of the Southwest? What does a focus on family and kinship as primary units of analysis contribute to our knowledge of and understanding about America's western past? How might an exploration of families and kinship in the American West enrich broader histories of the family, gender, and childhood in the United States? And, perhaps more modestly, what might such a collection contribute to the field of family history as a whole? Barclay's long search offers clues for pursuing answers to these questions: the entangled plotlines of "race," empire, and family. A brief discussion of each is in order.

One of the distinctive characteristics of the West in general is the constellation of ethnoracial groups who populated it and shaped its history. To be sure, the histories of race relations in the eastern and southern United States are not simple narratives, but the history of the West is significantly different in several respects. First there is the distinctiveness of the Native American groups that occupied the region. Although many Americans collapse all Native cultures into one category—Indians—anthropologists have long recognized the uniqueness of each Native society as a cultural system. Put simply, Navajos, Pueblos, and Comanches are not the same as Shawnees, Iroquois, or Cherokees. Second, whereas by the 1840s the powerful Native American nations in the East and South had either been vanquished, removed, brought to the brink of extinction, or some combination thereof, further west many indigenous peoples still held suzerainty over vast stretches of the western landscape, and in some instances they still possess significant portions of their homeland today. Third, the Southwest shares a border with Mexico. The long-term historical, demographic, cultural, economic, and political consequences of this fact, that the region was Spanish and later became Mexican and that large swaths of the social and physical landscape have been shaped by both the history and memory of these heritages, cannot be underestimated. Finally, both Native Americans and Mexican Americans remain concentrated in the western United States today, a legacy of the nation's racial history, including border construction. As of this writing the largest numbers of Native Americans live in five southwestern states—California, Oklahoma, Arizona, New Mexico, and Texas, in descending order. Mexican Americans, moreover, today constitute the largest single minority in the American Southwest.[3]

Although this volume focuses on interactions among Anglo-Americans, Hispanics, and Native Americans, it is important to acknowledge that the intercultural history of the West is not limited to these groups. Chinese immigrants in search of "Gold Mountain," Japanese farmers, African American "exodusters," Peruvian gold miners, and countless other sojourners all played their part in the western story. In this sense, the region was always the "geography of hope," a landscape invested with real and fanciful visions of opportunity and wealth, whether defined in terms of lost cities of gold, beaver pelts, bison hides, land speculation, freighting along the Santa Fe Trail, or staking out homesteads. Seeing the West as an intercultural meeting ground—where various peoples over time have sized one another up, traded, fought, bedded one another, and along the way indulged in all manner of domination, resistance, cultural exchange, and mutual accommodation—is central to this volume. As historian Patricia Limerick has observed, the West "was not where we escaped each other, but where we all met." Similarly, Peggy Pascoe asserts that historians should view the West as a "cultural crossroads rather than a geographic freeway . . . , and we need to focus on the interactions among the various groups of people who sought to control the region."[4] By exploring the West as a place where individuals and groups from different backgrounds engaged with one another through the processes of forging, sustaining, rending, scrutinizing, and regulating families, the authors of the chapters in this volume take this admonition to heart.

A second plotline revolves around the interconnected themes of conquest, empire, and colonialism. Imperialism and colonialism have taken on a range of forms around the globe. Such forms can be associated with particular places, distinct time periods, and specific imperial powers, but purveyors of colonial conquest and rule also frequently combined their various strategies, methods, ideologies, and goals. Daiva Stasiulis and Nira Yuval-Davis specify the characteristics of two key typologies of colonialism—extractive colonialism and settler colonialism. Extractive colonialism, they explain, relied on the "indirect control" of foreign colonial subjects by small groups of "primarily male administrators, merchants, soldiers, and missionaries" in order to facilitate the "appropriation of land, natural resources and labour" for the benefit of geographically distant colonial powers. In contrast, settler colonialism required the creation of "much more elaborate political and economic infrastructures" in order to achieve its chief aim of acquiring land for a large population of men, women, and children for permanent settlement. Settler colonialism demarked as racially inferior the indigenous peoples who occupied the land settlers desired and mandated their segregation, removal, and extermination, both biological and cultural. This central goal of eliminating or marginalizing racial "others" was pursued through warfare and other state-coordinated acts of violence and coercion, political exclusion, and economic exploitation, as well as allegedly more benign policies of cultural assimilation.[5] Broadly conceived, settler colonialism is conceptually compatible with the interpretive framework of "internal colonialism," which is characterized by settler and state policies designed to subjugate, marginalize, exploit, and culturally transform a conquered group—including its understanding of family and associated realms of intimacy.[6]

With these concepts in mind, let us again consider Bent's Fort. As already noted, from one perspective the great fort can be viewed as a cultural meeting ground between Anglo-American, Hispanic, and Indian traders and, on occasion, would-be intercultural marriage brokers. But from another perspective—and here we have the advantage of hindsight—the fort was also a signpost of American expansionism and settler and internal colonialism. Americans, of course, were not the first to cast imperial eyes on the Southwest, Spain being the first colonial power to lay claim to the region. Spanish conquest of the Southwest incorporated elements of both extractive and settler colonialism. While Francisco Vázquez de Coronado's *entrada* as far north as the southern plains in 1540 was an important moment in this regard, a more significant date is 1598, when Juan de Oñate led a colonizing party composed of soldiers, families, and missionaries into present-day New Mexico for permanent settlement. Although the Pueblo Rebellion of 1680 successfully rolled back Spanish colonization for twelve years, the Spanish returned and in the coming years exerted an immense cultural influence on the region and its peoples. During this period increasing numbers of Indians spoke Spanish, lived and worshipped in Catholic missions, and intermarried with their colonizers, giving rise to an increasingly mestizo society. In the end, Spain's imperial reach far exceeded its military and economic capabilities, paving the way for Mexico's independence in 1821. But Mexico's hold on the Southwest was to be short-lived. Political factionalism, economic crises, an inability to subdue powerful Indian nations on its northern frontier, failure to entice Mexican settlers to these same areas, and, finally, New Mexico's increased economic orientation toward St. Louis all contributed to Mexico's inability to hold on to the region.[7]

Enter the Americans. By 1840, the same year that Barclay went looking for a Cheyenne bride at Bent's Fort, Texas had already declared its independence from Mexico. The Texas development only reinforced what many Americans took for granted, that the West was destined to be part of what Jefferson called an "empire of liberty." In 1811, John Quincy Adams wrote to his father, "The whole continent of North America appears to be *destined by Divine Providence* to be peopled by one *nation,* speaking one language, professing one general system of religious and political principles, and accustomed to one general tenor of social usages and customs." These sentiments reached a rapturous crescendo during the war with Mexico, as reflected in the *Boston Times'* declaration that the territorial spoils of the war "must necessarily be a great blessing to the conquered."[8]

The fact that there were few moral qualms about the quest for empire flowed from the widely held belief that Americans were a chosen people, including the racialist belief that Anglo-Saxons were a race apart, superior in both their genetic and cultural makeup. As in other settler colonial societies, the plotline of empire intersected with discourses on race and racial hierarchies. Indeed, over the course of the nineteenth century the prevailing view of Indians was that they were little more than savages, who by the law of civilized progress must either adopt white ways or face the prospect of extinction. In the short term, the Indians' paganism, manner of subsistence, communal and tribal outlook, ideas about family and gender roles, and a host of other characteristics condemned them to removal and geographical concentration. The era of the Indian reservation was at hand.[9]

In the last quarter of the nineteenth century, reformers sought a long-term solution to the "Indian problem" by pursuing two policies designed to incorporate Indians into national life. The first was the General Allotment Act of 1887, a monumental piece of congressional legislation that broke reservations into individual allotments. By becoming private landholding farmers, supporters argued, former bison hunters would make the transition to farming and in the process acquire the habits and virtues associated with private property and possessive individualism.[10] A second policy called for the forcible removal of children from their "savage" parents and placing them in boarding schools, institutions designed to strip the rising generation of Indian youth from their cultural heritage while inculcating them with the knowledge, skills, and values appropriate for survival in a post-Indian world.[11] Central to both these policies was the determination to alter Native conceptions of family and kinship. Land allotment linked property ownership to the patriarchal family; boarding schools sought to shred children's attachment to ancestral understandings of belonging and connection.

Although racial thinking with respect to Mexicans was more complicated and subtle, in the end it was hardly less pejorative. Through miscegenation, or *mestizaje,* most Hispanics were by degrees a mixed-race population. And it was mainly on this issue that Anglo-Saxon fears and prejudices focused. Objections to the war with Mexico and the prospect of incorporating a large chunk of its conquered territory into the American system raised nativist alarms that Mexicans were a "mongrel race." One journalist of the day despaired that the geographical Mexican prize was of dubious worth: "It would likely prove to be a sickening mixture, consisting of such a conglomeration of Negroes, Rancheros, Mestizoes [sic] and Indians, with but a few Castilians."[12] As in the case of Indians, opinions differed as to whether Mexican inferiority was innate or amenable to environmental influences. Meanwhile, the negative stereotypes—that Mexicans were essentially indolent, shiftless, ignorant, dirty, immoral, vassals of popery, fit only for menial labor—poured forth. This racial stigmatization took concrete form in a dual labor system, anti-unionism, inferior segregated schools, and "Americanization" programs designed to alter Hispanics' perceived cultural inadequacies. For Mexicans, as for Indians, the promise of genuine citizenship was anchored to their acceptance of their colonizers' prevailing gender, racial, and moral codes, including dominant modes of family life. If the institution of the family was an essential source of moral character, the child's first window on home life and social living as well as the wellspring of identity, then surely, it was reasoned, society was justified in efforts to improve the Mexican family's suitability in the American fold. Toward this end, progressive reformers, fervent nationalists, teachers, essayists, and social workers all played a part.[13]

The third plotline that emerges from Barclay's story is that of the connection between the history of the West and the history of the family. In mapping some of the permutations of that connection across the changing western landscape over the course of the sixteenth through the twentieth century, the contributors to this volume deploy and elaborate upon two propositions that have been fundamental to the scholarly study of the family. Most basically, they all consider the family to be "a social institution of intrinsic importance."[14] The family "is a person's earliest and most important and continuing influence," explains historian Elliott West. "It is the innermost circle of a society's arrangement, and it has the prime responsibility for performing essential functions. The family reveals a lot about what people believe, about who controls whom, and about how they cope with change." Second, the contributors clearly demonstrate that meanings and experiences of family and kinship have varied considerably across time and place. As another historian, Kathleen N. Conzen, writes, "Societies determine for themselves what defines a family, who constitutes its members and what their responsibilities are to one another, how the family identity extends through marriage and consanguinity and across generations, on what basis a family is to be formed, and what societal functions it is meant to fulfill."[15] Taken together, West's and Conzen's observations reveal why the history of the family is such an essential vantage point for making sense of the West in general, and the Southwest especially, as a multicultural region where worlds of connection, obligation, and meaning were brought into contact and interconnection with one another.

The ethnocultural groups represented in this volume differed significantly in how they construed gender roles and relations, childhood and child rearing, the determination of lineage and kinship, the rituals of sexual intimacy, and the relationship between the public and the private. It followed that when these groups met, conflicts and negotiations over family life figured prominently in relation to larger struggles among individuals and groups for conquest and control, as well as for identity, dignity, autonomy, belonging, and survival. Yet western historians, when they have turned their attention to the family, have generally focused on the Anglo-American experience—stories of Anglo-American homesteaders, children coming of age, and pioneer women.[16] Similarly, when they have addressed the subject of minority experiences, the role and place of family and kinship have been given short shrift.[17] In attending to the multiple ways in which family relations have been conceptualized and lived by various groups of people in different times and places in the history of the Southwest, as well as attesting to the import of such relations, this volume marks a significant departure from earlier scholarship by western historians. At the same time, it attempts to contribute to broader efforts by those historians seeking to prioritize comparative and global perspectives on the family.[18]

Building on these fundamental propositions, all of the chapters in this volume explore the relationship between family life and larger structures of social and political power in specific times and places, including the role that families have played in producing, reproducing, mediating, or contesting the prevailing social order. Thus, they are all concerned with the dynamics between what Ann Laura Stoler refers to as "macropolitics," on the one hand, and the "microsites of familial and intimate space," on the other.[19] Along these same lines, the authors subscribe to historian Nara Milanich's assertion that the "new agenda for family history" must include investigations into how "the interpenetration of family and hierarchy" has changed over time and has been variously constituted in particular settings.[20] Accordingly, they endeavor to elucidate some of the ways in which families of various kinds have functioned as sites where authority in its many intersecting forms—state, religious, class, gender, racial, and generational—was stipulated and imposed, as well as resisted and transgressed.

Each of the three sections of this volume centers around a core theme and suggests a particular vantage point from which to approach questions about the relationship between love and power in the West. The first group of chapters probes the social and psychological experiences of individuals involved in intimate relationships inscribed by ethnocultural difference and hierarchy. The second section highlights the role of the law and other formal strictures, including religious doctrine, public policy, and professional expertise, in governing family life. The final group of chapters explores how cultural expectations for family relations were interpreted and negotiated among individuals and groups in specific times and places, as well as across historical eras. Although this organization is meant to offer readers one way of framing patterns regarding the collection's conceptual and methodological contributions, the themes of diversity, hierarchy, regulation, and cultural contestation cut across the sections, and, as outlined below, the chapters can be placed in conversation with one another in a myriad of potentially illuminating ways.

The interconnections between family and authority explored in these chapters all entwined against the larger backdrop of colonialism and the ethnoracial contacts that colonial encounters entailed. In all manner of colonial enterprises around the globe, intimate spaces and relationships became, as Margaret Jacobs writes, "small theaters of colonialism where colonial scripts were produced and performed."[21] So, too, in the American Southwest. As Ramón A. Gutiérrez, Tracy Brown, Cathleen D. Cahill, Monica Perales, and others show, the family lives of Native Americans and Hispanics were intensively scrutinized and most often found wanting by priests, colonial administrators, missionaries, settlers, and reformers, who possessed resolute notions about proper family form, gender roles and relations, sexual mores, child rearing practices, and the like. Colonizers' assessments of the families of the ethnoracial groups they encountered as barbaric, inferior, and uncivilized, as well as their determination to protect their own family order from possible threats of external violation and contagion, provided a prime motivation and justification for the elimination, exclusion, and exploitation of these groups. At the same time, transforming the families of Native Americans and Hispanics (and in the process reconstituting the subjectivities and allegiances of the individuals within them) became both an end and means of colonial conquest and control.

Even so, absolute imposition of one group's family ideology upon another group never constituted the whole story, at least partly due to fractures within the dominant group itself. Thus, Gutiérrez explores Spanish colonizers' evolving and competing conceptions of family as constituted by an authority relationship, biological kinship, co-residence, and spiritual connection, showing that tensions between secular and religious notions of family ties held mixed ramifications for the treatment of Native Americans in the Spanish Southwest. Brown suggests that Spanish authorities' attempts to regulate Pueblo sexual relationships in seventeenth-century New Mexico "waxed and waned based upon the strength of the personal commitment of individual governors and missionaries." Cahill documents a similar dynamic at play in the Indian school service at the turn of the twentieth century, finding that the U.S. government's intentions to reshape the family lives of Native Americans were compromised by the employees charged with implementing state policy, who often calculated family interest differently from officials in Washington. And Perales aptly demonstrates that the class assumptions and goals of those early twentieth-century Anglo reformers who sought to remake Mexican mothers according to Anglo domestic ideology conflicted with certain basic presumptions of that ideology, especially regarding mothers' work outside the home.

Furthermore, if colonial order could be imposed (albeit at times inconsistently and unevenly) through the realm of the intimate, it could also be negotiated and contested there as well. Writing about the resiliency of African American slaves in the antebellum South, Annette Gordon-Reed asserts, "Oppressed people do not always internalize the stories their oppressors tell about them. They often, in fact, develop their own internal narratives about who they are, ones that can be enormously self-regarding and vaguely, or even vigorously, contemptuous of their overlords."[22] And so it would be in the Southwest, a social and intercultural landscape where families were not only sites of domination and assimilation but also locations for resistance and strategic adaptation. As these chapters show, the stakes of the struggles over family life waged by Native Americans and Hispanics were especially high—power, citizenship, and identity itself—and the results were by no means uniform, conclusive, or unambiguous. Erika Pérez, for example, argues that while the practice of godparentage, or compadrazgo, served as an effective tool of conquest by the Spanish of the Native peoples of Alta California, this Catholic kinship system also provided some incentives for Indians to incorporate it to further the survival of families and communities. Anne F. Hyde's more speculative piece raises an intriguing set of questions about the possibilities for marriage and child rearing to promote accommodation and cooperation between ethnoracial groups as she considers the fate of mixed-race children across the West during a period of transition when racial lines were becoming increasingly hardened in the United States. What options, she wonders, were available for interracial couples in the post-1848 West to provide their mixed-race children with "networks of human connection and some measure of material comfort"? How did race, culture, gender, geography, and changing notions of family and childhood influence what these parents wanted for their children and how their children fared in the end? Hyde's search for answers to these and other questions, based on her study of several elite western families, begins to establish a framework for understanding this largely forgotten population.

In yet another crucial variation on the theme of the family as contested terrain, several contributors remind us that power dynamics operate not only between "the family" and larger social and political structures but also among family members themselves. That is, just as the world of macropolitics is not seamlessly unified, so the family is often marked by internal struggles and divisions, especially those arising out of gender and generational differences and hierarchy. Tracy Brown analyzes one such tragic case of intrafamily conflict, examining how an inter-Pueblo marriage descends into violence because the wife is unable to negotiate the differing kinship practices and gender expectations of two Pueblo traditions, which have been rendered increasingly incompatible under the influence of Spanish colonialism. Likewise, Donna C. Schuele finds that conflicts between siblings, which were in part the product of age and gender inequities, worked in conjunction with external pressures to divest one Mexican American family of its considerable property holdings in southern California during the mid-nineteenth century. In Pablo Mitchell's chapter, as well, we see that efforts by Mexican Americans to use the courts to reject Anglos' denigration of Mexican family life in the early twentieth-century Southwest also entailed a reinforcement of "patriarchy and heteronormativity" within the Mexican American family, whereby women and girls continued to be subordinated to the authority of Mexican men. In these and other analyses of "the interpenetration of family and hierarchy" contained in this volume, it is always worth attending to the multiple levels on which power relationships operated in any given context and to the differing perspectives *within* family, kinship, and cultural groups on the gains and losses associated with certain kinds of intimacies and with particular configurations of the relationship between the exertions of public power and the realms of private life.

This volume's contributors are also careful to consider the divergent perspectives of individuals involved in intimate encounters when exploring the role of affectivity in family life and its relationship to various forms of public power. The great "sentiment debate" has deep roots in the scholarship on the history of the family. Much ink has been spilled, for example, in deliberations over whether parents in medieval and premodern Europe and colonial America loved their children, given the high rates of infant mortality that characterized these periods, as well as over when romantic attraction supplanted economic considerations in the selection of marriage partners.[23] Although these questions are not without merit, the contributors to this volume are less concerned with whether family members in the past "really" loved one another than they are with the ways in which meanings and expressions of love and affection took shape in particular social and political contexts and with what their social, political, and personal effects were. We see, then, that as with the family itself, love assumed many forms within and between the groups living in the particular historical settings examined here—as protection, provision, compassion, reciprocity, spiritual guidance, obligation, deference, desire, sacrifice—and that it could work both to reinscribe various kinds of social authority and to challenge them. Readers will also find several examples in these chapters of groups and individuals deploying the naturalizing language of love and family in order to obfuscate and thereby bolster their control over others. The larger point is that although it is certainly possible for intimate encounters and family relationships to be utterly devoid of affection and characterized only by domination (and there is ample evidence of this in the following pages), it does not necessarily correlate that relationships entailing affection can be unmarked by the workings of social and political power, for, as Linda Gordon reminds us, "the supposedly private is also often very public."[24] As Joaquín Rivaya-Martínez reveals in his study of nineteenth-century Comanche captivity, Katrina Jagodinsky finds in her examination of three households in territorial Arizona that indentured Native American children, and Margaret Jacobs emphasizes in her analysis of the relationships between white women and their adopted Indian children at the turn of the twentieth century, love and power intersected with one another in the history of the American West in diverse, complex, and consequential ways.

To return to our original story, this was likely the case with Barclay and his prospective bride as well. The love that he professed to feel for her (and that perhaps was reciprocated by her as well) takes on its full meaning only when understood in relation to the social and political power dynamics at play in the context in which it was expressed. As already noted, this was a world in which such intercultural intimacies had long held out the promise of mutual economic and diplomatic benefit to Anglo fur traders and Native communities alike. But these relationships were now becoming increasingly stigmatized, with the burdens of their marginalization falling disproportionately on Native American women and their mixed-race children. However deliberately Barclay and the girl he went bargaining for reckoned with the larger forces that were transforming the world around them, these dynamics would have been deeply implicated in whatever sorts of affection the couple held for each other in the initial encounters that constituted their courtship and throughout the marriage that could have followed.

As suggested above, several of the contributors are especially interested in understanding the role children played and were made to play in interweaving the "tense and tender ties" that bound individuals and groups together within various colonial contexts throughout the history of the American West.[25] Several decades of scholarship in western women's history and gender history, along with more recent work on gender and colonialism, have begun to paint a fuller picture of the role of gender and of the experiences of diverse groups of women in the settling and unsettling of the American West.[26] Scholars are now increasingly turning their attention to children's experiences as equally significant objects of study. From the forays into this territory pursued by the contributors to this volume, we learn that because of both their impressionability and their vulnerability, Indian and Hispanic children were viewed by Anglo, Native, and Hispanic adults in a variety of ways, including as potential facilitators of intercultural cooperation, possibly dangerous disrupters of social boundaries and categories of racial difference, prime targets for assimilation, and crucial carriers of traditional culture. Although it is important to see how children were used and abused by adults to advance, mediate, and resist colonial rule, it is as important, if considerably more difficult, to track children's own actions, thoughts, and feelings in these endeavors. Here, Rivaya-Martínez, Jagodinsky, and Jacobs attempt to do just that, mining captivity narratives, oral interviews, memoirs, and legal records to trace what children said and did as they strove to make sense of and maneuver within and between the world of macropolitics and the world of the family, worlds in which they were often victimized and always constrained but never entirely powerless.

A final theme broached by the collection as a whole, and taken up explicitly by several of the contributors, centers on the politics of memory—on questions about how and why we remember the history of the family in the West as we do. Perhaps no entities in the United States have been subjected to greater mythologizing than "the West" and "the family"; consequently, scholars working in the fields of both family history and western history have taken on the task of debunking countless misconceptions about what historian Stephanie Coontz has succinctly termed "the way we never were."[27] Here, several contributors contemplate the relationship between these two potent arenas of mythmaking to probe what the mythology about western families, as well as what new perspectives on the history such myths have obscured, might reveal about the meanings of American national identity and belonging, race relations, and family values in the past and the present. Why, Anne F. Hyde asks, have the children of mixed-race families in the nineteenth-century West remained "hidden in plain sight" for so long? Likewise, Katrina Jagodinsky wants to know why popular and scholarly histories of Arizona's "founding fathers" have almost entirely ignored the Indian children those men indentured, exploited, and cared for, along with the mixed-race children some of them fathered. Subsequent generations of Arizonans and chroniclers of Arizona history, she concludes, have been both reluctant to acknowledge Indian children's mistreatment and unwilling to account for the affection that sometimes abided in territorial households because these realities ran counter to more palatable memories of pioneers "gentling" and "whitening" Arizona along its way into modern statehood. In the final chapter of the volume, Susan Lee Johnson analyzes the remaking of the iconic western individualist Kit Carson into a "family man" by two amateur female historians during the era of the Cold War. During this period, idealized versions of the white monogamous nuclear family and of the West as a proving ground for rugged masculinity and the virtues of American democracy were pervasively touted "as ramparts against changing times." Bernice Blackwelder's and Quantrille McClung's portraits of

Carson complicated these idealizations by documenting the intercultural intimate relations in which Carson and his extended family were involved and by placing these at the center of his life story and, by extension, at the center of western history itself. At the same time, Blackwelder interpreted Carson's intercultural marriages through the lens of racial hierarchy, and both historians disregarded evidence about members of the Carson clan engaging in violent conflict with one another and in sexual relationships outside marriage, thereby reinforcing certain crucial Cold War myths about the West and the family as well.

If the reinterpretation of the "great westerner" as a family man served Cold War culture in certain key ways, what sorts of cultural work do the chapters in this collection, with their focus on intercultural intimacies and the relationship between family life and structures of social power, perform in our own time? Even as Blackwelder and McClung were penning their midcentury tomes on Carson, a cluster of potent social, economic, and cultural changes were underway that would produce dramatic transformations in family life in the United States by the turn of the twenty-first century. Forces of global economic and technological change, unprecedented numbers of people on the move around the world, and social movements for civil, women's, children's, and gay rights have all contributed to the rise of what has been termed the "postmodern family." On the one hand, contemporary families in the United States are characterized by a growing diversity in racial and ethnic composition, increasing variety and fluidity in family form and family practices, and more genuine egalitarianism in gender and generational relations, all accompanied by signs of developing acceptance of differences in family life within the broader society. On the other hand, contemporary families are also marked by a great deal of instability, disruption, and uncertainty, and contests over "family values" have become a major polarizing force in American politics and the culture at large. Thus, as sociologist Judith Stacey explains, rather than representing something entirely new or wholly progressive, "the postmodern family condition incorporates both experimental and nostalgic dimensions as it lurches forward and backward into an uncertain future."[28]

A fuller, more nuanced examination of the history of the family in the American West, as pursued by the contributors to this volume, may open up some new possibilities for understanding postmodern family life and for responding to the challenges, anxieties, and tensions that have arisen in its wake. Certainly, this collection brooks little tolerance for the yearning for a singular ideal family that can be resurrected from the past as a cure for the very real sufferings currently experienced by so many families living in the United States.[29] American families have been characterized by greater diversity and have been interconnected in more complicated ways than idealizations of "the traditional family" have allowed. Recognizing this marks an important first step in relinquishing impossible dreams for family life and in seeing more clearly the legacies that the interpenetrations of love and power in the past have bequeathed to the present. At the same time, these chapters document what a powerful force the yearning for a normative standard of family life has been in bolstering and justifying hierarchy of many kinds. Its power over our collective imaginations should not, therefore, be underestimated. In the realms of family and kinship the West has long been a place where new possibilities collided with inherited scripts and codes for mapping human connections. It follows that we can recognize in the following stories some of the conflicts and uncertainties of our present age. And in so doing, we can see that we are not so distant from Bent's Fort as we might imagine.

NOTES

1. See George P. Hammond, ed., *The Adventures of Alexander Barclay: Mountain Man* (Denver, CO: Fred A. Rosenstock Old West Publishing, 1976), 53–67.

2. Ibid.

3. See www.census.gov/population/www/census2000/briefs/phc-t-18/index.html. For an analysis of Native American population figures, see Colin Calloway, *First Peoples: A Documentary Survey of American Indian History* (Boston, MA: Bedford/St. Martin's, 2008), 528–34. For Hispanic numbers, state distribution numbers are at www.censusscope.org.

4. Patricia Nelson Limerick, *The Legacy of Conquest: The Unbroken Past of the American West* (New York: W. W. Norton and Co., 1987), 291; and Peggy Pascoe, "Western Women at the Cultural Crossroads," in *Trails: Toward a New Western History*, ed. Patricia Nelson Limerick, Clyde A. Milner II, and Charles Rankin (Lawrence: University of Kansas Press, 1991), 46.

5. Daiva Stasiulis and Nira Yuval-Davis, "Introduction: Beyond Dichotomies—Gender, Race, Ethnicity and Class in Settler Societies," in *Unsettling Settler Societies: Articulations of Gender, Race, Ethnicity, and Class*, ed. Daiva Stasiulis and Nira Yuval-Davis (London: Sage Publications, 1995), 3. See also Margaret D. Jacobs, *White Mother to a Dark Race: Settler Colonialism, Maternalism, and the Removal of Indigenous Children in the American West and Australia, 1880–1940* (Lincoln: University of Nebraska Press, 2009), 2–3.

6. See Linda Gordon, "Internal Colonialism and Gender," in *Haunted by Empire: Geographies of Intimacy in North American History*, ed. Ann Laura Stoler (Durham, NC: Duke University Press, 2006), 427–51; and Gordon, *The Great Arizona Orphan Abduction* (Cambridge, MA: Harvard University Press, 1999), 179–85.

7. For the history and legacy of the Spanish and Mexican periods see David J. Weber, *The Spanish Frontier in North America* (New Haven, CT: Yale University Press, 1992); Weber, *The Mexican Frontier 1821–1846: The American Southwest under Mexico* (Albuquerque: University of New Mexico Press, 1982); John L. Kessell, *Spain in the Southwest: A Narrative History of Colonial New Mexico, Arizona, Texas, and California* (Norman: University of Oklahoma Press, 2002); John Chávez, *The Lost Land: The Chicano Image of the Southwest* (Albuquerque: University of New Mexico Press, 1984); and Juan Gómez-Quiñones, *Roots of Chicano Politics, 1600–1940* (Albuquerque: University of New Mexico Press, 1994.

8. Adams is quoted in Samuel Flagg Bemis, *John Quincy Adams and the Foundations of American Foreign Policy* (New York: Alfred A. Knopf, 1965), 182 (italics in the original); and the *Boston Times* in Rush Welter, *The Mind of America, 1820–1860* (New York: Columbia University Press, 1975), 69.

9. Roy Harvey Pearce, *The Savages of America: A Study of the Indian and the Idea of Civilization,* rev. ed. (Baltimore, MD: Johns Hopkins University Press, 1965), chapters 3–4; Bernard W. Sheehan, *Seeds of Extinction: Jeffersonian Philanthropy and the American Indian* (Chapel Hill: University of North Carolina Press, 1973), part 1; and Helen M. Bannan, "The Idea of Civilization and American Indian Policy Reformers in the 1880s," *Journal of American Culture* 1 (Winter 1978): 787–99.

10. D. S. Otis, *The Dawes Act and the Allotment of Indian Lands,* ed. Francis P. Prucha (Norman: University of Oklahoma Press, 1973); Prucha, *The Great Father,* vol. 2 (Lincoln: University of Nebraska Press, 1984), chapters 26 and 34; and Janet A. McDonnell, *The Dispossession of the American Indian, 1887–1934* (Bloomington: Indiana University Press, 1991).

11. David Wallace Adams, *Education for Extinction: American Indians and the Boarding School Experience, 1875–1928* (Lawrence: University Press of Kansas, 1995); Jacqueline Fear-Segal, *White Man's Club: Schools, Race, and the Struggle of Indian Acculturation* (Lincoln: University of Nebraska Press, 2007); and Jacobs, *White Mother to a Dark Race.*

12. Quoted in Reginald Horsman, *Race and Manifest Destiny: The Origins of American Racial Anglo-Saxonism* (Cambridge, MA: Harvard University Press, 1981), 239.

13. Interest in the Hispanic experience in the Southwest has generated a number of insightful historical studies too numerous to cite. Examples are David Montejano, *Anglos and Mexicans in the Making of Texas, 1836–1986* (Austin: University of Texas Press, 1987); George J. Sánchez, *Becoming Mexican American: Ethnicity, Culture and Identity in Chicano Los Angeles, 1900–1945* (New York: Oxford University Press, 1993); Neil Foley, *The White Scourge: Mexicans, Blacks, and Poor Whites in Texas Cotton Culture* (Berkeley: University of California Press, 1997); Laura E. Gómez, *Manifest Destinies: The Making of the Mexican American Race* (New York: New York University Press, 2007); and Katherine Benton-Cohen, *Borderline Americans: Racial Division and Labor War in the Arizona Borderlands* (Cambridge, MA: Harvard University Press, 2009).

14. Nara Milanich, "Review Essay: Whither Family History? A Road Map from Latin America," *American Historical Review* 112 (April 2007): 443.

15. Elliott West, *The Way to the West: Essays on the Central Plains* (Albuquerque: University of New Mexico Press, 1995), 85; and Kathleen Neils Conzen, "A Saga of Families," in *The Oxford History of the American West,* ed. Clyde A. Milner II, Carol A. O'Conner, and Martha A. Sandweiss (New York: Oxford University Press, 1994), 319.

16. Examples are John Mack Faragher, *Sugar Creek: Life on the Illinois Prairie* (New Haven, CT: Yale University Press, 1986); Faragher, *Women and Men on the Overland Trail* (New Haven, CT: Yale University Press, 1979); Dee Garceau, *The Important Things of Life: Women, Work, and Family in Sweetwater County, Wyoming, 1880–1929* (Lincoln: University of Nebraska Press, 1997); Elizabeth Hampsten, *Settlers' Children: Growing Up on the Great Plains* (Norman: University of Oklahoma Press, 1991); Cynthia Culver Prescott, *Gender and Generation on the Far Western Frontier* (Tucson: University of Arizona Press, 2007); Glenda Riley, *The Female Frontier: A Comparative View of Women on the Prairie and the Plains* (Lawrence: University Press of Kansas, 1988); and Elliott West, *Growing Up with the Country: Childhood on the Far-Western Frontier* (Albuquerque: University of New Mexico Press, 1989).

17. Important exceptions are Ramón A. Gutiérrez, *When Jesus Came, the Corn Mothers Went Away: Marriage, Sexuality, and Power in New Mexico, 1500–1846* (Stanford, CA: Stanford University Press, 1991); Anne F. Hyde, *Empires, Nations, and Families: A History of the North American West, 1800–1860* (Lincoln: University of Nebraska Press, 2011); Albert L. Hurtado, *Intimate Frontiers: Sex, Gender, and Culture in Old California* (Albuquerque: University of New Mexico Press, 1999); Sarah Deutsch, *No Separate Refuge: Culture, Class, and Gender on an Anglo-Hispanic Frontier in the American Southwest, 1880–1940* (New York: Oxford University Press 1987); and María Raquél Casas,

Married to a Daughter of the Land: Spanish-Mexican Women and Interethnic Marriage in California, 1820–1880 (Reno: University of Nevada Press, 2007).

18. For works that call for and illustrate global and comparative approaches to the study of family, kinship, and other intimate domains, see Ann M. Little, "Gender and Sexuality in the North American Borderlands, 1492–1848," *History Compass* 7, no. 6 (2009): 1606–15; Göran Therborn, *Between Sex and Power: Family in the World, 1900–2000* (New York: Routledge, 2004); Ann B. Waltner and Mary Jo Maynes, "Family History as World History," in *Women's History in Global Perspective*, vol. 1, ed. Bonnie G. Smith (Urbana: University of Illinois Press, 2004), 148–91; Paula S. Fass, "Children and Globalization," *Journal of Social History* 36 (Summer 2003): 963–77; Ann Laura Stoler, "Tense and Tender Ties: The Politics of Comparison in North American History and (Post) Colonial Studies," *Journal of American History* 88 (December 2001): 829–65; and Hugh Cunningham, "Histories of Childhood," *American Historical Review* 103 (October 1998): 1195–1208.

19. Ann Laura Stoler, *Carnal Knowledge and Imperial Power: Race and the Intimate in Colonial Rule* (Berkeley: University of California Press, 2002), 19.

20. Milanich, "Review Essay," 441.

21. Jacobs, *White Mother to a Dark Race*, xxxi.

22. Annette Gordon-Reed, *The Hemingses of Monticello: An American Family* (New York: W. W. Norton & Co., 2008), 288.

23. Milanich, "Review Essay," 448. For an early review of these debates in the literature, see Barbara J. Harris, "Recent Work on the History of the Family: A Review Article," *Feminist Studies* 3 (Spring/Summer 1976): 159–72. For a more recent review of and intervention in these longstanding debates, see Judith S. Graham, *Puritan Family Life: The Diary of Samuel Sewall* (Boston: Northeastern University Press, 2000), esp. 4–12, 61–108, and 167–80.

24. Gordon, "Internal Colonialism and Gender," 443.

25. Stoler, "Tense and Tender Ties."

26. For helpful overviews of this literature, see Little, "Gender and Sexuality"; Susan Armitage, "Turner's Ghost: A Personal Retrospective on Western Women's History," in *The Practice of U.S. Women's History: Narratives, Intersections, and Dialogues*, ed. S. Jay Kleinberg, Eileen Boris, and Vicki L. Ruíz (New Brunswick, NJ: Rutgers University Press, 2007); and Katherine G. Morrissey, "Engendering the West," in *Under an Open Sky: Rethinking America's Western Past*, ed. William Cronon, George Miles, and Jay Gitlin (New York: W. W. Norton & Company, 1992), 132–44. For important anthologies on the women's west, see Elizabeth Jameson and Sheila McManus, eds., *One Step Over the Line: Toward a History of Women in the North American Wests* (Edmonton: University of Alberta Press, 2008); Mary Ann Irwin and James F. Brooks, eds., *Women and Gender in the American West* (Albuquerque: University of New Mexico Press, 2004); and Elizabeth Jameson and Susan Armitage, eds., *Writing the Range: Race, Class, and Culture in the Women's West* (Norman: University of Oklahoma Press, 1997).

27. Stephanie Coontz, *The Way We Never Were: American Families and the Nostalgia Trap* (New York: Basic Books, 1992).

28. Judith Stacey, *In the Name of the Family: Rethinking Family Values in the Postmodern Age* (Boston: Beacon Press, 1996), 8. See also Stephanie Coontz, *The Way We Really Are: Coming to Terms with America's Changing Families* (New York: Basic Books, 1997).

29. Stacey, *In the Name of the Family*, 11.

PART ONE

Diverse Families and Racial Hierarchy

1

Breaking and Remaking Families

The Fostering and Adoption of Native American Children in Non-Native Families in the American West, 1880–1940

Margaret Jacobs

In the late nineteenth century, Mary Dissette, a single missionary and schoolteacher at Zuni Pueblo, adopted a Zuni girl named Daisy. After her tenure at Zuni, Dissette settled in Santa Fe, where she bought an adobe house and a large orchard with the intent of taking in "a dozen Indian girls from the different pueblos and teach[ing] them practical domestic industries, especially spinning, weaving, horticulture and poultry raising." Dissette asked the Women's National Indian Association (WNIA) for their help in establishing her home as a school. "It is because I know I can raise girls, Indian girls, to be true, loving, useful women, that I want to try my hands on more," Dissette told the WNIA. In 1904 she informed the WNIA that she had taken "legal control of three Indian waifs and placed two of them in the Albuquerque Boarding School." Ultimately, according to one of her friends, Dissette "adopted and educated out of her own slender earnings, five Pueblo Indian children."[1]

Over the last fifteen years, as I have researched white women's interactions with Indian people at the turn of the twentieth century, I have found many instances of white women like Dissette who adopted Indian children. In most cases, I have only the barest of references to such adoptions, usually told solely from the viewpoint of the white women themselves. I sense there are important stories to be told here, stories of love and intimacy in the forming of new families, but also stories of grief and loss in the breaking of Indian families. Such stories link love and power, the private and the public, the family and the state; they offer a poignant example of what noted scholar of colonialism Ann Laura Stoler calls the "intimacies of empire."[2] The federal government asserted such a degree of power over Indian peoples at the turn of the twentieth century that it could interfere even in the most intimate sites of Indian families; its power could and did sever ties of love. But love also complicated such brute power; many white women such as Dissette truly cared for the Indian children they adopted, and many Indian children loved their adoptive families.

Such stories of love and power connect the era of assimilation to the late twentieth century, when the fostering and adoption of Indian children within non-Native families had become a common practice. In 1969, at the request of the Devils Lake Sioux tribe of North Dakota to conduct an investigation, the Association on American Indian Affairs (AAIA) found that in most states with large American Indian populations, 25 to 35 percent of Indian children had been separated from their families and placed in foster or adoptive homes or in institutions such as boarding schools.[3] In a follow-up state-by-state statistical analysis of Indian child welfare conducted in 1976, the AAIA found that in every state with a significant Indian population, Indian children were placed in foster care or in adoptive homes at a per capita rate far higher than that of non-Indian children.[4]

The AAIA and many other Indian groups lobbied the federal government to enact legislation that would reverse this practice. The result was the Indian Child Welfare Act (ICWA) of 1978, which gave tribal courts jurisdiction over most cases involving the fostering or adoption of Indian children and prioritized the placement of Indian children with relatives, tribal members, or other Indian families.[5] Given the shockingly high estimates of Indian children who had been fostered or adopted outside their communities, and the significance of the ICWA, surprisingly little historical research has been done on this topic.[6]

In this chapter I explore the genealogy of this widespread practice and find that its roots extend deep into the late nineteenth century and are entangled with the intensive participation of white women in enacting assimilation policy. Many white women developed commonplace images of unfit Indian mothers and neglected Indian children and practiced a politics of maternalism that often included the informal adoption of Indian children. In most cases, white women had their own very personal and laudable reasons for adopting Indian children; they undoubtedly acted out of real love. Yet their participation in the pathologizing of Indian families and the removal of their children reinforced the power and the policy aims of the state, aims that threatened the viability of Native families and communities. Moreover, white women who wished to adopt Indian children benefited from the assimilation policies of the state, policies that promoted the removal of American Indian children to boarding schools and facilitated their fostering and adoption by non-Indian families. To exert its power, the state, through the Bureau of Indian Affairs (BIA), also found white women's interest in Indian children useful and exploited white women's maternalist impulses. Thus when white women and their families adopted Indian children, no hard and fast border existed between love and power; the two became inextricably muddled.

The practice of fostering and adopting out Indian children to non-Indian families created shifting intimate allegiances. Thus this chapter also attempts to understand this phenomenon from multiple perspectives: from that of the non-Native families who brought Indian children into their lives, from that of the children who were displaced from their Native families and communities but formed new intimacies, and from that of the Indian families and communities whose intimate relationships were profoundly disturbed. I begin with an overview of the white women who adopted Indian children at the turn of the twentieth century, how they obtained children, and what motivated them. I then turn to several case studies told as much as possible from the vantage point of Indian children. I end by briefly addressing the viewpoints of Indian families whose children were adopted.

ADOPTION PRACTICES

Adoption was not a new phenomenon to American Indian peoples. As historian Marilyn Irvin Holt writes, "It was a fiber of tribal life that intertwined the needs of an individual with a group."[7] In some cases, biological parents consented to have another family raise their child, often when a family had lost a child or when a medical practitioner healed a sick child. For example, Hopi Edmund Nequatewa's grandfather, who had "put a claim on [him] when [he] was sick," gained the right under Hopi custom to guide the boy's upbringing.[8] Moreover, it was common for grandparents and other extended family members to participate in the rearing of children so that they could easily step in should a child's biological parents die or be unable to care for them. Among the Navajos, for example, according to Left Handed, "'Mother' refers to a great many other women besides one's real mother. In fact, wishing to distinguish his [biological] mother from among all these other women, . . . a Navaho [sic] must state explicitly, 'my real mother,' or use some such . . . phrase as, 'she who gave me birth.'"[9] These intricate kinship systems assured that few Indian children were ever left truly orphaned.

The practice of non-Indian families adopting Indian children took on a quite different quality. Beginning in the colonial period, many non-Indian families adopted children primarily to fill labor needs.[10] Up to the late nineteenth century the adoption of Indian children by non-Indian families in the West grew out of the captive trade, practiced widely by many Native peoples, Spanish colonists, and subsequent Mexican and Anglo settlers. Early Mormon settlers in Utah, for example, adopted Indian children by purchasing them from Indian or Mexican slave traders or directly from their parents. In most cases the Indian children were required to pay back their purchase price through laboring for their Mormon families for up to twenty years.[11] Similarly, the 1850 Act for the Government and Protection of Indians enabled California settlers to adopt and indenture Indian children.[12] Military leaders also sometimes adopted Indian children in the early nineteenth century; most famously, after vanquishing a resistant band of Creeks in the Redstick Wars, Andrew Jackson adopted a Creek boy as a "trophy of war."[13] Some non-Indians may have sought guardianship of Indian children as a means of gaining property, too. In Washington territory, for example, four children of an Indian woman who had been widowed were appointed a white male guardian to oversee the property they had inherited, valued at about a thousand dollars.[14]

Although these earlier adoptions seem to have been based primarily on practical economic concerns and assertions of myriad forms of power—military, judicial, patriarchal—over Indian labor and lands, it would be a mistake to see them as relationships that tilted entirely toward power and involved no love, affection, or sentiment. As Sherry Smith finds in her book on army perceptions of American Indians in the nineteenth century, many army officers were moved by a sense of responsibility or compassion to take "orphaned" or lost Indian children into their families, temporarily or permanently, after battles against Indian peoples.[15]

By the late nineteenth century, many adoptive parents adopted children for more emotional reasons. This may have been due to a change in families and households that accompanied industrialization and the rise of the middle class: a shift from patriarchal utilitarian productive households to nuclear families with a smaller number of children. With this shift came a new emphasis on the family as a site for the fulfillment of sentimental needs and the investiture of middle-class women with new domestic duties and intensive maternal responsibilities. Although some families undoubtedly continued to adopt children to fulfill their labor needs, middle-class ideals about adoption gained increasing prominence. These ideals focused not only on the child that needed a home but also on the home and the mother that needed the child.[16]

Although most adoption historians characterize transracial adoption as a phenomenon of the 1960s and beyond, many white families and single white women were drawn to adopting Indian children in the late nineteenth and early twentieth centuries.[17] Military officers and their wives often had opportunities to adopt Indian children. In the case of the Lakota infant Lost Bird, or Zintka Nuni, Brigadier General Leonard Colby, Civil War hero and commander of the Nebraska National Guard, had been headquartered twenty-six miles south of the Pine Ridge Reservation when the Wounded Knee massacre of 1890 occurred. When he led his unit to Pine Ridge, Colby bargained to obtain the infant girl, recovered from under her dead mother's frozen body four days after the massacre, as "an Indian relic" and a gift for Clara, his wife of eight years. Before others could obtain the valued little girl (the Ghost Dance camp of Lakotas tried to keep her, Buffalo Bill Cody had tried to obtain her for a hunting buddy, and Cody's manager hoped to exhibit her in the Wild West Show), the general brought her to his home in Beatrice, Nebraska, and legally adopted her.[18]

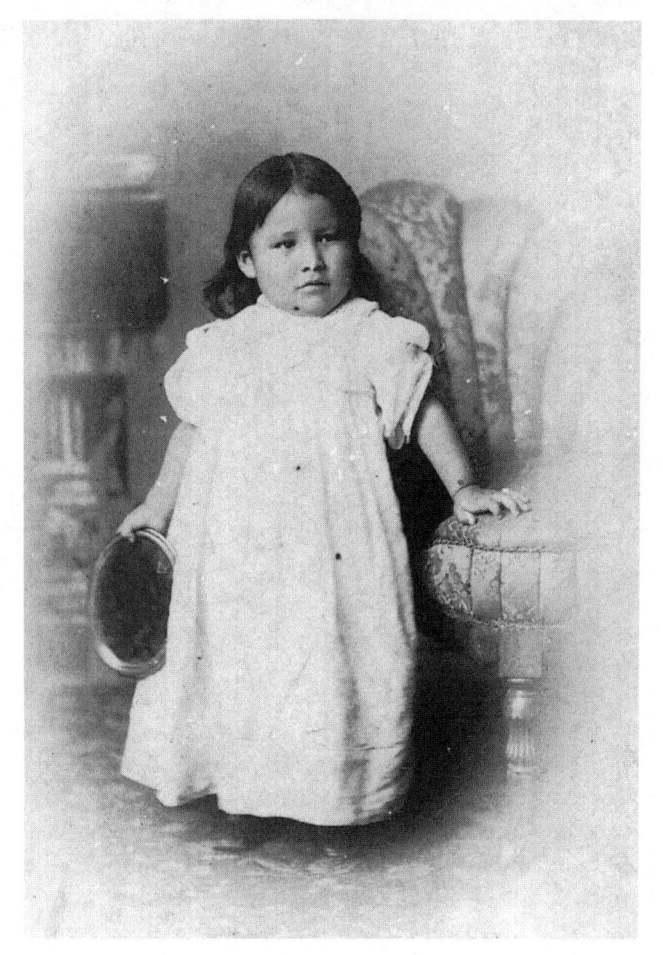

FIGURE 1.1. Zinka Nuni, ca. 1891. Courtesy of Wisconsin Historical Society, no. WHi-26606.

White women married to traders on Indian reservations also lived in close proximity to Indian people and in some instances adopted Indian children. Louisa Wade Wetherill, wife of the longtime trader John Wetherill, adopted two Navajo children, Betty and Frances, into their home at Kayenta, Arizona.[19] Betty Wetherill Rodgers, a Navajo woman who was born around 1915, experienced removal from her family first to a boarding school: "I was born at Lukachukai. . . . And then . . . , my Navajo family . . . , after I was a few years old, came to Kayenta. . . . And then I was taken from my Navajo people. Then, the government just went out and just took kids to put 'em in school. . . . I don't know why they picked me. I was just a baby. But I was placed at Tuba City.... I was there 'til I was about four." Rodgers adds, "They were very mean to us. When we'd run away, or even speak a word of Navajo, they'd just more or less beat us.... I never did like it there. They just treated us like prisoners or something."[20]

In the book she wrote with Frances Gillmor, Wetherill also spoke of tensions between the federal government and the Navajos over the Tuba City school. When fifty Navajo children showed up at a day school in Kayenta that could hold only thirty, the government insisted on sending the twenty extra children to the Tuba City boarding school. The Navajos opposed this and convinced Wetherill to teach them English at the trading post.[21]

In her interview, Rodgers claims that Louisa Wetherill visited the Navajo children at the Tuba City school frequently and was appalled at the treatment of the children. As Rodgers explains, "She came over there and found that they were treating the Navajo children real bad.... So she thought, 'Well, this is gonna stop!' So she went to Washington and told the president what was goin' on among the Navajos, and so she put a stop to all that. Everybody at Tuba then was fired and ran off." Thereafter, according to Rodgers, Wetherill's older daughter (Georgia Ida) became "matron to the Navajo girls.... She took care of us, 'cause she spoke the Navajo language pretty well herself."

Wetherill, however, tells a different story of how she adopted Betty. According to Wetherill, prior to Betty she had already adopted two other Indian children, Esther and Fanny, daughters of a Ute Indian woman captive—or slave, as Wetherill called her—who had married a Navajo man. The Wetherills had first adopted Esther from her Ute mother. Later, in the early 1920s, the Ute woman stopped the Wetherills as they were driving and complained to them that her Navajo husband was mistreating her and her daughter. The Wetherills "took the slave woman and her baby back with them. When the slave woman made arrangements to go to other hogans, and did not want the responsibility of her child, she begged them to take the baby as they had taken Esther for their own." The Wetherills, on their way to Tucson for Louisa to lecture at the university that winter, enrolled Esther at the Tuba City school and arranged for the baby, Fanny, to be boarded there as well. They picked the two girls up in the spring and took them back to the trading post in Kayenta. But Esther had contracted tuberculosis in boarding school, a fate that was all too common for many Indian children, and was later sent to a sanitarium in Phoenix, where she died. "With a heavy heart," laden with both guilt and grief, Wetherill agreed to adopt another child, Betty. As she describes it, "When in 1922, the authorities at Tuba City asked her to adopt a little girl away from the school who was unhappy there, she had the child brought home to [Kayenta]. Soon it was said in the hogans of the People that Asthon Sosi and Hosteen John [the Wetherills] had taken another

Navajo girl for their own. Betty and Fanny were the Wetherill's children, now that [their older children Ben and Georgia Ida] had married and were so much away."[22]

Though Betty Rodgers (and perhaps Louisa Wetherill as well) was critical of the care she received in boarding school, many female boarding school teachers also adopted children in their care. For example, Miss Hope Ghiselin, who taught Apaches at a BIA school in San Carlos, Arizona, wrote to the WNIA, "I came here in May [18]87 and have not ceased since then to beg first for one girl and then for another. Finally as an especial favor, Captain Bullis, our agent, gave me one for my last Thanksgiving Day gift." Ghiselin also "acquired" another child when the resident doctor asked her if she could take in an "orphan." "I named [her] ... Lizzie Owing for my mother, and hope if possible to have her always with me; I love her so."[23] No less a figure than Estelle Reel, superintendent of Indian education from 1898 to 1910, also adopted an Indian girl. Reel kept an "orphaned Aleut girl during the summers. The girl was attending Indian schools in Oregon and Washington."[24] Notably, Ghiselin, Reel, and many other white women who adopted Indian children were single.

Idealistic women reformers in the late nineteenth century were also drawn to adopting Indian children. Mary Duggan, a feminist and advocate for Indians in the late nineteenth and early twentieth centuries, lived with her brother, the physician Cornelius Duggan, on Riverside Drive in New York City. According to Bonita Wa Wa Calachaw, the Indian girl she adopted, Duggan was "a humanitarian. Always she was doing things for the *forsaken* Indian."[25] Duggan attended club meetings of "*Women* that called themselves the *New Thought members*" and took part in the Psychic Society.[26] By adopting Wa Wa Chaw, as she became known, Duggan seemed to believe she was fulfilling a higher purpose. As Wa Wa Chaw saw it, "Mother Mary Duggan Knew that when she took me in her *arms* that she was helping a common Cause."[27]

Although some white women (and men) legally adopted Indian children, the process by which the custody of an Indian child transferred from their Indian family to their white guardians was often informal. Although Lakota people had sought to keep Zintka Nuni, Leonard Colby was able to bargain for her and spirit her away to Beatrice, Nebraska. Nebraska law required the voluntary relinquishment of a child by its parents or guardian before adoption could take place, but the judge who approved her adoption by the Colbys did not require the presence or testimony of any Lakota relatives.[28] Colby had not taken pains to find the birth father of the child, and the judge seems to have assumed that both parents of Lost Bird had died. Neither Colby nor the judge considered Indian conceptions of adoption that would have placed Lost Bird with extended family members or other members of the tribe.[29]

In her oral history interview, Betty Rodgers describes the very casual process by which she began to live with the Wetherills at age four:

> So when summer came, my foster mother . . . Mrs. Wetherill, said, "I think I'll just take this little girl home." . . . Of course I was kind of shy and scared, you know, of the white people then. She asked me if I wanted to go home with her, and of course I didn't just right off say yes or nothing. She just said, "Well, you can just go home with us any time." So after a few weeks or so, one day she had sent for me, and there was her nephews, sons-in-law, . . . driving trucks, . . . carrying mail and carrying supplies . . . through the reservation. . . . So she told these guys to pick me up. So . . . one day one of 'em . . . said, "I'm takin' this little Navajo girl home. I'm taking her to Mrs. Wetherill at Kayenta." So . . . I thought, "Well, I guess it's all right," so I just went with him. . . . And that's when I started living with the Wetherills. . . . That was way back when I was four years old.

Although Louisa Wetherill's story of Betty's adoption differs, it is equally vague. The adoption is arranged through the boarding school and neither the authorities nor Wetherill mentions the wishes of Betty's parents and family.

Bonita Wa Wa Calachaw's adoption was equally ad hoc. She was allegedly born on Christmas Day in 1888 in the southern California desert to a woman who may have been a member of the Rincon band of the Luiseño people. According to Wa Wa Chaw, Mary Duggan was "passing through California on her way East and, having to make connections for her return home, had to wait for two or three days. . . . Wandering along the roads, . . . [she] stopped at a wooden *shack*. And in that *shack* was My real Mother Indian having *labor pains*. Mother Mary Duggan took things into her hands and in a few minutes I was born. Mother gave Me to her [Duggan]." Wa Wa Chaw concluded, "I was born of the curse of being poor, My real Mother having to part with a new born child."[30]

As these stories reveal, the adoption of Indian children seemed to take place offhandedly, with very little concern for the rights or feelings of Indian families. An attitude that Indian children were free for the taking seemed to prevail. For example, when Mrs. Oresmus Boyd, the wife of a cavalry officer, encountered Paiute and Shoshone Indians in Nevada, she wrote, "In one of their camps, I found a beautiful dark-eyed baby boy, to whom I paid frequent visits, which were at first well received. But one day I carried the child a neat little dress—my own handiwork—and before arraying baby in it gave him a bath, which evidently caused his mother to decide that I had sinister designs upon her prize, for on subsequent visits no trace of the baby could ever be found." Mrs. Boyd felt entitled to take over as mother of this boy. She felt sure that "had his sex been different I probably could have obtained complete possession; but boys are highly prized among the Indians."[31] Interestingly, while stationed in Arizona, Mrs. Boyd balked when local Pima and Maricopa Indian women admired her own child. "Every night when we pitched our tents," she recounted, "the [Indian] women would crowd about and indulge in ecstasies over the little white baby.... I never permitted any of them to touch baby, being afraid to do so."[32] Boyd's double standard seems to have been shared by a large number of white women reformers; white children belonged with and to their white mothers but Indian children would be better off under the care of white women.[33]

Why was the adoption of Indian children carried out in such a seemingly informal manner? Certainly, this was an era in which many adoptions were unregulated. It was not until 1929 that *all* states had enacted adoption laws that authorized courts to formally transfer the custody of children from their biological parents to their adoptive parents. Nevertheless, most states had enacted such laws by 1900.[34] It appears that even after 1900, however, adoptive parents rarely felt the need to apply for the legal custody of Indian children. This is likely due to the predominant ideas about Indian families in this era of assimilation policy. Arguing that Indian families stymied the assimilation of Indian children, many if not most government officials, missionaries, and reformers believed it best that Indian children be separated from their parents and families and institutionalized in boarding schools.[35] By 1902 about 17,700 Indian children attended one of the more than 150 federally run Indian boarding schools.[36] This practice created a climate in which the separation of children from their families became naturalized. Moreover, as with the case of Betty Rodgers above and the large numbers of white women schoolteachers who adopted Indian children, the removal of children to boarding school was closely linked to adoption in a very concrete way.[37]

In these instances it is quite difficult to ascertain the extent to which Indian parents gave genuine consent to the adoption of their children. In many cases they had not even consented to their children attending boarding schools. Over many decades, when many Indian parents proved unwilling to send their children to distant schools, the BIA had resorted to various coercive means, including trickery, threats, withholding rations, bribes, or the use of police or military force.[38] Once confined to a boarding school, an Indian child's status in relation to his or her parents became increasingly tenuous. Rarely could parents bring their children home when they wished. Thus the apparent ease with which many white women adopted Indian children was integrally related to existing practices of Indian child removal to boarding schools.

Moreover, the BIA's vision of the role of boarding school matrons and female teachers as surrogate mothers to removed Indian children led logically to the fostering and adoption of Indian children by white women teachers and white families more generally. As I detail in *White Mother to a Dark Race* and as Cathleen Cahill explores in this volume, the government deemed white women as the ideal caretakers for removed Indian children within the boarding schools. White women matrons and teachers would take the place of supposedly unfit Indian mothers, introducing Indian girls to appropriate domestic standards and maternal skills.[39]

It was thus no coincidence that a large number of white women teachers and matrons within the Indian boarding schools adopted Indian children.

In some cases, white women may have obtained at least informal Indian consent for the adoption of their children. Tesbah, a Navajo (Diné) woman, for example, after delivering a baby boy at home and laboring for several more days before delivering a baby girl in the hospital, believed, "The baby girl has killed me." She instructed her family, "Do not keep her in the family to raise with our other children, as she will bring bad luck to the family. Give her to the white people to raise." Tesbah died the next day and her infant boy a few days later. Kay Bennett, another Navajo woman, remembered, "A childless couple that ran a trading post had gladly accepted the baby girl to raise as their own."[40] In other cases, Indian families may have incorporated white women into their own kinship systems and therefore regarded them as appropriate adopters of their children. This may have been true for Louisa Wetherill, who learned the Navajo language and many facets of Navajo culture, attended Navajo ceremonies, and was adopted by the tribe. Unlike white women in other colonial settings, too, Wetherill did not object to close contact between the Navajo and her two birth children. "The People were their friends, the country of the People, their home," she explained. "And so familiar was the Navajo tongue to them that sometimes Little Girl [Wetherill's oldest daughter] . . . would fall naturally into the Navajo speech and would break off to ask in a puzzled fashion—'How do you say that in English?'"[41] In many instances, Navajo people living in the vicinity of the Wetherill trading post at Kayenta brought ill people to be nursed or cured by Asthon Sosi, or Slim Woman, as the Navajos called Wetherill, and Wetherill claims that she "became known as the Little Mother of the Navajos."[42] Documentary traces of Indian adoption suggest, however, that such voluntary relinquishment was less common than white women obtaining children through other means.

Although men such as Leonard Colby were sometimes involved in the adoption of Indian children, it was more often white women who initiated adoptions and cared for the children.[43] Middle-class gender and racial ideologies converged to influence white women to adopt Indian children. Ideals of maternalism extolled motherhood as women's highest calling and justified middle-class, and mostly white, women's political and social reform activity on behalf of other women. As Claudia Nelson explains, adoptive motherhood enabled women to gain public recognition and to signify their social, moral, and financial status.[44] Moreover, the power of maternalism may have swayed many single women (some of whom lived in long-term relationships with other women) to adopt children, a phenomenon that was socially acceptable before the 1920s. In many cases of Indian adoption, it was, indeed, single white women who adopted Indian children, usually Indian girls, perhaps signifying a means by which unconventional white women who had avoided marriage could still raise children. These white women were forming new families in the American West, maternalist families that were modeled on the utopian male-free communal families of Charlotte Perkins Gilman's *Herland,* not the patriarchal families from which most of these middle-class white women came.[45] Although such a move could be seen as radical, it could also be reconciled to more conservative views of women—that even a "spinster" felt the tug of maternity and needed to fill her God-given role.[46]

To some extent, practical considerations may have influenced single women in choosing Indian children. First, prospective adoptive parents complained that there was a "baby shortage" in this period, due in part to the reluctance of orphanages to place children up for adoption. Most children in orphanages were not true orphans, but rather children whose parents had fallen on hard times. Most social workers believed—at least when it came to white children—that they should be reunited with their birth parents if possible.[47] Many prospective adopters feared that if they adopted from an orphanage the birth parents would one day seek to reclaim their children. In addition, confusion and conflict between adoption laws and institutional policies could discourage those who obtained children from orphanages from legally adopting them. Some families also balked at the costs, $10 to $25, that were associated with legal adoption.[48]

By adopting Indian children, adopters could bypass such obstacles. First, because Indian parents and extended family members were often isolated on reservations and in many cases already cut off from their children, adoptive parents had less fear that Indian birth parents would reclaim their children. Second, as most adoptions became more formalized in the 1920s and '30s and social workers clamored for increased control over the placement of non-Indian adoptive children, the informal adoption of Indian children remained relatively free of state regulation and the intervention of child placement workers.[49] Moreover, many social service professionals became unwilling to place children with single women. Scholar Julie Berebitsky found that as sexual and gender norms changed in the 1920s to include the labeling and stigmatization of lesbianism, most child welfare workers opposed the placement of adopted children with single women.[50] The adoption of an Indian child would have been one way for a single white woman to circumvent such biases.

Intertwining racial and gender ideologies regarding Indian people as savages in need of rescue and white women as civilizers also played into white women's motivations for adopting Indian children. In the nineteenth century, courts routinely considered Indianness itself to be grounds for granting guardianship of Indian children to non-Indians. For example, in one probate case in Washington territory, a young white man who had fathered a child with an Indian woman petitioned the court to have his child apprenticed to another white man because he was "desirous of having [the] child protected and cared for and not permitted to become an Indian by living among them." The judge granted the petition without consulting with the child's Indian mother.[51] In several other cases, petitioners portrayed Indian women as unfit guardians for their own children and often accused them of having bad morals, including drinking alcohol, being promiscuous, and engaging in prostitution.[52] One court document portrayed an Indian woman as having no home, "and . . . now living on the beach, as is the manner of her people; and who is not a fit and proper person to have the care of guardianship" of her own daughter.[53]

White women often portrayed their adoption of Indian children as an act of rescue, welcomed by the child and often initiated by some family members. In the case of a Navajo girl known as Grace Segar, a missionary stated that "this young girl came to us at the age of about eight years, wrapped in an old blanket. She was given to us in all probability because her mother did not want her to become the plural wife of her stepfather."[54] Although it is possible that in some cases indigenous women may have used white women to protect or shelter their children, this type of statement was part of a larger maternalist discourse that commonly represented American Indian women and gender relations in a negative light.

Indeed, the rhetoric of rescue was based on and reinforced a pathological view of Indian families and Indian motherhood. Many white women missionaries, teachers, and reformers who encountered Indian peoples in the late nineteenth and early twentieth centuries regarded several facets of Indian family life—unfamiliar Indian gender relations, Indian women's active physical labor, and the presence of some polygamous unions, for example—as signs that Indian families were unfit to care for their children. Because Indian families did not always conform to the standard of the nuclear family customary among white middle-class Americans, many white women deemed indigenous children orphans. For instance, Mary Collins wrote for the WNIA publication, "Unfortunately, among [the Sioux] almost every woman and man is married more than once, and the children of these various marriages, though often both parents may be living, are really orphans."[55] White women rarely recognized the role that extended family members played in the upbringing of children. Thus when an Alaska Native girl's mother and father died, a reformer believed "she had no one to love her until one day, when she found her way into a mission school," where the teacher "kept her and took care of her as if she were her own daughter."[56]

Notions of rescue led many white women to support policies that called for the removal of Indian children to boarding schools and to believe that Indian children would be better off brought up in white families than raised among their own kin.[57] Despite the obvious ethnocentrism of white women's viewpoints, they saw themselves as racially enlightened and progressive. Compared to many Americans, perhaps they were. Susan B. Anthony, for example, objected to Clara Colby's decision to raise Lost Bird, or Zintka, partly on the basis that it would distract her from her suffrage activism, but also on the grounds that Zintka was an "untutored Indian girl." Other suffrage activists similarly disapproved of

Clara's adoption of an Indian child.[58] In the early twentieth century, when an increasingly shrill hereditarian and eugenicist discourse claimed that Indians and other "non-Aryan stock" were genetically inferior to the Anglo-Saxon "race," the stance of many white women who adopted Indian children was, in many ways, a refreshing alternative.[59]

Undoubtedly, most white women who adopted Indian children considered themselves to have the purest and most altruistic of motives; many, indeed, loved the Indian children they fostered and adopted. And it is likely that in many cases adopted Indian children gained greater access to education, healthcare, and an improved standard of living through living with white women. But it is also inescapable that white women's involvement in the adoption of Indian children inadvertently supported the state aims of undermining Indian identities and thereby consolidating control over Indian lands. In this era the government had adopted a number of measures to reduce the land base of Indian peoples and to sever the ties between generations, ostensibly in order to facilitate the assimilation of Indians. The Dawes Act, through the allotment of communally held land to individual Indians, transferred some ninety million acres of land to non-Natives for settlement and development. The network of boarding schools removed children during the most crucial years of their social and cultural upbringing and sought to undermine their Indian identities, identities that enabled them to claim land. The adoption of Indian children, although on a much smaller scale than the boarding schools, intersected with the state's assertions of power to obliterate Indian identities and extinguish Indian claims to land. In the late twentieth century, when fostering and adoption became common and was coupled with efforts to involuntarily sterilize Native American women, the federal government still seemed bent on destroying Indian identities and land claims.[60]

The promotion of the fostering and adoption of indigenous children was not limited to the American West. In other settler colonies and nations, including Canada and Australia, the practice was also widespread, suggesting that it is a phenomenon closely associated with the project of settler colonialism.[61] In settler colonies, colonizing powers have sought to engineer the transfer of land from indigenous peoples to settlers. To do so, they enact polices that promote the growth and expansion of the "white" settler population (as, for example, the Homestead Act did) as well as the elimination of the indigenous population.[62] Disease and military campaigns may have brought about the elimination of many indigenous people in the eighteenth and nineteenth centuries in the West (as in Canada and Australia), but such frontier violence became increasingly morally untenable. Policies that culturally eliminated Indian people through assimilation became the preferred method of enabling the dispossession of indigenous people in the late nineteenth century and beyond.[63] These policies increasingly enacted colonial relations on a most intimate scale—through sexual liaisons, but also through the rearing of children. It is important to keep this larger backdrop in mind as we study the adoptive families that white women and Indian children formed.

RELATIONS BETWEEN WHITE MOTHERS AND ADOPTED INDIAN CHILDREN

Obviously, many white women developed deep affection for the young Indian girls (and less often boys) they brought into their homes and with whom they created alternative families. For example, Mary Dissette told the WNIA in 1902 that "my own little Indian girl [Daisy] . . . is my greatest earthly comfort and blessing."[64] If we are to believe Dissette, her relationship with Daisy was mutually satisfying. In 1924 she told an associate, "I am just as fond of her as ever, and I believe she is just as devoted and loyal to me."[65] In 1904 she adopted another Indian girl, a three-year-old baby, which she put in the care of Daisy. Dissette wrote, "It is very gratifying to see Daisy's willingness to pass on to another helpless orphan the care and affection which she has had, and which have borne such rich fruit in her own transfigured life. Daisy assures me that her baby Dorothy will 'come out all right.'"[66] We need to know more from Daisy's point of view to truly understand the nature of this relationship, yet indigenous children's points of view are difficult to find.

One exception is that of Betty Rodgers, who was interviewed for United Indian Traders Association Oral History Project in 1999. Rodgers describes her life with the Wetherills briefly and in glowing terms: "Well, they raised me then, and took care of me, and treated me just like one of their own. . . . Her [Mrs. Wetherill's] kids was already grown men and women. . . . So I stayed there and she had another Navajo girl. Her name is Frances [Fanny]. . . . So it was her and I that were raised by Mrs. Wetherill. She tried to raise other Navajo kids, but they either died or didn't want to live with them or something. But anyway, we were very fortunate, me and her." Rodgers particularly recalled meeting "all kinds of great people. There were all kinds of artists, writers, painters, and movie stars. So many people like that, that I had met from the time I was growing up there, and it was really something, being with those people, because my foster father then used to take 'em on trips to the Rainbow Bridge." Rodgers and her sister Fanny went to grade school in Kayenta, which she remembered fondly: "We had it made then. We had this wonderful person that came there and taught us all of our grade years, 'til we finished the eighth grade." Rodgers and her sister then went to live with their adoptive sister in Mesa, Arizona, where they attended high school and she met her white husband, with whom she established a trading post on the Navajo reservation. In her interview, Rodgers emphasized love, not power.

Other adopted Indian children struggled much more than Betty Rodgers appears to; for Lost Bird, or Zintka Nuni, assertions of power were as common as expressions of love and affection in the Colby family. Zintka witnessed the gendered

FIGURE 1.2. Fanny and Betty Wetherill in the early to mid-1920s. John and Louisa Wetherill Collection. Courtesy of Harvey Leake.

power dynamics that rocked the relationship between her adoptive parents. General Colby adopted Lost Bird without consulting with his wife; in Washington, D.C., Clara Colby learned of the adoption by telegram three days after the fact. Clara Colby was an unusual woman; she was based with her husband at their home in Beatrice for six months of the year, where she edited the preeminent suffrage newspaper, *The Woman's Tribune*, but the rest of the year she worked as a lobbyist for woman's suffrage in Washington. Although General Colby ordered Clara home from her suffrage work to take care of the infant, Clara did not return until more than four months later. Throughout Zintka's life, Clara continued her suffrage activism, often leaving home for months at a time on speaking tours. Zintka shuttled between homes in Beatrice, Nebraska, and Washington. The Colbys hired a young woman, Maud Miller, to take care of Zintka. Maud became pregnant within a few years of beginning her employment. The father? General Colby. Clara and the general separated, after which he lived openly with Maud while failing to financially support Zintka. The general repeatedly tried to obtain a divorce from Clara, who finally agreed in the early 1900s. By this time Clara had moved to Portland, Oregon, to carry out her suffrage work. The general ignored his commitment to paying alimony and child support, and Clara and Zintka lived on the brink of poverty the rest of their lives. Through a complicated scheme, Maud inherited half a million dollars, after which the general married her.[67]

Despite the unsettled nature of Zintka's home life, real love and affection clearly existed between her and Clara. As a teenager, when she was in boarding school, Zintka wrote a series of poignant letters to Clara. "I must come home, for if I don't I shall die of grief," she wrote in one letter. Suffering from a series of health problems, Zintka declared, "You know precious I can not bear to have any take care of me when I am sick but you for when I am sick you know I always come and sit on your [lap] for you to hug." In a powerless situation—stuck in a boarding school against her will—Zintka used her expressions of love in hopes of swaying her mother to bring her home: "I have no one to love or to love me."[68]

Clara's love and affection were not enough to protect Zintka from other power dynamics. Widespread racial prejudice and discrimination contributed to Zintka's troubled experience. Whether in Beatrice, Washington, or the home of her cousins in Wisconsin, Zintka endured ostracism and ridicule from white children. One cousin taunted her, "Yer ma's a dirty squaw." Another purposely abandoned her in a violent storm. White girls at the public school in Beatrice openly shunned her. In segregated turn-of-the-twentieth-century Washington, she endured racial slurs.[69] Even from Clara she faced prejudice and confusing messages. In Washington, she found companionship among the children who played in the alley that ran behind her mother's home. When Zintka brought home a new black friend, her mother would not let her friend in the door and forbid Zintka from playing in the alley.[70]

From an early age Zintka learned the racial codes of her day. When the consul of Madagascar and his wife visited the Colbys in Washington, Zintka stared at them for many minutes and confided to them, "Don't worry, I'm not white either." She sought out others who were "not white." With Clara frequently gone, Zintka continued to make friends among African American children. When she attended the Pan-America Exposition in Buffalo in 1901, she spent hours with a group of Lakota dancers.[71]

Although Zintka sought out the company of Indians and especially Lakota people, her parents initially tried to prevent such associations. When she experienced troubles in public school and was then expelled from two private schools, Clara enrolled her at Bishop William Hare's All Saints School, a boarding school in South Dakota that catered primarily to white girls and the daughters of Native clergy. Yet, without financial support from the general, Clara could not afford to continue to send Zintka to the school. Moreover, Zintka was miserable there, at one point sending Clara a thirty-page letter requesting that she be allowed to leave the school.[72] Unable to pay the school fees, Clara then sent Zintka to a series of federal Indian boarding schools, all of which were free: the Chamberlain School in South Dakota, Chemawa in Salem, Oregon, and Haskell Institute in Kansas. When Zintka started writing in a kind of Indian slang from Chemawa, Clara feared that the boarding schools had been a bad influence on Zintka.[73]

As she grew older, Zintka rejected the assimilated identity her adoptive parents had promoted. She longed to find her relatives and to associate with members of her tribe. The only boarding school in which she felt at ease was Chamberlain, where she met children of her own tribal background.[74] Zintka ran away from Chemawa, making her way back to South Dakota in search of lost relatives. On many other occasions in her life she gravitated back to South Dakota, and for a year she lived with a Lakota couple who claimed her as their own and enabled her to attain an allotment of land on the Standing Rock Reservation. Zintka also took on a pan-Indian identity and became a professional Indian. She joined a number of Wild West shows, including Buffalo Bill Cody's, worked as the Indian mascot for the Nation of the Lakotah, a white sportsmen's club in Seattle, and journeyed to Hollywood to appear as an extra in several early silent movie westerns.[75]

Zintka rebelled against middle-class gender ideals as well. While in her father's care she became pregnant. He institutionalized her in the Milford Industrial Home, formerly the Nebraska Maternity Home, near Lincoln. Within a month of entering the institution Zintka delivered a stillborn infant, but her father refused to pay the fees for nursing school that would have allowed Zintka to leave the institution. Instead she was forced to stay there eleven more months. Subsequently she had a series of short marriages and had two more children. One of her husbands gave her syphilis, which blinded her in one eye within a few years. Living in dire poverty with a sick husband in the San Joaquin Valley in the late 1910s, one of her children died and she relinquished another to be adopted by an Indian woman in Los Angeles. She contracted the Spanish flu in 1920 and died soon after.[76]

In her adoptive family, Wa Wa Chaw similarly experienced both love and power. We have her diaries and autobiographical sketches, written in her unique voice, to give us a firsthand account of her experience. Mary Duggan and her physician brother, Cornelius Duggan, both agnostics, seem to have regarded raising their adopted daughter as a scientific experiment. According to Wa Wa Chaw, "Dr. Duggan had bought Me a chess board when I was five years old. This chess board was to become the system by which they were to train My Mind, every evening for 15 minutes.... The chess board played a secret part in the strange regulation of My young Life. I *have never been* a *little child.* They had from the beginning talked plain language and laid down the laws governing common sense." The Duggans also brought in a psychologist, Dr. Edward Campbell, to examine Wa Wa Chaw. "I Learned that Dr. *Campbell* was to take charge of My *Mental* attitude," Wa Wa Chaw wrote. "A fine gentleman. Dr. Campbell was a noted neurologist and *psychologist.* It seems that Mother's complaint was I did not talk. It was her wish that I learn to express My feelings a little more freely." Wa Wa Chaw keenly felt as if she were living under a microscope. As she describes it, "My youth was spent under the Observation lens of the Human Eye. The Scientific Mind of Men that *sought* out the *action* of *Causes.*"[77]

Wa Wa Chaw's Indian background as well as her unusual upbringing often led her to feel like a "freak" on display. "I wonder if you Know what it *means* to be constantly on *exhibition*," she wrote. "I discovered that the Indian is always *on* display of some kind. And without pay." At the age of eight or ten, Wa Wa Chaw addressed a women's rights convention on the plight of Indian women and "became [an] object of fame and curiosity." Even as a baby, the Duggans had treated Wa Wa Chaw as an object for exhibit: "They [the Duggans] told Me at the Age of 6 months how I entered a baby contest and won $500.00 for them. And how Mother would dress and undress Me."[78] Zintka had experienced similar sensations and had also "played Indian" in suffrage pageants. According to Renee Flood, she lived "forever a curiosity on public view"; whether Zintka was at home or traveling, "at every turn the child inspired crowds of gaping onlookers."[79]

Although the Duggans undoubtedly loved Wa Wa Chaw, her sense that she was part of an experiment and exhibition left her feeling neglected. "My Parrot had a Greater care taken with it [than] I was cared for," she wrote. Moreover, schooled at home, she was lonely for the company of other children. Wa Wa Chaw drew a sketch of herself reading the dictionary. Her caption read, "I never had any childhood Friends From the time I can remember. I have been surrounded By adults."[80]

Like Zintka, Wa Wa Chaw craved the company of other Indians. When she started piano lessons, she went to Philadelphia with her mother and met two Indian students from Hampton Institute. "Their company opened My Mind," she wrote. Like Zintka, Wa Wa Chaw learned racial ideologies early. "I often wondered how Mother ever went through all this suffering to keep an Indian alive," she pondered, "when the American has said the only good Indian was the dead Indian." At the age of ten, she "was told by another little girl Living in the same building: 'Indians don't belong here. Go somewhere else to Live.'" Like Clara Colby, Mary Duggan endured prejudice from other white women reformers for her adoption of Wa Wa Chaw. "One afternoon," Wa Wa Chaw writes, "I heard a friend of Mother make a remark about giving her Life for a *wild Indian*. I heard Mother say, 'My little girl isn't wild. I could not Live without her.'"[81]

As it was for Zintka and Clara Colby, the decision about whether the girl should attend a federal Indian boarding school was an issue for Wa Wa Chaw and Mary Duggan. Both Duggan and Colby corresponded with Richard Pratt, founder of the Carlisle Institute and staunch advocate for Indian boarding schools, who counseled both women not to send their charges to Indian boarding schools.[82] Although Pratt had pioneered the boarding school system for Indian children, he believed that Indian children ultimately should become fully assimilated into American society. Because Wa Wa Chaw and Zintka Nuni had already been raised within white families, he believed it would not be wise to place them in a segregated Indian-only setting.[83] Due to financial exigencies, Colby reluctantly sent Zintka Nuni to an Indian boarding school, but she feared that it would reverse her assimilation process. Duggan strongly opposed sending Wa Wa Chaw to boarding school for different reasons. She told Wa Wa Chaw that Indian students in the schools "are in a *prison,* you Know," and also referred to "the Great pain of *loneliness,* which was the Fate of every little boy and girl sent to these remote institutions with rules and laws somewhat like a prison for the Criminal inmate."[84]

Wa Wa Chaw shared her adoptive mother's dim view of the boarding schools, partly as a result of a trip Duggan and Wa Wa Chaw took together to the West, including many stops at Indian boarding schools: "After a visit to one of our boarding *schools* I learned that *children* in building 1 could not meet children in building 2," she wrote. "This seemed to be the *system* imposed, by the *order* of the Indian Bureau, to *Create loneliness*. I shall not forget how I *visited an Indian school* and found seven children made deaf because those in charge were allowed to beat them in one side of their *heads* and *ears.* When I complained the Agents molested Me." An orphaned Indian boy who was in an institution also contacted Wa Wa Chaw. "I was told these children were children born *syphilis-Germed,*" she recounted. "What this Black robe did not Know was that *one* of his youthful Victims was told to contact Me. Which the boy did. This boy ran away not because he was a *bad boy.* His *Mind* just could not accept the strange *Idea.* I asked him to talk so I could understand his troubled *Mind.* He said the Man in charge was guilty of *sexuality* and homosexuality."[85]

Like Zintka, Wa Wa Chaw sought to connect with Indian cultures and find her lost relatives throughout her life. She spent eight months living on the Wind River Reservation of Shoshones and Arapahoes in Wyoming. When she and Mary Duggan visited Sherman Institute, they gained clues to Wa Wa Chaw's heritage: "It seemed that My *real Mother's* Name *was Calac* Chaw. And a friend ... had contacted someone at the Indian *school,* who knew Mother Duggan and had some Knowledge of My Indian Mother and other *children.*" Yet although she searched for her family throughout her adult life, Wa Wa Chaw could never find her relatives. Her search experience suggests that she had been stolen or sold. While Wa Wa Chaw and Mary Duggan stayed with an Indian family in southern California, two Indian boys mysteriously disappeared. Although the local sheriff denied any knowledge of their whereabouts, Wa Wa Chaw found them in the nearby hospital. Both boys had been beaten so severely by a white man who had offered them each a nickel to deliver a letter that one died from his wounds and the other had to stay in the hospital for seven months. As she recalled, while she was at the hospital, "The Doctor asked Me what I was doing there. I told him I have tried to locate My own Mother who gave Me away. That I was born at Valley Center and instead Fate has changed My course." The Doctor said "in plain language to get out if I Knew what was good for Me. I did just that." According to Wa Wa Chaw, the incident

FIGURE 1.3. Bonita Wa Wa Calachaw with husband Manuel Nuñez, ca. 1920. Arthur and Shifra Silberman Native American Collection, Dickinson Research Center, Courtesy of National Cowboy and Western Heritage Museum.

"prevented My search for the Mother who gave birth to My body in this World. Valley Center was more than 75 Miles from where we were. So I returned *never* to Know her."[86]

Fiercely opposing assimilation, Wa Wa Chaw became an activist on behalf of Indian people. "Let every American Indian make it clear," she wrote, that "we are not interested in being made over as White Men or White Women. Nor of the White Race. We are what we are. Being Indians and members of the American Nations. And as Citizens we are seeking Justice within the law of our American Nation. Our youth must be given a chance to take part in all activity of our national Life." Wa Wa Chaw put her words into actions; during World War I she fought for the rights of Native Americans to serve in the armed forces.[87]

Unlike Leonard Colby with Zintka, the Duggans kept close control over Wa Wa Chaw's sexuality. When she reached the age of eighteen, they believed it was time for her to marry. When Manuel Nuñez, a Puerto Rican American, took an interest in Wa Wa Chaw, the Duggans hired private detectives to make sure he was suitable for their daughter, and Mary Duggan also took Wa Wa Chaw with her to Puerto Rico for three months that year to investigate his family background. Although Wa Wa Chaw was not particularly interested in Nuñez—she writes, "I was more interested in My reading and paints than in *Love*"—the Duggans regarded him as an ideal mate and promoted the marriage. The couple had a child, "Tee Tee Chaw," who died at age three, and they eventually divorced.[88] Like Zintka, Wa Wa Chaw became impoverished after leaving her adoptive family, especially after the death of Mary Duggan. Destitute after parting from her husband, she took to the streets of Greenwich Village, selling "Indian liniment" from "secret herbs" and her oil paintings.[89] However, Wa Wa Chaw survived, became a respected artist, and lived until 1972.[90]

ASSESSING INDIAN ADOPTION

In recent studies of transracial adoption, researchers have been particularly interested in determining whether these adoptions have been successful. Their success is assessed by the extent to which the children adapt to their families and whether they become "well-adjusted" adults.[91] By this standard, we would probably deem Betty Rodgers's adoption the most successful and Zintka Nuni's the least. This may have been due to the vagaries of family dynamics, but it was also related to whether the adoptive families enabled their Indian children to connect with Indian culture and family. In Betty Rodgers's case, her adoptive parents adopted another Navajo girl, spoke Navajo, maintained ongoing relationships with Navajo people, and lived on the Navajo reservation. As Rodgers characterized her, "My mother [Mrs. Wetherill] . . . thought the world of the Navajo people, just like they were her own, . . . or she was just a Navajo herself, really." Ironically, though Louisa's birth children learned the Navajo language, Betty did not. Nevertheless, she still resided with her family on the border between the Navajo and white worlds (or in a particular variety of rural, southwestern, hobnobbing-with-the-stars white world). Moreover, as evidenced by her empathy with Navajo families against the Tuba City boarding school, Louisa Wetherill did not support one of the primary planks of the assimilation agenda.

Unlike the Wetherills, the Colbys sought to prevent Zintka from mingling with Indian people. Supporting assimilation policy, they imbibed reformers' messages that the solution to the "Indian problem" was to Christianize, civilize, and Americanize Indian people. They undoubtedly believed that through bringing Zintka into their supposedly respectable and civilized middle-class family, they were saving her and helping to promote the cause of assimilation. At least at first, Zintka seemed to fulfill a symbolic role in their lives, as a trophy of war or living Indian keepsake for the general and as a badge of maternalist reform credentials for Clara.[92] Clearly, Zintka became much more to Clara, if not to Leonard. Clara struggled to support her daughter as Zintka experienced racism and longed to connect with her Indian family and community. Clara may have been as caught within the web of the intimacies of empire as her daughter, unable to find a way out of the tangled net of gender norms and ideals, racial ideologies, and settler colonial policies that limited her as much as her daughter.

In the case of Wa Wa Chaw and the Duggans, Mary Duggan shared Louisa Wetherill's aversion to Indian boarding schools and evinced real sympathy to Indian rights. Yet she and her brother's experimental approach to bringing up Wa Wa Chaw—and their residence in New York City—left Wa Wa Chaw isolated from her Indian roots until she was an adult. These are just three cases and cannot represent every adoption of an Indian child in the assimilation era. However, these cases do suggest that if the adoption of Indian children was meant to assimilate, it had many unforeseen consequences. In fact, the more a family concentrated on shielding an Indian child from contact with Indian people, the less likely that child was to adjust to her family and mainstream American society.

Yet the issue of Indian adoption should not focus only on adoptive families and adopted children. The question of whether adoptive Indian children "turned out well" rests on the assumption that assimilation was a legitimate enterprise and privileges liberal individualist values over community interests. A third perspective and experience must be taken into account. For while white women (and men) made new families, they inadvertently broke up many Indian families and damaged Indian communities.

In many cases, entire communities mourned for their lost children. When a group of Lakota ghost dancers visited Washington, D.C., and called on the Colbys, one elder, Kicking Bear, spent much time with Zintka. He gave the child a feather from his beaded cape and "put both his hands on Zintka's head and spoke in a low voice: then placed one hand on her chest and the other on her forehead, still continuing the invocation. Then he kissed his fingers, laid them on Zintka's mouth and back again on his own, after which he stood . . . with bowed head." Overcome with grief, Kicking Bear wept and could not raise his head.[93]

It is rare to find any account of birth mothers' points of view in archival or published sources. Sometimes we get a glimpse of the meaning of this adoption from reunions between birth mothers and child many years later. Betty Rodgers told her interviewer that she didn't see her Navajo mother again until the late 1930s, by which time Betty had a child of her own.

> My Navajo mother came to see me. She came to Kayenta, and she came in my foster mother's home. I guess I was up at my little house, takin' care of my baby and stuff. I went down to see Mother [Wetherill] most of the time through the day. So I walked in the house and I saw this Navajo woman sittin' there on the couch as I walked by—walked right by her to find Mother [Wetherill], see where she was. So I met her in the dining room, and [Wetherill] said, "Betty, do you know that woman sittin' in there on the couch?" And I said, . . . "No, I don't know her." So she went in there with me and said, "Well, that's your mother, Betty." And I said, "My mother?!" "Yes that's your mother." So she got up and stood up and I went over there and put my arms around her, and she cried. Of course she was just some other Navajo woman, is all I knew. . . . So I let her hold Betty, who is my oldest child. . . . I said, "Here's my baby, you can hold her." Oh, she was so proud of that! And she was sittin' there and cryin' and holdin' that baby in her arms and all that stuff.

Certainly, all adoption histories potentially involve the personal grief that Betty Rodgers's mother experienced. Ann Fessler's recent book *The Girls Who Went Away: The Hidden History of Women Who Surrendered Children for Adoption in the Decades Before Roe v. Wade* makes it clear that many young, white, middle-class women who were pressured to give up their babies in the post–World War II era suffered as a result of relinquishing their children. In these cases, social workers promoted the adoption of children born to unwed white mothers as a means to bolster postwar gender and class ideals. By relinquishing their children, unwed mothers could retain their middle-class status and regain their proper womanly role while simultaneously allowing another family to live up to the postwar family ideal.[94]

Yet the adoption of Indian children, when seen in the context of the long history of federal Indian policy, represented a qualitatively different affront. It involved a twisted tangle of racial and gender ideologies that left Indian communities vulnerable to losing their children. Indian women and families had three strikes against them. First, authorities and reformers believed that many if not most Indian families could not or would not conform to middle-class gender norms and thus were not fit to raise children. (Ironically, of course, many of the white women who adopted Indian children did not themselves live up to many gender norms of the time.) Second, the government and the reform movement believed that assimilation through the removal of Indian children was a necessary step toward the "civilization" of Indian people and the solution to "the Indian problem." Finally, the project of settler colonialism—the process whereby settlers took possession of land once claimed by Indian people—further justified the practice by which Indian children were separated from their families and adopted by white families. Although new gender and racial ideologies evolved in the post–World War II era, these three strikes would continue to haunt Indian families well into the late twentieth century, and the fostering and adoption of Indian children would become more commonplace. Together with the involuntary sterilization of many American Indian women in the postwar era, the continued removal of Indian children from their families represented a continuation of nineteenth-century policies that envisioned the eventual eradication of "the Indian problem" through the elimination of Indianness and Indian claims to land.

It was ultimately the power of the state over Indian families that led to the phenomenon of Indian adoption by non-Indian families. Yet, in these adoptive families, where the intimacies of empire were enacted on a daily basis, a fragile love could emerge to challenge the aims of the state colonial project and offer the potential of more equitable cross-cultural encounters. Fragile as it was, this love could not conquer all, but neither could the power of the state.

NOTES

1. *The Indian's Friend* 8, no. 10 (June 1896): 5; 15, no. 1 (September 1902); 16, no. 6 (February 1904): 5; 37, no. 2 (November 1924): 6. For more on Dissette, see *The Indian's Friend* 10, no. 2 (August 1898): 9–11, and my *Engendered Encounters: Feminism and Pueblo Cultures, 1879–1934* (Lincoln: University of Nebraska Press, 1999).

2. Ann Laura Stoler, "Tense and Tender Ties: The Politics of Comparison in North American History and (Post) Colonial Studies," in *Haunted by Empire: Geographies of Intimacy in North American History,* ed. Ann Laura Stoler (Durham, NC: Duke University Press, 2006), 23–67.

3. "Background on the Indian Child Welfare Act, H.R. 12533," *Indian Child Welfare Act of 1978: Hearings before the Subcommittee on Indian Affairs and Public Lands of the Committee on Interior and Insular Affairs, House of Representatives,* 95th Congress, Second Session on S. 1214, February 9 and March 9, 1978, Serial No. 96-42 (Washington, DC: U.S. Government Printing Office, 1981), 29.

4. Appendix G, "Indian Child Welfare Statistical Survey, July 1976, Association of American Indian Affairs," *Indian Child Welfare Act of 1977, Hearing Before the United States Senate Select Committee on Indian Affairs,* 95th Congress, First Session on S. 1214, August 4, 1977 (Washington, DC: U.S. Government Printing Office, 1977).

5. *Indian Child Welfare Act of 1978,* U.S. Code, vol. 25 (1978).

6. Important exceptions are Karen Balcom, "The Logic of Exchange: The Child Welfare League of America, The Adoption Resource Exchange Movement and the Indian Adoption Project, 1958–1967," *Adoption and Culture* 1, no. 1 (2008): 1–65; and Marilyn Irvin Holt, *Indian Orphanages* (Lawrence: University Press of Kansas, 2001).

7. Holt, *Indian Orphanages*, 23.

8. David A. Seaman, ed., *Born a Chief: The Nineteenth Century Hopi Boyhood of Edmund Nequatewa, as Told to Alfred Whiting* (Tucson: University of Arizona Press, 1993), 106.

9. Walter Dyk, "Preface," in *Left Handed, Son of Old Man Hat: A Navajo Autobiography* (1938; reprint, Lincoln: University of Nebraska Press, 1967), xii.

10. Claudia Nelson, *Little Strangers: Portrayals of Adoption and Foster Care in America, 1850–1929* (Bloomington: Indiana University Press, 2003), 2, 5, 9–32, 123; Barbara Melosh, *Strangers and Kin: The American Way of Adoption* (Cambridge, MA: Harvard University Press, 2002), 12–13, 15; and Julie Berebitsky, *Like Our Very Own: Adoption and the Changing Culture of Motherhood, 1851–1950* (Lawrence: University Press of Kansas, 2000), 19–20.

11. James F. Brooks, *Captives and Cousins: Slavery, Kinship, and Community in the Southwest Borderlands* (Chapel Hill: University of North Carolina Press, 2002). On Mormon participation in the captive trade, see Sondra Jones, "'Redeeming' the Indian: The Enslavement of Indian Children in New Mexico and Utah," *Utah Historical Quarterly* 67, no. 3 (Summer 1999): 220–41.

12. Clifford E. Trafzer and Joel R. Hyer, *"Exterminate Them": Written Accounts of the Murder, Rape, and Slavery of Native Americans during the California Gold Rush, 1848–1868* (East Lansing: Michigan State University Press, 1999), 157–58.

13. Renée Samson Flood, *Lost Bird of Wounded Knee: Spirit of the Lakota* (New York: Scribner, 1995), 70.

14. "Petition for Guardianship," Clallam County Probate Case no. 27, 1878, Washington State Archives, Northwest Regional Branch, Bellingham, Washington (hereafter WSA-NW). Thanks to Katrina Jagodinsky for sharing this and similar cases with me.

15. Sherry L. Smith, *The View from Officers' Row: Army Perceptions of Western Indians* (Tucson: University of Arizona Press, 1990), 72–74, 78.

16. Nelson, *Little Strangers*, 2, 5, 54–55, 117, 123; Melosh, *Strangers and Kin*, 12–13; and Berebitsky, *Like Our Very Own*, 21.

17. See, for example, Melosh, *Strangers and Kin*, 4, 158; and Sandra Patton, *BirthMarks: Transracial Adoption in Contemporary America* (New York: New York University Press, 2000), 37.

18. Flood, *Lost Bird*, 46–86. For more on other army officers who sought to adopt children, see Smith, *View from Officers' Row*, 73, 78.

19. Frances Gillmor and Louisa Wade Wetherill, *Traders to the Navajos: The Story of the Wetherills of Kayenta* (Albuquerque: University of New Mexico Press, 1953).

20. Interview with Betty Rodgers by Brad Cole, July 14, 1999, United Indian Traders Association Oral History Project, Cline Library, Special Collections, Northern Arizona University, Flagstaff, Arizona, www.nau.edu/library/speccoll/exhibits/traders/oralhistories/oralhist.html. All subsequent quotes from Betty Rodgers are from this interview.

21. Gillmor and Wetherill, *Traders to the Navajos*, 202–4.

22. Ibid., 230–32; quotes from 231 and 232.

23. *The Indian's Friend* 3, no. 3 (November 1890).

24. Lori Van Pelt, "Estelle Reel, Pioneer Politician," *True West* 47, no. 4 (April 2000): 53.

25. Stan Steiner, ed., *Spirit Woman: The Diaries and Paintings of Bonita Wa Wa Calachaw Nuñez* (San Francisco: Harper & Row, 1980), 2. The capitalization and emphases in Wa Wa Chaw's writing are part of her unique style.

26. Ibid., 8, 28, 29, 75.

27. Ibid., 3, 30.

28. Flood, *Little Bird*, 70–81; Title XXV, Probate Court, chapter II, Adoption of Children, Statutes of the State of Nebraska, 1891, 4th edition, 956–57.

29. Flood, *Lost Bird*, 79–80, 86.

30. Steiner, *Spirit Woman*, xii, xiii, 1, 3.

31. Mrs. Oresmus Bronson Boyd (Frances Anne Mullen Boyd), *Cavalry Life in Tent and Field*, with an introduction by Darlis Miller (Lincoln: University of Nebraska Press, 1982), 64–65.

32. Ibid., 150.

33. Sherry Smith notes that many army officers and their wives were drawn to Indian children. She also describes the mutual distrust of Indian and white families, both of whom feared "their children's admirers would steal them." Smith, *View from the Officers' Row*, 76–78; quote from 78.

34. Berebitsky, *Like Our Very Own*, 20–22.

35. See my *White Mother to a Dark Race: Settler Colonialism, Maternalism, and the Removal of Indigenous Children in the American West and Australia, 1880–1940* (Lincoln: University of Nebraska Press, 2009).

36. David Wallace Adams, *Education for Extinction: American Indians and the Boarding School Experience, 1875–1928* (Lawrence: University Press of Kansas, 1995), 57, 58.

37. The same was true for Canada. See Suzanne Fournier and Ernie Crey, *Stolen from Our Embrace: The Abduction of First Nations Children and the Restoration of Aboriginal Communities* (Vancouver: Douglas and McIntyre, 1997).

38. Jacobs, *White Mother*, particularly 149–92.

39. Ibid., particularly 193–228.

40. Kay Bennett, *Kaibah: Recollection of a Navajo Girlhood* (Los Angeles: Westernlore Press, 1964), 194, 196.

41. Gillmor and Wetherill, *Traders to the Navajos*, 51–56; quotes from 58. Wetherill became close friends with a Navajo man, Wolfkiller. She took down his life story in the Navajo language and translated it into English. Later her great grandson discovered it in her papers and had it published. See Louisa Wade Wetherill and Harvey Leake, *Wolfkiller: Wisdom from a Nineteenth-Century Navajo Shepherd* (Layton, UT: Gibbs Smith, 2007).

42. Gillmor and Wetherill, *Traders to the Navajos*, 197–98; quote from 200.

43. Melosh, *Strangers and Kin*, 2–3; and Berebitsky, *Like Our Very Own*, 8.

44. Nelson, *Little Strangers*, 188, 123; and Berebitsky, *Like Our Very Own*, 57, 79. For more on maternalism, see Jacobs, *White Mother*, 88–95.

45. Charlotte Perkins Gilman, *Herland, The Yellow Wallpaper, and Selected Writings* (1915; reprint, New York: Penguin, 1999).

46. Nelson, *Little Strangers*, 124–25, 128, 130; and Berebitsky, *Like Our Very Own*, 103–13.

47. Melosh, *Strangers and Kin*, 19–21; Berebitsky, *Like Our Very Own*, 18, 23, 31–35; and Regina Kunzel, *Fallen Women, Problem Girls: Unmarried Mothers and the Professionalization of Social Work, 1890–1945* (New Haven, CT: Yale University Press, 1993) 6, 14–17, 89, 49, 52–56, 128–30, 155.

48. See Berebitsky, *Like Our Very Own*, 33–34, 37–40, 43.

49. Nelson, *Little Strangers*, 2; Melosh, *Strangers and Kin*, 40, 109; and Berebitsky, *Like Our Very Own*, 129–37.

50. Nelson, *Little Strangers*, 125; and Berebitsky, *Like Our Very Own*, 102–26.

51. Whatcom County Probate Case no. 89, 1859, WSA-NW.

52. See Jefferson County Probate Index no. 2122, 1874, Clallam County Probate Case no. 27, 1878, and Clallam County Probate Case no. 18, 1876, WSA-NW.

53. "Petition for Appointment of Guardian," Skagit County Probate Case no. 2, WSA-NW.

54. *The Indian's Friend* 38, no. 3 (January 1926): 7.

55. *The Indian's Friend* 12, no. 12 (August 1900): 12.

56. *The Indian's Friend* 3, no. 3 (November 1890).

57. Jacobs, *White Mother*, esp. 87–148.

58. Flood, *Lost Bird*, 175, 130.
59. Melosh, *Strangers and Kin*, 39.
60. For more on the involuntary sterilization of Indian women, see Sally J. Torpy, "Native American Women and Coerced Sterilization: On the Trail of Tears in the 1970s," *American Indian Culture and Research Journal* 24, no. 2 (2000): 1–22; and Jane Lawrence, "The Indian Health Service and the Sterilization of Native American Women," *American Indian Quarterly* 24, no. 3 (Summer 2000): 400–419.
61. Fournier and Crey, *Stolen from Our Embrace*; Human Rights and Equal Opportunity Commission, *Bringing Them Home: Report of the National Inquiry into the Separation of Aboriginal and Torres Strait Islander Children from Their Families* (Canberra: Commonwealth of Australia, 1997).
62. Patrick Wolfe, "Land, Labor, and Difference: Elementary Structures of Race," *American Historical Review* 106, no. 3 (June 2001): 866–1006.
63. Jacobs, *White Mother*, esp. 25–86.
64. *The Indian's Friend* 15, no. 1 (September 1902).
65. Mary Dissette to Frederick Hodge, March 7, 1924, MS.7.MAI.1.163, Frederick Hodge papers, Braun Library, Autry National Center's Southwest Museum of the American Indian, Los Angeles, California.
66. *The Indian's Friend* 16, no. 6 (February 1904): 5.
67. Flood, *Lost Bird*.
68. Zintka Colby to Clara Colby, January 10, 1904, Box 2, Clara Bewick Colby Papers, Wisconsin State Historical Society, Madison (hereafter Colby Papers).
69. Flood, *Lost Bird*, 180–81, 203, 206–10, 214–16, 252.
70. Ibid., 158–59.
71. Ibid., 159–60, 205.
72. Zintka Colby to Clara Colby, March 17–20, 1904, Box 2, Colby Papers.
73. Zintka Colby to Clara Colby, September 22 and September 30, 1905, Box 2, Colby Papers; and Flood, *Lost Bird*, 217–20, 224–31, 233–35, 239, 242.
74. Zintka Colby to Clara Colby, January 9, 1906, Box 2, Colby Papers.
75. Flood, *Lost Bird*, 234, 246–50, 267–80.
76. Ibid., 253–58, 260–62, 274–76, 279–85, 289–90, 293, 297–99.
77. Steiner, *Spirit Woman*, 7, 8, 10.
78. Ibid., 16, xiii, xiv, 78.
79. Flood, *Lost Bird*, 116, 127, 285.
80. Steiner, *Spirit Woman*, 9, 21.
81. Ibid., 49–50, 71, 21, 14–15.
82. Ibid., 100; and Flood, *Lost Bird*, 217–18.
83. For a full picture of Pratt's views, see Richard Henry Pratt, *Battlefield and Classroom: Four Decades with the American Indian, 1867–1904*, with an introduction by Robert Utley (New Haven, CT: Yale University Press, 1964).
84. Steiner, *Spirit Woman*, 101, 114.
85. Ibid., 101, 129, 130.
86. Ibid., 107, 110–11, xiii, 112.
87. Ibid., 230, xiv.
88. Ibid., 74–76, 83–84; quotes from 75 and 76.
89. Ibid., xiv.
90. Wa Wa Chaw's artwork is finally gaining recognition. See Kathleen E. Ash-Milby, "Indian Identity and Evaluating the Past: Bonita Wa Wa Calachaw Nuñez and an Indian Princess Painter," in *Painters, Patrons, and Identity: Essays in Native American Art to Honor J. J. Brody*, ed. Joyce Szabo

(Albuquerque: University of New Mexico Press, 2001), 119–40. The National Cowboy and Western Heritage Museum in Oklahoma City held an exhibit of Wa Wa Chaw's paintings from September 19, 2009, through May 9, 2010.

91. For examples of these studies, see David Fanshel, *Far from the Reservation: The Transracial Adoption of American Indian Children* (Metuchen, NJ: Scarecrow Press, 1972); and Rita J. Simon and Howard Altstein, *Transracial Adoption* (New York: John Wiley and Sons, 1977).

92. Flood, *Lost Bird,* 114–15. In fact, Clara's friend Elaine Goodale Eastman wrote a fictionalized account of Zintka's life, *Yellow Star,* in which Zintka becomes an assimilated field matron (263).

93. Ibid., 133–34; quote from 134.

94. Ann Fessler, *The Girls Who Went Away: The Hidden History of Women Who Surrendered Children for Adoption in the Decades Before Roe v. Wade* (New York: Penguin Press, 2006).

2

Becoming Comanches

Patterns of Captive Incorporation into Comanche Kinship Networks, 1820–1875

Joaquín Rivaya-Martínez

On September 15, 1866, a Comanche named Kerno captured ten-year-old Bianca Babb during a raid in Wise County, Texas. Kerno placed Bianca in the care of his childless sister Tekwashana, whose husband had died in the course of the raid. Tekwashana tried to teach Bianca the Comanche language and manners. According to Bianca, "This woman was always good to me . . . she never scolded me, and seldom ever corrected me. . . . She was always very thoughtful of me and seemed to care as much for me as if I was her very own child. . . . I was made to know and realize that my life was to be a regular Indian life." However, Bianca's fictive kin did not always treat her like a blood relative. In times of scarcity, she wrote, "some member of the family would hand out certain portions of the dried meat to each member of the family, and many times they did not give me any, as long as two days at a time I would go hungry." Around April 1867, a man named Jacob Sturm exchanged Bianca for articles worth $333.[1] When Bianca showed her willingness to leave the Comanches, she remembered, "my Mother Squaw [Tekwashana] was crying. . . . She said if I wanted to leave her it was because I did not love her."[2] Bianca's ransom epitomizes the ambivalent nature of Comanche captivity.

This chapter explores the mechanisms by which Euro-Americans captured by Comanche Indians between 1820 and 1875 became incorporated into Comanche kinship networks.[3] Recent scholarship on the U.S. Southwest has brought attention to the widespread indigenous practice of taking captives and its enormous repercussions on the history of the borderlands.[4] Diverse authors have highlighted the importance of captives in the political economy of the Comanches, in Comanche relations with other groups, and for population replacement.[5] Little attention has been paid, however, to the experiences of the captives themselves.[6]

Much of what has been published on the subject is based on (auto-)biographical captivity narratives written by, on, and for Anglos.[7] Here I will use information from archival documents, ethnographic data, and linguistic evidence, drawing fundamentally upon some previously untapped testimonies of Hispanic captives, oral traditions and family histories obtained through personal interviews with descendants of both captives and captors. The quantitative data presented here comes from a sample of more than eight hundred individuals captured by Comanches between 1820 and 1875.[8]

Some of my interpretations of the captive experience depart from earlier explanations offered by scholars such as James Brooks or Pekka Hämäläinen, who tend to overemphasize materialistic considerations. Instead, I stress the multiplicity of Comanche motivations for taking captives and for their subsequent treatment of them, which certainly depended on Comanche labor needs but also relied on the weight of Comanche kinship traditions, reproductive considerations, the development of ties of affection between abductees and captors, and the individual performance of captives themselves. Pre-reservation Comanche practices of captivity and incorporation were the result of specific historical circumstances that gave rise to a peculiar rank society articulated to a large extent around kinship.[9] Within Comanche families, however, power and love intertwined in complex ways. The incorporation of captives often lasted many years, and it did not always culminate in de facto full-fledged membership in the family. Still, the stories of some captives reveal that in the nineteenth-century American West ethnic differences and hierarchies believed to be insuperable were sometimes permeable to relationships of love and affection even in the face of overwhelming adversity. In light of the evidence presented here, Hämäläinen's contention that Comanches "transformed themselves into large-scale slaveholders" must be called into question.[10]

Following my Comanche consultants' usage, I employ the term "full-blood" to refer to individuals whose known ancestry is entirely Comanche. "Comanche by birth" refers to both full-bloods and descendants from incorporated captives. I use "Euro-American," "Hispanic," and "Anglo" as cultural categories to designate groups irrespective of the genetic makeup of their members. By "Euro-Americans" I mean individuals born in European-speaking communities, including both "Hispanics" (individuals born in Spanish-speaking communities) and "Anglos" (non-Hispanic Euro-Americans). This distinction replicates an equivalent Comanche terminological differentiation between *yutaibo* (literally, ordinary non-Indian person) and *pabotaibo* (light-skinned non-Indian person).[11]

Between 1820 and 1875, the Shoshonean-speaking, equestrian Comanches (*Nʉmʉnʉʉ*) lived in residential bands of several dozen to a few hundred people spread widely over the Southern Plains and peripheral regions. Bands closely related by kinship ties and frequent interactions formed larger sociopolitical divisions. Comanches relied largely on hunting for their subsistence, whereas the acquisition of wealth depended fundamentally on raiding and trading.[12]

Comanche interpersonal relations were generally based on age, gender, kinship, and relative rank, which created a fluid system of inequalities. Status differences were neither permanent nor hereditary, depending primarily on the performance of each person, which the group reevaluated constantly.[13] Comanches were a caring, loving people to their own, particularly to their children. English-born captive Sarah Ann Horn put it thus: "The strength of their attachment to each other, and the demonstrations they give of the same . . . might put many professed christians [sic] to the blush!"[14] Similarly, in the words of Texan captive Theodore (Dot) Babb, "In their relations with one another they were considerate and tolerant, and did not fall out, fight, and kill each other as do the white men."[15]

An androcentric, martial ethos permeated most aspects of Comanche social life. Comanche males earned prestige and status through success on the warpath and generosity in the distribution of plunder. Women worked in a variety of household activities, some of which were physically demanding, including cooking, caregiving, gathering plants, working hides, making garments, carrying water, firewood, and the products of the hunt, packing and unpacking most household belongings when moving camp, and occasionally helping with the horses as well.[16] Comanches recognized the value of women's work and often rewarded outstanding female workers. Nevertheless, characteristically male activities, especially raiding, enjoyed more prestige than work traditionally performed by women. As Bianca Babb wrote, "If a man should ever do any work such as getting wood and water, [or] setting up tents[,] he would be ridiculed by all the rest of the tribe."[17]

Involvement with horses and Euro-American commodities made Comanches reliant on horse pastoralism and predatory expeditions starting around 1700. A growing competition over natural resources, horses, and trade boosted Comanche warfare and raids on other groups. Between roughly the 1740s and the 1850s, Comanches imposed their military and commercial hegemony over much of the Great Plains. To satisfy their want for livestock and prestige, Comanche warriors raided frequently in Texas and northern Mexico, where they acquired large numbers of horses, captives, and other loot.[18] The acquisition of individually owned horses, access to Euro-American commodities, and differential success in raiding and trading accentuated inequalities within Comanche society, which resulted in its stratification into three ranks: the wealthy *(tsaanaakatʉ)*, consisting largely of successful raiders and their immediate relatives; the poor *(tahkapʉ)*; and the extremely poor *(tʉbitsi tahkapʉ)*.[19]

Comanche raiders abducted children and young adult women from enemy groups, but they generally killed adult males on the spot.[20] Captives belonged to their captors, who sometimes gave them away to a relative or sold them to nonkin.

The receivers were usually childless couples or individuals in need of a caregiver. The status of a captive could change over time, from that of an enslaved outsider to that of a fully integrated adoptee.[21] Comanche language differentiates between the generic idiom *nʉ kwʉhupʉ*, meaning "my captive," which could be applied to any captive irrespective of status, and the noun *tʉrʉʔaiwapi*, meaning "slave" or "servant," which denoted an enslaved captive.[22]

Comanches captured outsiders for a variety of reasons, but they most commonly acquired captives for their labor. Servants could significantly lighten the workload of the women in the captor's household. Seizing an enemy under dangerous circumstances brought prestige to the captor, and so did the conspicuous display of captives. Comanches could also enhance their status and political influence by giving away, adopting, or marrying captives to replace deceased kin or augment the pool of dependable relatives and followers. Other important enticements to abduct outsiders were the possibilities that one might incorporate or sell them. Comanches also occasionally seized enemies to avenge the death of Comanche kinsfolk.[23]

Comanches generally subjected recently acquired captives to corporal and psychological trials to test their hardiness, personal character, and ability to obey orders and behave according to Comanche expectations.[24] The mistreatment also served to confuse the captives, create in them a dependence on their captors, and instill in them enough fear to prevent them from attempting to escape.[25] The early captivity of Macario Leal is typical.

Sometime in 1847 a Comanche party seized Macario, a boy some thirteen years old, on the outskirts of Laredo, Texas. During the next couple of days, as they traveled, the Indians whipped Macario repeatedly for failing to obey their orders. When the raiders arrived at their hideout, "they unhorsed him, stripped him, and he began to suffer the torment inflicted by the Indians." Days later, a similar scene took place when they returned to their main encampment. As Macario declared after his successful escape seven years later, "That night they gave him a dance that they formed around a big bonfire. Comanches forced him to participate in it with his brother's scalp, which one of the Indians had taken when they killed him. His assignment in that encampment was to become the tender of the [horse] herd, and, since he could not do it properly because there were too many animals, they punished him frequently; thus he learned their language in a year."[26]

In general, Comanches made chattel slaves of those captives whom they did not readily adopt. Masters could sell, inherit, give away, or even kill enslaved captives at will. Martina Díaz, captured at age sixteen near Laredo in December 1871, spent a year in captivity before she managed to escape. Interrogated by U.S. officials in 1873, she declared that "she was treated as a general servant in the camp, and was outraged by her captor," and when he died she "became a slave to his sister."[27] Deprived of any inherent rights or social standing, and lacking Comanche kin, enslaved captives were absolutely powerless.[28]

The outrages that enslaved captives suffered contrast sharply with the way that the Comanches treated one another. Comanche masters—or, more commonly, other members of their households—often forced enslaved captives to work until exhausted doing dangerous tasks, sometimes under severe weather conditions. They could beat their slaves, sometimes harshly, when they did not perform their chores satisfactorily or they failed to behave as expected. Occasionally captives froze to death while tending horses in the winter.[29] Five Hispanic boy captives, the oldest of whom was fifteen at the time of capture, declared in 1873 "that they were abused by the Indians, having little food and no clothing, left exposed to sun and cold, and worked to exhaustion in herding and cleaning horses. At times the captive boys were horsewhipped till the blood ran."[30] In the words of Texan captive Clinton Smith, in his camp, "All the captives were worked packing meat and washing the robes, sometimes working thus for two whole days; also cleaning and herding horses.... The Comanches are very rough with their captive boys and whip them terribly, sometimes killing them if they cry over the beating."[31] This maltreatment could last for as long as the captive remained in a servile position, sometimes the entire length of the captivity. Comanche slavery, however, was neither hereditary nor necessarily permanent.

Although the socialization of unincorporated captives depended largely on the individual character of their masters, it generally was significantly different from that of Comanche children. The manner in which this was probably most obvious to the captives themselves was the comparative lack of affection in their upbringing, especially in the case of the older captives. The use of violence in the education of Comanche children was extremely rare. In the words of Bianca Babb, "In all the time I was with them, I do not remember of seeing them correct or punish one." Instead, Comanches taught their offspring largely by word and example.[32] Captives with no Comanche kin could not count on the teachings of relatives whose contribution was paramount in the education of Comanche children. Moreover, much of the captives' learning took place at work, whereas Comanche children had to do relatively little work until they were in their teens.[33] The treatment could change over time, as ties of affection developed between captives and members of the families holding them, and as captives became increasingly acculturated. Both of these circumstances paved the way for their incorporation. Margaret Jacobs and Katrina Jagodinsky discuss similar processes involving adopted Indians and Indian servants, respectively, in this volume.

The ability to communicate and interact in culturally appropriate ways was a key factor conditioning the incorporation of noninfant captives. However, "communicative competence" was not the only requirement for an outsider to be accepted into the Comanche community, and birth was not a negligible factor.[34]

Euro-American captives had to adjust to new roles and behaviors in a highly nomadic camp lifestyle, and to the idiosyncrasies of their Comanche interlocutors. Captives had to assimilate quickly Comanche notions of childhood, adulthood, parenthood, family, and belonging. They also had to learn what types of speech suited each context. Captives had to remember, for instance, never to use the name of the dead in the presence of the deceased's relatives, and not to approach young individuals of the opposite sex without having been expressly authorized to do so.[35]

During the earliest stage of captivity, Comanches generally watched abductees closely and kept them apart from captives with the same ethnic background, only rarely permitting them to visit or even talk to one another. As Martina Díaz declared, "Captives were only allowed to use the Comanche language, and to talk . . . on current matters of the camp."[36] Repeated punishments for failing to communicate in Comanche and restrictions on captives' freedom of movement made learning the Comanche language and customs a matter of survival. Conversely, captives' good behavior generally resulted in the easing or removal of those restrictions.

To what degree captives assimilated Comanche culture depended fundamentally on their age at the time of capture. The captive's sex and the length of captivity were other important factors. Life experiences in the early years play a decisive role in shaping an individual's personality and self-identity. The capacity of most people to learn a language with native proficiency begins to decline at age six or seven, whereas the ability to become fluent in a language other than one's mother tongue decreases considerably after age twelve or thirteen.[37] Accordingly, Comanches had a preference for capturing children between five and twelve years old (more than 61 percent of all abductees), who were young enough to learn Comanche quickly and proficiently (see figure 2.1). Older captives spoke only broken Comanche and tried to run away much more often.[38] Occasionally, however, even people seized in their teens became proficient in Comanche.[39] In the case of young girls the acculturation process could be rather short, as it was encouraged by their constant involvement in female collective activities that were facilitated by fluent communication.[40] Most boy captives, in contrast, had to spend much of their time herding horses in relative isolation.

In tune with the androcentric nature of the Comanche ethos, over 66 percent of the captives in the sample were male (see figure 2.1).[41] Apparently, Comanche raiders had a preference for capturing boys between five and twelve years of age, who constituted over 46 percent of all abductees, whereas thirteen- to nineteen-year-old males comprised less than 14 percent. These figures contradict Hämäläinen's contention that "Comanches put special value on female captives" and adolescent males.[42] Arguably, on the farms and ranches where Comanches raided, boys working in the fields were easier prey than girls working nearer the

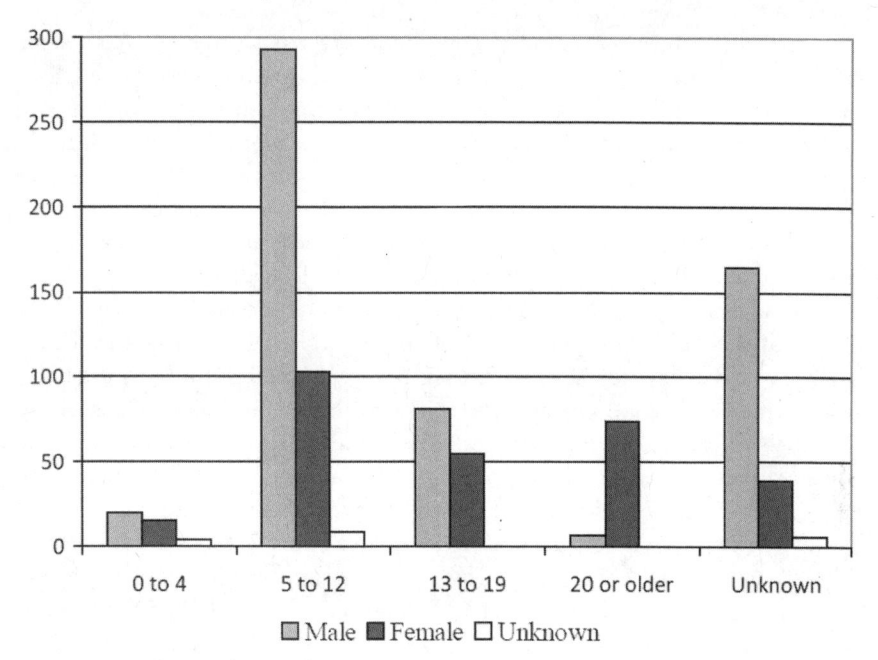

FIGURE 2.1. Captives' sex and age at capture

household. Most likely, though, their fondness for male captives was a consequence of the Comanches' constant demand for horse herding, a task customarily assigned to boys. Perhaps the apparent sexual selection was also due to the need to reach a balance in a society with a generally higher male mortality. However, Comanches dealt with this problem largely through polygyny (multiple-wife marriage), and postmortem levirate (the inheritance of widowed wives by a brother of the deceased husband).

The ease with which some captives adapted to Comanche culture puzzled many a Euro-American observer.[43] Thoroughly acculturated captives often opposed attempts to "redeem" them. Motherhood was likely one factor that deterred some female captives from leaving the Comanches willingly. Motherhood signaled an important promotion in the status of captive wives, and it creates strong emotional ties between mother and offspring. The stigma that frontier society ascribed to Euro-American women suspected of having sexual intercourse with Native males was probably another factor hindering women from leaving captivity, especially if they had become pregnant or had children in captivity.[44]

Comanches incorporated captives through adoption, marriage to a Comanche individual, or cooptation, that is, the acceptance of an outsider as an equal.[45] Incorporation could occur at any time, but only if the captive's overall demeanor or exceptional achievements proved that he or she was worthy of such a step. Generally, courageous captives who stood up for themselves fared better than those who did not.[46] Ultimately, though, incorporation depended upon the will of the masters, who often gradually gave their captives more freedom and rights over time.

Incorporation was not a communal decision, nor was it marked by a ceremony. Instead, it was realized in practice through private and public interactions (for example, addressing the captive as kin) that made evident to the larger Comanche community the captive's new status.[47] The extension of kinship terms to nonrelatives carried the expectation that both interlocutors (and their immediate kin) would behave to one another as if they were actual relatives.[48] Participation in rituals was another way of integrating captives into Comanche society. Comanches sometimes publicly honored captured women who became virtuous wives and honored captive men who had served admirably as warriors, for example by assigning them important roles in the preliminaries of the sun dance.[49]

Comanches often developed strong ties of love and affection with their captives, particularly with children.[50] This became particularly obvious upon the separation of some captives from their Comanche relatives. When Sarah Ann Horn was about to be sold in New Mexico, after about a year and two months in captivity, an old Comanche woman who had always been kind to her broke into tears and proceeded to paint Horn's "face, neck and arms, with a sort of red paint, which they thus use upon the persons of their friends, as one of the highest tokens of friendship."[51] Dot Babb, Bianca's brother, remembered the scene of his ransom with these words: "Not a few cried and wept bitterly, and notably one squaw and her son who had claimed me as son and brother and as such were my guardians and protectors, and to whose immediate family and household I had been attached.... The close companionship had cemented bonds of affection *almost* as sacred as family ties" (emphasis added).[52]

Michael Tate, Daniel Gelo, and Scott Zesch have suggested that Comanche captors had a premeditated intention to incorporate the people they kidnapped into their families.[53] Conversely, James Brooks and Pekka Hämäläinen emphasize the importance of captives in Comanche society as laborers and commodities.[54] Although both perspectives are correct to some extent, they ignore the existence in nineteenth-century Comanche society of different types of captives who were incorporated to differing degrees and were treated in various ways. Although captive labor was precious and captives certainly had value as potential commodities, materialistic considerations were never sufficient to reverse true adoptions, and Comanches were generally reluctant to let acculturated captives go. The few occasions when Comanches relinquished nonadopted acculturated captives, they did so under coercion or in exchange for full-blood Comanche prisoners, and generally after the captives' closest fictive male relatives had died.[55]

Comanches, especially childless families, could quickly adopt the infant captives, raising them as natural children, and expected them to reciprocate appropriately.[56] This required familiarity with the obligations, taboos, and avoidance rules that regulated Comanche kinship relations.[57] Adoptees had to stay away from siblings of the opposite sex, learn Comanche forms of courtship, intimacy, and marriage, and learn the appropriate ways of, and occasions for, showing affection or restraint. Married captives had to avoid joking with their parents-in-law and be willing to share their spouses with their siblings of the same sex through the widespread Comanche habits of the levirate (the sharing of wives among brothers), and the sororate (the marriage of several sisters to the same husband).

Comanche testimonies generally refer to adopted captives as the "children" of their adopters, and captives often referred to their Comanche relatives as parents or siblings.[58] Comanche parents sometimes referred to adoptees by adding the suffix *boopʉ*, "adopted," or *toyapʉ*, "lifted" or "claimed," to the regular terms for "son" (*tua*) and "daughter" (*petʉ*).[59] Adoptees could become favorite children in childless families even if they later had full-blood siblings. A favorite child rarely had to work, wore special garments, and could boss his or her siblings around. In addition, parents often made gifts in the honor of their favorite, whom everyone would treat with indulgence.[60] This institutionalized status was probably extended to Cynthia Ann Parker, whose Comanche name, Narua, literally means "favorite."[61]

Often Comanche masters addressed their captives as relatives, thereby distinguishing them from actual slaves, but continued to treat them as nonkin in some ways.[62] There is no specific Comanche term for this status, called "filial servitude" by several nineteenth-century observers. This status was generally extended to kidnapped children who had the potential to become acculturated, and whom Comanches thus considered prospective adoptees or wives.[63] Filial servants, irrespective of their age or sex, generally occupied the lowest sibling status in their households. Meaningfully, an older sibling could apply the term *tʉrʉʔaiwapi*, "slave," to a younger one, although "this was considered being particularly unpleasant."[64]

Sometimes the boundaries between adoption, filial servitude, and slavery blurred. Although the fictive parents of filial servants often treated them benevolently, other members of their household still might overwork, boss, or occasionally even abuse them. Furthermore, the extension of fictive kinship to captives did not automatically imply their acceptance as a full member by all Comanches. Bianca Babb, for instance, was clearly not treated as a slave. However, the facts that Bianca did not partake of the emergency food, that she often performed exhausting tasks in the company of a "regular servant," that she was eventually sold, and that her petition of an allotment of Comanche land was rejected indicate that her incorporation into Comanche society as an equal was never fully realized.[65]

In a sense, Comanche filial servitude was not unique. After all, children generally had a relatively low status everywhere in the United States in the nineteenth century, and they were expected to obey, defer to, and provide labor for their parents or other adult relatives. Children also often played significant economic roles in their households, particularly among the underprivileged.[66] Considering the foreign origin, lower status, more demanding roles, and occasional mistreatment of these semi-incorporated children compared to Comanches by birth, perhaps the closest parallel can be found in the detribalized Indian servants of the U.S. Southwest (see the contribution of Katrina Jagodinsky to this volume).

The status and treatment of nonadopted female captives depended fundamentally on whether their captors held them as potential wives or simply as menials or concubines.[67] They carried out the same tasks as Comanche women and became eligible for marriage once they learned the Comanche language and customs. Girls seized before age twelve often became acculturated and married Comanche men. Female captives, however, might continue to be treated as servants even after marriage, as was "Mexican" captive Francisca, who was reportedly "whipped, mistreated, and beaten all the time she was a captive and a wife in the Comanche tribe."[68]

The autobiographical story of Herkeyah is perhaps most illustrative in this regard. An acculturated captive named Toyop (Neck) captured Herkeyah in Mexico when she was a little girl. He was about to kill her when a widower named Wahaomo (Two Legs) "felt sorry for her and thought of his own children ... so he picked her up and put her on his mule." Sometime later, Wahaomo told Herkeyah "that when she grew up she would be his wife." He also told a niece of his who "was running his camp ... to be good to her (sometimes they were very mean to captives), and to look after her so no men would harm her." Wahaomo himself had to watch Herkeyah closely after a young man tried to steal her. Herkeyah's work was to look after Wahaomo's children, one of whom was crippled and needed to be carried on Herkeyah's back. Wahaomo "slept regularly with his former wife's younger sister," Puki, but he taught Herkeyah to hunt and treated her kindly. As a result, Puki "would take a stick from the fire and poke it at her in jealousy to scare her." When this happened the children regularly tried to help Herkeyah against Puki. In two years Herkeyah already "knew the language and was familiar with the customs."

When Herkeyah was about twelve years old, her captor, Toyop, lost his wife during a battle with U.S. troops, so he "begged Wahaomo to give her back to him" so that she could care for an aged male relative. Wahaomo consented and announced to his children that "their mother was going to leave," at which time both Herkeyah and the children cried. Toyop's family treated Herkeyah badly, beating her often.[69] Later, after some Osages killed Wahaomo, Herkeyah drifted to another band, which suggests that the death of a captive's protector could have major consequences.[70] Indeed, if an outsider killed a Comanche the relatives of the deceased might try to take revenge on some nonadopted captive of the same ethnic extraction as the killer, occasionally beating or even slaying the captive.

Meaningfully, a number of runaway captives decided to flee the Comanches because they felt threatened after the death of their immediate Comanche "kin." Herkeyah eventually married a Comanche named Tissypahqueschy, and later a second husband named Esahaupt, mothering children from both men.[71] It must be noted that divorce was rather common in pre-reservation Comanche society.[72]

Captive wives typically occupied the lowest rank in polygynous marriages, which enabled the full-blood wives to exploit them, sometimes pitilessly.[73] All co-wives were subservient to the husband, but they had differing status. The chief wife, usually the first to be married to a man and generally a Comanche by birth, exerted her authority over her junior co-wives and generally benefited from their labor. The same dynamic applied to every other wife in relation to those of inferior rank. A Comanche husband could sell his captive wife only if they had no children in common. Conversely, mothering could raise the status of captured wives within the family.[74] Rivalries among the full-blood wives could benefit a captive wife. More rarely, the latter could even rise to the position of chief wife, especially after having children. Therefore, although a captive co-wife could certainly alleviate the workload of the other wives, she was also a potential rival for the affection of the husband and for the status of chief wife. All things considered, a Comanche wife most likely would have preferred to have in the household a servant boy instead, whom she could put to use doing work typically assigned to women.[75]

Scholars have overemphasized the economic value of captured women as processors of bison hides in Comanche households.[76] Both Brooks and Hämäläinen contend that a correlation existed between Comanche involvement in the hide traffic, the supposed expansion of Comanche polygyny since the late eighteenth century, and purported peaks in Comanche raiding.[77] This theory is disputable on at least four grounds. First, the incorporation of seized enemy women into Comanche polygynous arrangements was common since at least 1750, that is, several decades prior to the boom of the hide trade on the Southern Plains. Moreover, this practice continued into the reservation period despite the disappearance of the bison and notwithstanding repeated U.S. attempts to suppress it.[78] Second, Comanches were not as involved in the bison hide trade as other Plains groups.[79] Indeed, horses were by and large the main commodity in Comanche transactions throughout the nineteenth century. Third, Comanches often assigned "female" tasks, including hide processing, to male captives, as Hämäläinen implicitly acknowledges.[80] Fourth, although older women also processed hides, the majority of female abductees were girls or young adults (see figure 2.1). Out of 141 female captives, only nine were twenty-six years or older at the time of capture.

All in all, Comanche polygyny and demand for captive women does not seem to have depended on the fluctuations of the hide market. Instead, Comanche interest in young adult women was most likely a function of their attractiveness and presumed fertility. Comanche captors, typically young men, rarely captured boys over fifteen years old, who accounted for less than 8 percent of all captive males (see figure 2.1). Conversely, Comanches relatively often captured women sixteen to twenty-nine years, a group that totaled 31 percent of all female captives. The fact that Comanches did not fully incorporate captive wives until they had children makes clear that they valued their reproductive capacity more than any physical work they could perform. Meaningfully, "barrenness on the part of a wife was considered a valid excuse for leaving her."[81] On the other hand, despite the Comanches' permanent need for herders, only rarely did they assign young female captives to help with the horses, typically doing so only when moving camp. On the other hand, Comanches systematically assigned captured boys to herd livestock, sometimes alone and often at considerable distances from camp. Such gendered discrimination can be explained as a deliberate decision to preserve the captured females' virginity and reproductive capacity, and hence their value, intact. Moreover, Comanches closely watched potential captive wives, and if someone raped a captive they generally abandoned or killed the victim.[82]

Success on the warpath was the overriding factor in the status of nonadopted male captives. Comanches systematically compelled male captives to take care of their livestock, and sometimes to break horses or do women's work, and occasionally they required skilled captives to repair guns, do silverwork, or make saddles. However, male captives could improve their social standing by showing courage and respect. Those who distinguished themselves in warfare generally enjoyed the same rights as Comanches by birth.[83]

Like Comanche-born youths, captured boys started to participate in raids in their teens, sometimes against their will. As Clinton Smith recalls, "All the boys over twelve years old were compelled to go with them in their stealing raids."[84] Comanche warriors took their captives along only once they had earned their trust, which was contingent on the captive's ability to communicate fluently in Comanche.[85] Captive boys often accompanied raiders to perform as servants and herders, particularly during their first raids. Perhaps the role most typically served by a captive during a raiding party, however, was that of cook. In spite of the low prestige associated with cooking, usually a woman's chore, the cook played a fundamental role in a raid by preventing the contamination of the warriors' supernatural power. Significantly, when the partition of the plunder took place, the leader of the war party could offer first choice to the cook.[86]

Nonadopted captives had slave status until marriage, but if they married Comanche individuals, they and their offspring got the same rights as full-bloods.[87] Raiding was the main avenue by which captives could acquire wealth, which in turn enabled them to acquire a wife and become fully accepted by the group, particularly if they married a full-blood.[88] What attached male captives most to Comanches, John Louis Berlandier noted, was the fact that "they may win the right to marry. When they manage that, they lose no time in taking several wives and settling down as if they had been born to the life."[89]

Given their relative lack of status, it must not have been easy for nonadopted male captives to marry full-blood Comanche women. At least occasionally, Comanches may have preferred as prospective son-in-laws poor young captives who lacked strong kinship ties in the community but had earned a reputation for being industrious. Sometimes the relatives of a Comanche girl arranged her marriage with an unwealthy male. In such cases, the son-in-law generally moved in with the bride's parents or moved near them. There he was expected to help tend his father-in-law's horses, receiving some in return, and to provide his mother-in-law with meat and hides. She reciprocated by making her son-in-law fine garments. This arrangement lasted only until the son-in-law accumulated enough property of his own, either through gifts or by raiding, which often occurred within a couple of years. According to Thomas Gladwin, a captive "made the most dependent, and hence reliable, son-in-law of all, though the lowered prestige of the resultant half-Comanche children was a deterrent to this practice."[90]

A brave captive who succeeded on the warpath became a *tekwʉniwapi* ("veteran," or "hero") who could lead a war party or even become headman of his own band.[91] Exceptional warrior captives could also achieve the prestigious status of club bearer, a position held by very few individuals and that entailed a leading role in ceremonial dances. Captives could also become powerful medicine men. All things considered, it is not surprising that some captives displayed daredevil performances on the warpath. Moreover, warriors of captive origin often participated in raids on the settlements of their original kinsfolk.[92]

Nevertheless, becoming a Comanche warrior must not have been easy for captives, especially for those who did not participate in the careful military training that Comanche boys typically received from male relatives.[93] Again, Macario Leal's experience is illustrative. Once Macario was able to communicate in Comanche, a leader called Bajo el Sol (Under the Sun), who presumably was Macario's master, took him on his first campaign. During an encounter with American soldiers on the Colorado River in 1848, Bajo el Sol threatened to kill Macario unless he brought him a soldier "by the hair." Macario received "several bullet shots in the shield and one in the leg" before he returned to the Comanches empty-handed. They scorned him and "he replied that he was afraid of" the Americans. Bajo el Sol "told him many curses and bad arguments," adding "now you will see what it is to be a man ... of the chosen ones." Then the Comanche leader "entered the fight with his lance[,] ... dismounted[,] ... received twenty something bullet shots, and returned grabbing an American by the hair." He presented the American to Macario to fight, but the soldier was so much taller that Macario could not even move his opponent. After the American hit Macario with his spur, Bajo el Sol himself knocked down and killed the soldier. In total, Macario was shot seven times during his seven-year captivity. During his last year of captivity some Comanches took him on a raid into Nuevo León. There they ran across some muleteers, killing all of them except one, whom they spared so that Macario himself could kill him. Macario, however, declined to execute the unfortunate Mexican, and the Indians thrashed him.[94]

A Comanche man could co-opt a male captive through a peculiar institution, the "true friendship" *(tʉbitsinahaitsinʉʉ)*, a relationship characterized by sharing, mutual joking, and a perennial commitment to help each other in all matters.[95] Like the Spanish institution of compadrazgo described by Ramón Gutiérrez and Erica Pérez in this volume, a true friendship created a strong and enduring bond between two individuals and their families even if the people involved were not related by blood. True friendships usually consisted of a Comanche by birth and a captive or half blood. By acquiring the status of true friend to a full-blood, a Comanche captive became integrated into the latter's kinship networks. True friends became closer than biological kin and addressed each other as *haitsi* (friend). This term, however, could index an asymmetrical relationship by which, on the warpath, the less prestigious, subordinate individual acted as a servant of the dominant friend in return for a share of the plunder. A man used terms for his true friend's relatives that equated him with a brother. They had to observe the customary Comanche practice of brother-sister avoidance and associated taboos with each other's sisters. Children of true friends could not intermarry either.[96]

True friends had great respect for each other. They could share their wives, and, in case of infidelity, they might collect *nanʉwokʉ* (damages for adultery) from the unfaithful wife together, splitting the payment between them. If one were about to leave in a war party without his true friend, he might publicly announce that he entrusted his wife to his friend, who must provide meat for her. Generally, however, true friends went on the warpath together. One could not retreat in battle leaving the other behind. If one of the friends was killed, his father treated the survivor as if he were an adopted son, and both families mourned the deceased equally.

Most full-bloods had more power than most captives. Meaningfully, Comanches made a terminological distinction between Comanches by birth and individuals who "lived like Comanches," that is, acculturated captives.[97] Apparently a Comanche by birth could take a captive's wife at will unless the latter were a brave warrior.[98] Captors might keep certain rights over their nonadopted captives, even after the latter got married. If a captive were living with his captor, the latter might take over the loot taken by the former in a raid, but "if the captive was brave and treated his captor and family with respect, he generally had full rights as a warrior." If a captive had a family of his own, he could keep the horses and other booty that he stole; otherwise, it went to the captor.[99] Captives, like other low-ranking individuals, could compensate for their relative lack of power by allying themselves with powerful people. For instance, a captive betrayed by his wife could recruit a brave warrior to collect *nanʉwokʉ*.[100]

The relative lack of status of Comanche captives and their descendants was to some extent a function of their relatively small kinship networks. In pre-reservation Comanche society, interpersonal relations between unrelated individuals were based on "pragmatic considerations of relative power."[101] This was generally measured in terms of one's war record and ability to mobilize support. Comanches recognized kin ties on both the paternal and the maternal sides. Marriages generally took place within the division but outside the band. Comanche spouses had two sets of relatives, biological and affinal, in two different bands. Conversely, captives incorporated through marriage (and their children) could only claim kinship in one band through the full-blood spouse or parent.

The lack of kin connections, status, and power made unincorporated captives preferred targets for the rage of a Comanche by birth. Full-bloods sometimes looked down on captives of their same gender incorporated into other families, and they occasionally disparaged them in public. These attitudes seem to have been more prevalent among men. The stigmatization of male captives was interrelated with Comanche notions of masculinity. A full-blood could insult an incorporated male captive by calling him *kwʉhʉpʉ*. This term, literally meaning "caught" or "captured," conveyed the ideas of both "captive" and "wife" and denoted a lack of status. It was thus sometimes applied derogatorily to incorporated captives.[102] Male captives were also generally suspected of having engaged in female tasks during their early captivity. Occasionally, captured boys who had to spend a great deal of time helping with women's tasks ended up learning the female talk, which was significantly different from the men's in lexicon, pronunciation, and inflection[103] In addition, some captives never spoke Comanche with native fluency, and thus their speech itself became a permanent marker of their foreign origin.

Although individuals of captive descent enjoyed the same rights as full-bloods and could attain high-status and even leadership positions, Comanche testimonies about Quanah Parker indicate that full-bloods continued to remember their mixed ancestry. Quanah, the son of Anglo captive Cynthia Ann Parker and Comanche leader (Peta) Nokona, became an influential leader in reservation times, having as many as five wives in 1900, and a total of eight throughout his life.[104] According to Herman Asenap, Quanah was unpopular among full-bloods in spite of having a "great heart." In the view of Comanche consultant Niyah, most "chiefs" were against Quanah because of his "great influence with the whites." According to Howard White Wolf, however, some also disliked Quanah because of his "white strain."[105] "Comanche blood" and "captive ancestry" are still recurrent themes in contemporary Comanche discourses on memory and identity, which corroborates that those factors played a significant role in the degree of acceptance or stigmatization of captives and their descendants in the past.[106]

Captives and individuals of captive ancestry frequently exhibited a great deal of solidarity and often developed strong friendships with one another.[107] Their closeness was probably a function of the difficulty of strengthening ties with full-bloods. Sympathetic captives occasionally comforted recently kidnapped ones when they arrived in camp for the first time.[108] After several months in captivity, Mrs. Horn's son, Joseph, told his mother that "he had changed masters, and that the people with whom he lived were kind to him and gave him plenty to eat," in spite of the scarcity of meat that the Comanches were suffering at the time. Joseph's new "mistress" was a Hispanic captive who had married a Comanche. Much to Mrs. Horn's relief, this woman "appeared of an amiable disposition, and seemed much interested" in Joseph's care.[109]

Captives, people of captive descent, and individuals of non-Comanche ancestry frequently married among themselves. Out of 116 recorded marriages involving captives, 67 involved a full-blood spouse.[110] Polygamy was comparatively uncommon among incorporated captives.[111] Two Hispanic captives, Asenap (Grey Foot) and Wissische (Curly), however, each had two wives. Typically, Wissische's wives, Asequitsquip and Nahhah, were also captives. Exceptionally, another "Mexican" captive named Titchywy had as many as five wives; four were half-Mexican sisters, the fifth a "Mexican" captive herself. To this day, the descendants of the *Wia?nɨtɨ*, or "Worn Away People," a local band whose members settled in the Walters area of southwestern Oklahoma around 1900, are considered people of "Mexican" captive ancestry. More than likely, their name alludes to the highly mixed descent of its members.[112]

The patterns of incorporation outlined here remained remarkably unaltered between 1820 and 1875. The steady population loss that Comanches experienced during that period as a consequence of epidemic outbreaks and almost constant warfare led to the suppression of the sacrifice of captives during mourning rituals, a practice last documented in the 1830s.[113] Overall, Comanches seized more Hispanics (over 82 percent of all captives) than Anglos (16 percent), particularly in the 1840s and 1850s, the two decades when they captured the largest number of captives (over 70 percent). During those decades, Comanches took advantage of the Mexican-American rivalry and the vulnerability of the underprotected northern third of Mexico to escalate their incursions, which became more frequent and larger in scale, into that region.[114] Conversely, the largest numbers of Anglos were seized in the 1830s, as well as in the 1860s and early 1870s, when Comanche raids into Texas were most common (see figure 2.2).[115] In a context of overall population decline, the proportion of captives and people of captive ancestry living in Comanche camps grew over the course of the nineteenth century. By the 1900s, captives and people of captive descent amounted to over 40 percent of the Comanche population.[116] Nevertheless, I have found no solid evidence sug-

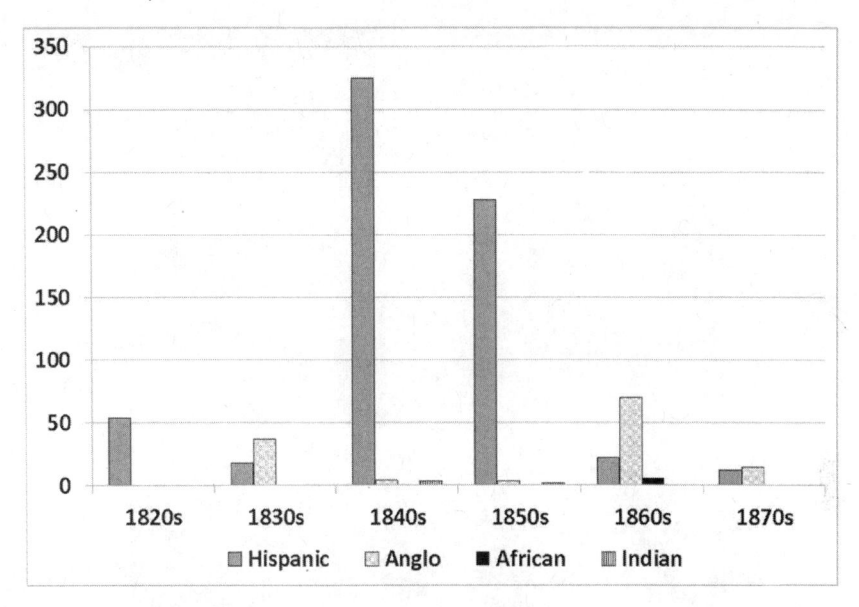

FIGURE 2.2. Captives' ethnic extraction by decade

gesting meaningful changes over time with regard to the preferred sex and age of captives, the rate of incorporation, attitudes toward captives, or the very meaning of captivity, probably because the expectations and needs around captives did not change significantly until the Comanches settled on reservations.

In 1875, in the wake of stunning Comanche population decline, the United States forced all Comanche bands to relocate to Indian Territory, mostly at the Kiowa-Comanche-Apache Reservation, in present-day southwestern Oklahoma. Reservation life and assimilation policies undermined Comanche traditional values and interfered with personal relationships, altering the kinship and behavioral patterns that constituted the backbone of pre-reservation Comanche society.[117] U.S. authorities compelled Comanches to stop raiding and release their non-Indian captives. Incorporated captives and their Comanche relatives pursued a variety of strategies to resist or circumvent these alienating impositions with unequal results. Generally, if the non-Comanche origin of a captive became apparent, the reservation agent offered the captive the option to stay with the Comanches.[118] Acculturated captives generally chose to stay with their Comanche relatives. Often, captives who were "redeemed," willingly or not, and returned to their biological kindred did not readapt to life in their communities of origin and sometimes died shortly after their return[119] Others, such as German-Texan Rudolph Fischer, managed to return to their Comanche kin and eventually

FIGURE 2.3. Semeno's tombstone in Highland Cemetery, Lawton, Oklahoma. Semeno ("Cartitlege" in Comanche) was captured somewhere in Mexico in the early 1870s when he was a young boy. He eventually married a Comanche woman called Patsebah. He was one of the captives who remained with the Comanches and received land at allotment time in 1901. Photograph by the author.

received land allotments in 1901.[120] All in all, more than forty captives who were still alive by 1901 received plots, and so did the descendants of these and other captives who had already died by then.[121]

The incorporation of captives into Comanche society between 1820 and 1875 was often an arduous process marked by deprivation, exploitation, and sometimes violence. Although Comanche families commonly adopted the youngest captives quickly, they often enslaved the older ones. In tune with their highly androcentric ethos, Comanches had a preference for capturing boys. However, both male and female captives had the potential for full incorporation, which generally was the culmination of a process initiated through the extension of fictive kinship to the captive, by which the captive gradually received more rights over time. Some captives already addressed as kin were actually in a situation of filial servitude, which was often a transitory phase that preceded their full incorporation. In a society marked by nonhereditary rank distinctions, the individual performance of captives and their sociocultural malleability could significantly influence their ultimate destiny. Although male captives could improve their condition through military success and marriage to Comanche women, motherhood granted power and introduced love in the lives of female captives. In a sense, forging Comanche families empowered captives. The status of many captives, however, remained ambiguous even after incorporation. Ancestry was an important factor in Comanche interpersonal relationships, which often placed captives at a disadvantage. Full-bloods generally had more power than captives and their descendants, whom they sometimes stigmatized. Conversely, captives and people of mixed descent built strong friendships and married among themselves frequently.

Although Euro-American captives had to acclimate themselves to Comanche cultural expectations and social conventions, often under harsh conditions, the guidance and affection that individuals of diverse ancestry dispensed to some captives mitigated the hardships of incorporation. Sometimes the relationship between captives and captors changed as dominance and authority gave way to affection and love. "Redemption" and the return to "civilization" sometimes turned out to be traumatic experiences in their own right. Some captives moved across cultural barriers that seemed insurmountable to their contemporaries. Their remarkable lives bear testimony to the violent past of the American West, but also to the adaptiveness and resilience of the human body and mind, and, in some cases, to the power of love.

NOTES

This essay benefits from research funded by the University of California Institute for Mexico and the United States (UC MEXUS), the Phillips Fund Grant, the American Philosophical Society, the Newberry Library, the Wenner-Gren Foundation for Anthropological Research, the UCLA Institute of American Cultures, the UCLA Department of Anthropology, and the UCLA American Indian Studies Center. The editors and other contributors to this volume provided insightful comments on earlier versions. I am also indebted to my Comanche consultants, particularly to the late Carney Saupitty Sr. and the late Ray Niedo.

1. Daniel J. Gelo and Scott Zesch, "'Every Day Seemed to Be a Holiday': The Captivity of Bianca Babb," *Southwestern Historical Quarterly* 107, no. 1 (2003): 39–44, 49–60; quotes from 56, 57, and 60.

2. Ibid., 65.

3. The earliest significant descriptions of Comanche captivity date from the 1820s. The year 1875 signals the beginning of the reservation period.

4. Gary C. Anderson, *The Indian Southwest, 1580–1830: Ethnogenesis and Reinvention* (Norman: University of Oklahoma Press, 1999); Juliana Barr, *Peace Came in the Form of a Woman: Indians and Spaniards in the Texas Borderlands* (Chapel Hill: University of North Carolina Press, 2007); James F. Brooks, *Captives and Cousins: Slavery, Kinship, and Community in the Southwest Borderlands* (Chapel Hill: University of North Carolina Press, 2002); and Victoria Smith, *Captive Arizona, 1851–1901* (Lincoln: University of Nebraska Press, 2009).

5. See, for instance, Anderson, *Indian Southwest*, 220–22, 39–40; Brooks, *Captives and Cousins*, 59–79, 160–207, esp. 180–93; Barr, *Peace Came*, 247–86; Brian E. Delay, *War of a Thousand Deserts: Indian Raids and the U.S.-Mexican War* (New Haven, CT: Yale University Press, 2008), 90–95; and Pekka Hämäläinen, *The Comanche Empire* (New Haven, CT: Yale University Press, 2008), 250–59.

6. The exception being Scott Zesch, *The Captured: A True Story of Abduction by Indians on the Texas Frontier* (New York: Saint Martin's Press, 2004).

7. The most reliable narratives of captivity among Comanches are Gelo and Zesch, "Bianca Babb"; T. A. Babb, *In the Bosom of the Comanches: A Thrilling Tale of Savage Indian Life, Massacre and Captivity Truthfully Told by a Surviving Captive* (Amarillo: n.p., 1912); Benjamin Dolbeare, *A Narrative of the Captivity and Sufferings of Dolly Webster Among the Comanche Indians in Texas with an Account of the Massacre of John Webster and His Party As Related by Mrs. Webster* (Clarksburg: M'Granaghan & M'Carty Printer, 1843); E. House, ed., *A Narrative of the Captivity of Mrs. Horn and Her Two Children with That of Mrs. Harris by the Comanche Indians* (St. Louis: C. Keemle Printer, 1839); and Rachel Plummer, *Rachel Plummer's Narrative of Twenty-One Months Servitude as a Prisoner among the Comanche Indians* (Houston: Telegraph Power Press, 1838).

8. The information on captives of indigenous background is too scant to be considered. For a summary of the information available on each captive, see Joaquín Rivaya-Martínez, "Captivity and Adoption among the Comanche Indians, 1700–1875," Ph.D. diss., University of California, Los Angeles, 2006, 417–519.

9. "Incorporation" refers to the process through which outsiders become integrated into a given social group.

10. Hämäläinen, *Comanche Empire*, 223.

11. Comanche Language and Cultural Preservation Committee (hereafter CLCPC), *Taa Numu Tekwapu?ha Tuboopu (Our Comanche Dictionary)* (Lawton, OK: CLCPC, 2003), 39, 59, 87; Carney Saupitty Sr., interview with the author, Apache, Oklahoma, July 14, 2005. For Comanche names, if available, I follow the spellings proposed in Thomas W. Kavanagh, *Comanche Political History: An Ethnohistorical Perspective, 1706–1875* (Lincoln: University of Nebraska Press, 1996; reprint, 1999); Thomas W. Kavanagh, comp. and ed., *Comanche Ethnography: Field Notes of E. Adamson Hoebel, Waldo R. Wedel, Gustav G. Carlson, and Robert H. Lowie* (Lincoln: University of Nebraska Press, 2008). For spellings of other Comanche words I follow CLCPC, *Dictionary*. I have adapted the spelling and accent marks of Hispanic names to contemporary standard Spanish.

12. Kavanagh, *Comanche History*, 28–62; Thomas W. Kavanagh, "Comanche," in *Plains*, ed. Raymond J. DeMallie (Washington, DC: Smithsonian Institution, 2001), 889–96.

13. Morris W. Foster, *Being Comanche: A Social History of an American Indian Community* (Tucson: University of Arizona Press, 1991), 23–30.

14. House, ed., *Captivity of Mrs. Horn*, 55.

15. Babb, *In the Bosom*, 101.

16. House, ed., *Captivity of Mrs. Horn*, 38–39.

17. Ibid.; Gelo and Zesch, "Bianca Babb," 59.

18. Diverse interpretations of these processes are offered in Rupert N. Richardson, *The Comanche Barrier to South Plains Settlement* (Austin: Eakin Press, 1996); Kavanagh, *Comanche History*; Gerald Louis Betty, *Comanche Society: Before the Reservation* (College Station: Texas A&M University Press, 2002); Hämäläinen, *Comanche Empire*.

19. Saupitty, interview with the author.

20. Josiah Gregg, *Commerce of the Prairies* (Norman: University of Oklahoma Press, 1954), 439.

21. My discussion of nineteenth-century Comanche captivity draws amply on Rivaya-Martínez, "Captivity." See also Ernest Wallace and E. Adamson Hoebel, *The Comanches: Lords of the South Plains* (Norman: University of Oklahoma Press, 1952), 241–42, 59–64, 71; Carl C. Rister, *Border Captives: The Traffic in Prisoners by Southern Plains Indians, 1835–1875* (Norman: University of Oklahoma Press, 1940); Michael L. Tate, "Comanche Captives: People between Two Worlds," *Chronicles of Oklahoma* 72, no. 3 (1994); Brooks, *Captives and Cousins*, 59–79, 160–207, esp. 180–93; Gelo and Zesch, "Bianca Babb," 35–49; Delay, *War of a Thousand Deserts*, 90–95; Hämäläinen, *Comanche Empire*, 250–59. The stories of some captives are told in Hugh D. Corwin, *Comanche and Kiowa Captives in Oklahoma and Texas* (Guthrie, OK: Cooperative Publishing, 1959); Jo Ella Powell Exley, *Frontier Blood: The Saga of the Parker Family* (College Station: Texas A&M University Press, 2001); Zesch, *The Captured*.

22. CLCPC, *Dictionary*, 35, 76; and Saupitty, interview with the author.

23. Rivaya-Martínez, "Captivity," 45–79.

24. Ibid., 222–37.

25. Tate, "Comanche Captives," 239.

26. Macario Leal, Felipe N. de Alcalde, and Juan N. Marichalar, "Declaración," Monterrey, May 12, 1854, Archivo Histórico Municipal de Monterrey-Principal 3, 7.

27. Thomas P. Robb, Richard H. Savage, and Thomas O. Osborn, "Report of the United States Commission to Texas, Appointed under Joint Resolution of Congress Approved May 7, 1872," Washington, D.C., June 30, 1873, 43rd Congress, 1st Session, H. Exec. Doc. 257, 25.

28. John C. Ewers, ed., *The Indians of Texas in 1830* (Washington, DC: Smithsonian Institution Press, 1969), 83.

29. Corwin, *Captives*, 217–28; and Rister, *Border Captives*, 142–43.

30. Robb, Savage, and Osborn, "Report," 25.

31. Ibid., 26–27.

32. The quotation is from Gelo and Zesch, "Bianca Babb," 63; and Wallace and Hoebel, *Comanches*, 123–24, 30.

33. Ibid., 124–30.

34. This view is contrary to that expressed in Foster, *Being Comanche*, 22.

35. Gelo and Zesch, "Bianca Babb," 58–59.

36. Robb, Savage, and Osborn, "Report," 25.

37. See the different contributions in David Birdsong, ed., *Second Language Acquisition and the Critical Period Hypothesis* (Mahwah, NJ: Lawrence Erlbaum Associates, 1999).

38. Saupitty, interview with the author.

39. Fernando González, "Deposition. Lampazos, Nuevo León, July 7, 1873," Archivo de la Secretaría de Relaciones Exteriores (hereafter ASRE) L-E-1589: 259v–263v; Leal, Alcalde, and Marichalar, "Declaración"; Dionisio Santos, "Deposition. Lampazos, Nuevo León, July 11, 1873," ASRE L-E-1589: 268–270v.

40. Gelo and Zesch, "Bianca Babb," 43; and Kavanagh, ed., *Comanche Ethnography*, 382.

41. Delores Titchywy, interview with the author, Walters, Oklahoma, July 17, 2005.

42. Hämäläinen, *Comanche Empire*, 252.

43. Ewers, ed., *Indians of Texas,* 119; José Francisco Ruiz, "Relación," in *Report on the Indian Tribes of Texas in 1828,* ed. John C. Ewers (New Haven, CT: Yale University Library, 1972); and Ernest Wallace, "David G. Burnet's Letters Describing the Comanche Indians," *West Texas Historical Association Year Book* 30 (1954): 130–31.

44. Gregg, *Commerce,* 249.

45. Ewers, ed., *Indians of Texas,* 119–20; Lawrie Tatum, *Our Red Brothers and the Peace Policy of President Ulysses S. Grant* (Lincoln: University of Nebraska Press, 1970), 59; and Kavanagh, ed., *Comanche Ethnography,* 327.

46. Dolbeare, *Narrative,* 22–23; Babb, *In the Bosom,* 38–40; Gelo and Zesch, "Bianca Babb," 41, 50; and Tate, "Comanche Captives," 239–40.

47. Gelo and Zesch, "Bianca Babb," 37.

48. Ibid.; and Thomas Gladwin, "Comanche Kin Behavior," *American Anthropologist* 50, no. 1, part 1 (1948): 78–80, 90–94.

49. Kavanagh, ed., *Comanche Ethnography,* 178, 82, 448.

50. Ewers, ed., *Indians of Texas,* 76; and Pedro Vial and Francisco Xavier Chávez, "Diario [of San Antonio de Béxar, November 15, 1785]," Archivo General de Simancas–Secretaría de Guerra 7031, 9, 2.

51. House, ed., *Captivity of Mrs. Horn,* 41–45.

52. Babb, *In the Bosom,* 56–58.

53. Gelo and Zesch, "Bianca Babb," 36–37; and Tate, "Comanche Captives," 242.

54. Hämäläinen, *Comanche Empire,* 223, 50–53; and Brooks, *Captives and Cousins,* 71, 367.

55. Wilbur S. Nye, *Carbine and Lance: The Story of Old Fort Sill* (Norman: University of Oklahoma Press, 1969); Thomas C. Battey, *The Life and Adventures of a Quaker among the Indians* (Williamstown, MA: Corner House Publishers, 1972), 82–83, 87; Esteban Herrera, "Deposition. Ciudad Guerrero, Tamaulipas, June 30, 1873," ASRE L-E-1589: 64v–65v; G. Marvin Hunter, *The Boy Captives* (San Saba, TX: San Saba Printing, 1927; reprint, 2002), 128; Kavanagh, *Comanche History,* 432, 34–37, 513–14 n. 21; and Tatum, *Our Red Brothers.*

56. Kavanagh, ed., *Comanche Ethnography,* 91.

57. Ibid., 351.

58. Ibid., 67, 351; and Babb, *In the Bosom,* 57, 108.

59. CLCPC, *Dictionary,* 89; and Saupitty, interview with the author.

60. Gladwin, "Comanche Kin," 81–84; quotes from 82.

61. Saupitty, interview with the author.

62. The fact that in some small-scale societies slaves can be addressed using kinship terms has sometimes blinded scholars to the subservient and powerless status implicit in their bondage. See Igor Kopytoff, "Slavery," *Annual Review of Anthropology* 11 (1982): 215; and Suzanne Miers and Igor Kopytoff, eds., *Slavery in Africa: Historical and Anthroplogical Perspectives* (Madison: University of Wisconsin Press, 1977), 24–26. Studies of Native American captivity are often stalled by similar pitfalls.

63. Gelo and Zesch, "Bianca Babb," 37; and Gladwin, "Comanche Kin," 78–80, 90–94. On "filial servitude" see Ewers, ed., *Indians of Texas,* 76–77, 83, 119; and Wallace, "Burnet's Letters," 130.

64. Gladwin, "Comanche Kin," 81–82.

65. Gelo and Zesch, "Bianca Babb," 39–44, 49–60.

66. See, for instance, Joseph E. Illick, *American Childhoods* (Philadelphia: University of Pennsylvania Press, 2002).

67. Kavanagh, ed., *Comanche Ethnography,* 380–86; House, ed., *Captivity of Mrs. Horn;* and Robb, Savage, and Osborn, "Report," 25–26.

68. Corwin, *Captives,* 7–8.

69. Kavanagh, ed., *Comanche Ethnography,* 380–86, quotes from 81–83 and 86.

70. Ibid., 384-85.
71. Ibid., 385-86; and Polly L. Murphy, ed., *Anadarko Agency Genealogy Record Book of the Kiowa, Comanche, Kiowa-Apache, and Some Twenty-Two Sioux Families, 1902* (typed transcription of the original documents held by the Niedo Comanche family, Lawton, OK), 122-23, 52-53.
72. Gladwin, "Comanche Kin," 86.
73. Ibid., 82; and Kavanagh, ed., *Comanche Ethnography*, 351.
74. Kavanagh, "Comanche," 894; and Kavanagh, ed., *Comanche Ethnography*, 363, 408.
75. Babb, *In the Bosom*, 38.
76. Anderson, *Indian Southwest*, 222; Brooks, *Captives and Cousins*, 179; and Hämäläinen, *Comanche Empire*, 252.
77. See Brooks, *Captives and Cousins*, 60, 64, 71-72, 179; and Hämäläinen, *Comanche Empire*, 247-50.
78. Felipe de Sandoval, report submitted to Vélez Cachupín, Santa Fe, March 1, 1750, Archivo General de la Nación—Provincias Internas 37: 103-106v; and Domingo Cabello, "Respuestas... sobre varias circunstancias de los indios Cumanches Orientales," Béxar, April 30, 1786, Bexar Archives 17: 417-19.
79. Kavanagh, *Comanche History*, 380-81.
80. Hämäläinen, *Comanche Empire*, 253.
81. Gladwin, "Comanche Kin," 86.
82. Kavanagh, ed., *Comanche Ethnography*, 380-86; Alice Marriott and Carol K. Rachlin, eds., *Plains Indian Mythology* (New York: Thomas Y. Cromwell Company, 1975), 123-24; and Nye, *Carbine and Lance*, 52.
83. Ruiz, "Relación."
84. Hunter, *Boy Captives*, 73.
85. Ewers, ed., *Indians of Texas*, 83; Hunter, *Boy Captives*, 73; and Leal, Alcalde, and Marichalar, "Declaración."
86. Corwin, *Captives*, 168.
87. Kavanagh, ed., *Comanche Ethnography*, 327.
88. Corwin, *Captives*, 95, 101, 22, 68.
89. Ewers, ed., *Indians of Texas*, 119; Kavanagh, ed., *Comanche Ethnography*, 279; and Ruiz, "Relación."
90. Gladwin, "Comanche Kin," 84, 89-90.
91. Kavanagh, ed., *Comanche Ethnography*, 33; "Diez y ocho caciques muertos," *El Registro Oficial. Periódico del Gobierno del Departamento de Durango*, April 8, 1854; Corwin, *Captives*, 170; Eugenio Fernández, letter to the Alcalde of Guerrero, Nava, July 21, 1839, Archivo General del Estado de Coahuila, Fondo s. XIX 1839, 2, 6, 7: 1-1v; Kavanagh, ed., *Comanche Ethnography*, 380; and Titchywy, interview with the author.
92. Kavanagh, ed., *Comanche Ethnography*, 31, 450-51; Kavanagh, *Comanche History*, 31; and William Courtney Meadows, *Kiowa, Apache, and Comanche Military Societies* (Austin: University of Texas Press, 1999), 303-5.
93. Wallace and Hoebel, *Comanches*, 126-27.
94. Leal, Alcalde, and Marichalar, "Declaración."
95. The term *tʉbitsinahaitsinʉʉ* can be broken down into its constituent morphemes: *tʉbitsi* (really), *nah* (with each other), *haitsi* (man's male friend), and *nʉʉ* (people). See CLCPC, *Dictionary*, 4, 23, 71.
96. My discussion of "true friendship" draws from Gladwin, "Comanche Kin," 91-92, and especially from diverse 1933 Comanche testimonies published in Kavanagh, ed., *Comanche Ethnography*.
97. Brooks, *Captives and Cousins*, 180-81.

98. Kavanagh, ed., *Comanche Ethnography*, 151, 191.
99. Ibid., 279.
100. Ibid., 294–97.
101. Kavanagh, "Comanche," 896.
102. Kavanagh, ed., *Comanche Ethnography*, 469–70.
103. LaDonna Harris, interview with the author, Albuquerque, New Mexico, July 8, 2005.
104. William T. Hagan, *Quanah Parker, Comanche Chief* (Norman: University of Oklahoma Press, 1993), 115.
105. Kavanagh, ed., *Comanche Ethnography*, 34, 70, 119, 291. On Cynthia Ann Parker and her son Quanah, see Exley, *Frontier Blood*; and Hagan, *Quanah Parker*.
106. Opal Gore, interview with the author, Lawton, Oklahoma, July 12, 2005; Harris, interview with the author; Ray Niedo, interview with the author, Indiahoma, Oklahoma, July 15, 2005; Saupitty, interview with the author; Carmelita Red Elk Thomas, interview with the author, Lawton, Oklahoma, July 15, 2005.
107. Corwin, *Captives*, 11, 95.
108. Kavanagh, ed., *Comanche Ethnography*, 380; House, ed., *Captivity of Mrs. Horn*, 37.
109. Ibid., 40.
110. Ibid., 168.
111. Ibid., 95.
112. CLCPC, *Dictionary*, 81; Kavanagh, ed., *Comanche Ethnography*, 291 n. 1; Lila Winstrand Robinson and James Armagost, *Comanche Dictionary and Grammar* (Dallas: SIL International and the University of Texas at Arlington, 1990), 148; and Titchywy, interview with the author.
113. Dolbeare, *Narrative*, 21; Ewers, ed., *Indians of Texas*, 117; and Ruiz, "Relación."
114. Cuauthémoc Velasco Ávila, "La amenaza comanche en la frontera mexicana, 1800–1841," Ph.D. diss., Universidad Nacional Autónoma de México, 1998; Isidro Vizcaya Canales, *Tierra de guerra viva: Incursiones de indios y otros conflictos en el noreste de México durante el siglo XIX, 1821–1885* (Monterrey: Academia de Investigación Humanística, A.C., 2001); Matthew M. Babcock, "Trans-national Trade Routes and Diplomacy: Comanche Expansion, 1760–1846," M.A. thesis, University of New Mexico, 2001; Brian E. Delay, "The Wider World of the Handsome Man: Southern Plains Indians Invade Mexico, 1830–1846," *Journal of the Early Republic* 27, no. 1 (2007); and Delay, *War of a Thousand Deserts*.
115. Gary C. Anderson, *The Conquest of Texas: Ethnic Cleansing in the Promised Land, 1820–1875* (Norman: University of Oklahoma Press, 2005); Richardson, *Comanche Barrier*; and Kavanagh, *Comanche History*.
116. This estimate is based on Murphy, ed., *Genealogy Record Book*.
117. See William T. Hagan, *United States–Comanche Relations: The Reservation Years* (Norman: University of Oklahoma Press, 1990).
118. Tatum, *Our Red Brothers*, 148–49.
119. Zesch, *The Captured*, 171–79, 198.
120. Ibid., 253–56.
121. Corwin, *Captives*, 168.

3

"Seeking the Incalculable Benefit of a Faithful, Patient Man and Wife"

Families in the Federal Indian Service, 1880–1925

Cathleen D. Cahill

Kidnapped. That was how Irene Stewart (Navajo) described her enrollment in the Indian Boarding School at Fort Defiance in 1913. Stewart's grandmother had left that morning to pick yucca fruit and cactus berries on the canyon rim above her home when the Indian Service policeman came to take Irene to school. Many Native families had similar stories of their children being taken away and enrolled in government boarding schools by force or through bribery, trickery, or threats.[1] Federal officials believed that these child removal policies—or what one policymaker dispassionately described as "the kindly cruel surgery which hurts that it may save"[2]—were a necessary part of solving "the Indian problem" by assimilating them into the citizenry.[3]

Administrators hoped that once children like Stewart were in the schools far away from their families and communities, the school employees—superintendents, principals, teachers, matrons, disciplinarians, and others—would serve as surrogate parents and teach the children everything about "civilization," including those things that white children had learned "at the fireside and in Christian homes."[4] Indeed, most administrators agreed with the logic behind the title of the 1896 report by the superintendent of Indian schools, "The School As a Home."[5] The commissioner of Indian affairs concurred: "When the closing hour has arrived teachers and pupils in white schools go to their homes and enjoy around the family circle those pleasures of home life which are characteristic of the American people. The Indian reservation school, on the other hand, must combine both the home and the school."[6] He highlighted the important role of the employees in creating those surrogate homes: "The Indian school is the Indian's home" and its success "is largely due to the earnest and faithful cooperation of these patient workers in this great field."[7] He urged employees to remember that they were competing with Native parents for their students' affections and that "unless the child is loved and can love unreservedly, he will never take a real heart interest in the school."[8]

The Indian Office's attempt to redirect the love and affection of Native children from their families to its employees reveals a strategy that scholars have termed "intimate colonialism." Anthropologist Ann Stoler has defined such tactics as "the production and harnessing of sentiment as a technology of the state." Other scholars have emphasized the focus on reproduction—both biological and social—that has often defined colonial agendas.[9] In the United States, intimate relationships played several important roles in federal theories of assimilation. Policymakers believed that assimilation's success hinged on transforming intimate relations among Native people so that they would no longer live in "tribal relations" but would conform to the middle-class Anglo norm of a nuclear family. This alteration would then become self-sustaining as newly trained Native mothers would reproduce their household configurations in the next generation, ultimately ending the need for federal oversight. Thus policymakers sought to use love as a form of power by harnessing ostensibly private relationships between parents and children in the service of the state.

This strategy made personnel a key component in the exercise of federal power. Administrators exhorted employees (especially married employees) to offer "object lessons" of "civilized" behavior through the example of their own conduct. They also urged personnel to develop with Native people—especially children—close personal relationships that would counteract and replace the authority of their family and community ties and lead them to enlightenment. In developing this strategy the Indian Office drew heavily on standard missionary procedures that emphasized both the role of individual contact and the example offered by Christian couples. One commissioner proudly proclaimed, "The little day school ... is a center from which the missionary spirit of a faithful teacher and his wife may be exerted upon old and young."[10] As I have explored elsewhere, this emphasis on personal connections sometimes led to intimate relationships between Indians and whites that policymakers had not anticipated.[11] In this chapter, however, I focus on the unintended consequences of building a workforce based on a family model.

The Indian Office needed its employees to serve as examples of "civilized" living in places where there were no white communities; it also needed to retain them in what were often isolated posts, so it sought incentives to keep them there. One key enticement was the policy of hiring married couples, including, eventually, Native couples. This was extremely unusual at a time when married middle-class women seldom worked for wages outside their homes, and spouses of any class rarely worked together except in their own households.[12] The employment of married couples has gone largely unnoticed by historians, and those who note it at all too often dismiss it solely as nepotism.[13] But to ignore this phenomenon is to overlook an important window into federal Indian policy.

The Indian Service's hiring of spouses clearly reveals the bureaucratic ramifications of a strategy of intimate colonialism. Policymakers hoped to use employees as living examples of a family ideal while simultaneously positioning those employees as federal fathers and mothers to Native wards. Administrators predicated their hiring strategies upon particular assumptions, but the differences between those assumptions and the reality of life on the reservations had a major impact on how employees put assimilation policy into practice. As the Indian Office struggled to bring its theory and reality into alignment, it demonstrated some flexibility and experimentation in its attempts to adjust its procedures to fit the needs of its employees. These examples offer a striking depiction of how personnel meaningfully influenced the shape of the nation's colonial bureaucracy.

Native children generally recognized and rejected these efforts to realign their affections from their parents and communities to Indian Service employees. Tsianina Lomawaima interviewed alumni from Chilocco Indian School in Oklahoma who emphasized precisely this point. Looking back on her boarding school experience, Vivian, a Choctaw student, said that "they tried to take the place of your home life but they can't." Noreen (Potawatomi) recalled that "the only time you saw your, talked with your matron was in a disciplinary area, you see, so you didn't *love* your matron [laughter]" (italics in original).[14] Moreover, many former students had traumatic memories of harsh physical and psychological treatment experienced in the schools that gave the lie to the Indian Office's language of affection.[15] Many remembered their days as punctuated by beatings, extreme manual labor, being locked up without food, and public humiliation. Everyday classroom experiences were often infused with casual abuse from white teachers. Irene Stewart recalled that, at the Fort Defiance School in Arizona, "the teachers were mean and strict. We were always being punished for not knowing our lessons. Once I was slapped in the face for gazing out the window." School records of multiple runaway efforts and attempted arsons further emphasize the students' intense resistance and unhappiness.[16]

Historians have greatly enhanced our understanding of how the Indian Office sought to disrupt Native families, and we know that the government's goal of assimilation failed in part because most Native children rejected the premise that Indian Service employees could replace their ties of affection with their families. But we know much less about those colonial agents and how their needs and desires influenced the implementation of the government's policies. It is the stories of the men and women whom it hired that this chapter seeks to reveal. In their actions, we see the multiple ramifications for the government of using a strategy that relied on changing intimate relationships through personal influence and example. In particular, we see that the Indian Office made faulty assumptions about the willingness of employees to sacrifice their own families to the goals of the service.

HIRING MARRIED COUPLES

The familial imagery in government reports was not merely a rhetorical device; instead the very structure of the School Service reflected the emphasis on the family. During the 1880s the Indian Office systematized its schools into three basic types: day schools, on-reservation boarding schools, and off-reservation boarding schools.[17] The smallest and simplest units of the system were the day schools, which students attended during the day before returning home to their families at night. These schools usually employed only two people, a teacher and housekeeper. By the 1890s the Indian Office stated that an "endeavor is made to fill them with a man and his wife," a trend that increased after the turn of the century. In 1889 the government ran 51 day schools, 7 of which were staffed by a spousal team. By 1900 that number had increased to 128, and married employees taught in 64 of them.[18] Employing couples reinforced both the idea of a family model and employees' ability to demonstrate the ideal household to their Native wards. The only task laid out for day school employees in the rules and regulations handbook, for example, was "to make their cottage a practical demonstration to the Indians of a neat and attractive home in the midst of orderly surroundings."[19] Indeed, the directive to have employees serve as object lessons of "civilized" homemaking was fundamental to their jobs and inseparable from their pedagogy.

The boarding schools also employed the family model, but it did so on a much larger scale. The superintendent, the official in charge, was most often a white man. He acted as a father figure to all of the schoolchildren as well as the employees.[20] He was complemented by the matron, the symbolic school mother "responsible for the management of all the domestic affairs of the school," including "oversight of the dormitories."[21] In 1895 Dr. Hailmann, the superintendent of Indian schools, reported, "The matron is beginning to feel that . . . she is a mother rather than a housekeeper; and she prides herself upon the title of 'school mother' and emphasizes that in her work."[22] Often the Indian Service hired actual husbands and wives as superintendent and matron, thus making the image of federal fathers and mothers even more explicit. In 1893, of the ninety-one boarding schools that reported, more than half had superintendents whose wives were also employed at the schools.[23]

Although the family model served as the Indian Office's guiding principle in hiring a workforce, other considerations encouraged the agency to employ large numbers of Native people. Though the hiring of Native people began as an effort to instruct indigenous men about market participation, the importance of gender roles during the assimilation era resulted in the hiring of numerous Native women as well. During the 1880s and 1890s the government instituted special hiring policies such as exemption from competitive civil service exams that theoretically gave Native employees an advantage over white applicants, who had to pass the exams to qualify for positions. According to the policymakers, hiring former Indian students offered an incentive to keep educated Indians from "returning to the blanket," as there were few other employment opportunities on most reservations. Officials also stressed that these employees offered good examples of "civilized" living to their fellow Indians. Finally, hiring Indians also saved money, as the Indian Office often paid its Native employees less than whites.[24]

As a result of these hiring policies, the percentage of Native employees in the Indian Service climbed steadily.[25] In 1888 the commissioner of Indian affairs reported that Indian employees constituted 15 percent of the School Service, and by 1895 that proportion had risen to 25 percent. In 1912 Commissioner Robert G. Valentine stated that Native employees made up almost 30 percent of the six thousand employees in both the school and agency services.[26] Although Native people were employed in both permanent and temporary positions, this chapter focuses especially on those who held permanent, skilled, and often white-collar positions, such as teacher, clerk, and superintendent as well as matron, seamstress, and cook. Regular positions were held on an annual basis and salaried. They often required their holders to move across the reservation system and serve at multiple posts. Many of these permanent employees had been trained in the federal school system and often subscribed to ideas of class based on Anglo standards, a value system that differed from traditional ways of assessing status. As Devon Mihesuah has argued, these stances tended to fall out along phenotypical lines, and many, though not all, Native employees were of mixed indigenous and white heritage. Nonetheless, the Indian Office regarded them all as "Indian" employees.[27]

The outcome of these hiring priorities was a highly unusual colonial workforce composed of married couples and women and men of both races. The number of married women, Native and white, employed by the Indian Service greatly outdistanced their proportion in the national workforce. For example, in 1885 a third of white women were married. The percentage of married Native women was slightly higher, at 36.7 percent. Nationally, by contrast, in 1890 only 14 percent of the female labor force was married, and few of those women were middle-class.[28] Even in other federal positions the number of married women was also smaller and more controversial than it was in the Indian Service. In her study of federal clerks in Washington, D.C., Cindy Aron found that two-thirds of the female clerks were single and many others were widowed. Struggling middle-class families, she argues, preferred to send their daughters out to work. Generally, only very desperate families would send a wife or mother to work for wages, as the non-wage-earning position of a woman in the home was the hallmark of middle-class respectability. There were also concerns that married women were taking jobs from needier workers, and during the 1870s various federal departments prohibited the employment of more than one family member, though as a whole the government did not specifically exclude married women from employment.

Significantly, the one other federal agency that looked similar in terms of the marital status and racial makeup of its workforce was the United States Philippine Service, founded in 1900. The personnel of this agency—whose goals were similarly colonial—mirrored that of the Indian Service. Not only did it employ large numbers of Filipinos,[29] but the Civil Service Commission favored women married to employees over single women for positions. It is striking that both colonial branches of the federal government had such similar policies regarding personnel.[30]

FEDERAL FATHERS AND MOTHERS

As employees filled the ranks of the Indian Service, the colonial theories under which they had been hired and their own motivations for taking employment often clashed. Employees placed the well-being of their own spouses, children, and family members ahead of the fictive kinship of assimilation theory. In many cases the Indian Office had to adjust its personnel policies in an effort to keep its programs functioning smoothly.

Initially, the government's desire to hire married employees to staff positions seemed beneficial to both the Indian Office and applicants. Couples actively sought the positions, and many candidly mentioned the economic benefits of spousal employment. For example, a number of white men asked for joint appointments, indicating that they approved of their spouses working. When Charles H. Groover of Leavenworth, Kansas, applied for a school superintendency in 1889, he added, "Should my application receive favorable consideration, I wish respectfully to submit the accompanying application of my wife Mrs. S[arah] H. Groover for the position of Matron or Assistant teacher in the same school with me."[31]

The desire of couples for joint positions was so great that at times it contributed to the service's personnel problems of excessive transferring and declinations of appointments as employees used their ability to accept or reject positions for leverage. In 1893 a reporter for the *New York Evening Post* investigated complaints by the commissioner of Indian affairs that the new civil service rules had resulted in "delays and hitches" in the staffing of the service. The reporter found that the majority of people declining their positions were women, particularly those appointed to matron positions (nineteen out of the forty-nine selected as eligible). He concluded, "Most of the cases where matrons have hesitated to accept have been where their husbands were eligible for appointments as superintendents, and had not yet been reached in the certifications. These women naturally desired to be assigned [to the] same schools with their husbands, and rather than be separated, declined their first offers with a view to a later certification to a place to which both could go."[32] In response, the Indian Office sought to make it easier for wives to be hired.

By 1903 the Indian Office had changed its appointment procedures to offer the wives of superintendents noncompetitive civil service exams for appointment as teacher or matron.[33] The Indian Office also used the inducement of spousal hiring to fill the less desirable remote and isolated positions, such as day school teachers and instructional farmers. Both of these positions had as its counterpart a female housekeeper, whose job included domestic instruction. It was assumed that the farmer or teacher's wife would serve as the housekeeper. For example, in 1910 the commissioner of Indian affairs wrote of one appointee that "in case the Farmer has no wife he is allowed to select some other member of the family" to serve in the position.[34]

As the number of employed couples increased, the trope of the superintendent's wife as troublemaker emerged in depictions of the service. Often the account charged that the superintendent or his wife was trying to drive away an innocent employee so that she could fill the position. This dynamic established the foundation for Minnie Braithwaite's entire memoir. The superintendent's wife, she wrote, "wanted my job and meant to get it. If one plan failed, she tried another. She always had another."[35] In 1917 the matron at the Chinle School in Arizona, Lucy Jobin (Chippewa/mixed), received a negative efficiency report from her superintendent that charged her with disloyalty. She fired back with several charges of her own, including that Mr. Garber was prejudiced toward Indian employees, but in particular that he had targeted her because she didn't "toady" to Mrs. Garber.[36]

An accusation that a superintendent's wife was behaving badly could also adversely affect her husband's position. David U. Betts, principal at the Yankton School, received negative reviews from both his superintendent and a special Indian agent sent to investigate the charges. Although most of the evidence revolved around Betts's behavior, both men also blamed his wife for problems at the school. The special agent noted that the employees were divided and pointed to the fact that "his wife is inclined to do much gossiping about the employees, and that adds fuel to the feeling."[37] Superintendent Estep complained, "If he stays I am going to eliminate Mrs. Betts from the equation. She puts him up to lots of the things he does and then comes to his defense most heroically.... She weighs about 180 and is about 300 horse-power when it comes to talking ... but she seems to have been raised on goat's milk and formed the habit of butting in on things that do not concern her."[38]

Women were certainly involved in the internal battles of the Indian Service, even the violent ones,[39] but it is unclear if superintendents' wives were more likely to cause trouble than others. Perhaps this theme contained some grain of truth because of the hierarchical nature of the service, or maybe superintendents' wives were easy marks. Whatever the case, the idea came to influence administrators. For example, the official who in 1926 filled out the efficiency report of Jerdine Bonnin (Wyandot/mixed)[40] commented positively that "Mrs. Bonnin is the wife of Superintendent [Leo] Bonnin.... She assumes no authority because of the fact that she is the Superintendent's wife."[41]

RESISTING ASSIMILATION

Although Native men rarely rose to the position of superintendent,[42] many indigenous couples did find employment in the bureaucracy and often used their jobs to maintain and protect their family and communal ties in direct opposition to the federal government's objective of breaking up tribal relations. The Indian Service's employment of Native people reveals the most intense conflict between federal goals and the desires of employees. Almost all Native employees rejected the totalizing goal of complete assimilation even as they may have embraced some aspects of white culture and society. The available evidence suggests that their employment offered them an economic survival strategy for adjusting to the changing world within which they lived.

The most basic reason Native people gave for their entrance into the Indian Service was economic survival. Their employment choices both on and off the reservation were limited, and Indian Service employment provided one of the few income sources on the reservations, which were often poverty-stricken areas. Indeed, salaries from service positions offered people a means to remain with their communities, or at least in Indian country. Like white employees, Native people also often emphasized their families and a desire for spousal employment in their applications. For instance, in her request Selma Kane (Pottawatomie) wrote that her husband's salary as engineer and blacksmith at the Shawnee Indian School was "small and we have quite a family to support."[43]

Because government policies sought to destroy indigenous family and community ties in the name of assimilation, keeping one's family together—especially one's extended family—carried greater political valence for Native employees than it did for white employees. Using the service to maintain those ties undermined federal goals. Maude Peacore (Chippewa) requested a transfer to the Seneca School in Oklahoma, explaining, "I have held the position here at Tomah School [in Wisconsin] as assistant seamstress for several years. When I came here my home was at Tomah, but now my relatives are in Oklahoma. I would like a position in an Indian school near their home."[44] Mrs. Harriet Chapman, a Native woman from northeastern California, responded that she would accept a transfer only if her son could receive the position of disciplinarian at the same school, as she did not want to leave him.[45] Many applicants indicated that they would accept positions in nearby states but refused to take those too far from their homes. For instance, Jessie Morago, a Native woman of mixed heritage from Lac du Flambeau, Wisconsin, asked, "Will you help me to get in some school in Wisconsin or as near the Wisconsin line in Minnesota?"[46]

Indigenous employees also used the flexibility offered by the civil service reinstatement policies to fulfill their kinship responsibilities and thus undermine assimilation policies. Civil service protocol granted all employees a grace period after resignation in which they could apply for reinstatement. White employees had one year, but the period was indefinite for Native employees. Indigenous personnel often took advantage of this policy, moving back and forth between work in the service and their other obligations, especially to family members. Lavinia Cornelius (Oneida) resigned several times to care for her sick mother, dying sister, and ailing father.[47] When Sarah Wyman's (Anishinabe) mother's health failed, she resigned and was reinstated twice.[48] Naomi Dawson Pacheco (Wyandot) resigned in 1909, writing of "being needed at home."[49]

A number of Native women employed by the service also became primary caregivers for nieces and nephews. It is possible that the women's steady employment made them best able to care for their family members, many of whom had lost their parents, but it also indicates that they remained connected to their extended families. These efforts stood in direct contrast to the government's goal of destroying Native kinship ties. And, as we will see next, Native employees also fought hard to protect their children.[50]

THE CHILDREN OF EMPLOYEES

As the Indian Office began to fill its ranks with married couples both Indian and white, another issue rose to prominence: the place of employees' children. Parents of both races wanted what was best for their offspring and manipulated their positions to help them. Although white parental ambition did cause some changes in federal policy, the actions of Native parents were more politicized and contested the raison d'être of federal Indian policy.

The office's ideal workforce was composed of childless couples who would spend all of their time looking after their Indian wards. The *Rules of the Indian School Service* demonstrates the expectation of full-time service that the Indian Office had for its employees. In 1892 they specifically stated, "No person should offer himself for a position in this service who is encumbered with the care of children."[51] A decade later they reiterated, "Employees are expected to devote their whole time and attention to the duties for which they are employed."[52] Yet the office was certainly aware that children might accompany employees, as it requested that job seekers list the number and age of the family members who would be with them at their posts.[53]

It is clear that the Indian Service only inconsistently followed its own rules regarding the employment of people with small children. Photographic evidence from the Indian schools also hints that many employees had their children with them. Native and white children appear in numerous staff photographs, suggesting that the white children had accompanied their parents to their post. Two different staff portraits from the Albuquerque Indian School portray small children, both white and nonwhite, sitting with the employees; the small number of children included in the photograph here suggests that they had a special relationship to the adults in the picture (see figure 3.1). Other children appear in photographs with the entire student body but are set off from the pupils by their clothing, placement in the images, or physical proximity to adults who are most likely their parents. The 1888 school picture from the Fort Simcoe School in Washington (figure 3.2) depicts several light-skinned children wearing refined clothing and sitting on the grass in front of the standing uniformed students. In a portrait featuring the 1909 Eastern Cherokee School community (not shown here), several adults—most likely staff members—are positioned on either side of the students, where they are tenderly caressing small children: a Native woman holds on her lap a small boy who, unlike the pupils, is not dressed in uniform, while on the other side another boy not in uniform stands in front of a Native man, and a white man rests his hand on the shoulder of a young, fashionably dressed girl.

For many Native parents, employment in the Indian Service offered not only a job but also a strategy for maintaining oversight of their children in opposition to the federal government's efforts to remove them. They often requested posts where their children were students or were eligible to enroll, thus undermining the government's ideas about separating Indian families. For example, Jessie Morago, from Lac du Flambeau, Wisconsin, requested a teaching position by saying, "I would like to get in a school where I could enroll my children; and yet not be a great ways from my home."[54] The widowed Lottie Smith Pattee (Eastern Band of Cherokee/mixed) hoped for a transfer from Chemawa School in Oregon to Haskell Institute in Kansas in order to enroll her son at the latter institution. Despite fond memories of her own experiences as a student at the boarding school in Hampton, Virginia, she had a different vision for her children's future. As she explained, "The time has come, when it is all I can do to discipline Fred. Perhaps there I could put him in school and yet be with him or near him so that my little family will not be entirely separated. That is what I dread."[55] In a second letter to the superintendent of Indian schools, Estelle Reel, Pattee reiterated her priority of keeping her family together, despite the service's rules about employees with small children: "Miss Folsom, she says for me to put Cora [her daughter] in some school and Fred too, as a great many Superintendents would not want employees with children. O! I can't think of giving up my little girls. . . . I want to keep [Cora] in the same school with me and if possible to room with me. . . . I feel like this: if I separate the two girls they will grow up strangers to each other. I think that I could watch over them better than a stranger."[56] In her statement, Lottie Smith Pattee rejected the premise of assimilation, insisting that she did

FIGURE 3.1. Faculty of the Albuquerque Indian School, 1883. Numerous staff photographs like this one include children whose small number suggest a closer relationship with the employees than a student/teacher relationship. The child in this image is most likely the son of one of the teachers in the photograph. Courtesy of National Archives, Denver Branch, no. NRG-75-AISP-17.

FIGURE 3.2. Yakima Indian employees and schoolchildren, Fort Simcoe, Washington, ca. 1888. The children sitting in front of the uniformed Native students are set off by their casual poses and dress, suggesting that they are not pupils but the children of faculty or staff members. Courtesy of University of Washington Libraries, Special Collections, NA4112.

not want her children to grow up without their family members, and that she, their mother, could raise them better than any surrogate stranger in a school.

Another employee, Sherman Norton (Hupa), also sought to use Indian Service employment to keep his family together, to supervise his children, and to keep them involved in the traditions of their community. In 1912 Norton, a former Chemawa student, returned with his three children to the Hoopa Valley Reservation in northern California and took a job as carpenter at the reservation boarding school.[57] During a dispute over his salary—Norton was being paid the "Indian" rate of $45 per month despite having previously served as temporary carpenter at the "white" rate of $60 per month—his superintendent described Norton as a man who held strong opinions about a wide range of reservation issues, especially the treatment of his children at the school. Norton, Superintendent Mortsolf wrote, had "interfered at times with the discipline in the school" and "complain[ed] considerably" about the treatment of his children. Moreover, he was "quite a talker, very critical of the management of the school," and had a "tendency to mix in reservation affairs."[58]

Like other superintendents who dealt with local "troublemakers," Mortsolf suggested transferring Norton to another reservation where he had no personal—or, more importantly, tribal—stake in governance.[59] For Norton, however, the ability to earn a living while remaining within his tribal community seems to have been precisely the benefit of an Indian Service job. He opposed a transfer for a number of compelling political, personal, and social reasons. Superintendent Mortsolf wrote, "Mr. Norton wants to be allotted at Hoopa, and is afraid if he goes away he will lose his rights." Moreover, Norton's wife, Ella, refused to leave her home in the valley. Also, his children were receiving an education at the agency boarding school but were able to attend Hupa cultural and religious events as well. In fact, the superintendent had complained that Norton had made a request to "take his oldest child, a girl about sixteen years of age, out [of school] to attend dances," most likely the Hupa ceremonial dances.[60]

The superintendent of Naomi Dawson Pacheco (Wyandot) tried to use her desire to remain near her family to force the outspoken Pacheco out of the service. He characterized the kindergarten teacher, whose husband worked as a baker at the Quapaw Agency in Oklahoma, as a good instructor, but claimed "her disposition to find fault and to antagonize those in authority over her offset her school room work." He disingenuously suggested a transfer, knowing, as he wrote to the commissioner, "Mrs. Pacheco's people live about four miles from the school.... It is probable that she would not accept a transfer to some other school."[61] Permanent Native employees such as Norton and Pacheco who were able to remain in their own communities were few and far between because the Indian Office found that they often became "troublemakers," using their language skills and bureaucratic knowledge to criticize administrators and stand up for their people. By 1912 the School Service's "Indian Application for Employment" form specified "it is not considered to be for the interest of the Service or the applicants to assign him to a position among his own people. Therefore the Indian Office looks with disfavor upon applications for appointment at home schools."[62] Even when Native employees were unable to remain on their own reservations, managing to keep their families together was a triumph in the face of intense federal efforts to disrupt the intimate ties between Native parents and children. Native employees maintained close contact with their children and had at least some supervision over the other employees when they worked in the same school.

Given that the stability of its workforce was one of the Indian Office's major priorities, and that frequent transfers were a significant problem, the government attempted to accommodate the concerns of its white employees, especially regarding the education of their offspring. The children of Native employees were often (though not always) eligible for enrollment in the schools at which their parents worked,[63] but white children were not allowed to enroll in Indian schools.

Those couples (and widows) who brought their progeny with them confronted the problem of their supervision during the day. Moreover, positions in the Indian Service demanded significant amounts of time outside regular working hours. Policymakers expected that employees would devote all of their energy to their jobs to the point of serving as surrogate parents to the government's Indian wards. Their own children were not part of that familial model of assimilation.

Many female employees had to choose between fulfilling their familial duties and employment obligations. Estelle Aubrey Brown, a single teacher at the Crow Creek Boarding School in South Dakota, contrasted the lot of two women at her school, one of whom was employed by the service and one of whom was not: "White children were not eligible to enter classrooms for Indian pupils. Mrs. Lake's two sons were pitiful. Her duties left her little time for her own children, who shared her one small room in boys' quarters." Standing in contrast to Mrs. Lake's experience was that of the superintendent's wife, who did not work: "More than many of us, she [Mrs. Hillyard] managed to display an equable happy spirit, perhaps because she was not an employee, or perhaps because she had the solace of her small son of 8 years whom she taught at home." According to Brown, the employees' children ironically suffered from a lack of education at the same time that their parents spent long hours teaching the Indian children.[64]

Indian schools, which were funded by either treaty stipulation, the proceeds of tribal land sales, or congressional appropriation, were intended only for Native children. White employees found it offensive that their children were not allowed to attend the schools and that, for most, there were few alternatives. For instance, Flora Gregg Iliff and her husband Joe, who had met while working at the Havasupi Agency in Arizona, had three children when they transferred to the Chilocco Indian School in Oklahoma. It was, Iliff wrote crossly in her memoir, "one of the largest in the U.S. Here the children of White employees attended public school. The free schooling granted Indian children was not available to those of White blood."[65] But the Iliffs were lucky in that there were established public schools in their community. Many employees were not so fortunate. A 1906 study by the Office of Indian Affairs (OIA) noted that only thirty-two reservations had public schools close enough for students to attend and that most of those were newly established.[66] Employees had to get creative with their educational solutions. At the Rosebud Reservation Agency in South Dakota, Dr. Clark testified that he built a private school for his children and those of the other employees, including Native employees. A teacher hired by the parents taught the fourteen pupils. There were some exceptions to the prohibition on employees enrolling their children in the school at which they worked, but they were often based on particular circumstances and likely the superintendent's willingness to bend the rules as well.[67] In 1900 a journalist reported that the Haskell Institute in Lawrence, Kansas, had "501 Indian students, besides a dozen white children of officers, admitted on sufferance but not regularly enrolled."[68]

Congress eventually passed legislation officially allowing white children to enroll in Indian Schools: one law in 1907 applied to day schools and another in 1909 involved boarding schools. In exchange, parents were required to pay tuition fees that would reimburse the fund from which the schools were maintained.[69] Although that legislation addressed concerns about younger children, parents still faced hard choices with their high school–aged children. Many strongly believed in upward mobility through education, and the lack of public high schools near most reservations bred discontent. What this meant for the service was a barrage of transfer requests, rejections of appointments, and outright resignations. For example, when offered a promotion to the position of day school inspector at Pine Ridge in 1916, William Blish hesitated, writing to the commissioner, "I was much in hopes that I might be so located that we might have our daughters at home until they had finished their high school." He further explained:

> I have three daughters, all of whom ought to be in school. They are not yet ready for college, but are beyond the place where they can be taught at home to advantage. Were I to go to Pine Ridge it would be necessary for me to send, at least, two of these girls away to school, just at the time when they most need the home, or of having my family live away from the reservation and being separated from them. The expense of either of these arrangements would be much more expensive than the increased salary could cover.[70]

Employees' concern for their children's education continued to cause disruptions in the work of assimilation. In 1928, *The Problem of Indian Administration*, the critical study of the Indian Service, was released. Based on extensive research, including numerous interviews with service personnel, the study concluded that family interests were a primary reason for employees' transfers or resignations. Summing up the section on personnel, it concluded, "To a certain type of employee, considerate of his wife and children, conditions of the home and access to schools mean even more than wages."[71]

END OF THE EXPERIMENT

By the second decade of the twentieth century, Indian Service salaries had stagnated and the practice of hiring married couples started to shift away from its ideological roots. This became even more pronounced after World War I, when appropriations for the OAI remained extremely low, making Indian Service salaries even smaller compared to nongovernmental positions. Under these conditions, more administrators turned to spousal hiring to augment the male head of household's salary. One commissioner noted, "The fact is the practice [of hiring wives] must be regarded largely as a means of paying the Farmers more."[72] Discussing the practicality of giving Frank Kyselka a raise, his superior offered a solution: "It has occurred to me that as a man and wife occupy these positions we might meet the demands of justice to some extent by increasing her salary."[73]

After World War I, the ideological reasoning behind this hiring practice seems to have been completely dropped by the Indian Office. Commissioner of Indian Affairs Charles Burke, who served from 1921 to 1929, failed to recognize the previous ideological emphasis on couples and saw only an embarrassing policy with implications of nepotism, petty corruption, and fraud. Testifying before the congressional appropriation committee in 1923, Burke's assistant commissioner, Mr. E. B. Meritt, conceded that many positions filled by wives were those that paid too little to be filled by other employees, but he added, "We are discouraging superintendents employing their wives in the service. We have found that it results in abuses." Several congressmen agreed with him.[74]

In 1925 Burke's administration issued circular number 2148 to agents and superintendents. The circular urged the reining in of hiring the wives of employees. According to the commissioner, "The main purpose ... was to terminate the practice of employing temporarily the members of the family of the employee when such employment was not in the interest of the service. ... This practice ... has caused a great deal of criticism both of the superintendent and the Office, and such employment must be restricted."[75] That same year Commissioner Burke further elaborated his opinion in response to Superintendent John Brown's request that his spouse be appointed as seamstress at the Phoenix School. Ignoring the ideological hiring of the past, the commissioner implied that spousal hiring had arisen as a result of the personnel shortages during World War I. He also revealed his assumptions about the gendered construction of labor, according to which men should be given available positions and married women should rely on their husband's salaries.

> I have been giving some thought to the practice that has arisen, apparently under exceptional circumstances, of employing the wives of Superintendents. ... I should like to discontinue this practice. ... It is realized that the difficulty of securing suitable instruction in the regular way has been unusual for some years past, but the prospects are now much more favorable. There should be no neglect of any opportunity to offer service to the many capable people now unemployed. ... I doubt the wisdom of giving preference to dependents of those now employed at good salaries. Of course, this practice cannot be wholly discarded at once, and there may be instances where little would be gained by attempting it, or where it should continue for a time on a temporary basis, but its elimination, I am convinced, will remove various embarrassing conditions and strengthen the Service.[76]

Commissioner Burke's statements demonstrate that the Indian Office was moving away from a policy that it had endorsed for over four decades and that had contributed to the unique makeup of the Indian Office's bureaucracy. Instead of emphasizing the importance of couples as object lessons for Indians to emulate, Burke focused on the "criticism" and "embarrassing conditions" that had resulted from spousal employment.

As policymakers developed federal Indian policy after the Civil War, they argued that Indian Service personnel would play a key role in transforming Native people. More than mere employees, they would be fathers and mothers to their Indian wards. This familial language ultimately suffused assimilation programs: schools were homes, employees were parents, Indians were children, and Washington, D.C., was the seat of the Great Father. This use of intimate colonialism with its ideological emphasis on social reproduction and gender roles set the stage for the creation of a unique federal bureaucracy full of women, Indians, and married couples.

The particular structure of the service's workforce holds major implications for our understanding of the development of the federal government, especially its administrative and ideological connections with other federal agencies. We need to consider, for example, whether the shape of the Indian Service influenced the government's administration of America's overseas colonies in the Philippines. Moreover, we are compelled to revise our existing accounts of the emergence of what Linda Gordon and Theda Skocpol, among others, have termed the "maternalist welfare state." Decades before the establishment of the federal Children's Bureau (1912) and the Women's Bureau (1920)—events that most scholars point to as the moments when women and women's concerns entered the federal bureaucracy—the Indian Service brought large numbers of women into the federal workforce.[77]

But examining the everyday experiences of those employees also reveals the currents and shoals—the assumptions, affections, and animosities—embedded in the government's hiring policies. As the Indian Office began to hire real people to fit its theories, tensions began to appear. Although it had initially appeared as though hiring married couples would benefit both the Indian Service and applicants, the couples' efforts to work together often undermined the service's goal of a stable workforce. White employees had taken positions in the Indian Service expressly for the benefit of themselves and their loved ones. While they hoped that the advancement of the Indians would parallel the good fortunes of their own kin, when circumstances forced them to choose between the two, their households took top priority. Like their white counterparts, many Native employees who had children of school age were deeply concerned about their educational prospects, and upward mobility through education was an important tenet. Indeed, many indigenous employees, especially those in permanent positions, did conform to the norms of the Anglo middle class, but they also tried to fuse those norms with their own cultural traditions to create a modern tribal identity. Their Indian Service positions offered them one strategy for maintaining their family ties in the face of hostile federal policies and endowed their decisions with great political weight.

The actions of its employees forced the Indian Office to adjust its positions. In some cases it created new rules to accommodate its personnel's concerns, such as changing the classification requirements for the wives of school superintendents or allowing white children to enroll in Indian schools. In other cases it worked to stop employee action that it perceived as detrimental to its goals, such as discouraging the hiring of Indian people on their own reservations or moving away from spousal hiring in the face of backlash against the employment of superintendent's wives. What this reminds us is that the actions of bureaucratic agents have a profound influence on the outcomes of their agencies, and in the Indian Service it was precisely those qualities of kinship that the service sought to incorporate that substantially interfered with its personnel's ability to carry out the policy of assimilation.

NOTES

1. Irene Stewart, *A Voice in Her Tribe: A Navajo Woman's Own Story*, ed. Doris Ostrander Dawdy (Socorro, NM: Ballena Press, 1980), 15. For more on the policy of child removal, see Margaret Jacobs, *White Mother to a Dark Race: Settler Colonialism, Maternalism, and the Removal of Indigenous Children in the American West and Australia, 1880–1940* (Lincoln: University of Nebraska Press, 2009); and Michael Coleman, *American Indian Children at School: 1850–1930* (Jackson: University Press of Mississippi, 1993).

2. *Annual Report of the Commissioner of Indian Affairs* (hereafter *ARCIA*) (Washington, DC: Government Printing Office, 1885), 114. Jacobs emphasizes the violence inherent in the ostensibly more beneficent programs aimed at indigenous children. See *White Mother to a Dark Race*.

3. As historians have demonstrated, the policy of assimilation could be many things to many people, and the fact that it facilitated land dispossession gave it many supporters. Brian Dippie, *The Vanishing American: White Attitudes and U.S. Indian Policy* (Middletown, CT: Wesleyan University Press, 1982), 163; Frederick E. Hoxie, *A Final Promise: The Campaign to Assimilate the Indians, 1880–1920* (Lincoln: University of Nebraska Press, 1984); David Wishart, *An Unspeakable Sadness: The Dispossession of the Nebraska Indians* (Lincoln: University of Nebraska Press, 1994); and David Wallace Adams, "Fundamental Considerations: The Deep Meaning of Native American Schooling, 1880–1900," *Harvard Educational Review* 58 (1988): 1–28.

4. *ARCIA*, 1899, 4.

5. *ARCIA*, 1896, 348. See also *ARCIA*, 1885, 114.

6. *ARCIA*, 1898, 10. See also *ARCIA*, 1899, 4; and *The Lake Mohonk Conference for the Friends of the Indian* (hereafter *Lake Mohonk*), 1895, 27.

7. *ARCIA*, 1899, 29.

8. *ARCIA*, 1896, 348. See also *ARCIA*, 1899, 4. The outing system under which Indian students lived and worked for white families was an extreme manifestation of this idea. See David Wallace Adams, *Education for Extinction: American Indians and the Boarding School Experience, 1875–1928* (Lawrence: University of Kansas Press, 1995), 155–62.

9. Ann Laura Stoler, *Carnal Knowledge and Imperial Power: Race and the Intimate in Colonial Rule* (Berkeley: University of California Press, 2002), 19, 7. See also "Empires and Intimacies: Lessons from (Post) Colonial Studies. A Round Table," *Journal of American History* 88 (2001): 829–97; Ann Laura Stoler, ed., *Haunted by Empire: Geographies of Intimacy in North American History* (Durham, NC: Duke University Press, 2006); Carol Summers, "Intimate Colonialism: The Imperial Production of Reproduction in Uganda, 1907–1925," *Signs* 16 (1991): 787–807; and the special issue of *Frontiers,* "Domestic Frontiers: The Home and Colonization," *Frontiers* 28 (2007). See also Jackie Thompson Rand, *Kiowa Humanity and the Invasion of the State* (Lincoln: University of Nebraska Press, 2008), 5–10.

10. *Rules for Indian Schools with Course of Study, List of Text-Books, and Civil Service Rules* (hereafter *Rules* 1892) (Washington, DC: Government Printing Office, 1892), 26–27. See also *Lake Mohonk,* 1893, 108.

11. See Cathleen D. Cahill, "'You Think It Strange That I Can Love an Indian': Native Men, White Women, and Marriage in the Indian Service," *Frontiers: A Journal of Women Studies* 29 nos. 2–3 (2008): 106–45.

12. On the rising numbers of single women in the workforce, see Joanne Meyerowitz, *Women Adrift: Independent Wage Earners in Chicago, 1880–1930* (Chicago: University of Chicago Press, 1988); Kathy Peiss, *Cheap Amusements: Working Women and Leisure in Turn-of-the-Century New York* (Philadelphia: Temple University Press, 1986); Angel Kwolek-Folland, *Engendering Business: Men and Women in the Corporate Office, 1870–1930* (Baltimore, MD: Johns Hopkins University Press, 1994); and Cindy Aron, *Ladies and Gentlemen of the Civil Service* (New York: Oxford University Press, 1987).

13. Although I am by no means denying that there was nepotism in the Indian Service, I am asserting that the wives of employees were also hired for ideological reasons. See, for example, Henry Edwin Stamm, *People of the Wind River: The Eastern Shoshones, 1825–1900* (Norman: University of Oklahoma Press, 1999), 77; and Adams, *Education for Extinction,* 66–67.

14. K. Tsianina Lomawaima, *They Called It Prairie Light: The Story of Chilocco Indian School* (Lincoln: University of Nebraska Press, 1994), 47–51; and Robert A. Trennert, *The Phoenix Indian School: Forced Assimilation in Arizona, 1891–1935* (Norman: University of Oklahoma Press, 1988).

15. See, for example, Myriam Vučković, *Voices from Haskell: Indian Students between Two Worlds, 1884–1928* (Lawrence: University Press of Kansas, 2008), 291 and 211–46.

16. Stewart, *A Voice in Her Tribe,* 17. See also Adams, *Education for Extinction,* 209–38.

17. Office of Indian Affairs, *Rules for the Indian School Service* (hereafter *Rules* 1898) (Washington, DC: Government Printing Office, 1898), 15; and Adams, *Education for Extinction,* 66.

18. *ARCIA,* 1889; and *ARCIA,* 1900, Appendix, "Employees of Indian Schools," 728–64.

19. *Rules* 1892, 29. See also *Rules* 1898, 20; and *Lake Mohonk,* 1891, 88.

20. *Rules* 1898, 8–9.

21. *Rules* 1892, 16–17; and Department of the Interior, *Regulations of the Indian Office, Indian Schools* (hereafter *Regulations*) (Washington, DC: Government Printing Office, 1928), 19.

22. *Lake Mohonk,* 1895, 27.

23. *Register of Officers and Agents, Civil, Military, and Naval, in the Service of the United States* (Washington, DC: Government Printing Office, 1893, 755–74. I have assumed that women listed as "Mrs." with the same last name as the superintendent were their spouse. *Rules* 1892, 16–17.

24. See Steven J. Novak, "The Real Takeover of the BIA: The Preferential Hiring of Indians," *Journal of Economic History* 50 (1990): 646; and Wilbert Ahern, "An Experiment Aborted: Returned Indian Students in the Indian School Service," *Ethnohistory* 44 (1997): 263–304. See also *ARCIA,* 1881, xii. See also *Annual Report of the Board of Indian Commissioners* (hereafter *ARBIC*) (Washington, DC: Government Printing Office, 1885), 17–18, 269, and 271. The Indian Office also saw employment

as a way to undermine traditional lines of authority. See *ARCIA*, 1880–81, xviii; and William T. Hagan, *Indian Police and Judges: Experiments in Acculturation and Control* (1966; reprint, Lincoln: University of Nebraska Press, 1980).

25. *ARCIA*, Appendix, "Employees of Indian Schools," 1888 and 1895.

26. This number includes only regular employees and does not count the very large number of Indians employed as temporary labor. *ARCIA*, Appendix, "Employees of Indian Schools," 1888 and 1895; *Report of the Executive Council on the Proceedings of the First Annual Conference of the Society of American Indians* (hereafter *SAI Conference Report*) (Washington, 1912), 27. In 1924 Commissioner Burke stated that about two thousand of the five to six thousand employees were Native and that they were "in every part of the service." *Interior Department Appropriation Bill* (Washington, DC: Government Printing Office, 1924), 136.

27. See Devon A. Mihesuah, *Indigenous American Women: Decolonization, Empowerment, Activism* (Lincoln: University of Nebraska Press, 2003), 62–80; and Mihesuah, *Cultivating the Rosebuds: The Education of Women at the Cherokee Female Seminary* (Urbana: University of Illinois Press, 1993).

28. It is unclear if widows were consistently listed as such or as married, but according to the records, only 3 percent of white women in the Indian Service were widowed, compared to 18 percent of women in the national population. Cahill, "Only the Home Can Found a State," Ph.D. diss., University of Chicago, 2004, 142.

29. Aron, *Ladies and Gentlemen of the Civil Service*, 46, 50–52; *31st Annual Report of the U.S. Civil Service Commission* (Washington, DC: Government Printing Office, 1904), 14–15; and Paul A. Kramer, *The Blood of Government: Race, Empire, the United States, and the Philippines* (Chapel Hill: University of North Carolina Press, 2006).

30. See U.S. Civil Service Commission, *Manual of Examinations* (Washington, DC: Government Printing Office, 1915), 130–131. See also *Annual Report of the War Department* (Washington, DC: Government Printing Office, 1903), 767.

31. Letters Received (LR), Record Group (RG) 75, National Archive and Record Administration, Washington, D.C. (hereafter NARA DC), #216, Application, Charles H. Groover, 1889. See also Victor Brown's request, February 10, 1908, Personnel File, Victor Brown, National Personnel Record Center (hereafter NPRC), St. Louis, Missouri.

32. Quoted in Herbert Welsh, *A Dangerous Assault upon the Integrity of the Civil Service Law in the Indian Service* (Philadelphia: Indian Rights Association, 1893), 4–7.

33. *Regulations*, 15.

34. See also Efficiency Report, December 20, 1921, Personnel File, Agnes Fredette, NPRC.

35. Minnie Braithwaite Jenkins, *Girl from Williamsburg* (Richmond, VA: Dietz Press, 1951), 61.

36. Letter, June 14, 1917, Personnel File, Lucy Jobin, NPRC. See also letter, September 18, 1911, Personnel File, Julia DeCora Lukecart, NPRC.

37. Letter, August 7, 1909, and letter, May 16, 1911, Personnel File, David U. Betts, NPRC; and letter, n.d., 1908, Personnel File, John H. Bailly, NPRC.

38. Letter, August 7, 1909, and letter, May 16, 1911, Personnel File, David U. Betts, NPRC.

39. See E. Jane Gay, *With the Nez Perces: Alice Fletcher in the Field, 1889–92*. ed. and introduction by Frederick E. Hoxie and Joan T. Mark (Lincoln: University of Nebraska Press, 1981), 7; and Adams, *Education for Extinction*, 70–82, on the incident at Duck Valley, Nevada.

40. Although the Bonnins were Native, white men made up the vast majority of superintendents hired by the Indian Service and thus most discussions revolving around the wives of superintendents involved white women.

41. Efficiency Report, 1926, Personnel File, Leo Bonnin, NPRC. See also letter, August 26, 1909, Personnel File, Homer Bibb, NPRC.

42. I have identified five Native men and one Native woman who served as superintendents during this period. For the problems they faced, see Cahill "You Think It Strange That I Can Love an Indian.'"

43. Letter, April 11, 1913, Personnel File, John A. Buntin, NPRC.

44. Letter, November 1, 1909, Personnel File, Maude Peacore, NPRC. See also Luther Standing Bear, *My People, The Sioux* (New York: Houghton Mifflin, 1928; reprint, Lincoln: University of Nebraska Press, 1975), 190, 234.

45. Letter, October 2, 1918, Personnel File, Harriet M. Chapman, NPRC.

46. Letter, November 5, 1917, Personnel File, Jessie Morago, NPRC. See also request for reinstatement, July 5, 1911; letter June 29, 1915, and letter, November 10, 1927, Personnel File, Madeline Jacker, NPRC.

47. Letter, July 1, 1925, Personnel File, Lavinia Cornelius, NPRC.

48. Wyman was from Isabella, Michigan, and thus most likely a member of the Saginaw Chippewa Tribe. Letter, October 24, 1912; letter, July 25, 1914; and letter, October 3, 1916, Personnel File, Sarah Wyman, NPRC.

49. Efficiency Report, April 1, 1913, letter July 9, 1909, and Request for Reinstatement, August 18, 1915, Personnel File, Naomi Dawson Pacheco, NPRC.

50. Efficiency Report, April 1, 1931, Lavinia Cornelius, NPRC; letter, November 1, 1909, and October 21, 1909, Personnel File, H. Courier, NPRC; letter, August 18, 1917, Personnel File, Madeline Jacker, NPRC; and letter, March 27, 1933, Personnel File, Harriet Kyselka, NPRC.

51. *Rules* 1892, 28. See also letter, March 5, 1919, Personnel File, Madeline Jacker, NPRC.

52. Indian Office, *Regulations of the Indian Office* (Washington, DC: Government Printing Office, 1904), 17. See also Scott Riney, *The Rapid City Indian School* (Norman: University of Oklahoma Press, 1999), 177–82.

53. See, for example, 1889 Application, Patrick Henry Hamlin, #1591, LR, RG 75, NARA DC.

54. Letter, November 5, 1917, Personnel File, Jessie Morago, NPRC. See also Indian Application for Appointment, n.d., and Efficiency Report, February 17, 1922, Personnel File, Addie Molzahn, NPRC; letter, May 2, 1914, Personnel File, Dollie Johnson, NPRC; Efficiency Report, May 1, 1926, Personnel File, Katie Brewer, NPRC; and letter, August 17, 1917, Personnel File, Elizabeth Morrison, NPRC.

55. Quoted in Virginia Moore Carney, *Eastern Band Cherokee Women: Cultural Persistence in Their Letters and Speeches* (Knoxville: University of Tennessee Press, 2005), 96.

56. Quoted in ibid., 97.

57. Letter, Jesse B. Mortsolf to Commissioner of Indian Affairs (hereafter CIA), October 15, 1915, folder: Carpenter, box 56, series 51, Hoopa Valley Agency, RG 75, National Archive and Record Administration, San Bruno, California (hereafter NARA SB).

58. Letter, Mortsolf to CIA, February 24, 1913, folder: Carpenter, box 56, series 51, Hoopa Valley Agency, RG 75, NARA SB; Edward Holden to CIA, March 26, 1914, folder: Carpenter, box 56, series 51, Hoopa Valley Agency RG 75, NARA SB; and Sherman Norton to CIA, June 17, 1913, folder: Carpenter, box 56, series 51, Hoopa Valley Agency, RG 75, NARA SB.

59. Letter, Mortsolf to CIA, October 17, 1915, Personnel Files, Sherman Norton, NPRC. See also Efficiency Report, January 17, 1914; letter, August 7, 1918; letter, August 7, 1918; Efficiency Report, May 1, 1918; and Efficiency Report, July 24, 1919, Personnel File, Naomi Dawson Pacheco, NPRC.

60. Letter, Mortsolf to CIA, October 17, 1915, folder: Carpenter, box 56, series 51, Hoopa Valley Agency, RG 75, NARA SB; and Industrial Survey, Sherman Norton, 1922, Hoopa Valley, Box 17, Entry 762, RG 75, NARA DC. Norton also actively participated in tribal affairs. Byron Nelson Jr., *Our Home Forever: The Hupa Indians of Northern California*, ed. Laura Bayer (Salt Lake City, UT: Howe Brothers, 1988), 146, 172.

61. Superintendent Mayer to CIA, July 12, 1918, Personnel File, Naomi Dawson, NPRC.

62. Application for Appointment, March 14, 1912, Personnel File, Nellie Santeo, NPRC.

63. Any Indian student could attend a school funded by the general fund, but schools funded by tribal land sales or treaties were generally limited to children from those tribes. See letter, May 9, 1914, Personnel File, Dollie Johnson, NPRC. Where their children were not eligible to attend the schools at which their parents worked, it appears as though Native employees turned to public schools in the area. I have especially found evidence of this for high school students, which may also reflect the lack of higher educational opportunities at most federal Indian schools. See letter, August 5, 1918, Personnel File, Dollie Johnson, NPRC; letter, April 30, 1918, NPRC; and letter, March 19, 1923, Personnel File, Harriet Kyselka, NPRC.

64. Estelle Aubrey Brown, *Stubborn Fool: A Narrative* (Caldwell, ID: Caxton Printers, 1952), 84-85.

65. Flora Gregg Iliff, *People of the Blue Water: My Adventures Among the Walapai and Havasupai Indians* (New York: Harper & Brothers, 1954), 264-65.

66. *ARCIA*, 1906, 47.

67. Testimony of Dr. Gates, *Indian Appropriation Bill: Hearings, 64th Congress, Second Session* (Washington, DC: GPO, 1917), 480.

68. A. O. Wright, "Contributions: An Indian School," *Wisconsin Journal of Education* 30 (1900): 83-85. See also Thisba Huston Morgan, "Reminiscences of My Days in the Land of the Ogallala Sioux," *South Dakota Historical Collections* 29 (1958): 46.

69. Laurence F. Schmeckebier, *The Office of Indian Affairs: Its History, Activities and Organization*, Institute for Government Research Service Monographs of the United States Government, No. 48 (Baltimore, MD: John Hopkins University Press, 1927), 482; and *Regulations*.

70. Letter, February 21, 1916, letter, January 17, 1916, and letter, July 11, 1916, Personnel File, William Blish, NPRC. See also letter, August 21, 1909, Personnel File, Charles M. Buchanan, NPRC. See also requests for transfer in Personnel File, John A. Buntin, NPRC.

71. *The Problem of Indian Administration* (Baltimore, MD: Johns Hopkins University Press, 1928), 160-62.

72. Letter, June 23, 1910, Personnel File, Agnes Reedy, NPRC.

73. Letter, December 9, 1920, Personnel File, Harriet Kyselka, NPRC. See also letter, January 28, 1913, Personnel File, John Buntin, NPRC; and letter, August 28, 1912, Personnel Folder, Michael H. Brown, NPRC.

74. *Interior Department Appropriation Bill, 1923*, Hearing before Subcommittee of House Committee on Appropriations, 67th Congress, 2nd Session (Washington, DC: GPO, 1922), 205-6.

75. Letter, CIA to J. Brown, September 17, 1925, Personnel Files, John Brown, NPRC. See also letter, CIA to Charles Burton, December 7, 1914, Personnel Files, Ella Burton, NPRC; and letter, Supt. Duclos to CIA, October 19, 1925, Personnel Files, Artie Peacore, NPRC.

76. Letter, CIA to J. Brown, September 17, 1925, Personnel Files, John Brown, NPRC; letters, March 8, 1917, and March 14, 1917, Personnel Files, Anna Paquette, NPRC; and letter, CIA to Jessie Scott, January 26, 1931, Personnel Files, Jessie Morago, NPRC.

77. Linda Gordon, ed., *Women, the State, and Welfare* (Madison: University of Wisconsin Press, 1990); Linda Gordon, *Pitied But Not Entitled: Single Mothers and the History of Welfare* (Cambridge, MA: Harvard University Press, 1994); Theda Skocpol, *Protecting Soldiers and Mothers: The Political Origins of Social Policy in the United States* (Cambridge, MA: Harvard University Press, 1992); Seth Koven and Sonya Michel, eds., *Mothers of a New World: Maternalist Politics and the Origins of Welfare States* (New York: Routledge, 1993). Margaret Jacobs has recently used the lens of maternalism in her comparative study of the United States and Australian policies aimed at Native children. See Jacobs, *White Mother to a Dark Race*. For additional sources on the maternalist welfare state, see Gordon, *Pitied But Not Entitled*, 55 n. 78.

4

Hard Choices

Mixed-Race Families and Strategies of Acculturation in the U.S. West after 1848

Anne F. Hyde

Senator Benjamin Davis Wilson's hands shook as he opened a letter from his wife, Margaret. He dreaded the news those pages would hold, and indeed he wept on that December night in 1870 over reports of his son's suicide in a downtown Los Angeles hotel. John Bernardo Wilson, his Juanito, was dead at twenty-five. Though his family had hired private tutors and sent him to fine Jesuit boarding schools, John never found a niche for himself in 1860s California. He worked in various Wilson family businesses, but, like many sons who bear too many expectations, he ran up debts and lost his family's trust. His father's business managers reported that John drank to excess, got into fights, and gambled away any money they gave him. Devastated by the loss of his son, Benjamin Wilson could only write as an epitaph, "Poor boy I loved him with all his faults."[1]

Other parents received similar crushing news about their sons. Some twenty-five years earlier John McLoughlin, the powerful leader who headed up the entire Columbia district for the Hudson's Bay Company, had to tell his wife, Marguerite, that their son had been murdered in 1842. Young John McLoughlin shared with young John Wilson a youthful history of bad behavior, trouble in school, drinking, and gambling. Another son, Charles Bent, distraught over the Sand Creek Massacre, ran away from his family, the Bents of Bent's Fort and the Cheyenne of southern Colorado. He joined the Dog Soldiers and spent a season burning forts and settlements on the central plains before his parents received word of his death at the hands of U.S. Army Scouts in 1867.[2] These scions of elite western families also shared the cultural fact of having parents from different ancestral backgrounds. It was common practice in the nineteenth-century West for Euro-American men to marry into powerful local families and become part of many generations of families who produced a world of mixed-race people in the American West. We have barely begun to see the outlines of this population and to understand its demographic power.

Several complex historical issues are illuminated by these stories of family tragedy: evolving attitudes toward race in the larger cultures around them that changed how mixed-race people were perceived; a shift in ideas about what families were and what role children should play in them; and a range of colonial practices imposed on people living in the post–Mexican War West. These ideological shifts undermined family efforts to protect children and legacies. The story gets more complex when we consider gender and geography. Daughters from mixed-race families fared better than sons, and some parts of North America remained easier for mixed-race people to navigate. This chapter first suggests the scope of mixed-race families in the post-1848 West, then explores four families to investigate strategies that parents used to acculturate and protect their mixed-race children. Finally, it assesses the impact of changing economies and hardening racial ideologies on the families that frame this chapter.

TRADE AND FAMILY: BUILDING EMPIRES IN THE NORTH AMERICAN WEST

For centuries, North America operated as a contact zone between peoples as the exploration, trade, and conquest that characterized the long colonial era mingled cultural groups. In particular, two centuries of trade left deep human traces along the rivers, mountains, and coasts. Looking carefully at the record we see that many—perhaps even most—male fur trappers, explorers, government agents, soldiers, and merchants who had dealings with Native Nations in the nineteenth century had relationships with women that resulted in children. Rather than treating these human connections as boys-will-be-boys frontier aberrations, we need to examine their long-term impact. Western couples gambled with these relationships and the children that came from them, as does every family that takes on the risk of reproducing. Scholars have tried to describe this risky racial frontier, but its significance has been only dimly recognized, especially in the region that became the United States. Because of the transience of the fur and hide trade, the number of people who participated only briefly or illegally, and the transborder nature of the business, estimating the number of people involved is tricky. Perhaps three thousand white men trapped and traded in the Rocky Mountains between 1810 and 1845.[3] The Great Lakes, Mississippi River, and Missouri River trades were far larger in terms of the longevity of the trade and number of furs that came out of those regions, so we can assume the labor required amounted to tens of thousands of people. If we add in the Arkansas River trade, the buffalo hide trade, and the cattle industries of the Mexican north, we have a truly large number of people. Moving beyond participants to their partners, extended families, and children becomes a dangerous exercise in guessing, but we can say that a lot of people were involved and that their presence marked the demographic profile of the North American West. Though this isn't news to people living in the region, scholars have just started to look, and mixed-race people appear everywhere—hidden in plain sight.[4]

Twenty and thirty years ago, in separate projects, John Mack Faragher and William Swagerty used LeRoy Hafen's compilation of mountain man biographies to analyze the families created by these men and their Native and mixed-race wives. Building on the work of Canadian historians who had examined the social history of the business that so dominated Canadian history, they wanted to see if those patterns held south of the Canadian border. Rather than the casual sex and brief marriages of convenience reputed to characterize this period in the trade, these two scholars found remarkable stability. Women and men of various ethnicities formed lasting relationships, had children, left personal and economic legacies to support these children, and cared for and worried about them.[5]

From the traders on the upper Missouri and Mississippi Rivers to the mountain men of the Rocky Mountains to the government agents, merchants, and soldiers along the Arkansas, we see visceral proof of cultural mingling. And these people and their extended families didn't just disappear. The traces they left in government records, business documents, and family letters and pictures, however, leave us with a lot of questions that Swagerty and Faragher encouraged others to ask. Were these fathers deadbeat dads who left their children behind, or was there a more complex range of relationships and family arrangements that came from such contact? How did communities incorporate mixed-race children and their families? What sort of challenges did these families face? Were these choices any simpler for Mexican, New Mexican, or Californio women who married Anglo men? What about Anglo women who married Native, Hispanic, or mixed-race men? How were their children perceived and received? Did girls have an easier time assimilating than boys? How did the evolving power of the North American state and new cultural ideas about race affect the choices people made in the fur trade world? The greatest challenge is learning how to see this West—a region long populated by Native and mixed-race people—as something more than an anomaly.[6]

To examine such questions, this chapter focuses on the period between 1840 and 1870, using the experiences of certain families to illuminate this mixed-race world we still barely see. The period was a complicated moment in several ways. Culture and the economy were reshaping fundamental ideas about family and race, while families evolved from being households with economic and political functions to being more emotionally focused "havens in a heartless world," to use Christopher Lasch's phrase. The families I describe here—complicated, extended, and built across cultures—were never simple nuclear families. Historians have learned over the past thirty years that looking for either progress or decline in how families operated in the past is treacherous and that there is no norm for what defines a family.

Another challenge is understanding parental ambitions. What did parents want for their children in this shifting world? How did culture or gender shape these hopes? Ultimately, what parents want to pass on to their children are networks of human connection and some measure of material comfort, but how these might be defined or achieved varies enormously. Like so many Americans, these middling to elite parents in the West that I examine believed in the power of their own nurturing and a formal education to give their children the tools and polish to succeed. It turns out that race, gender, and location mattered more than careful educational choices.[7]

This sort of analysis is fraught with difficulties because of the personal and intimate nature of the choices involved in marriage and parenthood. Attempting to understand why people form relationships in one's own family is hard enough, much less discerning motive for people living at least 150 years ago. In 1853, in the waning years of the Canadian fur trade, Chief Trader Robert Campbell risked making a judgment about the foolishness of men who married Native women: "It is too well known fact that few indeed of those joined to the ebony and half-ebony damsels of the north are happy or anything like it." He concluded with confidence that "none of them have pleasure, comfort or satisfaction of their Families."[8] Although it is dangerous to make judgments about individuals' happiness, we can see that the people in our examples did derive pleasure and comfort from their mixed-race families, but they took on new and very personal worries as the nineteenth century progressed. One of those new worries was race, or at least what race might mean for their children. Unevenly, but insidiously, any heritage not read as "white" became a source of shame for these children of the trade world.

Children have enormous social and economic impact because they become both a long-term responsibility of families and communities and a crucial investment in the future.[9] On frontiers and borders, children can take on the role of diplomatic markers as one group tries to make lasting connections with another. My examples are four large extended families, all of which had connections to the fur and hide trades and which formed relationships with people across cultural and ethnic boundaries. These people, quite different from each other though all from elite backgrounds, certainly do not represent the experiences of all mixed-race families, but their lives and choices reveal some patterns we should begin to trace. To help us examine the world that evolved out of the fur trade, we have Marguerite and John McLoughlin's part Cree children and part Chinook grandchildren; Henry Schoolcraft and Jane Johnston's part Ojibwe children; the complicated family of Benjamin Davis Wilson, Ramona Yorba, and Margaret Hereford; and, finally, William Bent and Owl Woman's Anglo-American and Cheyenne children born along the Arkansas River.

These families demonstrate the spread of a trading world that enabled people to make intimate connections across borders and cultures. They also bring into sharp focus the risks parents took because of their entanglement in the "tense and tender ties" of colonial practice that suffused trade. Westerners in these years made decisions about marriage partners, children's names, educations, and playmates with the demands of imperial political economies insidiously guiding each "choice."[10]

Instead of seeing these families as racial oddities, I see them as typical of the founding families of many western communities. The founders and leaders of western towns, territories, and states included people who came from this mixed-race world. Early governors of Michigan, Minnesota, New Mexico, Kansas, Missouri, Illinois, Arkansas, and Wisconsin; the first Anglo mayor of Los Angeles; and the founders of Detroit, Chicago, Denver, St. Louis, Kansas City, Santa Fe, and Austin all had roots in the fur trade, and most had intimate family connections with Native and mixed-race people. In spite of this long heritage of "ethnic mingling," as John Mack Faragher neatly describes it,[11] by the mid-nineteenth century Anglo-American cultural ideals had created a settler culture that replaced the colonial and imperial cultures that had previously characterized much of the West. This moment also involved a new calculus around race and what it meant, a change that had a great impact on mixed-race families as new western states and legislatures passed antimiscegenation laws and upheld them in the courts.

Unraveling the experiences of these parents and children is challenging for several reasons. Gender mattered, as Sylvia Van Kirk reminds us in her study of five fur trade families in Victoria, as "a complex interaction of gender and class dynamics ... enabled girls to transcend the racist climate of the colony more successfully than the boys."[12] The families in this chapter show these gendered differences, but we have to ask if we are imposing definitions of success that miss what these parents and children hoped for in this time and place.

Race led to another set of complications. Important differences characterize the way that Canada, the United States, and Mexico understood race and its relationship to marriage and families. Miscegenation was bad, but it could be forgiven with class and marriage more easily in Mexico and Canada than in the United States, with its complex racial baggage related to African chattel slavery. Recently, scholars of race have demonstrated that it took the full stretch of the nineteenth century for racialization to take on its meanest power. Until the end of the century, even in the United States, race had elasticity. Part of the problem here is figuring out whether nineteenth-century North America was a more or less racist place than twenty-first century North America. We can't trust our own eyes to look at the past because of the ways we see race now.[13]

THE MCLOUGHLINS OF FORT VANCOUVER

For an example of the messiness of determining who counted as "Indian" and how that came to matter, it is worth examining John McLoughlin, a longtime power broker in the Hudson's Bay Company's Columbia district, and his family. McLoughlin lived with his mixed-race wife, Marguerite, and their blended family of seven children at Fort Vancouver on the Columbia River. In 1846, after more than twenty years of ruling the region, the McLoughlins retired to settle on land in what had become the United States' Oregon Territory. After a very rocky start, during which his new Anglo-American neighbors denied him land and citizenship, John McLoughlin was forgiven for the transgressions of being Catholic and foreign, and eventually he became known as the father of Oregon. Marguerite McLoughlin, however, who was visibly Native, never became Oregon's founding mother. In the late nineteenth century she couldn't be forgiven for being an Indian, and her children would lose the rights she had to own property and to hold a place in elite society.[14]

Just how mixed this family was and how much that came to matter becomes evident in looking at what happened to John and Marguerite's children. The couple expected much of their children, who had been born into an elite and powerful family in the fur trade world. They shored up these expectations with careful and expensive education. Marguerite, who could not speak English and could not write in any language, insisted on literacy and a formal education for her children, who were taught to read and write in French and English when they were young. As adolescents, both the girls and boys attended boarding schools in Montreal, London, and Paris at enormous expense and family sacrifice. Sons received professional training in engineering, medicine, and business, and daughters received convent educations in preparation for life in western North America. It seemed, however, that blood trumped education in the settler culture that emerged there in the 1850s.

The eldest, Thomas McKay, from Marguerite's first marriage, married a Chinook woman named Timmee, the daughter of Concomely, a wealthy leader of the local Columbia River Chinooks, in 1824. She died in a malaria outbreak in the 1830s, but their son, William Cameron McKay, in theory the hereditary chief of the Chinooks, lived in Fort Vancouver with the McLoughlins until he went to school in New York in the 1840s. He received a medical degree from Willamette University in 1873 and served as a reservation doctor with the Umatilla people. After Timmee's death, Thomas McKay married a mixed-race woman named Isabelle Montour, daughter of a Fort Vancouver trapper. Thomas and Isabel had five children. Those children served as translators and "Indian scouts" during the Oregon Indian Wars and the Modoc War in 1860. One son, Donald McKay, operated an Indian show in the 1870s that promised audiences they could see "the

Donald McKay, Dr. McKay and Son.
WARM SPRING INDIANS.
HOUSEWORTH'S Celebrities, 9 & 12 Montgomery St., San Francisco.

FIGURE 4.1. Donald McKay, Dr. William McKay, and son posed in a photograph designed to show the civility of Oregon Indians in the 1870s. They were the grandsons of John and Marguerite McLoughlin and the sons of Thomas McKay and his Cree and Chinook wives. Even with their elite fur trade heritage, these mixed-blood sons struggled to find love and steady work in race-conscious Oregon. Courtesy of Oregon Historical Society, no. OrHi83306.

Man Who Captured Captain Jack and his Murderous Bands of Modocs."[15] These McKay sons stayed in the Pacific Northwest on the Umatilla, Warm Springs, and Colville Reservations and married Native women, if they married at all.[16]

The male McLoughlin children had a difficult time finding a place in the United States. Young John McLoughlin Jr. was killed by his own employees in a fight over Tlingit women at Fort Stickeen in 1842. In his account of the murder, H. H. Bancroft editorialized about his own feeling about mixed-race people: "I would rather be cursed than to mimic this man, John McLoughlin[,] who had such a vile copy of himself in the junior version."[17] David McLoughlin, the youngest child, trained for the foreign service in Paris but ended up working at Fort Vancouver with his father as a clerk and shipping agent. After his father's death in 1857, David went to British Columbia in hopes of finding gold. Somewhere on his travels he met Annie Grizzly, a Kootenai woman, and he married her in 1866. Technically their marriage was illegal because antimiscegenation laws, aimed at blunting the cultural legacies of the fur trade, had passed in Washington Territory. They had nine children, some of them named after McLoughlin family members: Margaret, Louisa, John, Angeline, and Eliza. David farmed on reservation land controlled by his wife's people and ran a store.

John and Marguerite's daughters had different experiences. In 1850 John and Marguerite's youngest daughter, Eloisa, married Daniel Harvey, formerly the manager of the Fort Vancouver farm but now her father's business partner. Eloisa's children went to Catholic schools in Oregon and California, and the girls married into elite Portland mercantile families and helped to found the Oregon Historical Society, thus displaying evidence of their solid American status.[18] Like the children of the fur trade aristocracy that Sylvia Van Kirk traced in British Columbia, the daughters in these families generally married white men—though some had French-Canadian last names, so their husbands may have been mixed race or connected to the racial mixing of the fur trade in ways not apparent to census takers. U.S. census forms between 1850 and 1880 had no category for mixed-race people of Native heritage: they were counted as either Indian or white. The sons, however, either never married or married women labeled as "Indian" in the census. Which of these children was happiest or most successful is, of course, impossible to determine. Children like David McLoughlin's offspring, who remained well integrated in their Native family networks, may have received immeasurable benefit and comfort from their families, while children who blended into white society in the Pacific Northwest may have suffered from dislocation and not-so-subtle prejudice. We don't know, but none of them had the future their parents envisioned.[19]

JANE AND HENRY: THE SCHOOLCRAFTS OF MICHIGAN

Jane Johnston and Henry Schoolcraft married on October 12, 1823, at Sault Ste. Marie in what is now the Upper Peninsula of Michigan. Their story clearly demonstrates the same tensions between parental ambitions and varying definitions of success that are described above. Living at a strategic site where Lake Superior joins Lake Huron, Jane and Henry hoped that a marriage joining Ojibwe, Irish, and Anglo-American families would be as powerful as the water that rushed past.[20] Their marriage reflected a confidence that evolved over several generations of mixed-race marriages in communities inhabited by Europeans and Native Americans in the fur-rich Great Lakes region. Jane's mother, Oshahgushkodanaqua, came from an elite Ojibwe family. At fourteen she had a vision about sharing a life with a white man, and her father, a local headman named Waubojeeg, arranged her marriage with an Irish trader named John Johnston, who had arrived at Lake Superior in 1791.[21]

John and Oshahgushkodanaqua, renamed Susan by her husband, had four sons and four daughters, whom they raised in a bilingual household. As devout Protestants and good Ojibwes, the children read Sir Walter Scott and learned to make moccasins and maple syrup. Their parents intended for them to take their place in elite fur trade society, where they could remain in the network of their mother's Ojibwe kin and have the financial security of employment in powerful fur trading companies. That ambition proved far more elusive than anyone would have imagined. The couple named their first daughter, born in 1800, Obahmwewageshegequay, or The Sound Stars Make When Rushing Through the Sky, and also Jane, for John's much-loved older sister. While the sons in the family went to boarding school in Montreal to perfect their Latin and French, Jane studied at home with her father and then, at the age of nine, went to Ireland to be educated and supervised by her Irish aunts.[22]

When poor but ambitious Henry Schoolcraft arrived in Sault Ste. Marie in 1820, Jane Johnston had become an accomplished writer and housekeeper, in both Anglo-American and Ojibwe eyes. Schoolcraft, a self-taught scientist and literary stylist, had failed completely in the glassmaking business and had left his home in upstate New York in a state of frustration and humiliation—a "ruined man" at age twenty-five. In grim economic times he hoped to find stable employment with a government salary. After a couple of trips to the Great Lakes, Schoolcraft decided that his economic future lay in the Indian Service and his literary ambitions in recording Native languages and stories. Like other Indian enthusiasts, he preferred Native people who spoke English and who lived in houses with chairs, tables, and bookshelves.[23]

John Johnston, lordly trader at Sault Ste. Marie, and his daughter Jane offered the key to these ambitions. Henry later described his relief at discovering "the polished circle of [Johnston's] household," where Schoolcraft could study the "manners, and customs, and ... curious philosophical traits of the Indian language" in the comfort of a parlor with people who understood the demands of scholarship. He admitted that he had found it "intolerable to converse with Indian traders and interpreters here, who have, for half their lives, been using a language without being able to identify with precision ... any of the first laws of

FIGURE 4.2. Jane Johnston Schoolcraft, 1800–1842. This painted miniature of Jane Johnston captures the woman of Ojibwe and Irish heritage as a winsome young lady of great accomplishment as a linguist and writer. The daughter of John Johnston, an Irish trader who spent his life on the Great Lakes, and Oshahgushko-danaqua, an elite Ojibwe, Jane would marry the Indian agent and scholar Henry Schoolcraft and become his interpreter of Native life. Courtesy of Bentley Historical Library, University of Michigan, Johnston Family Collection.

grammatical utterance." In the Johnston family he found proof of his beliefs about assimilation in "their agreeable, easy manners and refinement."[24]

Lewis Cass, then governor of Michigan Territory, decided that the Johnston trading post at Sault Ste. Marie would be an ideal site for an Indian agency, and Schoolcraft managed to be appointed as the new agent. His dual career desires—government service and a career in scholarship on Native languages and customs—seemed about to come to fruition. He wrote, almost giddily, in July of 1821, "I have in fact stumbled on the only family in North West America who could, in Indian lore, have acted as my guide, philosopher, and friend."[25]

Despite the fact they lived in the same house and ate their meals together, Henry and Jane wrote achingly stilted love notes to each other in the winter of 1822. Their prose demonstrated Jane's schooling in etiquette and Henry's painfully cold personality. One day Jane wrote, "Miss Johnston presents her compliments to Mr. Schoolcraft, & begs he will have the goodness to send her the sixth volume of Goldsmith." She added demurely, "Miss Johnson is sorry to interrupt Mr. Schoolcraft but hopes he will pardon the interruption."[26] A few months later we see how easily Henry took exception and how hard Jane had to work to avoid offending him. Jane apologized for her "mean attempt at wit" and for "wounding the feelings of one to whose superior understanding I have always looked up with a kind of pleasing awe and admiration." She also chided him a bit for his delicate ego and defended herself: "If you had listened, dearest Henry, to the explanation I was going to give you about the etiology of the word I put to you, you would have seen at once, that I could not have had the most distant idea of giving offence."[27]

Henry clearly resented her wit and intelligence—and her ability to speak several Native languages—even though these skills became a path to the success he so desperately desired. She tried to meet his never entirely articulated demands of piety, purity, domestic virtue, and intellectual attainment (as long as it never threatened his), but she never could. Schoolcraft viewed his life as a personal crusade to preserve Indian languages, to educate, convert, and civilize Indian people, and to demonstrate the potential of racial blending. His own family, both immediate and extended, became an experiment in what he would come to call "amalgamation."

Both parents worried about the challenges facing a mixed-race child after the birth of their first, William Henry Schoolcraft. The Johnston family provided a model, but the entire Sault Ste. Marie community and the larger world of various Native Nations and French and English traders interspersed among them served as a warning. Generations of mixed-race people lived on the shores of the Great Lakes, working as the labor force for the fur trade but also supplementing that work with farming, gathering, sugar production, fishing, and hunting. Many thousands of people lived in the mixed communities that characterized the Great Lakes and the river systems of the interior of North America, successfully raising families and participating in local and global economies, a world few residents of the United States, then or now, knew existed.[28]

The Johnston family represented the most elite group in this mingled world. Jane hoped that the wealth and skills of her Ojibwe family would sustain her own children. However, when Henry Schoolcraft became part of the family, he represented the leading edge of a powerful settler society that would see even the Johnstons as shiftless and barbaric. Even with their proud lineage, educations, and experiences, few of them succeeded on Anglo-American terms. Henry remained optimistic that his own mixed-race children would have a different reception because of his own influence. They would, in his view, be seen as exotic and capable, a "new American type," as he wrote hopefully in 1823.[29]

After this promising moment, hopes turned to ashes with the death of little Willy. Henry took Willy's death as "God's chastening rod" that had appeared to punish his family for adoring a child too much, a common response to a child's death in nineteenth-century America. Though Henry and Jane had two more children, Janee in 1827 and Johnny in 1830, Henry steeled himself against the dangers of emotional connection. Jane suffered enormously from losing Willy, especially when her father died soon after. To cope with the losses, she wrote verse that began and ended with these stanzas:

> Who was it nestled on my breast,
> And on my cheek kisses prest,
> And in whose smile I felt so blest,
>   Sweet Willy...
> But soon my spirit will be free,
> And I my lovely son shall see,
> For God, I know did this decree.
>   My Willy.

Henry published the poem in his memoirs, citing it as a "specimen of native composition" rather than remembering it as an emotional and personal response to his child's death.[30]

Henry's career continued to move forward. His success demonstrates the importance of his Ojibwe kinship networks, which would be equally important to his wife's siblings and his own children. As Michigan became a territory, the Johnston family's influence meant that John Johnston's mixed-race sons often held public office and received government positions. After his death, however, his children found it harder to make their way in the world. Susan Johnston continued to run the family business, but she also relied on her Ojibwe connections to fishing, trading, and sugar making. Henry Schoolcraft, acting as head of the Johnston family, ensured that his family made out handsomely when the United States government made land settlements with the Ojibwe in 1828, 1830, and 1835, and the

Johnstons received special compensation as "half-breeds" under other treaties. Schoolcraft helped pay for Jane's younger siblings' educations and supervised their choices in schools. He also practiced what we would now describe as nepotism, but deploying family connections was essential in the fur trade and the Indian Service in the nineteenth century. His brothers-in-law, George, William, and John Johnston, held numerous positions as subagents, traders, and carpenters at the Sault Ste. Marie and Mackinac agencies. His own brother, James Schoolcraft, arrived on their doorstep in 1830, married Jane's youngest sister, Anna Maria, and took up various paid government positions that Henry created.[31]

In 1834 Jane and Henry moved to the larger community of Mackinac. He wrote to Jane that summer expressing his fears about the Mackinac schools, where their children would "come into contact with children of bad language and low manners."[32] Even though his own career was proving satisfying and lucrative, as he rose from agent to superintendent of all of Michigan's Indians in 1836, Schoolcraft's anxiety over how to prepare his children for adult life emerged in a will he drew up in 1835. It stipulated that Janee should attend a female seminary "in the east" and that Johnny should attend college, where ideally he would study divinity.[33]

The Johnston family's dependence on Henry became a seriously liability when local and national political shifts made Henry's sinecure in the Indian Service vulnerable. His lax bookkeeping and his employment of his relatives made him a target for political housecleaning, and in 1840 Henry found himself without a government position for the first time in two decades. This setback came on top of a cataclysmic economic downturn in 1837. Henry had invested his personal savings, along with considerable cash settlements given to his Ojibwe Johnston relatives, in Detroit land schemes. They all lost every penny. In response to these double losses, Henry and Jane decided to move permanently to New York, where Henry could pursue his literary career and they could oversee their children's educations.[34]

Henry's white relatives, his brother James Schoolcraft and his brother-in-law John Hulbert, who were both married to Jane's sisters, kept their appointed positions, but the mixed-race Johnstons did not. This wasn't just about race—much of it was related to settling very old political scores on the Michigan frontier—but the Johnstons, especially Jane's brothers, never found good jobs after they were dismissed from their Indian Service positions. George Johnston, who described himself as "an Aborigine,"[35] had alienated himself from much of the Mackinac community—both Native and white—because of his occasional drunken brawls and his general air of haughty superiority. Educated in Montreal and trained for military service, he went into the family fur trade, but his career reflected the huge changes that had come to the trade after two hundred years. Similar to the strategies used by the McLoughlin and McKay children in the Pacific Northwest, George tried to trade independently, but like his brothers William and John, he would move between lower management positions with the American Fur

Company and government appointments. He had married Louisa Raymond, the mixed-race daughter of a French-Canadian trapper, and they had three children before her death in 1832. When George lost the position that his brother-in-law had secured for him and the money he had gotten from land claims, he never really recovered. Susan Johnston, their Ojibwe grandmother, stepped in and raised his children until George could put his life back together.[36]

Given this family turmoil, Jane had resisted the move to New York, and when Janee entered a female seminary in Philadelphia and Johnny (now called Johnston) was attending Round Hall School in Princeton, New Jersey, Jane was miserable.[37] Henry advised her to endure it for the sake of the children, and in a letter written in 1839 he warned her that "without education, children grow up, like the beasts that perish." He explained that they had a special parental responsibility because their children "were not simply of unmixed blood." Obviously worried, Henry continued that his "hopes for their success in life, are essentially based, on that mixture of Anglo-Saxon blood which they derive from their father" and "the western mind strongly exemplified in the Algic race" that was their mother's contribution. He feared that without careful training, "the result is want of foresight, and firmness—two traits that man cannot spare and excel in the sterner duties of human life."[38]

Henry, who did excel in the sterner duties, found himself in a very difficult situation when Jane died rather suddenly in 1842 while visiting her sister in Canada. Henry insisted on burying her in Canada, against the wishes of Susan, who desperately wanted her daughter to rest at Sault Ste. Marie. Henry inscribed Jane's mixed-race lineage on a large marble headstone, but he also wrote in stone that she was "carefully educated, of polished manners and true piety . . . fitted to adorn society."[39]

After Jane's death, her children rarely visited their Johnston family relatives, though George wrote encouraging letters to both children throughout their school years. The grandchildren of John Johnston and Oshahgushkodanaqua worked as teamsters, loggers, storekeepers, and servants in the world of the frontier Upper Midwest. The only land remaining in the family was Susan's sugar maple tract, which remained in probate until 1855 and then was condemned by the state for a railroad right-of-way.[40]

Henry Schoolcraft wanted to leave his mixed-race children with something more than worthless land. He continued to educate them and to find suitable employment and connections for them. In the end, Janee and Johnston may have done better had they been raised by their Ojibwe grandmother. Schoolcraft remarried in 1847 to a racist southerner named Mary Howard, who loathed Henry's children. Janee Schoolcraft finished school and moved to Washington, D.C., where her father had settled while petitioning Congress to fund his latest scheme, a great compendium of Indian history that would survey the status of all the living Native people in the greatly expanded United States that had taken shape in 1848. The vast project was undertaken by three white men who had mixed-race children: Henry Schoolcraft; Seth Eastman, army officer and artist of Indian America; and Henry Hopkins Sibley, who had once worked for Susan Johnston as a storekeeper and who was now governor of Minnesota.[41]

While he worked on the great tomes, Schoolcraft employed his entire family. Janee Schoolcraft, blonde and accomplished, worked as a copyist. She was briefly engaged to an old friend of her father's, the poet Charles Fenno Hoffman, before he was permanently institutionalized for depression. Though she may have dodged a bullet in this case, she never married. Johnston Schoolcraft, Henry's "darker Algic son," served as personal assistant on the Indian history project, which lasted through most of the 1850s, but he never found a job without the assistance of his father and he never married. He eventually served in the Union Army and died from wounds he received at Gettysburg.[42] Schoolcraft did get to spend his last years on a great literary project, but his lifetime experiment of racial mixing did not end as he had hoped.

THE WILSON FAMILY'S LOS ANGELES

How did the experiences of elite mixed-race families who emerged out of the fur trade in the Great Lakes and Pacific Northwest compare to those who lived other places and who mixed different races? The Wilson family of Los Angeles proved more successful than the McLoughlins or the Johnstons at protecting the fortunes they had created out of the fur and hide trade, land speculation, and mercantile endeavors. Benjamin Davis (B. D.) Wilson, a former fur trader turned landowner, had arrived in southern California in 1841. After the United States took California as part of the Mexican-American War and its treaty settlement in 1848, Wilson decided not to trust in the courts and the law to uphold his rights to a considerable amount of land granted to him by the Mexican government. Unlike many wealthy landowners, he would fare well in the courts, but he still invested in railroads and water companies to secure his investments. He hedged his bets in more intimate ways as well. Wilson had married into an old Californio family, the Yorbas, and took on the trappings of elite Mexican life. When his first wife, Ramona Yorba Wilson, died in 1849 he married an American widow named Margaret Sale Hereford, who had conveniently arrived on his doorstep. Financial success and remarriage, however, did not protect the Wilsons from the crises created by a changing world.[43]

Like the McLoughlins and the Schoolcrafts, the Wilsons believed that education would help their children develop the skills and personal connections to build lives in the new United States' California. Margaret and B. D. hired tutors to supplement their children's education in local schools that they founded and paid for. María de Jesus, Benjamin Davis Wilson's daughter from his first marriage to Ramona Yorba, became Sue Wilson when she went to boarding school in

FIGURE 4.3. John Bernardo Wilson, 1848–1870. With a slightly crooked smile, young Juanito posed for a formal photograph. Born into a Californio family as the son of Benjamin Davis Wilson and Ramona Yorba, he would grow into an unhappy man who never found a place in Anglo California. He committed suicide in 1870, breaking his father's heart. Courtesy of Huntington Library, San Marino, CA, PhotCL283.

San Francisco. Even though she was pressured to become a Protestant by her new stepmother, Margaret Hereford Wilson, with the support of her Yorba relatives she remained a practicing Catholic. She married James DeBarth Shorb, a gold rush emigrant to California, and had eleven children. Shorb, also a Catholic, became the son and partner that B. D. had always wanted, and he and his family built a house next door to B. D. and Margaret at Lake Vineyard. Sue, who looked "Mexican" (unlike her new Anglo stepfamily) but who spoke and wrote excellent English, seemed not to be burdened by racial markers. Her father's status and her husband's financial success allowed Sue and her children to move easily into the upper-class world of wealthy southern Californians but also to retain their ties to the Californio Yorba family through naming and godparenting. Even though Sue managed to cross growing ethnic divides, marriage between Anglos and Mexican Californians grew ever more rare.[44]

John Bernardo Wilson, later called Johnny, never seemed to find a place for himself. Refusing to go to school in the 1850s because he was teased about his poor English, he was tutored at home, then attended a Jesuit college near San Francisco. Like so many sons we have seen here, he ran up debts and lost his parents' respect when entrusted with family business matters. This is more than a trope about rich men's sons disappointing their families because of the ways in which new classifications involving race and gender affected cultural reception and self-perception. After these failures Johnny moved back to Los Angeles, where he lived on and off with his Yorba cousins and uncles, perhaps feeling more at home in that world. Then, in 1870, while B. D. was working on an appropriations bill in Washington, John killed himself in the Bella Union Hotel in downtown Los Angeles, which had once been owned by his father. John was buried in the Yorba family cemetery with his mother and his grandfather Bernardo, for whom he was named.[45]

THE BENT FAMILY OF ST. LOUIS AND COLORADO

As Benjamin Davis Wilson worried about how to consolidate his fortune and to protect his family in Southern California, other families worried about the same issues. The oldest children in the Bent family, having been born and raised in their father's great fort on the Arkansas River, about fifty miles east of the Rocky Mountains, headed east to school in 1854. They were the issue of a great diplomatic marriage between the Bent family of St. Louis and Santa Fe and the family of the greatest living Arrow Keeper of the Southern Cheyenne. William Bent built a great stockade on the banks of the Arkansas River and had conducted trade with many Native Nations in a free trade zone he had created with careful diplomacy and kin relations. He married Owl Woman in 1835 in a traditional Cheyenne ceremony and they had four children. The family lived both in her lodge in the Cheyenne camps and in the family quarters built in the fort. Bent's business extended for thousands of miles south into Comanche territory and north into Arapaho, Pawnee, and even Sioux lands and was bisected by the Santa Fe Trail. After Owl Woman died in 1847, her sister Yellow Woman or Island stepped into the role of Bent's wife and the children's mother, further extending the kinship network that supported the Bents' business and Cheyenne trade.[46]

After 1848, however, Bent and his Cheyenne kin recognized that their situation was rapidly changing. The gold rush of 1849 had brought a vast increase in traffic over the Santa Fe Trail as well as a terrible cholera epidemic. The Bent family fled with their children, seeing the rotting bodies of relatives as they headed north. After the family returned to the fort, Bent decided to move further up the river and blow up the old fort, which held so many memories. He also decided that his children needed a different education to provide them with more options as adults. He and Yellow Woman sent them east to the Missouri border, where the old Missouri River posts had evolved into thriving towns with large mixed-race populations. Most of the region's early founders had been involved in the fur trade and had married Native and mixed-race women. Seth Ward, Nathan and Alfred Boone, Ceran St. Vrain, Cyprian Chouteau, William Guerrier, Andrew Drips, Jim Bridger, William Bent, and Thomas Fitzpatrick, to name a few of them, knew that the familiar world of the fur trade would no longer support their children. As they looked for alternatives, they concluded, as did many middle-class and elite parents in the mid-nineteenth century, that formal education offered a ticket to mainstream success. Their children were educated at local boarding schools and at mission schools at Fort Osage and at Shawnee Mission. Catholic colleges in St. Louis provided further education for elite mixed-race and Native children. Mary, George, and Robert attended Mr. Huffacre's school for several years and boarded with the Alfred Boone family along with the mixed-race children of their father's old friends, Thomas "Broken Hand" Fitzpatrick and Ceran St. Vrain. The boys then went to college in St. Louis, where they were supervised by William's Aunt Dorcas.[47]

William Bent tried to provide his children with the materials for a prosperous future. He watched the brutal process of creating reservations for the Plains Nations and of keeping them there with military force. He settled onto a new ranch along the Purgatoire River while Bent's Fort slowly eroded back into the mud from which it had been built. Yellow Woman left Bent, moving permanently to the Cheyenne camps when her husband moved to the ranch. Even after his years as a successful trader and merchant, William died deeply in debt, leaving his children the Purgatoire ranch, its furnishings, some mules, and seventy-eight head of cattle. He also left them, after his last and most personal negotiation with the U.S. government, land along the Arkansas River especially designated for mixed bloods as part of reparations for the Sand Creek Massacre.[48]

William and Owl Woman's children did not benefit from their father's effort to create legacies of land and money, nor did education prove to be their ticket to mainstream success. The female children, however, seemed to have more options than the males. Mary Bent married an Anglo named Robinson Moore in 1860 and brought him to the Purgatoire ranch, where they spent their lives and raised a family. Though she was identified in both the Missouri and Colorado censuses as "Indian," Mary never let her children visit the Cheyenne camps. She baptized them in the Episcopal Church, and they blended into the rural communities that characterized southern Colorado. Julia Bent, the youngest daughter, married a mixed-race Cheyenne man, Ed Guerrier, who had served as an army interpreter. They hoped to remain on the Arkansas River reserve that Julia's father had negotiated for them, but all those lands had been preempted by white emigrants in the 1870s. They settled in Indian Territory with the Cheyenne and worked as teachers in the reservation schools.[49]

Even with the benefits of the Bent family name, land, and army service, the Bent boys grew into troubled men. Like Mary, Robert Bent came back to the ranch, in his case after serving in the Civil War on the Union side. He eventually married an Arapaho woman and moved to Indian Territory after his father died.[50] George Bent, after fighting with the Confederates and with the Cheyenne, married a Cheyenne woman named Magpie, the daughter of the leader Black Kettle, who led his people during the Sand Creek Massacre. George sold his land on the half-breed tract along the Arkansas to John Prowers, a white settler with a Cheyenne spouse, who would build a huge cattle empire on land William Bent had intended for the Cheyenne. After serving as a government interpreter and negotiator throughout the Plains Indian Wars, George and Magpie ended up on Cheyenne and Arapaho lands in Indian Territory. George married two other Cheyenne women, Standing Out Woman and Kiowa Woman, while living on the reservation, but drinking and gambling marred much of his adult life.[51]

The youngest Bent, Charles, became the family's angry young man. He witnessed the Sand Creek Massacre and vowed never to settle on a reservation or to see his white father again. Instead he became a famous Cheyenne Dog Soldier, raiding and burning settlements and military installations from Nebraska to Colorado in the 1860s. The "mongrel son of William Bent" became a frightening name used in newspaper articles that described the violent chaos of those years. For Cheyenne men joining the Dog Soldiers was certainly an honorable choice, but it was dangerous: Charles was killed by Kaw government scouts in 1867.[52] Whether the mixed-race Bents spoke English, went to college, owned land, or had influential friends didn't matter. They were labeled and recognized as "Indian" and thus couldn't become "settlers" or "pioneers"—the same lesson the McLoughlin children had learned in Oregon. They had families, communities, and heritages in Indian Territory, but they never enjoyed the same choices as their fathers and mothers about where to live, whom to marry, and how to name their children.

When B. D. Wilson and Ramona Yorba or Jane Johnston and Henry Schoolcraft chose to create families, they lived in times and places where mixed-race people had not yet been categorized. A generation later, however, marriages like theirs became discouraged or even illegal because racial categories had been created and the project of enforcing them had become central in U.S. culture. A settler culture, with rigid rules intended to benefit Anglo-American property holders, had replaced the more flexible categories that characterized trade culture. We have only a hazy view of a world of mixed-race people who filled western communities in the nineteenth century. We aren't used to looking for them, and we need to learn how to see them. My depiction of some families and my claim that they represent a common model isn't enough. Much work has been done on individual people and families, but we have no good idea of the scale of this mingled world, which couldn't simply have disappeared with conquest. We need to stop sketching and to start counting and filling out a more accurate view. This isn't easy, as the censuses and other government records deliberately erased mixed-race people. The children of the fur trade, however, did not disappear. They left important legacies in love and power that should shift how we understand our past and present.

NOTES

1. B.D. Wilson to Margaret Wilson, December 30, 1870, Wilson Papers, Box 14, Henry Huntington Library, San Marino, CA.

2. George Simpson to John McLoughlin, April, 27, 1842, in George Simpson, *An Overland Journey around the World in 1841 and 1842*, vol. 2 (Philadelphia: Lea and Blanchard, 1847), 181; George Bent, *Life of George Bent Written from His Letters, by George E. Hyde* (Norman: University of Oklahoma Press, 1968), 164–83; and Thom Hatch, *Black Kettle: The Cheyenne Chief Who Sought Peace, but Found War* (Hoboken, NJ: Wiley), 168–84.

3. Estimated in Harvey Lewis Carter and Marcia Carpenter Spencer, "Stereotypes of the Mountain Man," *Western Historical Quarterly* 6 (January 1975): 22.

4. Richard J. Fehrman, "The Mountain Men: A Statistical View," in *Mountain Men and the Fur Trade of the Far West*, 10 vols., ed. LeRoy R. Hafen (Glendale, CA: Arthur Clark, 1965–72), 10: 9–15; William R. Swagerty, "Marriage and Settlement Patterns of Rocky Mountain Trappers and Traders," *Western Historical Quarterly* 11 (April 1980): 159–80; and Susan E. Gray, "Meingun's Children: Tales from a Mixed-Race Family," *Frontiers: A Journal of Women Studies* 29, nos. 2 and 3 (2008): 146–49.

5. John Mack Faragher, "The Custom of the Country: Cross-Cultural Marriage in the Far Western Fur Trade," in *Western Women: Their Land, Their Lives*, ed. Lillian Schlissel, Vicki L. Ruiz, and Janice Monk (Albuquerque: University of New Mexico Press, 1988), 199–215; Swagerty, "Marriage and Settlement Patterns," 163–65; and Sylvia Van Kirk, "From 'Marrying-In' to 'Marrying-Out': Changing Patterns of Aboriginal/Non-Aboriginal Marriage in Colonial Canada," *Frontiers: A Journal of Women Studies* 23, no. 3 (2002): 1–11.

6. A generation of Canadian and American scholars, beginning with Sylvia Van Kirk, Jennifer Brown, and Jacqueline Peterson, followed by Susan Sleeper-Smith and Tanis Thorne, has investigated family formation in the fur trade. Historians have looked at families in the Indian Service, missions, mission schools, and other institutions in the nineteenth and twentieth centuries. Katherine Ellinghaus, *Taking Assimilation to Heart: Marriages of White Women and Indigenous Men in the United States and Australia* (Lincoln: University of Nebraska Press, 2006); Theda Purdue, *Mixed*

Blood Indians: Racial Construction in the Early South (Athens: University of Georgia Press, 2003); Margaret Jacobs, "The Eastmans and the Luhans: Interracial Marriage between White Women and Native American Men, 1875–1935," *Frontiers: A Journal of Women Studies* 23, no. 3 (2002); Carol Devens, *Countering Civilization: Native American Women and Great Lakes Missions, 1830–1900* (Berkeley: University of California Press, 2005); and Cathleen D. Cahill, "'You Think it Strange That I Can Love an Indian': Native Men, White Women, and Marriage in the Indian Service," *Frontiers: A Journal of Women Studies* 29, nos. 2–3 (2008): 106–45.

7. Jacqueline Peterson, "Women Dreaming: The Religiopsychology of Indian White Marriages and the Rise of a Metis Culture," in *Western Women: Their Land, Their Lives*, ed. Lillian Schlissel, Vicki L. Ruiz, and Janice Monk (Albuquerque: University of New Mexico Press, 1988), 49–68; Sylvia Van Kirk, "The Reputation of a Lady: Sarah Ballenden and the Foss-Pelly Scandal," *Manitoba History* 11 (Spring 1986): 4–14; and Van Kirk, "A Transborder Family in the Pacific North West," in *One Step Over the Line: Toward a History of Women in the North American Wests*, ed. Elizabeth Jameson and Sheila McManus (Edmonton, Alberta: Athabasca University Press, 2008), 81–93. The larger context of marriage in Canada has been examined in Sarah Carter, *The Importance of Being Monogamous: Marriage and Nation Building in Western Canada to 1915* (Edmonton: University of Alberta Press, 2008).

8. Robert Campbell to Governor George Simpson, August 31, 1853, quoted in Van Kirk, "The Reputation of a Lady."

9. Paula S. Fass and Mary Ann Mason, eds., *Childhood in America* (New York: New York University Press, 2000), 1–5; and Steven Mintz, *Huck's Raft: A History of American Childhood* (Cambridge, MA: Harvard University Press, 2004), 2–4.

10. Ann Laura Stoler threw down the gauntlet about North America as a true imperial overlord in "Tense and Tender Ties: The Politics of Comparison in North American History and (Post) Colonial Studies," *Journal of American History* 88, no. 3 (December 2001). Her critique there and in books, essays, and symposia that followed has shifted our simplistic view of the relationships between people on North American frontiers.

11. John Mack Faragher, "More Motley Than Mackinaw: From Ethnic Mixing to Ethnic Cleansing on the Frontier," in *Contact Points: American Frontiers from the Mohawk Valley to the Mississippi, 1680–1830*, ed. Andrew Clayton and Fredrika Teute (Chapel Hill: University of North Carolina Press, 1998), 309–13.

12. Sylvia Van Kirk, "Tracing the Fortunes of Five Founding Families of Victoria," *British Columbia Studies* 115/116 (Autumn/Winter 1997/98): 150.

13. Martha Hodes, *The Sea Captain's Wife: A True Story of Love, Race, and War in the Nineteenth Century* (New York: Norton, 2006), makes this point, while Peggy Pascoe's *What Comes Naturally: Miscegenation Law and the Making of Race in America* (New York: Oxford University Press, 2009) reminds us how rigid racial definition became in the twentieth century.

14. Dorothy Nafus Morrison, *Outpost: John McLoughlin and the Far Northwest* (Portland: Oregon Historical Society Press, 1999) is the most recent biography of McLoughlin, but the most important sources on his life are published letters, reports, and business correspondence, beginning with E. E. Rich, ed., *McLoughlin's Fort Vancouver Letters, First Series* (Toronto: The Champlain Society, 1941).

15. "Show Flyer, 1873," McKay Folder, Oregon Historical Society, Portland. For a larger context for these personal choices and career paths, see Philip Deloria, *Indians in Unexpected Places* (Lawrence: University of Kansas Press, 2004); and Cathleen D. Cahill's chapter in this book.

16. McLoughlin Family Clippings Files, McLoughlin House Museum, Oregon City, Oregon; John McLoughlin to James Douglas, March 1850, in *McLoughlin's Business Correspondence*, ed. William R. Sampson (Seattle: University of Washington Press, 1973), 140–42; Alberta Brooks

Fogdall, *Royal Family of the Columbia: John McLoughlin and His Family* (Fairfield, WA: Ye Galleon Press, 1978), 193, 232–36; and Richard Montgomery, *The White Headed Eagle, John McLoughlin: Builder of an Empire* (New York: Macmillan, 1934), 156–58, 199.

17. H. H. Bancroft, *The History of the Pacific States of North America*, vol. 22 (San Francisco: H. Bancroft and Co., 1882), 344.

18. McLoughlin Family Clippings Files, McLoughlin House; Burt Brown Barker, *McLoughlin Family Empire and Its Rulers* (Glendale, CA: Arthur Clark, 1959), 137–40; and Fogdall, *Royal Family of the Columbia*, 215–27.

19. Fogdall, *Royal Family of the Columbia*, 215–27; Van Kirk, "Tracing the Fortunes," 150; and "Instructions to Census Enumerators," 1860, 1870, and 1880 censuses, reproduced in U.S. Census Bureau, "Measuring America: The Decennial Censuses from 1790–2000" (2002), available at www.census.gov/prod/www/abs/ma.html (accessed September 14, 2009).

20. Marjorie Cahn Brazer, *Harps upon the Willows: The Johnston Family of the Old Northwest* (Ann Arbor: Historical Society of Michigan, 1993), 162.

21. Peterson, "Women Dreaming," 58–59; Anna Brownell Jameson, *Winter Studies and Summer Rambles in Canada* (New York: n.p., 1839), 214–15; and Brazer, *Harps upon the Willows*, 49–54.

22. Brazer, *Harps upon the Willows*, 75–82.

23. Henry Rowe Schoolcraft, *Personal Memoirs of a Residence of Thirty Years with the Indian Tribes on the American Frontiers* (Philadelphia: Lippincott, Grambo, and Co., 1851), 17–39; Richard G. Bremer, *Indian Agent and Wilderness Scholar: The Life of Henry Rowe Schoolcraft* (Mount Pleasant, MI: Clark Historical Library, 1987), 12–24; and Brian Dippie, *Catlin and His Contemporaries: The Politics of Patronage* (Lincoln: University of Nebraska Press, 1990), 182–85.

24. Schoolcraft, *Personal Memoirs*, 100, 107.

25. Bremer, *Indian Agent and Wilderness Scholar*, 96–97; Brazer, *Harps upon the Willows*, 153–154; Schoolcraft, *Personal Memoirs*, 92–93 and 107.

26. Jane Johnston to Henry Schoolcraft, December 26, 1822, Schoolcraft Papers, Library of Congress, Microfilm Version, Reel 18.

27. Jane Johnston to Henry Schoolcraft, January 27, 1823, Schoolcraft Papers, Reel 18.

28. Jacqueline Peterson, "Many Roads to Red River: Métis Genesis in the Great Lakes Region," in *The New Peoples: Being and Becoming Métis in North America*, ed. Jacqueline Peterson and Jennifer S. H. Brown (Lincoln: University of Nebraska, 1985); Bruce M. White, "The Woman Who Married a Beaver: Trade Patterns and Gender Roles in the Ojibwa Fur Trade," *Ethnohistory* 46 (Winter 1999): 109–47; Faragher, "More Motley Than Mackinaw," 311–15; and Susan Sleeper-Smith, *Indian Women and French Men: Rethinking Cultural Encounter in the Western Great Lakes* (Amherst: University of Massachusetts Press, 2001).

29. Brazer, *Harps upon the Willows*, xv; and Schoolcraft, *Personal Memoirs*, 189.

30. Brazer, *Harps upon the Willows*, 194–95; Schoolcraft, *Personal Memoirs*, 260–62; Karen Sánchez-Eppler, *Dependent States: The Child's Part in Nineteenth-Century American Culture* (Chicago: University of Chicago Press, 2005), 101–3, 131–44; and Jeremy Mumford, "Mixed-Race Identity in a Nineteenth-Century Family: The Schoolcrafts of Sault Ste. Marie, 1824–1827," *Michigan Historical Review* 25 (Spring 1999): 3–21.

31. Brazer, *Harps upon the Willows*, 207–8; and Bremer, *Indian Agent and Wilderness Scholar*, 180–86.

32. Schoolcraft, *Personal Memoirs*, 471; and Henry Schoolcraft to Jane Schoolcraft, July 10, 1835, Schoolcraft Papers, Reel 23.

33. Bremer, *Indian Agent and Wilderness Scholar*, 153.

34. Ibid., 202–6.

35. George Johnston to Henry Schoolcraft, February 12, 1827, Schoolcraft Papers, Reel 3.

36. Robert Stuart to Henry Schoolcraft, August 29, 1826, Schoolcraft Papers, Reel 3; and Brazer, *Harps upon the Willows*, 174–77, 187–90, 231, 250–52.

37. Jane Schoolcraft to Janee Schoolcraft, January 28, 1839, Schoolcraft Papers, Reel 28; Schoolcraft, *Personal Memoirs*, 626; and Bremer, *Indian Agent and Wilderness Scholar*, 217–19.

38. Henry Schoolcraft to Jane Schoolcraft, May 27, 1839, Schoolcraft Papers, Reel 8.

39. Brazer, *Harps upon the Willows*, 316.

40. Ibid., 332–35.

41. Dippie, *Catlin and His Contemporaries*, 165–68, 183–87, 205–7.

42. Bremer, *Indian Agent and Wilderness Scholar*, 255–77; and Dippie, *Catlin and His Contemporaries*, 192–95, 250–61.

43. Robert Glass Cleland, *The Cattle on a Thousand Hills: Southern California, 1850–1870*, 2nd ed. (San Marino: CA: Huntington Library, 1962), 108–11; Nat B. Read, *Don Benito Wilson: From Mountain Man to Mayor, Los Angeles, 1841 to 1878* (Santa Monica, CA: Angel City Press, 2008), 184–85; William Boardman to B. D. Wilson, June 12, 1860, Wilson Papers, Box 8; and Henry Markham Page, *Pasadena: Its Early Years* (Los Angeles: Lorrin L. Morrison, 1964), 8–17.

44. Read, *Don Benito Wilson*, 78–82; and Family Letters, 1856–57, Box 6, 1867–68, Box 13, Wilson Papers. There is a debate about the legality of such marriages. Even though no states made Hispanic-Anglo marriages illegal, they certainly discouraged them, according to both Albert L. Hurtado in *Intimate Frontiers: Sex, Gender, and Culture in Old California* (Albuquerque: University of New Mexico Press, 1979), 144–55; and Peggy Pascoe, *What Comes Naturally*, 122.

45. B. D. Wilson to Margaret Wilson, December 30, 1870, Box 14, Wilson Papers; Terry Stephenson, *Don Bernardo Yorba* (Los Angeles: Dawson's Books, 1963), 63; and Ann Laura Stoler, ed., *Haunted By Empire: Geographies of Intimacy in North American History* (Durham, NC: Duke University Press, 2006), 2–3.

46. David Fridtjof Halaas and Andrew E. Masich, *Halfbreed: The Remarkable True Story of George Bent* (Cambridge, MA: Da Capo Press, 2004), 1–7; David Lavender, *Bent's Fort* (Lincoln: University of Nebraska Press, 1954), 17, 43–62, 117–38, 347–49; Elliott West, *The Contested Plains: Indians, Goldseekers, and the Rush to Colorado* (Lawrence: University of Kansas Press, 1998), 63; and Samuel P. Arnold, "William W. Bent," in *Mountain Men and the Fur Trade of the Far West*, 10 vols., ed. LeRoy R. Hafen (Glendale, CA: Arthur Clark, 1965–72), 6: 62.

47. Halaas and Masich, *Halfbreed*, 76–80, 266–70; David Boutros, "Confluence of People and Place: The Chouteau Posts on the Missouri and Kansas Rivers," *Missouri Historical Review* 97, no. 1 (October 2002): 1–19; and Robert Campbell's Private Journal, *Bulletin of the Missouri Historical Society* 20 (July 1964).

48. Lavender, *Bent's Fort*, 325–26; LeRoy R. Hafen, *Broken Hand: The Life of Thomas Fitzpatrick, Mountain Man, Guide, and Indian Agent* (Denver, CO: Old West Publishing, 1973), 242–43; and Halaas and Masich, *Halfbreed*, 266–70.

49. Quantrille McClung, comp., *Carson-Bent-Boggs Genealogy* (Denver, CO: Denver Public Library, 1962), 95–101; Halaas and Masich, *Halfbreed*, 268–69; U.S. census, Jackson County, Missouri, 1860; U.S. census, Prowers County, Colorado Territory, 1870.

50. Halaas and Masich, *Halfbreed*, 270.

51. McClung, *Carson-Bent-Boggs Genealogy*, 95–101; Halaas and Masich, *Halfbreed*, 268–69, 296–307; and H. L. Lubers, "William Bent's Family and the Indians of the Plains," *Colorado Magazine* 13 (January 1936): 19–21.

52. Halaas and Masich, *Halfbreed*, 296–307; and Elliott West, *The Way to the West: Essays on the Central Plains* (Albuquerque: University of New Mexico, 1996), 116–24.

PART TWO

Law, Order, and the Regulation of Family Life

5

Family and Kinship in the Spanish and Mexican Borderlands

A Cultural Account

Ramón A. Gutiérrez

Open the newspaper. Turn on the television set. Listen to a radio broadcast just about any day of the week. What you will see and hear is a cacophony of voices telling us that increasingly the dominant way that residents in the American West think and talk about their most intimate relationships is in genetic terms. The mapping of the genome, the development of targeted gene therapies, and the proliferation of technologies capable of detecting DNA links are rapidly changing how we view the human body, how we define its relationship to others, and even how its disembodied traces in the form of saliva, hair strands, and fingernail clippings are tied to specific pasts and to particular presents. Recall, for a moment, how the veracity of former president Bill Clinton's 1998 assertion that he had not consorted with Monica Lewinski was legally challenged through an analysis of the DNA that Clinton had spewed on her dress. Eugene Foster and a team of researchers in 1998 reported in the journal *Nature* that a genealogical relationship had been found between the descendants of Thomas Jefferson and those of Eston Hemings, Sally Hemings's youngest son, based on a comparative analysis of Y-chromosome polymorphisms.[1] Project Innocence, an advocacy group for individuals who claim that they have been falsely imprisoned, has been assisting incarcerated women and men in proving their innocence by introducing DNA evidence as substantive parts of their legal appeals since 1992. Project Innocence boasts that it has freed 244 individuals, 17 of whom were on death row, through the use of genetic evidence.[2]

African Americans, most of them direct descendants of slaves, have been particularly eager to establish genetic connections to their remote African pasts. Slavery ripped many of them from their ancestral kinship groups, and over time what was left was knowledge of the fictive relatives they forged in the Americas. What they now seek is a deeper "truth," which they think genomic science holds. For almost a decade now Harvard professor Henry Louis Gates Jr., director of that university's W.E.B. Du Bois Institute for African and African American Research, has been selling African Americans such hopes in the form of personal genetic histories (PGH), promising to tell them where in Africa their ancestors are from. Much to Professor Gates's dismay, his own PGH tests produced contradictory results. One said he could trace his maternal ancestry to ethnic Nubians in Egypt some twenty to thirty thousand years ago, even before such ethnic categories could have existed. A second test confirmed categorically that his DNA could be traced back to Europe and showed he is just as genetically white as he is black.[3] Of course, Henry Louis Gates Jr. is not the only biological fundamentalist trying to recuperate ancestry for individuals who have no memory or mnemonics to help chart their genealogical ties. Log onto the Internet and perform a Google search on "DNA testing." You will find an array of profit-making companies—dnatribes.com, gtlDNA.net, Ancestry.com, DNAAncestryProject.com—promising, for a hefty price, to tell you whether the man you call "dad" and the woman you call "mom" naturally deserve those titles and, perhaps more importantly, to tell you where your ancestors originated twenty thousand years ago.

This fixation on the biological, with the singular importance placed upon nature in determining relatedness, is but one of the methods that has been used to define love and power over the centuries. Today we turn to science and genetics for answers, but in early modern Europe and the Americas, blood was the measure of connection. Great emphasis was placed upon the lineages through which blood had flowed historically, and this interest reached a particular obsession in the fifteenth century among the Spanish, who became intensely preoccupied with their *limpieza de sangre,* or their purity of blood. Through lengthy investigations and declarations Spaniards sought to prove that they and their ancestors were of pure blood, free of any ugly stain produced by mixing with heretics, Moors, Jews, and, in the New World, Indians.[4] Elaborate genealogies and family trees were only a few of the ways that blood's history was remembered and charted, particularly by royals. Blood was the fluid that culturally dictated how individuals so related should feel toward each other.

But blood is not the entire story. Intense emotional relationships between individuals not related by blood, such as between humans and animals and between humans and inanimate spirits, can be as potent. Today we refer to such relationships as "fictive," because we presume that the "real" nature of relatedness is to be found in blood, the female egg, and semen. One only has to look at adoption practices in our own culture to understand that relationships between parents and adopted children are just as significant and intense than those between parents and their natural progeny, and might be more so. Recall for a moment the disappointment that Leona Helmsley inspired in 2008 when she announced that she was leaving a large portion of her estate, valued at five to eight billion dollars, for the care of dogs; for her own dog she had established a twelve-million-dollar trust fund. Many pet lovers will undoubtedly agree that Helmsley, who was often called the "Queen of Mean" by employees at her New York City hotels, did a venerable if extravagant thing.[5] The Pueblo Indians of New Mexico would have understood Ms. Helmsley well. In the past and continuing to the present they, too, routinely offered food and prayers to the animals of their natural world, "adopted" them into their households as family members, and even entered into intimate communion with them to assure that their spirits did not cause any harm.[6]

What I propose here is that "real" and "fictive" understandings of kinship have long interacted in complicated ways, and I offer a history of the family as it developed in Europe, Spain, and the Spanish borderlands as a way of delving into the complexity of social reckoning over the ages. Today, when we think about the family, or *familia,* we equate it with our immediate blood kin, with a domestic unit that somehow harbors the individuals gathered in its intimate space from the trials and tribulations of the outside world. That which is within the family is private, within the isolating walls of the home, and devoid of strangers. But if we focus carefully on the historical genealogy of the word *familia* and on its ancient meanings, we will see that it was tied neither to biological relationships nor to a specific space such as a household or home. In classical Latin the word *familia* was used to refer to both persons and property. Historian David Herlihy has argued that ancient and medieval grammarians believed that the word entered Latin as a borrowing from Oscan, the language of a neighboring people. In Oscan *famel* meant "slave"; the Latin word for *slave* became *famulus.* "Fifteen freemen make a people, fifteen slaves make a family, and fifteen prisoners make a jail," wrote Apuleius, the second-century novelist. Ulpian, the second-century Roman jurist, further stated, "We are accustomed to call staffs of slaves families. . . . [W]e call a family the several persons who by nature of law are placed under the authority of a single person." What constituted *familia* was the relationship of authority that one person exercised over others; specifically, *familia* was the authority relationship that a master exercised over his slaves. The word *family* slowly evolved to describe the servants and staff members of lay and ecclesiastical officials. Thus as late as the nineteenth century the entourages of the popes of Rome, which included everyone from cooks to clerks to cardinals, were referred to collectively as *la famiglia pontífica,* or the pontifical family.[7]

The male who exercised authority over the *familia* was known as the *pater* (father), a role not associated with blood or genetic connection. The *paterfamilias* exercised absolute authority over those under his command; those under such supervision were a part of his *patria potestas.* Today we refer to a person's male biological parent as his or her father, though in Latin only the word *genitor* was used for this relationship. Gradually the meaning of the word *familia* extended to include not only slaves but also one's wife, children, and strays. Philology helps to explain how this occurred.

The 1984 edition of the Spanish Royal Academy's *Diccionario de la lengua española* lists thirteen different meanings and historical uses of the word *familia*. Family is:

> 1. A group of persons related to each other that live together under the authority of one. 2. The number of servants *[criados]* a person has, even if they do not live in his house. 3. The group of ascendants, descendants, collaterals, and affines in a lineage ... 6. The body of an order or religion or considerable part of one. 7. One's immediate kin ... 9. A group of individuals who share a common condition. 10. A large group of persons ... 13. (Biology and zoology) A taxonomic group that consists of several natural types that possess a large number of common characteristics.[8]

Explaining the word's usage, the *Diccionario* states that *en familia* (within family) means "without strangers, in intimacy." The definition of *familia* in the *Diccionario* succinctly summarizes how it evolved from an authority relationship over slaves to an insular, tightly knit group based largely on biological kinship, then to a private domestic institution centered around a hearth, before expanding its meaning as a capacious set of religious ties.

Many of the antique meanings of *familia* persisted into the seventeenth century, undoubtedly because of the revival of Roman juridical thought in canon law and in the legal institutions of Iberia's fifteenth-century kingdoms. Sebastián de Covarrubias's 1611 dictionary, *Tesoro de la lengua castellana o española,* defined *familia* as "the people that a lord sustains within his house."[9] Covarrubias concurred that *familia* was of Oscan etymology and explained that "although previously it had only meant a person's slaves," at the current time the word's meanings included the "the lord and his wife and the rest of the individuals under his command, such as children, servants, and slaves." Citing contemporary seventeenth-century usage, Covarrubias quoted the Siete Partidas, that legal code written by King Alfonso X of Castile in the later half of the thirteenth century, which stipulated that "there is family when there are three persons governed by a lord."[10]

The 1732 *Diccionario de le lengua castellana,* prepared by the Spanish Royal Academy for King Philip V, reproduced Covarrubias's definition of *familia* almost verbatim.[11] The only additional meaning of the word referred to "the body of a religion or a considerable part of it." As an example of its usage, it included the following: "Many are the Holy Families that occupy themselves seeking the salvation of souls." *Padre de familia* (father of the family) was "the lord of the house, even though he may not have any children. He is so called because he is obliged to exercise the role of father for everyone who lives under his dominion." *Hijo de familia* (child of a family) was that person "who has not taken the state [of marriage] and remains under the father's authority."

By the seventeenth century, both in Spain and in Spanish America, *familia* was a jural unit rooted in authority relationships born of servility and perpetuated through marriage. Family was tied to a particular place, to the house, or *casa*, in which the lord and his subordinates lived. The *casa* was a lord's domestic kingdom, much as the public realm was the king's. Authority, kinship, and space defined family at the most fundamental level.

The centrality of the *casa* as familial space had important ramifications for family structure. Every census, every demographic report, every civil and criminal investigation took this dwelling as the basic unit of analysis and implicitly assumed a set of authority relations therein. In early modern Spain and New Spain *casas* were large and small, rich and poor, nuclear and extended, but nonetheless equal in that everyone belonged to a household through marriage, consanguinity, or whatever circumstances befell orphans, slaves, and strays.

Spanish legal and philosophical tracts from the seventeenth and early eighteenth centuries equated kinship with consanguinity. The commingling of natural substance through procreation produced blood relations, which when conjoined with the authority of the pater were the cement that bound parents and their children as families in households. Ties of affinity created through marriage were important as well, but they were quite secondary in structuring the solidarities, obligations, and legal rights that family enjoyed.[12]

Juxtaposed to this restrictive secular notion of family rooted in authority, blood, and coresidence was a much more expansive religious theory of family and relationship advocated by the Catholic Church. According to Christian theology, every person had a body and soul and thus was both a natural and a spiritual being. Through baptism, the sacrament of spiritual regeneration, one was given full jural standing in the Christian community. According to theologians, baptism rivaled physical procreation itself, for as Saint Thomas Aquinas explained in the *Summa Theologica*, through baptism one is "born again a son of God as Father, and of the church as Mother." Once a person was incorporated in the mystical body of Christ through baptism, that person became a member of an extensive global community linked by spiritual kinship.[13]

These two diametrically opposed theories of kinship, one restrictive and the other expansive, one secular and the other religious, were at the center of much of the conflict that characterized relations between families and the Catholic Church in Western Europe from the sixth to the seventeenth centuries. Indeed, similar controversies would play out anew in the Americas as the juridical status of Native peoples was defined. In the long history of these disputes, the increasing power of families was what most bothered the church, undoubtedly reflecting its own hegemonic aspirations in society. The church was suspicious of the absolute authority a father could exercise over members of his household and thus constantly tried to set limits to that power. Tightly integrated families and households were developing into mighty lineages, kingdoms, and protonations, threatening the universal community the Catholic Church sought to create and control.

To weaken the power families had developed through such exclusivist practices as inbreeding during the Middle Ages, the church defined and sought to enforce an expansive theory of spiritual kinship in all realms of life. Relationships of the spirit, born of baptism, required Christians to act in certain ways; by getting individuals to behave in these prescribed ways, the church ultimately hoped to limit the power of fathers over their broods.

Marriage was the moment in the life cycle when a new family was created, thus ending a child's unmediated submission to the family's head. But matrimony, the ritual that socially sanctified the creation of family, was exclusively in the hands of the Catholic Church. To weaken the power of families, the church purposefully defined an expansive set of impediments that prohibited certain classes of persons from being joined sacramentally.

Of greatest importance to the church was the prohibition of incest, or marriage between close blood relatives. Starting at the Council of Elvira (ca. A.D. 300), the church began prohibiting marriage between persons related to the fourth degree of consanguinity (that is, three generations removed from the common ancestor). This prohibition was extended to the seventh degree of consanguinity at the Council of Rome (A.D. 1059). To understand how restrictive such a prohibition was, imagine a couple in each of six generations giving birth to two children. The consanguinity impediment eliminated 2,731 blood relatives of the same generation from choosing each other as mates. The church's intention was clear. By defining incest so broadly, it forced families to seek marriages for their children among much a wider group of people, thus hopefully weakening the concentration of familial solidarity and power.[14]

The power that fathers exercised within the family over wife, children, and slaves was itself a complex and contradictory issue for the church. The fourth commandment enjoined children to "honor thy father and mother," a stricture Saint Paul's Epistle to the Ephesians underscored when he urged Christians to obey God as wives, children, and slaves obeyed their masters: "Wives, submit yourselves unto your own husbands, as unto the Lord ... children, obey your parents in the Lord.... Servants, be obedient to them that are your masters... with fear and trembling ... with good doing service as to the Lord."[15] For Saint Paul, the kingdom of heaven was governed by rules identical to those that governed terrestrial kingdoms, or, as the Lord's Prayer put it, "on earth as it is in heaven." Nevertheless, the church simultaneously maintained a healthy skepticism about the untrammeled exercise of patriarchal power and through its theory of spiritual kinship and impediment to marriage consistently tied to limit its exercise. Parents were simply the earthly custodians of God's children, or so theologians and canon lawyers maintained.

The enforcement of an increasingly expansive set of incest impediments to marriage tempered secular solidarities rooted in kinship and naturally increased the church's power. The church also subverted parental and seignorial power from the Middle Ages to the present by maintaining that for a marriage to be legitimate its partners had to enter this sacramental state of their own volition, freely consenting, without fear or coercion. On this point canon law simply embraced the Roman legal maxim that *consensus facit nuptias,* or that consent constitutes the nuptial.[16]

Before the Council of Trent (1545–63), all that was theoretically necessary for two individuals to be joined validly was consent and conjugation. Canon lawyers maintained that because marriage was a natural bond, tangible evidence of a marital contract existed if there had been a mutual expression of consent signified by sexual intercourse and/or the exchange of gifts. Just as a person could be incorporated into the mystical body of Christ through a covert baptism to avoid persecution, so a man and a woman might similarly be secretly joined in marriage through consent and consort. But for such marriages to be considered legitimate in the eyes of the church, they also had to be ritually blessed and witnessed by a priest.[17]

The Council of Trent further elaborated ecclesiastical law by pronouncing that for a marriage to be valid and legitimate the ritual had to be performed by a priest who had to ascertain whether the partners were freely consenting. Since many marriages in early modern Europe and the Americas were arranged solely for the expansion and consolidation of family fortune, here was another mechanism by which the church could, and often did, undermine the exercise of paternal and seignorial control over children, servants, and slaves. If two individuals truly wanted to marry, whatever the parental objections, the church would marry them, just as it repeatedly refused to unite individuals it suspected were being forced against their will.[18]

SPANISH AMERICA

All of the concerns that had locked the church and families in struggle from the tenth century to the seventeenth in Iberia—the limits of paternal authority, the intensity of blood relations, the establishment and consolidation of families through marriage—were played out anew in Spain's colonial empire and renegotiated under different terms in the Americas with new colonial subjects. The nature of the contestation between patriarchs and priests was radically different in

Spanish America because the Catholic Church was juridically subordinated to the Spanish state as a result of a series of papal bulls collectively known as the Real Patronato (royal patronage). Dating from the final years of the Spanish reconquest of the Iberian Peninsula from the Moors, the Spanish crown proclaimed Catholicism the one and only true religion in the realm and promised to convert infidels in newly conquered territories, for which the pope granted to Spain's kings far-reaching rights over the regulation of the church. What the Real Patronato concretely meant for the regulation of family and marriage in Spanish America was that no separate form of civil law developed until the end of the eighteenth century. Family law was church law, a fact that persisted until the 1770s, when the "enlightened" Bourbon monarch, King Charles III, moved aggressively to secularize society and to limit the power of the Catholic Church in the regulation of everyday life.[19]

The conquest of the Americas and the extension of Iberian juridical forms into Spain's colonies presented the monarchy with new issues that would be resolved through the extension of antique principles. Perhaps the most nettlesome of all was the juridical status of the Indian. Did the Indians have souls? Were they born into a natural state of slavery? If so, did the authority a lord exercised over members of his household extend to those Indians who were awarded to the first conquistadores in tributary grants of entrustment known as *encomienda*?[20]

Flowing from the juridical definition of the Indian were other equally complex issues. Should Indians be allowed to establish families through marriage? If so, who were and were not appropriate partners? Should preconquest Native mating rites be deemed valid marriages? Would the church recognize them? Was the indigenous domestic hearth a moral terrain equivalent to the Spanish house?

Spanish theologians and jurists concluded that the Indians definitely had souls and, as newly conquered subjects, had to be baptized and incorporated into the faith. Indians could not be bought and sold as chattel, nor could they be incorporated into the household of an *encomendero* (the holder of an *encomienda*). Only indigenous peoples who already had been pressed into slavery by other pagans could be kept under its yoke. Indians who had resisted Christian advances and had been captured as prisoners of a putatively "just war" could likewise be enslaved, but only for a period of twenty years.

The nature of the relationship between an *encomendero* and the Indians "entrusted" to him produced long legal disquisitions. According to Spanish law Indians were considered free vassals who were under the age of majority. As "children," Indians required special protection and tutelage. Accordingly, indigenous towns and villages were entrusted to the Spanish conquistadores for Christianization and defense, for which Indians had to reciprocate with tribute payments in the form of foodstuff, hides and cloth, and often, though illegally, personal labor.[21]

In Spanish America *encomiendas* were brutally exploitative tributary relationships that quickly decimated the hemisphere's Native peoples. Stirred by the debates about the genocidal treatment of the Indians that Francisco de Victoria, Bartolomé de las Casas, and others provoked in Europe, the crown's conscience was moved. In 1542 it outlawed the distribution of new *encomiendas* and limited the number of generations extant ones could be inherited. These New Laws, as the legislation of 1542 was called, immediately sparked rebellions in Peru and other parts of the empire, slowing the law's enforcement and ultimately leading to the awarding of new *encomiendas* for the conquest of very peripheral, resource-poor areas such as the Amazon, Chile, Paraguay, and New Mexico.[22] In 1721 the institution was finally abolished, replaced by a rotational labor levy known in New Spain as the *repartimiento*.

Because Indians were considered children before the law, their marriages proved to be a complex issue. Since marriage was the sacrament through which families were formed, the church consistently proclaimed the right of Indians to marry freely and held that the canons of the Council of Trent would regulate their unions as well. It should be noted that the Council of Trent declared that mystical marriage and spiritual union with God was the highest form of love. The council's first marriage canon unequivocally stated that "whoever shall affirm that the conjugal state is to be preferred to a life of virginity or celibacy, and that it is not better and more conducive to happiness to remain in virginity or celibacy than to be married, let them be excommunicated." Matrimony, the council explained, had been instituted by Christ as a *remedium peccati,* a remedy for the sinfulness of lust, as a means of reproducing the species and educating children, and as an indissoluble state that conferred on a couple sanctifying grace so that they could endure the rigors of conjugal life.[23]

In the initial years of the conquest, before single Spanish women began arriving in the Americas in numbers that approximated those of single European men, marriage between Spaniards and Indians was encouraged by the church as the way to stem concubinage and the proliferation of defamed illegitimate mixed-blood children. By the 1550s, as the number of eligible European brides in central places increased, the incidence of Spanish-Indian marriages decreased, particularly among those elites who wanted their aristocratic privileges affirmed by legally proving their *limpieza de sangre,* or that their blood was pure of any ugly stain produced by mixing with Moors, Jews, heretics, or Indians.[24]

One of the most interesting problems the Spaniards had to adjudicate was the legal status of those unions established by Indians prior to their conversion to Catholicism. Polygamy was widely practiced in the Americas, particularly by the Native nobility. Which of a man's several wives would be deemed the Christian one? Pope Paul III (1534–49) quickly resolved the issue by proclaiming that by natural law the first woman who had intimate sexual contact with a husband had to be recognized as the legal wife. But if a man did not remember which of his several wives had been his first, he was free to choose the one with whom he would be sacramentally united in a lifelong monogamous union. This man then had to separate himself from the other women he had lived with, to dower them and any children they had produced, and to seek good husbands for his previous wives.

An equally complex problem for clerics was defining the indigenous residential unit that would be morally valorized as the familial home. Before the conquest the indigenous peoples of the Americas lived in a variety of domestic arrangements that were largely based on the gendered division of labor. Spaniards were accustomed to imagining the familial *casa* as the residential unit in which the biological ties of kinship were formed and in which feeding, socialization, sleeping, sexual activity, and ancestral rituals occurred. But indigenous peoples did not define the relationship between these functions and space in similar ways. Feeding, sleeping, sexual activity, and ancestral rites could occur in the same space but did not always. More often than not they took place in different sites. For example, among the nomadic Apache, for whom animal skins and natural vegetation provided their portable shelters, it was not uncommon for camps to have men's and women's huts and for a communal campfire or hearth to be used jointly by the women to cook and to feed both themselves and the men. Men spent large amounts of their time together on hunts, as did women, who would forage for seeds and plants. When men returned to their camps with meat, the foodstuffs were shared among all residents, sleeping quarters were segregated, and sexual rights to a wife were exercised in matrilocal space.[25] Joaquín Rivaya-Martínez's chapter in this volume describes the complexity of the Comanche camps and the sexual division of labor and space within them.

Similar arrangements existed among sedentary agriculturalists such as the Pueblo Indians of New Mexico and Arizona. Houses were owned by women, and within their walls resided grandmothers, mothers, and daughters. Sons and husbands provided these households with labor and meat but did not reside or sleep in them. Adult men lived in their own lodge houses known as *kivas,* in which they also ate when women delivered prepared food. Men who enjoyed sexual rights to one or several women would enter that woman's maternal house to enjoy such prerogatives at night, but by daybreak they returned to the men's lodge.[26]

One of the goals of Spanish colonization was to Christianize and Hispanicize the Indians, to restructure their societies to conform to Spanish familial and marital ideals. Church and state officials repeatedly congregated nomadic hunters and gathers with fluid housing arrangements into villages known as *reducciones* or *congregaciones* formed around nuclear households; indeed, habitation in durable houses was deemed a sign that Native peoples were civilized or were on the road to civilization. Whereas houses and huts previously had been segregated by sex, husbands were now forced to live with a wife under a common roof, thus fundamentally transforming the indigenous spatialization of kinship, residence, and sexual rights, and thus the fundamental structures of power.

Nomads, of course, vigorously resisted such attempts to congregate them as sedentary farmers dependent on imported European crops. The missions of New Mexico and Texas that ministered to the Utes, Navajos, Apaches, and Comanches failed miserably during the seventeenth and eighteenth centuries. The missions of Alta and Baja California devoted to the Christianization of nomadic Indians were ultimately more "successful" largely because of the extensive and sustained use of military force to curtail indigenous movement and apostasy, prompting Native American militants in the late twentieth century to refer to these missions as "concentration camps."[27] Christianity was an urban religion that flourished best in towns, and so it was relatively more successful among sedentary Indian groups who had been settled in town for several hundred years. Nevertheless, in those places where indigenous women had rights to property, under colonial rule these were systematically taken away and vested in men instead, quickly leading to the transformation of matrilineal forms of descent into patrilineal and patriarchal ones.[28] In his book *The Origin of the Family, Private Property and the State*, Friedrich Engels called this the historic overthrow of mother right by father right.[29]

SPIRITUAL FAMILY

The Catholic Church had long been suspicious of the strong blood ties that tightly bound elite families together and constantly militated to weaken them using its regulation of marriage and incest impediments as their bluntest instruments. Simultaneously the church also propagated its own superior theory of spiritual family through two institutions, compadrazgo and *cofradías*.

Compadrazgo

Unlike the natural family that was concerned with worldly authority, patrimonies, and bloodlines, spiritual family concerned itself primarily with the salvation of souls. Compadrazgo emerged in every part of the Spanish empire during the colonial period and continues to this day. Compadrazgo, often referred to in English as godparenthood or spiritual coparenthood, dictated that any Christian receiving the sacraments of baptism, confirmation, or matrimony had to be sponsored in these rites of incorporations into the Christian community by a set of godparents or coparents. Compadrazgo required three roles—parent (*padre/madre,* or father/mother), child (*hijo/hija,* or son/daughter), and godparents (*padrino/ madrina,* or godfather/godmother)—and created three sets of relationships: a natural kinship tie between a parent and child and two spiritual relationships, one between the child and his or her godparents and the other between the parents and the godparents. The godchild, depending on its sex, was referred to as an *ahijado* (male) *or ahijada* (female) by his or her *padrino* and *madrina*. The parents and godparents referred to each other as *compadres,* or coparents.[30]

Compadrazgo was rooted in a cultural conception of the person as both a natural and a spiritual being. Such dualistic notions of personhood were by no means unique to Spanish America. What was unique, maintains anthropologist Stephen Gudeman, was the belief that these two aspects of a person were quite distinct and as such had to "be entrusted to different sets of persons: the natural and the spiritual parents."[31] The profane secular world of kinship, that realm of existence deemed created through blood and substance and rooted in material life, belonged to the natural family. But before a person could enter into the Christian moral community, he or she had to be baptized. Through baptism a person attained juridical standing in the eyes of the church. Indeed, baptism prefigured the very death and resurrection of Christ, for through this sacrament one died to the world of nature and was reborn as a spiritual child of God as father and of the church as mother.

In the New Testament, Saint John articulated the foundation for this meaning of baptism through a set of questions Nicodemus posed to Christ.

> Jesus answered, and said to him: Amen, amen I say to thee, unless a man be born again, he cannot see the kingdom of God. Nicodemus saith to him: How can a man be born when he is old? Can he enter a second time into his mother's womb, and be born again? Jesus answered: Amen, amen I say to thee, unless a man be born again of water and the Holy Ghost, he cannot enter into the kingdom of God. That which is born of flesh, is flesh; and that which is born of Spirit, is spirit. (John 3:3–6)

The obligations of compadrazgo were initially primarily moral, but in time they also became material. Godparents were supposed to counsel and guide their godchildren, leading them to eternal salvation and God by ensuring that they complied with the laws of the church. Relationships between *compadres* were to be based on trust, tempering and displacing the values of the profane world marked by envy, greed, lust, suspicion, and war. But godparenthood could also entail material succor. If one's parents died, for example, it was the godparents' responsibility to care for the orphaned child. In times of economic distress or if there were a stark economic inequality between the godparents and their godchild, it was common for godparents to assist their coparents with resources, to guarantee loans, and to offer introductions, social connections, and even the marriage-validating gifts necessary for their godchild to marry well.

The dual definition of personhood as both spiritual and natural during the colonial period is clearly demonstrated in the baptism of captured indigenous slaves who were pressed into domestic servitude. In colonial New Mexico, for example, 3,294 Indian slaves were baptized between 1693 and 1849. In 280 of these baptisms the officiating priest recorded the names of the godparents and their exact relationship to the slave. Only 14 percent of the slaves also had their owners listed as their *padrinos*. A master/nonmaster combination served as godparents in 20 percent of these christenings, but in the majority of cases—65 percent, to be exact—no apparent relationship existed between the slave's godparents and their masters. A more striking pattern emerges in the godparenthood information on children born to slaves. Only in one out of 113 baptisms were the child's godparents also his or her parents' masters. Seven master/nonmaster combinations acted as godparents. In 92 percent of these baptisms, the child's *padrinos* were totally unrelated to the slave's master.[32]

Why were masters not preferred as baptismal godparents? Gudeman and Stuart B. Schwartz have proposed that the answer lies in the ideological clash between baptism and slavery.[33] In Christian theology a person is made of body and soul. Baptismal sponsorship creates a spiritual bond between the baptized person and the godparents that entails obligations of protection, instruction, and succor. Unlike slavery, a bond of domination over human volition expressed as control over another person's body and signified through servility, baptism bespoke an equality born of participation in the mystical body of Christ. When the church insisted that captives be baptized, two rather incompatible states—spiritual freedom and physical bondage—were brought together. The contradiction was resolved by the selection of a sponsor other than the slave master to witness the baptized person's liberation from original sin and rebirth into Christ's salvation. Masters themselves may have refused to serve as godparents, fearing that to do so would abrogate some of their temporal powers over the slave. And when slaves chose *padrinos* for their children, they invariably avoided selecting their owner to participate in their children's spiritual salvation.

The elaborate role that compadrazgo played in the Christianization of Alta California's Native peoples between 1769 and 1848 is excellently explored in Erika Pérez's chapter in this volume. When Indians were baptized or married at the Alta California missions they were not allowed to choose their own *padrinos*. Instead, the local mission father assigned them one from among the resident Spanish colonials. The duty of these godparents was to hasten the Christianization of the Indians, to lead them to moral lives, and to offer assistance in times of duress. In 1774, for example, Fray Junípero Serra reported that "out of the presidio [Monterey, California] come great heaps of tortillas sent by godfathers for their godsons, and even though each day a mighty cauldron of pozole is filled and emptied three times over, these poor little fellows still have a corner for the tortillas their godfathers send them."[34] The formal duties of spiritual coparenting were often at odds with colonial desires to extract Native wealth from the godchildren they imaged as inferior and uncivilized. Indeed, Pérez shows how compadrazgo created unequal relations between Indian godchildren and the Spanish/Mexican godparents. Native Americans were never allowed to serve as godparents for the Spanish colonists, and once Christianized Indians from Baja California were dispatched to Alta California to assist in the Christianization, these Indians began serving as godparents for locals and the assignment of Spanish colonial godparents all but ceased.

Several permutations of the ecclesiastical core of compadrazgo evolved in the Spanish borderlands of New Spain over time. Such modifications were frequently the result of the secularization of public life and the deeply rooted inequalities that marked relations between status and ethnic groups. At the end of the eighteenth century it was not uncommon for godparents to be selected to sponsor a variety of public community events. It was from among a town's elites that *padrinos* were frequently selected to serve as patrons for the celebrations associated with the town's foundation and the veneration of its patron saint. To this day, when cities such as Santa Fe, San Antonio, and Los Angeles celebrate the feast of their patron saint and their town's establishment, *padrinos* are chosen to bear the brunt of its costs.[35] Similarly, starting in the nineteenth century, when a person made, purchased, or was given an unconsecrated religious icon, godparents were chosen to sponsor the image's consecration, thus creating spiritual ties of trust and reciprocity. And undoubtedly to further similar aims in the present, throughout the Hispanic world parents still often select a set of *compadres* to underwrite a child's first haircut.

Cofradías

Cofradías (confraternities or brotherhoods) were a second institution organized by the Catholic Church in Europe and the Americas to deepen the importance of spiritual kinship and to temper the power of blood. The word *confraternity* and its Spanish equivalent, *cofradía,* derive from the Latin word *confrater* (cobrother). The idea behind the confraternity was that persons unrelated by blood should live together like brothers with a strong moral code of conduct guiding their daily affairs. Confraternities under ecclesiastical governance originated in Europe during the twelfth century as voluntary associations of the Christian faithful committed to acts of charity. In an era before social services were provided by the state, pressing social needs accelerated their formation. Victims of catastrophe, disease, or unemployment found succor through the works of mercy the confraternities performed, and by performing such acts members gained grace and indulgences, considered sure routes to personal sanctity and eternal salvation.[36]

Ecclesiastical law dictated that a confraternity was a group of men and women dedicated to the promotion of devotions to Christ, the Virgin Mary, the saints, and the poor souls in purgatory. *Cofradías* required episcopal sanction and were governed by statutes that described their rituals, membership and dues, required works of piety and mortification, and festival days of observance. Despite great differences in devotional practices, the common thread that bound most brotherhoods was their obligation to lead model lives of Christian virtue, to care for the physical welfare of the area's needy, to bury the dead, and to pray for the salvation of departed souls.[37]

The familial language that *cofradías* employed made them fitting outlets for the expression of broad-based social affinities. As equal members of the mystical body of Christ joined in spiritual brotherhood, residents of a community could, through acts of solidarity, put aside, if only momentarily, those enmities that typically marked the interactions among families, households, and clans in Europe and the Americas.

In Florida, New Mexico, Texas, and California, membership in one or more confraternities was often an essential part of the religious identity of every explorer, conquistador, colonist, and slave. As soon as a church was constructed and Mass was celebrated at any location, the establishment of confraternities soon followed. Although the form of Roman Catholic confraternities was remarkably uniform throughout the world, their meaning and significance were apparent only at the parish level, in the relationships confraternities had with each other.

Two types of *cofradías*—vertical and horizontal—existed side by side in most towns of any size. Vertical confraternities integrated a town's social groups, joining rich and poor, Spaniards and Indians, slaves and the free. By emphasizing mutual aid and ritually obliterating local status distinctions, these confraternities diffused underlying social tensions into less dangerous forms. In place of overt social antagonisms, parish confraternities squabbled over displays of material wealth, the splendor of their respective celebrations, and the precedence due a particular *cofradía* because of the sumptuousness of its rituals and the putative piety of its members.[38]

In Santa Fe, New Mexico, in Saint Augustine, Florida, and in San Antonio, Texas, vertical confraternities were formed shortly after these towns were established. Santa Fe, for example, had four such confraternities in 1729 dedicated to the devotion of the Blessed Sacrament, the Poor Souls in Purgatory, Our Lady of the Rosary, and Saint Michael. Fray Atanasio Domínguez reported in 1776 that the Santa Fe members of the Confraternity of Our Lady of the Rosary (also known as Our Lady of the Conquest) included soldiers, peasants, and aristocrats who communally celebrated the defeat of the forces of evil through the subjugation of the Pueblo Indians. On the feast days that commemorated the Virgin's conception, purification, nativity, and assumption, devotees carried her bejeweled and finely dressed statue through Santa Fe's streets while the royal garrison fired salvos. The celebration ended with dances, dramas, and bullfights.[39]

If vertical brotherhoods integrated disparate classes and social groups, horizontal confraternities mirrored a locale's inequalities based on race, honor, and property ownership. The social supremacy of the Spanish gentry was expressed through its opulent confraternity rituals. Dominated groups, such as Indians and slaves, equally expressed their dignity and collective identities with acts of piety that attempted to rival those of their oppressors.

For example, in Santa Fe during the eighteenth century a symbolic opposition existed between the Confraternity of Our Lady of the Light and the Confraternity of Our Lord Jesus Nazarene, also popularly known as the Brothers of Darkness. Governor Francisco Marín del Valle founded the former in 1760.[40] The confraternity owned a private chapel, which was the most ornate in town, with sumptuous furnishings, rich vestments for worship, and a large endowment of land and livestock. Its membership, which consisted of Santa Fe's elite Spanish families, numbered 236 in 1776. The brotherhood provided the local gentry with an institutional mechanism for negotiating conflict, organizing rituals that celebrated their spiritual bonds with celestial beings and more earthly ones, and with a way of avoiding contact with the town's lower classes during religious services.[41]

The Confraternity of Our Lord Jesus Nazarene, on the other hand, was composed primarily of *genízaros,* or detribalized Indian slaves.[42] Bound by their veneration of the passion and death of Jesus Christ, the Brothers of Darkness displayed their piety through acts of self-mortification, including flagellation and cross bearing, culminating each Good Friday with the mock crucifixion of one of its members. "The body of this Order is composed of members so dry that all its juice consists chiefly of misfortunes," wrote Fray Atanasio Domínguez, describing the poverty of the confraternity in 1776. It had no membership records, accounts, or endowments. Indeed, it had to borrow ceremonial paraphernalia from other confraternities to stage its prescribed rites.[43]

Cofradías were initially formed in Spanish America as a response to individual and collective needs for physical and spiritual succor. Though indigents were sometimes given meat from illegally slaughtered livestock and widows of soldiers killed in Indian warfare were regularly paid royal stipends, the church and state provided little else to indigents. The need to care for the poor, the sick, and the elderly gave rise to the confraternities of the Spanish borderlands. *Cofradía* statutes enjoined brothers to provide mutual aid in the form of charitable acts, religious instruction, and the burying of the dead. Given the high rates of mortality on the northern frontiers of New Spain and the limited access to the sacramental rituals of the Catholic Church, *cofradía* membership guaranteed at least a Christian burial. One of the greatest communal acts of brotherhood a member could perform was to participate in constructing a casket for a deceased cobrother, digging his grave, and praying for eternal peace for his soul.

SECULARIZATION OF MARRIAGE AND THE FAMILY

From 1492 until the middle of the eighteenth century, marriage and the definition of a family were strictly regulated by the Catholic Church, whose goal was tempering the secular, exclusivist kinship practices of biological families and extending what it considered to be its own superior notions of spiritual relatedness. Though there were several monarchical attempts to whittle away the church's power over family formation and marital regulation, those attempts proved minor and insignificant.

Not until the ascendancy of King Charles III to Spain's throne in 1759 did a civil law of family and marriage start to take form. Charles III initiated a far-reaching set of administrative, social, political, and economic reforms, collectively known as the Bourbon reforms. One of the monarchy's central objectives was to limit the power of entrenched interest groups, including the nobility, church, and guilds. King Charles III thus moved rapidly to end the church's monopoly over the regulation of private life. To accomplish this the crown began secularizing the missions throughout the Spanish empire, removing the Indians from ecclesiastical tutelage, declaring them fit to become independent Hispanic citizens, and transforming their communally owned land into private property, which quickly resulted in their transformation into a landless peasantry. The number of missionaries funded from the king's coffers to proselytize in Mexico, Peru, and their respective borderlands was sharply reduced, resulting in the formation of secular settlements without priests instead. The amount of land owned by the church and cultivated with unpaid Indian labor shrank significantly, as the crown strictly ordered clerics to justly compensate Indians for whatever work they performed. In 1776 a royal pragmatic on marriage was issued that required all children, under the pain of disinheritance, to obtain explicit parental consent to marry, thus curtailing the exercise of free will, which the church had long maintained as the requisite for the sacrament. The state increasingly expanded its role in marital formation, especially over its contractual and property aspects, limiting the church to the supervision of its ritual form and forcing clerics to serve simply as witnesses of the state's ultimate authority to regulate marriage.

The Bourbon reforms represented King Charles III's attempt to articulate an absolutist monarchy with clear lines of power, and accordingly to structure the family as a domestic monarchy in which a father's authority and power over the domestic hearth were comparable to the king's. The state's explicit aim was to deprive the church of its far-reaching powers in familial affairs and ultimately to subordinate the church to state power.

The result of the Bourbon reforms on family affairs and marriage in the Spanish borderlands was soon evident. By removing missionaries and by secularizing both the missions and society at large, the reforms reaffirmed the power of patriarchs as domestic lords. The authority exercised by the king was reproduced within the household. With the disappearance of the missionaries, too, the regulation of spiritual life increasingly fell to the community through its *cofradías* and compadrazgo. For example, today if one visits the Sanctuario de Chimayo in northern central New Mexico, about twenty miles north of Santa Fe, one will find that most of the rituals conducted at this shrine are performed by members of the Confraternity of Our Lord Jesus Nazarene, who venerate a statue of the crucified Christ known as Nuestro Señor de Esquipulas. At this shrine, the most frequently visited pilgrimage site in the United States and often called the "Lourdes of America," there is little ecclesiastical supervision of its public religious rituals. In fact, until 1929 the chapel was privately owned. Today pilgrims from around the world come there, as did Native Americans in prehistoric times, to seek a spiritual connection and a personal relationship with the gods.[44]

We can also very clearly chart the impact of secularization on confraternities. The Confraternity of Our Lord Jesus Nazarene, for example, started as a religious association but eventually became a secular political organization. The first observable change was a redefinition of the confraternity's sacral topography. Reporting on the condition of New Mexico's missions in 1776, Fray Atanasio Domínguez noted that the Confraternity of Our Lord Jesus Nazarene had separate altars in the churches of Santa Fe, Santa Cruz de la Cañada, Albuquerque, Tomé, and Abiquiu.[45] By 1814 the altar to Jesus Nazarene inside Santa Fe's parish church had been replaced by a freestanding chapel in the church's courtyard,[46] and by 1821 this chapel had been moved off church land and established as an independent *morada*, or chapel, on private property.[47] The confraternity maintained its own *moradas* without any form of ecclesiastical supervision, which itself became quite a bone of contention between the confraternity and the episcopal see.

Starting in 1836, the bishop of Durango, Mexico, who was in charge of New Mexico until 1848, continually tried to assert his authority over the confraternity by imposing the rule of the Third Order of Saint Francis. He failed to do so, claimed the bishop, because the confraternity's members were indifferent to the authority of his dictates.[48] In 1830 José de la Peña expressed succinctly why the church hierarchy found the Confraternity of Our Lord Jesus Nazarene so subversive. Peña wrote, "They have a constitution somewhat resembling that of the Third Order [of Saint Francis], but entirely suited to their own political views. In fact, they have but self-constituted superiors and as a group do as they please."[49] Fifty years later, in 1888, Archbishop Jean Baptiste Salpointe of Santa Fe similarly observed, "This society, though perhaps legitimate and religious in its beginning, has so greatly degenerated many years ago that it has no longer fixed rules, but is governed in everything according to the pleasure of the director of every locality; and in many cases it is nothing else but a political society."[50] Salpointe was indeed correct, for with the secularization of the missions the confraternities of the

Spanish and Mexican borderlands slowly began morphing into fraternal lodges, labor unions, mutual aid societies, livestock and irrigation associations, local cooperatives dedicated to various activities, and, ultimately, civil rights groups.[51]

Historical scholarship tells us that between the seventeenth century and the middle of the twentieth, marriages went from being arranged by kin, primarily to advance property and social alliances, to being governed by individual desires or love. Extended households governed by a paterfamilias and encompassing several generations gave way to the nuclear family headed by a husband and composed of a wife and children. Families shrank in size, and attention was increasingly focused on children. In earlier times the elderly lived with their children, divorce was rare, unmarried women infrequently gave birth, and patriarchal authority reigned supreme, but that is no longer so. Scholars locate most of these changes in the evolution of the organization of work, in the nature of industrialization and the sanitary revolution, and in changes in the devolution of property, particularly of family farms, which themselves accounted for rural-urban migration and changes in the sexual division of labor.

In this chapter I have tried to show how malleable an institution the family has been and how contestations over its form, its function, and its locale have been struggles over the power to regulate the formation and transmission of authority and wealth. When powerful Spanish families vied with the church over the latter's definition of incest, when the church elaborated alternative spiritual kinship structures in the form of compadrazgo and *cofradías* to weaken family blood ties, and when missionaries dictated how conquered indigenous people would live and love, what was at stake was how human reproduction would be harnessed for material gain. In ancient Rome *familia* was about slave labor. In the Spanish borderlands of the seventeenth and eighteenth centuries, as well as in what became the American West in the nineteenth century, family, too, was about the organization and reproduction of labor, both slave and free.

NOTES

1. Eugene A. Foster, M. A. Jobling, P. G. Taylor, P. Donnelly, P. de Knijff, Rene Mieremet, T. Zerjal, and C. Tyler-Smith, "Jefferson Fathered Slave's Last Child," *Nature* 396 (1998): 27–28.

2. See www.innocenceproject.org (accessed August 10, 2010).

3. Ron Nixon, "DNA Tests Find Branches but Few Roots," *New York Times*, November 25, 2007, available at www.nytimes.com/2007/11/25/business/25dna.html (accessed August 10, 2010).

4. María Elena Martínez, *Genealogical Fictions: Limpieza de Sangre, Religion, and Gender in Colonial Mexico* (Stanford, CA: Stanford University Press, 2008).

5. Stephanie Strom, "Leona Helmsley's Fortune May Go to Benefit Dogs," *New York Times*, July 2, 2008, available at www.nytimes.com/2007/11/25/business/25dna.html (accessed August 10, 2010).

6. Ramón A. Gutiérrez, *When Jesus Came, the Corn Mothers Went Away: Marriage, Sexuality, and Power in New Mexico 1500–1846* (Stanford, CA: Stanford University Press, 1991), 16.

7. David Herlihy, "Family," *American Historical Review* 96 (1991): 1–16; quotes from 2–3.
8. Real Academia Española, *Diccionario de la lengua española* (Madrid: Real Academia Española, 1984), 1: 630.
9. Sebastián de Covarrubias, *Tesoro de la lengua castellana o española* (Madrid: Por L. Sanchez, impressor del rey N.S., 1611).
10. *Las siete partidas del rey Don Alfonso el Sabio, cotejados con varios codices antiguos por la Real Academia de la Historia* (Madrid: Imprenta Real, 1807): ley 6, título 33, part. 7.
11. Real Academia Española, *Diccionario de la lengua castellana* (Madrid: Real Academia Española, 1732).
12. José María Imízcoz, ed., *Casa, familia y sociedad: Pais Vasco, España y América, siglos XV–XIX* (Bilbao: Servicio Editorial, Universidad del País Vasco, 2004); James Casey, *Family and Community in Early Modern Spain: The Citizens of Granada, 1570–1739* (New York: Cambridge University Press, 2007); and Francisco García González, *Las estrategias de la diferencia: familia y reproducción social en la Sierra: Alcaraz* (Madrid: Ministerio de Agricultura, Pesca y Alimentación, 2000).
13. Aquinas as quoted in Stephen Gudeman, "The Compadrazgo as a Reflection of the Natural and Spiritual Person," in *Proceedings of the Royal Anthropological Institute of Great Britain and Ireland* (1971): 43–49; quote from 49.
14. Jean-Louis Flandrin, *Families in Former Times: Kinship, Households, and Sexuality* (Cambridge: Cambridge University Press, 1979).
15. St. Paul's Epistle to the Ephesians 5:22–6:9.
16. Percy E. Corbett, *The Roman Law of Marriage* (Oxford: Oxford University Press, 1930), 24–67.
17. Jaime M. Mans Puigarnau, *Derecho matrimonial canónico* (Barcelona: Bosch, 1951), 87–146.
18. Jaime M. Mans Puigarnau, *Legislación, jurisprudencia y formularios sobre el matrimonio canónico* (Barcelona: Bosch, 1951–52), 26–67.
19. William Eugene Shiels, *King and Church: The Rise and Fall of the Patronato Real* (Chicago: Loyola University Press, 1961).
20. Lewis Hanke extensively describes these vigorous theological debates between Bartolomé de las Casas and Juan Ginés de Sepúlveda in *Aristotle and the American Indians: A Study of Race Prejudice in the Modern World* (London: Hollis & Carter, 1959).
21. Silvio Arturo Zavala, *La encomienda indiana* (México: Editorial Porrúa, 1992); and Eugenio Fernández Méndez, *Las encomiendas y esclavitud de los indios de Puerto Rico, 1508–1550* (Río Piedras: Editorial Universitaria de la Universidad de Puerto Rico, 1976).
22. Francisco de Victoria, *Political Writings*, ed. Anthony Pagden (Cambridge: Cambridge University Press, 1991), esp. 341–51; Bartolomé de las Casas, *A Short Account of the Destruction of the Indies*, trans. Nigel Griffin (New York: Penguin Books, 1992). On the promulgation of the New Laws, see Mario Góngora, *Studies in the Colonial History of Spanish America* (Cambridge: Cambridge University Press, 1975). On the awarding of *encomiendas* on the peripheries of the Spanish empire after 1542, see David H. Snow, "A Note on *Encomienda* Economics in Seventeenth-Century New Mexico," in *Hispanic Arts and Ethnohistory in the Southwest*, ed. Marta Weigle (Santa Fe, NM: Ancient City Press, 1983), 350–59.
23. James Mockett Cramp, *A Text-Book of Popery; Comprising a Brief History of the Council of Trent a translation of its doctrinal decrees, and copious extracts from the catechism published by its authority; with notes and illustrations: to which is added, in an appendix, the doctrinal decrees, and canons of the Council of Trent, in Latin, as published at Rome, anno Domini 1564: the whole intended to furnish a correct and complete view of the theological system of popery* (New York: D. Appleton, 1831), 322.

24. Karen Vieira Powers, *Women in the Crucible of Conquest: The Gendered Genesis of Spanish American Society, 1500–1600* (Albuquerque: University of New Mexico Press, 2005); and Juan Francisco Maura, *Women in the Conquest of the Americas,* trans. John F. Deredita (New York: Peter Lang, 1997).

25. Juliana Barr, *Peace Came in the Form of a Woman: Indian and Spaniards in the Texas Borderlands* (Chapel Hill: University of North Carolina Press, 2007), 69–108.

26. Gutiérrez, *When Jesus Came,* 1–36.

27. Rupert Costo and Jeannette Henry Costo, eds., *The Missions of California: A Legacy of Genocide* (San Francisco: Indian Historian Press, 1987).

28. For the experiences of the Spanish conquest among nomads, see Douglas Monroy, *Thrown Among Strangers: The Making of Mexican Culture in Frontier California* (Berkeley: University of California Press, 1990). The kinship transformations among the sedentary Pueblo Indians can be studied in Gutiérrez's *When Jesus Came,* esp. 77–84.

29. Friedrich Engels, *The Origin of the Family, Private Property and the State* (Chicago: C. H. Kerr & Company, 1902).

30. George M. Foster, "Godparents and Social Networks in Tzintzuntzan," *Southwestern Journal of Anthropology* 9 (1969): 261–78; and Sidney Mintz and Eric R. Wolf, "An Analysis of Ritual Co-parenthood *(Compadrazgo),*" *Southwestern Journal of Anthropology* 6 (1950): 341–68.

31. Gudeman, "The Compadrazgo as a Reflection," 45–72.

32. Gutiérrez, *When Jesus Came,* 181–82.

33. Stephen Gudeman and Stuart B. Schwartz, "Baptismal Godparents in Slavery: Cleansing Original Sin in Eighteenth-Century Bahia," in *Kinship Ideology and Practice in Latin America,* ed. Raymond T. Smith (Chapel Hill: University of North Carolina Press, 1984), 35–58.

34. Junípero Serra, *Writings of Junípero Serra,* ed. and trans. Antonine Tibesar, O.F.M. (Washington, DC: Academy of American Franciscan History, 1956), 71–73, as cited in by Pérez in chapter 10 of this volume.

35. Ronald L. Grimes, *Ritual and Conquest: Public Ritual and Drama in Santa Fe, New Mexico* (Ithaca, NY: Cornell University Press, 1976).

36. George M. Foster, "Cofradía and Compadrazgo in Spain and Spanish America," *Southwestern Journal of Anthropology* 9 (1953): 1–28.

37. There is an extensive literature on the origins and organization of confraternities in Spain and their transport to the Americas. See Alicia Bazarte Martínez, *Las cofradías de españoles en la ciudad de México (1526–1869)* (México, DF: Universidad Autónoma Metropolitana, 1989); Archivo General de Indias, *Signos de evangelización: Sevilla y las hermandades en Hispanoamérica* (Sevilla: Ministerio de Educación y Cultura, 1999); Pilar Martínez López-Cano, Gisela Von Wobeser, and Juan Guillermo Muñoz, eds., *Cofradías, capellanías y obras pías en la América colonial* (México, DF: Universidad Nacional Autónoma de México, 1998); Lara Mancuso, *Cofradías mineras: religiosidad popular en México y Brasil, siglo XVIII* (México, DF: El Colegio de México, 2007); and Albert Meyers and Diane Elizabeth Hopkins, eds., *Manipulating the Saints: Religious Brotherhoods and Social Integration in Postconquest Latin America* (Hamburg: Wayasbah, 1988).

38. Julio Caro Baroja, *Razas, pueblos y linajes* (Madrid: Revista de Occidente, 1957). For an excellent study for the ways in which Italian Americans still maintain their confraternity rituals in New York, see Robert Orsi, *The Madonna of 115th Street: Faith and Community in Italian Harlem, 1880–1950* (New Haven, CT: Yale University Press, 1985). See also Thomas A. Tweed, *Our Lady of the Exile: Diasporic Religion at a Cuban Catholic Shrine in Miami* (New York: Oxford University Press, 1997).

39. Eleanor B. Adams and Fray Angélico Chávez, eds. and trans., *The Missions of New Mexico, 1776: A Description by Fray Atanasio Domínguez* (Albuquerque: University of New Mexico Press, 1975), 18.

40. Anton Von Wuthenau, "The Spanish Military Chapels in Santa Fe and the Reredos of Our Lady of Light," *New Mexico Historical Review* 10 (1935): 175-94.

41. Eleanor B. Adams, "The Chapel and Cofradía of Our Lady of the Light in Santa Fe," *New Mexico Historical Review* 22, no. 3 (1947): 327-41.

42. Marta Weigle, *Brothers of Light, Brothers of Blood: The Penitentes of the Southwest* (Albuquerque: University of New Mexico Press, 1976).

43. Adams and Chávez, *The Missions of New Mexico*, 18.

44. Ramón A. Gutiérrez, "El Santuario de Chimayo: A Syncretic Shrine in New Mexico," in *Festivals and Celebrations in American Ethnic Communities*, ed. Ramón A. Gutiérrez and Genevieve Fabre(Albuquerque: University of New Mexico Press, 1995), 71-86.

45. Adams and Chávez, *The Missions of New Mexico*, 29, 80, 150.

46. Spanish Archives of New Mexico, microfilm reel 21, frame 686; Weigle, *Brothers of Light*, 44.

47. Richard E. Ahlborn, *The Penitente Moradas of Abiquiu* (Washington, DC: Smithsonian Institution Press, 1968); Bainbridge Bunting, "Penitente Brotherhood *Moradas* and Their Architecture," in *Hispanic Arts and Ethnohistory in the Southwest*, ed. Marta Weigle (Albuquerque: University of New Mexico Press, 1983), 31-80.

48. Weigle, *Brothers of Light*, 31; and Elizabeth Boyd, *Popular Arts of Spanish New Mexico* (Santa Fe: Museum of New Mexico Press, 1974), 49.

49. Peña quoted in Jean Baptiste Salpointe, *Soldiers of the Cross: Notes on the Ecclesiastical History of New Mexico, Arizona, and Colorado* (Banning, CA: St. Boniface's Industrial School Press, 1898), 161.

50. Salpointe quoted in Laurence Lee, "Los Hermanos Penitentes," *El Palacio* 8 (1920): 5.

51. For a history of how confraternities evolved into labor unions and political parties in Europe, see Mary Ann Clawson, *Constructing Brotherhood: Class, Gender, and Fraternalism* (Princeton, NJ: Princeton University Press, 1989). For the evolution of confraternities in the American West, see José Amaro Hernandez, *Mutual Aid for Survival: The Case of Mexican Americans* (Malabar, FL: Robert E. Krieger Publishing, 1983). The Alianza Hispano-Americana became the biggest of these mutual aid societies in the American West. For the Alianza's history, see Olivia Arrieta, "La Alianza Hispano-Americana, 1894-1965: An Analysis of Collective Action and Cultural Adaptation," in *Nuevomexicano Cultural Legacy: Forms, Agencies, and Discourse*, ed. Francisco A. Lomelí, Víctor A. Sorell, and Genaro M. Padilla (Albuquerque: University of New Mexico Press, 2002), 35-60.

6

Love, Honor, and the Power of Law

Probating the Ávila Estate in Frontier California

Donna C. Schuele

On October 19, 1850, with the assistance of a scribe, elite ranchero Antonio Ygnacio Ávila prepared his last will and testament. In earlier days, it might have been remarkable only that Ávila was not on his deathbed when he executed his will. But fall 1850 marked a time of significant legal change and uncertainty in the new State of California. The inaugural legislature officially established California as a common law jurisdiction, the American conquest having already weakened the force of Mexican civil law in practice. Although the state constitution guaranteed protection of community property rights, providing some stability to married Californios such as Ávila, there was no telling how an Anglo-dominated legislature would effect that mandate. Thus, as the scribe recorded Ávila's testamentary wishes, even the basics were in flux. If Ávila had been relying on Mexican social and legal structures to guarantee a smooth transference and maintenance of his family's wealth, he would be sorely disappointed. Just one month into California's statehood, American probate law was unsettled, so Ávila could not know how his will would be interpreted, or even what property would be considered part of his estate. But Ávila's window of testamentary capacity was probably closing quickly, and at stake was a 22,500-acre rancho and thousands of head of cattle to pass down to a wife and numerous children and grandchildren.

Certainly it was never Ávila's wish that his family lose its legacy. He had established and operated Rancho Sausal Redondo in an era of patriarchal authority and family unity, and the various Spanish/Mexican social structures—religious, economic, legal, and governmental—supported that arrangement. But the next generation found a way to escape their fathers' hold through the secularization of mission lands, which allowed self-interested agendas to replace collective goals.

FIGURE 6.1. Painting of Antonio Ygnacio Ávila by Henri Penelon. Courtesy of Seaver Center for Western History Research, Los Angeles County Museum of Natural History.

When the American era ushered in an even more fundamental individuality, reflected throughout society and especially in the law, it proved irresistible to Californios. Now freer to pursue their own interests, some embraced the American system of law and legal processes, perhaps without appreciating its potentially destructive force. For the Ávilas, the years surrounding Antonio Ygnacio's death in 1858 were the occasion of the perfect storm, leaving them particularly vulnerable to the effects of the Americanization of law and society. In a culture in which Californio status hinged on a family's landholdings and American status was tied to individual economic wealth, the Ávilas' loss of Rancho Sausal Redondo marked the swift decline of one of the most elite families of Los Angeles.[1]

THE ÁVILA FAMILY

In the early 1780s Don Antonio Ygnacio Ávila was born in Mexico into what became one of the founding families of the pueblo of Los Angeles. His life in Alta California was shaped by the needs of imperial Spain—Ávila apprenticed as a blacksmith, served in the military, and held local government positions. With the demand for artisans decreasing and land rights expanding after Mexican independence, Ávila devoted himself to ranching and continued to serve as a government official. In return, Spain and then Mexico gave him permission to graze his cattle on land known as Rancho Sausal Redondo, an area encompassing today's Los Angeles International Airport. In 1826 he built an adobe and stocked the rancho with about three thousand head of cattle. The Mexican government confirmed 22,500 acres to him in 1837, awarding him ownership rights to the land.[2]

In 1803 Antonio Ygnacio married Rosa Ruiz, from another founding family, who gave birth to upward of a dozen children. Five daughters and four sons lived into adulthood: Francisca, Ascención, Juan, José Martín, Rafaela, Concepción, Pedro, Pedro Antonio, and Marta.[3] Among elite Californios, large families were considered a fulfillment of duty to church and nation and thus were a mark of status.[4] These families existed within a patriarchal structure particular to and deeply embedded within the Spanish/Mexican culture. Mexican Californian patriarchy included a set of values known as the "honor/shame complex," according to which, historian Louise Pubols notes, "male honor ideally rested on a set of positive accomplishments—the ability to show force of will and command over others, the ability to protect and provide for one's dependents, and respect for the rank of other powerful men—whereas female virtue depended on a more passive ability to show submission to husbands, fathers, and elders, strict adherence to sexual propriety, and respect for social decorum." But also, in this dynamic of father-elder dominance, " one's generation . . . [was] at least as important as one's gender in determining relationships of rights, obligation, and dependence," such that "at every

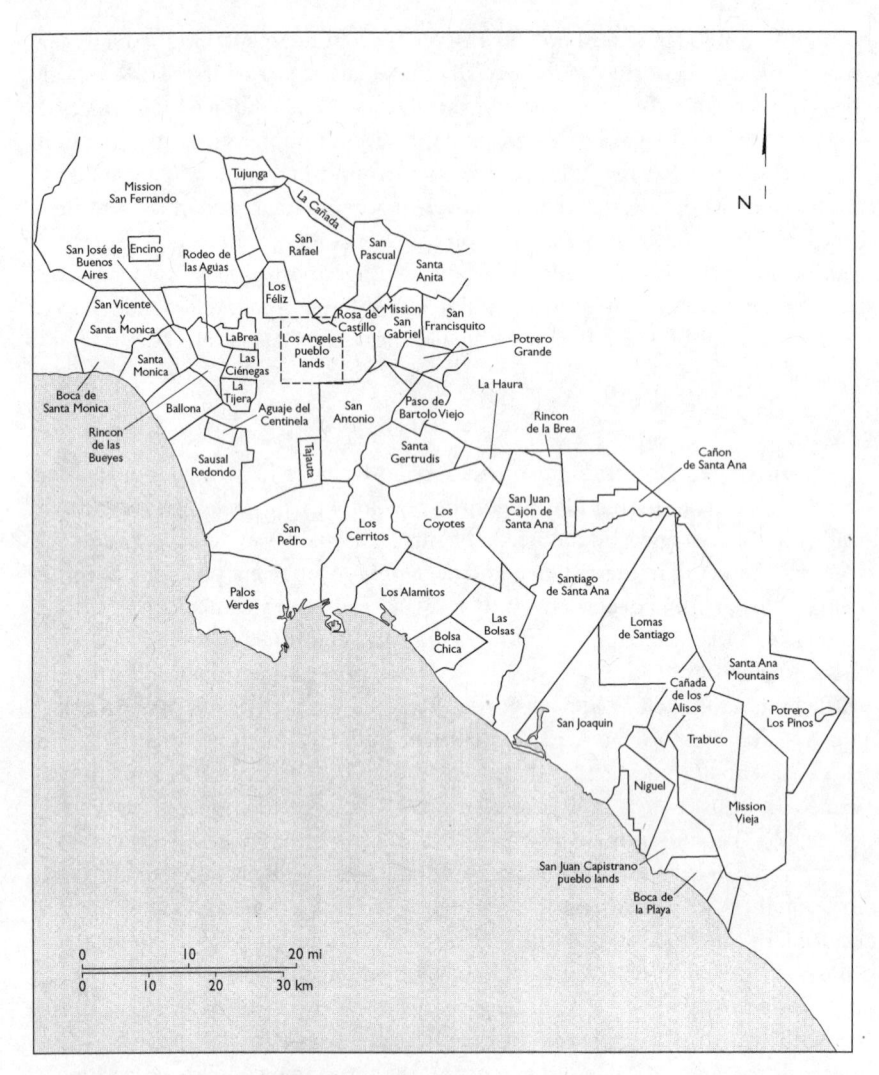

MAP 6.1. Land grants in Mexican Califonia

level of society, a person's age and stage in the life cycle further ranked him or her in family and community hierarchies of deference and authority."[5]

Although the contours of patriarchy were always under negotiation within families, its framework was based in the ancient concept of *patria potestas* (paternal authority), whereby male heads of household exercised complete authority over dependents, and obligations of parental respect and obedience prevailed into children's adulthood. Both age and marital status determined the nature and extent of children's independence. Single daughters and sons, no matter their age, remained subject to their father's authority during his lifetime except under certain conditions such as emancipation or the father's incapacitation. The legal regime supported the *patria potestas* requirement that children under the age of majority, twenty-five, gain their father's consent to marry or risk being disinherited. Once married, however, children were released from some paternal authority, no matter their age.[6]

In Mexican Californian society, hierarchically defined by landholdings and the distinction between *gente de razón* (people of reason, i.e., Californios) and *gente sin razón* (people without reason, i.e., Indian peoples), the doctrine of *patria potestas* ensured that children's marriages were not disruptive of family unity, and arranged marriages were the norm. Spanish concerns about marriages between unequals were expanded in the Americas to include concerns about wealth, and landed fathers focused on creating unions that would bolster kinship networks and increase the family's economic position. In addition, Pubols notes, "fathers claimed a special interest in controlling the marriages and sexuality of girls because ... a father's masculine honor ... depended on his ability to protect his wife and daughters from sexual dishonor." On the other hand, the Catholic Church's sacramental approach to marriage required consent by both parties, at least theoretically protecting children from being forced into unwanted unions.[7]

Under Mexican law, property might nominally be owned jointly by married couples or by individual members of a family, but the patriarchal structure guaranteed that family members would act predictably and in unison and not compete against each other. Ranchos were operated under a single manager, father or brother, "enabling the extended kin network to consolidate its holdings and direct management from a single source, and thus to increase its economic power." Culture and economy thus dictated that married children, both sons and daughters, remain on the rancho under the watchful guise of the patriarch.[8]

As each of his children matured, Antonio Ygnacio found his ability to exercise his paternal prerogative shifting. His first two daughters, Francisca and Ascención, married in a double ceremony in 1825, when Antonio Ygnacio's patriarchal authority and his status in the community were rising, and he chose well. Each wed into founding families of Los Angeles, the Sepúlveda and Sánchez families, whose patriarchs, similar to Ávila, engaged in ranching and held various governmental posts. Seven years later Antonio Ygnacio's eldest son wed into the Yorba family, which held one of the largest and earliest Spanish land concessions. Through these marriages, Antonio Ygnacio's children demonstrated a strong commitment to strengthening the family kinship network and economy. Upon these and subsequent weddings, Antonio Ygnacio presented each child with a gift of cattle, no doubt assuming that the stock would continue to graze on his land, further integrating his now-emancipated children in the family economy. In the mid-1830s the married Juan and his unemancipated, unmarried brothers, Pedro and Pedro Antonio, were working Rancho Sausal Redondo alongside their father, aided by a new brother-in-law.[9]

Around the time that Juan married, however, a tension inherent in patriarchal authority threatened to disrupt the Californio family economy. As adults, second-generation native sons yearned to escape their fathers' control, establish themselves as patriarchs, and gain the honor that would come with the position. A change in inheritance law after independence, however, left eldest sons vulnerable. No longer would they be the sole beneficiary of their fathers' land; now, property would descend equally to all children in the family. Any rebellion by this next generation was thus dangerous to the family economy. "When a son came of age and struggled to become an independent patriarch," Pubols argues, a "family could split apart at that moment, and the careful webs of alliances and obligations unravel."[10]

The secularization of the missions from 1829 to 1846 provided an opportunity for the younger generation to free themselves from the restrictions of patriarchal authority and economy without rejecting the system altogether. When the territorial legislature ordered so-called vacant mission lands to be granted according to Mexican colonization laws, notwithstanding earlier mandates to provide mission lands to Indians, "the floodgates opened, and scores of new grants, carved from mission estates, transferred to the hands of the native sons each year thereafter."[11] Thus the second generation was released from the strictures of patriarchy and gained the prerogatives of patriarchy at the same time.

Ironically, native sons gained this independence through family ties to the commissioners appointed to administer the mission lands, and the Ávila family's pattern of marriage and land acquisition in the 1830s reflected this new reality. Francisca's father-in-law, Francisco Sepúlveda, was appointed one of the commissioners of the deteriorating Mission San Juan Capistrano, sixty miles to the south of Los Angeles, and he was extremely generous to those connected to his family. Juan, who was newly married, and Francisca's husband, José Sepúlveda, received permission to graze their cattle on the mission lands in the early 1830s. A few years later Francisco opened the door to official grants, which accelerated once the Mexican government established a new pueblo in the early 1840s. José received his first grant in 1837 and added to that in 1842 to create the 49,000-acre Rancho San Joaquin. That same year Juan, along with his now-widowed sister Ascención, gained the 13,000-acre Rancho Niguel.[12]

As opportunities opened up for the second generation, the ability of patriarchs to use their children's marriages to bolster the family economy declined. The next few marriages connected the Ávilas with other founding families, but ones that were landless and thus less elite. Perhaps Antonio Ygnacio was most concerned with adding hands to work Sausal Redondo, yet the outcomes of these unions were less predictable, and later ones highlighted the social disruption that was creeping into Californio society. Rafaela married Emidgio Vejar around 1835, but her new husband quickly moved from working Antonio Ygnacio's rancho to joining his brothers-in-law in the new pueblo. He gained one of the last land grants, to the 6,600-acre Rancho Boca de la Playa, before the American conquest in 1846.[13]

It was the wedding of sixteen-year-old daughter Concepción in 1836 that seemed to set the family on an unfortunate path. Concepción was married to her first cousin, Servulo Varelas, whose landless family had spiraled downward after the death of his mother, Antonio Ygnacio's sister, when he was very young. Servulo's father was subsequently unable to control the sexuality of his two motherless daughters, who went on to have more than a dozen out-of-wedlock children between them. One was even publicly branded *mala vida* (living a bad life) just prior to Servulo's marriage. Antonio Ygnacio most likely was acting out of a sense of patriarchal responsibility to provide a better life for his nephew, who had yet to adopt a profession, yet it is hard to believe that Concepción would have any enthusiasm for sacrificing her virtue in the face of the shameful status of the Varelas family.[14]

The Ávilas would soon become connected through marriage with another equally notorious family. Widower José Martín remarried in the early 1840s to a widow who also traced her roots to early settlers, but her family had been shamed in 1836, when her sister was executed by vigilantes for having abetted her lover in killing her elite ranchero husband. Perhaps by this point Antonio Ygnacio had given up on finding honorable spouses among the local population. Pedro wed an outsider from Monterey in 1841, but he, too, could not escape social disorder. He fathered an illegitimate child in 1845, and the marriage appeared to be over by the American period.[15]

By the mid-1840s, Antonio Ygnacio's children who had wed well were living a day's ride from Rancho Sausal Redondo. Pedro and José Martín were the only married children connected to the rancho, their life circumstances leaving few options but to remain reliant on their father. Unmarried Pedro Antonio and Marta, still under the age of majority, also resided with their parents, although Pedro Antonio may have been emancipated by then. Most likely, Concepción and her husband were also tied to the rancho.[16]

At some point in the later 1840s, Antonio Ygnacio's mental and physical capacities began to diminish, probably due to a stroke. It appears that in 1848 he ceased engaging in business transactions and resigned as *juez de campo,* by then unable even to mount a horse. Tenets of *patria potestas* dictated that Marta, as the only unmarried daughter, would become her father's caretaker. Although Marta's marriageable years ticked by, no doubt her father would have opposed any union that interfered with her filial duties. Marta's life changed dramatically, however, soon after her father executed his will in 1850. By early March 1851, Antonio Ygnacio, Rosa, and Pedro Antonio were residing with Juan in San Juan Capistrano. Marta, now past the age of majority under Mexican law, married the month before at the nearby rancho of her cousin.[17]

Over the next seven to eight years, Antonio Ygnacio's health declined but the fortunes of the Ávila family improved. In 1851, her marriage apparently having ended, Concepción offered her fourteen-year-old daughter Ysabel in marriage to Ygnacio del Valle, son of the owner of the 48,000-acre Rancho San Francisco and Los Angeles' last alcalde. He was twenty-eight years Ysabel's senior. This union, perhaps born out of desperation, subsequently provided a home for Concepción, Antonio Ygnacio, and Rosa. Pedro continued operating Rancho Sausal Redondo, acting as his father's de facto agent in matters involving ownership of the land. The cattle boon brought on by the gold rush provided a considerable economic cushion, no doubt allowing the family to ignore the factors that were pushing it apart. Antonio Ygnacio passed away in 1858 at del Valle's Los Angeles Plaza adobe at age seventy-five, leaving what seemed to be a significant estate.[18]

THE WILL CONTEST

Rosa presented her husband's will to the Los Angeles County Probate Court and petitioned to be appointed coexecutor along with sons Juan and Pedro Antonio. Gone were the days of "the civil-law easy-going, not judicially supervised, settlement of the affairs of a decedent" during the Mexican period. The State of California had established an estate administration process based on "the Anglo-American concept of fiduciary management under a close judicial supervision." The new system not only decreased the executors' control, but it also allowed for individual interests to trump those of the family.[19]

Exploiting a contradiction in the law's notice requirement, Marta delayed the proceedings long enough to formulate a challenge to the validity of the will. During the Mexican period, Californianas had a long history of seeking judicial resolution of disputes through procedures that respected Californio social and family hierarchy.[20] If Marta believed that resort to Anglo-American legal process would result in a similar experience, then she sorely underestimated the bite of the adversarial system.

Marta's claims centered on a lifetime gift of cattle to her brother Juan, which was memorialized in the will. Antonio Ygnacio recounted entrusting eight hundred head to Juan in 1842, praised him for increasing the herd to two thousand over the next eight years, and declared that any further increase in the herd during his lifetime would belong to Juan.[21] With a cattle market focused on hides and tallow and Antonio Ygnacio in failing health, the gift may have seemed reasonable at the time. However, the 1850s were boon years for southern California rancheros, as the gold rush set off an unprecedented market for beef soon after the will was executed. Moreover, Antonio Ygnacio survived an additional eight years. From the vantage point of 1858, Antonio Ygnacio's gift to Juan now looked scandalously generous, and even detrimental to the family's interest.

It may have been the gift's violation of Californio family economy norms that motivated Marta to seek its avoidance, but she had to present her arguments in the context of American legal culture and doctrine. Nineteenth-century American law was increasingly individualistic; it cared little about family cohesion and filial respect once children reached adulthood, and the doctrine of *patria potestas* was irrelevant. In the American law of estates, the measure of the validity of a gift or a testamentary bequest was not its accordance with family interests. Instead the focus was on the mental capacity and the state of mind of the individual donor.[22]

Having closely witnessed her father's declining health, Marta contended that the lifetime gift to Juan was void, either because by 1850 her father lacked the capacity to make the gift or because Juan procured the gift through fraud. In addition, Marta argued that the will itself was void due to lack of testamentary capacity or Juan's fraud and undue influence. According to Marta, by 1850 Antonio Ygnacio had already been "incompetent by reason of mental imbecility and unsoundness of mind to transact any business or to make said will" for several years. She acknowledged that Juan had become his father's agent some time before the will was executed, but she argued that this arrangement resulted from Antonio Ygnacio's diminished capacities rather than any agreement between the two. If so, American law might provide Juan with the value of his services, but that figure would not be tied to the increasing value of the cattle.[23]

Alternatively, Marta contended that Juan had committed fraud by underreporting by 2,500 head the number of Antonio Ygnacio's cattle that had been born on Rancho Niguel between 1842 and 1850, prior to the gift.[24] Such an underreporting would allow Juan to lay claim to significantly more cattle and profits between 1850 and 1858 than he otherwise would be entitled to. Should Marta prevail, the excess cattle and profits would become a part of her father's probate estate, to be divided among her and her siblings. Marta's focus on this personal property, in the context of the vast real property included in this estate, reflected both the culture and economy. Unlike Anglos, Californios had not commodified their land, and livestock was seen as families' source of wealth. Even so, it is hard to imagine that this lawsuit was really about additional cattle.

Evidence of fraud on Juan's part was circumstantial at best. The day before his father died, Juan sought and received a conservatorship over Antonio Ygnacio. Perhaps he suspected that his sister was prepared to contest his handling of their father's affairs and worried that his informal management would not withstand American judicial scrutiny. And certain provisions in the will looked questionable.

For example, the unequal treatment of the siblings was explained as "justice in favor of those who have been most meritorious," a statement certain to exacerbate rather than temper hard feelings. Moreover, in imploring the siblings not to cause trouble over the uneven treatment, the will made a pointed reference to Juan: "I wish, and it is my will that no one disturb him for reason of the increase [in the herd] nor for other cause whatsoever, since I am satisfied that he has conducted himself very well." According to Marta, these provisions were Juan's idea, "the better to conceal his frauds ... and to protect himself," and adopted by Antonio Ygnacio only because of his "imbecility" and vulnerability to Juan's influence.[25]

Juan Ávila was probably the last Californio his countrymen would expect to be accused, by a younger sister no less, of dishonorable behavior. By 1858 he was one of the most elite and wealthy members of San Juan Capistrano. If anyone exemplified a *gente de razón*, it was Juan, who had a reputation as a man of reason, a man of his word. Elite Californios embraced a sense of reciprocity and obligation, where wealth was merely the means to act honorably. Acting in a self-interested, acquisitive way was unacceptable.[26]

It would be difficult to explain Marta's radical step of suing her eldest brother if there had not been some sort of estrangement in the family, including a breakdown in the patriarchal structure so crucial to Californio culture and economy. Certainly, the decampment to San Juan Capistrano in the mid-1830s of those siblings who wed well, the series of odd and even shame-ridden marriages of other siblings beginning around the same time, and Antonio Ygnacio's declining health in the 1840s indicate that the family had ceased operating as a patriarchal unit long ago, the dysfunction perhaps temporarily masked by a booming cattle market in the 1850s. The gift to Juan may have simply been the breaking point, while Marta's marriage, coming so soon after the execution of Antonio Ygnacio's will, may hold other clues.

Perhaps Marta had married against her family's wishes and, unable to stop the wedding, they responded by ostracizing her. Marta's husband, Juan Nepomuceno Padilla, was essentially an outlaw. Having emigrated from Mexico to San Francisco in the mid-1840s, he became embroiled in the Bear Flag Revolt in 1846. When two Americans were killed and mutilated under his command, Padilla fled for his life to southern California. He hid out for two years, returned north in 1848 to sell his interests in two ranchos, and headed south again in 1850 flush from the land sales, marrying Marta soon afterward.[27]

If Marta had hoped to marry Padilla during his first stay in Los Angeles, Antonio Ygnacio may have had the power to block the wedding, and at least he could have threatened her with disinheritance. But by 1851 there was little the patriarch could do. First, with the institution of American law, including civil marriage and a lower age of majority, Marta would have met the qualifications to marry without parental consent. Second, although American law would not have stopped Antonio Ygnacio from disinheriting his daughter, he probably lacked the mental capacity to alter his will after its execution. More to the point, Antonio Ygnacio's incapacitation prevented him from exercising any authority over Marta's choice of spouse.

Yet, under the dictates of *patria potestas*, Marta would not have been left to her own devices once her father became disabled. Instead, eldest son Juan would have stepped into the shoes of his father, and Juan Padilla might not have been his first choice of spouse for his youngest sister. Notwithstanding his elite status, Juan Ávila was known for his lack of involvement in the political and military skirmishes that marked the nineteenth-century history of Alta California, which positioned him to deliver the "flag of truce" to the American military headquarters in Los Angeles.[28] Simply put, Juan Ávila and Juan Padilla were on opposite sides of a determinative issue.

Surprisingly, however, Juan and his wife, Soledad, served as witnesses to the Ávila-Padilla wedding. Perhaps the family was relieved that Marta could find any spouse at such an advanced age and thus was willing to overlook Padilla's pedigree. But worth considering is a darker possibility: that this marriage was actually arranged by the eldest son over his sister's objections. Perhaps Juan was worried that his sister would remain economically dependent on the family, but more likely he was nervous that the social and legal changes wrought by the American conquest had left this particular family ill equipped to guard the sexuality of an unmarried, legally emancipated adult daughter. After all, he had only to look at his deceased aunt's family, the Varelases, to see the manifestations of a lack of parental control over daughters.[29]

On the one hand, Marta's choice to sue her brother can be explained by the Americanization of law and society in post-statehood Los Angeles. Mexican law gave wives as much of an identity before the law as husbands, and women were not shy about defending their rights, but the law had not permitted family members to sue each other.[30] These women thus may have been uniquely positioned to take advantage of the individualistic nature of American law in order to act on a modern sense of rights contrary to the Californio tradition of family unity. Such an explanation situates Marta's lawsuit as an attempt not only to gain a better deal for herself (and her siblings) than if she had she kept quiet, but also as an attempt to undermine her brother's public reputation and eliminate his ability to control the administration of the estate.

But the work of historian Miroslava Chávez-García offers another explanation. Californio patriarchy was not marked merely by a daughter's obedience to her father. It was also defined by a reciprocity of obligations insisted upon by Californianas not afraid to resort to official enforcement. As Chávez-García notes, daughters seeking to hold their fathers accountable were attempting not to overthrow the system of patriarchy, but instead "to challenge patriarchal authority figures who had failed to behave according to the gender and social roles prescribed for them." Perhaps this lawsuit, then, was not only an action against a dishonorable, self-interested brother but also a move against a father who had fallen down in his duties to his youngest daughter. But if Marta saw herself as acting out of filial duty, it is worth noting that she received no assistance from her other siblings.[31]

Only niece and nephew Juana and Guadalupe Sánchez, heirs of their deceased mother, Ascención, joined in the will contest. Perhaps they, too, were motivated to expose Juan as a fraud. Although their mother had been listed as a cograntee of Rancho Niguel, it is unclear whether Juan ever considered his sister a true joint owner. Circumstances instead point to his having used Ascención to gain a double allocation of mission lands. Although thwarted, he may have kept her on as a coapplicant in order to cover up the plan. In any event, there is no indication that any share of Rancho Niguel devolved to Ascención's children, notwithstanding that the eldest son, Tomás, served as administrator of the estate.[32] This lawsuit may have been Juana's and Guadalupe's first opportunity to challenge their uncle's failure during the Mexican period to recognize their rights in Rancho Niguel.

Yet even if Marta was motivated by Californianas' traditional use of the courts, her case was facilitated by changes in the law a few years after statehood that gave children an individualized present interest in their father's estate. The new order provided a greater incentive to contest a parent's will and allowed children to do so during the lifetime of their widowed mother. Meanwhile, the will challenge would take place not in the conciliatory setting of the Mexican dispute resolution process but in the adversarial setting of the Anglo-American legal system, which cared little about the cost of a lawsuit—financial, emotional, or otherwise. Marta probably had no idea what she was getting into when she hired an American lawyer to represent her interests in an American court.[33]

The will contest would be tried before a jury in District Court. In the end, the battle over jury instructions proved determinative. Marta focused primarily on the issue of whether her father lacked testamentary capacity, almost ignoring the more incendiary charge that Juan had engaged in dishonest behavior. She suggested that her father lacked capacity if he did not fully understand "the whole of said will in all its parts and the results" that would flow from its provisions. Juan countered that Antonio Ygnacio would have had to have been "totally deprived of reason" and that "embecility of mind" was not sufficient cause for voiding the testament. Juan's position allowed him to ignore just how disabled his father had become by 1850. Perhaps Juan sought a shred of pride for the old man, grasping for any outcome that would preserve his father's memory as the hero Juan believed him to be. Even twenty years after his death, he reverently remembered his father as a good horseback rider, implausibly asserting that it was "a faculty which he did not lose up to the last moment of his life."[34]

Occupying the bench was Judge Benjamin Hayes, who would choose the instructions to be submitted to the jury. Hayes accepted Juan's suggestion over Marta's, even though Marta's represented the more common standard of testamentary capacity. Nonetheless, the first jury deadlocked in late 1858. After a second trial, before an all-Anglo jury, a verdict was reached the following April. The jury found that in fact Antonio Ygnacio was of "sound and disposing mind" when he executed his will, and that he did not do so "under undue influence or restraint" or "under fraudulent representation." But perhaps there was more to this verdict than the jury simply applying law favorable to Juan. Given that filial obligations and a sense of a family economy were less central to the American experience, American jurors might have seen the cattle gift as an appropriate reward for Juan going above and beyond what would be required of an American son.[35]

Tragically, the cattle that were so valuable at the start of the will contest disappeared at the same time that the contest itself saddled the estate with ever increasing legal bills. As the demand for beef increased in the 1850s, Californios had responded by increasing the size of their herds. Disaster ensued when Midwestern producers tapped into the California market, breaking the Californios' monopoly, and then a disastrous two-season drought in 1863–64 caused a mass starvation of cattle. Meanwhile, although he was wealthy enough to bear the cost of defending himself against the lawsuit, Juan had his lawyers bill the estate for $1,200. In a cash-poor economy, debts for estate administration would eat away at the estate itself, requiring the sale of assets. To avoid this result, the executors obtained an order that Marta, her niece, and her nephew cover the estate's legal costs. In the California Supreme Court, the contestants unsuccessfully appealed the jury verdict but successfully challenged the order to pay costs. These actions further drove up the costs of administration and established a pattern that was to haunt the estate until the end.[36]

A LEGACY LOST

That Marta stood nearly alone in the will contest while Juan prevailed might have cemented his role as the family's new patriarch. Instead, Juan distanced himself from his mother and siblings afterward, the contest appearing to have exacted a significant psychic toll. Once the will was admitted to probate, Juan declined to serve as an executor because it would be "inconvenient" and he sold off his interest in the estate to Rafaela's husband. Although his life in San Juan Capistrano had all the trappings of a Californio ranchero and Juan became known as one of the wealthiest in the community, his sense of family seemed to become Americanized, focused primarily on his wife and children.[37] There's no indication that he cared about the fate of Rancho Sausal Redondo.

Meanwhile, Marta, who might have been ostracized for suing her eldest brother, reunited with her sister Concepción upon being widowed, relying on Concepción's ties to the del Valle family. Although other Californios suffered irrecoverable ranching losses in the mid-1860s, Ygnacio del Valle consolidated his land holdings and moved his family from the pueblo to Rancho Camulos, where he became a hugely successful citrus farmer. Concepción and Marta were absorbed into that household along with Pedro's daughter, Susana.[38]

Yet Marta, too, sold her interest in her father's estate just after the will contest concluded. Unlike her brother, however, she sold to an outsider, Scotsman Robert Burnett. When he purchased the adjacent rancho the following year, a plan dangerous to the Ávila family's interests emerged. Under Mexican law, Burnett would have had no incentive or opportunity to buy into the Ávila estate. Mexican law discouraged the alienability of granted land in order to keep the ranchos intact and in the family. The land could pass only through inheritance to family members, typically the children. Once the land became co-owned, further restrictions kept the grant intact. The widow, who took her share as common property, was given a use right in the children's share. No matter their age, children had to wait until their mother's death to assert any legal control over their share. And joint owners could assert only an undivided interest; they had no claim to particular acreage. Nor would there be any motivation to make a claim. In a grazing economy where land was plentiful, it was more important to assert ownership over a particular animal.[39]

By the time of Antonio Ygnacio's death, the California legislature had upended this scheme. The law eliminated the widow's use rights and now permitted actions for partition, allowing one co-owner to seek a particular piece of the land or to ask the court to sell the property and divide the proceeds. Only the inability to divide or sell the property would stop a partition, an unlikely circumstance with unimproved acreage. That the property may have been more valuable if kept intact was irrelevant. These changes in the law severely undermined the unity of family interest that permeated Californio culture. Now, individual interests in a rancho were more marketable, to more people, earlier in an heir's lifetime. The law thus facilitated heirs such as Marta and Juan in distancing themselves from their families and from what could be an arduous probate process, even if doing so was not in the best interests of the family.[40]

The threat of a Burnett partition action now hovered over the estate, but Burnett appeared to value more the legal right of standing, which allowed any interest holder, no matter how insignificant, to invoke the oversight of the court in an estate's administration. Each time this oversight was invoked, the costs of administering the estate would rise. The power of the court to order cash payments for legal fees was magnified in the cash-poor economy of southern California, and Californios had to sell assets of the estate to pay these costs. Consequently, for a relatively modest sum, Burnett was able to buy his way into a position where he could affect the devolution of the entire rancho.[41]

The costs of the will contest bore down on the estate just as the cattle market began collapsing in the early 1860s. To meet these obligations, Pedro Antonio first sold livestock, which brought in less than the appraised value. This pressure only increased once his mother died the following year. In 1865, he began selling off real property in order to cover the additional expenses of administering her estate. This move required an order of sale from the court. Any stakeholder could oppose the sale, further increasing the costs of administration. Indeed, Burnett contested Pedro Antonio's petition, relying on ambiguities in Antonio Ygnacio's will that were born of the uncertainty surrounding American adoption and implementation of the Mexican-based marital property law. His arguments went nowhere in the probate court, but his appeal to the California Supreme Court succeeded in stopping a piecemeal sale.[42]

The court's reasoning, while faulty, provided only a temporary roadblock to the sale, which was all that Burnett needed. His actions drove the costs of administration even higher, and the estate's debts now amounted to nearly $8,400. Pedro Antonio had no choice but to liquidate all of the real estate, and he filed yet another petition for order of sale in January 1868. Hearing no opposition, the court ordered the sale of "all that certain lot or parcel of land known as the Sausal Redondo rancho," these cryptic words not even beginning to capture the Ávila family's loss. On the appointed day, April 18, 1868, Burnett, living on the adjoining rancho, was ready to purchase all 22,500 acres, which he did for $29,550.[43]

A few years after Burnett purchased Rancho Sausal Redondo, Antonio Ygnacio's grandson hatched a plan to return the property to the family. Tomás Sánchez, Ascención's son, had been elected sheriff of Los Angeles County from 1860 to 1867, one of fewer and fewer Californios to hold a government position in the rapidly anglicizing Los Angeles. Adopting Ávila as his middle name, he became the face of his family's interests, notwithstanding that his uncles were still alive. The terms of patriarchy were now being negotiated on an American stage, where generational status mattered less and positions of public leadership and honor would be claimed by those garnering the most votes. After convincing his aunts, uncles, siblings, and cousins to quitclaim to him their interests in the rancho, he filed suit against Burnett, alleging a fraudulent conspiracy between him and Pedro Antonio to run up expenses of administration in order to trigger a sale of Sausal Redondo. The lawsuit failed.[44]

In pursuing his claim, Sánchez ignored the fact that the first step down the path to losing the land was not an outsider's wrongdoing, but rather a daughter's unwillingness to swallow what she perceived as an injustice inside her own family.

Whether she perceived the injustice as to her, her father, or her family generally, we will never know. However, had Sánchez recognized Marta's role, he would have had to admit that, years before Antonio Ygnacio's death, his family had already experienced a fatal weakening of the patriarchy, honor, and devotion to unity so crucial to holding the rancho enterprise together.

Antonio Ygnacio could claim his patriarchal prerogative handily in the 1820s, at a time when his position in the community was rising and his children's chances were tied to their father's status and wealth. By the 1830s, however, native sons hungering for their own land and independence and unwilling to wait for their parents' deaths found conspirators in government officials seeking to wrest control of mission lands from the Catholic Church. The result was not only a significant weakening of paternal authority but also a devaluing of honor, especially as it related to the common good. Acquisitiveness, greed, and duplicity marked the land grab at San Juan Capistrano, instilling a new sense of individuality.

Looking forward from his grandfather's death, Tomás Sánchez would have seen how vulnerable his family was to further erosion, now by the Americanization of law and society, which explicitly supported a system in which individual interests trumped collective goals. Although his Aunt Marta may have hoped to use the American legal system to restore family unity by ousting a dishonorable brother, it proved to be too blunt an instrument to save Rancho Sausal Redondo.

By 1868 modern American social forces had eroded the meaning that Californios attached to their land. It was, instead, a commodity, and a grandson's nostalgic yearning was not enough to keep the cause of Sausal Redondo alive. Those family members who had struck out on their own had done well. Those who had put their efforts toward the common good, meanwhile, were left with little more than the few dollars doled out from the sale of the Ávila legacy, their position in society auctioned off to the highest bidder.

NOTES

Funding for this chapter was provided by the Huntington Library and the Historical Society of Southern California. The author thanks Nadar Albawadi and John Chen for their research assistance.

1. On the adoption of common law and community property law at statehood, see Donna Clare Schuele, "A Robbery of the Wife: Culture, Gender, and Marital Property in California Law and Politics, 1850–1890," Ph.D. diss., University of California, Berkeley, 1999, chapter 2. For legal practices during the American conquest, see David Langum, *Law and Community on the Mexican California Frontier: Anglo-American Expatriates and the Clash of Legal Traditions, 1821–1846* (Norman: University of Oklahoma Press, 1987). For the development of law from the Spanish/Mexican periods through early statehood, see Richard R. Powell, *Compromises of Conflicting Claims: A Century of California Law, 1760 to 1860* (Dobbs Ferry, NY: Oceana Publications, 1977). Regarding the customary practice of deathbed wills, see Sylvia Marina Arrom, *The Women of Mexico City, 1790–1857* (Stanford, CA: Stanford University Press, 1985), 115, 315 n. 30. Leonard Pitt's pathbreaking book *The*

Decline of the Californios: A Social History of the Spanish-Speaking Californians, 1846–1890 (Berkeley: University of California Press, 1966) depicts this community as somewhat passive victims of American legal processes. Newer scholarship, such as Lisbeth Haas, *Conquests and Historical Identities in California, 1769–1936* (Berkeley: University of California Press, 1995); Miroslava Chávez-García, *Negotiating Conquest: Gender and Power in California, 1770s to 1880s* (Tucson: University of Arizona Press, 2004); and Carlos Manuel Salomon, *Pio Pico: The Last Governor of Mexican California* (Norman: University of Oklahoma Press, 2010), demonstrate Californios' proactive use of the American legal system to litigate disputes, notwithstanding catastrophic results.

2. The spelling of Californios' names was variable in the nineteenth century. I have chosen to use Ávila, except when referring to specific documents employing an alternative spelling. For Ávila's early life, see Hubert Howe Bancroft, *The Works of Hubert Howe Bancroft*, vol. 19 (San Francisco: A. L. Bancroft & Co., 1885), 349–50 n. 25, 351, 566, 664–65 n. 24, 736; Mardith K. Schuetz-Miller, *Building and Builders in Hispanic California, 1769–1850* (Santa Barbara, CA: Santa Barbara Trust for Historic Preservation, 1994), 16, 27, 32, 54–55; Orange County Genealogical Society, *Saddleback Ancestors: Rancho Families of Orange County, California* (Santa Ana, CA: Aladdin Litho & Art, 1969), 20 (hereafter *Saddleback Ancestors*); and Alfonso Yorba, trans., "Don Juan Ávila's 'Notas Californias,'" *Orange County History Series*, vol. 3 (1939): 1–6 (hereafter "Juan Ávila Testimonio"). Ávila served most notably as *juez de campo* (judge of the plains, charged with resolving disputes over cattle ownership) almost continuously from 1835 to 1848. See Bancroft, *Works of Hubert Howe Bancroft*, vol. 19, 350–51, 706; and Bancroft, *The Works of Hubert Howe Bancroft*, vol. 20 (San Francisco: The History Co., 1886), 634–35. The Spanish and Mexican governments designated artisans such as Ávila for land use rights, and in March 1822 Antonio Ygnacio received one of the earliest grants, which offered ownership rights upon investment in the land. See Schuetz-Miller, *Building and Builders in Hispanic California*, 32; and W. W. Robinson, *Ranchos Become Cities* (Pasadena, CA: San Pasqual Press, 1939), 130–33.

3. For demographic information regarding Ávila family members, see The Huntington Library, *Early California Population Project Database*, 2006 (hereafter *ECPP*), Santa Barbara Presidio Marriage Record no. 00053 and San Gabriel Mission (hereafter SG) Baptismal Record nos. 04121, 04424, 05129, 05667, 06734, 07120, and 07339; Estate of Antonio Ygnacio Abila, Case No. 116, Los Angeles County Probate Court Records, The Huntington Library, San Marino, California (hereafter Ávila Probate); *Padilla v. Abila*, District Court Case No. 585, filed November 15, 1858, Translation of Will of Antonio Ygnacio Abila, filed December 6, 1858, collection in The Huntington Library, San Marino, California (hereafter Will Translation); Marie E. Northrop, *Spanish-Mexican Families of Early California: 1769–1850, Volume I* (Burbank: Southern California Genealogical Society, 1986), 53–56, 291–92; *Saddleback Ancestors*, 20–21. Records reflect that the Ávila family and others used the names Ascensión and Concepción interchangeably. Based on the references in Antonio Ygnacio's will, I use Ascensión to refer to the older daughter, who married Pedro Sánchez, and Concepción to refer to the younger daughter, who married Servulo Varelas. See Will Translation.

4. Louise Pubols, *The Father of All: The de la Guerra Family, Power, and Patriarchy in Mexican California* (Berkeley: University of California Press, 2009), 30. See also Gloria E. Miranda, "Hispano-Mexican Childrearing Practices in Pre-American Santa Barbara," *Southern California Quarterly* 64 (Winter 1983): 309; and Chávez-García, *Negotiating Conquests*, 20, 23 (noting the critical value of reproduction during the lull in colonization from 1790 to 1830).

5. Pubols, *Father of All*, 8. See also Douglas Monroy, *Thrown Among Strangers: The Making of Mexican Culture in Frontier California* (Berkeley: University of California Press, 1990), 140–42.

6. Pubols, *Father of All*, 26, 58, 123, 177; Arrom, *Women of Mexico City*, 57–58, 69; and Richard Griswold del Castillo, *Los Angeles Barrio: A Social History* (Berkeley: University of California Press, 1979), 64–65. Prior to reaching the age of majority, even married children were subject to guardianship for legal transactions. *Patria potestas* also gave fathers control over their children's property, as well

as the right to use physical punishment or take legal action against their children. Reforms adopted in some Mexican jurisdictions in the 1820s and '30s to reduce the authority of fathers appear not to have taken hold in Alta California. See Arrom, *Women of Mexico City*, 58, 69, 92.

7. On the distinction between *gente de razón* and *gente sin razón* in Alta California and the issue of marriage between unequals, see Haas, *Conquests and Historical Identities*, 2, 29–32; Monroy, *Thrown Among Strangers*, 22–23, 139–40; Gloria E. Miranda, "Gente de Razón Marriage Patterns in Spanish and Mexican California: A Case Study of Santa Barbara and Los Angeles," *Southern California Quarterly* 63 (Spring 1981): 8; Arrom, *Women of Mexico City*, 148; and Pubols, *Father of All*, 26, 121. On arranged marriages and the family economy, see Pubols, *Father of All*, 36–37, 120, 122–23; Griswold del Castillo, *Los Angeles Barrio*, 65; Monroy, *Thrown Among Strangers*, 140, 159; and Miroslava Chávez, "'Pongo mi Demanda': Challenging Patriarchy in Mexican Los Angeles, 1830–1850," in *Over the Edge: Remapping the American West*, ed. Valerie J. Matsumoto and Blake Allmendinger (Berkeley: University of California Press, 1999), 274–75. Fathers might arrange marriages without their children's knowledge, but some daughters successfully appealed to religious authorities to block undesired pairings. See Monroy, *Thrown Among Strangers*, 140; and Chávez-García, *Negotiating Conquests*, 278. Daughters were more vulnerable after Mexican independence weakened church authority, but most were willing participants in arranged marriages because they identified with their families' interests and saw these marriages as a long-term benefit. See Pubols, *Father of All*, 124, 126.

8. Pubols, *Father of All*, 36–37; Griswold del Castillo, *Los Angeles Barrio*, 65.

9. Francisca married José Sepúlveda, son of Francisco Sepúlveda, and Ascención married Pedro Sánchez, son of Vicente Sánchez, at the ages of eighteen and sixteen, respectively. Juan married Soledad Yorba, daughter of José Antonio Yorba, at the age of twenty. Ascención and Pedro resided with his father. ECPP SG Marriage Record nos. 01737, 01738, and 01887; Northrop, *Spanish-Mexican Families, Volume I*, 307, 311, 369–70; Will Translation (memorializing wedding gifts of cattle); Historical Society of Southern California, "Padron de la ciudad de Los Angeles y su jurisdiccion," *Southern California Quarterly* 18 (September/December 1936): 116, 134 (hereafter "1836 Padron"); and J. Gregg Layne, comp., "The First Census of the Los Angeles District," *Southern California Quarterly* 18 (September/December 1936): 92–93.

10. Pubols, *Father of All*, chapter 4; quote from 150.

11. Ibid., 181–82, 187.

12. For the role of Francisco Sepúlveda in the secularization of the mission, see Zephyrin Engelhardt, O.F.M., *San Juan Capistrano Mission* (Los Angeles: Standard Printing Co., 1922), 120, 129–30; and Haas, *Conquests and Historical Identities*, 47 (noting that all but one grant of San Juan Capistrano Mission lands went to family members of the administrators). For José Sepúlveda's grant, see *Saddleback Ancestors*, 84, 103–6; and Haas, *Conquests and Historical Identities*, 47. For the grant of Rancho Niguel, see Haas, *Conquests and Historical Identities*, 45–47; and Chávez-García, *Negotiating Conquests*, 57.

13. Rafaela married Emidgio Vejar around the age of sixteen. See Schuetz-Miller, *Building and Builders in Hispanic California*, 56; ECPP Los Angeles Plaza Church (hereafter LA) Baptismal Record no. 00483; and Northrop, *Spanish-Mexican Families, Volume I*, 54. For Emidgio's grant, see *Saddleback Ancestors*, 96–98. José Martín married Maria Ygnacia Feliz at the age of twenty-three but was widowed less than two years later, in 1840. ECPP SG Marriage Record no. 01887, LA Death Record no. 00496; and Northrop, *Spanish-Mexican Families, Volume I*, 54, 150.

14. On Concepción and Servulo's marriage, see Northrop, *Spanish-Mexican Families, Volume I*, 54. Shortly before the wedding, both Servulo and his father were listed as "flagrantly" having no profession. See "1836 Padron," 134; and Layne, "First Census," 82. For information on the Varelas daughters and their children, see ECPP SG Baptismal Record no. 08237, and LA Baptismal Record nos. 00196, 00234, 00379, 00558, 00936, 01158, 01283, 01619, 01636, and 01657; Historical Society of

Southern California, "The Los Angeles Padron of 1844, As Copied from the Los Angeles County Archives," *Southern California Quarterly* 42 (1960): 395 (hereafter "1844 Padron"); Maurice H. Newmark and Marco R. Newmark, eds., *Census of the City and County of Los Angeles, California, for the Year 1850* (Los Angeles: Times-Mirror Press, 1929), 62, 66 (hereafter *1850 Census*); Marie E. Northrop, *Spanish-Mexican Families of Early California, Volume III: Los Pobladores de la Reina de Los Angeles* (Burbank: Southern California Genealogical Society, 2004), 184; Northrop, *Spanish-Mexican Families, Volume I*, 327; and Chávez-García, *Negotiating Conquests*, 46. For a discussion of the negative effect of Californio daughters' sexual impropriety and out-of-wedlock births on the reputation of the entire family, see ibid., 26, 45. The label *"mala vida"* was an attempt by authorities outside the family to control women's sexuality and to provide examples to other women. See ibid., 47–48.

15. José Martín married Maria del Pilar Villa around 1841 or 1842, possibly to legitimate their first-born child. See *ECPP* SG Marriage Record no. 08528 and LA Death record no. 00496; and Northrop, *Spanish-Mexican Families, Volume I*, 54; and Northrup, *Spanish-Mexican Families, Volume III*, 279. For the execution of Maria del Rosario Villa, see Chávez-García, *Negotiating Conquests*, 43–45. Pedro wed Juana Nepomucena Altamirano at age twenty in 1841. *ECPP* SG Marriage Record no. 01925 and Baptismal Record nos. 08528 and 01529; Northrop, *Spanish-Mexican Families, Volume I*, 54; and *1850 Census*, 75.

16. See "Juan Ávila Testimonio," 20 (referring to having returned his brothers Pedro and Pedro Antonio to "their rancho," presumably Sausal Redondo, after a battle in January 1847). Pedro Antonio did not formally marry until just after his father's probate closed in 1868, at the very late age of forty-four years old, but it appears that he began cohabitating with his future wife by 1860. Northrup, *Spanish-Mexican Families, Volume I*, 54; and *United States Federal Census*, 1860, Los Angeles, Los Angeles, California, roll M635_59, p. 500, image 500, accessed via Ancestry.com (hereafter *1860 Census*). Although the mother would by default become the guardian of any minor children upon the death of the father, Antonio Ygnacio's will appointed Francisca guardian of Marta's property "if she is not married and still a minor" at his death. See Arrom, *Women of Mexico City*, 70; and Will Translation.

17. See the painting of Antonio Ygnacio Ávila by Henri Penelon, reproduced as figure 6.1, depicting a frail, elderly Antonio Ygnacio grasping a cane while one corner of his mouth twists downward unnaturally. Regarding the possibility that Ávila became disabled around 1848, see Northrop, *Spanish-Mexican Families, Volume I*, 55 (noting that he resigned as *juez de campo* in 1848); Account of Antonio Ygnacio Abila with Abel Stearns, 1844–50, Box 2, del Valle Family Papers, Seaver Center for Western Research, Natural History Museum of Los Angeles County (hereafter del Valle Family Papers), which shows Juan Ávila's involvement in overseeing the account as of August 3, 1848; and Abel Stearns Collection 1, The Huntington Library. For information on the Ávila family in early 1851, see *1850 Census*, 67, 75, 104, 108. On Marta's marriage, see Los Angeles Plaza Church Marriage Record no. 209. Many thanks to Steven Hackel for providing this reference.

18. On Ygnacio del Valle and his marriage to Ysabel Ávila, see Margie Brown-Coronel, "Beyond the Rancho: Four Generations of del Valle Women in Southern California, 1830–1940," Ph.D. diss., University of California, Irvine, 2011, 50–54; Funeral Announcement of Antonio Ygnacio Abila, Box 4, del Valle Family Papers; *1860 Census*, Los Angeles, Los Angeles, California, roll M653_59, p. 345, image 345. Regarding Pedro's assertion of typical rights of ownership, see Mortgage, Pedro Ávila to Teodosia Saiz, December 12, 1854; *Lanfranco v. Abila*, Case No. 380, First District Court, Los Angeles County, Abstract of the Title to the Ranchos Sausal Redondo and La Centinela, 25, 26 (hereafter Abstract of Title); Robert G. Cowan, *Ranchos of California* (Fresno, CA: Academy Library Guild, 1956), 38, 195–96, 437; Robert Cameron Gillingham, *The Rancho San Pedro* (Los Angeles: Cole-Holmquist Press, 1961), 121, 180, 195–96, 242; and "The Avila Heirs," *Los Angeles Times*, September 9,

1895. On Antonio Ygnacio's wealth, see Robert Glass Cleland, *Cattle on a Thousand Hills: Southern California, 1850–1870* (San Marino, CA: Huntington Library, 1941), 158.

19. Petition to Admit Will to Probate and for Appointment of Executors, Notice of Hearing, October 4, 1858, Ávila Probate; and Powell, *Compromises of Conflicting Claims,* 178.

20. Motion to Dismiss, October 15, 1858, and November 1, 1858; and Opposition to Probate of Will, November 1, 1858, Ávila Probate.

21. The will stated, "On the Ranch of my son Juan, I placed eight hundred (800) head of meat cattle. Eight years ago and through the cares of this good son who has worked in the increase and preservation of this stock with his own horses and servants, I had wherewith to maintain me the greater part of my old age, with my family; and which to pay many of my debts... which all of my family is informed, and I declare that my aforesaid son Juan has paid part of my liabilities with his own money, and that only by his care and expenses has my cattle been able to amount at this date to the amount of two thousand head." See Will Translation.

22. For the evolution of domestic relations law in nineteenth-century America, see Michael Grossberg, *Governing the Hearth: Law and Family in Nineteenth-Century America* (Chapel Hill: University of North Carolina Press, 1985).

23. Motion to Dismiss, Exception to Court's Decision to Admit Will to Probate, November 1, 1858, Ávila Probate.

24. Ibid.

25. Guardianship of José (Antonio Ygnacio) Abila, Case No. 115, Los Angeles County Probate Court Records. The Probate Court granted Juan a temporary appointment as conservator. For will provisions, see Will Translation.

26. Monroy, *Thrown Among Strangers,* 136–40 ("the amount of *honor* one had made a reputation, not the amount of money") (italics in original). Regarding Ávila's reputation and wealth, see Bancroft, *Works of Hubert Howe Bancroft,* vol. 19, 736; Anita L. Alexander, "Life of Don Juan Ávila, 'El Rico,'" *Orange County History Series* 3 (1939): 33, 40; Marjorie Tisdale Wolcott, ed., *Pioneer Notes from the Diaries of Judge Benjamin Hayes, 1849–1875* (Los Angeles: Priv. Print, 1929), 113 (hereafter *Diaries of Judge Hayes*); and *Saddleback Ancestors,* 22–26.

27. Bancroft described Padilla as a "Mexican barber of no influence or standing whatever" who was a saloonkeeper in San Francisco when he served briefly and controversially as an alcalde in 1845. See Bancroft, *The Works of Hubert Howe Bancroft,* vol. 21 (San Francisco: The History Co., 1886), 666–67 n. 12, 765; and Bancroft, *The Works of Hubert Howe Bancroft,* vol. 22 (San Francisco: The History Co., 1886), 160. For Padilla's role in the Bear Flag Revolt, see ibid., 160–66, 173; Barbara R. Warner, *The Men of the California Bear Flag Revolt and Their Heritage* (Spokane, WA: Arthur H. Clark Pub., 1996), 243–46; and Rose Marie Beebe and Robert M. Senkewicz, *Testimonios: Early California through the Eyes of Women, 1818–1848* (Berkeley, CA: Heyday Books, 2006), 28–29. Neither did Padilla enjoy a good reputation with regard to his land grants. The United States Supreme Court accused him of forgery and deemed his testimony to the Land Commission not credible, although by the later 1850s he was considered a respected member of the Los Angeles community. *Salmon v. Symonds,* 30 Cal. 301 (1866); *U.S. v. Galbraith,* 63 U.S. 89 (1859); and Griswold del Castillo, *Los Angeles Barrio,* 154–55.

28. On the place of an eldest son, see Monroy, *Thrown Among Strangers,* 141. Regarding Juan's noninvolvement in military and political matters, see Bancroft, *Works of Hubert Howe Bancroft,* vol. 19, 736; *Diaries of Judge Hayes,* 114; and *Saddleback Ancestors,* 22. Regarding Ávila's role in the American victory at Los Angeles, see "Juan Ávila Testimonio," 17–21.

29. Los Angeles Plaza Church Marriage Record no. 209. The record notes that an impediment had to be overcome before the couple could marry. The impediment may only have been pro forma, as the Catholic hierarchy required verification of single status from Mexico City before émigrés could marry. On the other hand, the impediment might have indicated Marta's lack of consent to

the marriage, and perhaps she capitulated later. Interestingly, the wedding did not take place at the Plaza Church but instead at the San Juan Capistrano rancho of the Ávilas' first cousin, who was particularly close to Juan, which may have allowed the event to be kept more private. Ultimately, the marriage was not a happy one. See *People v. Juan N. Padilla,* Case No. 537, Los Angeles County Criminal Cases, collection in The Huntington Library, San Marino, California (charging Padilla with having committed armed assault and battery on Marta in January 1861). Thanks to Erika Pérez for bringing this case to my attention.

30. Haas notes Californianas' sense of entitlement to the land, which "rested, in part, on the fact that Spanish and Mexican law gave them the right to control their property and wealth and to litigate on questions related to their person, their families, and their holdings." See Haas, *Conquests and Historical Identities,* 81; also Arrom, *Women of Mexico City,* 307 n. 69.

31. Chávez-García, *Negotiating Conquests,* xviii, 26. Nevertheless, women often failed in these actions, as "courts interpreted the law in ways that reflected deeply rooted gender biases."

32. "The Avila Heirs," *Los Angeles Times,* September 9, 1895. Land grants to women were uncommon. Juan and Ascensión originally requested a grant of more than seventy thousand acres, nearly twice the amount that could be granted to an individual. When the mission Indians contested the application, the grant was reduced. Robert H. Becker, *Designs on the Land: Diseños of California Ranchos and Their Markers* (San Francisco: Book Club of California, 1969), *diseño* 37. Although Ascensión allegedly built a home for herself and her children on Rancho Niguel in 1842, as of 1844 she was living with her deceased husband's parents. See Haas, *Conquests and Historical Identities,* 47; and "1844 Padron," 400.

33. The goal of the Mexican dispute resolution system was to do the least harm to the community, even if that meant shortchanging an individual. See Chávez-García, *Negotiating Conquests,* 66. For changes in inheritance law, see Powell, *Compromises of Conflicting Claims,* 200. On Mexican property and inheritance law, see Arrom, *Women of Mexico City,* 63, 67–68, 91. Although Anglo members of the Los Angeles bar were quite willing to represent Californios, most lawyers were handicapped by their inability to speak Spanish. Marta's attorney, Jonathan Scott, was one of the few who knew the language. See Griswold del Castillo, *Los Angeles Barrio,* 116–17.

34. Until 1862 the probate court was powerless to convene a jury, so issues of fact were certified to the district court for resolution. See D. P. Belknap, *The Probate Law and Practice of California, containing all the provisions of the codes, of 1871–72, and other statutes relating thereto* (San Francisco: Bancroft Co., 1873), 2, 8. For jury instructions, see Proposed Jury Instructions and Contestant's Instructions, December 10, 1858, *Juan Abila v. Juan Padilla,* Case No. 585, District Court of the State of California, First Judicial District (hereafter Will Contest). For Juan's recollections of his father, see "Juan Ávila Testimonio," 1.

35. In considering whether judicial bias played a role in this case, it is hard to determine which side was in the better graces of the judge. Hayes knew Juan well, often partaking of his generous hospitality on his travels as a district judge, but Marta was represented by Jonathan Scott, who had been in practice with Hayes before he became a judge. *Diaries of Judge Hayes,* 113; and W. W. Robinson, *Lawyers of Los Angeles: A History of the Los Angeles Bar Association and of the Bar of Los Angeles County* (Los Angeles: Los Angeles Bar Association, 1959), 33–37, 43. For results of the trials, see Petition for Special Letters of Administration, January 11, 1859, Ávila Probate; Verdict, April 27, 1859, Will Contest. Although the first jury summons contained a few Californio names, the second jury was assembled from a nearly all-Anglo panel. With Antonio Ygnacio's lengthy deterioration more likely to be known in the Californio community, an Anglo jury favored Juan. The experience in the second trial is consistent with Griswold del Castillo's larger finding that Californios and Mexicans "were conspicuously absent on [Los Angeles] juries." See Griswold del Castillo, *Los Angeles Barrio,* 117–18.

36. Notice of Appeal, June 20, 1859, Ávila Probate; *Abila v. Padilla,* 14 Cal. 103 (1859) (upholding the jury verdict); Judgment for Costs, February 18, 1860, Ávila Probate; Notice of Appeal, March 14, 1860, Ávila Probate; and *Abila v. Padilla,* 19 Cal. 388 (1861). On the collapsing cattle market, see Griswold del Castillo, *Los Angeles Barrio,* 42.

37. Renunciation of Juan Abila, May 13, 1859, Ávila Probate. In 1860 Juan exchanged his interest in Rancho Sausal Redondo for his brother-in-law Emidgio Vejar's nearby rancho. Deed, Juan Abila to Emidgio Vejar, August 16, 1860, Abstract of Title, 53; and W. W. Robinson and Doyce Blackman Nunis, *Southern California Local History: A Gathering of the Writings of W. W. Robinson* (Los Angeles: Historical Society of Southern California, 1993), 302–3. Juan did not house his parents or siblings after 1851. By 1860 his household consisted of his wife, his children, his wife's relatives, and various Indian servants and laborers. Ten years later he appeared to be living alone, having been widowed in 1867, and later he lived with his adult daughter. Like most Californios, his wealth decreased over time. See *1852 California State Census,* roll 2, p. 54, line 30, accessed via Ancestry.com (hereafter *1852 Census*); *1860 Census,* San Juan, Los Angeles, California, roll M653_59, p. 477, image 477; and *1870 United States Federal Census,* San Juan, Los Angeles, California, roll M593_73, p. 624A, image 625, accessed via Ancestry.com (hereafter *1870 Census*); *Saddleback Ancestors,* 22–26.

38. *1852 Census,* roll 2, p. 84, line 30; *1860 Census,* Los Angeles, Los Angeles, California, roll M653_59, p. 362, image 362; *1870 Census,* Township 1, Santa Barbara, California, roll M593_87, p. 428A, image 320; *1880 United States Federal Census,* Saticoy, Ventura, California, roll 86, p. 246A, image 0068, accessed via Ancestry.com (hereafter *1880 Census*); and Brown-Coronel, "Beyond the Rancho," 92–96.

39. Deed, Juan N. Padilla and Marta Abila de Padilla, his wife, to Robert Burnett, July 15, 1859 (selling the interest for $4,000); Deed, Joseph Lancaster Brent to Robert Burnett, November 16, 1860, Abstract of Title, 22–23, 48–49; Petition to Revoke Order of Sale, April 25, 1865, Ávila Probate; and Haas, *Conquests and Historical Identities,* 49–50, 64.

40. Haas, *Conquests and Historical Identities,* 64; and Schuele, "A Robbery of the Wife," chapter 2.

41. Inventory and Appraisement, June 22, 1859; Order for Sale of Personal Property, February 22, 1860; and Petition for Approval of Final Accounting, May 16, Ávila Probate.

42. Burnett had an initial order of sale for the rancho set aside due to lack of notice and other defects in 1865. Petition for Order of Sale, March 2, 1865; Petition to Revoke Order of Sale, April 25, 1865; and Order Vacating Order of Sale, May 1, 1865, Ávila Probate. Pedro Antonio succeeded in having a second order of sale granted the following year, which Burnett appealed to the California Supreme Court. Amended Petition for Order of Sale, April 22, 1866; Order of Sale, September 24, 1866; and Notice of Appeal, October 15, 1866, Ávila Probate. At first Francisca also objected to the sale of the rancho. See Contest to Accounting and Petition for Executor for Sale of Real Estate, May 10, 1866, Ávila Probate.

43. *Abila v. Burnett,* 33 Cal. 658, 666–67; Second Amended Petition for Order of Sale, January 17, 1868; Order of Sale, March 9, 1868; Return and Account of Sale, April 23, 1868; Administrator's Final Accounting, May 6, 1868 (showing that Rancho Sausal Redondo sold for nearly $23,000 over its appraised value), Ávila Probate; and Deed, Pedro Antonio Abila to Robert Burnett, May 8, 1868, Abstract of Title, 67. As Haas notes of outsiders such as Burnett, "their ability to invest in land and other economic ventures contrasted sharply to the situation of most Californios, the majority of whom lost their ranchos during the 1860s.... The new migrants, with their regenerative wealth (money to loan and to invest in land, farming, livestock, and other capital ventures), gained substantially during this decade." See Haas, *Conquests and Historical Identities,* 66.

44. Maurice H. and Marco R. Newmark, eds., *Sixty Years in Southern California, 1853–1913, Containing the Reminiscences of Harris Newmark,* 3rd ed. (Boston: Houghton Mifflin, 1930), 275; *Sánchez v. Burnett,* 17th District Court, Los Angeles County, December 15, 1868, removed to U.S. District Court, Case No. 881, July 20, 1870, Abstract of Title, 74, 86–92. For various quitclaim deeds, see ibid., 69–73.

7

"Who has a greater job than a mother?"

Defining Mexican Motherhood on the U.S.-Mexico Border in the Early Twentieth Century

Monica Perales

In 1929, Ruby Jane Simmons, adult home economics instructor at the Smelter Vocational School in El Paso, Texas, wrote an article extolling the virtues of the school. She framed the advantages of vocational training by emphasizing the critical role that mothers play in the maintenance and functioning of the home. "Who has a greater job than a mother," wrote Simmons, "who cares for her children day and night every day?" More important, Simmons noted the dire consequences that resulted when mothers failed in their missions: "If [the children] are sick, if they get dirty, if they do not eat at the appropriate time the adequate and necessary foods, if the boys are ill-behaved and the girls not very good, if they do not have success in their life and they are unhappy in love . . . *the fault lies with the mother more than anyone else*" (emphasis added).[1] Simmons's words were entirely consistent with the prevailing attitudes at the heart of Progressive-era reform that, among many other things, urged the Americanization of millions of seemingly inassimilable immigrants arriving in urban centers across the country.[2] Although Simmons's ideas were not uncommon for that time, perhaps the publication in which they were printed was. Simmons's article appeared on the pages of the *Hoja Parroquial de Smelter*, the Spanish-language newsletter distributed weekly to the working-class parishioners of the San José del Rio Catholic Church in the Mexican barrio of Smeltertown. By the time the article was published, the *Hoja Parroquial* had become a source of parish and community information for the largely Catholic barrio and emerged as an important tool by which the parish priest—a Spaniard named Father Lourdes Costa— exerted considerable influence over his parishioners. The article encouraged women to enroll in classes and other activities sponsored by the vocational school, which he described as "the best in the territory of our Smelter parish."[3]

The publication of Simmons's article in the Spanish-language weekly suggests that teaching Mexican women how to be "good mothers" was of vital concern to various groups in El Paso in the early twentieth century. Anglo and Mexican reformers, middle- and upper-class writers and columnists, and medical experts focused on teaching Mexican mothers in the border city childcare and child rearing techniques and time-saving homemaking skills. These lessons also contained important messages about appropriate gender roles, moral values, notions of respectability, and racial and class boundaries. Drawing from writings by American educators and reformers and women's advice columns in local Spanish-language newspapers and vocational journals, this chapter illuminates the multivocal discourse surrounding Mexican motherhood in the border city. More important, it contends that El Paso represented a crossroads of maternal discourse and that these various writings were fundamentally influenced by parallel national projects that placed women and mothers at the center of defining citizenship in both the United States and Mexico.

In this period women in both countries came under greater scrutiny, as federal, state, and local agencies launched broad campaigns to reduce infant mortality and implement the techniques of scientific motherhood, contributing to what historian Alexandra M. Stern calls the "nationalization of women."[4] Anglo and Mexican writers and reformers played key roles. Both sought to provide information regarding children's health and nutrition as well as general advice on housekeeping and home economics. For Anglo instructors, improving the Mexican home through its mothers also reinforced the image of Mexican woman as domestic laborer. Local ethnic Mexican newspapers and journals aimed their messages at a larger working- and middle-class readership and highlighted similar themes of scientific motherhood and the careful management of the home in service to the nation. Like middle-class U.S. writers, their advice columns (including translated versions of U.S. women's columns) also cultivated notions of domesticity and respectability directed at Mexican mothers and housewives. The advice promised a middle-class ideal that was, for many working Mexican mothers, a mere illusion. Yet they also promised to elevate the image of Mexican families in the face of racial discrimination in U.S. cities. In the end, these writers reveal how motherhood defined the racial, class, and gender boundaries of Mexicanness and Americanness, even as they left Mexican women to make sense of deeply conflicting messages about how to be a "good" mother.

MOTHERHOOD AND THE STATE
IN THE BORDERLANDS

Motherhood is more than a private, intimate relationship; it is an important site wherein the very meanings of nation and citizenship are defined. Familial and gender relations served as models against and through which the United States imagined itself as a nation, thereby placing women and families at the center of nation building, class formation, and determining the boundaries of civic inclusion.[5] The early nineteenth-century concept of "true womanhood" defined women's ultimate personal and civic role as the submissive guardian of the domestic realm; by the end of the century, it served to justify women's public activism.[6] Spanning the late nineteenth and early twentieth centuries, the Progressive era represented a concerted effort by reformers at the local, state, and national levels to bring about sweeping political, social, and economic change in American society. Rapid industrialization, urban growth, rising immigration rates, and the related problems of deplorable working and living conditions and poverty emerged as important targets. Drawing upon their accepted roles as mothers and nurturers, and influenced by their racial and class privilege, maternalist reformers directed their energies toward helping to alleviate these societal ills, creating what one historian has called a "female dominion in the mostly male empire of policymaking."[7] Some women, guided by the desire to improve the social and moral welfare of immigrant communities, worked as Protestant missionaries and Americanization instructors to transform immigrant families into American ones, targeting women in general, and mothers and wives in particular.[8] Others worked to place the mission to save mothers and babies on the national agenda. Their efforts represented a legitimate concern about the health and welfare of women and infants. However, they also carried implicit (and sometimes explicit) assumptions about the normative American family. The ideal family was one in which mothers exhibited total devotion to their children and homes while remaining economically dependent on the wages of the male breadwinner. As a result, African American, Native American, and immigrant mothers—who faced a variety of class and racial barriers to full citizenship—were deemed unsuitable and "un-American" by comparison.

Maternal and infant well-being was more than an act of kindness; it was a vital state interest. In making good mothers, clean homes, and healthy children, reformers were making good Americans, too, thereby setting the bar for determining civic belonging. In the intercultural West, the process of making good American mothers and families was far from painless. As historian Margaret Jacobs has shown, Indian child removal policies aimed at "fixing" indigenous families asserted and enforced the authority of the federal government "not only in the halls of governance or on fields of battle, but also in the most intimate spaces of homes, schools, and missions where colonialism's power and hierarchies were constituted and reproduced."[9] The chapters in this volume by Cathleen D. Cahill and Pablo Mitchell also show how the state (in the form of federal Indian schools and the court system, respectively) transformed, monitored, and imposed order on families of color in ways that reified social and racial hierarchies. Intervention into Mexican households—from federally funded child-health campaigns and statistics reporting to county-supported vocational schools—also reveals how Mexican families came under the scrutiny of the state on both sides of the Rio Grande. The motivations behind these efforts reveal how motherhood rested at the border of maternal love and state power, and they suggest the wider implications of events unfolding in El Paso in the early decades of the twentieth century.

Perhaps nowhere is the project of defining national boundaries and belonging more apparent than at the border, a place where what is "American" and what is "Mexican" are continually defined and redefined in practical and personal ways. Here, Mexican women—in their labor, domestic activities, and reproductive capacities—have historically served to set the boundaries of national belonging and exclusion. In the past and continuing into the present, Mexican women have been viewed with suspicion, either as a class "likely to become a public charge," in the parlance of early twentieth-century immigration laws, or as "hyper-fertile baby machines" that constitute a perceived social crisis in recent times.[10] Mexican mothers—and discourses about their mothering abilities or lack thereof—further illuminate national anxieties about race, labor politics, and citizenship. As Linda Gordon revealed in her account of the placement of Irish foundling children in Mexican homes in Arizona in 1904, poverty, race, and labor conflict undermined the suitability of Mexican women as adoptive mothers to "white" children.[11] At the same time, the family has also been viewed as one of the most basic sources of support and sustenance among people of Mexican origin in the United States, thus making motherhood central to defining the contours of community life.[12] A flourishing scholarship on Chicanas has revealed how women transformed "traditional" roles as wives, mothers, and daughters to create political, social, and economic spaces for themselves and their families.[13] In selectively choosing from the lessons and public and educational services intended to remake their families, Mexican mothers challenged the notion that their families were deficient, unhealthy, and, ultimately, un-American.

In order to fully understand the multiple meanings of Mexican motherhood in the borderlands, it is critical to take a broader view. Anglo reformers were not the only ones concerned with motherhood in this period. As Ann S. Blum has argued, in Mexico, family and childhood served as important categories through which class boundaries were imagined, but they were also models for shaping the postrevolution state. Children "carried the family forward, representing optimism and regeneration," she writes, and the concept of family provided "political legitimacy" and continuity to the government.[14] Throughout the 1920s and 1930s, following a nearly decade-long revolution, the Mexican government launched a sweeping nationalist project aimed at modernization and unification. Central to this monumental task was the "rationalization of domesticity" and the creation of government-sponsored educational and public health programs designed to teach impoverished (and largely indigenous) mothers how to "produce healthy, efficient, patriotic citizen workers" for the service of Mexico.[15] The rise of the eugenics and puericulture movements in Mexico culminated in the creation of state agencies, federal legislation, and medical organizations designed to promote "responsible motherhood" and involved "rescripting the behavior of mothers on behalf of the post-revolutionary state."[16] While the Mexican medical and educational communities reformulated what motherhood meant to the Mexican nation, a politically situated and vocal middle-class and exile population living in El Paso also worried about what Mexican motherhood meant in the lives of Mexicans living on the U.S. side of the border. Though a strong current of condescension sometimes shaped their views, Mexicans of the so-called better classes possessed a sense of duty to improve the lives of the less advantaged and to preserve a sense of Mexican national identity and affinity among a population under the strong influence of Americanization in the public schools, on the job, and through popular culture. Like their American counterparts, Mexican writers and reformers viewed mothers as key to promoting nationalistic ideals and, over time, asserting rights and respectability. On both sides of the border, then, reformers and writers operated according to the premise that good mothers were not born, they were made through careful instruction. This chapter thus attempts to examine the overlapping and intersecting interests that sought to define the image of Mexican motherhood in a border city.

AMERICAN MOTHERS, MEXICAN WORKERS

Largely Anglo and middle-class, Progressive-era maternalists used the language of motherhood not only to justify their own participation in the political arena, but also to press for solutions to the problems affecting women and children. One area of special concern was mother and infant care. According to a 1912 report, as many as a quarter of a million infants in the United States died before the age of one every year, and complications from childbirth were the second leading cause of death among women between the ages of fifteen and forty-five.[17] In dealing with the problem of infant mortality, solutions that addressed the deeper environmental and social conditions that affected the welfare of children soon gave way to more narrowly conceived solutions that saw mothers as the root of the problem and pointed specifically to the pathology of poor, urban families who were often immigrants.[18] The emergence of pediatrics as a medical specialty, the growing popularity of the scientific management of childbirth and child rearing, and the proliferation of advice columns related to such topics reflected the general trend toward "scientific motherhood" in the late nineteenth and early twentieth centuries.[19] Equating "good mothering" and scientific management of the home, activists, doctors, social workers, and teachers advocated the education of mothers in modern maternity practices and infant care as vitally necessary "to both women's sense of dignity and to the well-being of the nation."[20]

The Act for the Promotion of the Welfare and Hygiene of Maternity and Infancy (the Sheppard-Towner Act) epitomized this approach.[21] Passed in 1921 and administered by the Children's Bureau, the Sheppard-Towner Act coordinated efforts between federal and state governments to provide funding and programs in infant and maternity care. An annual appropriation of more than $1.2 million was given in grants to states to organize child health care conferences, provide prenatal counseling and advice to mothers, establish prenatal and infant health care centers, and provide home visits and demonstrations on infant care by certified nurses and health practitioners. In some states, nutritionists gave women instruction on proper diet during pregnancy as well as the importance of breast-feeding to babies' health. For women not reached through the conferences, health officials sent out monthly prenatal letters to expecting mothers.[22] In addition to providing much-needed preventative and prenatal care, education, and hands-on instruction, the Sheppard-Towner Act also attempted to standardize maternity practices and focused on the training and regulation of midwives.[23] Though severely underfunded from the start, the Sheppard-Towner Act established the role of the state in promoting better motherhood, as well as the right of its paid agents to intrude into the homes and lives of the recipients of its benefits. Framed within the prevailing discourse of scientific management and professionalization, as well as the class and racial assumptions of its administrators, the Sheppard-Towner Act had as its main objective fighting infant mortality and ignorance through education, not charity, one mother at a time.

The Sheppard-Towner Act also emphasized instruction for mothers and young women as a means of preventing disease and creating a better class of mothers more generally. Various states instituted "mothers' clubs" and classes, as well as "little mother's clubs" for girls as young as ten, led by nurses and other health practitioners. The purpose of these clubs and classes was clear—to teach young girls the scientific techniques of mothering at an early age in the hopes of bettering the nation's mothers. "The course usually covers the routine care of the baby and the pre-school child," explained one report. The classes covered topics such as "the bathing, dressing and feeding of the baby; regulation of his habits; methods of preparing formulas; diet of the preschool child; and prevention of children's diseases."[24] Reformers also pushed for the inclusion of similar courses in public schools, for they argued that they "should show results 5 or 10 years hence not only in lowered infant mortality rates but in better physical condition of little children."[25] Women and girls learned to prepare layettes, properly bathe babies, and make suitable cribs out of boxes or baskets. Nutrition and preventative care were also priorities. Local parent-teacher associations also coordinated their efforts with state health boards to implement "Get Ready for School Campaigns," which included health exams for children entering school and follow-up appointments with parents. Passed in Texas in 1923 with the support of groups such as the Women's Legislative Council, the Texas Congress of Mothers and Parent-Teacher Associations, the Texas League of Women Voters, and the Texas Woman's Christian Temperance Union, the Sheppard-Towner Act managed to reach mothers in nearly every corner of the vast state.[26] By the end of the 1926 fiscal year, the state had conducted more than five hundred child health conferences and eighty prenatal conferences and had established 135 child health centers and thirteen prenatal centers. More than four thousand girls participated in little mothers' classes, and more than a thousand women enrolled in similar mothers' classes. Home visits exceeded eight thousand, and almost six hundred midwives enrolled in classes, with 162 completing a ten-lesson course, thereby improving "the midwife situation" across the state.[27] Guided by the belief that "the health of the mother and the child spells the source of our nation," the Sheppard-Towner Act made great strides in the improvement of infant care. It also set into play wide-ranging programs that defined the role of motherhood in the United States and connected "good mothers" to the building of a stronger nation, attempting to stamp out not only disease and mortality but also bad mothering practices in the process.[28]

Long before the passage of the Sheppard-Towner Act, local reformers and city health officials in El Paso focused on mothers as a means of addressing public health. The influx of thousands of Mexicans in the 1910s taxed the city's already overcrowded barrios, which received few services. Infectious diseases were of particular concern, as the city's boosters had carefully cultivated El Paso's image as a health oasis.[29] Efforts to curb the spread of contagion took many forms, but before long, public health concerns became entwined with popular anxieties about the Mexican population.[30] As in other cities, poverty and poor health came to be deeply entwined with notions of racial difference and marked entire communities as unworthy of civic inclusion.[31] In particular, El Paso's infant and child mortality rates were among the worst in the nation (close to three times the national rate) and were especially high in the barrios.[32] Mexican mothers and their supposed lack of proper training became targets of efforts to reduce infant and child death rates. The Woman's Charity Association, a private philanthropic organization of middle-class women, launched the Save the Babies campaign in 1910. Under the guidance of H. Grace Franklin, a graduate of the New York Training School for Nurses and a veteran of similar maternalist efforts on New

York's Lower East Side, the El Paso Save the Babies campaign grew to encompass the School for Mothers, home nurse visits, and the distribution of clean milk and other much-needed items.[33] After establishing roots in El Paso's Mexican barrios in the early 1900s, Methodist missionary women opened the Rose Gregory Houchen Settlement House in 1912, providing classes in domestic arts, a kindergarten, and showers for residents in their efforts to effect "Christian Americanization."[34] In 1920 they opened the Freeman Clinic, the first permanent clinic to offer prenatal, infant, and child health care services in the barrio.[35] In order to reach the children, services such as the School for Mothers and Houchen and its clinic had to reach the mothers first.

In June 1910, Franklin, director of the School for Mothers, made a clear connection between infant mortality and Mexican mothers' deficiencies. According to Franklin, by stressing follow-up visits and preventative care, the School for Mothers provided an essential service to poor infants "at the mercy of ignorant mothers."[36] "Often a mother becomes careless," she explained, "and only by close watching is it possible to keep the babies well and strong." Although the work of the school had increased the number of return visits at the county dispensary and reduced the rate of infant deaths, one of the greatest benefits was the work done with the women. "More important than the actual saving in baby lives, is the teaching of mothers how to adjust their homes and incomes to the needs of the children," she explained. The school sponsored "housewives' clubs" for both girls and women that trained Mexican women in household management and child care techniques. Franklin's request for donations of household items such as kitchenware, bathtubs, toothpaste and toothbrushes, soap, baby clothing, and large dolls for demonstrations suggests that the School for Mothers provided hands-on training in almost every aspect of domestic life.

Franklin was certainly worried about infant and public health, but her comments also reveal a larger concern about Mexican mothers. To be fair, Franklin cited poverty, poor sanitation, and the lack of ventilation in tenement apartments as sources of unhealthy barrio conditions. At the same time, however, she claimed that "ignorant" Mexicans presented a very real peril to American health. She argued that "the Mexicans coming into the United States, ignorant of all sanitation and hygiene, are a menace to any community and it is up to that community to educate them while young, so that the next generation will be a cleaner, healthier race."[37] The fact that her article mentions only women and girls, not men or boys, reflects the central role that present and future mothers played in ensuring public health, in her estimation. The "menace" of uneducated Mexican mothers was a real threat to American homes. Disease-carrying flies from open sewers in barrios spread germs to the food eaten "by these people," and then made their way from the barrios to the tables in Anglo households. A problem faced by Mexican mothers thus became a problem for the entire city. "El Paso must face her problem, she cannot shift the burden with a shrug of her shoulders," Franklin warned.[38] Franklin saw her job as so vital to the welfare of the city that she took to wearing a police badge to get her message across, despite the fact that she was not a public safety official.[39] That Franklin recognized the power of police authority to persuade her charges speaks to how some viewed motherhood as falling within the purview of state control.

Training Mexican women in child rearing and household duties also had economic value, underscoring the fundamental contradiction between the ideal of middle-class domesticity and the realities of a border labor system. Although good middle-class Anglo mothers were expected to remain devoted to the home, good Mexican mothers were also being prepared for the wage labor force. In a city that by the early 1900s had already come to rely on Mexican women as domestic laborers, training Mexican women in "American" ways of housekeeping in their own homes had the added benefit of preparing Mexican women to enter the labor force as maids and nannies in private homes. By the early 1900s, domestic labor in the border city had become firmly identified as Mexican women's work.[40] According to one historian, more than 1,500 women with Spanish surnames worked as domestics in 1920.[41] In 1930, the number of Mexican women employed as servants, housekeepers, and laundresses in the city's many professional laundries had grown to nearly 3,300. Of all female workers in occupations categorized as "domestic and personal service" (a group that included hairdressers, waitresses, nurses, and hotel keepers), Mexican women constituted a full 78 percent.[42] One contemporary observer recalled just how common Mexican maids were in El Paso in the early part of the century. "Owing to the large Mexican majority ... almost every Anglo-American family had at least one, sometimes two or three servants: a maid and laundress, and perhaps a nursemaid or yardmen [sic]. The maid came in after breakfast and cleaned up the breakfast dishes, and very likely last night's supper dishes as well; did the routine cleaning, washing and ironing, and after the family dinner in the middle of the day, washed dishes again, and then went home to perform similar service in her own home."[43] As both the numbers and memories suggest, training Mexican mothers did more than address the city's public health. It ensured the economic health of the border economy as well.

This economic benefit was certainly not lost on reformers, who looked to Mexican women not only to turn their sons and husbands into good, clean American workers but to become workers themselves as well. Recognizing the reality of the El Paso economy, Franklin noted that "if El Paso wishes to improve her servant class, she must improve the homes from which this class comes."[44] Houchen's courses in cooking, sewing, and maintaining a clean household improved the daily lives of Mexican families, but they also made for more efficient workers in Anglo homes as well.[45] Women at the Smelter Vocational School in El Paso, which established a girl's school and women's programs in 1924, received education in "household service, dressmaking, parental training, nursing, personal hygiene, cooking, household care and clothing."[46] Their education had immediate economic benefits. "Training in cooking and service to the community are combined," explained the *Vocational News,* as young women in the cooking classes prepared lunch for the two hundred students at the local elementary school.[47] Moreover, classes at the girls' school were conducted in a house "fitted up like a model home," where the students gained practical training in "how to cook a meal, how to make beds, [and] how to take care of a baby," while others received lessons in dressmaking.[48] Good mothers were not born, they had to be made, and thus instruction such as that imparted at Houchen and the Smelter Vocational School and at other schools across the Southwest intended to train modern American mothers. More important, by teaching Mexican mothers and girls how to set a proper table, to make nutritious American meals, and to care for the home and children in the "American" way, they guaranteed a pool of labor to fill a specific economic niche, as well as a permanent domestic labor force skilled in the methods Anglo households found desirable.[49]

MEXICAN MOTHERHOOD: A VIEW FROM THE SPANISH-LANGUAGE PRESS

Following the end of the revolution in 1920, Mexico turned to the task of reuniting a divided nation. One of the objectives of this nationalist project was to incorporate the rural indigenous population into the national body through educational programs that stressed modernity, national unity, and *mestizaje.*[50] Consistent with the responses to urban conditions and public health in Europe and the United States and the general shift toward modernization, Mexico also focused on health and sanitation, immunization programs, improving the nation's food and milk supply, and the creation of a new department of public health.[51] As in the United States, women and families were both targets and agents of change. As early as 1915 the governor of Yucatán implemented reforms that included the first compulsory coeducational schools in the region among the Maya to promote literacy, to educate them on the goals of the revolution, and to transform them into "productive" citizens.[52] Young women educated in the United States worked in rural schools, as well as in vocational schools in Mérida and Mexico City. Like their counterparts in the United States, these schools "prepare[d] women for the home so that they could comply with their 'elevated mission' of mother in a 'rational and scientific manner.' "[53] Following the revolution, Mexican eugenicists played an important role in rebuilding a healthy nation, literally and figuratively, extending the reach of the state into the private lives and homes of Mexico's citizens. Enforcing "responsible motherhood" encompassed everything from sending visiting nurses into homes, encouraging doctor-supervised births and the removal of midwives, the passage of laws requiring medical examinations before marriage to prevent the spread of venereal disease and the passing of defective traits, and, in extreme cases, forced sterilization of "unfit" mothers.[54] In addition to organizing "sanitary brigades," which conducted outreach work with mothers and children in Mexico City, the School Hygiene Service published instructional guides on the cleanliness of one's person and home and used radio broadcasts to reach the masses.[55] Consistent with the emphasis on medicine, President Lázaro Cárdenas (1934–40) launched an educational campaign to end poverty that favored scientific management of the family over charity, challenging the authority long held by the Catholic Church.[56] In brief, the modernization of Mexico not only involved the subordination of the family and all its members to the interests of the nation, but it also gave women a discrete role to play in the making of those modern citizens.

Developments in Mexico shaped how borderlands residents viewed mothers and motherhood. This influence can be found on the pages of Spanish-language press, which played a vital role among Mexicans living in U.S. cities. According to Nicolás Kanellos, the press "assumed an importance parallel to that of the church and the mutualist society in providing leadership, solidifying the community, protecting it and furthering its cultural survival." Furthermore, the press acted as "purveyors of education, culture and entertainment."[57] Owned and operated by politically and economically advantaged Mexican exiles and members of the Mexican American middle class, these newspapers often betrayed their class sensibilities. This self-described group of *gente decente* (literally, "decent people") viewed their working-class compatriots through the prism of a fluid class- and race-based social hierarchy that separated those with education, good manners, respectability, and, in the case of women, domesticity from the crude, uncultured *gente corriente* (common people).[58] Writers in the Spanish-language press used their columns and editorial pages, as well as short stories called *crónicas*, to satirize the declining cultural integrity and nationalism among Mexicans living in the United States.[59] They saw a population that was increasingly falling victim to American popular culture, giving up the proper Spanish language for tacky border slang and turning away from their Catholic faith.[60] Though they often looked down on their working-class compatriots with disdain, they also provided critical leadership, defending all Mexicans against discrimination encountered in U.S. cities. Elite and middle-class Mexican women, for example, organized clubs to address the needs of poor families, guided by the principles of traditional female benevolence, cultural redemption, and moral uplift.[61] With readerships that extended beyond class boundaries, Mexican newspapers became a critical voice of, and for, Mexicans living in the United States.

Tapping into the discourse of scientific motherhood prevalent in both Mexico and the United States, articles in Spanish-language newspapers and journals focused on training young women in basic infant care. Like the lessons from U.S. women's programs and schools, these writings presumed a basic lack of knowledge among poor women and reflected a general Progressive trend. In fact, they often came from similar sources. One lengthy article titled "Advice for Mothers" appeared in *El Hogar,* a journal published by an agricultural and vocational college in Ciudad Juárez, just across the border from El Paso. The practical advice ranged from how to put a baby down to sleep, to appropriate schedules for breastfeeding, to the dangers of overfeeding. The article also prescribed a carefully calculated daily schedule for feedings and bathing, basic rules about sanitizing baby bottles and spoons, suggestions for avoiding diaper rash, and rules about required immunizations.[62] *El Hogar* also published articles by doctors from the Mexican Department of Public Health on the prevention of contagious diseases such as whooping cough, precautions against food-borne diseases, and advice for families on how to rid their homes of common pests.[63] In the same way that American schools stressed modern child-rearing practices, the Juárez vocational school targeted the mother as a key weapon in the fight against childhood diseases and infant mortality, and, by extension, as a means of reinforcing the nation through raising healthy Mexican citizens.

Readers of the regular women's column in *El Continental,* "Buzón femenino," also received information on basic child and maternity care. Sometimes these columns were translated versions of ones that had previously been published in English. Hertha Chessire's piece published in July 1936 offered advice to convalescing mothers. Describing the period after the birth of her own "Juanito," Chessire emphasized the importance of nutrition for the mother to regain her strength after childbirth, and also for the ultimate health of the infant.[64] Other advice came from Mexican medical professionals. An article by Dr. Oscar O. Carrera cautioned expectant mothers to "consider the doctor as her best friend and her only advisor." Like public health officials in the United States and Mexico, Carrera criticized midwives for their "rudimentary knowledge and dirty hands" and urged women instead to turn to a medical doctor to oversee her pregnancy.[65] Importantly, both articles place high importance on professional maternity care. In describing her experience at what was likely a hospital, Chessire detailed the instruction and care provided by nurses, who helped prepare her to care for her baby at home. Each morning the nurse prepared the baby's bath, carefully laying out his clothing and checking the temperature of the water. "With enthusiasm I followed all the nurse's movements [and] she promised me that when I was strong enough, she would let me bathe him myself and in that way practice for the time when I took him home," Chessire elaborated. Her comments suggest that this kind of careful infant care—such as the basic act of preparing and bathing one's child—was not something a woman simply knew how to do. Such knowledge could only come from highly trained professionals. Likewise,

Carrera is highly critical of the untrained midwives popular throughout Mexico, across different regions and socioeconomic classes; a good mother, he argues, gets quality prenatal care from a medical doctor.

The lessons in mothering appearing in the Spanish-language press also dealt with a variety of child-rearing dilemmas and suggest how mothers were considered responsible for imparting a sense of respectability to their families. The implicit messages about the social meaning of Mexican motherhood are especially illuminating. Perhaps most important, teaching cleanliness was considered of paramount importance to raising a respectable family. Personal hygiene was a favorite theme among Americanization agents, who assumed that Mexicans lacked knowledge of basic cleanliness. Spanish-language writers, however, focused on the impression that unkempt children reflected upon their family's respectability. In the regular column "The Cultivation of Beauty," author Mme Qui Vive provided women with general beauty tips and advice. In one piece she addressed the importance of raising clean children. "When we see a little girl of four or five years of age, with dirty fingernails, we do not have a good impression of her mother," she writes.[66] To this end, she reminded mothers that children of this age are fully capable of dressing themselves and keeping their nails and hands clean if taught properly. The point here is not just a critique of young girls "who do not even know how to put on their own socks," but a more pointed criticism of the mother who spoils or coddles her children. More than teaching personal care, the mother is imparting critical lessons in self-respect and confidence, she adds. "[Children] should be taught from infancy, and from the time they are children they will learn to abhor filth." Mme Qui Vive goes so far as to recommend keeping a space in the bathroom that the child can access easily (admittedly a problem in the poorest barrios, where outhouses prevailed). In that space the child could keep her personal items, as well as little gifts such as a bottle of lotion or tins of cream and powder, which would inspire her to focus on her personal presentation.

Clean households were also of vital importance, and once again mothers played a key role in this effort. The column "For the Housewife" was filled with handy household tips on maintaining an orderly home. Advice included recipes and cooking tips, home remedies, and other household hints. Nearly every column contained suggestions to make the homemaker's cleaning duties easier. Readers were instructed, for example, that water and vinegar was the best solution for cleaning glass, crystal, and even furniture. They also learned the best methods for polishing brass, silver, and pewter, for stretching the household dollar by repairing tablecloths, curtains, and even aluminum cookware, and for keeping linens crisp and white. Epsom salt could prevent colors from running in the laundry, and a little salt could keep the coffee percolator fresh and help with dreaded caked-on stains on casserole dishes. Lavender and a carbolic solution helped keep ants away.[67] In a similar fashion, America Bustillos's report of a

Cornell University study that linked housework to women's health and beauty focused on the side benefits of maintaining a clean home. If done properly, many everyday household tasks such as sweeping, mopping and polishing floors, making beds, and fluffing cushions not only contributed to a proper and clean household but also had the added benefit of strengthening the waist, improving flexibility, slimming the hips, and maintaining joint flexibility and health.[68]

The wisdom imparted through these articles can be read on numerous levels. At the very least, they suggest the importance placed on maintaining a clean home and the duty that fell on the shoulders of mothers and housewives in the border city. The articles certainly provided a set of valuable tips that probably did make household duties easier to accomplish. Advice on how to stretch a dollar was likely welcome in all families, especially as the Great Depression wore on and economizing became a necessity. The question of audience and purpose can be extended further. El Paso's Mexican elite and middle class were certainly aware of the economic character of the city in which they lived, and it is quite possible that they, too, made use of a Mexican maid or two in their own homes. Perhaps these columns also, like the vocational programs at El Paso's schools, functioned to train a pool of domestic workers that consisted of their working-class readership and to maintain a class divide even as they aimed to provide education and uplift. And what of the women who read these columns? Such time-saving tips may have also helped Mexican domestics finish their jobs quickly, so they could return to their own families and domestic duties. Perhaps adopting the household tips and advice on creating an ideal home allowed working women the opportunity to make their homes into replicas of middle-class domesticity. This was admittedly a difficult task given the meager incomes on which Mexican families subsisted. Freshly pressed white linens and finely polished silverware, well-behaved and clean children, and stylish meals even on a budget held out the promise of respectability to many Mexican mothers just trying to get by.

BORDERLANDS RESPONSES

Anglo and Mexican reformers and writers developed an idealized notion of Mexican motherhood, clearly demonstrating that they viewed Mexican mothers as not only the root of myriad problems but also the source of change. The degree to which Mexican women accepted these lessons and the ideology behind them is much harder to measure. On the one hand, maternalist efforts in El Paso likely contributed to the decline of infant and child mortality rates (although El Paso's rates still surpassed national averages). Mexican women made use of the medical services these various organizations provided. By 1920, the number of patients seen at the clinic housed at the county courthouse doubled, and within a decade there were several new clinics throughout the county and city providing healthcare and information for Mexican mothers (albeit on a segregated basis).[69] The Freeman Clinic proved so successful that in 1930 it added a six-bed maternity ward; in 1937, construction began on the much-expanded Newark Methodist Maternity Hospital, which continued to provide free immunizations, pregnancy tests, and prenatal instruction for women in the barrio.[70] Mexican women also enrolled in courses at the Smelter Vocational School and Houchen, but how they used their training is not known. Although it is possible that the new recipes and housekeeping techniques taught at these institutions replaced older ones in use by Mexican women, it is more likely that women incorporated the lessons they deemed useful in their daily lives and dismissed those that seemed impractical or unappealing.[71] Some Mexican mothers took advantage of the health and educational services at Houchen but forbade their children from playing on the new playground there as a means of rejecting the center's proselytizing message.[72] In other cases Mexican women questioned intrusions into their bodies and families. In Los Angeles throughout the 1920s, Mexican women remained wary of birthing options offered at county health clinics and hospitals, and they continued to use the services of midwives.[73] Although observers had much to say about what Mexican mothers *should* do, these women chose to act in ways that made sense in their own lives. Mexican mothers transformed the meanings of these prescriptive lessons.

A closer reading of themes in Spanish-language articles also suggests that the emphasis on clean and respectable Mexican families perhaps served as a borderlands response to prevailing racial discrimination in El Paso. The large numbers of Mexican immigrants entering El Paso in the early twentieth century long represented a Mexican "problem" to city leaders, the medical community, and reformers. By the 1930s the crisis had reached a fevered pitch. Mexicans, once welcomed as cheap labor, had now come to be viewed as foreigners stealing jobs from "real" Americans and as liabilities on already-taxed relief rolls. The Immigration and Naturalization Service raided barrios in cities with significant Mexican populations, rounding up hundreds of individuals who simply appeared to be Mexican. By 1933 and 1934, these deportation dragnets had spread to cities across the country.[74] A combination of formal deportations and popular pressure forced anywhere from 365,000 to 600,000 Mexicans and Mexican Americans voluntarily and involuntarily to "repatriate" to Mexico during the Great Depression.[75] Once the busiest port of entry into the United States, El Paso had earned the distinction of being one of the main points of departure for repatriates by the 1930s. For Mexicans who stayed in El Paso, the economic conditions facing Mexican workers created even greater challenges. The city's business, labor, and city leaders advocated stronger border regulations, pushed for the dismissal of Mexicans from jobs that could go to unemployed American workers, and argued for the exclusion of Mexicans from relief rolls.[76]

In 1936 racial tensions were further inflamed when the El Paso city registrar and city health officer—following the lead of the U.S. Census Bureau and other Texas cities—attempted to reclassify Mexicans as "colored" for the purpose of reporting infant mortality rates.[77] Such a move was a statistical sleight of hand; by removing the extremely large number of Mexican deaths from the tally, the city's overall infant mortality rate "improved" radically. Mexican and Mexican American activists, including the editor of *El Continental*, protested the action as an affront not only to Mexicans' racial status but also to international relations. In the end, city officials wrote the incident off as a misunderstanding, asserting that doctors and midwives, not the health department, made determinations about reporting race on birth and death records.[78] Still, poor mothering skills labeled Mexicans as racially and socially "other." Repatriation and reclassification efforts threatened Mexicans' already tenuous position in the border city. In a world where everything Mexican was devalued and Mexicans were deemed unworthy of civic inclusion (and could be forcibly removed from the nation regardless of citizenship status), being able to claim a place in society mattered in practical ways. Having clean homes and clean children may, on some level, have proved that Mexican families were not unlike American ones.

LOST IN TRANSLATION

As strong as the lure of domestic respectability may have been, economic necessity weighed heavily on the minds of Mexican mothers and was also reflected in the opinions of prominent columnists. In December 1935 *El Continental* ran a translated version of prominent advice columnist Dorothy Dix's latest column, which recounted the story of Ernesto and Lucia. The young couple was so intensely in love that they ignored their family's warnings about the difficulties of marriage, especially during the economic downturn, and eloped. At first they were happy, but soon Ernesto lost his job as a result of the depression, and Lucia, who became pregnant, had to leave hers as well. Ernesto, "a strong young man, full of energy and ambition," worked in whatever job he could find to bring money home to his wife and child, but he could find no steady work. At last he was offered a job, but it required him to leave some earnest money as a deposit. Because the family found themselves in such dire economic straits, he begged his wife Lucia to return to work so they could earn the money for the deposit. Lucia refused. In her mind, her duties as a mother were clear. "She allege[d] that she could not leave her child in a stranger's hands, and that she could not remotely dream of leaving her daughter with a wet nurse," Dix wrote. Lucia argued that "she could hurt herself, or they might give her inadequate food, or she could contract a contagious disease, or only God knows what dangers she could be exposed to. And to add the last grain of dust in the barrel, she tells [Ernesto] that her primary duty is to tend to her baby and that the duty of the husband is to support the home and the wife's to keep it."[79]

It would appear that Lucia had learned her lessons about motherhood well, as she placed the care of her child and of the household first. She worried about her baby's health and nutrition, as both American and Mexican medical professionals advised, and she also subscribed to the notion that a mother's most important duty was to maintain the home. Dix, however, advised otherwise. "It is our particular opinion," she wrote, "that Ernesto is right." Lucia's obligation, Dix reasoned, was to help Ernesto, even if it meant working outside the home and leaving the baby in a stranger's hands. Given the conditions wrought upon families across the country during the Great Depression, it probably comes as no surprise that an advice columnist such as Dorothy Dix would advise women to enter the labor force. By temporarily supporting her husband, Lucia would allow him to find permanent labor and thereby retain his role as the breadwinner of the family. Yet the meaning of the column is transformed in translation. To a Mexican audience, Dix's advice sent a mixed message about the role that Mexican mothers needed to play. Sadly, the dream of middle-class respectability was just within their reach, but at the end of the day, Mexican mothers were necessary workers in their families and in a border economy.

In the first decades of the twentieth century, Mexican motherhood proved to be a hotly contested topic in the U.S.-Mexico borderlands. In El Paso, the definition of a "good" Mexican mother depended upon one's perspective. For Anglo reformers, city leaders, and Americanization agents, Mexican mothers alternately represented a menace to American health and society and a potential source of labor. From a Mexican perspective, Mexican motherhood needed molding, but it also presented a way to claim inclusion at a time when the position of Mexicans in American society was especially fragile and under question. In this way, Mexican motherhood became a contentious site where ideas about nation, belonging, and citizenship were debated in personal ways. Far from being isolated, ideas about the quality and importance of Mexican motherhood on both sides of the border were deeply interconnected. The United Sates and Mexico engaged in national projects that increasingly placed women and mothers at the center of defining a healthy citizenry, and the state—from federal legislators down to the local schools—took notice of the critical role that mothers play. Much research remains to be done to further tease out the connections between these processes and examine how Mexican motherhood mattered in a borderlands milieu. In the end, however, it is clear that although there were disagreements about the particulars, many voices in this border city agreed that no one had a greater job than a mother.

NOTES

1. *Hoja Parroquial de Smelter* no. 40, October 6, 1929, Aguilar family personal collection, El Paso, Texas. All translations of Spanish-language materials are my own. Material on the Smelter Vocational School originally appeared in Monica Perales, *Smeltertown: Making and Remembering a Southwest Border Community* (Chapel Hill: University of North Carolina Press, 2010).

2. See Richard Hoffstadter, *The Age of Reform: From Bryan to FDR* (New York: Alfred Knopf, 1955); Robert H. Wiebe, *The Search for Order, 1877–1920* (New York: Hill and Wang, 1967); and Paul Boyer, *Urban Masses and the Moral Order in America, 1820–1920* (Cambridge, MA: Harvard University Press, 1978).

3. *Hoja Parroquial de Smelter* no. 40, October 6, 1929.

4. Alexandra M. Stern, "Responsible Mothers and Normal Children: Eugenics, Nationalism, and Welfare in Post-revolutionary Mexico, 1920–1940," *Journal of Historical Sociology* 12, no. 4 (December 1999): 369.

5. Mary Beth Norton, *Founding Mothers & Fathers: Gendered Power and the Forming of American Society*, 1st ed. (New York: Alfred A. Knopf, 1996); Linda K Kerber, *Women of the Republic: Intellect and Ideology in Revolutionary America* (Chapel Hill: University of North Carolina Press, 1980); and Mary P. Ryan, *Cradle of the Middle Class: The Family in Oneida County, New York, 1790–1865* (Cambridge: Cambridge University Press, 1983).

6. Barbara Welter, "The Cult of True Womanhood: 1820–1860," *American Quarterly* 18, no. 2 (Summer 1966): 151–74.

7. Robyn Muncy, *Creating a Female Dominion in American Reform, 1890–1935* (New York: Oxford University Press, 1991), xii. The literature on women in the Progressive era and maternalism is extensive. For a brief overview, see Rima D. Apple and Janet Golden, eds., *Mothers and Motherhood: Readings in American History* (Columbus: Ohio State University Press, 1997); Linda Gordon, *Pitied but Not Entitled: Single Mothers and the History of Welfare, 1890–1935* (Cambridge, MA: Harvard University Press, 1994); Molly Ladd-Taylor, *Mother-Work: Women, Child Welfare, and the State, 1890–1930* (Urbana: University of Illinois Press, 1994); Richard A. Meckel, *Save the Babies: American Public Health Reform and the Prevention of Infant Mortality, 1850–1929* (Baltimore, MD: Johns Hopkins University Press, 1990); Peggy Pascoe, *Relations of Rescue: The Search for Female Moral Authority in the American West, 1874–1939* (New York: Oxford University Press, 1990); Charlotte J. Rich, *Transcending the New Woman: Multiethnic Narratives in the Progressive Era* (Columbia: University of Missouri Press, 2009); and Sandra Schackel, *Social Housekeepers: Women Shaping Public Policy in New Mexico, 1920–1940*, 1st ed. (Albuquerque: University of New Mexico Press, 1992).

8. On Americanization programs and Mexican women, see George Sánchez, "'Go after the Women': Americanization and the Mexican Immigrant Woman, 1915–1929," in *Unequal Sisters: A Multicultural Reader in U.S. Women's History*, 2nd ed., ed. Vicki L. Ruíz and Ellen Carol DuBois (New York: Routledge, 1994), 284–97; Vicki L. Ruíz, *From Out of the Shadows: Mexican Women in Twentieth-Century America* (New York: Oxford University Press, 1998); and María E. Montoya, "Creating an American Home: Contest and Accommodation in Rockefeller's Company Towns," in *Memories and Migrations: Mapping Boricua and Chicana Histories*, ed. Vicki L. Ruíz and John R. Chávez (Urbana: University of Illinois Press, 2008), 13–43. On Americanization in the West, see Frank Van Nuys, *Americanizing the West: Race, Immigrants and Citizenship, 1890–1930* (Lawrence: University of Kansas Press, 2002); and Pascoe, *Relations of Rescue*.

9. Margaret D. Jacobs, *White Mother to a Dark Race: Settler Colonialism, Maternalism, and the Removal of Indigenous Children in the American West and Australia, 1880–1940* (Lincoln: University of Nebraska Press, 2009), 10.

10. Yolanda Chávez Leyva, "Cruzando la Linea: Engendering the History of Border Mexican Children during the Early Twentieth Century," in *Memories and Migrations: Mapping Boricua and Chicana Histories*, ed. Vicki L. Ruíz and John R. Chávez (Urbana: University of Illinois Press, 2008), 71–92; Eithne Luibhéid, *Entry Denied: Controlling Sexuality at the Border* (Minneapolis: University of Minnesota Press, 2002); Elena Gutiérrez, *Fertile Matters: The Politics of Mexican-Origin Women's Reproduction* (Austin: University of Texas Press, 2008); and Denise A. Segura and Patricia Zavella, eds., *Women and Migration in the U.S.-Mexico Borderlands: A Reader* (Durham, NC: Duke University Press, 2007).

11. Linda Gordon, *The Great Arizona Orphan Abduction* (Cambridge, MA: Harvard University Press, 1999).

12. See, for example, Albert Camarillo, *Chicanos in a Changing Society: From Mexican Pueblos to American Barrios in Santa Barbara and Southern California, 1848–1930* (Cambridge, MA: Harvard University Press, 1979); and Richard Griswold del Castillo, *La Familia: Chicano Families in the Urban Southwest, 1848 to the Present* (South Bend, IN: Notre Dame University Press, 1984).

13. For studies that examine Mexican women, see Ruíz, *From Out of the Shadows*; Deena González, *Refusing the Favor: The Spanish Mexican Women of Santa Fe, 1820–1880* (New York: Oxford University Press, 1999); Sarah Deutsch, *No Separate Refuge: Culture, Class, and Gender on an Anglo-Hispanic Frontier in the American Southwest, 1880–1940* (New York: Oxford University Press, 1987); and Gabriela Arredondo, *Mexican Chicago: Race, Identity and Nation, 1916–1939* (Urbana: University of Illinois Press, 2008).

14. Ann S. Blum, *Domestic Economies: Family, Work, and Welfare in Mexico City, 1884–1943* (Lincoln: University of Nebraska Press, 2009), 130.

15. Mary Kay Vaughan, "Modernizing Patriarchy: State Policies, Rural Households, and Women in Mexico, 1930–1940," in *Hidden Histories of Gender and the State in Latin America*, ed. Elizabeth Dore and Maxine Molyneux (Durham, NC: Duke University Press, 2000), 196. See also Nichole Sanders, "Improving Mothers: Poverty, the Family, and 'Modern' Social Assistance in Mexico, 1937–1950," in *The Women's Revolution in Mexico, 1910–1953*, ed. Stephanie Mitchell and Patience A. Schell (Lanham, MD: Rowman & Littlefield, 2007), 187–203; Stephanie J. Smith, "Educating the Mothers of the Nation: The Project of Revolutionary Education in Yucatan," in *The Women's Revolution in Mexico*, 37–51; and Patience A Schell, "Of the Sublime Mission of Mothers of Families: The Union of Mexican Catholic Ladies in Revolutionary Mexico," in *The Women's Revolution in Mexico*, 99–123.

16. Stern, "Responsible Mothers and Normal Children," 375.

17. "The Maternity and Infancy Act in Texas, Commonly Known as the Sheppard-Towner Act," *Maternity and Infancy Number Quarterly Bulletin*, Texas State Board of Health, Austin, Texas, December 1923, 7; Belle Christie Critchett Papers, 1915–1968, MS 386, C. L. Sonnichsen Special Collections Department, University of Texas at El Paso Library (hereafter Critchett Papers), Box 9, folder 19.

18. Meckel, *Save the Babies*.

19. Meckel, *Save the Babies*; and Muncy, *Creating a Female Dominion*.

20. Ladd-Taylor, *Mother-Work*, 5.

21. For the history of the hotly contested passage of the Sheppard-Towner Act, see Ladd-Taylor, *Mother-Work*; Meckel, *Save the Babies*; and Muncy, *Creating a Female Dominion*.

22. Department of Labor, Children's Bureau, Publication 178, "The Promotion of the Welfare and Hygiene and Maternity and Infancy, United States, The Administration of the Act of Congress of November 23, 1921, for the Fiscal Year Ended June 30, 1926," 1–14, Critchett Papers, Box 10, folder 24.

23. Ibid., 4.

24. Department of Labor, Children's Bureau, "The Promotion," 19–20.

25. Ibid., 20.

26. "The Maternity and Infancy Act," 8.

27. Department of Labor, Children's Bureau, "The Promotion," 26–27, 68–69.

28. "The Maternity and Infancy Act," 7. Despite resulting in many gains and the creation of new professional opportunities for women as administrators, nurses, social workers, and educators, the Sheppard-Towner Act was repealed in 1929. Opposed by professional medical organizations such as the American Medical Association, challenged by right-wing critics, who viewed it as a step toward socialism, and up against the antifeminist rhetoric of the 1920s, the original bill failed to fundamentally alleviate the social conditions of poverty and access that placed poor women and their infants in danger. Still, scholars note how the Sheppard-Towner Act represented both the pinnacle and nadir of the American maternalist movement. See Meckel, *Save the Babies;* Ladd-Taylor, *Mother-Work;* and Muncy, *Creating a Female Dominion.*

29. Alexandra Stern, *Eugenic Nation Faults and Frontiers of Better Breeding in Modern America* (Berkeley: University of California Press, 2005), 61; and Dr. Hugh Crouse, "With Every Natural Resource Plus Climate El Paso Becomes Not Only Great Tourist Point but Stands Out in the Nation as a Health Resort," *Greater El Paso,* March 1920. For an excellent discussion of the evolution of public health policy in El Paso, see Ann R. Gabbert, "Defining the Boundaries of Care: Local Responses to Global Concerns in El Paso Public Health Policy, 1881–1941," Ph.D. diss., University of Texas at El Paso, 2006.

30. As early as 1910 the U.S. Public Health Service implemented medical inspections and quarantine procedures at the El Paso border crossing to address health concerns. A fear of typhus in 1919 led to raids in the city's barrios and the demolition of Mexican homes. See Gabbert, "Defining the Boundaries of Care"; Stern, *Eugenic Nation,* 59; and David Dorado Romo, *Ringside Seat to a Revolution: An Underground Cultural History of El Paso and Juárez, 1893–1923* (El Paso, TX: Cinco Puntos Press, 2005), 234.

31. See Natalia Molina, *Fit to Be Citizens? Public Health and Race in Los Angeles, 1879–1939* (Berkeley: University of California Press, 2006); Nayan Shah, *Contagious Divides: Epidemics and Race in San Francisco's Chinatown* (Berkeley: University of California Press, 2001); and Stern, *Eugenic Nation.*

32. Gabbert, "Defining the Boundaries of Care," 389.

33. Ibid., 377–79, 397–98.

34. Eve Carr, "Missionaries and Motherhood: Sixty-Six Years of Public Health Work in South El Paso," Ph.D. diss., Arizona State University, 2003, 13.

35. Carr, "Missionaries and Motherhood," 145–46; and Ruíz, *From Out of the Shadows,* 135–36.

36. H. Grace Franklin, "Present Care for Babies Prevents Future Worries," *El Paso Times,* June 20, 1910.

37. Ibid.

38. Ibid.

39. Gabbert, "Defining the Boundaries of Care," 389.

40. Vicki L. Ruíz, "By the Day or the Week: Mexicana Domestic Workers in El Paso," in *Women on the U.S.-Mexico Border: Responses to Change,* ed. Vicki L. Ruíz and Susan Tiano (Boston, MA: Allen & Unwin, 1987), 61–76; Mario T. García, "The Chicana in American History: The Mexican Women of El Paso, 1880–1920, A Case Study," *Pacific Historical Review* 49, no. 2 (May 1980): 315–37; and Yolanda Chávez Leyva, "'Faithful Hard-Working Mexican Hands': Mexicana Workers During the Great Depression," *Perspectives in Mexican American Studies* 5 (1995): 63–77.

41. García, "The Chicana in American History," 326.

42. U.S. Census Bureau, 15th Census, Population Abstract, vol. 4, table 12, "Males and Females 10 years old and over in selected occupations by color, nativity and age for cities of 100,000 or more, 1930," p. 1590.

43. Quoted in García, "The Chicana in American History," 326–27.

44. Franklin, "Present Care for Babies."

45. Carr, "Missionaries and Motherhood," 136–37.
46. "Smelter School Aid to Students," *Vocational News*, April 22, 1932, 4, Perales Family Personal Collection, El Paso, Texas (hereafter PFPC).
47. "Smelter Prepares Lunch for 200 Every School Day," *Vocational News*, April 22, 1932, 4, PFPC.
48. "A School Where They Don't Give a Hoot for Grades," *El Paso Herald Post*, February 14, 1931, El Paso Vertical File, El Paso Public Library.
49. As sociologist Mary Romero observes, although domestic work has been a profession that has served as a temporary alternative for many immigrant women, this has not been the case for Latinas, who often find themselves locked in domestic labor and with fewer options. Mary Romero, *Maid in the U.S.A.* (New York: Routledge, 1992).
50. Michael C Meyer, *The Course of Mexican History*, 7th ed. (New York: Oxford University Press, 2003), 550–52.
51. Meyer, *The Course of Mexican History*, 562; and Vaughan, "Modernizing Patriarchy," 196.
52. Smith, "Educating the Mothers of the Nation."
53. Ibid., 40.
54. Stern, "Responsible Mothers and Normal Children," 375–78.
55. Ibid., 373–76.
56. Sanders, "Improving Mothers," 187–203.
57. Nicolás Kanellos with Helvetia Martell, *Hispanic Periodicals in the United States, Origins to 1960: A Brief History and Comprehensive Bibliography* (Houston, TX: Arte Público Press, 2000), 7.
58. See William E. French, *A Peaceful and Working People: Manners, Morals, and Class Formation in Northern Mexico* (Albuquerque: University of New Mexico Press, 1996); Gabriela González, "Carolina Munguía and Emma Tenayuca: The Politics of Benevolence and Radical Reform, 1930s," *Frontiers: A Journal of Women Studies* 24, nos. 2–3 (Spring 2004): 200–229; Margaret Chowning, *Wealth and Power in Provincial Mexico: Michoacán from the Late Colony to the Revolution* (Stanford, CA: Stanford University Press, 1999); and Leticia Garza-Falcón, *Gente Decente: A Borderlands Response to the Rhetoric of Dominance* (Austin: University of Texas Press, 1998).
59. Nicolás Kanellos, "A Socio-Historic Study of Hispanic Newspapers in the United States," in *Recovering the U.S. Hispanic Literary Heritage*, ed. Ramón Gutiérrez and Genaro Padilla (Houston, TX: Arte Público Press, 1993), 116. See also Magdalena L. Barrera, "Of *Chicharrones* and Clam Chowder: Gender and Consumption in Jorge Ulica's *Crónicas diabólicas*," *Bilingual Review* 29, no. 1 (2008): 49–65.
60. It is important to note that although many exiled Mexican elites maintained a strong affiliation with Catholicism, the overall role of the church within Mexico was more complicated. The revolution and subsequent governments espoused a strong anti-Catholic position, and the social and educational reforms enacted as a result were decidedly secular in nature. See Schell, "Of the Sublime Mission."
61. González, "Carolina Munguía and Emma Tenayuca."
62. *El Hogar* 44, no. 2 (February 1928): 27–29, C. L. Sonnichsen Special Collections Department, University of Texas at El Paso Library.
63. Antonia Ursúa, "La tos ferina," *El Hogar* 47, no. 6 (June 1931): 14–16; Adolfo Arreguín, "Las verduras y sus peligros," *El Hogar* 47, no. 7 (July 1931): 7–9; "La higiene y las enfermedades," *El Hogar* 47, no. 7 (July 1931): 10–12; and Adolfo Arreguín, "Las moscas," *El Hogar* 47, no. 8 (August 1931): 13–15.
64. Hertha Chessire, "Después del nacimiento," *El Continental*, July 13, 1936, 3.
65. Oscar O. Carrera, "La prevención en el embarazo," *El Continental*, June 18, 1936, 6.
66. Mme Qui Vive, "El cultivo de la belleza," *El Continental*, March 27, 1938, 9.

67. *El Continental,* November 22, 1936; May 2, 1937; June 6, 1937; June 13, 1937; September 12, 1937; September 19, 1937; September 26, 1937; October 3, 1937; October 15, 1937; October 21, 1937; and June 3, 1938.

68. *El Continental,* September 24, 1936, 6.

69. Gabbert, "Defining the Boundaries of Care," 449–50.

70. Ruíz, *From Out of the Shadows,* 36.

71. Perales, *Smeltertown,* 185–222.

72. Carr, "Missionaries and Motherhood," 138.

73. Molina, *Fit to Be Citizens,* 100–105.

74. Francisco Balderrama and Raymond Rodríguez, *Decade of Betrayal: Mexican Repatriation in the 1930s* (Albuquerque: University of New Mexico Press, 1995), 55.

75. Camille Guerin-Gonzales, *Mexican Workers and American Dreams: Immigration, Repatriation, and California Labor, 1900–1939* (New Brunswick, NJ: Rutgers University Press, 1996), 94; Rodolfo Acuña, *Occupied America: A History of Chicanos,* 3rd ed. (New York: Harper Collins, 1988), 202; and Mae Ngai, *Impossible Subjects: Illegal Aliens and the Making of Modern America* (Princeton, NJ: Princeton University Press, 2004), 72.

76. Chávez Leyva, "Faithful Hard-Working Mexican Hands."

77. Mario T. García, "Mexican Americans and the Politics of Citizenship: The Case of El Paso, 1936," *New Mexico Historical Review* 59, no. 2 (April 1984): 187–204; Gabbert, "Defining the Boundaries of Care," 420–70.

78. García, "Mexican Americans and the Politics of Citizenship," 189–93.

79. *El Continental,* December 4, 1935, 3.

8

Borderlands / *La Familia*

Mexicans, Homes, and Colonialism in the Early Twentieth-Century Southwest

Pablo Mitchell

Two decades ago Gloria Anzaldúa published Borderlands/La Frontera: The New Mestiza. A foundational text in borderlands studies, Anzaldúa's masterful work combines prose and poetry in its exploration of intersecting forms of oppression along the U.S.-Mexico border. In her poem "To live in the Borderlands means you . . . ," Anzaldúa identifies multiple dimensions of violence and dispossession in the Southwest. On one level are "border disputes," conflicts between nation-states, and the work of agents of the state such as immigration officials, who produce a region where living on the borderlands is, in Anzaldúa's words, "to be stopped by la migra at the border checkpoints." Colonialism occupies a similar plane, stretching broadly in time and space to encompass the lives of the *"hispana india negra española,"* as well as "the india in you, betrayed for 500 years."[1]

Betrayals and state-inspired violence and exclusion are matched in the poem by assaults inflicted on a more domestic, familial scale. Anzaldúa sees the family as a source of terror analogous to state and colonial rule. At home, she writes, is "the mill with razor white teeth." "Enemies are kin to each other," she continues, "you are at home, a stranger." Even making bread, a task so often invoked as nurturing and safe, is transformed as traumatic: "pound you pinch you roll you out / smelling like white bread but dead." And yet, in the poem, the borderlands are also a place of hope, creativity, and transformation. "To live in the borderlands," Anzaldúa suggests, "means to put chile in the borscht, eat whole wheat tortillas, speak Tex-Mex with a Brooklyn accent." Resistance, in both the poem and the book, is thus deeply rooted in the borderlands, as are the traumas of the state, of colonialism, and of the family.[2]

Writing in the late twentieth century, Anzaldúa highlighted themes pertinent to a previous era as well. In the early twentieth century, Anglo elites targeted Mexican communities, and Mexican families, from multiple perches. The denigration of Mexican families was, in fact, an integral feature of an Anglo colonial order that had persisted in the Southwest since the mid-nineteenth century.[3] So, too, did Mexican families during the period contain many of the inequities, especially in terms of gender and sex, that Anzaldúa would note decades later. Although Mexicans were stalwart defenders of their families in the face of Anglo attacks, their responses to such critiques by Anglos were not unrelated to the asymmetries of power dividing and pervading Mexicans' families. This chapter will argue, in other words, that Mexicans' counterhegemonic claims of family respectability and decency were grounded in a form of heteropatriarchy that privileged female inferiority and subservience, marital reproduction, and fraternal order.[4]

I will explore such contestations over domestic space through the use of criminal appeals cases involving Mexicans in the early twentieth-century Southwest. Between 1900 and 1930, the ethnic Mexican population of the United States grew from 400,000 to 1.4 million.[5] Every year, tens of thousands of Mexicans left their hometowns and villages and made the arduous journey across the U.S.-Mexico border. Decades-long modernization efforts led by Mexican president Porfirio Díaz, bolstered by the ample support of American politicians and business leaders, had wreaked havoc on the Mexican countryside. Subsistence agriculture was increasingly unsustainable during the Díaz presidency, and Mexican rural inhabitants found migration, whether to cities within Mexico or to foreign lands, to be the best option in hard times.

The same forces of modernization that sought to undermine subsistence agriculture, of course, also enabled Mexican villagers to travel far from their homelands, as Mexican migrants took advantage of newly constructed, often American-financed, railroad lines within Mexico to make the journey to the north and to the United States. Mexican migrants also fled the violence and chaos of civil war in Mexico after a series of armed uprisings eventually toppled the Díaz regime and the country suffered through years of turmoil and dislocation. Drawing Mexicans to the United States was the promise of jobs. The borderlands economy boomed in the early twentieth century, especially in the areas of agriculture, led by California and Texas, and railroad construction. Mexican communities subsequently expanded in big cities and small towns stretching from the border states to the industrial Midwest.

Although Mexicans, whether newcomers or natives to the region, faced multiple hardships in the Southwest (including racialized wage scales, vicious anti-immigrant attacks from newspapers, politicians, and the broader Anglo public, inferior housing, and segregated schools), they nonetheless possessed important advantages as well. In the early twentieth century Mexicans were designated by

TABLE 8.1 Spanish-surnamed defendants appealing criminal convictions to higher courts, 1900–1930

	Cases with Spanish-surnamed appellants	Total criminal appeals
California Supreme Court	41	950
California Court of Appeals (1905–1930)	167	2,972
Arizona Supreme Court	78	531
New Mexico Supreme Court	114	411
Texas Court of Criminal Appeals	749	17,034

SOURCE: LexisNexis Legal Database, accessed December 2009 to November 2010.

the U.S. census as members of the "white" race and could own land, vote, testify against Anglos in courts, and marry other "whites." As appeals cases suggest, Mexicans also claimed important rights as citizens in Anglo-dominated courtrooms, namely the right to appeal criminal convictions or unfavorable decisions in civil trials to higher courts.

Mexicans convicted of a variety of crimes, ranging in severity from murder, assault, and rape to minor theft and possession of liquor, initiated appeals cases across the region in the early twentieth century (see table 8.1). Many of the cases involved crimes against other Mexicans, but a significant number of the appeals, including some successful ones, involved Anglo victims. In 1904, for instance, Aniceto Guerrero, who was originally convicted of stealing a hog from an Anglo neighbor, appealed his conviction on theft charges to the Texas Court of Criminal Appeals and won his case. In the 1920s in Los Angeles, Marina Torres, though unsuccessful in her appeals process, asked the California higher courts to review her conviction on the charge of enticing Dorothy Hall, a sixteen-year-old "American" girl, into prostitution. Especially notable in this respect were the successful appeals of their assault convictions by Pedro Barstado, Saturina Garza, and Blazeo Pedro in Texas in 1905. The three men were convicted of severely beating their former employer, Tom Gallamore, after Gallamore first refused to pay the men and then shot Barstado outside a Taylor County drugstore. The three men successfully appealed their convictions and were granted new trials.[6]

Regardless of the identity of the victim, however, the context of the appeals is significant. Mexicans appealed convictions within a period of widespread hostility to immigrants in general, and Mexicans in particular. In the midst of anti-immigrant legislation such as the 1924 National Origins Act, antilabor crusades targeting "foreigners," specific (and often violent) anti-Mexican campaigns such as the forcible removal of Mexican miners from Bisbee, Arizona, in 1917, the Anglo terror inflicted on south Texas Mexicans in the 1910s, and the repatriation campaigns of the late 1920s and 1930s, significant numbers of ordinary Mexicans turned to the Anglo-dominated American legal system with a reasonable expectation of success. Whether convicted of murdering another Mexican, illegally selling liquor, enticing an Anglo "girl" into prostitution, or severely beating an Anglo employer, Mexican appellants turned to the appeals process because at a fundamental level they believed—not inaccurately—that it was their right to do so.[7]

Such cases offer vivid and revealing accounts of Mexicans' engagement with the American legal system.[8] This is especially true when the case files include the transcripts of trials, which can often extend over one hundred of pages of witness testimony. In such trials, Mexican witnesses for both the defense and the prosecution spoke publicly, and often quite assertively, before an audience of jury members, lawyers, judges, and courtroom observers. They described their families and homes, their work experiences, their journeys to and within the United States, and their neighborhoods and communities. Although often deferential and submissive on the witness stand, Mexican witnesses could also openly spar with attorneys, refusing especially to concede to negative depictions of their homes and their families. In doing so in the Anglo-dominated space of courtrooms, Mexican women and men further asserted rights and status associated with citizenship and American belonging.

I will suggest that such claims of rights resulted at least in part from Mexicans' peculiar status as American colonial subjects. American colonial rule in the Southwest is pronounced: it is evidenced in the appropriation and exploitation of Mexican and Native American property and resources, the enduring U.S. military presence, the resettling, with ample government help, of Anglo families into new homes within this newly occupied land, and the dependence on the easily exploitable labor of subjugated and impoverished colonial subjects. For Mexicans specifically, American settler colonialism was underway in Texas, New Mexico, and California well before the Treaty of Guadalupe Hidalgo in 1848, and Mexican loss of land accelerated throughout the remainder of the nineteenth century, as did the reliance on the labor of Mexican women and men in the expanding agricultural, ranching, and industrial economies of the West. Exploitation and subordination did not cease with increased immigration from Mexico in the early twentieth century. In fact, historians have used terms such as "imported colonialism" and "colonized labor" to describe Mexican immigration to the United States over the course of the past century.[9]

In asserting their rights in the American legal system, Mexicans exposed a critical tension within the American colonial endeavor: dispossession and the many traumas of occupation were accompanied by the promise of citizenship and eventual, though distantly imagined, civic inclusion. American colonial order, that is, though committed to vast seizures of land, the overthrow of Native economies and cultures, and the supremacy of Anglo America, nonetheless also promoted itself as inclusionary. Turn-of-the-twentieth-century American colonial subjects (Native Americans, Hawaiians, Puerto Ricans, Filipinos, Mexicans) were depicted by a range of colonial elites as potentially achieving citizenship as long as they cultivated an assortment of correctly managed attributes, including civilized demeanor, deference to Anglo-American superiority, and proper gender and sexual comportment.[10]

Families and domestic life were especially important in this respect. Assessing families and domesticity—determining proper sexual behavior, gender roles, reproduction, and parenting—was, in fact, at the heart of colonial rule. The racial taxonomies that sustained colonial projects depended on highlighting the proper heteropatriarchal families of colonial elites and disparaging the home lives of colonial subjects. Colonial reports from a range of settings were filled with colonizers' accounts of the improperly, even dangerously, constituted living arrangements and family relations of colonial subjects. And yet the proper families of particular colonial subjects, most frequently defined as controlled by men and based on church- or government-sanctioned marriage, could be described by colonial elites in positive terms and at times celebrated as examples of the civilizing potential of colonial rule. Competing portrayals of Mexican families (whether disparaging accounts by Anglos or the occasional spirited defense of one's home by a Mexican witness) thus must be understood as developing within a context of American colonial rule.[11]

This chapter will begin by offering examples of the negative portrayals of Mexican families by Anglos. Next it will turn to more positive depictions of families by Mexican trial participants, followed by an examination of the exclusions and inequities, largely in terms of gender and sex, embedded in such claims of respectability. The chapter will conclude by suggesting that both Mexicans' use of the American legal system to defend their rights and the trial participants' frequent emphasis on extending patriarchy and sexual propriety have roots in the persisting American colonial domination of the borderlands.

CRITIQUES OF MEXICAN HOMES

Criticism of Mexican homes and families could take many forms in the courtroom. Trials often depicted a sharp divide between Anglo and Mexican homes. During Alma Carrillo's trial for murdering her husband in rural California in 1929, an Anglo witness was asked to describe the home of the Carrillo family. "Kind of a shack of a house?" the prosecutor asked Mrs. E. W. Leininger, a neighbor of the Carrillos. "Well, yes," she answered. "Dilapidated in places?" the prosecutor asked. "Yes, quite dilapidated now," Mrs. Leininger answered. "These people had all the resemblance of being very poor people?" the prosecutor continued. "Well, yes," she answered.[12] In turning down Alvino Méndez's appeal of a murder conviction in the beating death of Mike Farnesaro in California's Imperial Valley in 1923, the opinion filed by the California supreme court repeatedly differentiated between the "ranch" of the unfortunate Farnesaro family, as well as the nearby "ranch house" of the Sample family, from the "shacks" occupied by Mexican workers. At the time of the attack, the court noted, "sixteen Mexicans were occupying a shack upon the Farnesaro ranch a quarter mile north of the place where the decedent [Farnesaro] was living and were employed upon the Sample ranch."[13] Criticisms of Mexican homes could extend to entire neighborhoods as well. Samuel Ginsberg, a merchant testifying in defense of Cruz Vicuña during his trial for murder in Los Angeles in 1930, described Vicuña in a positive light, as a "law-abiding citizen," yet at the same time perpetuated a common image of Mexican neighborhoods as overcrowded and unfamiliar. Asked if he knew any of Vicuña's neighbors, Ginsberg answered, "I know several of them" and identified one man, a "Mr. Espinoza." "Anybody else?" the prosecutor asked. "Well," Ginsberg paused, "a lot of Mexicans live together down there." "I know a few," he continued, "I don't know them all." Acquainted to a certain extent with Mexican communities ("I understand Spanish," he told the court), Ginsberg nonetheless accentuated racial difference in his testimony, portraying large numbers of anonymous Mexicans clustered together in congested living quarters.[14]

Anglo trial participants also tended to dwell on the nonnuclear domestic arrangements of Mexican families, highlighting the presence and residence of stepbrothers and stepsisters, stepfathers, cousins, aunts and uncles, and grandparents in the home. During the 1911 trial of Frank Ramírez for raping the fourteen-year-old sister of his wife in Stockton, California, witnesses were repeatedly asked to enumerate the occupants of the house, which included Ramírez, his wife, their two children, and her sister (Carmelita Salazar, the victim of the attack), as well as several other members of the extended family. Ramírez's wife described the household as consisting of her "three brothers, and my sister, my mother and my stepmother and me and my husband." The defense, anxious to suggest that someone other than Ramírez had raped Carmelita Salazar, further cast aspersions upon the reputation of the home by asking Ramírez's wife if she had ever seen "a prostitute at [the home] associating with Carmelita?"[15] It is not surprising, of course, that sex crime trials, especially those involving attacks in the home, would tend to focus on members of the household, or that the defense would look for possible attackers other than the defendant. Nonetheless, such depictions of Mexican homes as ramshackle abodes filled with extended kin reflected a broader Anglo current of thought about the inferior state of Mexican domesticity in the region.

Among the prominent Anglo critiques were those of Progressive-era reformers, largely Anglo women, who sought to remake Mexican homes in Anglo images through numerous settlement-house-style programs across the region. Historian María Cristina García has described the establishment of the Rusk Settlement

House in Houston, which in 1907 began to offer "cooking classes, sewing classes, recreational activities for children and teenagers, and a social club for young women" to an increasingly ethnic Mexican population in the city. Though she acknowledges that the exclusively Anglo staff ("Mexican Americans," she notes, "did not join the staff until the 1950s") provided much-needed services to the impoverished Mexican community, García is clear that a primary, and persistent, goal of the program was to transform—and, in the eyes of Anglos, improve—the homes of Mexican families. Other historians have noted similar sets of initiatives targeting Mexican domesticity throughout the region during the period.[16]

DEFENDING MEXICAN HOMES

Just as Mexicans throughout the Southwest struggled mightily to defend themselves and their families against such interventions, critiques of Mexican families did not go unchallenged in courtrooms. Mexican witnesses, for instance, described multiple occasions on which extended kin networks provided important sources of support during times of special need. During the trial of Eulogio Castro, who was accused of raping the goddaughter of his wife, Elvira Salazar, in San Bernardino, California, in 1899, the accuser's aunt described how different family members had helped to raise her niece after the death of the girl's mother seven years earlier. "I was present at her birth," Manuela Quintana, the sister of the girl's dead mother, told the court; "she was born at Yucaipa." According to Quintana, after her mother's death, the girl "went to live at Castro's because Mrs. Castro is her godmother and when Mrs. Salazar died they took her to raise." Elvira Salazar lived with her godmother and her husband for seven years, until she became pregnant, allegedly after being forced to have sex with the husband of her godmother, Eulogio Castro, and fled the home. After leaving the Castro home, Elvira Salazar took up residence at the home of her aunt, Manuela Quintana.[17]

At times, Mexicans' claims of family respectability proved persuasive to the American courts. In 1920, for instance, Tomás Gutiérrez filed a petition asking that his two daughters, aged one and three, be returned to him. According to the higher court's opinion, "the mother is dead, and the children had for some time been in the immediate care of the maternal grandmother, with the father's consent, and under an arrangement whereby he paid for their upkeep." After a dispute between Tomás Gutiérrez and the girls' grandmother, Gutiérrez assumed custody of his daughters: "He at first kept them at his home, with the help of a woman he employed, but later sent for and paid the transportation of a brother and his family, who lived in New Mexico, to come to San Diego and live with him and make a home for himself and the children." The juvenile court in San Diego, however, ordered that the children be taken from Gutiérrez and declared wards of the state. The court "place[d] them in the custody of the probation officer under the immediate care of the grandmother." Gutiérrez subsequently appealed the order to California's Court of Appeal.[18]

In its decision in favor of Gutiérrez and reversing the lower court, the higher court lauded Gutiérrez as "an industrious man, earning good wages, affectionate with the children, spending his money freely to provide for them, and able and willing to care for them." While the court agreed with the judge in the lower court that the grandmother provided the children "better attention and more wholesome surroundings" than the newly constituted household of their father—suggesting that nonnuclear families were frowned upon by the courts—there was nothing in the case, according to the judge in the higher court, to "justify depriving the father of the custody of his children." The court added a sharp note in conclusion: "The juvenile court law certainly does not contemplate the taking of children from their parents and breaking up family ties merely because, in the estimation of probation officers and courts, the children can be better provided for and more wisely trained as wards of the state. Probably from the mere consideration of healthful and hygienic living and systemic education and training this would be true in the cases of thousands of families of wealth and respectability." Though clearly differentiated from "families of wealth and respectability," members of the Gutiérrez family were nonetheless portrayed by the California higher court as similar to a broader group of Americans and deserving of the right to raise their own children.[19]

Mexican witnesses also described their homes, in contrast to Anglo depictions, as clean and properly ordered. During a 1906 rape trial in California, Altagracia Enríquez, whose niece had been attacked in the home, resisted efforts to portray her household as unseemly and unkempt. When the defense attorney asked her at one point about the bed in her family's home, Enríquez was adamant in her response. "Your bed there in the cabin," the lawyer asked, "do you use sheets on it or is it just quilts or blankets, or do you use sheets on your bed?" He had prefaced the question by stating that he did not "want to harass [her] or annoy [her] at all, or reflect on [her] condition," but that his question had "a purpose in it." Enríquez answered flatly, "We have two sheets and two pillows and [a] quilt on top." "This man," she added, referring disdainfully to the defendant, "didn't even consider or respect the fact that it was the couch of a married couple." In Enríquez's clever response, she contrasts the decency of her own home (appropriate bedding, appropriate marital condition) to the actions of the defendant and his attorney, both of whom—literally, in the case of the defendant, by attacking her niece in her home; figuratively, in the case of his lawyer, by impugning her home's propriety—sullied her household.[20]

In another case, from Texas in 1922, a Mexican witness who was defending her brother against a charge of attempted rape described their home as more American than Mexican. Celia Castañeda testified that her brother, Domingo Brown, had been at the family home the entire evening of December 19, 1919, the night he was accused of sneaking into the bedroom of a neighbor and attacking her in her bed. That night, according to Castañeda, "we were making some cakes and fixing things for Christmas time." "My brother was there too," she said. "He went to bed at 11 o'clock and then me and my sister, my young[er] sister, went to bed at one o'clock." "My family always cooked up things to celebrate Christmas," she added. "We celebrate like you all do here, we do not celebrate like they do in Mexico." In her testimony Castañeda did more than simply provide an alibi for her brother. She presented herself and her sister as properly domestic in cooking for the family in preparation for a holiday. Significantly, she placed this domesticity in national terms. Rather than following Mexican traditions and practices, she affiliates herself and her family with American customs.[21]

REINFORCING HETEROPATRIARCHY

By claiming to have properly ordered families and domestic spaces, Mexicans challenged one of the foundations of colonial rule in the Southwest: the notion that Anglo families were superior to Mexican and other non-Anglo families. At the same time, family was also a critical site in the maintenance of social divisions within Mexican communities. Hierarchies based on gender were among the most persistent of such divisions. The subordination of women was especially visible in matters related to sex. Trial transcripts suggest the existence of a powerful sexual double standard whereby the sexual practices and desires of women and girls were carefully monitored while male sexuality was left relatively unsupervised and unfettered.

Take, for instance, the practice of female chaperonage, the escorting, often by male family members such as uncles, brothers, or cousins, of young, unmarried women to events outside the home. Throughout the region, Mexicans turned to the family to cushion themselves against the pervasive inequities of Anglo rule. Chaperonage was one such attempt to shield vulnerable members from perceived social dangers. As Vicki Ruíz and others have maintained, female chaperonage could also mask imbalances of power within Mexican communities, especially inequities of gender. On a basic level, Mexican men and boys were not supervised by other men, or by women, when they left the home. Female chaperonage thus obviously constrained the sexual freedom of *mexicanas*. But it also, under the guise of protection from sexual danger, severely limited their geographic movement and underscored the notion that the proper place for women was in the home. Finally, chaperonage allowed parents and guardians some control over the courtship and marriage partners of young women, helping them to screen out unacceptable candidates and reinforce their power over marital decisions.[22]

Mexican trial participants recounted practicing forms of chaperonage and overseeing the behavior of young women and girls during visits to the homes of other families and outings to nearby movie theaters and dances. Take, for example, the trial of Rudolfo Rodríguez in Texas in the early 1920s. Rodríguez was convicted of raping his fourteen-year-old daughter, Natalia Rodríguez, and was sentenced to five years in the Texas state penitentiary. According to the trial transcript, several months after the original attack Natalia Rodríguez married José Mata, and six months later she gave birth to a child. At that point Rodríguez accused her father of raping her some thirteen months earlier. Although Natalia Rodríguez asserted that her father was the father of the child, the defense claimed that Rodríguez and her eventual husband had had sex before their marriage and that Mata was the father.[23]

Testimony on both sides of the aisle explored notions of proper courtship and chaperonage. Natalia Rodríguez told jurors that she had only met José Mata in person on a handful of occasions and had communicated with him largely through letters left for each other in the hollow trunk of an oak tree. Even when the couple met in person, Rodríguez testified, they were never alone with each other. Although on one occasion Rodríguez and Mata met at a fence along the road outside her home, "my sisters could see where I was," Rodríguez stated. "I did not go anyplace where they could not see me."[24]

Rudolfo Rodríguez, on the other hand, told jurors that he had discovered his daughter and José Mata "close to the house, about ten yards, he was on the outside of the wire fence, and she was on the inside." "I don't know what they were doing," he continued, "probably talking as they were close together." Rodríguez admonished Mata for not coming directly to the house but instead leaving his horse on a nearby road and walking across a pasture to meet the young woman. "I told him these actions of his were dishonoring my home," Rodríguez recalled. "I told him," he continued, "if that was the way he was going to do toward that young lady, that he would not make a good husband for her, that he was trying to dishonor her, that if he wanted to speak to her, for him to come by way of the road and come to the house, and if I was there he could talk to her, but if I was not there, no." Rodríguez added that he told his daughter "that any time I would catch either of the grown girls talking to any one out in the pasture, I would not permit them to be in the house any longer." Although the opposing sides of the case were divided over the origins of Rodríguez's pregnancy, both shared an understanding of female chaperonage and its role in limiting the sexual freedom and mobility of Mexican women.[25]

Closely related to the subordination of women through practices such as chaperonage was the fraternal bonding of men. Although Mexican women could be accorded respect on the witness stand, laudatory comments were largely reserved for men. In the predominantly male courtroom—populated with male judges, lawyers, and police officers and usually male jurors—men often saluted, and were saluted by, other men. Further hierarchically dividing Mexican men and women was the occasional formation of interracial bonds between Mexican and Anglo men. One such bond, of course, was a result of the legal process itself, as almost exclusively Anglo lawyers collaborated with Mexican male defendants in developing a legal strategy. Another bond linked Anglo and Mexican civic elites in locations where Mexicans exerted sufficient authority and political and economic power. In *New Mexico v. Juan Lujan,* for instance, a seduction trial from northern New Mexico in 1916, several of the Mexican witnesses were introduced as "Don," a title suggesting considerable deference and respect. In his opening statement to the jury, W. G. Ward, the district attorney representing the prosecution, noted that Juan Lujan and Josefita Martínez were cousins and had lived in the same house for several years during their childhood. The house, he added, was "the house of the grandfather—Don Ramón Martínez." "Don," as a signal of respect and deference, was used often during the trial to identify Ramon Martínez and other high-status Mexican men.[26]

This system of patriarchy, whereby older elite men, Anglo and Mexican alike, assumed the authority to make decisions about important aspects of women's lives, rendered Mexican women like Josefita Martínez, the woman who brought the seduction charges against Juan Lujan, marginal. During his opening statement, the attorney, Ward, likely referred to Martínez as "Don Martínez" in an attempt to compensate for the shortcomings in the reputation of Josefita Martínez, Martínez's granddaughter and the state's main witness. "We will show to you by evidence that we believe to be entirely credible, the evidence of the young woman herself," Ward continued, "that the seduction was accomplished as a result of a promise of the defendant to marry this young lady." Ward finished outlining the state's case against Juan Lujan and then made a curious admission. "There will be a great deal of detail," he told the jury, "and there will no doubt be some contradictions, which appear in almost every case." In other words, Ward found the evidence of Josefita Martínez to be "entirely credible" but acknowledged to the jury the existence of contrary accounts. Contradictions notwithstanding, Ward appealed to the men of the jury, "I know you gentlemen will pay, as you have done in other cases, the most careful attention to the evidence." In other words, jurors may find reasons to doubt the full story put forth by Josefita Martínez, but as "gentlemen" they would decide the case correctly. Although the high status and respect accorded Mexican families like the Martínezes and Lujans was clearly exceptional in the early twentieth-century Southwest, the extent to which such families adhered to heteropatriarchal norms (fraternal bonds, diminution of women) is instructive. In the same fleeting moments when Mexicans did manage to garner respect and dignity, much of the weight of those claims of sexual propriety rested on a vision of social order and hierarchy that favored men over women.[27]

Discussions of normal and abnormal sex offered Mexican witnesses another opportunity to present themselves as members of decent families. In 1891, Juan Mesa was accused of attempting to rape Alice Westfall one summer evening in southern California. Mesa and Westfall were neighbors and had been, according to Mesa and others, romantically involved. That night the couple was on a walk together when, according to Westfall, Mesa pushed her into the bushes and tore off her clothes before she managed to escape and summon the police. During the subsequent trial, Dolores de Valenzuela, Mesa's mother, was the second witness called by the defense. Valenzuela's distaste for both Westfall and her mother was barely concealed as she recounted a conversation between the families one evening before the attack. "Mrs. Westfall said it was good for them to marry," she recalled. "I told my son," she testified, "it was better for us to go home." But Valenzuela was not opposed to marriage in general; she was opposed to her son marrying Alice Westfall. She remembered telling her son, "This lady wants you to marry her daughter and you are a poor Californian, and I don't want you to marry her because she goes out nights and goes around; that is all I have to say." Though the transcript does not indicate if Valenzuela testified in Spanish, "Californian" was likely the English translation of the Spanish *californio*, the term identifying native Californians of Mexican, or Spanish Mexican, descent. Through much of the nineteenth century in California, daughters of elite Mexican families had married male Anglo newcomers, forming family alliances and facilitating the transfer of land and wealth into the hands of Anglo men. Referring to her son as a "poor Californian" tidily reverses the scenario so that the family seeking an alliance for their daughter is Anglo and the prospective groom is Mexican.[28]

Of far greater concern for Valenzuela than cross-cultural romance is the sexual comportment of her potential daughter-in-law. Valenzuela tells her son that she objects to his marriage to Westfall "because she goes out nights and goes around." Westfall was sexually intemperate, in other words, refusing to stay at home at night with her family, and she was promiscuous, in space as well as sex, "going around" to various locations and, presumably in Valenzuela's estimation, to various men besides her son. Of course Valenzuela, who seemed to love her son and want to defend him, had a considerable stake in portraying Alice Westfall as sexually profligate. Namely, challenging Westfall's sexual reputation could undermine her rape accusation against Valenzuela's son. Still, Valenzuela actively upholds a sexual double standard that views female sexual freedom with special disdain. It is notable that the mother of a "poor Californian" would present herself and her family as sexually respectable (especially by accentuating the value of marital reproductive sex) and an Anglo like Alice Westfall as sexually aberrant.[29]

Similar denunciations of nonnormative sex occurred in the case of *California v. Jesse Martínez*. In 1919 in Oakdale, California, Jesse Martínez was convicted of raping his neighbor, twelve-year-old Catharine Medina. During the trial, Catharine's stepmother, Evaline Medina, who had adopted the girl ten years earlier, contradicted her stepdaughter's account and testified in support of Martínez's innocence. According to Evaline, her stepdaughter had tried to hide her clothes from her parents and when confronted with the soiled laundry, "just soaked from head to foot with puss [sic]," had claimed that a man named Joe Paris had assaulted her. Evaline then asked the girl whether Jesse Martínez had attacked her. According to Evaline, Catharine replied, "No, honest to God Lena, he never did." Evaline went on to testify that the girl frequently lied to others and was in general "a very bad girl."[30]

Evaline also testified in some detail about Catharine's acts of masturbation dating back a full decade. "She was always abusing herself," Evaline told the court. Barely a week after she joined the Medina family, the three-year-old girl was discovered "abusing herself" with "a stick." She supposedly continued the practice for years to come. Asked whether she attempted to prevent the girl's masturbation, Evaline answered, "I sent for the doctor at one time." Prosecutors, undoubtedly concerned that the victim's stepmother so forcefully contradicted their case against Jesse Martínez, in turn implied that Evaline herself was romantically involved with Martínez, suggesting that her affection for him prompted her to accuse her stepdaughter of fabricating the rape charges.[31]

More striking is Medina's condemnation of her stepdaughter's supposed sexual excesses. This rare example in the court record of Mexican female desire is multiply demonized in the trial. Female masturbation is associated with lies and deception, rendered pathological and medically unhealthy ("I sent for the doctor at one time"), and placed in direct opposition to heterosexual sexual intimacy. In addition to denouncing so vividly female masturbation and its suggestion that female sexual pleasure and desire could exist outside the boundaries of heterosexual coupling, the trial reveals once again the unequal status of Mexican women and girls. Somebody, after all, sexually assaulted twelve-year-old Catharine Medina, and her family proved unable, or unwilling, to protect her.

TEXAS V. TANIS CABANA

As the criminal cases I've briefly discussed suggest, the multiple dimensions of heteropatriarchy were closely related and often overlapped and intersected over the course of an individual trial. Such was the case in the 1927 trial of Tanis Cabana. Cabana, a Mexican tenant farmer from rural Texas, was accused of statutory rape for sexually assaulting his thirteen-year-old neighbor, Luisa Estraca. During the subsequent trial, Estraca testified that Cabana had cornered her on repeated occasions in buildings outside her home and forced her to have sex with him. Estraca had become pregnant and stated unequivocally that Cabana was the father. Cabana repeatedly denied his guilt, claiming that he had never attacked her. In fact, he said, an accident years earlier had rendered him incapable of having sex with anyone, including his wife of many years. The jury, however, did not seem to be persuaded by Cabana's case and found him guilty of statutory rape.

Cabana subsequently appealed his conviction, arguing that the trial judge had disallowed important testimony in his defense, and the Texas Court of Criminal Appeals ultimately ruled in Cabana's favor and awarded him a new trial.[32]

The transcript of the trial suggests that Mexicans in Texas, as those elsewhere in the Southwest, were clearly subjects of Anglo rule. Lawyers and judges during the trial proceedings and subsequent appeal were exclusively Anglo, and, although the jury list from the trial is unavailable, it is almost certain that all twelve jury members were also Anglo.[33] Anglo witnesses moreover consistently highlighted the racial differences separating Anglos from Mexicans and made clear that Mexicans were inferior members of Anglo-ruled Texas. Emblematic was testimony that occurred near the end of the trial. Dr. H. LaForge, a practicing physician in the area, had been asked to attest to Tanis Cabana's sexual capacity, since Cabana had argued in his defense that a years-old accident had rendered him impotent and thus incapable of sexually assaulting Luisa Estraca. LaForge was also asked to testify to the general health of Cabana as well as his wife. The defense attorney asked LaForge to speculate as to the age of Cabana's wife. LaForge's answer is revealing, both in its offhand racism and in the extent to which no one in the courtroom refuted or challenged his remarks. "I would judge that this woman that I examined night before last was somewhere in the neighborhood of between forty-five and fifty," he said, "just judging from her looks." "You can't tell a thing on earth about a Mexican's age just from looking at one of them," he added, "but I would judge her to have been between forty-five and fifty." Dr. LaForge was not the only influential Anglo to draw a sharp distinction between "Mexicans" and "Americans" during either the trial or the subsequent appeals process, but his comment was certainly the trial's most vivid, and most biting, example of Mexican otherness and racial distinctiveness.[34]

At the same time, the trial record reveals that Mexicans were not entirely powerless within the American legal system and could on occasion turn the law to their own advantage. Luisa Estraca and her grandparents, who were her guardians, clearly considered it well within their rights to bring criminal charges against Tanis Cabana. Estraca was a prominent witness during the trial and showed few signs of being intimidated by the Anglo-dominated court atmosphere. The same was true of her uncle and grandparents, all of whom appeared confident and composed when they took the witness stand during the trial. For his part, Tanis Cabana maintained his innocence throughout the trial and refused to accept the jury's guilty verdict. Although he was clearly a man of limited means, he managed to cobble together enough money to finance a successful appeals process, and ultimately he convinced a higher court to grant him a new trial.

The testimony of Luisa Estraca reflects Mexicans' ability occasionally to receive concessions and decent treatment in American courts. Estraca, who testified with one of her two children, allegedly fathered by Tanis Cabana, sitting on her lap, began her testimony by describing the details of the attack. When asked next about the date of the attack, she answered, "This happened during cotton chopping time, the last cotton chopping time." Luisa's direct testimony ended with her assertion that she had never had sexual intercourse with her uncle, Florentino Estraca, or two other men, identified as Eusebio Zapata, who lived with the family for a period, and her neighbor, Faustino Ramírez. "No one has ever had intercourse with me except Tanis Cabana," she stated.[35]

Luisa Estraca's cross-examination by defense attorney Sid Malone was relatively short. She was first asked to identify the doctor that she had seen during her pregnancy. Her testimony next turned to the matter of the clothes that she wore during grand jury proceedings and her uncle Florentino's refusal to allow her clothes to be entered into evidence. Malone also asked Estraca to identify the individuals who accompanied her to the Mathis movie theater. In his cross-examination of the prosecution's star witness, the district attorney therefore seems to have limited his questions to the clothes Estraca wore in court, the doctor who attended her pregnancy, and a list of fellow moviegoers.[36]

What is especially significant about Estraca's testimony is what she was not asked to describe. Missing is any mention of Tanis Cabana or attention to Estraca's own account of the attack. The defense, in fact, apparently chose not to challenge Estraca's accusation of rape in any substantive way. They may have concluded that Estraca was a compelling and sympathetic witness and judged an attack on her sexual reputation to be less than judicious, even though it would take place in an Anglo-dominated courtroom. Whatever their reasoning, the defense seems to have approached Estraca with a degree of caution and care that was often reserved for privileged white women on the witness stand. The defense strategy is, of course, hard to discern in detail; however, there was clearly a reluctance to challenge in a straightforward manner Luisa Estraca's sexual propriety. Given the broad association of Mexicans with excessive and untoward sexuality, such reluctance speaks to the uneasy balance in the trial between denunciations of Mexicans on the one hand, and their limited civic acceptance on the other.

That Luisa Estraca emerged relatively unscathed from her cross-examination and was deemed credible, as evidenced by her attacker's subsequent conviction, may reflect her and her family's broader adherence to norms of heteropatriarchy. Recall that Estraca appeared on the witness stand with one of her children on her lap, demonstrating to the court her nurturing qualities and her commitment to motherhood. Likewise, witnesses from the family repeatedly sought to describe their home as proper and respectable. Like their counterparts throughout the region, the Estraca family relied on extended kin networks for much-needed support during trying times. The trial's second witness, for example, was the seventy-six-year-old grandmother and guardian of Luisa Estraca, also named Luisa Estraca. In English, apparently without the use of a translator, the grandmother described the arrival of their granddaughter (the daughter of their son, Santiago Estraca) into the family. "She was a year and two months and a half old when she came to me," she said, "and was very little and nursing at the time." "Her mother died," she continued, "and when her mother died, why, they gave her to me." "She is my daughter by raising," she added. Estraca also told the court that her granddaughter seldom strayed far from family and home. "My granddaughter," she said, "never visited anybody but the neighbors there close." "She did not attend dances," she testified, though "sometimes she would go with her father when he would go to town." "By her father," she clarified, "I mean Fermín, my husband." Estraca thus defended her family as supportive in times of need and committed to practices, such as chaperonage, that curtailed the sexual agency and freedom of young women.[37]

A related theme, the fraternal bonding between Mexican and Anglo men—and the implied, if not overt, subordination of Mexican women—was also expressed during the trial proceedings. Arthur Coffin, Dean Miller, and W. V. Wright all testified in defense of Tanis Cabana. Coffin told the jury that he considered Tanis Cabana to be "truthful" and to have a "good reputation." "I am a man of family," the next witness, Dean Miller, said, "and so is Mr. Coffin." "We both have little girls in our family," he continued, before describing his relationship with Tanis Cabana. "I have known this defendant since 1890," he said, "ever since I was about eight years old." "I know his reputation," he added, "and that reputation is good." W. V. Wright, a butcher and part-time farmer, next testified that he had known Cabana for nearly three decades and considered him to be a man of good reputation. Under cross-examination by the defense, Wright described also knowing Fermín Estraca, Luisa Estraca's grandfather. "I have known old man Fermín Estraca ever since 1911 or 1912," he said, continuing, "I think he is a pretty good old man." The testimony of prominent Anglo men, whether they were attesting to the character of Tanis Cabana or that of Fermín Estraca, evoked an interracial setting of jointly laboring Anglo and Mexican men, a setting that served to bolster the reputation of Mexican men.[38]

Dean Miller's seemingly offhand comment about himself and Arthur Coffin—"we both have little girls in our family"—is worth noting as well. The suggestion, of course, is that as fathers of daughters, the men were especially attuned to the vulnerability of girls to sexual assault and the need to provide sexual protection. By testifying in support of Tanis Cabana, the Anglo men demonstrated a shared (by themselves, as well as by Cabana) patriarchal duty to oversee and protect girls and women. Missing from the historical record is Estraca's reaction to such posturing about the protection of girls. Despite her family's attempts at protection, in fact, Estraca suffered the greatest trauma of any of those involved in the trial, first in the reported sexual assaults by Tanis Cabana and second in the public description of the assaults she was compelled to provide on the witness stand. Even if Cabana was indeed innocent of the charges against him, it is clear that some man—her grandfather, her uncle, or a neighbor—committed statutory rape against Estraca.

Mexican challenges in the courtroom to denigrations of their homes and families were thus laced with heteropatriarchy—claims of female inferiority, cross-cultural fraternal bonds, the privileging of marital reproductive sex, and disdain for nonnormative sex. This chapter has argued that a significant number of Mexicans in the early twentieth-century Southwest (including those involved in trials for sexual crimes) considered themselves fully entitled to rights and privileges within the American judicial system. But why? Why did Mexicans place such faith and material resources in the law (appealing a conviction required enough money to hire lawyers and create a transcript of the trial, as well as pay other expenses)? How did members of a group so reviled throughout the region—in Anglo newspapers, government reports, and political diatribes—testify with such confidence and aplomb in the courts? Some taking such liberties were also, of course, convicted sexual criminals, a demonized group of convicted child rapists, prostitutes, and committers of sodomy, seduction, and incest.

It may be fruitful to view such Mexican claims to rights and citizenship through the lens of colonialism and American empire. That otherwise ordinary Mexicans (nonelite, working-class, and of limited political influence) would affiliate themselves with the courts and demand the rights and respect accorded full citizens points to a wider colonial tradition of disenfranchised and subordinate groups turning to the courts to address grievances and inequalities.[39] Margaret Jacobs, quoting Ann Laura Stoler, has identified a critical dynamic in colonial relationships. There is, she says, "a common 'tension of empire' between 'a form of authority simultaneously predicated on incorporation and distancing.'" In her study of the removal of indigenous children from their homes in Australia and the United States, Jacobs highlights a movement from "the 'inclusionary impulses' of benevolent humanitarian rhetoric to the 'exclusionary practices' of segregating indigenous peoples and declaring them a menace."[40] This tension between inclusion and incorporation, on the one hand, and exclusion and distancing, on the other, is readily apparent in the lives of Mexicans in the Southwest in the early twentieth century.

Here, sex, family, and domesticity are critical. One of the premises of many forms of colonialism is that sexual propriety—as judged, of course, by colonial officials and their emissaries—is a central component of acceptance into citizenship. Those demonstrating such propriety by following and upholding heteropatriarchal norms can move significantly closer to full civic inclusion. I suggest that this expectation—that sexual decency in the home would translate to dignity and respect in the courts and possibly beyond—is reflected in the testimony of many of the Mexican trial participants discussed in this chapter. During the

Cabana trial, for example, the Estraca family, especially the grandmother, Luisa Estraca, was adamant in defense of the family's sexual propriety. Others supported the family's claims to sexual decency; Eusebio Zapata, for example, testified that, despite the fact that they slept on the floor together, nothing improper occurred between Florentino Estraca and his niece. The Estraca family in turn expected to be treated with dignity in the courts. And, to an extent, that expectation was fulfilled. Recall, for instance, the younger Luisa Estraca's respectful treatment while on the witness stand. In similar cases throughout the region, Mexicans reinforced their claims to citizenship by highlighting their commitment to heteropatriarchal norms.

Recognizing the persistence of colonial rule in the Southwest, as well as the salience of heteropatriarchal norms in Mexican claims to citizenship, opens some important new vistas in both Latina/o history and broader U.S. history. In terms of Latina/o history, the enduring reality of colonial rule in the Southwest raises an obvious point of comparison with other American colonial enterprises, especially those elsewhere in Latin America. Historians have often explained Mexicans' relative privileges within Anglo-dominated racial hierarchies in the Southwest (they were exempt from laws banning marriages with "whites" and allowed to own land, to become citizens, to vote, to run for office, and to testify against Anglos) by pointing to their relative whiteness. Other scholars, however, have emphasized the role of colonialism in the lives of Latina/o groups in the United States. Frances Aparicio, for instance, describes "analogous colonialism" as a potential bridge between groups as distinct as Central Americans, Puerto Ricans, Cuban Americans, and ethnic Mexicans in the United States. Underscoring Mexicans' status as colonial subjects offers a much-needed point of historical comparison, juxtaposing the colonial experience of Mexicans in the early twentieth century with the more widely understood intensification and formalization of American empire in the aftermath of the Spanish American War of 1898.[41]

Besides suggesting a critical link between ethnic Mexicans and Puerto Ricans and other Latina/o groups in the United States, this perspective can also help explore an important question in America in the twentieth, and twenty-first, centuries: how is social inequality maintained in a regime of legal equality? Like Puerto Ricans elsewhere in the country, who became U.S. citizens in 1917, Mexicans in the early twentieth-century Southwest (widely reviled elsewhere, yet compelling a relative degree of respect in the courthouse) derived their vexed position from the disjuncture between their legal citizenship and their cultural marginalization. The status of Mexicans differed in this respect from that of African Americans, who suffered through much of the twentieth century from dual disenfranchisement, both legal and cultural. When the African American freedom struggle of the mid-twentieth century finally succeeded in abolishing many forms of legal inequality, the status of African Americans came to bear a striking resemblance to that of other American colonial subjects such as Mexicans, Puerto Ricans, Filipinos, and even Native Americans: legally equal, yet culturally inferior to Anglo-Americans.

As I have argued in this chapter, Mexican trial participants often extolled their own adherence to heteropatriarchal norms in their struggle for recognition as full citizens. According to this strategy, when sexual norms were assiduously maintained and performed, legal equality could potentially be paired with social equality. Sexual normativity, that is, could become an avenue to social equality. In closing, I'd like to suggest that such a deeply colonial process—especially the reification of heteropatriarchal families as key to eventual civic inclusion—may be as relevant to the American present as it is to the American past. Perhaps American colonialism has expanded as much inward (domestically, as it were) as outward in the last half century. Sexual normativity, that is, especially in terms of the celebration of heteropatriarchal families, long one of the principal requisites for the inclusion of colonial subjects into positions of status and authority, has in recent decades become no less critical to the overcoming of racial barriers to citizenship and the claims by non-Anglos to inclusion in the Anglo-dominated American body politic. The post–civil rights era in America, in other words, may have opened a door to new, expanding forms of colonial order and domination, occurring as much within the nation as in foreign and distant lands.

Stranded on the periphery of this process, of course, are those defined as—or who define themselves as—sexually aberrant, the border dwellers, in Gloria Anzaldúa's famous phrase, "the squint-eyed, the perverse, the troublesome, the mongrel, the mulato, the half-breed, the half dead."[42] Following the beacon of heteropatriarchy certainly offered rewards to Mexican communities, but these rewards were not distributed equally. Anzaldúa describes the effects of these inequities in the poem quoted at the beginning of this chapter. The hundreds of Mexicans who appealed convictions to higher courts in the early twentieth-century in the Southwest are important examples of the depth and persistence of Mexican challenges to Anglo dominance in the region. The trial record is also, however, a stark reminder of the failings inherent in claims of citizenship that seek distance from nonpatriarchal, nonnormative, queer forms of sexuality. Decades before Anzaldúa's poem was written, Mexican women and men described these failings—of love, of protection, of family, of the home—with a poignant (and pointed) clarity.

NOTES

1. Gloria Anzaldúa, *Borderlands / La Frontera: The New Mestiza* (San Francisco: Spinsters / Aunt Lute Book Company, 1987), 194–95.

2. Ibid. In her comment about "put[ting] chile in the borscht," Anzaldúa slyly adds a touch of cold war politics.

3. I use "colonialism" here as opposed to "imperialism" following Lanny Thompson, who "distinguish[es] between colonialism (the expansion of a people through settlement), and imperialism (the expansion of a state through political domination)." Although the extensive involvement of the United States in Mexican politics and economic development in the late nineteenth and early twentieth centuries appears decidedly imperial in nature, Mexican immigrants encountered what I believe to have been a distinctively colonial landscape when they crossed into the United States. See Lanny Thompson, "The Imperial Republic: A Comparison of the Insular Territories under U.S. Dominion after 1898," *Pacific Historical Review* 71, no. 4 (November 2002): 535–74; quote from 540, n. 10. See also Patrick Wolfe, "Land, Labor, and Difference: Elementary Structures of Race," *American Historical Review* 106 (June 2001): 866–1006.

4. "Heteropatriarchy" summarizes an interrelated set of inequalities that are often left unrecognized or are seen as natural and eternal. The principle heteropatriarchal hierarchies are male over female, heterosexual over homosexual, married over unmarried, and reproductive sex over nonreproductive intimacy. Heteropatriarchal societies tend to see civic leadership, authority to distribute societal resources, and political and economic success as "naturally" belonging to those demonstrating a commitment to heterosexual marriage, reproductive sex, and ultimately the authority of men over women. See Andrea Smith, "Heteropatriarchy and the Three Pillars of White Supremacy: Rethinking Women of Color Organizing," in *Color of Violence: The Incite! Anthology*, ed. Andrea Smith, Beth E. Richie, and Julia Sudbury (Cambridge: South End Press, 2006), 66–73. Both Mexican and dominant Anglo forms of heteropatriarchy value marital, reproductive sex, male authority, and limitations on female sexual activity. The two forms of heteropatriarchy are not identical, however. The appeals cases that I will analyze in this chapter, for instance, suggest that Mexican communities tended to value domestic arrangements with extended families more than strictly nuclear family formation, one of the pillars of Anglo heteropatriarchy.

5. Myron P. Gutmann, Robert McCaa, Rudolfo Gutierrez-Montes, and Brian J. Gratton, "The Demographic Impact of the Mexican Revolution in the United States," Texas Population Research Center Papers 1999–2000, 4; and Elliott Robert Barkan, *From All Points: America's Immigrant West, 1870s–1952* (Bloomington: Indiana University Press, 2007), 199.

6. *Texas v. Anesetto [sic] Guerrero*, Texas Court of Criminal Appeals, 1904; *California v. Marina Torres*, California Supreme Court, 1924; *Texas v. Saturina Garza*, Texas Court of Criminal Appeals, 1905; *Texas v. Blazeo Pedro*, Texas Court of Criminal Appeals, 1905; *Texas v. Pedro Barstado*, Texas Court of Criminal Appeals, 1905.

7. For recent discussions of these events, see Katherine Benton-Cohen, *Borderline Americans: Racial Division and Labor War in the Arizona Borderlands* (Cambridge, MA: Harvard University Press, 2009); Benjamin Heber Johnson, *Revolution in Texas: How a Forgotten Rebellion and Its Bloody Suppression Turned Mexicans into Americans* (New Haven, CT: Yale University Press, 2003); and Natalia Molina, *Fit to Be Citizens? Public Health and Race in Los Angeles, 1879–1939* (Berkeley: University of California Press, 2006).

8. Historians must approach such records with caution, of course. Most trial participants have considerable interest in the outcome of a trial. Witnesses testify *for* the defendant or the prosecution, while lawyers draft arguments and induce testimony in the service of a particular verdict or outcome. At the same time, the success or effectiveness of individual arguments is frequently difficult to assess. Case files often do not include the names of jurors, much less present their reasoning for deciding in favor of one verdict over another. A guilty verdict in a rape trial, for instance, could be the result of any number of factors (credibility of victim, persuasiveness of evidence, lack of credibility of defendant, absence of alibi, errors on the part of defense lawyers), and the historical record often offers few clues beyond the trial transcript itself to suggest which factor, or factors, convinced the jury of the guilt of the accused in the end. Appeals records are additionally complex in that the

outcome of the trial was a conviction of the defendant, who then initiated the appeal of the conviction. Appeals cases are thus especially revealing in terms of arguments that did *not* prove persuasive to a particular jury. On the other hand, from the prosecution's perspective, appeals cases present arguments that on some (not insignificant) level worked with a jury. That being said, the clear interest that trial participants have in the outcome of a trial should not dissuade historians from the careful and measured use of legal records of the sort I examine in this chapter.

9. I am following the lead of other historians who have remarked on this lingering colonial presence in the region in the twentieth century. Vicki Ruíz, for instance, describes Mexicans in the early twentieth century as "inheriting a legacy of colonialism wrought by Manifest Destiny," that is, stretching back to the middle of the nineteenth century. Vicki L. Ruíz, *From Out of the Shadows: Mexican Women in Twentieth-Century America* (New York: Oxford University Press, 1998), 7. See also Mae M. Ngai, *Impossible Subjects: Illegal Aliens and the Making of Modern America* (Princeton, NJ: Princeton University Press, 2004), 29; Gilbert G. Gonzalez, *Guest Workers or Colonized Labor: Mexican Labor Migration to the United States* (Boulder, CO: Paradigm Press, 2006), 5; Ramón A. Gutiérrez, "Internal Colonialism: An American Theory of Race," *Du Bois Review* 1, no. 2 (2004): 282; and Linda Gordon, "Internal Colonialism and Gender," in *Haunted by Empire: Geographies of Intimacy in North American History*, ed. Ann Laura Stoler (Durham, NC: Duke University Press), 427–51.

10. See Margaret D. Jacobs, *White Mother to a Dark Race: Settler Colonialism, Maternalism, and the Removal of Indigenous Children in the American West and Australia, 1880–1940* (Lincoln: University of Nebraska Press, 2009); Sally Engle Merry, *Colonizing Hawaii: The Cultural Power of Law* (Princeton, NJ: Princeton University Press, 2000); Laura Briggs, *Reproducing Empire: Race, Sex, Science, and U.S. Imperialism in Puerto Rico* (Berkeley: University of California Press, 2002); Eileen J. Suárez Findlay, *Imposing Decency: The Politics of Sexuality and Race in Puerto Rico, 1870–1920* (Durham, NC: Duke University Press, 1999); and Paul A. Kramer, *The Blood of Government: Race, Empire, the United States, and the Philippines* (Chapel Hill: University of North Carolina Press, 2006).

11. See all the sources cited in the previous note. For example, writing about Hawaii, Sally Engle Merry notes "the willingness of early missionaries and the government they created to welcome all peoples who were willing to transform their bodies and their lives—their cultural selves—in accordance with principles of Christian piety and comportment into the community of the 'civilized.'" Engle Merry, *Colonizing Hawaii*, 23.

12. *People v. Alma Carrillo,* Court of Appeal of California, 1929, 13.

13. See, for example, the descriptions of homes in *People v. Alvino Méndez,* Supreme Court of California, 1924.

14. *People v. Cruz Vicunia [sic],* Court of Appeal of California, 1930, 239.

15. *People v. Frank Rameriz [sic],* Court of Appeal of California, 1911, 174.

16. María Cristina García, "Agents of Americanization: Rusk Settlement and the Houston Mexicano Community, 1907–1950," in *Mexican Americans in Texas History, Selected Essays,* ed. Emilio Zamora, Cynthia Orozco, and Rudolfo Rocha (Austin: Texas State Historical Association, 2000), 121–37. For more recent discussions of Anglo views of Mexican domesticity, see Monica Perales's chapter in this volume; Ruíz, *From Out of the Shadows;* Stephanie Lewthwaite, *Race, Place, and Reform in Mexican Los Angeles: A Transnational Perspective, 1890–1940* (Tucson: University of Arizona Press, 2009); and Molina, *Fit to Be Citizens?*

17. *People v. Eulogio Castro,* Supreme Court of California, 1901, 30, 31, 38.

18. *People, on Behalf of Guadalupe and Elvira Gutiérrez, Alleged Wards, etc., Respondent v. Tomás Gutiérrez,* Court of Appeal of California, 1920.

19. Ibid.

20. *California v. Álvaro Fernández,* Court of Appeal of California, 1906.

21. *Texas v. Domingo Brown,* Texas Court of Criminal Appeals, 1922, 28.

22. Ruíz, *From Out of the Shadows*, 71.
23. *Texas v. Rudolfo Rodríguez*, Texas Court of Criminal Appeals, 1921, 9.
24. Ibid., 39–41.
25. Ibid., 9, 39–41.
26. *New Mexico v. Juan Lujan*, Supreme Court of New Mexico, 1918, 22, 4.
27. Ibid.
28. *People v. Juan Mesa*, Supreme Court of California, 1892. See María Raquél Casas, *Married to a Daughter of the Land: Spanish-Mexican Women and Interethnic Marriage in California, 1820–1880* (Reno: University of Nevada Press, 2007); and Miroslava Chávez-García, *Negotiating Conquest: Gender and Power in California, 1770s to 1880s* (Tucson: University of Arizona Press, 2004).
29. *People v. Juan Mesa*.
30. *California v. Jesse Martínez*, Court of Appeal of California, 1919.
31. Ibid.
32. *State of Texas v. Tanis Cabana*, Live Oak County Texas, 1927. For changing age of consent laws in the United States, see Mary E. Odem, *Delinquent Daughters: Protecting and Policing Adolescent Sexuality in the United States, 1885–1920* (Chapel Hill: University of North Carolina Press, 1995).
33. According to Clare Sheridan, Mexicans in Texas were effectively barred from serving on juries until the 1950s. "While not prohibited by law from serving," she writes, "they were almost universally excluded on the grounds that they were not qualified to serve." Sheridan, "'Another White Race': Mexican Americans and the Paradox of Whiteness in Jury Selection," *Law and History Review* 21, no. 1 (Spring 2003): 112. Women were similarly not allowed to serve on juries in Texas until 1954. See www.tsl.state.tx.us/exhibits/suffrage/aftermath/page1.html (accessed January 28, 2010). Thanks to Crista DeLuzio for bringing up this point. See also Gretchen Ritter, "Jury Service and Women's Citizenship before and after the Nineteenth Amendment," *Law and History Review* (Fall 2002), www.historycooperative.org/journals/lhr/20.3/ritter.html (accessed January 28, 2010). For important overviews of race relations in Texas during this period, see David Montejano, *Anglos and Mexicans in the Making of Texas, 1836–1986* (Austin: University of Texas Press, 1987); and Neil Foley, *The White Scourge: Mexicans, Blacks, and Poor Whites in Texas Cotton Culture* (Berkeley: University of California Press, 1997).
34. *State of Texas v. Tanis Cabana*, 45–46.
35. Ibid., 16–17.
36. Ibid., 17–18.
37. Ibid., 7–9.
38. Ibid., 31–38.
39. See Briggs, *Reproducing Empire*; Suárez Findlay, *Imposing Decency*; Engle Merry, *Colonizing Hawaii*, 220; and Philippa Levine, *Prostitution, Race, and Politics: Policing Venereal Disease in the British Empire* (New York: Routledge, 2003), 222.
40. Jacobs, *White Mother to a Dark Race*, 48.
41. Frances R. Aparicio, "Jennifer as Selena: Rethinking Latinidad in Media and Popular Culture," *Latino Studies* 1 (2003): 90–105. See also Ian Haney Lopez, *White by Law: The Legal Construction of Race* (New York: New York University Press, 2006); Laura E. Gómez, *Manifest Destinies: The Making of the Mexican American Race* (New York: New York University Press, 2007); Sheridan, "Another White Race"; Clare Sheridan, "Contested Citizenship: National Identity and the Mexican Immigration Debates of the 1920s," *Journal of American Ethnic History* 21, no. 3 (Spring 2002): 3–35; and Ariela Gross, "Texas Mexicans and the Politics of Whiteness," *Law and History Review* 21, no. 1 (Spring 2003): 195–205.
42. Anzaldúa, *Borderlands/La Frontera*, 3.

PART THREE

Borderland Cultures and Family Relationships

9

Intimate Ties

*Marriage, Families, and Kinship
in Eighteenth-Century Pueblo Communities*

Tracy Brown

The New Mexican pueblo of Cochiti was rocked by a shocking and unusual murder in the spring of 1773.[1] On the morning of April 16, María Francisca and her mother, María Josefa, asked María Francisca's husband, Agustín, to accompany them on a trip to the mountains outside Cochiti. The Jemez Mountains, which sit just northwest of the pueblo, have long been visited by residents of Cochiti, who gather plants for "food, medicine, raw materials for basketry, dyes, and other purposes" there.[2] On this day, the women told Agustín that they were making the trip to search for roots with which to dye clothing. Although root gathering was not a task typically performed by males in Pueblo communities, the two women convinced Agustín to accompany them by telling him they needed assistance in carrying the plants they planned to collect.[3] Perhaps Agustín also agreed to go because he wished to protect his wife and mother-in-law from being kidnapped or killed by Navajo or Comanche raiders—a common fear at Cochiti in the 1770s.[4]

Whatever his motivation for accompanying the women, the trio started out for the mountains early in the morning, "sneaking away" while everyone else in the pueblo was cleaning the acequia. Once in the mountains, Agustín asked his wife to delouse him. He put his head in her lap, in the folds of her skirt, and quickly fell asleep. It was at this point that María Francisca took the tie with which her husband had fastened his braid and placed it around his neck. She took one end of the hair tie, her mother took the other end, and the two women proceeded to strangle Agustín. María Josefa then took a large knife and stabbed him in the neck and side.[5] It was in this moment that love and violence were strangely juxtaposed.

To explain the disappearance of Agustín, María Francisca told Cochiti authorities that they had gone to the mountains on Friday, April 16, but that Agustín had not returned with them. Upon hearing this, the captain of war ordered local resident Lorenzo Chayu to search for Agustín. Chayu soon located Agustín's body; he did not touch the body, but returned to the pueblo to report what he had found. Eventually, the body was brought to the father of the church at the pueblo, and both María Francisca and her mother were questioned about what had happened.[6]

In numerous declarations to the *alcalde mayor* taken after Agustín's body had been found, María Francisca admitted that she had planned her husband's murder with her mother, and she provided a motive for the crime. She explained that after marrying Agustín in the church at Nambé on January 26,[7] she was "brought to"—or forced to take up residence at—Tesuque.[8] This violated the promise her husband had made to her when they married that he would not remove her from her home community. Agustín's home pueblo, Tesuque was across the Rio Grande from María Francisca's home, and its people spoke a different language from the people of Cochiti. María Francisca was clearly afraid that she would be forced to live there after her marriage, a fear that apparently was founded despite Agustín's promise to her.

Agustín had also promised to love her and treat her with tenderness, but, according to María Francisca, "in all of this he had failed."[9] This failure was symbolized by his inability or unwillingness to provide for her materially. Prior to the murder, María Josefa asked her daughter if "her husband had given her shawls, belts and shoes." When María Francisca replied that he had not, her mother sympathized with her, saying, "You poor little thing, he has given you nothing."[10] María Francisca stressed in her declarations that her husband had left her "without aid or shelter" and that, due to this cruelty and her mother's growing anger over her treatment, she decided to murder him.[11] After initially telling her not to do it, her mother agreed to assist her with the murder.[12] After the declarations were taken, and with the permission of the father of the church, the *alcalde mayor* and his assistants had Agustín's body disinterred to determine his exact cause of death. The officials determined that his stab wounds were serious enough to cause his death.[13]

This case is unusual for a number of reasons. It is one of only a few murder cases involving Pueblo people for which there is documentation, and it is the only one that involves Pueblo women as perpetrators of the crime. It is also unusual in that it gives rare insight into changing Pueblo perceptions of coupling and uncoupling (the "marital tie"), kinship, and the rights, responsibilities, and duties that men and women assumed when they formed consensual unions with one another.[14] By the eighteenth century, a complex mix of both traditional and imposed kinship systems and beliefs concerning marriage and the family structured family life in Pueblo communities of New Mexico. These beliefs and systems of descent shaped perceptions of how families were to operate and what character intimate relations between men and women were supposed to assume. In the case that is the center of analysis in this chapter, María Francisca, from the matrilineal pueblo of Cochiti, married Agustín, from the bilateral pueblo of Tesuque. Both had to some degree adopted Spanish beliefs concerning kinship, marriage, and the family. This, then, was an intercultural or mixed marriage, one that crossed the boundaries of three separate kinship systems (Spanish and those systems found at Cochiti and Tesuque) and two different cultures (Pueblo and Spanish). Because of the differing expectations created by the kinship systems and cultural traditions at play in these mixed marriages, conflict and violence was a clear possibility, as I demonstrate below.

This analysis of Pueblo kinship, intimate relations, and family practices not only demonstrates that family life in what was to become the American West was "intercultural" in character even in the eighteenth century; it also reveals that Indian peoples were forced to negotiate numerous structures of social and political power whose purpose was to regulate intimate relations. In the case of Pueblo people in particular, kinship, intimate ties, and the family form were of course regulated by the traditions of their home communities, but Pueblo people were also under compulsion to adopt Spanish beliefs concerning these matters. Spanish authorities clearly saw the altering of Pueblo kinship and marriage practices as central to their mission to "civilize" Pueblo people, to make them as "Spanish" as possible, and to incorporate them into the state as vassals of the crown and members of the Catholic Church.[15] Pueblo people in mixed marriages thus found themselves negotiating a tricky terrain of competing structures of power (Spanish and Pueblo) and altered definitions of family, intimate relations, and kinship. In the final section of this chapter, I argue that such intercultural relationships were not uncommon in colonial New Mexico. Clearly, María Francisca and Agustín were not alone in struggling to bridge the differing cultural forces in their lives and in their marriage.

The vast majority of women in unhappy marriages in colonial New Mexico did not murder their husbands to end their relationships. There may have been other factors influencing María Francisca than the ones presented here: she may simply have been disturbed or afraid to face the sanctions—shaming, public gossip, or even corporal punishment—that a separation or divorce might have brought about. Unfortunately, there is no evidence in the record of the case to suggest what factors other than kinship practices were operating in María's life to shape her perception of her marriage and her options for ending it. What I am suggesting here is not that the kinship practices of the Spanish and the two pueblos in question were the only factors underwriting María's behavior, only that kinship was one of those factors. Because there are so few facts in the case to work with, other interpretations of María Francisca's behavior are possible.

THE REGULATION OF PUEBLO
INTIMATE RELATIONS

That instilling a commitment to Christian marriage was important to even the earliest of Spanish residents is made clear by Fray Alonso de Benavides's comments on the matter. His memorial concerning his missionizing efforts in New Mexico was first published in 1630 and revised in 1634. In it, he told a story about an old Taos woman who attempted to pollute the minds of young women who were living with their husbands as the church dictated.

> In particular, she sought to pervert certain good Christian women who lived alone with their husbands, as our holy mother church commands. In order to pervert them to her will she invited them to go out to the country and both on going and returning, all day long, she preached her loathsome ideas to them. But the good Christian women never wanted to agree with her, and while returning to the pueblo in the afternoon, the sky being clear and calm, a bolt of lightning from the heavens struck and killed her in the midst of the good Christians whom she was trying to corrupt and teach such bad doctrine.[16]

After her death, according to Benavides, everyone flocked to the church, where the father taught about the sacrament of holy matrimony. The result: "Those who were living in secret concubinage got married."[17] Whether this story is true or simply a fantasy concocted by the father in order to make the missionary enterprise in New Mexico look more successful than it actually was, it does show that the marital practices of Pueblo peoples were of concern to Spanish authorities in New Mexico.[18]

After the Pueblo Revolt of 1680 and the Spanish reconquest of New Mexico in 1692, Spanish civil authorities and Franciscan friars tried to impress upon the Pueblos how important it was for them to marry in the church or to return to the people they had married before the 1680 revolt. Friars noted that there was very little interest in marriage in the pueblos, and that few who had separated from their spouses were inclined to reunite with them. In 1694, Fray Miguel de Trizio reported that in Santo Domingo, "neither voluntarily nor after my having spoken to them many times in the church have any of them come to me to request the holy sacrament of matrimony and thereby leave their evil condition."[19] Other friars had little better news to report in that year. At Zia and Santa Ana, Fray Juan Alpuente reported that although a few inhabitants had asked to be married, and a few who had been living with women other than their wives had returned to their wives, "there are others who neither leave their present condition nor marry, no matter how much the father tells them to do so, and that is the largest portion of them."[20] Friars thus complained in 1696 that the Pueblos continued "in their depraved concubinage."[21] Those that did agree to marry were typically Pueblo officials, who, according to the friar at Pecos, were "men who would likely attempt to ingratiate themselves with the Spanish authorities."[22]

Efforts to put an end to Pueblo cohabitation continued into the eighteenth century. In 1706, members of the Santa Fe town council *(cabildo)* wrote a letter of support for Governor Cuervo y Valdés in which they said that he "dealt with public sin effectively"—especially cases of cohabitation, some of which were seven, nine, or even eleven years old.[23] Governor Flores Mogollón issued a detailed order concerning marriage in Pueblo communities in April of 1714.[24] The governor was upset to discover that many married Pueblo couples lived separately after being married in the church.[25] This would not do: couples were supposed to live in the same house. The husband was supposed to "feed and maintain" his wife and assist her in her work.[26] The wife was supposed to care for her husband and the house. Flores Mogollón ordered the missionary fathers to unite all couples living apart and his *alcaldes mayores* to announce the order in their jurisdictions. The penalty for not following this order was fifty lashes in the pillory and two months in prison for the first offense; for the second, the person would be sent to a workshop *(obraje)* for four years of hard labor. At the end of the document are notations from the governor's *alcaldes mayores* that this order was indeed read at the Tewa pueblos, at Taos and Picuris, at Isleta, Laguna, Acoma, and Halona (Zuni), and, finally, at San Felipe, Santo Domingo, and Cochiti.

The governor's assistants, such as the *alcaldes mayores,* also policed Pueblo communities to try to stop cohabitation. Ramón García Jurado functioned as *alcalde mayor* for the Keres jurisdiction (Zia, Santa Ana, and Jemez pueblos) between 1727 and 1732. His willingness to police Pueblo intimate relationships is evidenced by the fact that he investigated Juan Galvan and Juana Hurtado for cohabitation in 1727 at Zia,[27] and he patrolled the pueblos in his jurisdiction to prevent that practice. He was still patrolling pueblos for cohabitation in 1732. In an investigation into his labor abuses,[28] Governor Cruzat y Góngora's assistant, Antonio de Uribarrí, prepared an interrogatory that included a question that asked whether or not García Jurado had punished "public sin."[29] In the actual interviews, Uribarrí reworded the question to ask specifically if García Jurado had investigated whether people were cohabitating. Numerous Pueblo declarants verified that García Jurado had patrolled their pueblos to try to catch people cohabitating outside marriage and to punish them.

One year after García Jurado was investigated for labor abuses in the Keres jurisdiction, Bernabe Baca, the *alcalde mayor* of Acoma and Laguna, was investigated for the same issue. As in the García Jurado investigation, several declarants were asked if Baca had administered justice in the pueblos and if he had prosecuted "public sin."[30] The *cacique* (town chief) of Acoma complained that Baca was not fulfilling his duties because not only had he failed to assist the father of the mission in directing them toward "the road to heaven" so that they would not "lose their souls," but he had also failed to punish those living in "concubinage."[31] Baca retorted in his written statement that the charges that the people of

Acoma and Laguna made were false and that they lied about him precisely because he did punish some of them for living together outside marriage, and he even made a few of them marry.[32]

Thus, although there is some evidence that Spanish authorities attempted to regulate Pueblo intimate relations, that evidence is spotty. The spotty nature of the evidence, however, does not necessarily reflect a disinterest in Pueblo marital practices and beliefs by the Spanish authorities. Much documentation is missing from the colonial archive of New Mexico,[33] and evidence of regulation may have been more complete at some point in the past. This regulation was carried out by those Spanish authorities that had most contact with Pueblo people: the governor's *alcaldes mayores,* the local face of secular authority, and missionaries, who lived in Pueblo communities. I would argue, however, that this regulation waxed and waned based upon the strength of the personal commitment of individual governors and missionaries to wipe out practices such as cohabitation. For example, Governor López de Mendizábal (1659–61) refused to punish Pueblo people who were living together outside marriage.[34] His efforts must be compared to those of someone like Fray Benavides, who was keenly interested in eradicating "concubinage" from Pueblo communities. The result was that the amount of regulation of Pueblo kinship and marital practices and beliefs and family life rose and fell across the eighteenth century, depending upon the proclivities of those Spanish officials and missionaries that were in power.

Even with a strong personal commitment to eradicating practices such as cohabitation, however, Spanish authorities and missionaries lacked the resources to carry out full-scale morality campaigns. The province of New Mexico was located on the far northern frontier of New Spain, thousands of miles from any center of Spanish power or resources. Spanish government in New Mexico was thus skeletal at best: it consisted of the governor and his assistants, who worked with very little financial support or bureaucratic assistance. The same can be said of the missionary enterprise in New Mexico: it was run with a skeletal bureaucracy and little financial support. This made the consistent regulation and monitoring of Pueblo social life difficult at best. Thus, Pueblo ability to successfully resist the imposition of Spanish norms concerning marriage was in part due to the fact that state power was weak in colonial New Mexico, making it difficult for Spanish officials to impose beliefs and force social change in Pueblo communities.

MARITICIDE AT COCHITI

Despite the discontinuous nature of Spanish regulation of Pueblo family life, there is evidence that such efforts had begun to shape Pueblo perceptions of intimate relations by the late eighteenth century. Understandings of kinship, postmarital residence, and the expectations of the rights and duties of spouses in marriage all show evidence of the impact of Spanish ideologies in the investigation of Agustín's death.

Kinship and the Marital Tie in Pueblo Communities

In order to understand why María Francisca murdered her husband Agustín, it is necessary to discuss the intercultural character of their marriage. Two kinship systems existed in Pueblo communities at the time of Agustín's murder in 1773. The western New Mexican Pueblo communities of Hopi, Zuni, Acoma, and Laguna, and the Keresan communities (including Cochiti, María Francisca's home) in eastern New Mexico were matrilineal and matrilocal; descent was calculated through the female line and couples were expected to live with the wife's family after marriage. However, the eastern Tanoan Pueblo communities (including Tesuque, Agustín's home) were bilateral and bilocal—that is, men and women in those pueblos calculated their descent through both their mothers and fathers and couples could choose to live with either the wife's or the husband's family after marriage.[35] Language determined where bilaterality as opposed to matrilineality was practiced in the eastern pueblos: the Keresan-speaking communities were matrilineal, whereas the Tano communities were bilateral.[36] In short, in 1773 Pueblo communities were not united either by language or by common kinship systems.

María Francisca and Agustín came from two different pueblos that did not share the same language or practice the same system of descent. The fact that Agustín and María Francisca's marriage was a "mixed" one was one of the sources of their difficulties. In matrilineal and matrilocal pueblos such as María Francisca's home pueblo of Cochiti, marriage or partnership was not "necessarily intended to last for life."[37] This was reflected by the ease with which men and women formed and broke up their partnerships. According to early Spanish observers at Zuni, a western matrilineal pueblo, "when a man wished to marry, arrangements were made by those who governed. Men indicated whom they wanted to marry by weaving a blanket and placing it in front of the woman. This made her his wife."[38] According to another observer in New Mexico in 1601, if a man liked a woman, he spoke with her and gave her some blankets. She then took him to her house, "for the women own the houses," and they lived together for several months. If she got pregnant, then they might stay together for life. If not, the couple broke up and she made her availability known by wearing several roses in her hair.[39]

Both men and women seemed to have been free to dissolve such arrangements; in fact, Spaniards noted that "if a woman no longer wished to be married, she [simply] piled her husband's belongings outside the home and he returned to his parents' dwelling."[40] The explanation for the ease with which such unions were formed or broken up lies with the fact that the marital tie itself was not strong in matrilineal communities like Cochiti. Marital ties are typically weak in matrilineal and matrilocal societies, because descent is traced through the mother.

This means that in a marriage the father does not have a strong claim to children, for children belong to the wife and the wife's family; in fact, "strong ties between husbands and children" threaten kinship groups organized via matrilineal descent. So, too, do strong ties between husbands and wives.[41]

Since husbands have weak status and paternity is not an issue in matrilineal groups, there is no need to "tie a woman permanently in marriage to a man."[42] Women living in matrilineal groups are typically free to enter and leave marital unions, and their sexuality is generally less controlled than, for example, in patrilineal societies, in which paternity of children is an issue. There is not much to tie a husband to a wife either. With no claim to children and no status in the family that he marries into, men, too, are free to enter and leave such marital unions. That this was true for matrilineal Pueblo communities even into the twentieth century is made clear by ethnographers familiar with their kinship practices. Fred Eggan notes that, in mid-twentieth-century Hopi communities, "the relations between spouses are nonreciprocal, tenuous, and brittle, in contrast to the enduring relations between relatives by blood."[43]

Matrilocal residence also weakens marital ties. In communities with matrilocal residence, a husband moves in with his wife's family. If the marriage does not take, it is the husband who leaves and typically returns to his mother's home. According to Ramón Gutiérrez "[Pueblo] men moved from house to house according to their stage of life. During childhood boys lived with their mothers, and at adolescence they moved into a kiva to learn male magical lore. When they had mastered these skills, and were deemed worthy of marriage by their kin, they took up residence in their wife's home. A man nonetheless remained tied to his maternal home throughout his life. For important ceremonial events, men returned to their maternal households."[44] As a result of men's close, lifelong link to the maternal household, some Spanish observers argued that "the Pueblo Indians had . . . no home life"—in other words, husbands and wives did not share strong marital ties within a jointly managed home. Their orientation was always toward their mothers' households, not toward the tie that existed between them. The fact that males had heavy ceremonial duties outside the household only further weakened their ties to their wife and her family: "The men lived somewhat apart and concentrated their activities in their respective kivas, from which the women were more or less banned."[45] Males had strong positions in their mother's household due to their descent from them, but in their wife's household, where the tie was strictly a marital tie, not blood tie, husbands held a weaker status.

Matrilineal households are typically described as being "female-dominated," so it is no surprise to find such a characterization in the literature concerning the historic Pueblos. According to Gutiérrez, the matrilineal household in Pueblo communities such as Cochiti was "preeminently a female domain of love and ritual."[46] Because these communities were matrilineal, women "owned the domestic hearth, exercised authority over those that lived within it, and at death passed on the edifice to their daughters. The female household head was custodian of its rights and possessions: the agricultural plots their husbands and sons worked, all food and seed reserves, and the sacred fetishes and ritual objects of the clan." Spaniards noticed this dominance over the household by women. Spaniards that accompanied Juan de Oñate to New Mexico in 1598 noted that Pueblo men "did not reach any decision without consulting the women and getting their opinion."[47] Fray Alonso de Benavides noted in 1634 that the woman "always commands and is the mistress of the house, and not the husband."[48]

Late nineteenth-century observations of Cochiti do not contradict the early postcontact descriptions given by Spaniards concerning the ways in which matrilineality and matrilocality structured Pueblo life in matrilineal communities. In 1897 Frederick Starr, an observer of late nineteenth-century Cochiti life, wrote, "Among the Cochitis, the woman is boss. The high offices are held by men, but in the household and in the councils of clans, woman is supreme.... She has been the arbiter of destinies of the tribe for centuries."[49] According to Charles Lange, women were still influential in mid-twentieth-century Cochiti society. "In reference to one specific inquiry as to whether it would be permissible to do something, several men—council members, at that—stated without hesitation that they saw no reason for not doing it. 'But don't let that old lady see you,' they warned, pointing with their lips at a particular home. The implication was quite clear that if this woman had raised an objection, these officials would have been forced to rescind their permission."[50]

Postmarital Residence in Pueblo Communities

During the 1773 investigation into the death of Agustín, it became clear that one of the reasons that María Francisca was unhappy was because she was forced to move to Tesuque after her marriage to Agustín. That María Francisca had left Cochiti to live with her husband at Tesuque indicates that the couple did not have a "typical" Cochiti marriage. If they had, Agustín would have moved to Cochiti to take up residence with María Francisca and her mother. Instead, María Francisca complained in her declarations that she had been "brought" to Tesuque[51] after her marriage to Agustín, despite the fact that her husband had promised not to do so.[52] She explained that "when Agustín had sought to marry her, he promised that he would not remove her from her pueblo."[53] To make matters worse, Cochiti officials also pressured her to live in Tesuque: both she and Agustín were told to leave the pueblo and return to Tesuque by April 18.[54] Thus, she explained, she had killed Agustín so that "she would not have to return to Tesuque."[55] María Josefa, María Francisca's mother and accomplice in the murder, gave the same reason for killing Agustín: when asked what was her motive for the crime, she replied, "because he wanted to take her daughter to Tesuque."[56] The implication of this testimony is that Agustín had to promise María Francisca that he would not remove her from her pueblo to get her to agree to marry him. Agustín must have understood that it was Cochiti tradition for a newly married couple to live with the wife's family, and he appears to have promised his wife that they would follow that tradition.

Although the fact that María Francisca came from a matrilocal pueblo explains why she was distressed at having to move to Tesuque after her marriage, it does not explain why Agustín broke his promise to her. There was a rigidity to his actions that is not explained by an adherence to Tesuque practices alone, especially since postmarital residence was flexible at Tesuque. Why did he feel the need to force his wife to move to Tesuque, when he could see that she did not want to, and when the postmarital residence rules of his own community allowed for matrilocality? Although Cochiti officials appear to have played some role in forcing María Francisca to stay in Tesuque after her marriage, both daughter and mother made it clear in their declarations that it was Agustín who had initially forced María Francisca to move. He, not Cochiti officials, was the focus of their anger. It is likely that Agustín was motivated to behave in the way that he did for a number of reasons. I would argue that his "strong-arming" María Francisca into moving to Tesuque was due in part to the influence of Spanish patriarchal, patrilineal norms concerning family formation and marital ties. Whether it was intentional or not, the actions of Cochiti officials appear to have reinforced these norms.

Spaniards calculated descent bilaterally, as did the Tano pueblos such as Tesuque. Unlike Tesuque, however, there was a strong patrilineal bias to this calculation within the families of colonial Spanish New Mexican society. Children calculated their descent through both their mothers and fathers, and females as well as males inherited property from both of their parents. But male children, especially male children of the upper class, were favored in terms of inheritance and property. In other words, bilateral descent calculation was enshrined in law,[57] but in everyday life Spaniards practiced patrilineality: male children received land, property, and other forms of wealth at the expense of female children because it was believed that they carried on the family line.[58]

Furthermore, Spanish families were patriarchal in character: paternal authority governed them. In colonial New Mexico, as in Latin American more generally, Spanish law made it clear that both women and children were under the guardianship of the father in families. Both male and female children were legally under the control of their fathers as long as they were single and lived under their roof, no matter what their age. The only way a father's control was rescinded was by legal emancipation via marriage or voluntary or court-ordered emancipation.[59] As far as wives were concerned, "in return for the support, protection, and guidance her husband was legally required to provide, a wife owed him nearly total obedience. Compelled to reside with him, she became subject to his authority over every aspect of her life, relinquishing sovereignty over most of her legal transactions, property, and earnings, and even her domestic activities."[60] This does not mean that all women in Spanish society were subject to this paternal authority at all times in their lives. Widows, for example, were sometimes able to escape this authority: after their husbands died they exercised "complete sovereignty over their legal acts."[61] If they were wealthy because they used or controlled community property from their marriage or valuable dowries, they might be quite powerful in Spanish society.[62]

Very little is known about how bilaterality functioned in Pueblo communities—much less than is known about matrilineality. In general, however, there is little archaeological or documentary evidence to suggest a strong commitment to an ideology of male dominance in Pueblo families before Spanish contact. As I have already discussed, many communities were matrilineal and matrilocal in orientation; in those communities, women (and children) were not under the control of husbands or fathers. Although there is no colonial-period eyewitness testimony regarding how bilateral descent functioned in the eastern pueblos, there is no evidence to suggest a strong ethic of male control in bilateral families either.[63] Thus, although both the pueblo of Tesuque and Spanish society in New Mexico were bilateral in the calculation of descent, they did not share the strong bias toward male inheritance and leadership in families found in Spanish society. Bilaterality allowed flexibility in postmarital residence and thus alone would not have caused Agustín to force María Francisca to live at Tesuque. Bilaterality with some commitment to an ideology of male dominance and control, however, might.

Agustín's insistence that his wife live with him at Tesuque bespeaks a particularly patriarchal attitude, a commitment to the idea of a husband's power over his wife. He wanted to live in his home community. Since wives were compelled to live with their husbands in patriarchal families, it may be that Agustín felt justified in forcing María Francisca to do as he wanted. This commitment to male dominance may have resulted in part from his adoption of Spanish attitudes concerning the proper roles of men and women in marriages and families, since there was no such tradition of male control at Tesuque or in other Pueblo communities. Adopting such Spanish attitudes would have been easy for Agustín because he lived in Tesuque, a pueblo that had "become more accepting of the colonists' patrilineal and patrilocal ways" due to its close geographic proximity to Santa Fe.[64] Although it is impossible to reconstruct exactly who lived or spent time in Tesuque in the early 1770s due to scant archival evidence, it is clear that he was influenced by Spanish practices and beliefs because he married in the Catholic Church. He, like María, was a convert to Christianity. Because Tesuque was close to Santa Fe, there clearly would have been Spaniards living near or passing through the community on a regular basis. At the very least, Agustín would have had regular contact with the priest from Nambé, of which Tesuque was a visiting station, and he could have learned Spanish modes of authority from him. Both Agustín and María Francisca, then, felt the influence of a third system of descent in their already "mixed" or intercultural marriage.

Material Support in Pueblo Intimate Relations

Analyzing the second cause of María Francisca's unhappiness—Agustín's inability or unwillingness to materially provide for her—illustrates that Agustín was not the only person in the marriage to adopt Spanish attitudes about intimate relations and family to a degree. There is no evidence that in matrilineal Cochiti society husbands were expected to provide materially for their wives as an indication of their love and respect for them. Fred Eggan described long-standing attitudes toward material support of family members at Hopi, a matrilineal pueblo, in the mid-twentieth century: "In Hopi . . . the women own the houses and the crops. A husband has the economic obligation of helping to support not only his wife but the whole household, and, as such, his efforts are often criticized, with resultant separations."[65] If a separation happens, both the husband and wife have their mother's family to fall back on: the husband can simply return to his family, and the wife (and children, if there are any) "can fall back on the larger family for economic support until remarriage."[66] The only time that this might not be the case is if, for some reason, the wife has no male relatives on the mother's side to rely upon (for example, brothers or coresident brothers-in-law); then, the wife might find herself economically dependent upon her husband, although this rarely seems to be the case for Hopi women.[67]

Early Spanish observers of Pueblo life commented that men cultivated corn to support their wives and children.[68] But because wives in matrilineal communities were firmly ensconced in their mothers' families, they did not need to rely solely on their husbands for such support. In other words, a husband's material support of his wife was deemphasized in matrilineal pueblos. It does not make much sense, then, to argue that such support was *the* (or even *a*) symbol of the husband's respect and love for his wife in matrilineal pueblos. In these communities, love and respect must have been measured in different terms, if they were measured at all. Yet María Francisca complained that Agustín had failed to provide her with "aid and shelter," and specifically he had not given her shawls, belts, and shoes.[69] This issue was important enough to be a topic of discussion between María Francisca and her mother. María Josefa specifically asked her daughter if Agustín had indeed provided these things, and upon finding out that he had not, María Josefa expressed sympathy.[70] Thus, according to her lawyer's statement, María Francisca "found herself without aid or shelter, and due to this cruelty . . . she did the only thing she could."[71]

Not providing shawls, belts, and shoes seems a trivial complaint; however, it was most likely meant to be a metaphor for Agustín's inability to provide for her more generally. This attitude about material support reflects the orientation of someone who had acclimated at least somewhat to Spanish New Mexican society, not someone who adhered strictly to an ethic of matrilineality. Women in Spanish New Mexican society were essentially the wards of their husbands; as such, they were dependent upon their husbands for material support. It was the duty of the patriarch to provide for his family, including his wife. María Francisca clearly looked to Agustín as her provider, as did women in Spanish families of the period. She seems to have taken to heart the idea expressed in proclamations such as the one Flores Mogollón issued in 1714 and read aloud in Pueblo communities: that it was the husband's duty to "feed and maintain" his wife. It is not clear why Agustín failed to provide materially for María Francisca. Nonetheless, it is clear that María Francisca expected Agustín to support her and was extremely unhappy when he did not.

The fact that María Francisca did, ultimately, move to Tesuque points to an acclimation to Spanish beliefs and practices concerning marriage and family life as well. In Spanish New Mexican society the wife owed her husband "nearly total obedience" in return for material support.[72] As I discussed above, women were not the wards of husbands in Pueblo matrilineal society, nor is there any evidence to indicate that they were wards of their husbands in bilateral society either. María Francisca, however, appears to have believed that she lived under these conditions. As a good and "obedient" wife, she felt compelled to move to Tesuque even though she did not wish to do so.

Murder in Matrilineal Societies

María Francisca's desire for material goods and her "obedience" to Agustín are not the only evidence that suggests that she had assimilated Spanish beliefs about marriage. Given the way in which matrilineality and matrilocality structured the marital tie between men and women at Cochiti during the colonial period, María Francisca's solution to the problems in her marriage—the murder of her husband—also reflects this acclimation. If María Francisca were operating according to the belief that the marital tie between she and Agustín could easily be broken, as was typical in matrilineal and matrilocal societies, she would not have needed to murder her husband to put an end to their relationship. Obviously María Francisca must have been very unhappy to have committed such an act, but, more than this, she must have felt that she had no other way to end the relationship. Such a feeling about marriage would not be logical in a matrilineal society, in which it was easy to end intimate relationships. It is not too difficult to understand, however, how a woman might feel trapped in a relationship in a patriarchal, Catholic society, where there was no way to legally or morally end an unhappy marriage. In other words, María Francisca's actions and feelings appear to reflect a perception of marriage that more closely resembled a Spanish, Catholic union than a union created in a matrilineal and matrilocal society. When Agustín forced her to move to Tesuque and then failed to fulfill his duties toward her, she killed him in order to terminate the relationship.

This, of course, was an extreme action to take. As was acknowledged at the beginning of this chapter, other factors may have motivated María Francisca to make the choices that she did. Were the case richer in detail, a more complete picture of what happened might be painted. However, more information would not, I believe, negate the importance that perceptions of kinship, marriage, and family played in shaping María Francisca's behavior. Such perceptions formed, I would argue, a "background script" to her thought processes: she was not always consciously aware of them, yet they shaped her daily actions and thinking nonetheless.

In January of 1779 both María Francisca and her mother were shot and then hung in the gallows of Santa Fe after spending almost six years in prison while lawyers debated the proper sentence for their crime.[73] María Francisca and Agustín's actions and beliefs reveal the difficulties inherent in intercultural marriages in eighteenth-century Pueblo communities. Agustín's forcibly moving María Francisca to Tesuque and her begrudging obedience in this matter, María Francisca's complaints that Agustín did not provide properly for her despite the fact that husbands did not traditionally do so at Cochiti, and her decision to murder Agustín to end the unhappy marriage when divorce was typically an easy affair all reflect two individuals trying to navigate the difficult terrain of a marriage structured by competing and conflicting beliefs concerning kinship, intimate relations, and family life. Three systems of descent—matrilineality, bilaterality, and bilaterality with a "patrilineal twist"—all operated within the marriage. Spanish and Pueblo beliefs and practices concerning intimate relations and family life also influenced María Francisca and Agustín. Given this complicated mix of beliefs and practices, it is not surprising that conflict arose. Different and conflicting systems of descent and cultural traditions structured their perceptions of what a proper marriage was supposed to be. Due to their inability to reasonably resolve the conflicts that arose, María Francisca decided to murder her husband with the help of her mother.

PUEBLO MARRIAGE RATES IN THE EIGHTEENTH CENTURY

I conclude this chapter with a brief discussion of Pueblo marriage rates in the Catholic Church as well as the incidence of other types of intimate relationships formed by Pueblos to give some sense of the degree to which mixed marriages and family forms—as evidenced in María Francisca and Agustín's relationship—might have existed in Pueblo communities. By examining these intimate relationships it becomes clear that the experience of María Francisca and Agustín was not anomalous in colonial Pueblo society and that many couples faced similar difficulties in forming and maintaining intercultural relationships.

The most obvious place to look for evidence of intercultural relationships is the marriage registers of the local parishes that served Pueblo communities. Here one might find evidence of Pueblos who had to some degree assimilated Spanish beliefs and practices concerning kinship, marriage, and the family into their lives and were thus faced with challenges similar to those confronted by María Francisca and Agustín. The difficulty with this argument is that research into the Archdiocese of Santa Fe's marriage registers indicates that only a few Pueblos married in the Catholic Church in the eighteenth century.[74] Certainly, there was resistance in Pueblo communities to the adoption of Spanish norms concerning family, kinship, and marriage, which resulted in low marriage rates in the Catholic Church. Furthermore, racism prevented a vast majority of Spaniards from considering Pueblo people as acceptable marriage partners, making Spanish-Pueblo marriage an extremely rare event in colonial New Mexico. As Gutiérrez notes, marriage in colonial New Mexico was generally "isogamic—like married like."[75] Spanish New Mexicans were generally very status conscious. Marrying a Pueblo Indian—a person of a "lower" race—had deleterious effects on an individual's social standing in the Spanish communities of New Mexico. The very small number of Spanish-Pueblo marriages in the Archives of the Archdiocese of Santa Fe marriage registers reflects this fact.[76]

This does not, however, mean that few Pueblos were "Catholic" or had accepted Spanish beliefs concerning marriage, the family, and kinship to at least some degree. Informal intimate relationships between Spaniards and Pueblos were far more common in colonial New Mexico than church-sanctioned marriages and could be vectors for the adoption of Spanish beliefs.[77] I noted at the beginning of this chapter that missionaries found that few Pueblo people wished to return to marriage or get married after the reconquest of New Mexico in 1692. Things did not change as the century progressed. In 1760 Fray Sanz de Lezaún reported that cohabitation was very common among Pueblo peoples.[78] Kessell, citing an entry from the baptismal register from Pecos in 1804, writes that Fray Diego Martínez Arellano complained that "all the Indians ... live publicly in concubinage because the officials, both Spaniards and Indians, tolerate it."[79] In 1820 Fray Guevara made the same complaint when he wrote that, even at this late date, Pueblo men were in "commerce with many women."[80] Some of these relationships inevitably involved Pueblos and Spaniards. This is clear given the large number of people of Spanish and Pueblo descent that resided in New Mexico after conquest.[81] Pueblo individuals could adopt Spanish ideas concerning kinship and family, even if their relationships with Spaniards were never formalized within the Catholic Church. Low marriage rates thus cannot simply be interpreted as meaning that few Pueblos adopted Spanish norms, because Pueblos who had adopted these norms did not, for the most part, marry in the church.

Many Pueblo unions were intercultural even if they lacked the element of Spanish influence. The case of María Francisca and Agustín demonstrates that Pueblos who married persons residing outside their home communities might also face competing ideas and practices concerning intimate relations, kinship, and family life. Even if María Francisca and Agustín had not married in the Catholic Church and were not influenced by Spanish norms concerning marriage, family, and kinship, they still came from communities that did not share the same system of descent or language. Some Pueblos also married non-Pueblo Indians (Navajo, Apache, Ute, or Comanche) who resided either inside or outside their communities. These types of intercultural marriages—between individuals of different Pueblo communities or even different Indian groups—appear with some regularity in the Archdiocese of Santa Fe marriage registers.[82] Of course, just as with Spanish-Pueblo marriages, there were intimate unions between individuals of different pueblos or different Indian groups that were formed outside the Catholic Church and are therefore not accounted for in the Archdiocese marriage registers.

Spanish observers of Pueblo community life thus were correct to complain throughout the colonial period that Christian marriage rates were low while cohabitation rates were high. However, as I have demonstrated here, although rates of formal marriage in the church can give some indication of the number of intercultural marriages and families that existed in Pueblo communities in the eighteenth century, such statistics do not tell the whole story. There are any number of ways a marriage or a union could have been mixed, and not all of the unions between "Hispanicized" or acculturated Pueblos, Pueblos of different communities, or even different Indian groups can be accounted for with statistical data based on the archdiocese's marriage registers. Thus, although no overall, concrete statistic of the incidence of Pueblo mixed marriages and unions in the eighteenth century can be offered, it appears from the available data that they were not uncommon. This means that many Pueblo couples found themselves negotiating the same or similar rocky terrain of competing value systems that María Francisca and Agustín faced. Love, power, and the daily struggle to negotiate the competing political and social structures that regulated intimate relationships were common themes in the lives of Pueblo people. What sets the case of María Francisca and Agustín apart is not that they formed a mixed union, but that María Francisca chose to resolve the difficulties inherent in such unions in an atypical way.

The complex mix of practices and beliefs concerning kinship, marriage, and family life that existed in Agustín and María Francisca's relationship, and the relationships of many other Pueblo couples, arose in part as a result of Spanish colonization. After 1539 Pueblos had to negotiate numerous structures of political and social power that sought to regulate intimate relations and family life in their communities. Because Spanish authorities were never able to eradicate and replace Pueblo traditions completely, Pueblo and Spanish practices and beliefs intersected in Pueblo communities and individuals. As the Cochiti murder investigation reveals, individuals such as Agustín and María Francisca adopted some Spanish beliefs concerning marriage, kinship, and family life as a result of the Spanish authorities' efforts to eradicate "concubinage," but that did not mean they simply disregarded Pueblo traditions. Pueblos of the eighteenth century led syncretic lives and lived in diverse, even "cosmopolitan," communities, in addition to creating intercultural marriages and families. In the case of Agustín and María Francisca, Pueblo and Spanish beliefs and practices did not mesh well, and the resultant clash of ideas ultimately led to murder. If María Francisca had chosen to resolve her unhappiness with her marriage to Agustín according to the norms of her own community, such an extreme action would not have been necessary.

NOTES

1. This case is located at the Spanish Archives of New Mexico, reel 10, frames 752–88 (hereafter SANM reel number: frame number). The sentence in the case appears at SANM 10: 859–66. Brief discussions of this case, many of which focus on the peculiar sentencing of the accused, appear in Charles Cutter, *The Protector de Indios in Colonial New Mexico 1659–1821* (Albuquerque: University of New Mexico Press, 1986), 75; Ramón Gutiérrez, *When Jesus Came, the Corn Mothers Went Away: Marriage, Sexuality, and Power in New Mexico, 1500–1846* (Stanford, CA: Stanford University Press, 1991), 191, 205; John Kessell, *Spain in the Southwest: A Narrative History of Colonial New Mexico, Arizona, Texas, and California* (Norman: University of Oklahoma Press, 2002), 290–92; and Robert Torrez, *Ufos over Galisteo and Other Stories of New Mexico's History* (Albuquerque: University of New Mexico Press, 2004), 67–70. John Kessell provides a longer and more detailed narration of the case in "Death Delayed: The Sad Case of the Two Marías, 1773–1779," *New Mexico Historical Review* 83, no. 2 (2008): 157–70.
2. Charles Lange, *Cochiti: A New Mexico Pueblo, Past and Present* (Albuquerque: University of New Mexico Press, 1990), 149.
3. For a brief discussion of Pueblo gender roles, see Cheryl J. Foote and Sandra K. Schackel, "Indian Women of New Mexico, 1535–1680," in *New Mexico Women: Intercultural Perspectives*, ed. Joan Jensen and Darlis Miller (Albuquerque: University of New Mexico Press, 1986), 18–21.

4. According to Elizabeth John, New Mexico governor Pedro Fermín de Mendinueta had waged war against the Navajo by early 1774. He expected the pueblos of the Keres district, including Cochiti, to help carry out these campaigns. Just three months after Agustin's murder took place, five hundred Comanches raided Cochiti. Elizabeth John, *Storms Brewed in Other Men's Worlds: The Confrontation of the Indians, Spanish and French in the Southwest, 1540–1795* (College Station: Texas A&M Press, 1975), 474–75. See also James Brooks, *Captives and Cousins: Slavery, Kinship and Community in the Southwest Borderlands* (Chapel Hill: University of North Carolina Press, 2002).

5. SANM 10: 756, 762, 764.

6. SANM 10: 753–55. No last names are provided for any of the defendants.

7. Tesuque was a "visiting station" of Nambé, which means that the missionary who resided at Nambé was responsible for all official church business from Tesuque. Kessell, "Death Delayed," 163.

8. SANM 10: 756.

9. SANM 10: 767.

10. SANM 10: 762.

11. SANM 10: 768.

12. SANM 10: 756.

13. SANM 10: 758.

14. "Kinship" here refers specifically to the calculation of descent. "Marriage" is used to refer to both the tie between husband and wife that was sanctioned by the Catholic Church as well as any of the more informal intimate relationships that may have occurred between men and women in colonial New Mexico. I also use "cohabitation" and "intimate relations" or "relationships" to refer to those partnerships not sanctioned by the church. "Families" and "family life" are used to reference the social group composed of spouses or partners and their children as well as the relationships that existed between members of this group.

15. "Civilizing" Native peoples was central to Spanish state-making practices in the colonial period. In addition to being seen as immoral, marital and kinship practices such as polygyny, cohabitation, matrilineality, and the like were targeted for change because authorities believed the continuation of indigenous practices destabilized the Spanish state. State making was accompanied by efforts to remake the very personhoods of Indian people; as such, their sexuality and intimate practices came under scrutiny. On remaking the personhoods of Indian people as part of state-making practices, see Irene Silverblatt, "Becoming Indian in the Central Andes of Seventeenth-Century Peru," in *After Colonialism: Imperial Histories and Postcolonial Displacements*, ed. Gyan Prakash (Princeton, NJ: Princeton University Press, 1995). For more general comments on the Spanish focus on sexuality and gender in their efforts to "civilize" Native people, see Susan Kellogg, *Weaving the Past: A History of Latin America's Indigenous Women from the Prehispanic Period to the Present* (New York: Oxford University Press, 2005), 71–81; and Karen Vieira Powers, *Women in the Crucible of Conquest: The Gendered Genesis of Spanish American Society, 1500–1600* (Albuquerque: University of New Mexico Press, 2005), 52–62.

16. Frederick Hodge, George Hammond, and Agapito Rey, *Fray Alonso de Benavides' Revised Memorial of 1634* (Albuquerque: University of New Mexico Press, 1945), 159.

17. Ibid.

18. Benavides wrote the memorial for the king of Spain in part to convince him that the missionary enterprise in colonial New Mexico was a worthy one. Because of the need to justify continued financial support for his missionizing efforts in New Mexico, Benavides is known to have inflated the numbers of Pueblos baptized, as well as "elaborated" upon many of the details of his experiences in New Mexico. See ibid., 12; and Peter Forrestal, trans., *Benavides' Memorial of 1630* (Washington, DC: Academy of American Franciscan History, 1954), x.

19. J. Manuel Espinosa, *The Pueblo Indian Revolt of 1696 and the Franciscan Missions in New Mexico: Letters of the Missionaries and Related Documents* (Norman: University of Oklahoma Press, 1988), 129.

20. Ibid., 131.

21. Ibid., 221.

22. Jim Norris, *After "the Year Eighty": The Demise of Franciscan Power in Spanish New Mexico* (Albuquerque: University of New Mexico Press, 2000), 37.

23. Archivo General de la Nación, tomo 36, folio 2, Cabildo letter, September 15, 1706, France Scholes transcription, p. 5.

24. SANM 4: 1014–17.

25. This may indicate a continuation of the post-reconquest state of affairs—that missionaries were unsuccessful in uniting married couples that had split apart after the 1680 revolt.

26. SANM 4: 1014–17.

27. The case is at SANM 6: 524–41.

28. The case is at SANM 6: 1010–1127.

29. SANM 6: 1026.

30. The case is at SANM 7: 216–57. For questions about "public sin," see frames 225 and 232.

31. SANM 7: 235–36.

32. SANM 7: 246.

33. Henry Putnam Beers, *Spanish and Mexican Records of the American Southwest: A Bibliographical Guide to Archive and Manuscript Sources* (Tucson: University of Arizona Press, 1979).

34. France Scholes, *Troublous Times in New Mexico, 1659–1670* (Albuquerque: University of New Mexico Press, 1942).

35. Alfonso Ortiz, who was an anthropologist and member of the pueblo of San Juan, states that there has never been a tradition of unilineal descent—meaning the calculation of descent through one line rather than two—among the Tewa, the language group to which Tesuque belonged: "There is no evidence in the ethnographic record to indicate they ever had a unilineal rule of descent." See Ortiz, *The Tewa World: Space, Time, and Being and Becoming in a Pueblo Society* (Chicago: University of Chicago Press, 1969), 58, 6, 130. Edward Dozier, another Pueblo anthropologist, states that, in the Tanoan pueblos like the Tewa, "unilineal organizations appear not to have been important in the past and certainly not at present. . . . Tanoan Pueblos classify kin bilaterally on a principle of generation, emphasize age, and generally ignore sex distinctions. There is no evidence of a former lineage or clan system in the kinship terms or in the network of social relations among the kin group." See Dozier *The Pueblo Indians of North America* (New York: Holt, Rinehart, and Winston, 1970), 165. When and why matrilineality as opposed to bilaterality developed in Pueblo communities is debated by Fred Eggan, *Social Organization of the Western Pueblos* (Chicago: University of Chicago Press, 1950); and Robin Fox, *The Keresan Bridge: A Problem in Pueblo Ethnology* (New York: Humanities Press, 1967).

36. There are four unrelated languages spoken in the Pueblo communities of Arizona and New Mexico: Hopi, Zuni, Keresan, and Tanoan. Both the Tanoan and Keresan language have numerous branches. See Kenneth Hale and David Harris, "Historical Linguistics and Archaeology," in *Handbook of North American Indians: Southwest,* ed. Alfonso Ortiz (Washington, DC: Smithsonian Institution, 1979), 170–77.

37. Foote and Schackel, "Indian Women," 27.

38. Mamie Tanquest-Miller, *Pueblo Indian Culture as Seen by the Early Spanish Explorers,* USC School of Research Studies, no. 18, Social Science Series, no. 21 (Los Angeles: University of Southern California Press, 1941), 8.

39. George Hammond and Agapito Rey, eds. and trans., *Don Juan de Oñate: Colonizer of New Mexico, 1595–1628* (Albuquerque: University of New Mexico Press, 1953), 2: 636.

40. Foote and Schackel, "Indian Women," 27.

41. Linda Stone, *Kinship and Gender: An Introduction,* 3rd ed. (Boulder, CO: Westview Press, 2006), 126. Of course, this does not mean that fathers and children did not love or feel connected to

one another, only that, *structurally,* the place of the father and husband in matrilineal families can be problematic.

42. Ibid., 155.
43. Eggan, *Social Organization of the Western Pueblos,* 44.
44. Gutiérrez, *When Jesus Came,* 15–16.
45. Adolph Bandelier quoted in Lange, *Cochiti,* 368.
46. Gutiérrez, *When Jesus Came,* 14.
47. Hammond and Rey, *Don Juan de Oñate,* 2: 635.
48. Quoted in Gutiérrez, *When Jesus Came,* 15.
49. Quoted in Lange, *Cochiti,* 368.
50. Ibid., 369.
51. SANM 10: 756.
52. Kessell says he "spit in the face of a matrilocal society" ("Death Delayed," 162).
53. SANM 10: 767.
54. SANM 10: 762. No explanation for the actions of the Cochiti officials is provided in the documentation. Pueblo individuals were not simply free to move from community to community. For example, at marriage a couple was supposed to notify the father where they were to reside, in the woman's house or the man's house. Census books were then altered to indicate their choice of residence. Missionaries kept close tabs on couples so that they could check up on them to make sure they were living together after marriage and could locate them if necessary to punish them (Archives of the Archdiocese of Santa Fe, reel 48: frames 747–48). Furthermore, missionaries were not allowed to marry individuals from other pueblos without first notifying and receiving permission from the nonresident's missionary (ibid., frame 753). Pueblo authorities, like the missionaries, kept track of who was in their communities as a matter of routine. Cochiti officials may have wanted to deter nonresidents such as Agustín from spending long periods of time in the pueblo. It may also have been that María Francisca was a "troublemaker" and Cochiti officials were using her marriage to Agustín as an excuse to remove her from the pueblo.
55. SANM 10: 763.
56. SANM 10: 765.
57. Susan Kellogg, *Law and the Transformation of Aztec Culture, 1500–1700* (Norman: University of Oklahoma Press, 1995), 105–6.
58. That, in reality, Spaniards practiced patrilineality in New Mexico is made clear by Gutiérrez, *When Jesus Came,* 230. Linda Stone argues that there is very little difference between a bilateral descent calculation with a patrilineal bias and patrilineal descent calculation. Stone, *Kinship and Gender: An Introduction,* 174.
59. Silvia Marina Arrom, *The Women of Mexico City, 1790–1857* (Stanford, CA: Stanford University Press, 1985), 57–58.
60. Ibid., 65.
61. Ibid., 58.
62. On women and property in New Mexico, see Rosalind Rock, "'Pido y Suplico': Women and the Law in Spanish New Mexico, 1697–1763," *New Mexico Historical Review* 65, no. 2 (1990): 145–59; Rosalind Rock, "Mujeres de Substancia—Case Studies of Women of Property in Northern New Spain," *Colonial Latin American Historical Review* 2, no. 4 (1993): 425–40; Yolanda Leyva Chávez, "'A Poor Widow Burdened with Children': Widows and Land in Colonial New Mexico," in *Writing the Range: Race, Class and Culture in the Women's West,* ed. Elizabeth Jameson and Susan Armitage (Norman: University of Oklahoma Press, 1997), 85–96; Richard Ahlborn, "The Will of a New Mexico Woman in 1762," *New Mexico Historical Review* 65, no. 3 (1990): 319–55; Myra Ellen Jenkins, "Some Eighteenth-Century New Mexico Women of Property," in *Hispanic Arts and Ethnohistory in*

the Southwest, ed. Marta Weigle (Santa Fe: Ancient City Press, 1983): 335-45; and Angelina Veyna, "'It Is My Last Wish That...': A Look at Colonial Nuevo Mexicanas through Their Testaments," in *Building with Our Own Hands: New Directions in Chicana Studies,* ed. Adela de la Torre and Beatríz M. Pesquera (Berkeley: University of California Press, 1993), 91-108.

63. I draw this conclusion based on my own research using the colonial-period documentation concerning gender relations in Pueblo communities. Archaeologists have argued that there is a lack of evidence for "clear-cut, intensive male domination" in precontact Southwestern societies, but that, where power differentials existed, women "were more likely to suffer from lack of power than males" (Patricia Crown, "Gendered Tasks, Power, and Prestige in the Prehispanic Southwest," in *Women and Men in the Prehispanic Southwest: Labor, Power, and Prestige,* ed. Patricia Crown [Santa Fe: School of American Research Press, 2000], 13). Suzanne Fish argues that "there is no comprehensive and well-recorded patrilineal system of kinship, tenure, and inheritance in the Southwestern ethnographic record comparable to the matrilineal systems of Hopi and Zuni." See Suzanne Fish, "Farming, Foraging, and Gender," in *Women and Men in the Prehispanic Southwest: Labor, Power, and Prestige,* 185. I have found evidence in my own research for male preeminence in the political and economic spheres of Pueblo life but not in their intimate relationships.

64. Kessell, "Death Delayed," 162.
65. Eggan, *Social Organization of the Western Pueblos,* 34.
66. Ibid., 34-35.
67. Alice Schlegel, "Sexual Antagonism among the Sexually Egalitarian Hopi," *Ethos* 7, no. 2 (1979): 132.
68. Tanquest-Miller, *Pueblo Indian Culture,* 16.
69. SANM 10: 768, 762.
70. Ibid.
71. SANM 10: 768.
72. Arrom, *Women of Mexico City,* 65.
73. The sentence appears at SANM 10: 864-66. Both women were assigned representation by the governor of New Mexico. Their *curadores* submitted statements of defense to the governor at the end of May 1773. From there, papers were sent to lawyers in Chihuahua for a decision on what sentence to give the two women, a process that took six years to complete. For a complete account of the process, see Kessell, "Death Delayed," 161-67.
74. My own research using New Mexico censuses and the marriage registers from the Archdiocese of Santa Fe indicates that marriage rates in Pueblo communities rarely rose above 10 percent between 1750 and 1811. For a list of eighteenth-century censuses, see Gutiérrez, *When Jesus Came,* 173. The marriage registers for Pueblo communities are located on reels 26-33 of the Archives of the Archdiocese of Santa Fe microfilm (hereafter AASF reel number: frame number).
75. Ibid., 285; Andrew Knaut, *The Pueblo Revolt of 1680: Conquest and Resistance in Seventeenth-Century New Mexico* (Norman: University of Oklahoma Press, 1995), 136-51.
76. I could only locate ten such marriages in all of the marriage registers for Pueblo communities of the eighteenth century. Some of these marriages involved non-Pueblo Indian people (e.g., Apaches) and Spaniards.
77. Gutiérrez, *When Jesus Came,* 285.
78. Charles Hackett, ed. and trans., *Historical Documents Relating to New Mexico, Nueva Vizcaya, and Approaches Thereto, to 1773,* vol. 3 (Washington, CD: Carnegie Institute, 1937), 475.
79. John Kessell, *Kiva, Cross, and Crown: The Pecos Indians and New Mexico, 1540-1840* (Albuquerque: University of New Mexico Press, 1979), 421.
80. AASF 45: 299.

81. There are no formal statistics concerning how many children of Spanish and Pueblo descent were born in colonial New Mexico. It is not possible to construct such statistics because missionaries were not consistent in noting the race or status of children born in their parishes. Nevertheless, the consensus is that the birth rate of people of mixed Spanish and Pueblo ancestry was quite high. See Knaut, *The Pueblo Revolt of 1680,* 139. On the issue of illegitimacy in colonial New Mexico more generally, see Gutiérrez, *When Jesus Came,* 156, 94–202; and Brooks, *Captives and Cousins.*

82. According to my own research using the marriage registers, these types of marriages ranged from a high of twenty-eight in San Ildefonso between 1700 and 1820 to a low of one in Galisteo between 1776 and 1820 and in Zia between 1697 and 1767. In other words, at Galisteo a mixed marriage between individuals of different pueblos, or different Indian groups, occurred on average once every forty-four years, while at San Ildefonso such marriages occurred once every four years (AASF 26–33).

10

The Paradox of Kinship

Native-Catholic Communities in Alta California, 1769–1840s

Erika Pérez

On August 30, 1778, Antonio Cota, a San Diego presidio soldier from Villa del Fuente, Sinaloa, married María Bernarda Chigila, an Indian woman from the *ranchería* Puituida. The couple exchanged their vows at Mission San Juan Capistrano before Guillermo Carrillo, captain of the mission guard, Joseph Antonio Peña, a soldier, Pedro Ompsil, a mission Indian, and other neophytes.[1] By July of 1780, the couple's daughter, María Antonia Marcela, had been sponsored for baptism by soldier Francisco Lopes and Feliciana Arballa.[2] The Cotas produced two more children, María Gregoria Matilde Cota and Nabor Antonio Cota, baptized in 1785 and 1787, respectively, at Mission San Diego.[3] Spanish Mexican soldiers and settlers—known as *gente de razón* (people of reason), a designation that applied to Spanish Mexicans but not California Indians—served as the children's godparents. Antonio and María Cota's mixed offspring themselves sponsored local Indian converts for sacraments, and this continued exposure to both their mother's Indian community and their father's Spanish network aided in their development of a mestizo (Spanish Indian) identity.[4]

Throughout the Mexican and early American periods, the Cota family's association with Indians continued.[5] Antonio Cota's grandson, José María Uribes, later repeated the pattern of his grandparents by marrying an Indian named María Clara at Mission San Juan Capistrano on February 24, 1851.[6] Antonio Cota's niece, María Ignacia Jacinta Cota, daughter of Roque Jacinto Cota and his wife, Juana María Verdugo, married an Indian soldier from Mexico City, Francisco Bruno Garcia, at Mission San Gabriel on August 22, 1793.[7] Although some Cota family members comfortably associated with Indian neophytes, others were far less accepting of intimate connections with Native peoples. Despite having cousins and relatives who intermarried with and sponsored local Indians, soldier Valentín Cota was the catalyst of the Chumash Revolt of 1824 after he ordered the whipping of an Indian from Mission La Purísima Concepción. Chumash peoples responded to their mistreatment by revolting at three missions, including Mission San Buenaventura, where Valentin's great-uncle, Pablo Antonio Cota, served in the mission guard and as *padrino* (godfather) to fourteen converts from 1782 to 1787.[8]

The Cota family's intimate ties with Indian peoples reveal that interethnic contact was fraught with conflicting emotions and uncertain outcomes.[9] Even the existence of compadrazgo relationships between Spanish Mexican godparents and Indian godchildren did not always guarantee kind treatment by members of the same family, or, more broadly, by Spanish Mexican society. By the Mexican period social and economic gaps had widened, further dividing the *gente de razón* and Indians. Although the Cota family's intermarriage with and sponsorship of Indians reflect the fluidity that existed in the early Spanish period, Valentín Cota's violence and other incidents of hostility by Spanish Mexicans point to lost opportunities for mutual understanding. Nevertheless, more congenial encounters reveal the potential of kinship and compadrazgo to stabilize interethnic relations. The linking of kinship and evangelization in Alta California also accelerated the development of new indigenous-Catholic communities. Catholic godparenting practices and Indian puberty rituals shared commonalities that bound communities and families closer together. However, converted Indians who shaped and reproduced compadrazgo networks were not wholly assimilated, nor were their traditions completely annihilated. Compadrazgo, as a socioreligious institution, embodied contradictions, accelerating conquest and Hispanicization while also providing narrow openings for continuity in Native kinship practices and gender roles.

My analysis of kinship led me to examine subjugated peoples and their negotiations with colonial power from the bottom up.[10] For example, Baja Indian godparents were both cultural brokers and agents of "cycles of conquest" in Alta California.[11] Baja Indians functioned as servants, catechists, interpreters, and godparents, channeling invaluable information to Franciscan missionaries to better frame their spiritual agenda. However, their deployment was fraught with inconsistency as they were relegated to an inferior social status at the same time that they modeled the benefits of Christianity. Ironically, the presence of Baja Christian Indians and their social stigmatization may have reified their own sense of indigeneity and that of local neophytes. As Baja Indians married, reproduced, and sponsored Alta Californians, they augmented and melded into existing indigenous communities, contributing to the diversity of indigenous California.

Iberian godparenting traditions, which involved enlisting a *padrino* (godfather) and a *madrina* (godmother) from blood relations or close family friends, were tested in Alta California through the establishment of compadrazgo ties between Spanish Mexicans and Indians who previously held no affective connections. Customarily, a *padrino* or *madrina* spiritually guided their godchild and might rear the child in the event of the biological parents' death. Biological parents and spiritual coparents memorialized their bond through Catholic ritual, during which they acknowledged each other as *"compadres."* Spanish Mexican soldiers, artisans, and female kin sponsored Alta California Indians for Catholic sacraments and helped indoctrinate them. However, the relationships of social equality and familiarity typical of Iberian compadrazgo did not exist between Spanish Mexicans and neophytes.[12]

As becoming a godparent did not require literacy, being a man, or belonging to a particular racial or ethnic group, the influence of godparentage reached different segments of society. In Alta California this spiritual role demanded only a rudimentary knowledge of Catholic doctrine, and the majority of individuals in newly established Catholic communities either served as godparents or had godparents. However, the constant rotation of Spanish soldiers and artisans throughout Alta California might have undermined the influence of Spanish Mexican *padrinos* in the daily lives of their Indian godchildren. Despite the tenuousness of interethnic godparentage, compadrazgo entailed new expressions of obligation on the part of Spanish Mexican godparents who, in exchange for material incentives and spiritual knowledge imparted to neophytes, received social deference from their Native godchildren. This relationship of reciprocity and obligation was a colonizing tactic essential for replacing other traumatic memories of Spanish violence, specifically the rape and murder of Native Californians, which limited the success of spiritual and military conquest.

The historic flexibility in definitions of the family, as Ramón Gutiérrez describes in his chapter in this volume, legitimizes kinship studies in the Spanish borderlands, which requires an understanding of regional variations among Native populations, differences in missionary groups and evangelization techniques, and the reach of colonial domination and control. To understand changes and continuity in Native kinship in Alta California over time, some background in pre- and early contact cultural traditions is needed.

PRECONTACT MARRIAGE AND KINSHIP IN NATIVE CALIFORNIA

The intimate lives of Native peoples in Alta California embodied a multitude of relational expressions that were validated through rituals and cultural practices. Marriage was shaped by factors such as socioeconomic status, clan identification, and kinship taboos. Among the Juaneños, Luiseños, Serranos, and Gabrielinos, a man indicated his interest in a woman, either personally or through his family, by providing ritual gifts such as deer meat and perhaps his labor to her family. Offerings varied, but lavish gifts were not a prerequisite for marriage. Diegueño and Gabrielino parents informed their daughter of a suitor's interest; if she rejected a viable suitor, her family might encourage her to accept his proposal. Families occasionally prearranged marriages. Some Juaneño, Serrano, and Gabrielino children, for example, were promised to each other at birth or in their infancy by their parents, who raised them to have frequent contact, thus facilitating familiarity and acceptance of the marriage arrangement. Occasionally marriages were also arranged by village elders or intermediaries entrusted with this task.[13]

Native family units among the Cahuilla, Serrano, and Diegueño were typically nuclear, patrilineal (tracing descent through the father's line), and patrilocal (residing among the husband's family). Southern Californians often bestowed upon their children names from a collection common to the father's family line. Although the majority of Native couples in southern California lived near the husband's family after marriage, Native practices allowed for some flexibility, including matrilocal residency (living among the bride's family). Chumash commoners and some Diegueños practiced matrilocal residency, while Chumash elites remained patrilocal. Family units varied but often consisted of an adult couple, with a male as head of household, their unmarried offspring, and possibly a son with his wife and children. Other families consisted of two brothers, their wives and offspring, or an adult couple, their unmarried children, and a husband's elderly parents or unmarried siblings.[14]

Flexibility in marital expressions, including sororal polygyny (marriage of a man to sisters) and levirate unions (marriage of a widow to her dead husband's brother), facilitated the sharing of resources and preserved kinship obligations. This continuity was especially important following the death of a spouse, an event that could potentially disrupt or sever existing kinship ties. Among the Serrano, for example, polygyny was also allowed in special circumstances stemming from infertility in a first marriage.[15] Marriage variations also reflected political functions. Elites and tribal leaders among the Gabrielinos and the Chumash relied upon polygyny to solidify political connections with other groups.[16] Intermarriage involving sisters from a different clan or tribe fostered mutual obligations strengthened by familial bonds. Plural marriages yielded access to the productive labor of multiple females, which enhanced the prestige of elite males, who were responsible for the distribution of goods and foods during ceremonies. As these examples illustrate, the preservation of kinship obligations and procreation were core values among the peoples of southern California, and marital expressions were changeable according to demographic stresses and political considerations.[17]

Exogamy (marriage outside one's own group) was common among most southern California groups, with the possible exception of the Serranos, who married within their clan or lineage group. Those Luiseños, Cahuillas, Cupeños,

Serranos, and Diegueños who belonged to the same clan, such as the Wild Cat or Coyote clan, addressed each other with terms that suggested filial ties, such as "cousin" or "sister." Membership in the same clan was considered as legitimate as immediate blood ties, and it was believed that clan membership indicated some prior blood connection to even the remotest of clan members.[18]

Native kinship and family identifications were adjustable when internal tensions and demographic obstacles developed. In extreme circumstances, lineage rules shifted to allow individuals or family groups to claim new lineage identities. Although it was rare, individuals could reject patrilineal association and identify with their mother's lineage. Individuals and small family groups might claim new ancestral associations in reaction to intracommunity hostilities. Clans might also dissolve over time due to exogamic marriage rules that introduced new lineages into a family or community and possibly diluted the original clan. As these examples illustrate, Native peoples severed and forged affective ties, relying upon flexible kinship practices to regenerate and reconstitute families and communities. Following the arrival of Spanish Mexican invaders, Native peoples relied upon this survival skill to sustain and create familial relationships in the face of new challenges.[19]

COMPADRAZGO, POWER, AND PARALLELS

In the late eighteenth century, the Spanish crown established a mission system and presidios (military garrisons) along the Pacific coast of Alta California to establish a settler buffer zone. This buffer would protect valuable silver mining settlements in northern New Spain and possibly discourage the imperial designs of Russia, France, and England. After the first mission was established in San Diego in 1769, Franciscan missionaries began enticing and coercing indigenous peoples into the missions and introducing them to the Catholic faith. Franciscans targeted young children in particular, as they presented fewer challenges for spiritual indoctrination and cultural reform than adults. Infants and young children were baptized immediately, while the baptism of adolescents and adults was delayed until they received training in the basic tenets of the Catholic faith.[20]

Catholic sacraments such as baptism and marriage relied upon the sponsorship of godparents, who would instruct Indian neophytes in the faith and help found new Catholic communities. Although spiritual coparents were usually blood relatives or close family friends, in the earliest stages of the missions' founding in Alta California, godparents were primarily drawn from a pool of Spanish Mexican soldiers and their wives residing at presidios, missions, and pueblos. Gradually, Indians participated in compadrazgo in greater numbers and began to help interpret the faith to newer members of mission communities.[21] Because unhealthy conditions resulted in high death rates in these communities, compadrazgo took

FIGURE 10.1. Photograph of a baptismal font from the Mission San Luís Obispo in the early 1900s. Baptismal fonts such as this one symbolized both a threat to culture and community through conquest and a new tool for ritual ceremonialism and the regeneration of kinship ties. Courtesy of Braun Research Library Collection, Autry National Center, P.26983A.

on greater importance by serving as a potential safety net for orphaned godchildren, who by custom were adopted by blood relatives or godparents. Godparentage, according to Catholic doctrine, was as significant as blood ties, and marriage taboos excluded godparents as potential mates, as clan and lineage taboos governed the marriages of Native Californians.

Despite the potential of compadrazgo to forge a sense of community, the institution reflected colonial imposition in Alta California; more plainly, it was a "social barometer" for interethnic encounters.[22] Prior violent acts by the Spaniards undoubtedly coerced Native responses to compadrazgo and their adoption of Catholic kinship practices. Similarly, some Spanish Mexican inhabitants who feared displeasing the missionaries were persuaded to take on the sponsorship of Indians. These *gente de razón*, themselves racially mixed and ambitious for upward mobility, instituted social distance from California Indians and did not appear to view Native peoples as true *compadres* or *comadres*, terms of affection that memorialized the compadrazgo relationship. If the parents of someone baptized were unconverted, the potential for cultural convergence between Indian and Spanish Mexican *compadres* remained limited. Since Indian neophytes were perpetually developing their knowledge of Catholic doctrine, Christianized Indians never served as godparents for *gente de razón*.[23] Interethnic compadrazgo bonds allowed power to flow along a vertical social plane in Alta California by joining those of disparate class and ethnic backgrounds rather than those of the same social or class standing.[24]

Although social disparity existed in early compadrazgo relationships between Indians and Spanish Mexicans in Alta California, the institution offered advantages for those on the lower rung of the relationship. Parents sometimes sought out godparents of higher socioeconomic standing to secure material benefits for their children.[25] In Mexico, slaves of African ancestry tried to enlist wealthy godparents, hoping to gain emancipation for their offspring.[26] Similarly, in California, Indian parents sometimes realized benefits after baptizing their children. "Out from the presidio come great heaps of tortillas sent by godfathers for their godsons," reported Franciscan Junípero Serra to Father Guardian Francisco Pangua in 1774. "And even though each day a mighty cauldron of pozole is filled and emptied three times over [at the mission], these poor little fellows still have a corner for the tortillas their godfathers send them," he continued.[27] Indian parents realized that goods or food might be funneled through *padrinos* and *madrinas* and could be shared by the godchild with the rest of the family. A year later, Father Serra reported to Viceroy Bucareli that "heaps of remnants given in exchange, or as gifts by godfathers to their spiritual sons," were a welcome aspect of compadrazgo, and that sometimes godchildren received fresh clothing for baptism.[28]

Ritual aspects of compadrazgo and sponsorship for Catholic sacraments resonated for Native peoples of both sexes. Ceremonial participation by Native peoples in southern California was common, and women were more actively involved in tribal ceremonies than their counterparts in northern and central California. Traditional sponsorship rituals of adolescent initiates existed among indigenous peoples before the arrival of Spanish colonizers. During puberty rites, for example, men and women supported individuals of the same sex and guided them through an initiation process, imparting gender-specific *ayelkwi* (sacred knowledge and power) to prepare adolescents for adult responsibilities.[29]

One sponsored practice among southern Californian Indians involved the imbibing of hallucinogenic beverages. The *toloache* ceremony (known as *Mani* among the Luiseño), which required initiates to drink a jimsonweed concoction, was an important milestone in a Luiseño's life. Men from the community assisted the boys through the practice, which induced visions. Luiseño elders taught the *toloache* initiates songs of their god, Chungichnish, and both boys and girls were subjected to lengthy orations. Among the Gabrielinos, the *maanet* (datura) ceremony (known as the *pem-pa-wvan kiksawal* ceremony among the Cahuilla) also required the participation of older community members who supervised physical tests and shared with inductees their knowledge of rituals, songs, and other practices.[30]

Diegueño, Luiseño, Cahuilla, and Gabrielino girls were also subjected to elaborate puberty ceremonies that required the oversight of sponsors. Among the first three indigenous groups, adult men and women performed special dances to commemorate young girls reaching the age of maturity, usually considered to be the onset of menarche. Gabrielino girls also underwent a ceremony after reaching puberty, during which their torsos were buried under heated sand. Later they were sung to by older women, who supervised a dance in their honor. Cahuilla informant Ruby Modesto, a *pul* (medicine woman), reported that girls in her tribe occasionally underwent the *kikisulem* ceremony, stating, "It was unusual, but sometimes a girl would go through this initiation with the boys. She would be accompanied by a lady relative who would guide the young shamaness."[31]

The implementation of sacred religious artifacts in Catholic rituals was also familiar to Native Californians. Colorful vestments, silver chalices, and oils lent Catholic rituals a ceremonial quality that was not dissimilar to the blessed feathers, deer hooves, and sand paintings used by Native spiritual leaders. Catholics held baptismal ceremonies in front of families and neighbors and assigned those baptized a new Christian name, sometimes in honor of a saint. This mirrored the Chumash naming ceremonies, which relied upon a group of older men called the *'alchuklash* to determine a child's name based on the timing of birth and the lunar calendar. Bestowed soon after birth and in front of relatives, Chumash names acknowledged reverence for the child's birth planet. Gabrielino grandparents named newborns of the same sex and also factored astrological indicators in the selection.[32]

Despite cultural parallels between Spanish and Native practices, sustained contact between unconverted and missionized Indians discouraged the latter's complete assimilation. Missionaries reporting about San Diego neophytes in 1814 claimed, "They find it difficult to learn to speak Spanish at this mission, since each year pagans arrive to become Christians and the greater number of these are old people." New converts reintroduced indigenous languages and traditional practices to their mission community, and Alta Californians such as the Diegueños remained "devoted to the preservation of the customs of their ancestors." Consequently, Catholic Indian participation and the reproduction of compadrazgo networks probably combined Hispanic and indigenous elements to maintain precontact kinship ties. Native cultural practices that coexisted with Spanish norms were more protected from the power of the missionary gaze and reform than those that opposed them.[33]

Native perspectives on compadrazgo are difficult to discern because of the lack of Native-authored sources and oral histories indicating their impressions of godparentage. Missionaries and observers frequently remarked upon Native resistance to certain Hispanic cultural practices and the Natives' attachment to premarital sex, polygyny, Indian divorce, traditional healing practices, and dances. However, among the six volumes of correspondence from mission presidents Junípero Serra and Fermín Francisco de Lasuén, other missionary-authored texts, one Native-authored text by Pablo Tac, and oral histories from Native witnesses that I consulted, I did not come across a single reference to compadrazgo as unwelcome or rejected among converts. That compadrazgo generated no record of conflict lends credence to the theory that it was accepted by some indigenous peoples as a new vehicle for familial expression.[34]

California Indians transported their precontact kinship bonds to the missions, despite missionary efforts to eradicate what they perceived as deviant practices such as polygyny. On May 23, 1811, Lucio Cuinasum, a forty-two-year-old man from Pimicha, and his thirty-eight-year-old wife, Lucia Sunabam, presented themselves for baptism at Mission San Gabriel. The couple had a son named Luís Judaibit, age eleven, baptized that same day. Luisa Minadbam, of *ranchería* Jonomonai, was noted in the mission register as *"la mujer segunda"* (the second woman or wife) of Lucio prior to conversion. She, too, was baptized on May 23, along with the couple's children, Luís Nemainit and Flora Toyabam, the latter of whom was baptized alongside her husband, Flor Mole. Notably, the family was recorded in the mission register in sequence, with the three parents and all their offspring intermingled as a family cluster. Also, all were sponsored by the same Gabrielino godmother, María Manuela of Juyubit. Although missionaries viewed the conversion of a patriarch and his selection of one wife for Catholic marriage as a success in eliminating polygyny, indigenous families used baptism to honor and preserve extended families intact. Significantly, the baptism of Lucio and his family was not an isolated example. Other polygynous family baptisms in southern California reveal the desire of Native peoples to sanctify preexisting bonds through the use of a Catholic custom.[35]

Ironically, the mission system, which required the ongoing presence of Native peoples, created conditions that led to its own demise. Disease, declining fecundity, and high mortality rates coupled with the psychological trauma of missionization and forced cultural reform devastated mission communities and discouraged other Natives from converting. Consequently, from 1813 onward, Franciscans utilized military campaigns to capture runaways and unconverted people from the interior. Although missionization always raised the specter of violence, Franciscan efforts to persuade non-Christians to convert voluntarily gave way to force. This transition undoubtedly shaped how new arrivals viewed Catholic practices such as compadrazgo and their implementation.[36]

As evidenced by family baptisms, indigenous peoples resisted complete assimilation by viewing Catholic practices through their own lenses and investing Catholic ritual with meanings that may have countered missionary goals of spiritual indoctrination and Hispanicization. Paradoxically, symbols of spiritual conversion such as baptism and godparentage held the potential to carve out narrow spaces for Native cultural persistence; simultaneously, Catholic rituals such as compadrazgo fulfilled some of the emotional, psychological, and ceremonial needs of neophytes coping with Spanish Mexican domination.

NATIVE PEOPLES AND GODPARENTING PATTERNS

Catholic missionaries idealized the spiritual family as consisting of a father, a mother, and a child, an imitation of the biblical family of Mary, Joseph, and the baby Jesus. However, on-the-ground factors such as skewed sex ratios among the *gente de razón* during the early Spanish period (with men outnumbering women), a mission's proximity to a neighboring pueblo, and the demographic instability of a mission Indian community influenced a mission's ability to adhere to the compadrazgo ideal. Baptism records from Mission San Gabriel for the period of 1771 to 1821 reveal a tendency for godparent assignments to be based on the gender of the neophyte. In my sampling for this mission in the years 1771–74, 1780–81, and 1790–91, male Indian neophytes were predominantly assigned *padrinos*. Among female Indian neophytes, godfathers were prominent in the mission's founding period, but ten years later, in 1780–81, *madrinas* made up 95 percent of their sponsors, and they accounted for 80 percent in 1790–91. By the end of the eighteenth century, godfathers formed an almost negligible percentage of sponsors of female Indian neophytes.[37] Franciscan appointments of a same-sex godparent thus paralleled the assignment of sponsors for Native puberty rites, with sponsors in both practices offering cultural instruction in gender roles to adolescents.

During the transition from Spanish to Mexican control, intimate interactions between *gente de razón* and Native peoples continued through godparenting. Mission San Gabriel reflected a shift away from same-sex sponsorship to the Catholic ideal of dual sponsorship, one godmother and one godfather, often a married couple or unmarried individuals related to each other by blood. This trend was most evident for male Gabrielinos, who were assigned two godparents at a rate of 61.5 percent in 1830–31 and 57.5 percent in 1840–41, while females reached rates of

36.5 percent and 40 percent. This contrasts markedly with Gabrielinos of both sexes during the Spanish era, who received two godparents at a peak of only 4.5 percent of the baptisms that I sampled.[38] One explanation for this shift in godparenting at San Gabriel was the demographic stability attained by the *gente de razón* population at the neighboring pueblo of Los Angeles by 1815. The equalizing of sex ratios allowed these men and women to participate in godparenting more equally. By comparison, the closest *gente de razón* neighbors to Mission San Juan Capistrano were a good twenty leagues away at the San Diego presidio. Consequently, missionaries there relied primarily upon Native sponsors for Catholic sacraments, and these converts probably achieved greater success in retaining their culture than those at other southern California missions. These divergent patterns among southern California missions reveal that nuances in godparenting were shaped by a multitude of factors.[39]

At the turn of the nineteenth century, southern California missions experienced a virulent period of disease, death, and infertility. In 1798 Mission San Luís Obispo's hospital was filled with diseased neophytes, while Mission San Buenaventura was quarantined in response to a smallpox threat after the arrival of an infected ship upon the shores of Chumash territory.[40] Two years later Mission San Gabriel Indians complained of devastating afflictions such as side pains and pneumonia. One missionary sadly recorded, "The epidemic continues at San Gabriel. From the beginning of November up to the twentieth of this month there have been one hundred and twenty deaths."[41] Further south, Mission San Juan Capistrano experienced the loss of 115 souls in 1800 alone, and in 1806 the death rate nearly doubled, with 213 perishing. In 1812, missionaries reported to the Spanish government that no natural population increases occurred at San Gabriel, stating that "the number of dead persons is duplicated to that of the born," while at San Diego "deaths exceeded baptisms" between 1810 and 1814, with 118 deaths and 75 baptisms recorded for 1814 alone.[42]

This spike in mortality rates affected sponsorship patterns and led to a rise in deathbed baptisms. Usually these baptisms were of individuals who had incomplete spiritual training. Often these people lived in the outlying *rancherías* and summoned a missionary or catechist to administer last rites and baptism before taking their final breath. Such occasions did not allow for a full ceremony to be performed, as was typical of church baptisms. During the years 1800 and 1801, Mission San Gabriel experienced a significant jump in deathbed baptisms, as evidenced by the fact that the baptisms of one out of every three Indian males were recorded without godparents. This number is startling when compared to sample clusters from the same mission shortly before and after those lethal years: in 1790–91, 13 percent of male baptisms were deathbed, while only 0.5 percent of male baptisms were similarly administered in 1810–11. Among neophyte women, 11.5 percent were baptized in danger of death in 1790–91 and 1 percent in 1810–11, a drastic reduction from a rate of 41 percent baptized on their deathbed in 1800–1801.[43] As the data for the early 1800s reveals, Gabrielino women were more likely to die younger and at a greater rate than Indian men; women were especially vulnerable to complications arising from venereal diseases such as syphilis. Compadrazgo statistics such as those presented here are more than just abstract numbers; they provide texture to the names listed in mission registers and point to the fears that existed within the mission walls and in neighboring villages. Kinship analysis traces the effects of demographic annihilation brought on by ecological and microbial revolutions and the willingness of Native peoples to undergo baptism, hoping to survive by accessing missionary power or out of fear that they would not go on to the afterworld without it.[44]

Following early conquest, as conversions increased, new community roles emerged for Native peoples. Neophyte catechists, interpreters, and godparents represented new Catholic religious and social functions that provided respect and visibility. As catechists instructed unconverted Indians in their native tongues about Catholic doctrine, godparents sponsored fellow Indians for Catholic sacraments. Frequently, precontact indigenous leaders retained prominence after missionization.[45] Fray Fermín Francisco de Lasuén, mission president in the late eighteenth and early nineteenth centuries, commended José María, a chief of the Chumash at Mission Santa Bárbara, for facilitating the Chumash's integration into the missions, stating, "He collaborates in bringing about the subjection, pacification, and education of those who are Christians, and the conversion of the pagans. He is beloved by the whole nation."[46] At San Juan Capistrano one missionary reported that "instruction was given [to neophytes] in their own language by a blind prayer-leader from San Juan Capistrano Mission, a native of this place."[47] Native women as well as men participated as spiritual guides in keeping with traditionally gendered leadership roles.

The existence of Native female clan or village leaders among southern California societies was commonly reported. One Chumash woman, Encarnación, oversaw four channel islands and exercised authority over male captains. As late as 1869, a woman named Pomposa became the *wot,* or village chief, among the Chumash. The daughter of Chief Luís Francisco of the S'apwi *ranchería,* Pomposa ascended to power through her lineage. Among the Cahuilla, some women became *puls,* or medicine women, though it was far more common for men to fill this role. Female shamans existed among the Luiseños, but whether this practice traces from the precontact era or was a response to demographic pressures associated with missionization is unclear. Luiseño informant Albaña revealed that her great aunt was a shaman, probably during the late mission era.[48] Just as demographic or special circumstances elevated Native women to positions of power in their respective societies, historical shifts likewise contoured godparenting patterns in Native communities in Alta California.

Tenuous health conditions and high mortality rates at missions led to the occasional feminization of godparentage during Spanish rule. At Mission San Buenaventura, for example, disease and the resulting deaths led to godmothers representing 63 percent of all sponsors for Indian males during the years 1797–99. This signified a considerable jump from ten years earlier, when godmothers sponsored only 5 percent of male neophyte baptisms.[49] One explanation for this trend was a temporary higher ratio of Chumash women to men over the age of twenty-five among neophytes from the Santa Bárbara Channel Islands. This ran contrary to patterns exhibited for the mission system as a whole, which witnessed greater mortality among young Indian women.[50] In addition to the greater number of women and high disease and mortality rates, traditional respect for female authority among the Chumash also contributed to this spike in female participation in compadrazgo.[51] Finally, these statistical patterns applied to a significant number of Chumash people and represented at least one-fourth of the total missions in Alta California.[52]

Because of the flux that resulted from high disease and mortality rates, revered Native sponsors served as spiritual parents to a large number of their people and increased their arenas of authority from the precontact era. From 1808 to 1815 one *madrina* from the Jautbit *ranchería,* Ana María, served her Mission San Gabriel community by sponsoring 202 neophytes. Sponsoring another 178 converts at the same mission from 1802 to 1821 was Benito José, originally from Yabit.[53] Farther south at Mission San Diego, Indian Thomas Locau was a spiritual guide to more than sixty converts between 1786 and 1804.[54] Finally, María Serafina Hilachap, the wife of Indian captain Francisco Canuch, was godmother to twenty-four San Diego converts in the 1780s and 1790s. As Canuch's wife, this *madrina* achieved a degree of esteem among her people prior to European contact and was among the earliest elites to convert at this locale. María Serafina's visibility as a godmother of Kumeyaay and other Diegueño peoples, even after her husband's death, signifies a continued respect for female authority in community functions after missionization.[55] However, the elevation of ordinary men and women such as Ana María and Thomas Locau to the role of godparent reflected new openings for commoners in mission communities that subverted old class delineations.[56]

Although baptismal records reveal feminization trends in godparenting, marriage sponsorship during the Spanish and Mexican periods appears to have been dominated by men. In the mission registers of southern California, named marital investigation witnesses who contributed information on betrothed couples and listed as ceremony witnesses were exclusively male in my samplings and general review of records. This is consistent with patterns exhibited in colonial Mexico in the eighteenth century, when women experienced marginalization as witnesses in marriage matters, including their own betrothals. Mirroring this trend, at Mission San Juan Capistrano, Pedro Ompsil from the Captivit *ranchería* and two male Baja Indians, Remigio and Saturnino, witnessed dozens of marriages between 1777 and 1800.[57] Native women were noticeably absent as named witnesses in the San Juan Capistrano and San Diego marriage records. The pervasiveness of male witnesses implies that this activity conferred a degree of political authority that only men retained within the mission system.[58] In all likelihood, women attended marriage ceremonies but did not participate as prenuptial investigation witnesses. Even if women provided information relevant to marriage matters, Franciscan recordings of women's presence at marriage ceremonies varied considerably across the missions in southern California.[59]

Distinctions in female and male participation in baptismal and marriage sponsorship in mission-era communities fell along gendered lines similar to those that existed in Native puberty sponsorship, diplomatic marriage negotiations, and child-rearing responsibilities. Because Native women were associated with child rearing while men arranged political negotiations, including marriage alliances, these Native gender roles corresponded with the cultural assumptions of Franciscans and were not targeted for reform.[60] In their adoption of Catholic sponsorship practices, Native peoples participated in the oversight of their intimate relationships, but this oversight resulted in little change with respect to the division of certain community functions by sex. Despite colonial subjugation and intrusion in other areas of the intimate lives of Natives, converts incorporated Catholic cultural attributes that supported their own values. This selective process was a useful strategy for survival. What Alta Californians did not anticipate, however, was the need to incorporate new groups of Indians into existing families, communities, and kinship networks.

CONVERSION FROM BELOW? BAJA INDIANS AS CULTURAL MEDIATORS IN CALIFORNIA

On September 30, 1768, an expedition headed by Captain Fernando de Rivera y Moncada, the Loreto presidio commander, set out for Alta California with a group of "25 soldiers, three mule drivers and a goodly number of Indians [forty-four] on foot," the latter entrusted with the care of the horses and other animals being transported to the new mission stations.[61] The group rested at Mission San Fernando de Velicatá in northern Baja and waited for provisions before resuming their journey on March 24, 1769.[62] Thirty of the forty-four Baja Indians deserted the expedition, deciding to remain near their ancestral homelands. A second overland expedition consisting of Junípero Serra, Don Gaspar de Portolá, settlers, soldiers, and forty-two Baja California Natives set out from San Fernando de Velicatá on May 15, 1769. Out of this group, another thirty Baja Indians deserted before arriving in San Diego on July 1, 1769. In total, twenty-six Baja neophytes eventually migrated northward to Alta California.[63]

Following their arrival in San Diego, a party that included fifteen Baja Indians departed to establish a foothold in Monterey. Remaining in San Diego was another group that included eleven Baja Indians.[64] These Cochimí-speaking assistants, predominantly from Missions San Francisco de Borja Adac, Santa Gertrudis de Cadacamán, and Santa Rosalia de Mulegé, had barely experienced conversion themselves. Missions Santa Gertrudis and San Borja were established in 1751 and 1762, respectively, shortly before the Jesuit expulsion from the Spanish colonies and only a few years before the journey to Alta California.[65] Realizing the sacrifices made by his Native contingent that had left their kin and ancestral homeland, Junípero Serra believed that they should receive rewards for their contributions to the colonizing efforts in Alta California. Serra maintained that "those families and unmarried Indians who, with so much trouble on my part, have been brought from California, to set up this Mission of San Diego, and to work in it . . . should be given, for their encouragement, an allotment of the provisions, however small it may be; or that they should be returned to their former missions."[66] Although some of the Baja Indians ghosted away, a good many chose to remain. It is unclear if they expected to remain in Alta California for life or planned eventually to return to their homeland. Orphan boys such Fabián, Gaspar, José, and Saturnino probably assumed that they would remain in the care of the Franciscan fathers. Families such as José and his wife, Sinforosa; Esteban and his wife, Clara, and daughter, Brígida; Nicolás and his wife, Gertrudis; Antonio and his wife, María Salomé; and José Borgino and his wife, Gertrudis, were convinced that better conditions existed in Alta California than in their homeland of Baja California and were rotated throughout the upper missions, where they sponsored Alta California Natives, occasionally remarried to local Indians, and expanded their families.[67]

The presence of Cochimí-speaking peoples in late eighteenth- and early nineteenth-century southern California was multifaceted. Although these Indians achieved an elevated status superior to that of new converts because of their prior conversion, these Christians also embodied Hispanic cultural mores such as monogamy and consecrated marriage. Baja Indians were utilized to alleviate interethnic tensions and suspicions that arose between the Spanish and indigenous Alta Californians. In a lengthy letter to Viceroy Antonio María de Bucareli y Ursua dated March 13, 1773, Father Junípero Serra outlined his vision for Baja Christians. He wrote, "Two purposes will be accomplished. The first will be that there will be an additional two or three Indians for work. The second, and the one I have most in mind, is that the [Alta Californian] Indians may realize that, till now, they have been much mistaken when they saw all men, and no women, among us; that there are marriages, also among Christians."[68] As Serra indicated, transferring Christianized married couples from Baja California was not only inspired by labor needs in Alta California but was also a symbolic gesture to convince Native Alta Californians of their benevolent intentions.[69]

In the Spanish era, Baja Indians, more commonly referred to as Californios or Yndios Californios, were assigned by Franciscans to sponsor the early baptisms and nuptials of their neophyte neighbors. These Native Christians sustained constant intimate contact with new converts, especially since many chose to remain in Alta California for the remainder of their lives. Ironically, interethnic contact between Baja and Alta California Indians through marriage, sexual intimacy, and godparenting forged new family ties that arguably reinforced a sense of indigeneity. Consequently, Baja Indian reinforcement of Spanish power juxtaposes their assistance in regenerating Native communities, underscoring the contradictory ramifications of colonization.[70]

The acceptance of the Cochimí among Alta Californians is difficult to assess, but there is some indication that Baja Indians were better received than the Spaniards. According to Serra's reporting at Mission San Diego in 1773, "there was quite a commotion among the new Christians, and even among the gentiles; they did not know what to make of these [Baja] families, so great was their delight. Just to see these families was a lesson as useful to them as was their happiness at their arrival."[71] Whether the San Diego neophytes and unconverted peoples of that region were truly "delighted" or "happy" about the presence of Baja Indians or simply curious is unclear. Nevertheless, the presence of a new indigenous group certainly caused a degree of excitement and possibly alleviated some of the concerns among those contemplating baptism.

The potential impact of Baja Christians on conversion efforts was shaped by their communication with Alta Californians. From outward appearances, the diversity of Alta Californians presented a barrier to their acceptance of Baja people. The Chumash alone maintained at least six dialects, while the Cahuilla developed regionally varied dialects depending on their residence in the mountain, pass, or desert areas. The Alta and Baja groups, however, shared some cultural similarities. Like the Alta California women, Cochimí women were responsible for the majority of food production and child rearing and had access to leadership roles. Cochimí men were hunters, and Baja people were generally patrilineal and patrilocal, as were the Alta Californians. Finally, the Cochimí organized themselves in small bands or villages, like Alta Californians, and engaged in ceremonial exchanges and trade with other groups.[72]

In the precontact and postmission eras, large interethnic and intervillage fiestas connected an array of southern California lineage groups and societies to commemorate the naming of a new leader, births, deaths, marriages, and other events. Ceremonies included diverse groups from neighboring and distant regions. Cahuillas, Luiseños, Serranos, and Gabrielinos, for example, ritually distributed shell money, demonstrating the expansive potential of ceremonial exchanges to cross linguistic, cultural, and geographic distances. These exchanges required a basic degree of communication and mutual understanding of ritual protocol. This process and existing cultural commonalities facilitated the incorporation of the Cochimí, who held kinship ties with fellow Yuman speakers, including the Diegueños, Kumeyaay (Kamia or Kamiai), Pa-ipai, and Tipai peoples of lower southern California.[73]

Intimate interactions between Baja and Alta California Indians extended to include their mixed offspring. At least eighteen children of Alta and Baja Indian parentage were baptized in southern California missions.[74] The flow of affection and kinship extended horizontally, as Gabrielinos, Diegueños, Chumash, and Juaneños linked themselves to Baja Indians. In 1781, for example, Nicolás José, a respected leader and local convert at Mission San Gabriel, became a godfather to the son of his own *padrino*, José María Borjino.[75] In 1786 Indian leader Guillermo Paat of Mission San Juan Capistrano sponsored for baptism María Estefania, the daughter of Saturnino and Brigida of Mission San Borja. Unfortunately, María Estefania fell victim to the difficult conditions of mission life and died at the age of seven, further connecting Alta and Baja people in their shared grief.[76]

Despite their status as Christians and their work on behalf of the Franciscans, Baja Indians endured socioeconomic marginalization by the *gente de razón*. Father Lasuén lamented this state of affairs in a letter dated August 3, 1775, to the father guardian of the San Francisco College, Fray Francisco Pangua. In the letter he related the mistreatment of the Baja Indians: "By reason of their love for me, they became exiles from their own land.... [T]o their toil is due if not all, at least the greater part, of what the mission produces and what it needs for its sustenance. Despite all this, they are treated like stepchildren. Not only do they fail to receive the big returns that were promised when they were recruited, but they work much harder and receive less in return than in their own country."[77] As Lasuén pointed out, not only were Baja Christians made material promises that remained unfulfilled, but they were treated worse than the new Christians despite years of service to the missions. Lasuén further remarked, "Their discontent, I think, will not be so great if they can be spared the discovery that there are some missionaries who find it difficult to extend to them the same treatment and to show them the same affection that they give to the natives of their own missions."[78] The Cochimí, having established long-standing relationships with the original founding missionaries of the Baja peninsula, the Jesuits, found the attitudes of their new spiritual guardians in Alta California less accepting.

Just as Baja Indians who had arrived in Alta California in the eighteenth century participated in community formation, so did their countrymen who arrived subsequently, from the 1810s through the 1840s. These Christians originated from Cochimí strongholds such as Missions San Miguel Arcangel, San Joseph, and San Fernando de Velicatá, situated in the northernmost reaches of the peninsula.[79] Regardless of the timing of their arrival, Baja Indians intermarried with Alta Californian Christians, overcoming differences in language and indigenous practices. María del Carmen Chica from Mission San Miguel in Baja married her beloved, Juan María Dominguez, a local Indian from the Qulugat *ranchería*, on May 8, 1825, at San Gabriel. On the eve of the American invasion, Baja Indians continued to forge affective ties with Alta Californians. Widow Natividad of Mission San Miguel remarried Eleuterio, a Chumash man, at Santa Inés on May 3, 1843. Eleuterio's parents, residents of Mission La Purísima Concepción, had died previously, and their mutual loss may have bonded Natividad and Eleuterio, who recognized such events as a common reality of mission life. The two forged a family unit in the hope of creating new loved ones and a brighter future.[80]

Despite their station as spiritual guides to new converts, Baja Indians found adhering to Hispanic ideals such as monogamy to be a challenge. The married Indio Californio Saturnino had an illegitimate son, Simpliciano, in March 1786 by a San Juan Capistrano woman named Catharina Anapua. Catharina may have turned to Saturnino during an emotional time after suffering the loss of her husband. Sadly, Simpliciano survived only seven months, dying in October 1786. Saturnino and his Baja wife, Brigida, baptized their daughter, María Estefana, on December 26, 1785, so Brigida and Catharina were pregnant by Saturnino at the same time. Four years later, a then-widowed Saturnino fathered another child, a daughter named María Petra, by a Juaneño woman. Saturnino must have terminated his relationship with Catharina, as he and María Purificación Albeque were indicated as the legitimate parents of María Petra, suggesting that they were married at the time of her birth. Within an eight-year span, Saturnino lost his son, his wife, and then his daughter María Petra.[81] Saturnino's persistence in marrying and fathering children despite these experiences shows his determination to endure life's sorrows and to continue seeking intimate connections with others.

As mission records suggest, Christianized Indians from Baja participated in Spanish efforts to convert and acculturate Alta Californians. However, their inability to integrate with *gente de razón*, despite years of Christianization, illustrated to new converts that full spiritual and social equality remained unattainable. Their social marginalization probably compelled Baja neophytes to retain their Indian identities because of a greater affinity with Alta Californian practices and their acceptance by local Indians. Baja Christians integrated into local Native networks through intimate relations with local peoples and helped new indigenous kin adapt to changing realities. The precontact flexibility of Native kinship structures allowed for the inclusion and acceptance of the Cochimí, who, along with Alta Californians, found new meanings of family, community, and love.

Kinship in Spanish and Mexican southern California was shaped by both colonizers and the colonized. Despite compadrazgo's potential as a tool of domination and control, Indians were also incentivized to adopt it to further their survival.

Godparentage touched a number of Catholic Californians, Indian and Spanish Mexican alike, and their participation crossed gender, class, ethnic, and racial lines. Compadrazgo was a paradox, a tool of power and love, but always adaptive and enduring. This practice was molded by the hands and hearts of women as well as men, but it remains a mystery in many respects. Nevertheless, the value of kinship as an analytical tool for historical analysis opens up innovative possibilities for exploring the intersection of intimacy, colonial authority, and interethnic relations in other areas of the Spanish borderlands.

NOTES

1. Mission San Juan Capistrano (hereafter MSJC) Marriages I, Film 1290448, no. 26, Latter-day Saints Los Angeles Family History Library, West Los Angeles, California (hereafter LAFHL); Marie E. Northrop, *Spanish-Mexican Families of Early California: Los Pobladores de la Reina de los Angeles* (Burbank: Southern California Genealogical Society, 2004), 3: 1. Northrop lists María Bernarda's Native name as Chujila.

2. MSJC Baptisms, 1777–1938, Film 1290447, no. 264, LAFHL.

3. Northrop, *Spanish-Mexican Families*, 3: 1.

4. Godparents Database, The Huntington Library, Early California Population Project, 2006 (hereafter ECPP).

5. The Spanish period is 1769–1821, the Mexican 1822–48, and the American after 1848.

6. Northrop, *Spanish-Mexican Families*, 3: 2.

7. Ibid., 23.

8. Maynard J. Geiger, O.F.M., ed. and trans., *Fray Antonio Ripoll's Description of the Chumash Revolt at Santa Barbara in 1824* (Santa Barbara, CA: Mission Santa Barbara, 1980), 11. For José Valentin Cota, great-nephew of Antonio Cota, see Northrop, *Spanish-Mexican Families*, 3:19, 31, 270. See also Santa Bárbara Presidio Marriages Database no. 99, ECPP. For Pablo Antonio Cota's Chumash godchildren, see Mission San Buenaventura (hereafter MSBV) Baptisms, 1782–1873, Film 913170, esp. nos. 2, 7, 33–34, 43, 64, 88, 107, 190, 194, 203, 212, 242, and 247, LAFHL.

9. I define intimacy as sexuality, marriage, friendship, love, or other relationships that generate familiarity and knowledge among rival groups of people. See, for example, Ann Laura Stoler, *Carnal Knowledge and Imperial Power: Race and the Intimate in Colonial Rule* (Berkeley: University of California Press, 2002); Sylvia Van Kirk, *Many Tender Ties: Women in Fur-Trade Society, 1670–1870* (Norman: University of Oklahoma Press, 1980); Jacqueline Peterson and Jennifer S. H. Brown, eds., *The New Peoples: Being and Becoming Métis in North America* (Winnipeg: University of Manitoba Press, 1985); and Alberto L. Hurtado, *Intimate Frontiers: Sex, Gender, and Culture in Old California* (Albuquerque: University of New Mexico Press, 1999).

10. Colonial scholars debate whether the voices of colonized or subaltern peoples are recoverable because of the influence of colonialism. See Gayatri Spivak, "Can the Subaltern Speak?" in *Marxism and the Interpretation of Culture*, ed. Cary Nelson and Lawrence Grossberg (Urbana: University of Illinois Press, 1988). For works presenting Native perspectives in Alta California, see Steven W. Hackel, "The Staff of Leadership: Indian Authority in the Missions of Alta California," *William and Mary Quarterly* 54, no. 2 (April 1997): 347–76; James A. Sandos, "Christianization among the Chumash: An Ethnohistoric Perspective," *American Indian Quarterly* 15, no. 1 (Winter 1991): 65–89; and George Harwood Phillips, *Chiefs and Challengers: Indian Resistance and Cooperation in Southern California* (Berkeley: University of California Press, 1975).

11. The first Spanish conquistadors manipulated intertribal rivalries and enlisted the aid of indigenous allies. In northern New Spain missionaries relied upon Christianized Tlaxcalans and Indians from central Mexico to target new groups for conversion. See Bernal Díaz del Castillo, *The Conquest of New Spain*, trans. J.M. Cohen (London: Penguin Books, 1963), 87; and Edward H. Spicer, *Cycles of Conquest: The Impact of Spain, Mexico, and the United States on the Indians of the Southwest, 1533–1960* (Tucson: University of Arizona Press, 1962), 289.

12. For compadrazgo in Iberian and American contexts, see Sidney W. Mintz and Eric R. Wolf, "An Analysis of Ritual Co-Parenthood (Compadrazgo)," in *Marriage, Family, and Residence*, ed. Paul Bohannan and John Middleton (Garden City, NY: Natural History Press, 1968), esp. 334; Manuel L. Carlos and Lois Sellers, "Family, Kinship Structure, and Modernization in Latin America," *Latin American Research Review* 7, no. 2 (Summer 1972): 95–124; Stephen Gudeman, "The Compadrazgo as a Reflection of the Natural and Spiritual Person," *Proceedings of the Royal Anthropological Institute of Great Britain and Ireland*, no. 1971 (1971): 45–71; Ramón A. Gutiérrez, *When Jesus Came, the Corn Mothers Went Away: Marriage, Sexuality, and Power in New Mexico, 1500–1846* (Stanford, CA: Stanford University Press, 1991); and James F. Brooks, *Captives and Cousins: Slavery, Kinship, and Community in the Southwest Borderlands* (Chapel Hill: University of North Carolina Press, 2002).

13. For Juaneño marriages, see Alfred B. Kroeber, *Handbook of the Indians of California* (Berkeley: California Book Co., 1953), 646. For Luiseño practices, see ibid., 688. For southern California marriages in general, see ibid., 839. For Gabrielino marriages, see William McCawley, *The First Angelinos: The Gabrielino Indians of Los Angeles* (Banning and Novato, CA: Malki Museum Press and Ballena Press, 1996), 154–55. For Serrano courtship and marriage, see Ruth Fulton Benedict, "A Brief Sketch of Serrano Culture," *American Anthropologist* 26, no. 3 (July–September 1924): 371; Maynard Geiger et al., "Questionnaire of the Spanish Government in 1812 concerning the Native Culture of the California Mission Indians," *The Americas* 5, no. 4 (April 1949): 488 (hereafter "Questionnaire"); and Maynard Geiger and José Ma. de Zalvidea, "Reply of Mission San Gabriel to the Questionnaire of the Spanish Government in 1812 concerning the Native Culture of the California Mission Indians," *The Americas* 12, no. 1 (July 1955): 80 (hereafter "Reply").

14. For patrilineal inheritance among the Acâgchemem (Juaneños), see Lisbeth Haas, *Conquests and Historical Identities, 1769–1936* (Berkeley: University of California Press, 1995), 17. For Cahuilla and patrilineal descent, see Kroeber, *Handbook*, 705. For Diegueño residency and lineage practices, see ibid., 719. For Serrano descent, residency, and marriage, see Benedict, "A Brief Sketch," 371–72; and Katharine Luomala, "Flexibility in Sib Affiliation among the Diegueno," *Ethnology* 2, no. 3 (July 1963): 285, 291. For Chumash residency and class differences, see John R. Johnson, "Secrets of Chumash Social Life," originally printed in *Bulletin of the Santa Barbara Museum of Natural History* 188 (November/December 1996): 1, and reprinted on the Santa Barbara Museum of Natural History website, www.sbnature.org/crc/330.html (accessed November 7, 2009).

15. For levirate practices and sororal polygyny, see Kroeber, *Handbook*, 839. For the Gabrielino emphasis on procreation during marriage, see McCawley, *First Angelinos*, 155. For Serrano polygyny in cases of infertility, see Benedict, "A Brief Sketch," 371.

16. For polygyny and class, see Lowell John Bean, *Mukat's People: The Cahuilla Indians of Southern California* (Berkeley: University of California Press, 1972), 80. See also Claude N. Warren, "The Many Wives of Pedro Yanunali," *Journal of California Anthropology* 4, no. 2 (Winter 1977): 245–47; McCawley, *First Angelinos*, 92, 153; and Kroeber, *Handbook*, 834.

17. For polygyny debates among anthropologists, see Douglas R. White and Michael L. Burton, "Causes of Polygyny: Ecology, Economy, Kinship, and Warfare," *American Anthropologist* 90, no. 4 (December 1988): 882. According to the authors, fraternal interest groups and class differentiation contributed to polygyny. These existed among the Chumash and Gabrielino who practiced polygyny. See also Kroeber, *Handbook*, 556, 834.

18. Bean, *Mukat's People,* 94–96; Luomala, "Flexibility," 286, 296, 299. For Serrano endogamy and the Coyote and Wildcat clans, see Kroeber, *Handbook,* 837; and Benedict, "A Brief Sketch," 368–69, 371–72. I am using the term *clan* to indicate a lineage or kin group.

19. Luomala, "Flexibility," 288–96, 298.

20. Virginia M. Bouvier, *Women and the Conquest of California, 1542–1840: Codes of Silence* (Tucson: University of Arizona Press, 2001), 33–34; and Steven W. Hackel, *Children of Coyote, Missionaries of Saint Francis: Indian-Spanish Relations in Colonial California, 1769–1850* (Chapel Hill: University of North Carolina Press, 2005), 134–35.

21. Haas, *Conquests and Historical Identities,* 21.

22. William M. Mason, *Early Dominguez Families and Settlement of the Rancho San Pedro,* ed. Judson A. Grenier (Carson: California State University, Dominguez Hills and the Carson Companies, 1991), 10.

23. In my sampling of southern California mission records, I have not come across any Indians named as the only godparents for a *gente de razón* child. For interethnic and Indian godparentage at San Juan Capistrano, see Haas, *Conquests and Historical Identities,* 21, 24.

24. For vertical and horizontal flow in compadrazgo relationships, see Mintz and Wolf, "An Analysis of Ritual Co-Parenthood," 329. For Iberian and Spanish colonial compadrazgo, see George M. Foster, "Cofradía and Compadrazgo in Spain and Spanish America," *Southwestern Journal of Anthropology* 9, no. 1 (Spring 1953): 9.

25. Foster, "Cofradía and Compadrazgo," 3.

26. William M. Mason, *The Census of 1790: A Demographic History of Colonial California,* Ballena Press Anthropological Paper 45 (Menlo Park, CA: Ballena Press, 1998), 60.

27. Junípero Serra, *The Writings of Junípero Serra,* ed. Antonine Tibesar, O.F.M., 4 vols. (Washington, DC: Academy of American Franciscan History, 1955–56), 2: 71–73.

28. Ibid., 2: 307.

29. Edward D. Castillo, "Gender Status Decline, Resistance, and Accommodation among Female Neophytes in the Missions of California: A San Gabriel Case Study," *American Indian Culture and Research Journal* 18, no. l (1994): 68. For Acâgchemem (Juaneños) seeking baptism to acquire *ayelkwi,* see Haas, *Conquests and Historical Identities,* 20.

30. Constance Goddard DuBois, "The Religion of the Luiseño Indians of Southern California," *University Publications in American Archaeology and Ethnology* 8, no. 3 (1908): 74, 79–80. For Gabrielino practices, see Kroeber, *Handbook,* 856, 858; McCawley, *First Angelinos,* 151–52. For Cahuilla, see Ruby Modesto and Guy Mount, *Not for Innocent Ears: Spiritual Traditions of a Desert Cahuilla Medicine Woman* (Arcata: Sweetlight Books, 1980), 40. Also, A. L. Kroeber, "Ethnography of the Cahuilla Indians," University of California Publications in American Archaeology and Ethnology 8, no. 2 (1908): 66.

31. For girls' adolescence ceremonies in southern California, see Kroeber, *Handbook,* 861–62, 864–65. For Cahuilla examples, see Modesto and Mount, *Not for Innocent Ears,* 40.

32. For Chumash naming practices, see Fernando Librado Kitsepawit, *The Eye of the Flute: Chumash Traditional History and Ritual as Told by Fernando Librado Kitsepawit to John P. Harrington,* 2nd ed., ed. Travis Hudson et al. (Banning, CA: Malki Museum Press, 1981), 18–19. For Gabrielino practices, see McCawley, *First Gabrielinos,* 150. See also Thomas C. Blackburn, "Ceremonial Integration and Social Interaction in Aboriginal California," in *Native Californians: A Theoretical Retrospective,* ed. Lowell J. Bean and Thomas C. Blackburn (Socorro, NM: Ballena Press, 1976), 229, 231–33, 240–43.

33. Geiger, "Questionnaire," 487, 489.

34. See Serra, *Writings;* Fermín Francisco de Lasuén, *The Writings of Fermín Francisco de Lasuén,* 2 vols., trans. Finbar Kinneally (Washington, DC: Academy of American Franciscan History,

1965); Gerónimo Boscana, *Chinigchinich: A Revised and Annotated Version of Alfred Robinson's Translation of Father Gerónimo Boscana's Historical Account of the Belief, Usages, Customs and Extravagancies of the Indians of this Mission of San Juan Capistrano Called the Acagchemem Tribe*, annotated by John P. Harrington (Banning, CA: Malki Museum Press, 1978); Juan Cortés, *The Doctrina and Confesionario of Juan Cortés*, ed. and trans. Harry Kelsey (Altadena, CA: Howling Coyote Press, 1979); Geiger, *Fray Antonio Ripoll's Description*; José Señán, "The Ventureño Confesionario of José Señán, O.F.M.," ed. Madison S. Beeler, *University of California Publications in Linguistics* 47 (Berkeley: University of California Press, 1967); Pablo Tac, *Indian Life and Customs at Mission San Luis Rey*, ed. and trans. Minna and Gordon Hewes (San Luis Rey, CA: Old Mission, 1958); Fernando Librado, *Breath of the Sun: Life in Early California as Told by a Chumash Indian, Fernando Librado to John P. Harrington*, ed. Travis Hudson (Banning and Ventura, CA: Malki Museum Press and Ventura County Historical Society, 1979); Librado, *Eye of the Flute*.

35. Mission San Gabriel Arcangel (hereafter MSG), Baptisms 1771–1819, Film 2643, nos. 4988–94, LAFHL. For Lucia, probably another daughter of Luisa and Lucio, see no. 4671, ibid.; and MSG Baptisms Database, ECPP. For *madrina* María Manuela, see MSG Baptisms Database, no. 1367, and Marriage Database, no. 690, ibid.

36. On military raids, see Sherburne F. Cook, *The Conflict Between the California Indian and White Civilization* (Berkeley: University of California Press, 1976), 200–201.

37. MSG, Baptisms 1771–1819, Film 2643, LAFHL; MSG Baptisms Database, ECPP. Percentages are based upon statistics compiled for the Spanish period covering 1771–74, 1780–81, 1790–91, 1800–1801, and 1810–11. Samples were also compiled for the late Spanish and Mexican period, covering 1820–21, 1830–31, and 1840–41.

38. For dual godparent assignments, see MSG, Baptisms 1771–1819 and 1820–1908, Films 2643 and 2644, respectively, LAFHL; and MSG Baptisms Database, ECPP.

39. For *gente de razón* sex ratios in Los Angeles, see Mason, *Census of 1790*, 76. According to Mason, the ratio of adult *gente de razón* men to women stabilized between 1810 and 1815. For distances between missions, pueblos, and presidios, see Lasuén, *Writings*, 2: 23.

40. Lasuén, *Writings*, 2: 87, Lasuén letter to Don Diego de Borica, June 20, 1798.

41. Ibid., 2: 178, Lasuén letter to Fray José Gasol, December 29, 1800. See also letters dated 1798 referencing sickness at Missions San Gabriel and San Luís Obispo in ibid., 2: 78, 139.

42. For the San Juan Capistrano deaths, see Haas, *Conquests and Historical Identities*, 22–23. For missionary responses to conditions at Mission San Gabriel, see Geiger and Zalvidea, "Reply," 81. The English translation is mine. For conditions in San Diego, see Geiger, "Questionnaire," 488.

43. MSG, Baptisms 1771–1819, Film 2643, LAFHL; MSG Baptisms Database, ECPP.

44. For the impact of ecological and microbial revolutions on Native responses to colonization, see Hackel, *Children of Coyote*, chapter 3; and David Igler, "Diseased Goods: Global Exchanges in the Eastern Pacific Basin, 1770–1850," *American Historical Review* 109, no. 3 (June 2004): 693–719. For female mortality rates and mission sex ratios, see Cook, *Conflict*, 29.

45. For Native leaders seeking baptism at Mission San Juan Capistrano, see Haas, *Conquests and Historical Identities*, 20.

46. Lasuén, *Writings*, 2: 18, Lasuén letter to Marqués de Branciforte, April 25, 1797.

47. Ibid., 2: 87, Lasuén letter to Don Diego de Borica, June 20, 1798.

48. For Chumash female leaders, see Librado, *Eye of the Flute*, 15, 100 n. 16, and 101 n. 30. For Cahuilla female leadership, see Modesto and Mount, *Not for Innocent Ears*, 1, 26; for Luiseños, see DuBois, see "Religion," 111; and for Juaneños, see Haas, *Conquests and Historical Identities*, 17–18.

49. MSBV Baptisms, 1782–1873, Film 913170, LAFHL.

50. Cook, *Conflict*, 29. Per Robert Jackson, the ratio of females to males increased from 1:1.05 in 1798 to 1:0.91 in 1810. After 1820 the population of women and children declined at a faster rate than

that of men, and he attributes most deaths to disease. See Robert H. Jackson, "The Population of the Santa Barbara Channel Missions (Alta California), 1813–1832," *Journal of California and Great Basin Anthropology* 12, no. 2 (July 1990): 270–71, esp. table 2. For missionization's impact upon Gabrielino women, see Castillo, "Gender Status Decline," 67–93.

51. For matrilocal residency, sex ratios, and mortality among Chumash islanders, see John R. Johnson, *An Ethnohistoric Study of the Island Chumash* (M.A. thesis, University of California, Santa Barbara, 1982), 166. For class differences in residency practices, see Johnson, "Secrets of Chumash Social Life," 1. Per Johnson, elite chiefs were patrilocal, but the majority of Chumash were matrilocal.

52. Campbell Grant, "Chumash: Introduction," in *Handbook of North American Indians*, ed. Robert F. Heizer (Washington, DC: Smithsonian Institution, 1978), 505–6. The five Chumash missions were San Luís Obispo, Santa Bárbara, San Buenaventura, Santa Inés, and La Purísima Concepción.

53. MSG, Godparents and Baptisms Databases, ECPP. See baptisms nos. 00583 and 02113 for Benito José and Ana María, respectively.

54. See Mission San Diego (hereafter MSD), Godparents Database, ECPP.

55. See various baptisms from September 10, 1786, to July 27, 1799, listing *madrina* María Serafina (Hilachap), MSD Godparents database, ECPP. For Francisco Canuch (Januch) and María Serafina's marriage, see MSD Marriages Database, no. 21, ibid.

56. Hackel, "Staff of Leadership," 347–76.

57. MSJC Marriages, 1777–1915, Reel 1290448, Item 2, LAFHL. For Saturnino, marriage no. 1 (January 23, 1777). For Remigio, marriage no. 135. For Pedro Ompsil, see entry no. 28 (February 9, 1777), MSJC Baptisms, 1777–1938, Reel 1290447, LAFHL.

58. MSD baptisms for 1777, 1780, and 1790–91 and marriages for November 10, 1775–77, 1780–81, 1790–91, and 1800, MSD Baptisms and Marriages Database, ECPP, 2006. San Diego sacramental records indicate that Spanish soldiers figured prominently as godfathers and marriage witnesses until approximately 1777, when neophytes increasingly replaced them as sponsors. For the declining value of women's testimony in marriage matters, see Patricia Seed, "Marriage Promises and the Value of a Woman's Testimony in Colonial Mexico," *Signs* 13, no. 2 (Winter 1988): 273. The witnessing of marriages indicated Indian leadership and political authority. See Hackel, "The Staff of Leadership," 368 n. 95.

59. Johnson, *Ethnohistoric Study*, 118–19.

60. Castillo, "Gender Status Decline," 67–93.

61. Serra, *Writings*, 1: 41; Rose Marie Beebe and Robert M. Senkewicz, eds., *Lands of Promise and Despair: Chronicles of Early California, 1535–1846* (Santa Clara, CA: Heyday Books, 2001), 114.

62. Serra, *Writings*, 1: 61.

63. Ibid., 1:39–123; and Beebe and Senkewicz, eds., *Lands of Promise and Despair*, 115.

64. Beebe and Senkewicz, eds., *Lands of Promise and Despair*, 115.

65. Harry W. Crosby, *Antigua California: Mission and Colony on the Peninsular Frontier, 1697–1768* (Albuquerque: University of New Mexico Press, 1994), 179, table 7.1. For comparisons of the Cochimí, Guaycura, and Pericú in Baja and their receptivity to conversion, see ibid., 93, 101–2, 114–16, and 181.

66. Serra, *Writings*, 1: 283–85.

67. For the seven families and four orphans who accompanied the Franciscans to Alta California, see Lasuén, *Writings*, 1: 33, "Conveyance of San Borja Mission," June 15, 1773. Missions San Gabriel and San Juan Capistrano, established in 1771 and 1776, respectively, had a large number of Baja Indians, although Missions San Buenaventura and Santa Bárbara, which were established later, did not.

68. Serra, *Writings*, 1: 311.

69. Spicer, *Cycles of Conquest*, 289.

70. On Indian participation in assimilationist enterprises, see Cathleen D. Cahill's chapter in this volume.

71. Serra, *Writings*, 1: 311.

72. For Chumash dialects, see Kathryn A. Klar Mealiffe, "The Language of the Chumash Islanders," appendix in Johnson, *Ethnohistoric Study*, 1–2. For Cahuilla, see Kroeber, *Handbook*, 693–94. For Cochimí culture, see Bárbara O. Reyes, *Private Women, Public Lives: Gender and the Missions of the Californias* (Austin: University of Texas Press, 2009), 20–25, 44.

73. For the ceremonial complex in Alta California, see Blackburn, "Ceremonial Integration," 229, 231–33, and 240–43. For the Cochimí relation to other Yuman-speaking people, see Kroeber, *Handbook*, 709–10; and Reyes, *Private Women, Public Lives*, 20–25, 44.

74. Baptisms Database, ECPP; MSJC Baptisms, 1777–1938, Film 1290447; MSG Baptisms I, 1771–1819, Film 2643; MSG Baptisms II, 1820–1908, Film 2644; and MSD, Extracts of church records, 1775–1888, Film 944282 Item 11, LAFHL.

75. Steven W. Hackel, "Sources of Rebellion: Indian Testimony and the Mission San Gabriel Uprising of 1785," *Ethnohistory* 50, no. 4 (Autumn 2003): 652. Nicolás José sponsored Basilio de Jesus, baptized April 10, 1781, the child of José María Borjino and Gertrudis María of Mission San Borja in Antigua California. See MSG Baptisms Film 2643, no. 582, LAFHL.

76. MSJC Baptisms, Film 1290447, no. 668, LAFHL; MSJC Baptisms Database, ECPP. See also Mintz and Wolf, "Analysis of Ritual Co-Parenthood," 329.

77. Lasuén, *Writings*, 1: 49.

78. Ibid., 1: 50.

79. Serra, *Writings*, 1: 291–93.

80. For the marriage of María del Carmen Chica and Juan María Dominguez, see MSG Marriages Database, no. 1568, ECPP. For Natividad and Eleuterio's marriage, see La Purísima Concepción Marriages Database, no. 1087, ibid.

81. For Simpliciano's baptism and parentage, see MSJC Baptisms Database, no. 694, ECPP. Brigida was Saturnino's wife. For María Serafina, see baptism no. 668, ibid. For María Petra's legitimacy and parentage, see baptism no. 964, ibid. For Brigida's death, see MSJC Deaths Database, no. 159, ECPP.

11

Territorial Bonds

Indenture and Affection in Intercultural Arizona, 1864–1894

Katrina Jagodinsky

Borderlands families have never had it easy, and the second half of the nineteenth century was no exception. In an act of love and power, American and Hispano families reached out to Indian women and children to ease their borderlands burdens. Lieutenant Colonel King S. Woolsey left his central Arizona ranch in 1864 to kill Apaches and claim land; he returned from his campaign with a ten-year-old Yaqui girl as his personal consort. Lucía Martínez bore the Colonel's children and harassment until his death in 1879. The territorial patriarch left his illegitimate children no inheritance, but he had indentured them, ironically making them eligible for $1,000 from his estate. Woolsey's compatriot Jack Swilling had brandished a gun to uphold slavery, claim Western lands, and make "good Indians," but when his Mexican, American, and O'odham friends staged the Camp Grant Massacre in the spring of 1871, he stayed home with his Mexican wife, four American children, and four Apache wards. Swilling indentured one of these Indian minors, but he most likely did so to protect him from his neighbors' anti-Apache sentiments. Josefína and Miguel Gonzales Roca indentured three-year-old Teutílla in 1869. Of elite families in Mexico and Chile, the Rocas had been nursed and cared for by *criadas*—mestizo servants—and they wanted the same for their children. When they indentured the Apache toddler, they both continued a longtime Hispanic tradition of dependence upon racially inferior domestics and secured a future of white privilege for their new family.

This chapter focuses on intercultural households to examine linkages between bonds of indenture and ties of affection, between exploitative labor and love, and between questionable paternity and patronage. Though Woolsey, Swilling, and Roca have been chronicled as Arizona's territorial fathers, the profiles offered here emphasize their participation in the indenture system and their roles as heads of hierarchical households. By constructing histories from the evidence that others have ignored or obscured, this chapter addresses not only territorial Arizonans' intimate dependence on racial others but also the legacies of those intimacies in the state's historiography.

Between 1864, when Arizonans held their first legislative session, and 1894, when Phoenix Indian School administrators initiated a southwestern model of the "outing system," citizens used the indenture of American Indian children to strengthen their tenuous claims to the contested borderland territory. Legislators regulated domestic sites through the Howell Code, the body of law passed in 1864 that governed intercultural households. The Howell Code privileged white patriarchs, though not all Arizona heads of household claimed their racial and sexual privileges equally. Home to Mexicans, Europeans, Americans, Confederates, free blacks, Chinese, and Indians, the territory fostered racial ambiguities that senators sought to clarify in the Howell Code.[1] Citizens' dependence on nonwhite labor complicated official efforts to discourage intercultural intimacies. Working together often meant living together, which usually led people to share stories and secrets, germs and jokes. The three households analyzed here demonstrate that where there was exploitation, there was also affection—sometimes mutual, sometimes not—and that the indenture of minor Indians was merely one phase in a long history of labor and intimacy in the Southwest.[2]

Arizona's territorial senators did not create a coercive Indian labor market; rather, they formalized what had been an extralegal trade that featured interracial intimacies. The southwestern slave market connected Comanches and Seris, Utes and Pueblos, Mormons and Catholics; it predated the Arizona legislature and continued nearly into the twentieth century. Americans, Indians, and Mexicans who participated in this market targeted women and children for their reproductive and acculturative capacities, even as they murdered captives' male relatives in the struggle for frontier dominance. Slavers took advantage of racial ambiguity and sold Mexicans as Indians, redeemed Indians as white Mexicans, and tattooed Indianness onto white slaves. Though tribes often enslaved enemy tribal members, they sometimes incorporated them into their own families, linking exploitative labor and fictive kinship, as shown in Joaquín Rivaya-Martínez's study of Comanche enslavement in this volume. Hispanos did the same, drawing indigenous slaves into a complex caste system where they intermarried with free laborers and served elites as *criados*. As long as this system remained extralegal, American officials struggled to deter intercultural bonds that often formed as a result of the slave trade. Such widespread *mestizaje* made it difficult to distinguish citizen from subject, patriarch from peon, respectable from rogue. In an unregulated market, territorial Arizonans bought laborers for companionship as well as for apprenticeship; they bought children to replace those who had died;

they bought their way into an intercultural network that blurred the bonds of affection and indenture.[3]

In July of 1864, Lucía Martínez escaped Apache slavers. Just ten years old, the Yaqui girl outwitted her captors and began the more than two-hundred-mile trek from the central Arizona highlands to her southern Sonora home. Only a few miles into her escape, however, Lucía encountered Alabama-native Lieutenant Colonel King Woolsey leading an anti-Apache expedition along the Black River. The Colonel claimed the child for himself and took her back to his ranch, Agua Fria, near the territorial capital of Prescott. When he returned from his violent campaign, Woolsey's neighbors elected him to serve in the territory's first legislative session.[4]

On November 10, 1864, King Woolsey and his fellow senators approved a nearly five-hundred-page legal code addressing the civil and criminal conduct of all men and women, minors and adults, citizens and subjects. Known as the Howell Code, it defined deviant and acceptable behaviors and put into place the rules that made public the private details of territorial Arizonans' lives. The federal government had withheld citizenship status from Native peoples, but Woolsey and his peers constructed a broad range of laws to circumscribe the daily interactions between indigenous and newcomer westerners. The Howell Code codified racial and gender hierarchies that were widely contested throughout the ethnically diverse and demographically imbalanced territory, so that Arizona might become recognizable as a modern state ruled by respectable white men. When Woolsey signed the Howell Code, he affirmed his claims to young Lucía Martínez's body and labor.[5]

William T. Howell, appointed territorial Arizona justice, drafted a set of laws in anticipation of the 1863 Organic Act making the region a United States territory. Howell found the laws of California suitable to the social customs and racial hierarchies endorsed by Arizona's Anglo elites, so he adopted most of the neighboring state's legal code. Its peonage and indenture laws offered little protection to non-Anglos, but California law favored white women's property and marital rights. Howell continued the trend away from coverture but offered women few political rights, and overall the code upheld white male supremacy in the application of criminal and civil law, particularly where women's bodies were concerned.[6]

Arizona legislators, like many of their western and southern counterparts, fixed the age of sexual consent for all females at ten years, defining girls as potentially sexually active prior to menarche, but they set girls' marriageable age at sixteen. Females over ten years old who withheld consent had to prove sexual assault through evidence of physical injury, could not deny their husbands sexual access, and faced a prison term of at least five years if they terminated a pregnancy.[7] Between 1864 and 1871, the span of years Lucía spent under Woolsey's custody, nonwhite Arizonans could not testify in criminal cases against white men, rendering nonwhite sexual assault victims silent if their attackers were white. After 1871, legislators granted all residents the right to testify in criminal trials, though no indigenous woman testified against a white defendant until 1913 and nonwhites remained barred from testimony in civil trials until 1912.[8]

Arizona's pioneer fathers continued to have sex on their mind when they passed a provision banning mixed-race marriages.[9] Though Indians, Mexicans, and Anglos lived in close proximity, legislators ensured that sexual relations among these groups would remain illicit. Indigenous women could not use the courts to uphold the spousal rights that American women enjoyed, and Mexican women depended upon judges' discretion to enjoy white marital privileges since they might easily be seen as Indian.[10] Importantly, the miscegenation law did not make interracial intercourse criminal: the code simply put the burden of illegitimate progeny on the mother, deviating from the common-law presumption of patrilineality. This seemingly race-neutral move, very familiar to legislators from slaveholding families, kept property in the hands of white fathers who practiced procreative sex with racially ambiguous and socially vulnerable women.[11]

Legislators' concerns regarding miscegenation in the territory stemmed from their exposure to *mestizaje* under the intertribal slave trade in the southwestern borderlands.[12] The first territorial governor recognized that citizens' dependence upon Indian labor could foster interracial promiscuity. In his 1864 address to the legislature, Governor John Noble Goodwin advised Woolsey and other politicians to regulate such relations as he simultaneously linked Indian servitude to the ongoing Apache wars. "In the fierce conflicts for life waged . . . with the . . . Apaches, some young persons have been captured, and . . . placed in families as servants. . . . I can suggest no better enactment . . . than a system of apprenticeship similar to that existing in most of the states."[13] The territorial indenture system, then, constituted a pivotal shift between an extralegal slave trade and institutionalized unfree labor while also serving to discourage interracial bonds of affection. As the Woolsey, Swilling, and Roca households illustrate, however, not all Arizonans used indenture to distance themselves from minor Indians or to discontinue pre-American labor systems.[14]

Elected officials wrote a provision entitled "Of the Support of Minor Indians" in response to Governor Goodwin's concern for young Apaches. The law declared that "any person into whose care or custody shall come any captive Indian child of a hostile tribe, or any minor Indian child of other than hostile tribes, shall, within twenty days thereafter, produce such child before the judge of probate or a justice of the peace . . . and may apply to . . . have such Indian child bound to him until he shall arrive at the age of twenty-one years; and if a female, at the age of eighteen years."[15] The "Minor Indian" law did little to protect the welfare of indigent children, as did other western laws regulating minors, indenture, and guardianship. Just a year after the Emancipation Proclamation had freed black slaves and the California legislature had dismantled its own Native indenture system, Arizona lawmakers institutionalized the region's tribal slave trade by legalizing the abduction and forced labor of minor Native Americans. Between 1864 and 1873, legislators barred citizens from adopting Indian children and required that heads of households with Indian minors in their custody apply for a bond of indenture within twenty days of taking custody. When they wrote an adoption law in 1873, the legislature failed to mention indigenous children at all and upheld the "Minor Indian" law for fourteen more years, suggesting that they believed white minors should be adopted while Native wards should be indentured. The law granted local justices of the peace the authority to place Indian children in non-Indian households until the age of majority (eighteen for females and twenty-one for males) in exchange for good treatment, food, and clothing. Despite the governor's suggestion to borrow apprenticeship models from other states, the code did not make basic education or occupational training a component of indenture, leaving it to household heads to determine the most suitable work for young Native Americans.[16]

That Arizona citizens were at war with the indigenous population during the indenture period of 1864 to 1887 explains why Indian children were so widely available to settler-colonists and indicates that the statute regarding minor Indians was part of an extermination campaign waged against Native families. Woolsey captured Lucía while hunting Native Americans, Swilling described his orphans as children of "a tribe hostile to the Territory," and the Rocas called Teutílla a "captive Apache," making the children suitable subjects for servitude and linking indenture to anti-Indian sentiments. Geronimo's 1886 surrender marked an official end to the Indian wars in the territory, and when the 1887 Allotment Act held out the promise of citizenship to Native people, the territorial legislature repealed the indenture clause. Victoria Smith's study shows, however, that citizen families continued to capture indigenous children after 1887 without formally adopting them, indicating a continued interest in nonwhite child labor after the legislative assembly proscribed the practice.[17]

Arizonans could also use the Howell Code's statute on minor Indians to exploit Native women's reproductive and productive labor and continue an antebellum legacy of white men's sexual access to laboring women.[18] Reproductive labor included domestic management of the household: food preparation, child care, material maintenance, and emotional support.[19] Some masters also demanded sexual services. Having silenced indigenous voices through the witness exclusion provision and having legally defined Indian girls over ten as sexually available, the Colonel and his colleagues ensured that household heads enjoyed relatively free access to their servants' bodies with no concern for the support of illegitimate and mixed-race descendants.[20] The law upheld white men's demands on subordinates' bodies and then required women to bear children that would likely become servants rather than heirs.

Perhaps because he had a hand in drafting the Howell Code, King S. Woolsey applied most exactingly the aspects of the law that allowed him to exploit Lucía Martínez and their daughters' labors. The westering man made his wealth farming on Akimel O'odham lands, convinced his neighbors of his Union loyalties by supplying the U.S. military with foodstuffs during the Civil War, and earned his rank of lieutenant colonel by murdering Native Americans. He served as senator on and off between 1864 and 1877 before losing an 1878 bid to become a territorial delegate to Congress. Known to his servants as "Mr. King" and to his admirers as "the Colonel" or "the Honorable Mr. Woolsey," the southern frontiersman remains fondly remembered among Arizona history enthusiasts.[21]

From the age of ten to eighteen, Lucía Martínez served her master and his guests, who described Woolsey's ranch, Agua Fria, as a "little frontier establishment" that was organized according to the plantation model that Woolsey imported from the South. Woolsey's staff cook described the racialized table he and Lucía prepared each day: "First, there's the black men, i.e., Mexicans, the herders; then there's the white men, i.e. the carpenters, masons, etc.; then there's Mr. King, i.e. Woolsey and his friends; and last, I and . . . the Indian girl, an Apache captive . . . , and the dogs."[22]

Bound to serve the needs of male and female guests legally and socially designated as her racial superiors, Lucía Martínez found herself in the midst of the southwestern peonage market despite her escape from the Apaches. The Colonel's household bore strong resemblance to a southern plantation in a borderlands context, and he might have had no qualms about enjoying both the sexual and servile labors he expected of his Yaqui servant if he had grown up among men who fathered slaves.[23] Indeed, the laws he signed into place defined Lucía as sexually available and silenced her resistance to sexual advances. She gave birth to her first daughter at age twelve or thirteen, her second at fifteen, and she bore a son at seventeen. The Maricopa, Mexican, and O'odham men working for the Colonel may have recognized Lucía's subordinate and sexually vulnerable status as a component of the peonage and slave market, which relied heavily on women's reproductivity to forcibly cement kinship alliances. As Joaquín Rivaya-Martínez and Victoria Smith have found, female slaves who became mothers rarely escaped.[24] The full range of the Yaqui girl's experience may be difficult for historians to ascertain, but certainly the men she lived with made significant claims on her productive and reproductive labor.

By the summer of 1871 Lucía could bear no more. She had just given birth to a lame son when the Colonel married Mary H. Taylor of Georgia, thus ensuring his access to yet another woman's domestic and bodily services. Martínez fled the ranch for Yuma a month after Woolsey and Taylor's wedding. The founding father detained their three- and five-year-old daughters but allowed her to take their infant son, Robert. The girls' mother fought for her children, filing a suit of habeas corpus for their custody through a Yuma proxy. Probate Justice John T. Alsop agreed that Clara and Johanna were too young to leave their mother, but he approved the Colonel's application for indenture and guaranteed the girls would serve their father once they reached a "suitable age."[25]

In January 1879, when Johanna was thirteen and Clara ten, Woolsey visited Yuma and put his daughters—but not his son—into the orphanage at St. Joseph's Church. The Colonel had recently lost his campaign for territorial delegate and was now preparing to plant two thousand acres of wheat. Such a venture required that Woolsey increase his labor crew and domestic staff at his new Agua Caliente ranch southwest of modern-day Phoenix. Rather than putting his indentured daughters to valuable reproductive labor, as he had Lucía, the patriarch took the girls away from their Yaqui mother and put them under the care of the Catholic Church, using indenture as a way to sever the bond of affection between mother and children. He would not bring them into the home he shared with his wife, but neither would he allow his illegitimate family to remain together in Yuma. Almost fifteen years after he had abducted Lucía and just six months after he had taken her daughters from her, the Colonel suddenly died of apparent heart trouble. Soon the women he had mastered would face each other in probate court.[26]

The girls remained at St. Joseph's Catholic Church near Yuma, but Lucía once again fought for her daughters' few rights under the Howell Code. Woolsey's death constituted a forfeit of the $1,000 indenture bond he had signed in 1871 that required him to provide for the girls' sustenance while they were under his custody. Though the senator had not taken direct custody of his daughters, he had assumed responsibility for them once he put them in St. Joseph's, and he remained financially accountable for their care up to $1,000. The promise of payment on the bond, of course, helped Lucía find lawyers willing to assist her. The former legislator's widow challenged her husband's illegitimate family but lost because they made no inheritance claims. The nuns who cared for Clara and Johanna also sued Woolsey's estate for expenses incurred on his daughters' behalf, and the rancher's widow paid them what was owed "with the proviso that no acknowledgment of the legitimacy or adoption of any children [was] intended" by her payment.[27]

As she finessed Arizona's legal system to serve her daughters' interests, Lucía, now twenty-six, showed the same fortitude that she had displayed at ten years old, when she had escaped her Apache captors. Though the probate judge granted guardianship of Woolsey's daughters to the Sisters of St. Joseph's Church, Lucía managed to regain custody of them within a year. When the 1880 census agent came to her door in Yuma, the Yaqui woman claimed Mexican ethnicity for herself and her children, ensuring that none of them would be bound under the Howell Code statute on minor Indians again and that they would be listed as white on the census. She also claimed that she was a widow, and the Martínez family was again intact and looked remarkably ordinary on paper.[28]

Though Woolsey's biographers have romanticized or obscured his relationship to Lucía and his children, the Colonel's contemporaries criticized his treatment of them. When he ran for territorial delegate in 1878, a scathing editorial published in Yuma's *Arizona Sentinel* denounced Woolsey for abandoning Lucía, Clara, Johanna, and Robert to the "charity of strangers" while he amassed his own fortune on the backs of others.[29] When he died in 1879, the frontier hero's mourners acknowledged the surviving children but implied that they were the product of Woolsey's childless marriage to Mary Taylor—an implication that must have made her blood boil, since she had fought so hard to deny them in court. Such editorializing illustrates nineteenth-century Arizonans' ambivalence toward the exploitative nature of the Colonel's relationship to his children. He had clearly used indenture to keep minor Indians close to him rather than to deter interracial intimacy. When Clara died in 1947, an obituary declared simply that she was born on "February 4, 1867, at the Woolsey ranch north of Prescott and was the daughter of the late Lt. Col. King Sam Woolsey."[30] Eighty years after her birth, Clara Martínez had transformed from an Indian servant girl to a fondly remembered pioneer descendant.

The media's treatment of the senator and his children shows that many nineteenth-century Arizonans endorsed the racial and sexual hierarchies codified in the Howell Code but remembered ties of affection rather than bonds of indenture. Woolsey's reputation as a pioneer father was protected by twentieth-century Arizonans who preferred to interpret the settlement collected by Clara and Johanna as an inheritance rather than a hard-fought indenture payment, and the laws that barred Woolsey's daughters from claiming an inheritance were easily forgotten by those who romanticized the bonds between Lucía and Woolsey as ties of love rather than power. These accounts suggest not only that the pioneer from Alabama wanted to marry Lucía and was tragically thwarted by the miscegenation law, but also that the courts upheld his daughters' claims to Woolsey's estate as heirs. Both interpretations fail to note that the territorial legislator voted in support of the miscegenation and indenture laws and that his children made claims against his estate based upon their indenture contract rather than upon his paternity. These biographers also disregard Lucía's remarkable use of the legal system to challenge the Indian killer's custody of his daughters, a bold move indicating that if there was any affection in their relationship, it was not shared.[31]

Jack Swilling's use of the Howell Code statute on minor Indians differed vastly from that of his neighbor, though he and Woolsey otherwise had much in common. Both men had left their southern families seeking military adventure in the West and had led anti-Apache expeditions in Arizona. These territorial fathers lived and worked closely among the Maricopas and O'odham in the Salt River Valley and, with the extensive aid of Mexican and Indian laborers, achieved their wealth through a variety of agricultural, mining, and commercial pursuits.

Both frontiersmen served political office, though Swilling proved less able to maintain the genteel demeanor and polished reputation necessary to achieve political prominence among territorial elites.[32]

"Tragic Jack," as one of his biographers called him, settled in Arizona after his fellow Confederates were forced out of the region, and in 1864 he married Trinidad Escalante of Hermosillo, Sonora, shortly after they met in Tucson. Though the Treaty of Guadalupe Hidalgo had defined ethnic Mexicans as white citizens—just after they had defined themselves as mestizo during their War for Independence—making this union legal under the Howell Code, Trinidad's views on her own racial status differed. "I don't claim to be white . . . they don't call Mexicans white; I come from Sonora and they call me Mexican."[33] Legally white but racially ambiguous, Trinidad Escalante bore five children to her husband during their fourteen-year marriage, and between 1864 and 1872 Jack Swilling brought at least four minor Indians into their home. Described as a home open to their Hispanic and indigenous laborers, the multiethnic Escalante-Swilling household represents a stark contrast to Woolsey's plantation model of the southwestern intercultural household.[34]

In the seven years that Lucía Martínez and her three children lived on Woolsey's rigidly ordered ranch, they and the other laborers never appeared in census records as members of his household. Guests described a full working ranch of Mexican and Anglo workers, a cook, and domestics, but Woolsey appeared in the 1864 special territorial census as a single farmer worth $9,000. Jack Swilling, on the other hand, listed his Mexican wife, American children, and Indian wards along with a myriad of laboring men as household members—a radical departure from other household heads who reported Indian minors as "servants" and "laborers." The only marks that distinguished Swilling's Apache wards from his American children in the 1870 census were the "W" and "I" entered in the enumerator's shaky hand.[35]

Trinidad and her husband reportedly hosted the first Catholic mass said in Phoenix and offered their home for use as the 1868 polling place for that settlement (Swilling was elected as justice of the peace in that election). Jack encouraged many to join his ditch-digging efforts and became known as the "father of Phoenix," even as some of his actions perturbed his Anglo neighbors. Learning of traditional O'odham irrigation methods, Woolsey's neighbor orchestrated a plan to irrigate the Salt River Valley and make the region more suitable for large-scale agriculture. His multilingual laborers called him Don Juan Capistrano for his reputation of dealing harshly with the culpable and gently with the vulnerable.[36]

An enigmatic man, Justice Swilling alternately upheld and broke down racialism in the Southwest: he served the Confederate Army but worked side by side with Pima laborers; he killed Apaches for the Arizona Volunteers yet refused to indenture the indigenous minors who lived with his own children; and he married a

Mexican who denied her own whiteness. Unlike Woolsey's racially and sexually segregated ranch, the Swilling-Escalante settlement reflected the intimate and fluid nature of intercultural labor and kinship that must have characterized other southwestern households. Life might very well have been different for Lucía had Woolsey married a woman like Trinidad before he found the ten-year-old Yaqui girl in Arizona's highlands.

Jack Swilling's intercultural promiscuity did not serve him particularly well; perhaps he displayed too much love and not enough power. After irrigating Phoenix he lost control over the town site, and when his property ended up being four miles from the city center, he lost money. Despite his heroic contributions to Arizona's military and agricultural history, "Tragic Jack" suffered from an addiction to morphine and alcohol that stemmed from an 1854 head injury. His familiarity with racial inferiors combined with his intoxicated outbursts drove a friend to question the emotional man's suitability as a guardian of Indian children.

John Ammerman, whose marriage Jack had officiated just two years earlier, filed a habeas corpus petition against Swilling for Apache minors Guadalupa and Bonifácio Woolsey in July 1871, just days after Lucía claimed her own children in the same courtroom. Perhaps Jack Swilling took the Apache Woolseys from his neighbor's ranch to ease Mrs. Woolsey's settlement into her new borderlands home. In any case, Ammerman's petition represented an appropriate course of action for citizens concerned about Native American minors in white households who had not been reported within twenty days of being taken into custody, as required under the Howell Code statue on minor Indians. Ammerman dropped the petition when Jack filed an indenture for another Apache minor, Guillermo (Gavílan) Swilling, a boy he favored enough to pass onto him his surname. In filing this legal claim to Guillermo's services, Jack effectively barred other neighbors and "friends" from interfering with his Native wards during the aftermath of the Camp Grant Massacre, during which American, Mexican, and O'odham men killed more than 140 Apaches camped along Aravaipa Creek. In the months that followed, Camp Grant survivors shared concerns that kidnapped Apache "boys will grow up slaves, and ... girls, as soon as they are large enough, will be diseased prostitutes to get money for whoever owns them."[37] Swilling's indenture of Gavílan may have been a protective gesture meant to shield his indigenous children from the anti-Apache sentiment growing among his neighbors.[38]

That Justice Swilling favored Guillermo was made most evident in a studio photograph taken of the boy and his patron around 1875. The photo offers a range of interpretive possibilities. Viewed as a portrait of father and son, the image seems to highlight the tension between miscegenation laws and the persistence of interracial intimacies as the two stare into the camera with remarkably similar gazes. The veteran casually grips his weapon over his shoulder with the confidence of a father who had taught his adolescent son to shoot straight and true,

FIGURE 11.1. Jack Swilling with his Apache ward Guillermo Swilling, ca. 1875. Courtesy of Arizona State Library, Archives and Public Records, History and Archives Division, Phoenix, no. 98-003.

while his ward clutches his weapon with the timidity of a boy about to prove himself a man in one shot. Biographer Al Bates claims that Trinidad explained the photo as a family joke, meant to poke fun by overplaying Jack's desperado image and posing Guillermo as his fierce Indian bodyguard. Regardless of the justice's intent, the image clearly depicts the slippage between bonds of indenture and bonds of affection that the Howell Code aimed to discourage. Jack and Guillermo Swilling's bond is so readily apparent, in fact, that historians celebrating Arizona's

FIGURE 11.2. Portrait of Jack Swilling with Guillermo Swilling removed, ca. 1890. Courtesy of Arizona State Library, Archives and Public Records, History and Archives Division, Phoenix, no. 98–002.

past as one in which Anglo "pioneers . . . toiled and suffered *gentling* the Arizona Territory" (emphasis added) prefer a cropped version of the photograph that erased the Apache boy from this image (the only one of Jack Swilling) in order to remove evidence of extralegal intimacies and inside jokes that deflated territorial racialism.[39]

Though the tragic hero's excised portrait is widely circulated, and many tout him as the father of Phoenix, few historians have proven willing to address the intercultural complexities depicted in these photographs or the privileges of whiteness upheld in the Howell Code. In their biographies, Bates and Wilson recognize Guillermo's presence in Swilling's household, though neither acknowledges Bonifácio and Guadalupa Woolsey or Mariana, the three other Indian children who appeared in Swilling's census records. Bates claims that the Confederate indentured Guillermo because adoption was not allowed under the legal code until 1873, supporting the notion that Jack used indenture as a protective and paternalist measure.[40]

Swilling died in Yuma prison in 1878, falsely charged with armed robbery. The circumstances of his arrest indicate that well-placed officials wanted the renegade tried regardless of his innocence. His tragic end was the result of flouting his fellow citizens' interest in white supremacy: he lived intimately with Apaches and Mexicans, used indigenous methods to irrigate metropolitan Phoenix, and poked fun at miscegenation and hysteria about hostile Indians. From his prison deathbed Swilling wrote an open letter to his fellow Arizonans. Appealing to the mercy of his peers, he wrote, "From the Governor down to the lowest Mexican in the land have I extended my hospitality, and oh, my God, how am I paid for it all. Thrown into prison . . . [t]aken from my wife and little children who are left out in this cold world all alone. Is this my reward for the kindness I have done to my fellow men?"[41] Swilling decried those who repaid him for his interethnic intimacies with false imprisonment. After his death, Trinidad struggled to care for her four American children, one of them born the year of Jack's death. The widow suffered financially and could barely support her own children, let alone her husband's Apache wards. She married German immigrant Henry Shumaker after 1887, but the Indian children raised in her Salt River Valley home disappeared after Jack's death, an ephemeral legacy of Arizona's intercultural past.[42]

Josefína and José Miguel Gonzales Roca's household in territorial Tucson offers yet another model of indenture within Arizona's intercultural families. Whereas Woolsey and Swilling were free to form multiethnic households because their whiteness was unquestionable, Roca used the racial and sexual hierarchies within his household to bolster his family's perceived whiteness in the presidio. Nicknamed *"el Chileño orgulluso"* for his nationalist pride, Roca was the son of a wealthy transnational merchant based in Concepción, Chile. After a French education and a brief but wild youth among well-connected schoolmates in Hermosillo, Roca married Josefína Mariana Haro y Samaniego, who was from an elite Sonoran military family. The couple suffered vandalism and lost $20,000 of goods and property during the French intervention and moved to the United States in 1864, making their way to the American pueblo in 1867.[43] When they arrived in Tucson, the Rocas anglicized their names to appear less Mexican and more white—though not necessarily American. José Miguel Gonzales y Roca became Miguel Gonzales Roca and Josefína Mariana Haro de Gonzales became Josefína Roca.[44]

The Rocas would have eight children, and Miguel bragged that each of them was born under a Chilean flag that he draped ceremoniously over his wife's birthing bed while she strained in the throes of labor. Though Josefína's children were born American citizens, her husband never relinquished his foreign citizenship. Tucson Hispanics enjoyed substantial political influence between 1869 and 1877 under territorial governor Anson P. K. Safford, and the Rocas managed to increase their family's status into the twentieth century, even if they are not now widely remembered as an important Hispanic family. The maintenance and display of a patriotic household staffed by racially inferior laborers, in addition to a significant name change, allowed the Rocas to cultivate their political and social influence in an increasingly Anglophile city.[45]

Roca's upper-class Latin American background instilled in him an interest in the preservation of whiteness and male dominance within multiethnic households that he shared with the senators who enacted the Howell Code. The Chilean caste system favored elites who enjoyed the services of racially other wet nurses, domestics, and field-workers. Unlike the slave labor systems familiar to Woolsey and Swilling, the South American model recognized (but did not always uphold) the legal rights of unfree laborers and did not criminalize manumission or *mestizaje.* Born seven years after the abolition of slavery in independent Chile, *el Chileño orgulloso* brought with him to Tucson a sense of his own white and patriarchal superiority that he shared with Anglo territorial elites, even if he also recognized his laborers' rights to fair—though not equal—treatment.[46]

In indenturing Teutíla in 1869, Roca both continued a Chilean tradition and demonstrated his conformity to Arizona's social institutions. Under the *criada* system of lifelong servitude, the lower caste remained subject to exploitation by elite whites, and a system of servant child distribution emerged in the newly independent and abolitionist Chile, where Roca was raised. In a society bounded by "relations of dependence,"[47] wage-earning mothers often placed their children as domestics, or *criados,* in elite homes. A lifetime of servitude represented the best such mothers could provide for their children, and elite families took in minor servants to display their philanthropic patronage of lower castes. When the merchant indentured three-year-old Teutíla in 1869, the minor Apache joined three other female servants in the Roca household.[48]

The family successfully displayed both their wealth and whiteness through Teutíla's servitude. A destitute minor, three-year-old Teutíla likely had few options, and the merchant's family proved its wealth by promising to provide her fifteen years of food and clothing in exchange for her obedience and faithfulness. The indenture record described the economic contract between the merchant and the captive as a sentimental bond, suggesting that the indigenous girl would work in exchange for her master's "kindness." Such an arrangement likely appealed to the elite sensibilities of *el Chileño orgulloso,* and the bond allowed Roca to prove himself a charitable member of Tucson's white society. The Howell Code's statute on minor Indians required that probate judges inquire into the suitability of indenture petitioners. The Roca family may have sought this judicial stamp of respectability as a means to highlight their whiteness. The contract also allowed Josefína Roca to establish herself among the settlement's female elites as she signed the legal document alongside her husband, representing her vested interests in the domestic affairs governed by the Howell Code. In signing together, the Rocas agreed to uphold white supremacy by pledging to benefit from nonwhite labor, and they recognized the separate spheres of influence characteristic of Victorian gender roles: Josefína would manage the domestic laborers as Miguel exercised authority over the legal contracts that bound them. In conforming to intercultural household order within territorial Tucson, the mercantile family could afford to display their flamboyant Chilean national pride without risking their claims to wealth and whiteness.[49]

The Roca family's use of multiethnic laborers reflected their shifting needs for reproductive and productive labor between 1870 and 1880. Renamed Tontíllar Roca, the girl worked under *criada* Juana Castillo's direction in 1869, while Castillo's seven-year-old son Prudencio probably aided eighteen-year-old *criado* Reyno Moreno. Tontíllar attended at least two births and watched over four children while she lived with the Rocas in the 1870s. Just a child herself, the Apache minor must have grown attached to the Roca women and children that she was contracted to care for. By 1880, Josefína's daughters were old enough to help manage the family's domestic economy, and the servant staff had changed. Tontíllar had disappeared but had been replaced by a twenty-six-year-old Native American woman named Andrea, who likely devoted much of her attention to Josefína's three-year-old granddaughter. Four men joined Andrea: an Indian laborer her age, two white laborers, and a fourteen-year-old boy working in the store. Andrea and the other *criados* were all from Mexico. This creative mix of paid and unpaid, female and male, and domestic and commercial laborers further demonstrates a Hispano influence on indenture in the Roca's multiracial and multigenerational household.[50]

Racialized shifts in territorial politics required *el Chileño* to solicit white allies actively in order to ensure the continuation of his family's prominence in Tucson. Josefína hosted local lawyers, bankers, and publishers for lavish dinners during which she displayed her family's wealth through her servants' obedience and her daughters' propriety. While nonwhite *criados* waited on them, the Roca daughters flirted with their brothers' American friends visiting from preparatory school. By hosting dinner parties that featured nonwhite servants, the Rocas proved their ability to manage relations of dependence within their home and illustrated their willingness to participate in racial and sexual hierarchies outside their home during a crucial time in Arizona's Hispanic history. Each of these private events provided public evidence of the Rocas' conformity to American racialism, thus performing their whiteness within an increasingly segregated borderlands community. As Josefína and Miguel invited citizens to scrutinize their racially stratified household, they sealed their status on the upper rungs of the territory's racially stratified society.

The use of nonwhite labor within the Roca household proved the merchant's respectability and allowed him to escape the racial degradation that befell many Mexican families in turn-of-the-century Tucson. When Miguel died in 1886, his daughter Erminía married Ben Heney, who briefly served as mayor of Tucson in 1909. Heney's son Lautaro served as Tucson city councilman from 1933 to 1939, and in 1935 his granddaughter Frecia received a personal invitation to dine with President Franklin Roosevelt. Lautaro's son Paul actively served Arizona's Latino community during his impressive legal career.[51]

Sometime after his death, the merchant's family donated his flag stand to the Arizona Pioneers' Historical Society to honor the banner of Chileño paternity that the first generation of American Rocas had been born under. Whether archivists viewed the artifact as evidence of an Apache *criada*'s care for a Mexican woman bearing American children to a Chilean father is difficult to say, but they likely saw its connection to both love and power.[52] Considering the notoriety of Roca's children and grandchildren in comparison to the relative obscurity of Woolsey's and Swilling's children, surprisingly little has been written about Tucson's Chilean patriarch. Yndia Smalley Moore, Josefína and Miguel's granddaughter, served as director of the Arizona Pioneers' Historical Society from 1959 to 1964 but did not use the post to celebrate her Hispano past. Instead, she and her father, George Smalley, wrote a memoir that emphasized an Anglo family history. Yndia's cousin, Paul Roca, researched and wrote about Mexico's Jesuit past but saved his own genealogy for short letters that inadvertently found their way to the Arizona Historical Society.[53] Family documents contain letters written by Miguel Roca in 1885 that seem to indicate he planned to kill himself, which might explain why his descendants—though proud to claim a pioneer past—chose not to emphasize him in their family histories. No one described Teutílla's care for the children or the family's reliance on nonwhite labor either, but having *criadas* they could ignore marked the Rocas as a white family of privilege.

Lucía, Clara, and Johanna Martínez, Guadalupa and Bonifácio Woolsey, Mariana, Guillermo Swilling, and Teutílla Roca were not the only Indian women and children drawn into the bonds of indenture and affection that characterized the intercultural labor market in territorial Arizona. The families claiming indigenous minors' labor under the Howell Code rarely acknowledged the contributions of these unfree members of their households. Colonel Woolsey, "Tragic Jack," and *el Chileño* felt no need to explain the presence of Native children in their homes, most likely because their contemporaries asked no questions. Louis

John Frederick Jaeger, a prominent ferryman in Yuma, indentured a Native American girl named Mary at her mother's request around 1871 and drew no one's attention in doing so. In 1871, Carmena Campbell, a wealthy Arizona divorcee, indentured Indian girl Susan in Maricopa County. The same Maricopa County probate judge bound Indian boy Jim to Richard DeKuhn in 1873.[54]

Relationships between Native minors and their masters were sometimes exploitative and sometimes affectionate, but in any case they were usually overlooked. The reasons territorial Arizonans ignored Indian servants are difficult to determine, but the presence of these children in territorial Arizona is undeniable. Census records may show only a handful of indigenous wards serving Hispanic and Anglo households between 1860 and 1880, but men like Woolsey told half-truths to those collecting census information, and servants like Teutílla looked Mexican to enumerators. That Mariana and Gavílan are the only children featured in this chapter who actually appeared as "Indian" in census records proves the fallibility of census data in chronicling Native American labor in multiethnic households. In browsing census records between 1860 and 1880, it becomes clear that enumerators and reporters creatively and inconsistently documented ethnic identities and household relations throughout the territory. Given such widespread misreporting, it is surprising that any evidence of minor Indian servitude exists at all. Such unreliable data makes it difficult to know how common the Woolsey, Swilling, and Roca families were, but their very insignificance to contemporaries and chroniclers indicates the normalcy of indigenous laborers.

The Howell Code's statute on minor Indians represents territorial Arizonans' management of the intertribal slave trade that indigenous and Hispanic actors once dominated. The institutionalization of white male privilege that justified nonwhite exploitation under the guise of a free labor system marked a significant step in state formation. Legislating citizen Arizonans' subordination of indigenous people defined as enemies of the state proved an effective method of controlling and consuming Native American resources, including Indian child labor. Additional provisions of the Howell Code ensured there would be few consequences for those who overstepped the intimate bounds of the law, and where interracial intimacies occurred, they could be defined as illicit and illegitimate.

Mixed-race and indigenous Arizonans lived and worked in close proximity to Americans throughout the territorial period, even as official policies sought to maximize the social and geographic distances between them. The boarding school system satisfied those who feared alcoholism and miscegenation as the byproducts of interracial intimacy, as well as others convinced that reservation seclusion fostered indolence and savagery. The Phoenix Indian School (PIS), established in 1891, provided a compromise between citizens' reliance on Indian women's and children's labors and legislators' discomfort with unregulated multiethnic households by putting Native children into institutions rather than families.

Carlisle Indian School founder Richard Pratt proposed the outing system as a way to institutionalize familial relations and ease assimilation. Though he feared Westerners would abuse Native domestics, Pratt believed that putting Indian students into white households for short periods would enhance boarding schools' curricula. In 1894 the outing system—as it was applied in Arizona—put the regulation of citizen use of indigenous women and children's bodies under federal and philanthropic, rather than local and civil, jurisdiction. Although a continuation of the exploitation of Native American labor practiced under the indenture system, outing policies proposed strict segregation of minor Indian supervision by sex, thereby empowering matrons such as Trinidad Swilling and Josefína Roca while discouraging abusive patriarchs such as Woolsey.[55]

The outing system allowed PIS administrator Harwood Hall to bind minor Indians to the relations of dependence defined in the Howell Code without the risk of affectionate bonds being formed through indenture and guardianship arrangements. Brief exposure to domestic, agricultural, or industrial labor would train PIS students to serve their white superiors, while the interventions of field matrons and school supervisors would train citizen Arizonans to distance themselves from Native subordinates—lessons that Woolsey and Swilling had failed to learn but that the Rocas had mastered. In 1895, Hall wrote that in "reference to [the] feasibility of placing Indian pupils in white families, I have the honor to state that we have quite a number of pupils 'working out,' there being a larger demand for the pupils than we possibly can fill at this time."[56] Within a year, Hall was bragging, "[had] I 500 Indian girls and boys of sufficient size and training, capable of understanding English to the extent of doing what they are told, I am sure places could be secured in this thickly settled valley inside ten days."[57] Clearly, Native indenture had fallen out of favor, but the demand for minor Indian labor increased in step with the Anglo population.

Territorial Arizona's indenture period reflects the pivotal transition between the extralegal traffic in minor Indian labor prior to 1864 and the institutional traffic in minor Indian labor after 1894. Though reformers intended to guard indigenous children from abuse and exploitation, the outing system continued to vest in citizen Arizonans an unquestioned authority over Native American women's and children's bodies and ensured that non-Indian households benefited from their labors. Once integrated into the progressive model of federal Indian policy, the indigenous labor market shifted from an extralegal slave trade to a curriculum of dependent relations within one generation. That dramatic change likewise transformed Clara Martínez, indentured daughter of an Apache slave, to Clara Woolsey, favored daughter of a pioneer Indian fighter. Gavilán Pollero, minor child of a "hostile Indian tribe," became Guillermo Swilling, Native sidekick to a territorial desperado. And Apache toddler Teutilla became Mexican *criada* Tontíllar Roca.

These transformations reflect the creative chronicling of Arizona's intercultural households as "gentling" institutions rather than legislated sites that linked exploitative labor with intercultural intimacy. Ironically, the Howell Code ensured that Indian women and children nurtured and cared for citizens, while white heads of households craved the company of their Indian subordinates despite territorial senators' efforts to deter bonds of affection through the indenture mandate. Clara's decision sometime after 1880 to take her father's surname, Guillermo's staged jest as Swilling's bodyguard, and Tontíllar's pledge to serve the Rocas faithfully all posed problems for nineteenth-century legislators and continue to do so for twenty-first-century historians. Senators barred Clara Martínez from inheriting her father's wealth but not from inheriting his pioneer legacy. The Howell Code's statute on minor Indians disarmed Gavílan Pollero's Apache family members, but Jack Swilling put a gun in Guillermo's hands. The Pima County probate judge would not have accepted Teutílla's testimony against the Rocas, but he accepted the three-year-old's oath of indenture to them. Explicitly drafted in the interests of white patriarchy, the territorial legal code could not stand up to the everyday intricacies within territorial borderlands communities. Bonds of affection, though not always mutual, blurred the indenture contracts that made Arizona's Indian children vulnerable—and forgettable—members of white pioneer households.

NOTES

1. In 1864 the native-born white population in Arizona was not over 600, and ethnic Mexicans made Arizona's white population more like 6,500, a slim majority over the territory's 4,000 "civilized" Indians. These demographics threatened Arizona's prospects for statehood. See Thomas Edwin Farish, *History of Arizona: Volume II* (Phoenix, AZ: Filmer Brothers Electrotype Co., 1915), 322–23; and Katherine Benton-Cohen, *Borderline Americans: Racial Division and Labor War in the Arizona Borderlands* (Cambridge, MA: Harvard University Press, 2009), 7–16.

2. James F. Brooks, *Captives and Cousins: Slavery, Kinship, and Community in the Southwest Borderlands* (Chapel Hill: University of North Carolina Press, 2002); and Karl Jacoby, *Shadows at Dawn: A Borderlands Massacre and the Violence of History* (New York: Penguin Books, 2008).

3. Brooks, *Captives and Cousins*; Juliana Barr, "From Captives to Slaves: Commodifying Indian Women in the Borderlands," *Journal of American History* 92, no. 1 (June 2005): 19–46; Albert Hurtado, "'Hardly a Farm House—A Kitchen without Them': Indian and White Households on the California Borderland Frontier in 1860," *Western Historical Quarterly* 13, no. 3 (July 1982): 245–70; Margot Mifflin, *The Blue Tattoo: The Life of Olive Oatman* (Lincoln: University of Nebraska Press, 2009); and Victoria Smith, *Captive Arizona, 1851–1900* (Lincoln: University of Nebraska Press, 2009).

4. John Goff, *King S. Woolsey* (Cave Creek, AZ: Black Mountain Press, 1981), 48.

5. William T. Howell, *Howell Code Adopted by the First Legislative Assembly of the Territory of Arizona, 1864* (Prescott: Office of the Arizona Miner, 1865); and Martha Hodes, ed., *Sex, Love, Race: Crossing Boundaries in North American History* (New York: New York University Press, 1999).

6. John S. Goff, "William T. Howell and the Howell Code of Arizona," *American Journal of Legal History* 11, no. 3 (July 1967): 221–33.

7. An excellent discussion of age of consent laws and their reform can be found in Leslie K. Dunlap, "The Reform of Rape Law and the Problem of White Men: Age of Consent Campaigns in the South, 1885–1910," in *Sex, Love, Race: Crossing Boundaries in North American History*, ed. Martha Hodes (New York: New York University Press, 1999), 352–72. Although Arizona's age of consent law did not differ radically from those already in place in other parts of the country, the statute remains worthy of scrutiny. When combined with the witness exclusion law and the minor Indian indenture provision, the age of consent law made Indian minors particularly vulnerable to the sexual desires of citizens around them because this legal triad abolished their ability to give or withhold consent.

8. Albert Hurtado, *Intimate Frontiers: Sex, Gender, and Culture in Old California* (Albuquerque: University of New Mexico Press, 1999), 21–44; Howell, *Howell Code*, 75, 76, 237, 444; and John P. Hoyt, *The Compiled Laws of the Territory of Arizona, Compiled and Arranged by Authority of an Act of the Legislative Assembly, Approved February 9, 1877* (Detroit: Richmond, Backus & Co., 1877), 50. See also *Fernandez v. State of Arizona* (1914), Case No. 360, Arizona Court of Appeals, Division One, Criminal Files, Briefs and Records, Arizona State Library, Archives and Public Records (hereafter ASLAPR). This case is discussed at length in the author's dissertation, Katrina Jagodinsky, "Intimate Obscurity: American Indian Women in Arizona Households and Histories, 1854–1935," Ph.D. diss., University of Arizona, 2011.

9. Howell, *Howell Code*, 230.

10. Martha Menchaca, "Chicano Indianism: A Historical Account of Racial Repression in the United States," *American Ethnologist* 20, no. 3 (August 1993): 583–603; and Peggy Pascoe, "Race, Gender, and Intercultural Relations: The Case of Interracial Marriage," *Frontiers: A Journal of Women Studies* 12, no. 1 (1991): 5–18. Both Menchaca and Pascoe illustrate that Mexican women faced discrimination under miscegenation laws even though they were legally white because jurists could use phenotypes to rule that they were in fact Indian and therefore banned from intermarrying with whites—which could include other Mexicans.

11. Kathleen Brown, *Good Wives, Nasty Wenches, and Anxious Patriarchs: Gender, Race, and Power in Colonial Virginia* (Chapel Hill: University of North Carolina Press, 1996); and Jennifer Morgan, *Laboring Women: Reproduction and Gender in New World Slavery* (Philadelphia: University of Pennsylvania Press, 2004).

12. Some legislators likely brought to Arizona miscegenation fears shaped under antebellum and reconstruction contexts similar to those discussed in Peggy Pascoe, *What Comes Naturally: Miscegenation Law and the Making of Race in America* (New York: Oxford University Press, 2009), and applied "commonsense" definitions of race such as those described in Ariela J. Gross, *What Blood Won't Tell: A History of Race on Trial in America* (Cambridge, MA: Harvard University Press, 2008).

13. George H. Kelly, *Legislative History: Arizona, 1864–1912* (Phoenix, AZ: Manufacturing Stationers, 1926), 6.

14. Sondra Jones, "'Redeeming the Indian': The Enslavement of Indian Children in New Mexico and Utah," *Utah Historical Quarterly* 67, no. 3 (1999): 220–24; and Michael Magliari, "Free Soil, Unfree Labor: Cave Johnson Couts and the Binding of Indian Workers in California, 1850–1867," *Pacific Historical Review* 73, no. 3 (August 2004): 349–89.

15. Howell, *Howell Code*, 428.

16. Stacey Leigh Smith, "California Bound: Unfree Labor, Race, and the Reconstruction of the Far West, 1848–1870," Ph.D. diss., University of Wisconsin—Madison, 2008, 411; Hoyt, *Compiled Laws of Arizona*, 315; and James A. Bayard, *Revised Statutes of Arizona* (Prescott, AZ: Prescott Courier Print, 1887), 567.

17. Smith, *Captive Arizona*.

18. In *Laboring Women*, Morgan argues that sexual and economic access to laboring women's bodies constitutes a fundamental component of American masculinity.

19. Evelyn Nakano Glenn, "From Servitude to Service Work: Historical Continuities in the Racial Division of Paid Reproductive Labor," *Signs* 18, no. 1 (Autumn 1992): 1.

20. That male servants bore no children as a result of sexual assault and were also barred from testifying against their masters makes it virtually impossible to determine the frequency of sexual exploitation of Indian boys indentured under the Howell Code, although in theory the sodomy law, outlined in the same article as the rape statute, would have applied to them.

21. Goff, *King S. Woolsey*, 54–73.

22. John Nicolson, ed., *The Arizona of Joseph Pratt Allyn, Letters From a Pioneer Judge: Observations and Travels, 1863–1866* (Tucson: University of Arizona Press, 1974), 81.

23. Kirsten Fischer, *Suspect Relations: Sex, Race, and Resistance in Colonial North Carolina* (Ithaca, NY: Cornell University Press, 2002), 98–158.

24. See Joaquín Rivaya-Martínez's chapter in this volume and Smith, *Captive Arizona*.

25. Census data gathered for this chapter has been accessed through Ancestry.com and can be reviewed through both the name search and browsing features. Citation information provided by Ancestry.com is given here for those without access to the online database, which requires a subscription. *Tenth Census of the United States, 1880* (Washington, DC: National Archives and Records Administration, 1880), Roll T9–37; Goff, *King S. Woolsey*, 18–20, 74–82; "Henry S. Fitzgerald, Guardian of Clara and Johanna Woolsey, Minors, vs. M. W. Kales, Administrator of the Estate of King S. Woolsey, Deceased" (May 1880), Case No. 146 in MSS 110, Benjamin Sacks Collection of the American West (hereafter Sacks), Series 1, Box 30, Folder 8, Arizona Historical Foundation (hereafter AHF); and "Lucia Martinez vs. Thomas Barman, K.S. Woolsey, John Ammerman, and Mrs. Ammerman" and "Lucia Martinez and King Woolsey," Maricopa County Probate Court Record Book (1871–74), 6–8 and 15, Record Group (hereafter RG) 107, Maricopa County, Subgroup (hereafter SG) 8, Superior Court, ASLAPR.

26. Civil Case No. 146, RG 107, SG 8, ASLAPR; "In the Matter of the Estate of King S. Woolsey (1879)," Maricopa County Superior Court Civil Case No. 32, RG 107, SG 8, ASLAPR; and Goff, *King S. Woolsey*, 65–73, 78–79.

27. Civil Case No. 32, RG 107, SG 8, ASLAPR.

28. *Arizona Sentinel*, November 19, 1880, in Sacks, MSS 110, Series 1, Box 30, Folder 8, AHF; "Clara Woolsey vs. M. W. Kales, Administrator" (1880), in Sacks; *Phoenix Herald*, October 24, 1881, in Sacks, MSS 110, Series 1, Box 30, Folder 8, AHF; and *Tenth Census*, Roll T9–37. Though the 1930 census schedules are the only forms that offer an option to report Mexican ethnicity, territorial Arizona enumerators often wrote "M" or "Mex" to indicate Mexican ethnicity, and Arizonans listed as "W" for white can be identified as ethnic Mexicans through Sonoran birthplaces listed in the census.

29. "Editorial," *Arizona Sentinel*, October 5, 1878, in Sacks, MSS 110, Series 1, Box 30, Folder 8, AHF.

30. *Arizona Republic*, July 27, 1947, in Sacks, MSS 110, Series 1, Box 30, Folder 8, AHF.

31. Goff, *King S. Woolsey*, 80–81; and James M. Barney, "Col. King S. Woolsey, Famous Arizona Pioneer: The Story So Far, Vol. 8," *The Sheriff* (1948), in the James M. Barney Collection, MSS 4, Box 1, Folder 7, AHF.

32. Albert R. Bates, *Jack Swilling, Arizona's Most Lied About Pioneer* (Tucson, AZ: Wheatmark, 2008); Michael R. Wilson, *Tragic Jack: The True Story of Arizona Pioneer John William Swilling* (Guilford, CT: Two Dot, 2007); and Earl Zarbin, *The Swilling Legacy* (Phoenix, AZ: Salt River Project, 1984).

33. "Statement of Mrs. Trinidad Shoemaker (formerly Mrs. Jack Swilling)," p. 5, CM MSM 667, Arizona Collection, Hayden Library, Arizona State University Department of Archives and Special Collections.

34. Wilson, *Tragic Jack,* 11; and Bates, *Jack Swilling,* 55, 59.

35. United States Department of Census, *Federal Census—Territory of New Mexico and Territory of Arizona: Excerpts from the Decennial Federal Census, 1860, for Arizona County in the Territory of New Mexico, the Special Territorial Census of 1864 Taken in Arizona and Decennial Federal Census, 1870, for the Territory of Arizona* (Washington, DC: United States Government Printing Office, 1965); and *Ninth Census of the United States, 1870* (Washington, DC: National Archives and Records Administration), RG 29; Roll M593–46, p. 103, image 194.

36. Zarbin, *Swilling Legacy,* 6–7; and Bates, *Jack Swilling,* 54–55.

37. Jacoby, *Shadows at Dawn,* 247. Jacoby also demonstrates that Americans shared similar fears (223).

38. Zarbin, *Swilling Legacy,* 3; Wilson, *Tragic Jack,* 42; and "A. J. Ammerman vs. J. W. Swilling," Maricopa County Probate Court Record Book (1871–74), 4–8, RG 107, Maricopa County, SG 8, Superior Court, ASLAPR. These probate records indicate that there was some relationship between John Ammerman and King Woolsey as well, since Ammerman sued Swilling for Bonifácio and Guadalupa Woolsey, and Lucía Martínez named Ammerman in her suit against Woolsey for custody of Clara and Johanna Woolsey. Ammerman may have been seeking custody of Indian children associated with Woolsey as a favor to the Colonel, who was unwilling to keep them after his marriage to Mary Taylor. Swilling's indenture of Guillermo Swilling immediately followed Woolsey's indenture of Clara and Johanna Martínez. See "Indenture of Guillermo Swilling," Maricopa County Probate Court Record Book (1871–74), 16–17, ASLAPR.

39. "Photograph of Jack Swilling, an Early Settler of Phoenix (Ariz.), and a Native American Man," ca. 1875, RG 99, SG 12, Historical Photographs, ASLAPR; and Bates, *Jack Swilling,* 59.

40. Bates, *Jack Swilling,* 59; and Wilson, *Tragic Jack,* 11.

41. Farish, *History of Arizona, Volume II,* 256.

42. Wilson, *Tragic Jack,* 63–85.

43. José Luís Blasio, *Maximilian, Emperor of Mexico: Memoirs of His Private Secretary,* trans. Robert Hammond Murray (New Haven, CT: Yale University Press, 1934); Egon Corti, *Maximilian and Charlotte of Mexico,* 2 vols., trans. Catherine Alison Philips (New York: Alfred A. Knopf, 1928); and Bertida Harding, *The Phantom Crown: The Story of Maximilian and Carlota of Mexico* (New York: Halcyon House, 1934).

44. Letter by Paul M. Roca in Miguel Gonzales Roca Hayden Bio File, Arizona Historical Society (hereafter AHS).

45. George H. Smalley with Yndia Smalley Moore, ed., *My Adventures in Arizona: Leaves from a Reporter's Notebook* (Tucson: Arizona Pioneers' Historical Society, 1966), xi, xii, 39; Bernice Cosulich, *Tucson: The Fabulous Story of Arizona's Ancient Walled Presidio, 1692–1900's* (Tucson: Arizona Silhouettes, 1953), 206; James E. Officer et al., *Arizona's Hispanic Perspective: Research Report Prepared by the University of Arizona, May 17–20, 1981* (Phoenix: Arizona Academy, 1981), 68, 78; Laura E. Gómez, *Manifest Destinies: The Making of the Mexican American Race* (New York: New York University Press, 2007), 109; and *Tenth Census,* Roll T9–36, p. 327, image 0669.

46. Mark A. Burkholder and Lyman L. Johnson, *Colonial Latin America,* 3rd ed. (New York: Oxford University Press, 1998), 116–32, 194–219; and Maria Eugenia Chaves, "Slave Women's Strategies for Freedom and the Late Spanish Colonial State," in *Hidden Histories of Gender and the State in Latin America,* ed. Elizabeth Dore and Maxine Molyneux (Durham, NC: Duke University Press, 2000), 108–26.

47. Nara Milanich, "The *Casa de Huerfanos* and Child Circulation in Late-Nineteenth-Century Chile," *Journal of Social History* 38, no. 2 (Winter 2004): 311–40.

48. Smalley, *My Adventures in Arizona,* xii; "Case No. 41.5 (1869)," Box 88, RG 110, Pima County Probate Records, 1864–1924, ASLAPR; *Ninth Census,* RG 29, M593–46, p. 56, image 106.

49. "Case No. 41.5 (1869)."

50. *Ninth Census,* RG 29, Roll M593-46, p. 56, image 106; and *Tenth Census,* Roll T9-36, p. 327, image 0669.

51. Officer et al., *Arizona's Hispanic Perspective,* 73-82; Smalley, *My Adventures,* 38; Thomas E. Sheridan, *Los Tucsonenses: The Mexican Community in Tucson* (Tucson: University of Arizona Press, 1986), 215, 120; and MS 1374, Heney Family, Box 1, Folder 13, and Paul McLennan Roca Hayden Biofile, AHS.

52. According to archivists at the Arizona Historical Society, the flag stand has been lost.

53. See Miguel Roca Hayden Biofile and MS 1374, Heney Family, Box 1, Folder 1, AHS.

54. Case No. 37, Record Group 114, Yuma County Superior Court Probate Division and Maricopa County Probate Court Record Book (1871-74), 575, RG 107, Maricopa County, SG 8, Superior Court, ASLAPR.

55. David Wallace Adams, *Education for Extinction: American Indians and the Boarding School Experience, 1875-1928* (Lawrence: University of Kansas, 1995), 162-63; Margaret D. Jacobs, "Working on the Domestic Frontier: American Indian Domestic Servants in White Women's Households in the San Francisco Bay Area, 1920-1940," *Frontiers: A Journal of Women Studies* 28, no. 1/2 (2007): 165-99; Robert Trennert Jr., *Phoenix Indian School: Forced Assimilation in Arizona, 1891-1935* (Norman: University of Oklahoma Press, 1988); Robert Trennert Jr., "From Carlisle to Phoenix: The Rise and Fall of the Indian Outing System, 1878-1930," *Pacific Historical Review* 52, no. 3 (August 1983): 267-91; and Robert Trennert Jr., "Victorian Morality and the Supervision of Indian Women Working in Phoenix," *Journal of Social History* 22, no. 1 (Autumn 1988): 113-28.

56. Harwood Hall to Commissioner of Indian Affairs, January 16, 1895, in Robert Trennert Papers, Box 2, Folder 2, Labriola National American Indian Data Center, Arizona State University Library, Archives and Special Collections Division (hereafter Labriola Center).

57. Harwood Hall to Commissioner of Indian Affairs, January 11, 1896, in Robert Trennert Papers, Box 2, Folder 3, Labriola Center.

12

Writing Kit Carson in the Cold War

"The Family," "The West," and Their Chroniclers

Susan Lee Johnson

In the early 1950s, on the first television that many families owned, a buckskin-clad Kit Carson galloped across the West and through the 1880s with his Mexican pal El Toro. The black-and-white syndicated program, *The Adventures of Kit Carson*, must have irritated Bernice Blackwelder and Quantrille McClung as much as it enthralled young viewers.[1] Indeed, the show would have annoyed any viewer conversant with the history of western North America.[2] Amateur historians, Blackwelder and McClung were captivated by the real Carson. The program would have annoyed them not least because it was set in the 1880s. The actual Carson died in 1868, leaving little substance to fill a saddle two decades later. And El Toro never lived. Kit's closest Mexican companion was his wife, Josefa Jaramillo, who expired a month before her husband. Had the couple been resurrected to ride again in the 1880s? After all, Kit had been born on Christmas Eve, and perhaps, like Jesus, he rose from the dead. And maybe, since the moral economy of the Western dictated that men rode with men, Josefa got a makeover, rolled back the stone, and charged out as El Toro, the bull.[3]

It was a bother, the West of the Western. When Quantrille McClung saw another inaccurate portrayal of Carson on the TV show *Death Valley Days*, she was peeved. She immediately telephoned Bernice Blackwelder and found her friend "in the same state and for the same reason." McClung wrote a letter of protest to the network, CBS, and then dashed off a note to Marion Estergreen, a Carson devotee in New Mexico, suggesting that Estergreen enlist the aid of the man who ran the Kit Carson Home and Museum in Taos. "I consider it unpardonable to present programs that so distort history," McClung declared.[4]

For McClung and Blackwelder, the moment to set the record straight came in 1962. They had spent years working in libraries and archives and had exchanged hundreds of letters with Carson descendants, Carson enthusiasts, and each other. The West of the Western and the West of history were due for a showdown. Blackwelder and McClung took aim and fired. Early that year, an Idaho-based publishing house, Caxton Printers, released Blackwelder's biography *Great Westerner: The Story of Kit Carson*.[5] A few months later, the Denver Public Library published McClung's precisely titled *Carson-Bent-Boggs Genealogy: Line of William Carson, Ancestor of "Kit" Carson, Famous Scout and Pioneer of the Rocky Mountain Area, with the Western Branches of the Bent and Boggs Families, with Whom "Kit" Was Associated, and the Line of Samuel Carson, Supposed to Be a Brother of William Carson*.[6] Yet even as the gun smoke cleared, another shot rang out, seemingly from the same end of the dusty street. Marion Estergreen, it turned out, was packing too. Much to Blackwelder's dismay, Estergreen published a competing biography the very same year called *Kit Carson: A Portrait in Courage*.[7] The West of history was winning.

But the West of history itself was also changing. So was the West of the Western. And so was the wider landscape in which western history enthusiasts as well as producers of film and television Westerns did their work. It was a landscape in which civil rights struggles, the Cold War, and the shifting contours of city life loomed large. McClung and Blackwelder lived this changing landscape. It touched everything from the tables where they typed their books to the paths their letters traced across the miles to the way they made sense of Carson and the western past.

Few today have heard of these women. Their work is out of print, gathering dust on library shelves. McClung, a lifelong resident of Denver who lived from 1890 to 1985, was a librarian and genealogist. Unmarried, McClung liked to refer to herself as an "old maid." Blackwelder was born in Kansas in 1902 as Bernice Fowler, but she spent most of her adult life in Chicago and Washington, D.C. Married but childless, she died in 1986, having worked as a voice instructor, radio and theater performer, and Central Intelligence Agency employee. Nonetheless, Blackwelder called herself a "housewife." On the stage where historical knowledge was produced, these women were bit players, all but lost among the legions of amateurs and academics who wrote about the West. They were minor historians. But just as minor writers produce literature from a vantage point that provides a critical view of the literary canon and the process by which it is constituted, so do minor historians produce work that brings into bold relief the hierarchies that attend the production of historical knowledge.[8] Embracing McClung and Blackwelder's minor status, then, this chapter highlights their contributions and places those contributions in historical context.[9]

The year 1962 represents a key moment in the lives of Blackwelder and McClung, of western history as a field of inquiry, of the Western as a form of popular culture, and of the nation itself. Not only did McClung and Blackwelder publish their books that year, but academics and amateurs joined forces to establish the Western History Association, the first professional organization devoted to the West and its past. The founding of this association marked the beginning of the end of the reign of history buffs—amateurs like Blackwelder and McClung—in the field. Meanwhile, Westerns were only beginning to fade from their glory days, when they had dominated both big and little screens, providing a visual feast of western men and western landscapes to viewers nestled in theater seats and on living room sofas across the country and around the world. At the same time, national events and trends were pulling in different directions. On the one hand, the Cuban Missile Crisis evoked an older Cold War United States, in which frontier heroes such as Carson were celebrated and "the family" was enshrined as a truly natural human collectivity that could be opposed to the unnatural collectivism promoted by communists. On the other hand, nascent movements for civil rights evoked a nation in the midst of racial and sexual change, creating an atmosphere in which frontier heroes—and nuclear families— would fall from grace. At the same time, suburbanization was accelerating, stirring cities and their suburbs into a bubbling cauldron of political economy that left some metropolitan residents longing not just for a rural past but for a past of unexplored frontiers and undetermined futures: in a word, for the West.

In 1962, McClung, who was seventy-two, lived a secure if spartan retirement from librarianship, dwelling in a downtown Denver apartment and working as an independent genealogist. Blackwelder, at sixty, lived a more insecure and inconstant—but, for now, comfortable—existence in suburban Washington, D.C., even owning a home there. She helped her husband, Harold, in his business ventures but also carved out time for her work as an independent historian. Out of these daily worlds, McClung and Blackwelder produced novel visions of Kit Carson, visions that were based on hard historical research, to be sure, but also on their experiences as differently situated white women in a Cold War United States that vaunted "the family" and "the West" as ramparts against changing times. They remade Carson from a lone frontiersman who helped win the West for white America to a family man, the head of an expansive household who, despite his small stature, threw a protective arm around kinfolk of color. In the process, these women created a vision of the nation that served Cold War culture, itself a locus of contradiction, conflict, and change.

BEGOTTEN, AND MADE

The Kit Carson who appeared on the pages of Blackwelder's biography and McClung's genealogy was something of a new man. He was, predictably, the "great westerner" of Blackwelder's title. And he was, in McClung's rendering, the "famous

FIGURE 12.1. Kit Carson, 1840s. Courtesy of Taos Historic Museums.

scout and pioneer of the Rocky Mountain area." But he was also, less predictably, a man connected, and intimately so, to a whole host of people with whom he had seemed more loosely associated in the past: New Mexican *hispanos,* the Indigenous peoples of the plains and mountains, and, especially, women of many descriptions. McClung drew out these connections in the stark outline form of the genealogist, creating almost two hundred pages of charts that traced the "begats": the parents and the parents' parents, the children and the children's children, the cousins, the aunts, and the uncles of Kit Carson, Josefa Jaramillo, and scores of others related by birth and marriage. Blackwelder, in prose that was surprisingly stirring for a first-time author whose life had been filled with other pursuits, drew the connections through well-researched, if sometimes embellished, stories of meeting and parting, romance and estrangement, birth and death.

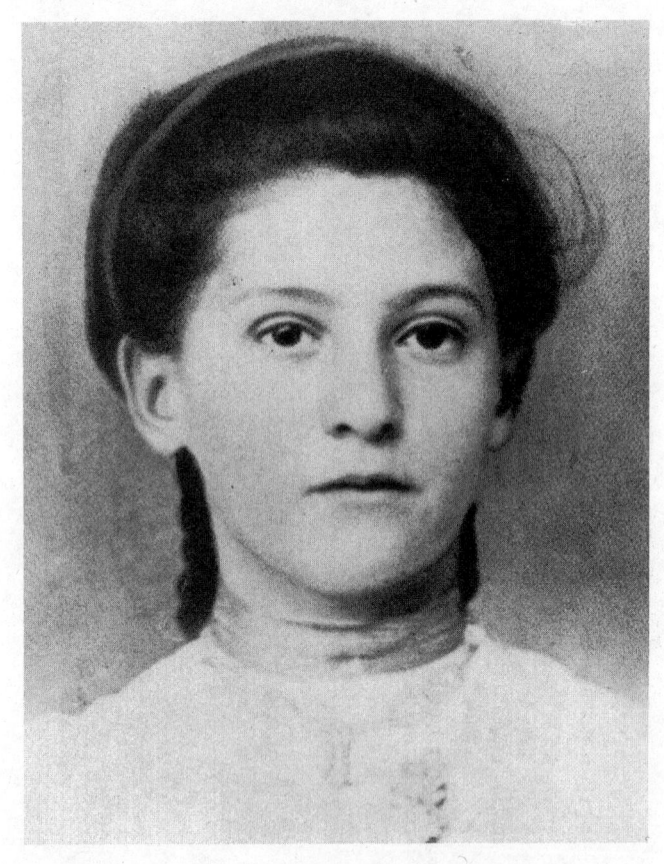

FIGURE 12.2. Josefa Jaramillo, 1840s. Courtesy of Taos Historic Museums.

First, then, the begats: The *Carson-Bent-Boggs Genealogy* opens with a brief Carson family record that McClung received from one of Kit and Josefa's grandsons. That record starts with William Carson, Kit's paternal grandfather, an eighteenth-century Scots-Irish migrant to Pennsylvania and then the western Piedmont in North Carolina. The rest of the volume presents McClung's own genealogical research. That work, however, begins right where the family record began: with William Carson.[10] It follows fathers and their wives and children down through the decades and across space, as the Carsons migrated from North Carolina to Kentucky to Missouri and, finally, to the Mexican North in the heyday of the fur trade and the Santa Fe trade. Tracing male lines of descent more thoroughly than female lines was a habit among genealogists, following broader cultural and legal practices that identified men as heads of families and by which women routinely took their husbands' names at marriage.[11]

As the title suggests, the *Carson-Bent-Boggs Genealogy* was not limited to the Carson family. McClung, when she worked as a librarian, had helped to develop the Genealogy Division of the Denver Public Library, and her interest in Carson began, she recalled, when "a lady in North Carolina wrote asking my help in relating her Carson line to that of the 'Kit' Carson family." Realizing that no complete genealogical record existed for the Carsons, McClung decided to compile one herself.[12] Over time, she found Carson was so linked to the famous Bent brothers, especially Charles and William, and to Thomas Boggs that it would be useful to include their family lines as well.[13] The Bents, along with Céran St. Vrain, were proprietors of Bent's Fort along the Santa Fe Trail, the trade route that tied the northern territories of Mexico to the western territories of the United States starting in the 1820s and culminating in the U.S. conquest of the 1840s, when Charles Bent became the first American governor of New Mexico. Thomas Boggs was younger and came to New Mexico later, but he, too, helped tighten the bonds that were creating a U.S. Southwest.

What McClung's genealogy revealed more clearly than earlier works, however, was that Carson, Boggs, and the Bents shared more than Missouri origins and adult lives spent on the borderlands of commerce and war between the United States and Mexico, a borderlands occupied by Native peoples. McClung showed that each of these men had intimate relationships with either American Indian women or Spanish Mexican women or both; that the women were often related to one another; and that these relationships produced mixed-race and ultimately bicultural children who lived out their lives in the West.[14]

At least that is what leaps out now when one scans the *Carson-Bent-Boggs Genealogy*. When Blackwelder anticipated her friend's book in the 1950s, however, she wrote simply, "I am eager to see the completed work and know it will be a real contribution to information about a truly American pioneer family."[15] Unlike Blackwelder, McClung was not given to verbal flourish. Indeed, she eschewed narrative prose altogether; when McClung wanted to include a brief sketch of the Carson family in her genealogy, she asked Blackwelder to write it.[16] Although it was Blackwelder who called the subjects of McClung's work "a truly American pioneer family," given the women's close collaboration, it is no stretch to assume that McClung shared her friend's estimation of this kin network.

In what sense, then, might McClung and Blackwelder have seen the Carson, Bent, and Boggs families as "truly American"? Those who populate the genealogy constitute a striking mix: Arapahos, Cheyennes, other Indigenous peoples, Spanish Mexicans (people of Spanish and often American Indian and even African descent, many of whom downplayed or even denied their non-European ancestry), Anglo Americans (here, mostly people of English and Scots-Irish descent), as well as various and sundry human amalgamations. If this group of people was not just American but hyper-American, by what processes did they achieve their Americanness? With McClung's genealogy as a guide, we might conclude that they gained this identity by meeting, by recognizing one another as different but also desirable, by making mutual accommodations appropriate to existing social relations of power, and, ultimately, by losing markers of difference in a manner that created a singular place called the American West. Except when they did not. So, on the one hand, Josefa Jaramillo and Kit Carson meet. Kit converts to Catholicism and finds himself called Cristobal. He marries Josefa, and she bears the children they conceive, children who answer, depending on circumstances, to names like Julián or William, Josefita or Josephine. Eventually, however, they become Carsons all, with no more Spanish given names or surnames to twist the tongues of "truly American" readers.[17] On the other hand, there is William Bent, who goes west and finds himself called Little White Man by Cheyennes and Lakotas. He meets and marries Owl Woman, who is Cheyenne. Owl Woman bears their children, children with names like Mary and Robert and George and Julia. But Mary and Robert and George and Julia do not become Bents all. Instead, they follow distinct paths through an ethnoculturally complex and constantly changing West; they grow old and die on ranches and reservations alike. If the Carson family story, as one can divine it from McClung's genealogical charts, is the typical trail to a truly American identity, the routes taken by Owl Woman and her children reached the destination well enough to fit in the same book.[18]

If McClung and Blackwelder agreed that McClung was producing a genealogy of "a truly American pioneer family," they may have understood the phrase somewhat differently. McClung was not one to draw the curtain on a historical drama like the one played out by William Bent and Owl Woman, even if she might not give it center stage. (By contrast, later in life, Blackwelder worked on a biographical dictionary of western men from which she consciously excluded Indians.)[19] When Blackwelder told McClung that she thought the genealogy would be "a real contribution to information about a truly American pioneer family," McClung's book was not yet published. Blackwelder may not have realized how significant a place the Bent and Boggs family lines would occupy in the finished product. The "truly American" clan in Blackwelder's mind may have been the Carson family more narrowly defined. It is, in fact, the Carson lineage that is the most elaborately traced in the *Carson-Bent-Boggs Genealogy*, but, as even the title suggests, McClung's American family may have been a bit more expansive than Blackwelder's. McClung did not comment on how this relatively inclusive historical impulse reflected her own understanding of human difference. But such an impulse was not incompatible with the goals of early civil rights movements that called for equality under the law, universal human rights, and disaffirmation of those presumed differences that informed hierarchies of race, gender, and sexuality—even if some later came to critique the unintended normative and assimilationist outcomes such goals could produce.[20]

One dimension of the Carson family story, however, remains mostly hidden in the genealogy, and that is the frequency with which those represented on its pages lived alongside enslaved people, generally African Americans or American Indians. These Native and black people were bound to labor through one of two systems of slavery that pervaded North America into the nineteenth century: the enslavement of African-origin and African-descent people rooted in the East, and the enslavement primarily (though by no means exclusively) of Native people that increasingly was localized in the West.[21] Scant traces of black slaves do appear in the *Carson-Bent-Boggs Genealogy*. For instance, McClung reproduces a North Carolina will written in 1836 by Kit Carson's uncle Andrew, in which Andrew bequeathed ten slaves to his offspring.[22] Absent in the genealogy, however, is any indication that those Carsons who left the southern backcountry for the lower Missouri River frontier in the early nineteenth century took slaves along with them—that is, any indication that Carson himself grew up alongside African American children and among white slave owners.[23]

More completely obscured in the genealogy is the western system of slavery by which *hispanos* in New Mexico purchased Native people, often from rival Indian groups, incorporating the captives into their households as servants and often "adopting" them as family members, or *criados,* as they were called.[24] Although Carson did not take black slaves with him in 1826 when he ran off from Missouri at the age of sixteen and headed for New Mexico, he did, once he married Josefa Jaramillo in 1843, live in a household that "adopted" Indigenous people.[25] McClung probably understood little of this western slave trade and the practices of bound labor it generated. Even if she encountered evidence of it in the course of her research—such as baptismal records for the three Navajos raised in the Carson household—she might not have recognized its meaning. Yet this, too, was part and parcel of a "truly American" clan.

These are some of the ways that McClung saw and did not see the Americanness of her historical charges. But in what sense did she see these people as constituting "a family"? First, the phrase suggests a single entity: just one family. But the very presence of three surnames in the genealogy's title announces that multiple families populate the text. The table of contents pluralizes the problem, with chapters entitled "Wood Family," "Boone Carson Intermarriages," and "Jaramillo-Vigil Ancestry." Of course one always finds multiple surnames in a genealogy: people marry and names proliferate. But the three surnames of this book's title—Carson, Bent, and Boggs—were linked in ways that, on the one hand, exceed conventional definitions of family ties and, on the other, bring to mind not fathers and husbands but mothers and wives and lovers and children.[26]

Before people with the last names Carson, Bent, and Boggs settled in the borderlands, there was but one family relation among them (as genealogists reckon such relations). Juliana Bent—a sister of Charles and William—had married Lilburn Boggs. Lilburn became governor of Missouri years later, and later still he went west to California. But Juliana died young, after she bore two children. Lilburn Boggs then married Panthea Boone, a granddaughter of frontiersman Daniel Boone. Panthea had ten children. One of those children, Thomas Boggs, migrated first to California and then to New Mexico. It was Tom Boggs who befriended Kit Carson, thus earning the name Boggs a place in McClung's work.[27] So, when Carson, Boggs, and the Bent brothers lived in Missouri, the only genealogically legible connection among them was this: Tom Boggs's father had been married to Charles and William Bent's sister before she died. Boggs's mother was not a Bent, but a Boone. And Boggs was almost a generation younger than the other three men; he was a toddler when Carson started down the Santa Fe Trail. What connected these men at first were patterns of residence and migration and the frontier economies that encouraged them now to stay put, now to move on. It was what happened once they came of age and went west that made the men kin.

What made them kin were intimate partnerships with women and an expansive sense of responsibility for children. It started around 1840, when Carson, having lost his first wife, the Northern Arapaho woman Singing Grass, married the Southern Cheyenne woman Making Out Road. Making Out Road seems to have been a sister of Owl Woman, who had married William Bent.[28] McClung probably never suspected that Making Out Road and Owl Woman were sisters; if she had, she would have called attention to the tie. At any rate, Carson and Making Out Road's marriage did not last, and soon Carson cast his lot with Josefa Jaramillo of Taos. Already, Charles Bent was living with Josefa's older sister, Ignacia. When Bent was killed in the 1847 uprising of *hispanos* and Pueblo Indians against U.S. rule in New Mexico, Kit and Josefa took in Charles and Ignacia's daughter. Later still, a now grown-up Tom Boggs married another of Ignacia's daughters, Rumalda. Then, when Josefa and Kit both died suddenly in 1868, Tom and Rumalda assumed responsibility for the seven Carson children.[29] It was women—Cheyenne and *hispana*—and the babies they bore who made William Bent, Kit Carson, Charles Bent, and Tom Boggs kin.

SOULS LOST IN PURGATORY

If McClung the genealogist tells a spare tale of an expansive American family made kin through the daughters of the country, Blackwelder the biographer narrates an elaborate saga of a strange son of the frontier—small of stature, soft of voice, but somehow still "the greatest Westerner of all."[30] Like the *Carson-Bent-Boggs Genealogy*, Blackwelder's *Great Westerner* is a family tale.[31] It is also a romance. But for Blackwelder, both family and romance are perpetually deferred by the racial responsibilities of westering, and the tragic end comes too soon. Part of the difference between the two books is one of genre: genealogy resists narrative and biography demands it; genealogy tracks connections and biography trails the individual. The rest of the difference lies in the two women who created these texts. And there were crucial similarities, too, reflecting Blackwelder and McClung's long collaboration and the shared circumstances in which they wrote history.

Great Westerner is a work of narrative grace that grips the reader like a rousing patriotic song, rich with tales of adventure but always situating those adventures in meditations on Carson's sterling character and his strong family ties. It opens flushed with sensuous anticipation: "Missouri's hardwoods were tingeing, bittersweet pulsed languorously in the underbrush, and September waited quietly, expectantly." Gazing out at this landscape from his work at a saddler's bench is an "ordinary-looking youth, clothed like any border boy in nettle shirt and linsey-woolsey from his mother's loom, quiet and undersized." The boy, of course, is Kit Carson, and he is watching as freight wagons assemble for their annual trek to northern Mexico. He is facing west, "as all Carson men had since the first one left Dumfriesshire, Scotland, to find greater freedom in North Ireland."[32] From his mother's loom and his father's longing comes a slight border boy, all dressed down and ready to go.

Blackwelder establishes much of import in this opening, crafting key characteristics for Carson that give coherence to all that follows. Kit's body and voice mark the improbability of his rise to fame: He is small and hushed. But he is also hardwired for westering, a trait passed down from father to son, the reward for which is freedom. Blackwelder drives these points home again and again: Kit "stood only five-feet-six"; he was a "scrappy little leader." She also quotes contemporaries who remarked on Kit's stature: for example, General William Tecumseh Sherman, on first meeting Kit, declared that he was shocked to set eyes on such a "small stoop-shouldered man."[33] As for Kit's voice, Blackwelder describes it as "gentle," "high-pitched," and "almost feminine."[34] In other words, Kit's manhood was not secured by his body or his voice; it would have to be won.

For all his freedom, Blackwelder's Carson is a family man: an ardent suitor, a devoted husband, and a father who delights in his children. Blackwelder was proud of this depiction. Years after *Great Westerner* was released, while acknowledging that each book on Carson "contributed something," she wrote that she believed hers showed "more of his personality and his home life than any other."[35] Over the years Carson called many places home: he lived in forts and towns and camps; he slept in tents and tipis and adobes alongside any number of human companions. But for Blackwelder, home life connoted the presence of women. Children sweetened the deal.

In *Great Westerner*, then, Carson's home life does not begin until he woos and wins the young Arapaho woman Singing Grass. In Blackwelder's telling, it is a swashbuckling courtship in which the diminutive Carson stands his ground against a rival suitor, a burly French Canadian. The scene of the fight is a fur trade rendezvous—the annual Rocky Mountain trade fair that drew trappers, traders, and Native people—and when Kit rides away from the gathering in 1835, Singing Grass is "beside him to be his companion in the wilderness, his wife, his warmth and comfort." Singing Grass cures animal skins, gathers greens, and gives birth to Adaline, the couple's daughter. The little family prospers in the mountains until the decline of the beaver trade leads Carson to Bent's Fort, on the plains, where he works as a buffalo hunter. There Singing Grass suddenly dies, ending for Kit what Blackwelder calls "a genuine happiness."[36]

Little Adaline lives, however, and Blackwelder says that the women of Bent's Fort assumed responsibility for her care. Those women probably included the Native and mixed-blood wives of trappers and traders; perhaps some *mexicanas*; and also Charlotte Green, an enslaved black woman owned by the Bent brothers.[37] The women no doubt eventually included Kit's second wife, but Blackwelder was never convinced that Carson married the Cheyenne woman Making Out Road. She argues in a footnote that the relationship "was vigorously denied by Kit."[38] Carson's second marriage dismissed, Blackwelder then narrates the doting father's decision to take Adaline east to be educated among his Missouri relatives.[39]

Carson does seem to have told his niece that he had never been married to Making Out Road.[40] Since the publication of *Great Westerner* more than one historian has surmised that Carson lied to his *hispana* kinswomen about Making Out Road. A male relative, by contrast, confirmed the marriage.[41] Blackwelder probably did not know of this confirmation, and she trusted the niece's report. But Blackwelder surely did know that a Cheyenne woman named Sitting in the Lodge had told ethnologist George Bird Grinnell about Carson's relationship with Making Out Road in 1917, and that other elderly Cheyennes remembered it as well.[42] Blackwelder did not credit Cheyenne memories.

Carson's marriage to Making Out Road presented Blackwelder with problems of evidence, to be sure. It also presented problems of narrative. Put simply, the thread of Blackwelder's story that follows Carson's intimate life is in part a tale of racial ascent by association, an ascent that helps fit Carson for the title "great westerner." The thread leads directly from Singing Grass to Josefa Jaramillo, and Making Out Road would have frayed it. Blackwelder does not minimize Carson's attachment to Singing Grass, whom she calls a "bronze-skinned beauty."[43] But Singing Grass is the love of Kit's younger years. Josefa is the love of his later years, and, unlike Singing Grass, she is propertied and European. According to Blackwelder, Kit and Josefa met in the home of Ignacia and Charles Bent:

> Doña Ignacia Bent was a handsome woman and her home one of the most attractive in Taos. Rich rugs of Eastern import and native bright-striped serapes brought color to the rough floors and heavy hand-hewn furnishings. Ornate religious articles and sconces of hammered tin reflected soft candlelight in an atmosphere of quiet serenity. Here Kit Carson met and fell in love with Ignacia's sister Maria Josefa, a fourteen-year-old dark-eyed beauty. Kit, approaching thirty-three, was a man of some importance in the West and in spite of that fact that he had spent most of his years living in a very primitive manner, possessed a natural dignity that impressed young Josefa. Her family—the Castilian Jaramillos and Vigils—made no objection to Kit's suit though he had no fortune to offer and Josefa chose to accept the gentle man whose destiny of fame appeared certain.[44]

For Blackwelder, then, Carson marries into a family of means with Spanish, not Mexican, origins—that is, a white family, not one with *mestizo,* to say nothing of *mulato,* ancestors, Josefa's dark eyes notwithstanding. And the family is not just generically Spanish but rather Castilian—that is, identified with the old kingdom of Castile, which united with Aragon to create modern Spain and provided the Spanish state with its primary language.

The Jaramillo and Vigil families dated back to the 1690s in New Mexico; their forebears were among those sent to reestablish Spanish settlement there after the Pueblo Revolt of 1680 had expelled the first colonizers. Josefa's ancestors hailed from Mexico City and Zacatecas, respectively. Having spent five generations in the north and as many as five more generations further south in colonial Mexico, the Jaramillos, the Vigils, and all those families with whom they intermarried were long residents of the New World.[45] While Spanish Mexican families of some means struggled to preserve their *limpieza de sangre,* or purity of blood, sexual ties with Indigenous people, both coerced and consensual, went to the heart of the colonial project. Furthermore, slave traders brought some two hundred thousand Africans to Mexico during the colonial era. If every one of Josefa's forebears over two centuries succeeded in avoiding close contact with Indian and black people in New Spain, and if their pursuit of blood purity extended backward in time through Spain's complicated Mediterranean past, then perhaps they earned the label Castilian. But in the eighteenth century, some fifty years before Josefa was born, intermarriage in New Mexico was on the rise, such that whole new peoples found themselves incorporated under the label *Españoles.* Meanwhile, the Spanish crown began selling certificates that allowed people to "cleanse" themselves of "impure" ancestry (generally Indian or African), obscuring a past of racial mixing. Just how Spanish the leading *hispano* families of New Mexico were remains an open question.[46]

These insights, of course, depend on scholarship that was unavailable to Blackwelder in 1962. And her designation of the Jaramillos and Vigils as Castilian, at any rate, is largely a narrative device, no doubt abetted by the defensive response of some *nuevomexicanos* to the Anglo American conquest that began with the arrival of men like Carson in the nineteenth century and then continued into the twentieth, when they reinvented themselves as "Spanish Americans" to avoid the anti-Mexican racism of Anglo newcomers and the U.S. government alike.[47] The device ultimately serves Blackwelder's story of Carson himself, who, in spite of his recent "primitive" life in the mountains and on the plains, is destined for greatness. And everyone around him, including Josefa and her parents, seems to know it. In this telling, then, as Carson matures, so do his desires, from the more primitive yearnings of youth to the more civilized longings of adulthood.

If Kit has a happy family life with Singing Grass in *Great Westerner*, his home life with Josefa is exuberant, at least when he is home. He is not there often. By Blackwelder's account, Kit's early marriage to Josefa depends on brief conjugal visits as he passes in and out of New Mexico while engaged in other pursuits: escorting *nuevomexicano* wagons along the Santa Fe Trail, guiding famed explorer John C. Frémont on his western expeditions, and generally helping to secure the borderlands for the United States before and during the U.S.-Mexico War, despite Kit's residence in Mexican territory and his marriage to a Mexican citizen.[48] One key visit comes in 1847, during the war, while Josefa is living at the Bent home in Taos. U.S. soldiers have marched into New Mexico and established rule with Charles Bent, Josefa's brother-in-law, as governor. When the main detachment of troops departs for the California front, northern New Mexico erupts in protest over the U.S. occupation. Pueblo Indians and *hispanos* alike descend on the Bent home, killing Bent as well as Pablo Jaramillo, Josefa and Ignacia's brother, and one of their Vigil uncles. The womenfolk use kitchen tools to dig through an adobe wall and then hide themselves in a neighbor's house disguised as Indian servants grinding corn. Local volunteers and U.S. troops chase the insurgents, who take refuge in the mission church at Taos Pueblo, until the soldiers lay siege to the adobe structure, killing 150 and subjecting the leaders to a makeshift trial presided over by Bent's closest associates. All the while, Carson is en route from California to Washington, D.C., carrying government dispatches, oblivious to the bloodshed in Taos. But his travels take him through New Mexico, where he hears the news and rushes to Josefa's side. He stays a few days, and then he is off again for the nation's capital.[49]

Much of *Great Westerner* reads like this, with Kit chasing around North America and Josefa living in Taos with her relatives. Once, Kit checks in on Adaline, his daughter by Singing Grass, who is attending a female seminary in Missouri. By then, Kit and Josefa have been married for six years but have spent less than six months together. Soon Josefa bears their first child, who lives only a short time. After this loss Josefa gives birth every two or three years, until there are seven children. Now and then Kit lives with his family, even for months at a time. They take up residence on a ranch, Kit having finally "established a home worthy of his aristocratic wife." He brings Adaline, now an "attractive, well-schooled young woman with pale copper-tinted skin," to this home. The family is also together in Taos, where Kit works as Indian agent to Pueblo, Ute, and Apache peoples. When the Civil War breaks out, however, Kit becomes an officer with the New Mexico Volunteers in support of the Union cause, and he takes his family to the headquarters in Albuquerque. There, Blackwelder says, he is a "most unsoldierly officer," who romps "on the floor with his children swarming over him, searching for candy in the pockets of his uniform." But then Kit is relocated to Fort Union, on the plains along the Santa Fe Trail, and Josefa returns to Taos. The rest of the war finds Carson fighting Confederate incursions from Texas and, most important, Native peoples as yet unaccustomed to U.S. rule.[50]

Carson's participation in the Civil War–era Navajo campaign would soon become the touchstone for a wholesale reevaluation of his legacy.[51] Blackwelder could not have known this in 1962. The campaign must have given her pause, however, since *Great Westerner* depicts Carson as "devoted to achieving a lasting peace with the Indians and providing for their welfare," and as an admirer of Navajos in particular. The problem, as Blackwelder lays it out, is that Navajo raiders have plagued the villagers of the upper Rio Grande, both *hispanos* and Pueblo Indians. Navajos raided for livestock, particularly sheep, but also for human captives, who could be used as servants, incorporated into families, or sold in the borderlands slave trade. What Blackwelder does not say, and may not have known, is that raiding was a two-way street: Pueblo Indians and *hispanos* alike also plagued Navajos, participating in a wider political economy of exchange and violence that had evolved over two centuries. The U.S. government, a newcomer on the scene, came down on the side of the villagers, and Colonel Carson, under the direction of General James Carleton, was the officer in charge.[52]

It is their plan, as Blackwelder puts it, "to force the Navajos into submission by systematically destroying their crops and driving off their sheep." And Carleton wants to move the Navajos out of their homeland to the spot in eastern New Mexico known as the Bosque Redondo. In Blackwelder's telling, Carson proceeds with his grim duty, but "not without regret." In the end, Carson achieves "victory almost without bloodshed," and eight thousand Navajos begin their Long Walk to the Bosque Redondo. Blackwelder acknowledges that the Bosque experiment was disastrous for the Navajo people. At the same time, she contends that it was "a great heartache" for Carson and Carleton. Still, it is heartache of a different sort that prompts Kit first to request reassignment at a post where his family can be with him and then to try to resign his command. Officials will not accommodate him, though, so "in spite of his personal feeling," he stays with the army. One last campaign rounds out his career, this one against Comanches and Kiowas. Then Kit receives his highest reward; he is brevetted brigadier general.

Finally, he is reassigned to Ute country at Fort Garland, north of Taos in the San Luis Valley. There Josefa joins him, as do the children, who run around the fort, in Blackwelder's words, "like a small tribe of untamed savages, completely adored by their father."[53]

This, then, is a final moment of family fare for Carson, for his health is slowly failing as the result of an old injury. But he has achieved the fullness of Blackwelder's title, *Great Westerner*. He is still, of course, a short fellow (Josefa is "slightly taller"), but now his body is "stout" and "solidly built."[54] His voice is still soft, but it commands "respect and attention," and with it he speaks English, Spanish, French, "and many Indian languages."[55] From a slight border boy—a provisional American, a provisional man—Kit has evolved into a brigadier general who bests even a Civil War officer as renowned as William Tecumseh Sherman. When Carson negotiates with the Utes alongside Sherman, the Union hero remarks, "Those redskins think Kit twice as big a man as me."[56] Carson has also evolved from a lad who loves a "bronze-skinned beauty" and sires a child with "pale copper-tinted skin" to a mature man who marries an "aristocratic," "Castilian" woman (even if she can, inexplicably, pass for an Indian servant when necessary). Granted, Kit and Josefa's children are boisterous: Blackwelder calls them "untamed savages," while Sherman says they are "as wild and untrained as a brood of Mexican mustangs."[57] These are racialized references that might seem to disrupt the narrative of racial ascent that Blackwelder plots for Carson. But her use of them may well draw on an educational theory that had passed into popular thought by the mid-twentieth century. According to recapitulation theory, youngsters, and particularly boys, benefit from a wild youth, because a child's growth must recapitulate the development of the "white race" from savagery to civilization. Children who act like "untamed savages" and "Mexican mustangs" can expect, with proper grooming, to learn the habits of civilization over time.[58] In this sense, then, the racialized references to Kit and Josefa's rowdy offspring neatly fit Blackwelder's larger story.

The devil of that story, however, is in the human details. Blackwelder spares nothing in the denouement. Rather than remain at a remote post like Fort Garland, Josefa suggests that the family join her niece Rumalda, who is now married to Tom Boggs, in southeastern Colorado. The couple has settled on land Tom claimed for Rumalda as an heir to the Vigil and St. Vrain Grant, one of the last extravagant land grants of the Mexican era. The spot is not far from Carson's old haunt, Bent's Fort, on a tributary of the Arkansas called the Purgatoire, known to Rumalda and Josefa as *Rio de las Animas Perdidas en Purgatorio* (River of Souls Lost in Purgatory). The family moves to the settlement at Boggsville. Meanwhile, Kit is appointed superintendent of Indian affairs for Colorado, in which capacity he accompanies Ute leaders east to negotiate a new treaty. The trip wearies Kit, who returns to Colorado unwell. Josefa meets his stagecoach heavy with child. Five days later she gives birth. Ten days after that, Josefa, Kit's "beautiful beloved," is dead. Kit lives for a month, cared for by a doctor, his niece, and her German-born husband. Then, one afternoon, the German cooks Kit a supper of buffalo and chile and gives him a pipe of tobacco. Kit relishes the fare, but then, suddenly, he cries out his dying words, "Doctor, *Compadres, Adios!*"[59]

This closing episode explains the epigraph Blackwelder chose for her book, a quotation that seems misplaced when one first cracks the cover of *Great Westerner*. The epigraph comes from Blackwelder's fellow Kansan Eugene Fitch Ware, a nineteenth-century politician and poet:

> Time is pursued by a pitiless, cruel oblivion,
> Following fast and near.[60]

The words evoke a foreboding and fatalism that do not characterize *Great Westerner* until the final passage. There, Carson has become "the greatest Westerner of them all," which, if westering is a quintessentially American habit, means that he has become the greatest American. He even consumes unique products of the Americas in the moment before his death: buffalo, chile, and tobacco.[61] What is more, each of these products is linked to one of the many peoples of the Americas: buffalo with Indian hunters, chile with Mexican farmers, and tobacco with African slaves. Carson absorbs them all. But pitiless, cruel oblivion chases him down. He dies the father of a "truly American pioneer family" with whom he has never really lived.

Both Blackwelder and McClung spun tales about Carson that bespoke a family romance. But McClung, the genealogist, was more taken by the web of western connections that enveloped Carson in a variegated human frontier fixed in place by female moorings. Blackwelder, the biographer, was keen on creating a new American man, one who resolved the tensions of an older, remembered empire through his own racial ascent but who also balanced newer, Cold War ideals for white, middle-class, heterosexual manhood—competing ideals that cherished both breadwinning providers and engaged, affectionate husbands and fathers.[62] Blackwelder's melancholy conclusion suggests that rhetorical equipoise could not, in fact, answer the riddles of injustice, inequality, and imperialism. No wonder she never wrote another book.

WESTERNS, WESTERNERS, AND WESTERN HISTORIANS

There were probably other reasons, too. When McClung and Blackwelder began their research in the 1950s, they were among thousands of history enthusiasts who worked on western topics without the benefit of advanced degrees or academic affiliations. Meanwhile, there were hundreds of degreed western historians working in colleges, universities, libraries, museums, and historical sites and societies. But as a senior scholar recalls, "in American academic circles," western history "was not considered mainline in the 1950s."[63] No professional organization of U.S. western historians existed. In the post–World War II era, then, the history of the West was largely the domain of amateurs. The majority of these history buffs were men, and almost all were white. There were exceptions, such as the well-published Mari Sandoz, daughter of Swiss immigrants and author of the biography *Crazy Horse*. Earlier in the century there was Delilah Beasley, African American clubwoman and author of *The Negro Trail Blazers of California*.[64] But the exceptions proved the rule: western history was a wide-open field for well-read amateurs who had the time and resources to devote to their hobby, and most such enthusiasts were white and male.[65] It was in this milieu that Blackwelder and McClung embarked on their Carson projects.

These western history buffs were an organized bunch. It all started in Chicago, where in 1944 a small group of men established The Westerners. The founding members of this first chapter named themselves the Chicago Corral. Word of The Westerners traveled, and soon men in Colorado's capital formed the Denver Posse. Most of the subsequent chapters that formed took on the "corral" or "posse" title, organizing in cities like St. Louis, New York, Tucson, Spokane, and Washington, D.C., and also statewide, in Wyoming and South Dakota. Within a decade of the Chicago Corral's founding, Westerners from all over began to meet annually at an Inter-Posse Rendezvous.[66]

Most of the corrals and posses did not admit women. The New York Posse was the first to break the mold; the wives of two of the men as well as Mari Sandoz herself were among the founders. As a Westerners' chronicler wrote in 1957, "There were a lot of wranglers in the Corrals and Posses further west who damn near moved camp over this, but it wasn't too long before the men stopped airin' their lungs and the whole outfit . . . is now bridle-wise. After all, one can't say 'No' to a Mari Sandoz!"[67] Nonetheless, The Westerners remained a heavily male group. As late as 1970, a founder explained, "The Westerners are bunches of males mostly, who meet monthly usually, to chomp and chat—then, after a speech on Western history to haze or praise the speaker."[68] The *Chicago Tribune* put it bluntly: "This is a stag outfit."[69] Meanwhile, Chicago's corral was bursting; according to the *Tribune*, the growing membership included "lawyers, artists, doctors, anthropologists, geologists, bank presidents, industrialists, and advertising men." In other words, this was a middle- and upper-middle-class organization. The members met monthly at the Merchants and Manufacturers Club, finding "a happy escape from current problems by thumping a hairy-chested past."[70] Predictably, then, the Chicago Corral was not among the first to go coed. Even a designated "ladies' night" in 1952 drew criticism. The gathering featured a display of Native women's traditional clothing in a show dubbed "America's First Fashions." One man grumbled, "It's bad enough to have a ladies' night... but to have a dress parade is too much. What is this? A knitting society?"[71]

Thus, when McClung and Blackwelder began their work in the 1950s, they were amateur historians in a field where amateurs predominated, which could have worked to their advantage. They were also white in an arena that assumed whiteness as a ticket of admission. But the flip side of that ticket said that white men ought to be admitted first. Well-educated, well-established men would be most at home on this range, where they offered one another a backslapping welcome to each chest-thumping roundup.

But change, of a sort, was on the horizon. In 1961 a small group of white men, mostly academics, met in Detroit at the annual conference of the Mississippi Valley Historical Association, forerunner of the Organization of American Historians, the leading professional group for U.S. historians. The western historians who huddled there were promoting, as Robert Utley recalls, a "regional association of specialists, such as already existed for the South, the Midwest, and elsewhere."[72] Utley himself was strategically positioned in this, since he had begun but not finished a Ph.D., choosing instead a career with the National Park Service.[73] His ties to both professors and buffs were an asset in building a new organization that drew on the strength of The Westerners but also appealed to degreed scholars working in academia. Those who met in Detroit in the spring of 1961 announced a fall gathering in Santa Fe, where the call for a new association would "spontaneously" arise.[74]

Organizers expected ninety registrants at the First Conference on the History of Western America in Santa Fe. Three hundred showed up, filling La Fonda, the grand hotel on the plaza at the end of the Santa Fe Trail. The location of this gathering (in the midst of Pueblo Indian country and at the heart of the old Mexican North) and the conference program distributed to participants (the cover featured a "prairie schooner lady" replete with rifle) suggested that a newer day might dawn in western history. To contemporary eyes, a "Southwestern Borderlands" session and ethnologist John Ewer's adaptation of the "marginal man" concept in "Mothers of the Mixed-Bloods: The Marginal Woman in the History of the Upper Missouri" look promising. But of the twenty-five papers presented, none were by women or people of color.[75]

Of more lasting impact than the sessions themselves was an evening business meeting, which staged the call for a new organization. Liquor lubricated the proceedings, and a consensus emerged. A "quiet dinner" of organizers followed. All of the men who dined, save Utley, had doctorates, most were professors, and some were active in The Westerners. Ray Allen Billington, the era's best-known western historian, agreed to serve as the new group's first president.[76] The actual founding of the Western History Association (WHA) came a year later, in 1962, at the Second Conference on the History of Western America in Denver. Reflecting the organization's commitment to bringing academics and buffs together, the first publication of the WHA was not a dense scholarly journal but a slick illustrated magazine called *The American West*.[77] Over time, professional historians would assume greater control over the WHA, and hence over the field of western history. But for now, a gentlemanly bargain kept the stags grazing more or less amiably in the same glen.

Unlike most early chapters of The Westerners, the WHA did not exclude women, though many of us who joined in later decades believe that a hot western sun of white male privilege bathed our organizational forebears in its glow.[78] The earth did not begin to turn until the 1970s, and the changed angle of light was not fully apparent until the 1980s.[79] In the meantime, as one white woman in the field put it, "There were very few of us, and we were treated like morons by most male historians."[80] Still, the WHA's open membership policy mattered. Blackwelder, who lived in suburban Washington, D.C., could not have joined The Westerners' Potomac Corral. She could, and did, become a charter member of the WHA.[81] McClung did not join, perhaps because her own work identity was less as a historian and more as a librarian and genealogist, and her chief organizational tie was to the Colorado Genealogical Society.[82]

WHA members or not, Blackwelder and McClung were marginal figures in the field. Indeed, they were minor historians, walk-ons whom few of the major actors even noticed. That is why they were so important to each other; they took one another seriously and thrived on their collaboration. Yet they—and Blackwelder especially—remained aware of their status as women working in western history (and, like most white people, oblivious to the privilege afforded by race). The first time Blackwelder sent her Carson biography out for consideration, an editor returned it, recommending that she rework it as a "youth book."[83] Irked by the suggestion, she revised the manuscript and sent it to Caxton Printers.[84] She told McClung, "I know there is a good and authentic story there," but, she continued, "perhaps it [is] too ladylike for a Wild West thriller."[85] Such protests notwithstanding, the psychic damage was done, and even though there is no indication that Blackwelder originally intended her work for young readers, ever after that initial rejection and revision, she clung to the notion that hers was "a story rather than a history book." In retrospect she insisted that she had always "had in mind the young adult," and she claimed that she would be satisfied if the book found a place in "school libraries."[86] Feigning low expectations, Blackwelder inoculated herself against the disappointment that might follow any woman—even a married white woman of the appropriate class—who ventured into the gendered space of the American West.

Blackwelder's rivalry with the woman who published a competing Carson biography in 1962 opens another window onto these dynamics. In 1961 Blackwelder wrote that she had heard about "some woman in Taos" who was also writing a book about Carson.[87] The woman was Marion Estergreen, and her *Kit Carson: A Portrait in Courage* was published by the University of Oklahoma Press shortly after Blackwelder's book was released.[88] Like Blackwelder, Estergreen was an amateur historian. Unlike Blackwelder, Estergreen won a contract with a university press and published under a gender-ambiguous name, M. Morgan Estergreen.[89] Blackwelder and Estergreen were not strangers; they had met and cooperated with one another on commemorations of Carson. Blackwelder felt that her relationship with Estergreen had soured years earlier when Estergreen asked for comments on a short Carson piece she had written. "I answered her honestly and offended her I suppose," Blackwelder griped to McClung about Estergreen, "as she has been very cool to me ever since."[90] By the time both Blackwelder and Estergreen published in 1962, the breach was complete, and Blackwelder told McClung that she "wondered what Kit was thinking about the old hens fighting over his memory."[91] Blackwelder held that Estergreen got key details of Carson's life wrong.[92] But it was also clear that, try as she might to be fair to Estergreen, Blackwelder did not like her rival. "She has worked so hard on every Carson project and is a very pleasant and attractive person," Blackwelder wrote of Estergreen, and then turned the knife: "The last time I saw her, she said she expected to be married to a very wealthy man who was travelling in Europe. . . . I think she has a vivid imagination."[93]

In calling her struggle with Estergreen a hen fight, Blackwelder abased not only Estergreen but also herself, trivializing not just their differences but the very intellectual work that animated both women. In suggesting that Estergreen's romance with an affluent, worldly man was a flight of fancy, Blackwelder hurled the ultimate insult one white, middle-class, heterosexual woman could fling at another. Both aspersions bespoke a cultural conservatism about women and their worth, a language so pervasive in this era that many women themselves were experts in its grammar. But Blackwelder's resentment stemmed, too, from a root of bitterness about how that language circumscribed her own life chances, especially as a woman working in western history.[94] When Estergreen published under the gender-ambiguous name Morgan and with a university press renowned for its western history list, she increased the chances that the very people who were gaining ground in the field—white male professors—would take notice. And, indeed, Estergreen's *Kit Carson* was available in a handsome paperback edition for over four decades, while Blackwelder's *Great Westerner* went out of print in just eight years.[95] Estergreen won the hen fight in part by passing as a rooster.

Nonetheless, there was one thing on which all creatures great and small—amateurs and professionals, lowly hens and high-stepping roosters—could agree: historians told the truth about the western past.[96] In this, historians set their West, the West of history, in opposition to the West of the Western. This habit of opposition developed in part because the field of western history had lagged at the same moment that film and television Westerns—oaters, as they were called—reached the height of their popularity.[97] Western history lagged because decades of criticism had battered the founding argument in the field, the frontier thesis. Frederick Jackson Turner had declared in 1893, "The existence of an area of free land, its continuous recession, and the advance of American settlement westward, explain American development." Turner's thesis fell on hard times, especially during the Depression, when the agony of many Americans seemed better explained by such forces as urbanization and industrialization.[98] Meanwhile, in the mines of myth and memory, the West maintained its luster, and purveyors of popular culture tapped that bright vein with a vengeance. Between 1935 and 1959, the percentage of Westerns as a proportion of all Hollywood films produced each year never dipped below 20 percent. The peak years came in the decade after 1945, when at least a quarter of features made annually were Westerns.[99] No other single film genre could match these proportions. The new medium of television followed suit; in 1958, for instance, seven of the top ten Nielsen-rated series were oaters. As one scholar argues, "No television program genre, not even the situation comedy, ever became so dominant at any given moment in time as the Western during the late 1950s and early 1960s."[100]

Raw numbers and relative proportions, however, do not reveal the changes that were taking place within the genre. Some film Westerns began to take a darker, more complicated view of the frontier. The most famous of these anti-Westerns was *High Noon* (1952), which, through Gary Cooper's character, critiqued not only the "civilizing" projects of the Old West but also the conformist, anticommunist politics of the Cold War.[101] Two years later, *Johnny Guitar* did likewise, this time with a butch-looking Joan Crawford wielding the gun. Then, in 1956, came *Giant*, a Texas epic in which neither Rock Hudson as cattle king nor James Dean as oil baron holds a sustainable vision of the West's riches. In a striking critique of regional racism, *Giant* ends with a new take on the wealth of Texas: a scene of two toddlers—cousins—in a playpen, one a towheaded Anglo and the other a dark-eyed *mestizo*. Television Westerns changed as well. The early 1950s saw a preponderance of morally simple action shows like *The Adventures of Kit Carson* and *The Lone Ranger*, which appealed to youngsters. The late 1950s and the 1960s witnessed series like *Gunsmoke* and *Bonanza*, dramas capable of moral complexity and geared toward adult audiences.[102]

As intricate, multiple, and mutable as Westerns were, they had weak links to the actual western past. It was those tenuous ties that bothered the historically minded, who, for better and worse, saw themselves as engaged not in acts of representation but in acts of recuperation. In the view of most historians, producers of popular culture created stylized images of the past; historians re-created what really happened. It would be decades before historians would start to recognize that their own practices were also representational. In the meantime, historians could envision themselves as rescuing the West from the Westerns.[103] For instance, academic Ray Allen Billington sniffed, "To a generation of Americans bred on television and cinema 'westerns,' ... the West is to be enjoyed rather than understood." Enjoyment was kid stuff.[104] For their part, The Westerners, not unfairly, boasted that they had preserved the field of western history at a time when even academics had shied away, and well before the explosion of film and TV Westerns. A founder states, "In [the 1940s], there was no subculture or public of Western buffs. The dime novel era was over, steel-eyed William S. Hart's fans were of Boy Scout age, and college catalogs attest that Western history was scantily accepted by academics. TV's 'oaters' were yet to be, and the Western History Association was almost two decades in the future."[105] The resurgence of western history, first among amateurs and then among the academics, would wean the Boy Scouts from their oaters for a manly meal of meat and potatoes—and no skipping the vegetables.

McClung and Blackwelder ate at a table nearby, even if the men of The Westerners who gathered to "chomp and chat" in Chicago and the WHA organizers who sat down to a "quiet dinner" in Santa Fe rarely glanced their way. So identified were these two women with the larger recuperative project of the historian—the sober reconstitution of a lost world that little resembled the West of the Western—that they barely realized the contribution their work had made. Seeing themselves as engaged in a broader contest between the truth of history and the sham of popular culture, they did not recognize that their achievements were partly in the realm of representation. They succeeded in domesticating a key icon of the western past, in tying Kit Carson tightly to the people who populated his everyday world—and not just the explorers, warriors, and soldiers featured in earlier accounts, but also the wives and children and brothers-in-law that in fact anchored Carson in the borderlands and kept him coming back, and back, and back again, until he finally spoke his dying words in Spanish to a German-born kinsman who understood him, as they rested not far from the old traders' fort where Kit had once held an Arapaho and then a Cheyenne woman in his arms, the same arms that shouldered a gun trained on Navajo people. No one at an Inter-Posse Rendezvous, no one at the Santa Fe conference, and no Saturday matinee Western had done that.

THE COLD WAR, THE COLOR LINE, AND THE CUL-DE-SAC

If the fortunes of western history as a field of inquiry and of the Western as a form of popular culture provide one context for Blackwelder and McClung's remaking of Carson, then the social, political, and economic dynamics of the postwar era provide another. The Cold War standoff between the capitalist United States and the communist Soviet Union fostered multiple cultural byproducts.

For McClung and Blackwelder's work, two of these were most relevant: the promotion of the heterosexual, nuclear family as both a locus of and a metaphor for national security, and the idealization of the West and its past as a sort of savings bank where American character might safely be deposited to earn interest against attempts at assassination, foreign or domestic. Just as important, the civil rights movements among minoritized populations in the United States both appropriated and challenged Cold War dogma, leavening lumpish notions of "the family" and "the West" and creating conditions for social change—and for conservative resistance to change. These dynamics, as well as the twin processes of suburban growth and urban decay, with all of their racial impetus and consequence, did not just shape Blackwelder and McClung's work casually, the way a cloudy day affects one's mood. The climate of the Cold War United States poured down on these women and saturated their daily lives, providing, in some ways, the elements for a good intellectual yield and, in others, the kind of weather that dampened creativity and left crops waterlogged.

The material conditions of Blackwelder's life, for example, reflected postwar trends. When she was working on *Great Westerner,* Bernice first lived with her

FIGURE 12.3. Bernice Blackwelder and Harold Blackwelder, 1970s. Quantrille D. McClung Papers, Western History Collection, Courtesy of Denver Public Library.

husband, Harold, on a cul-de-sac in a residential neighborhood of Arlington, Virginia, outside Washington, D.C.[106] The four-room half-duplex was small, and when they were preparing to move to nearby Alexandria in 1957, Bernice reported happily that she would now have space for her notes and books: "Will be wonderful to spread out a little more as now I will . . . have a room for assembling all this material." The new house—a one-story brick rambler that appears to have been financed with a GI loan—gave her the proverbial room of her own.[107] Like other postwar white married couples, Harold and Bernice benefited from federal housing policy, which underwrote mortgages for single-family suburban homes. Such loans went hand in hand with racial discrimination by the Federal Housing Administration and the Veteran's Administration, which endorsed racially segregated neighborhoods. This left poor people and people of color, often living in rentals, overrepresented in the cities, and more prosperous white people, most of them home owners, overrepresented in the suburbs.[108] It was a vicious cycle of suburban development and urban decline, since suburbs boasted property owners who created a strong tax base, while the urban tax base lagged, leaving city dwellers hurting for services and amenities that the affluent took as their due.[109] In the years that they lived in Arlington and Alexandria, the Blackwelders were in the thick of all this.

But they were not secure in this world. Bernice's changing fortunes were tied to those of her peripatetic husband. In 1960, with Bernice's help, Harold opened a restaurant called The Country House. Once this enterprise was up and running, Harold took over operations and Bernice declared, "I am now free to pursue my own interests."[110] Less than two years later, however, Harold opened a takeout food business, and Bernice was responsible for making the pastries they sold.[111] This enterprise must have faltered, because within months Bernice was worried that they might have to sell their house. She wrote to McClung in the summer of 1962 that she hoped she would still be in Alexandria in the fall: "Expect to be as I will not be too easily moved from this home." That was the last letter she posted from the East.[112] A real estate listing tucked in some family papers shows that she and Harold put the house up for sale soon thereafter.[113] Suburban dreams could die hard.

McClung never had those dreams, or, if she did, she did not have the resources to pursue them. In 1947 health problems had forced her to retire early from librarianship. McClung reported that her "modest affairs" were in a bank trust that allowed her "a small sum each month"; she also enjoyed a "small pension from the City" and kept a savings account for emergencies.[114] She seemed content to live in the city of her birth, renting an apartment that allowed her to walk to the Denver Public Library and the Colorado Historical Society. In 1962, she moved to a new apartment, just a half-dozen blocks from the building where she lived in the 1950s.[115] The neighborhood was predominantly white. In this era, Denver was a largely segregated city, and it remained so because of restrictive

FIGURE 12.4. Quantrille McClung, 1970s. Courtesy of *The Colorado Genealogist* 37, no. 2 (Summer 1976).

real estate covenants and, after legal challenges to such covenants, because of discriminatory practices by banks, realtors, and white property owners. In 1950, for example, almost 90 percent of African Americans in Denver lived in the Five Points area, more than a dozen blocks northeast of McClung's apartment. By 1960 the black population had grown, and some families had moved east toward the Park Hill area, but this was even further from McClung's home. Denver's ethnic Mexican population, which included *hispanos* with origins in New Mexico as well as Mexican immigrants, similarly lived in separate areas, especially to the north and west and along the South Platte River.[116] Still, McClung was probably more likely to encounter people of color in downtown Denver than Blackwelder was in suburban Arlington and Alexandria.

Both women must have been aware that racial change was brewing. They had lived through the upswing of activism that followed World War II among virtually all racialized minority peoples in the United States, including American Indians, Asian Americans, African Americans, and Latinos. Denver, for example, with its substantial ethnic Mexican population, was home to active chapters of the American GI Forum and the League of United Latin American Citizens.[117] But no movement was more visible to white Americans nationally than that of black civil rights activists, whose attack on the legal basis for discrimination and segregation, exemplified most famously in the 1954 U.S. Supreme Court case *Brown v. Board of Education,* had turned toward direct action of the sort associated with the Montgomery bus boycott of 1955–56 and the student sit-ins in the years that followed. Virginia, where the Blackwelders lived, participated in the "massive resistance" that southern states mounted to civil rights.[118] Nonetheless, McClung and Blackwelder were silent about all this in their correspondence, perhaps because they were just getting to know one another; they introduced themselves by letter in 1956, and by 1962 they had met face-to-face only twice.[119] The purpose of their correspondence in these years was to exchange research information; only later would the two women grow close and write freely about other areas of their lives. For white women who collaborated on research and were not yet trusted friends, perhaps it was white racial etiquette, itself an element of racial privilege, that dictated their deafening silence about the changes that were beginning to wrench the U.S. social order.[120]

But, as their depiction of Carson demonstrates, there was no aspect of that social order that did not pervade their thinking. The *Carson-Bent-Boggs Genealogy* and *Great Westerner* told tales about race as much as they told family stories, and those tales probably would have been different if the books had been written before the postwar civil rights movements flourished. Indeed, the books themselves constitute the best evidence McClung and Blackwelder left behind of their encounter with racial change. The evidence suggests that the two women met the challenge of civil rights in similar and different ways. Neither of them obscured

Carson's marriages to Singing Grass or Josefa Jaramillo, though both largely ignored his relationships with slaves. Civil rights organizations had been campaigning against miscegenation laws for decades, even if the U.S. Supreme Court would not declare such laws unconstitutional until five years after Blackwelder and McClung published their books.[121] The message of these campaigns seems to have reached both women, but in unequal measure. McClung was little fazed by Carson's mixed marriages, while Blackwelder felt compelled to arrange those nuptials along a continuum of ascending whiteness. Carson's connections to slavery, however, must have been disconcerting for both women. Blackwelder erased them altogether, while McClung documented only the slaveholding of Carson's forebears. By 1962, the history of slavery was an embarrassment to many white Americans, better forgotten or pushed far back in time, the easier, perhaps, to dismiss demands made by the descendants of slaves in the present.[122]

By contrast, McClung and Blackwelder reflected openly on the geopolitics of the Cold War, which, in fact, bolstered interest in all things western and so helped to nurture a market for the books they were producing.[123] The prospects for nuclear war proved particularly discomforting. In 1958, for instance, Blackwelder wrote to McClung that she wondered "what good it really is to dig into the past and unearth little nobodies when it is now a possibility that we may all be blown to nothing."[124] McClung replied, "Yes, in view of the possibilities of world destruction, genealogical research seems silly."[125] When *Great Westerner* was released in 1962, no less a cold warrior than former president Dwight Eisenhower sent Blackwelder his congratulations. Blackwelder—a Republican, a fellow Kansan, and a trained singer—had worked for the Eisenhower administration and had even performed at a party for his inauguration. The note he sent was in part political payback. But Eisenhower loved the frontier, and so the focus of *Great Westerner* mattered.[126] Just as Cold War politics laid out a welcome mat for work on the West, it also placed limits on where and when that work could proceed. In May of 1958, McClung was invited to a Carson family reunion in Kansas, where she might have gleaned information for her genealogy. But, she told Blackwelder, "I did not feel like spending my own money to go and I did not want to be on the road at such a dangerous time."[127] Lack of funds was a perennial theme for both women, but the danger McClung felt that May was particular. She was no doubt referring to international tensions created by the ongoing Cuban Revolution and, most immediately, by Vice President Richard Nixon's ill-fated tour of Latin America, where violent anti-U.S. protests prompted Eisenhower to send troops to Caribbean bases.[128]

The clearest indication of how Cold War culture shaped these women and the work they did, however, lies in their representation of Carson as a family man. And their subtle disagreements about what fit in a family story remind us that the idea of "family" was a flashpoint for debate as much as it was a cultural fund for the discipline of nonconformists. Blackwelder and McClung's crisis of representation started in 1957, when they heard rumor of murder and mayhem among Kit Carson and Josefa Jaramillo's offspring. One story had their son Cristobal shooting his in-laws, the parents of his wife, Lupe. After the shooting, Cristobal was said to have run off to escape authorities. While he was gone, Lupe reportedly had a baby who could not have been her husband's, though the child came to be called Kit Carson III.[129] A second story had Kit and Josefa's son Julián killing his wife Pasqualita's father.[130] McClung and Blackwelder found plausible the story of Lupe's parents' murder as well as the related tale of Kit III's illegitimacy. They dismissed the tale of Julián shooting his father-in-law. But they stopped short of working to confirm or discredit these stories. Blackwelder was blunt: as for "the family scandal," she wrote, "I believe we should keep the closet doors tightly shut." McClung was equivocal: "Accounts of the supposed Carson homicides just show how incorrect stories get around and how hard it is to clarify them."[131] Given how diligently they worked to clarify other aspects of Carson family history, however, their decision to maintain a public silence about such stories is notable. Not all tales had a place in the family room; some belonged in the closet.

It was not just murder that counted as scandal, as Kit Carson III's alleged illegitimacy suggests.[132] In the years to come, Blackwelder and McClung's crisis would grow as they encountered more evidence of sexual relationships outside marriage in the Carson family circle. This information was just beginning to surface as they completed their books. The main case in point was what McClung called the "mystery of the Rumaldas."[133] Recall that Tom Boggs married a woman named Rumalda, the daughter of Ignacia Jaramillo, Josefa's sister. This Rumalda, born about 1831, was Ignacia's child from her first marriage. Yet early on, Blackwelder and McClung ran across references to another daughter of Ignacia's named Rumalda. Bent descendants told McClung that this Rumalda was the child of Ignacia and Charles Bent, born in the summer of 1847. But in one Bent family Bible, the marriage records had been erased, and a second Bible listed this Rumalda's year of birth as 1850. If Rumalda the younger was indeed born in 1850, she could not have been the daughter of Charles Bent, because he was murdered in the January 1847 uprising against U.S. rule in New Mexico. A birth date of 1850 would have given the second Rumalda an amazingly long gestation, so long as Charles was considered her father.[134] In 1958, McClung wrote confidently that she thought she would be able "to clear up the mystery of the Rumaldas in the Bent and Boggs families."[135]

In fact, when McClung published her genealogy in 1962, the mystery was only half solved. In an entry for the Bents, McClung repeats the contention of some family members that Rumalda the younger was born in Taos six months after the 1847 death of her father Charles. But McClung also spells out the inconsistencies in Bent family Bibles that point to an 1850 birth date for this Rumalda, and thus a different father.[136] In an appendix, McClung goes on to quote from a court decree that not only listed just three children of Charles Bent, none of them named Rumalda, but also explained that these three were his "*natural* son and daughters... by him begotten upon and conceived and born of Ignacia Jaramillo."[137] In other words, Ignacia and Charles themselves might never have married. This and other such plots would thicken after McClung and Blackwelder published their books, as more clues surfaced and as attitudes about sexuality changed, until even the tale of Carson's three marriages would no longer seem to be the whole story of his intimate life. By 1969, Blackwelder would write to McClung in defense of the man she had portrayed in *Great Westerner:* "There is nothing gained by passing on 'gossip' of Kit's amorous associations.... To me he was a devoted family man and a great humanitarian."[138] Meanwhile, McClung went about her genealogical business, quietly hinting at how complicated domestic life in the nineteenth-century borderlands could be.

In different ways, the Cold War love affair with the family permeated each woman's work. After all, this was the era in which the fight against communism and the search for security in idealized heterosexual homes intertwined to produce a dominant discourse of "domestic containment," which, of course, obscured the actual complexity and diversity of both politics and intimate life in the United States.[139] It was hard to write a family history when so much of what swirled around folks like the Carsons also gusted up against conventional definitions of the family. Such definitions were informed by prescriptions for sexual intimacy: it should happen only in the context of marriage.[140] They were also informed by assumptions about nurturance and affection: these were the natural currency of family ties. Tales of murder and nonmarital sex alike gave pause. Regardless, Blackwelder (deliberately) and McClung (ambivalently) made of Kit Carson a family man who fought for America, a fellow any cold warrior could love.

All of this was not a little ironic, since neither Blackwelder nor McClung lived in idealized Cold War family forms. Blackwelder came closest, with her marriage of many years, but she had no children. Apparently, she had wanted to conceive; she once said that whenever she walked her dog, she wished she could "hang a sign on herself that read, '*We tried.*'" That way, "people wouldn't keep remarking that [I] should be pushing a baby carriage instead of walking a dog."[141] McClung, by contrast, expressed no regret about her own situation. She lived alone, suffering periodic bouts of ill health. As she told another genealogist, a woman in an abusive marriage, "Thank God, I never had to cope with a husband! Life has been difficult without that complication!"[142]

Of course, neither McClung nor Blackwelder was of the generation toward which Cold War prescriptions about the primacy of the family and women's place in it were directed; in the 1950s McClung was in her sixties and Blackwelder in her fifties.[143] They came of age with different expectations for white, middle-class women—expectations that arguably allowed them to envision more independent lives.[144] Nonetheless, although they were not among the principle targets of Cold War precepts, Blackwelder and McClung imbibed enough of postwar cultural conversations to produce a Kit Carson for the era. The subtle differences in the family man each crafted no doubt reflected their own desires, politics, and access to privilege, both sexual and racial. Blackwelder, a married white women who wanted but could not have children and whose politics tended toward the conservative, was the most taken with the idea of Carson as a loving husband and father, and she felt most compelled to create for his mixed marriages a trajectory toward whiteness. McClung, a contentedly single woman whose closest ties had always been to other white women, who shunned politics, and who never voiced the racial animosity that Blackwelder would later come to express, was curious about the intimacies represented by Carson's relationship with Josefa Jaramillo and William Bent's with Owl Woman, even as she kept men like Carson and Bent at the center of her genealogical story.[145] Thus, McClung and Blackwelder's focus on the family, the era's bulwark against foreign communists and domestic deviants, was not the same, though it displayed, shall we say, a certain kinship. Nothing served Cold War culture better, however, than their refurbishing of an old western hero into a white man who stood above all those around him but now stood connected to them, too. Theirs was a view from behind the color line in the Cold War cul-de-sac, a street with no outlet, only a distant view of a western past.[146]

NOTES

1. On *The Adventures of Kit Carson,* see www.tv.com/the-adventures-of-kit-carson/show/6301/summary.html (accessed January 30, 2007); Richard W. Slatta, ed., *The Mythical West: An Encyclopedia of Legend, Lore, and Popular Culture* (Santa Barbara, CA: ABC-CLIO, 2001), 79; Gary A. Yoggy, "Prime Time Bonanza! The Western on Television," in *Wanted Dead or Alive: The American West in Popular Culture,* ed. Richard Aquila (Urbana: University of Illinois Press, 1996), 160–95, esp. 163.

2. The show also would have outraged Navajos, the most vigorous critics of Carson because of his role in the dispossession of the Diné in the 1860s, but reservation-dwelling Navajos did not have access to television in the 1950s.

3. The pairing of an Anglo Kit Carson and a Mexican El Toro was reminiscent of the radio and then television series *The Lone Ranger,* which featured the white Lone Ranger and his American Indian sidekick, Tonto. See Slatta, ed., *Mythical West,* 213–15. In *Playing in the Dark: Whiteness and the Literary Imagination,* Toni Morrison describes the role of all such Tonto figures: "to do everything possible to serve the Lone Ranger without disturbing his indulgent delusion that he is indeed alone" ([1992; New York: Vintage, 1993], 82). Thanks to Ned Blackhawk for this reference.

4. Quantrille McClung to Marion Morgan Estergreeen, June 11, 1964, Quantrille McClung Papers, Denver Public Library (hereafter cited as McClung Papers). Their conversation continues in Estergreen to McClung, June 14, 1964, and McClung to Estergreen, June 20, 1964, McClung Papers.

5. Bernice Blackwelder, *Great Westerner: The Story of Kit Carson* (Caldwell, ID: Caxton, 1962).

6. Quantrille D. McClung, comp., *Carson-Bent-Boggs Genealogy: Line of William Carson, Ancestor of "Kit" Carson, Famous Scout and Pioneer of the Rocky Mountain Area, with the Western

Branches of the Bent and Boggs Families, with Whom "Kit" Was Associated, and the Line of Samuel Carson, Supposed to Be a Brother of William Carson (Denver, CO: Denver Public Library, 1962).

7. M. Morgan Estergreen, *Kit Carson: A Portrait in Courage* (Norman: University of Oklahoma Press, 1962).

8. On "minor writers," see Antoinette Burton, *The Postcolonial Careers of Santha Rama Rau* (Durham, NC: Duke University Press, 2007). I thank Burton for sharing her work with me before publication.

9. This chapter derives from a book manuscript in progress tentatively titled "A Traffic in Men: The Old Maid, the Housewife, and Their Great Westerner."

10. McClung, comp., *Carson-Bent-Boggs Genealogy*, 3–9, 11.

11. "A Traffic in Men" examines the genealogical literature that shaped McClung's practice, emphasizing the gender, racial, colonial, regional, and national assumptions that characterized such texts. Genealogical practice has changed, of course, and the changes began even before websites such as Ancestry.com transformed the field. See, e.g., Christina Schaefer, *The Hidden Half of the Family: A Sourcebook for Women's Genealogy* (Baltimore, MD: Genealogical Publishing, 1999); and Sharon DeBartolo Carmack, *A Genealogist's Guide to Discovering your Female Ancestors: Special Strategies for Uncovering Hard-to-Find Information about Your Female Lineage* (Cincinnati, OH: Betterway Books, 1998).

12. Quantrille D. McClung, "Genealogy in the Denver Public Library," *Colorado Genealogist* 29, no. 4 (December 1968): 89–94; McClung to Blackwelder, February 25, 1956, McClung Papers. The Denver Public Library's Genealogy Division is now part of the Western History and Genealogy Department, the collections having been merged in 1995. See http://history.denverlibrary.org/about/index.html (accessed February 23, 2007).

13. McClung to Blackwelder, June 30, 1957, McClung Papers.

14. For more on the children of such families, see Anne F. Hyde's chapter in this volume.

15. Blackwelder to McClung, October 30, 1956, McClung Papers.

16. Bernice Blackwelder, "Kit Carson and Family," in McClung, comp., *Carson-Bent-Boggs Genealogy*, 66–67.

17. This attempt to craft a narrative from McClung's genealogical charts gives me pause, given McClung's own narrative reticence. But it is the case that the *Carson-Bent-Boggs Genealogy* follows Carson's intimacies with Singing Grass (Northern Arapaho), with Making Out Road (Southern Cheyenne), and especially with Josefa Jaramillo; she traces the children of Carson and Jaramillo through their own, often-interethnic marriages; and she ends with mostly non-Spanish-surnamed descendants. She also traces those Carsons who did not intermarry with either Indians or *hispanos*. Over half of the genealogy (111 of 181 pages) is devoted to tracing "the line of William Carson" (Kit's grandfather) and "the line of Samuel Carson" (Samuel may or may not have been William's brother, and thus may or may not have been Kit's great-uncle). By contrast, McClung devotes one page to Josefa's ancestry among the Vigil and Jaramillo families (compare the four pages devoted to intermarriages between Kit Carson's and Daniel Boone's kin).

18. Bent had another mixed-blood child, Charles, not mentioned above because he was most likely the son of Bent's second wife, Yellow Woman. Yellow Woman was Owl Woman's sister, whom Bent married after Owl Woman died. Here again, I am locating a story in McClung's genealogy when she eschewed explicit storytelling. But it is clear that Bent's intimate life and the fate of his children interested McClung, and that she relied on historical as well as genealogical sources to tell the tale. Bent's lineage fills only four pages, but those pages are more densely annotated than most. McClung, comp., *Carson-Bent-Boggs Genealogy*, 98–101.

19. Blackwelder to McClung, April 12, 1969, McClung Papers.

20. Thanks to Crista DeLuzio for pointing this out. The literature that tracks changes over time (and across space) in civil rights movement strategies and goals is vast. Relevant titles include

Gary Gerstle, *American Crucible: Race and Nation in the Twentieth Century* (Princeton, NJ: Princeton University Press, 2001); Thomas Sugrue, *Sweet Land of Liberty: The Forgotten Struggle for Civil Rights in the North* (New York: Random House, 2008); Robert Self, *American Babylon: Race and the Struggle for Postwar Oakland* (Princeton, NJ: Princeton University Press, 2003); Mary Dudziak, *Cold War Civil Rights: Race and the Image of American Democracy* (Princeton, NJ: Princeton University Press, 2000); Taylor Branch, *Parting the Waters: America in the King Years, 1954–63* (New York: Simon and Schuster, 1988); David Gutiérrez, *Walls and Mirrors: Mexican Americans, Mexican Immigrants, and the Politics of Ethnicity* (Berkeley: University of California Press, 1995); John D'Emilio, *Sexual Politics, Sexual Communities: The Making of a Homosexual Minority in the United States, 1940–1970* (Chicago: University of Chicago Press, 1983); and Nan Alamilla Boyd, *Wide Open Town: A History of Queer San Francisco* (Berkeley: University of California Press, 2003).

21. This generalization simplifies a more complicated range of slaveries in North America. For the development of racial slavery in the East, see, e.g., Ira Berlin, *Many Thousands Gone: The First Two Centuries of Slavery in North America* (Cambridge, MA: Harvard University Press, 1998). Indian slavery was once continental in scope; only in the nineteenth century was it becoming a western phenomena. See, e.g., Alan Gallay, *The Indian Slave Trade: The Rise of the English Empire in the American South, 1670–1717* (New Haven, CT: Yale University Press, 2002). Work on western slavery is cited below.

22. McClung, comp., *Carson-Bent-Boggs Genealogy*, 13, 42, 168–71.

23. Evidence of slaveholding appears in the Carson Family Papers, Missouri Historical Society, St. Louis.

24. Pekka Hämäläinen, *Comanche Empire* (New Haven, CT: Yale University Press, 2008); Ned Blackhawk, *Violence Over the Land: Indians and Empires in the Early American West* (Cambridge, MA: Harvard University Press, 2006); James Brooks, *Captives and Cousins: Slavery, Kinship, and Community in the Southwest Borderlands* (Chapel Hill: University of North Carolina Press, 2002); Estevan Rael-Gálvez, "Identifying and Capturing Identity: Narratives of American Indian Servitude, Colorado and New Mexico, 1750–1930," Ph.D. diss., University of Michigan, Ann Arbor, 2002; and Ramón Gutiérrez, *When Jesus Came, the Corn Mothers Went Away: Marriage, Sexuality, and Power in New Mexico, 1500–1846* (Stanford, CA: Stanford University Press, 1991).

25. See the synopsis of the Carson *criados* in Marc Simmons, *Kit Carson and His Three Wives: A Family History* (Albuquerque: University of New Mexico Press, 2003), 100–102. The analysis by Hämäläinen, Blackhawk, Brooks, Rael-Gálvez, and Gutiérrez makes sense of such households. The Bents also trafficked in captives, including Mexican captives sold to them by Comanches. See George Hyde, *The Life of George Bent Written from His Letters*, ed. Savoie Lottinville (Norman: University of Oklahoma Press, 1968), 68–69. On captives among Comanches, see the chapter by Joaquín Rivaya-Martínez in this volume.

26. McClung, comp., *Carson-Bent-Boggs Genealogy*.

27. Ibid., 95,104–10. Juliana Bent's first name is sometimes given as "Juliannah" or "Julia Ann."

28. Ibid., 69–70. On the relationship between Owl Woman and Making Out Road, see Elliott West, *The Way to the West: Essays on the Central Plains* (Albuquerque: University of New Mexico Press, 1995), 123, and *Contested Plains: Indians, Goldseekers, and the Rush to Colorado* (Lawrence: University Press of Kansas, 1998), 210. A full account appears in Ida Ellen Rath, *The Rath Trail* (Wichita, KS: McCormick-Armstrong, 1961), 10–14, which is based on a number of sources, including the recollections of Cheyenne relatives and descendants. Charles Rath married Making Out Road years after she divorced Carson.

29. McClung, comp., *Carson-Bent-Boggs Genealogy*, 71–83, 88–95, 101–3, 106–8.

30. Blackwelder, *Great Westerner*, 365.

31. In this, McClung and Blackwelder anticipate Kathleen Neils Conzen's argument in "A Saga of Families," in *The Oxford History of the American West,* ed. Clyde Milner, Carol O'Connor, and Martha Sandweiss (New York: Oxford University Press, 1994), 315–57.

32. Blackwelder, *Great Westerner,* 13.

33. Ibid., 48, 77, 209–10, 221.

34. Ibid., 48, 269.

35. Blackwelder to McClung, July 14, 1969, McClung Papers.

36. Blackwelder, *Great Westerner,* 61–65, 85–90; quotes from 64, 90. Blackwelder calls Carson's rival Shunar, though his name was probably Chouinard. She claims that Carson killed Shunar, while others say the man survived. See, e.g., Harvey Carter, *"Dear Old Kit": The Historical Christopher Carson* (Norman: University of Oklahoma Press, 1968), 63–65; Simmons, *Kit Carson and His Three Wives,* 8–10.

37. Blackwelder, *Great Westerner,* 88, 90; cf. Simmons, *Kit Carson and His Three Wives,* 33. On Charlotte Green, see William W. Gwaltney, "Beyond the Pale: African-Americans in the Fur Trade West," www.coax.net/people/lwf/FURTRADE.HTM (accessed March 19, 2007). On women at the fort generally, see George Bird Grinnell, "Bent's Old Fort and Its Builders," *Collections of the Kansas State Historical Society, 1919–1922* 15 (1923): 28–91, esp. 52, 56, 60, 61.

38. Blackwelder, *Great Westerner,* 100 n. 4. Blackwelder cites Stanley Vestal, *Kit Carson: The Happy Warrior of the Old West* (Cambridge, MA: Riverside Press, 1928), as the source for information about Carson's second marriage. Stanley Vestal was the pen name of Walter S. Campbell, who interviewed Cheyenne and Arapaho people for the book. These interviews notwithstanding, the biography takes literary license with Carson's life and vexes historians with its lack of documentation. For a typical historian's rant against Campbell, see Carter, *"Dear Old Kit,"* 24–27.

39. Blackwelder, *Great Westerner,* 98–99.

40. Blackwelder refers to a letter from Teresina Bent, Ignacia Jaramillo's daughter, who apparently wrote, "Uncle Kit was very angry when [a man who had interviewed him] said that he was married to a Cheyenne woman named Making Out Road. He said there was no truth in that story." Blackwelder cites as the source for this letter *The Real Kit Carson* by Marion Estergreen (Taos, NM: El Crepúsculo, 1955). Estergreen, in turn, vaguely cites "a letter from Teresina Bent Scheurich" (pp. iv–v and bibliography, n.p.). Estergreen repeats this quotation in *Kit Carson* without clear attribution, but in her bibliography she refers to the "collected letters" of Teresina Bent Scheurich that were then "owned by Blanche C. Grant" (77, 305). Blanche Chloe Grant was a Vassar-educated Taos-based artist and writer who edited the first published version of Kit Carson's dictated autobiography, *Kit Carson's Own Story of His Life, As Dictated to Col. and Mrs. D..C. Peters about 1856–57, and Never Before Published* (Taos, NM: n.p., 1926). Teresina Bent's letters have never surfaced. See Estergreen, *Kit Carson,* viii.

41. Carter, *"Dear Old Kit,"* 82, and "Kit Carson," in *The Mountain Men and the Fur Trade of the Far West,* 10 vols., ed. Leroy Hafen (Glendale, CA: Arthur H. Clark Co., 1968), 6:105–31, esp. 26 n. 116; Simmons, *Kit Carson and His Three Wives,* 38–39. The male relative was Jesse Nelson, husband of another of Kit's nieces. Nelson's statement appears in Notebook 8, p. 83, of Francis W. Cragin Papers, Starsmore Center for Local History, Colorado Springs Pioneers Museum, Colorado Springs, Colorado.

42. Grinnell, "Bent's Old Fort," esp. 37. Blackwelder cites this source. Grinnell also wrote *The Fighting Cheyennes* (New York: Charles Scribner's Sons, 1915); and *The Cheyenne Indians: Their History and Ways of Life,* 2 vols. (New Haven, CT: Yale University Press, 1923).

43. Blackwelder, *Great Westerner,* 62.

44. Ibid., 97–98.

45. Fray Angélico Chávez, *Origins of New Mexico Families: A Genealogy of the Spanish Colonial Period,* rev. ed. (Santa Fe: Museum of New Mexico Press, 1992), 198–200 (Jaramillo), 311–12 (Vigil);

María C. Martínez et al., *María Josefa Jaramillo, Wife of Kit Carson: Her Descendants, Ancestors and Primos* (n.p., 2003), iii, xii–xiii.

46. See, e.g., Gutiérrez, *When Jesus Came*, esp. 190–206, 285–92; Ross Frank, *From Settler to Citizen: New Mexican Economic Development and the Creation of Vecino Society, 1750–1820* (Berkeley: University of California Press, 2000), esp. 178–81; Quintard Taylor, *In Search of the Racial Frontier: African Americans in the American West, 1528–1990* (New York: W. W. Norton, 1998), 29–32, 35–37.

47. Pablo Mitchell, *Coyote Nation: Sexuality, Race, and Conquest in Modernizing New Mexico, 1880–1920* (Chicago: University of Chicago Press, 2005); John Nieto Phillips, *The Language of Blood: The Making of Spanish-American Identity in New Mexico, 1880s–1930s* (Albuquerque: University of New Mexico Press, 2004); Charles Montgomery, *The Spanish Redemption: Heritage, Power, and Loss on New Mexico's Upper Rio Grande* (Berkeley: University of California Press, 2002); Deena González, *Refusing the Favor: The Spanish-Mexican Women of Santa Fe, 1820–1880* (New York: Oxford University Press, 1999), esp. ix–x, 123–24; and Sarah Deutsch, *No Separate Refuge: Culture, Class, and Gender on an Anglo-Hispanic Frontier in the American Southwest, 1880–1940* (New York: Oxford University Press, 1987), vii, 136–37.

48. Blackwelder, *Great Westerner*, 115–204.

49. Ibid., 204–9. For an account of this rebellion, see Laura Gómez, *Manifest Destinies: The Making of the Mexican American Race* (New York: New York University Press, 2007).

50. Blackwelder, *Great Westerner*, 210–314, esp. 235, 243–44, 260, 303, 305; quotes from 243, 260, 303.

51. I cover the reevaluation of Carson's legacy that started in the later 1960s, as well as Blackwelder and McClung's response to it, in "A Traffic in Men."

52. Blackwelder, *Great Westerner*, 313, 317–21; quote from 313. On Navajo-*hispano*-Pueblo relations, see Brooks, *Captives and Cousins*, esp. 80–116, 208–16, 234–57; Peter Iverson, *Diné: A History of the Navajos* (Albuquerque: University of New Mexico Press, 2002), 21–34; Frank McNitt, *Navajo Wars: Military Campaigns, Slave Raids, and Reprisals* (Albuquerque: University of New Mexico Press, 1972); and David Brugge, *Navajos in the Catholic Church Records of New Mexico, 1694–1875*, 2nd ed. (1969; Tsaile, AZ: Navajo Community College Press, 1986).

53. Blackwelder, *Great Westerner*, 317–55; quotes from 318, 321, 325, 328, 339, 350. In this characterization of the Carson children Blackwelder may have drawn on remarks by William Tecumseh Sherman; see below.

54. Ibid., 243, 269, 293.

55. Ibid., 269, 355.

56. Ibid., 352.

57. Ibid., 350, 353.

58. On recapitulation theory, see Gail Bederman, *Manliness and Civilization: A Cultural History of Gender and Race in the United States, 1880–1917* (Chicago: University of Chicago Press, 1995), esp. 92–94. My understanding of how the idea of recapitulation continued to circulate past the time when it was advanced by educational theorists has been enhanced by Paul Schwinn's undergraduate seminar paper, "Class, Character, and Cultural Epochs: Manliness, Adolescence, and the Boy Scouts of America," University of Wisconsin–Madison, 2003. Schwinn is now in the Ph.D. program at UCLA. Even among developmental psychologists, recapitulation theory broadly defined retained influence. See John Morss, *The Biologising of Childhood: Developmental Psychology and the Darwinian Myth* (Hove, UK: Lawrence Erlbaum, 1990). Thanks to Crista DeLuzio for this reference.

59. Blackwelder, *Great Westerner*, 355–65; quotes from 362, 364. Blackwelder misstates the Spanish name of the river as El Rio de las Perdida en Purgatorio. English speakers called it the Picketwire. Other biographers count the number of days between Kit's arrival, Josefita's delivery, Josefa's

death, and Kit's death differently, but everyone agrees that it all happened very quickly. See, e.g., Estergreen, *Kit Carson,* 273–78; Thelma Guild and Harvey Carter, *Kit Carson: A Pattern for Heroes* (Lincoln: University of Nebraska Press, 1984), 281–83; Simmons, *Kit Carson and His Three Wives,* 141–44. On the Vigil and St. Vrain and other grants, see LeRoy Hafen, "Mexican Land Grants in Colorado," *Colorado Magazine* 4, no. 3 (May 1927): 81–93; Joseph Van Hook, "Mexican Land Grants in the Arkansas Valley," *Southwestern Historical Quarterly* 40, no. 1 (July 1936): 58–76; Howard Lamar, "Land Policy in the Spanish Southwest, 1846–1891: A Study in Contrasts," *Journal of Economic History* 22, no. 4 (December 1962): 498–515, and *The Far Southwest, 1846–1912: A Territorial History,* rev. ed. (1966; Albuquerque: University of New Mexico Press, 2000); and María Montoya, *Translating Property: The Maxwell Land Grant and the Conflict over Land in the American West, 1840–1900* (Berkeley: University of California Press, 2002).

60. Blackwelder, *Great Westerner,* title page. Ware wrote poetry under the name Ironquill. See *Rhymes of Ironquill* (Topeka, KS: T. J. Kellam, 1885).

61. Most biographers say that Carson's last supper included buffalo and coffee, followed by a smoke. See Carter, *"Dear Old Kit,"* 177–78; Estergreen, *Kit Carson,* 278. The chile may be Blackwelder's invention. The sources she cites do not mention chile: Albert Thompson, "The Death and the Last Will of Kit Carson," *Colorado Magazine* 5, no. 5 (October 1928): 183–91; H. R. Tilton, *The Last Days of Kit Carson* (Grand Forks, ND: Holt Printing, 1939). It is, of course, plausible that the German husband of *hispana* Teresina Bent prepared the steak New Mexican-style, with chile. The chile reappears, entirely undocumented (and now as "red chili"), in Hampton Sides, *Blood and Thunder: An Epic of the American West* (New York: Doubleday, 2006), 395.

62. On those ideals, see Jessica Weiss, *To Have and to Hold: Marriage, the Baby Boom, and Social Change* (Chicago: University of Chicago Press, 2000). Thanks to Margaret Jacobs and Crista DeLuzio for posing questions that helped me clarify this argument.

63. Howard R. Lamar, "Much to Celebrate: The Western History Association's Twenty-Fifth Birthday," *Western Historical Quarterly* 17, no. 4 (October 1986): 397–416, esp. 397. See also Ray Allen Billington, "The Santa Fe Conference and the Writing of Western History," in *Probing the American West: Papers from the Santa Fe Conference,* ed. K. Ross Toole et al. (Santa Fe: Museum of New Mexico Press, 1962), 1–16, and "The New Western Social Order and the Synthesis of Western Scholarship," in *The American West: An Appraisal,* ed. Robert G. Ferris (Santa Fe: Museum of New Mexico Press, 1963), 3–12.

64. Julie Des Jardins, *Women and the Historical Enterprise in America: Gender, Race, and the Politics of Memory, 1880–1945* (Chapel Hill: University of North Carolina Press, 2003), esp. 28, 114–17. In addition to *Crazy Horse: The Strange Man of the Oglalas* (New York: Knopf, 1942), Sandoz is known for novels like *Old Jules* (Boston: Little, Brown, 1935) as well as histories like *Cheyenne Autumn* (New York: McGraw Hill, 1953). Against enormous odds, Beasley published *The Negro Trail Blazers of California: A Compilation of Records from the California Archives in the Bancroft Library at the University of California, in Berkeley; and from the Diaries, Old Papers and Conversations of Old Pioneers in the State of California* (Los Angeles: Times Mirror, 1919). Other early women in the field include Grace Hebard, Angie Debo, and Juanita Brooks. Hebard and Debo both had doctoral degrees, while Brooks had a master's degree. Of these historians, only Hebard enjoyed an ongoing university faculty position (even though Debo won a prize from the American Historical Association for *The Rise and Fall of the Choctaw Republic* [Norman: University of Oklahoma Press, 1934]). Brooks, a devout Mormon, was ostracized within the Church of Jesus Christ of Latter-Day Saints for her book *Mountain Meadows Massacre* (Stanford, CA: Stanford University Press, 1950), which exposed the church's role in the 1857 massacre; see Des Jardins, *Women and the Historical Enterprise in America,* 96, 101–17. On Hebard, see Virginia Scharff, *Twenty Thousand Roads: Women, Movement, and the West* (Berkeley: University of California Press, 2003), 94–114. See also Shirley Leckie and Nancy Parezo, eds., *Their Own Frontier:*

Women Intellectuals Re-Envisioning the American West (Lincoln: University of Nebraska Press, 2008), esp. Leckie and Parezo, "Introduction"; Leckie, "Angie Debo: From the Old to the New Western History"; and John Wunder, "Mari Sandoz: Historian of the Great Plains."

65. The overwhelming presence of men among amateur western historians is in marked contrast to the more general trend examined by Bonnie Smith, in which women created a separate world of amateur history even as university men professionalized the historical discipline, infusing it with deeply masculine assumptions. See her *The Gender of History: Men, Women, and Historical Practice* (Cambridge, MA: Harvard University Press, 1998).

66. See J. E. Reynolds, *History of The Westerners*, reprinted from The Westerners Brand Book No. 7, Los Angeles Corral (Glendale, CA: n.p., 1957); *The Westerners: A Mini-Bibliography and a Cataloging of Publications, 1944–1974*, no. 1 (Glendale, CA: Arthur H. Clark, 1974); Leland D. Case, "The Westerners: Twenty-Five Years of Riding the Range," *Western Historical Quarterly* 1, no. 1 (January 1970): 63–76. On the Inter-Posse Rendezvous, see LeRoy Hafen, *The Joyous Journey of LeRoy R. and Ann W. Hafen: An Autobiography* (Glendale, CA: Arthur H. Clark; Denver: Old West Publishing, 1973), 274–75, 285–86, 299; and Case, "The Westerners," 71.

67. Reynolds, *History of the Westerners*, n.p. (page 10).

68. Case, "The Westerners," 63.

69. Charles Collins, "Bookman's Holiday," *Chicago Tribune*, April 30, 1946; cf. Irene Steyskal, "Friends of the Middle Border to Hold Party," *Chicago Tribune*, July 7, 1946.

70. Frederick Babcock, "Among the Authors," *Chicago Tribune*, October 1, 1944; Lloyd Wendt, "Way Out West in Modern Chicago," *Chicago Tribune*, October 26, 1947. Some chapters drew on a slightly different membership base, but the class position of members was quite uniform. For example, Washington, D.C.'s Potomac Corral included employees of the National Park Service and other government agencies. Robert Utley, *Custer and Me: A Historian's Memoir* (Norman: University of Oklahoma Press, 2004), 57, 113; Mike Lawson, "Mr. Case Comes to Washington: A Retrospective on the Founding of the Potomac Corral," www.potomac-corral.org/pdfs/Potomac_Corral_Retrospective.pdf (accessed March 30, 2007).

71. John Randolph, "Chicago Posse Sees Styles of Old West," *Chicago Tribune*, November 25, 1952. The Denver Posse also held "ladies' nights"; see Hafen, *Joyous Journey*, 248, 259–60.

72. Utley, *Custer and Me*, 87–89; quote from 88.

73. Utley recalls his efforts "to keep one foot in each of two worlds" in ibid., 87.

74. Ibid., 89.

75. Ibid., 89–90. The program is reproduced following page 216 in Toole et al., eds., *Probing the American West*; the cover features "Prairie Schooner Lady" by artist Don Louis Perceval. Ewers's paper appears on 62–70. The "marginal man" theory was developed by Robert Park and Everett Stonequist to make sense of people situated between cultures, societies, or races. See esp. Park, "Human Migration and the Marginal Man," *American Journal of Sociology* 33, no. 6 (May 1928): 881–93, and *Race and Culture* (Glencoe, IL: Free Press, 1950); and Everett Stonequist, *The Marginal Man: A Study in Personality and Culture Conflict* (New York: Charles Scribner's Sons, 1937).

76. Utley, *Custer and Me*, 89–90. Cf. Hafen, *Joyous Journey*, 302. Billington is best known for *Westward Expansion: A History of the American Frontier* (New York: Macmillan, 1949), which appeared in new editions a half-dozen times over the next half century. See also Billington, "The Frontier and I," *Western Historical Quarterly* 1, no. 1 (January 1970): 4–20.

77. The 1962 conference papers appear in Ferris, ed., *The American West*. On the WHA and the *American West*, see 252–53. See also Utley, *Custer and Me*, 90–91, 110; Lamar, "Much to Celebrate"; and Billington, "New Western Social Order."

78. Our belief is based on stories that circulate about our bolo-tied forebears, including one told about a WHA conference where, as an older male publisher put it to two younger men in the field,

"part of the festivities was a 'busload of chippies' unloading at the convention hotel." Since the old days at the WHA are not quite over yet, I will follow the practice of journalists rather than historians here and protect my sources.

79. I discuss these changes in "A Traffic in Men."

80. Personal communication from Janet Lecompte, November 3, 2001. Lecompte wrote *Pueblo, Hardscrabble, Greenhorn: The Upper Arkansas, 1832–1856* (Norman: University of Oklahoma Press, 1978), and *Rebellion in Río Arriba, 1837* (Albuquerque: University of New Mexico Press, 1985). She excluded historian LeRoy Hafen from her indictment. Her assessment of Hafen is consistent with his own self-presentation in *Joyous Journey*.

81. About the WHA, Blackwelder wrote, "Difficult to believe it was 16 yrs ago that Dr. John Porter Bloom came to our house in Virginia and told me I owed him $5.00 as he had signed me as a charter member!" (The visit must have taken place in 1961 or 1962.) Blackwelder to McClung, November 18, 1976, McClung Papers. Bloom, the first WHA secretary-treasurer and also a member of The Westerners' Potomac Corral (see Lawson, "Mr. Case Comes to Washington," 6), has only vague memories of Blackwelder. Personal communication from John Porter Bloom, November 27, 2001.

82. McClung's ties to this organization are evident in *The Colorado Genealogist*, from 1, no. 1 (October 1939), where she is listed as vice president and executive board chair, to 46, no. 3 (August 1985), where a memorial appears.

83. Blackwelder to McClung, October 18, 1958, McClung Papers.

84. Blackwelder to McClung, January 3, 1959, and September 24, 1960, McClung Papers. Blackwelder's publisher, Caxton Press, provided me with a copy of her author file, for which I am grateful. My thanks especially to Scott Gipson, a descendant of J. H. Gipson, president of the press when *Great Westerner* was published.

85. Blackwelder to McClung, October 18, 1958, McClung Papers.

86. Blackwelder to McClung, September 24, 1960; May 19, 1962, and February 20 and July 14, 1969, McClung Papers.

87. Blackwelder to McClung, [n.d., ca. January 1, 1961], McClung Papers.

88. Estergreen, *Kit Carson*.

89. The University of Oklahoma Press generously provided me with a copy of Estergreen's author file, which shows that it was the publisher's idea for Estergreen to use the gender-ambiguous name "Morgan." An interoffice memo written by editor Herbert Hyde informs coworkers of the title chosen for the book and adds, "The author is in no way to be identified as a woman" (H. Hyde to G. Bradley and D. Palmer, November 15, 1961, Author File for Marion Estergreen, University of Oklahoma Press, Norman [hereafter cited as Estergreen Author File]). Although it was the publisher's idea, Estergreen acquiesced: "I am still in favor of your suggestion that the book will carry more weight if my name is 'M. Morgan Estergreen'" (Estergreen to Savoie Lottinville, April 12, 1960, Estergreen Author File). Later, when working on a new edition, Estergreen reversed herself: "Is there any way you can give me my full by-line ... in the second edition? If this cannot be done, can I be identified as a woman in the back cover by saying 'she lives in Taos'[?] You mentioned years ago that more men will buy the book if they think a man wrote it. I don't agree!" (Estergreen to Lottinville, March 23, 1963, Estergreen Author File). The publisher replied, "Only women change their minds! I don't think you should make the change in the character of your authorship.... [It] would only create confusion. If you want to do it, however, and feel strongly about it, I see no reason why not" (Lottinville to Estergreen, April 10, 1963, Estergreen Author File). The author's name was not changed.

90. Blackwelder to McClung, April 1, 1962, McClung Papers. Estergreen's earlier short piece was published as *The Real Kit Carson*.

91. Blackwelder to McClung, June 8 and August 24, 1962, McClung Papers.

92. See Blackwelder to McClung, April 1, May 1, and August 24, 1962, McClung Papers.
93. Blackwelder to McClung, June 8, [1962], McClung Papers.
94. I borrow "root of bitterness" from *Root of Bitterness: Documents of the Social History of American Women,* 2nd ed., ed. Nancy Cott, Jeanne Boydston, Ann Braude, Lori Ginzburg, and Molly Ladd-Taylor (Boston: Northeastern University Press, 1996), revised from the first edition edited by Cott (New York: Dutton, 1972).
95. A letter returned to the University of Oklahoma Press as undeliverable informed Marion Estergreen's daughter in 2005 that *Kit Carson: A Portrait in Courage* was out of print. Dale Bennie to Sheryl Marian Estergreen-Groce, July 25, 2005, Estergreen Author File. Estergreen died in 1984 (Social Security Death Index, Ancestry.com, accessed February 14, 2007). Blackwelder reported in 1970 that Caxton was closing out her book (Blackwelder to McClung, January 22, 1970, McClung Papers).
96. Apologies to James Herriot, *All Creatures Great and Small* (New York: St. Martin's Press, 1972).
97. Westerns were called oaters because horses, the key animal prop in the genre, like oats. In the press, the first use of the term was in *Time Magazine,* December 9, 1946, though it was already in use in the film industry.
98. This simplifies a more complex process ably analyzed by Billington, "Santa Fe Conference," "New Western Social Order," and "Frontier and I"; William Cronon, "Revisiting the Vanishing Frontier: The Legacy of Frederick Jackson Turner," *Western Historical Quarterly* 18, no. 2 (April 1987): 157–76; and William Cronon, George Miles, and Jay Gitlin, "Becoming West: Toward a New Meaning for Western History," in *Under an Open Sky: Rethinking America's Western Past,* ed. Cronon, Gitlin, and Miles (New York: W. W. Norton, 1992), 3–27.
99. See Edward Buscombe, ed., *The BFI Companion to the Western* (London: Atheneum, 1988; New York: Da Capo Press, 1991), 427; and John Lenihan, "Westbound: Feature Films and the American West," in Aquila, ed., *Wanted Dead or Alive,* 109–34.
100. In television, the peak came in 1959, which featured the largest number of Western series ever—forty-eight in all. At no time between 1952 and 1970 did the number of TV Westerns aired dip below ten per year. See Buscombe, *BFI Companion,* 428; Yoggy, "Prime Time Bonanza!" 160.
101. *High Noon* also featured a resourceful *mexicana* business owner played by Katy Jurado. Synopses of all films mentioned in this paragraph appear in Buscombe, *BFI Companion,* 263–64, 269, 277. See also Lenihan, "Westbound."
102. *Gunsmoke* remains tied with *Law and Order* as the longest-running prime-time drama in the history of U.S. television (1955–75). *Bonanza* ran 1959–73. For synopses, see Buscombe, *BFI Companion,* 399, 401, 407, 413. See also Yoggy, "Prime Time Bonanza!"
103. For an analysis of the way in which such oppositional thinking continued among a later generation of western historians, see Stephen Tatum, "The Problem of the 'Popular' in the New Western History," in *The New Western History: The Territory Ahead,* ed. Forrest Robinson (Tucson: University of Arizona Press, 1997), 153–90.
104. Billington, "Frontier and I," 18.
105. Case, "The Westerners"; quote from 69. William S. Hart was a cowboy star from an earlier generation of Westerns.
106. The address was 865 South Harrison Street. *Lusk's Northern Virginia Real Estate Directory Service* (Washington, DC: Rufus S. Lusk & Son, 1955 and 1962); *Plat Book of Arlington County, Virginia* (Philadelphia: Franklin Survey Co., 1952).
107. Blackwelder to McClung, October 3 and November 5, 1957, McClung Papers; Virginia Woolf, *A Room of One's Own* (London: Hogarth Press, 1929). Information about the Alexandria house and loan comes from a real estate listing in a set of materials loaned to me, in an act of great generosity, by Blackwelder's niece, Doris Lance of Alpena, Michigan (hereafter cited as Blackwelder Family Papers).

Nonetheless, I am not certain that the GI loan designation on the real estate listing is accurate. I have not found any evidence that either Harold or Bernice Blackwelder was in the military. GI loans derived from the mortgage program for veterans associated with the GI Bill of Rights, or the Servicemen's Readjustment Act of 1944. Bernice did work for the federal government in the 1950s, when she was employed by the Central Intelligence Agency (I discuss her CIA work in "A Traffic in Men"), but I have found no indication that CIA employees benefited from the GI Bill or similar legislation. It is possible, then, that the financing designated on the Blackwelders' real estate listing was in error, and that the mortgage derived from a Federal Housing Administration (FHA) loan. On federal housing loans administered by the Veterans Administration and the FHA, and their many exclusions, see, e.g., Self, *American Babylon*, esp. 42, 97–99, 104, 117; David Freund, "Marketing the Free Market: State Intervention and the Politics of Prosperity in Metropolitan America," in *The New Suburban History*, ed. Kevin Kruse and Thomas Sugrue (Chicago: University of Chicago Press, 2006), 11–32; Thomas Sugrue, *The Origins of the Urban Crisis: Race and Inequality in Postwar Detroit* (1996; Princeton, NJ: Princeton University Press, 2005), esp. 43–47, 59–72, 182; Becky Nicolaides, *My Blue Heaven: Life and Politics in the Working-Class Suburbs of Los Angeles, 1920–1965* (Chicago: University of Chicago Press, 2002), esp. 179–81, 188–93, 226, 230; Lizabeth Cohen, *A Consumers' Republic: The Politics of Mass Consumption in Postwar America* (New York: Knopf, 2003), esp. 122, 123, 137–41, 147, 170, 199, 204–5, 214; and Margot Canady, "Building a Straight State: Sexuality and Social Citizenship under the 1944 GI Bill," *Journal of American History* 90, no. 3 (December 2003): 935–57. Thanks to Jennifer Holland and Camille Guérin-Gonzales for information about GI loans.

108. These suburbs were not all middle-class. See, e.g., Nicolaides, *My Blue Heaven*.

109. This simplified summary of city/suburb relationships is based on Sugrue, *Origins of the Urban Crisis*; Self, *American Babylon*; Freund, "Marketing the Free Market"; Cohen, *Consumers' Republic*; Arnold Hirsch, *Making the Second Ghetto: Race and Housing in Chicago, 1940–1960* (1983; Chicago: University of Chicago Press, 1998); and Kevin Kruse and Thomas Sugrue, "The New Suburban History," in Kruse and Sugrue, eds., *New Suburban History*.

110. Blackwelder to McClung, September 24, 1960, McClung Papers.

111. Blackwelder to McClung, April 1, May 1, and June 8, 1962, McClung Papers.

112. Blackwelder to McClung, August 24, 1962, McClung Papers. After this letter there is a three-year gap in the correspondence between McClung and Blackwelder. I explain this gap in "A Traffic in Men."

113. Real estate listing for 7300 Yellowstone Drive, Alexandria, Virginia, Blackwelder Family Papers. A current map shows that this address is in a residential neighborhood on a street with no outlet to a major thoroughfare. See http://maps.google.com (accessed May 2, 2007).

114. McClung to Blackwelder, January 18, 1975, McClung Papers.

115. McClung lived at 975 Washington Street and then 1285 Clarkson Street. Her residences can be tracked through the McClung Papers and the *Colorado Genealogist*, which lists addresses for genealogical society members.

116. Stephen Leonard and Thomas Noel, *Denver: Mining Camp to Metropolis* (Niwot: University Press of Colorado, 1990), 374–75, 389–93. See also Tom Romero, "Of Race and Rights: Legal Culture, Social Change, and the Making of a Multiracial Metropolis, 1940–1975," Ph.D. diss., University of Michigan, 2004, and "Our Selma Is Here: The Political and Legal Struggle for Educational Equality in Denver, Colorado, and Multiracial Conundrums in American Jurisprudence," *Seattle Journal of Social Justice* 3, no. 73 (2004): 73–142. The latter focuses on legal struggles for educational equality that occurred later, but those struggles reflected residential segregation in Denver. There is limited background on ethnic Mexicans in Denver in Ernesto Vigil, *The Crusade for Justice: Chicano Militancy and the Government's War on Dissent* (Madison: University of Wisconsin Press, 1999).

117. Leonard and Noel, *Denver*, 394. See also Vigil, *Crusade for Justice*.

118. See esp. Clive Webb, ed., *Massive Resistance: Southern Opposition to the Second Reconstruction* (New York: Oxford University Press, 2005); and William H. Chafe, *The Unfinished Journey: America Since World War II*, 4th ed. (1986; New York: Oxford University Press, 1999), 146–76. On the West, where African Americans more often lived alongside other racialized peoples, see Taylor, *In Search of the Racial Frontier*, 278–310.

119. See Blackwelder to McClung, n.d. [ca. January 5], 1970, McClung Papers.

120. Although the context differs, Timothy Tyson, *Blood Done Sign My Name* (New York: Three Rivers Press, 2004), provides insight into white racial etiquette in this period. McClung and Blackwelder would not explicitly discuss racial matters until later, when they both began to live in closer proximity to people of color and when movements for racial justice advanced, forcing the women to foreground views and experiences they had left in the background before. Race surely structured their lives in this earlier period, but—since one of the benefits of whiteness has long been the ability to live in blissful ignorance of privilege and of the effects that privilege has on racialized others—at the time, they said little about it. I discuss their later conversations in "A Traffic in Men."

121. Peggy Pascoe, *What Comes Naturally: Miscegenation Law and the Making of Race in America* (New York: Oxford University Press, 2009).

122. Although it is about another time and place, Michael Salman's *The Embarrassment of Slavery: Controversies over Bondage and Nationalism in the American Colonial Philippines* (Berkeley: University of California Press, 2001) informs my thinking here. Salman draws from a remark in Orlando Patterson, *Slavery and Social Death: A Comparative Study* (Cambridge, MA: Harvard University Press, 1991), ix.

123. See Richard Slotkin, *Gunfighter Nation: The Myth of the Frontier in Twentieth-Century America* (New York: Atheneum, 1992).

124. Blackwelder to McClung, March 6, 1958, McClung Papers.

125. McClung to Blackwelder, March 10, 1958, McClung Papers.

126. Blackwelder to McClung, May 19 and August 24, 1962, and December 11, 1970, McClung Papers. I discuss Blackwelder's connection to the Eisenhower administration in "A Traffic in Men."

127. McClung to Blackwelder, May 28, 1958, McClung Papers.

128. See Alan McPherson, *Yankee No! Anti-Americanism in U.S.-Latin American Relations* (Cambridge, MA: Harvard University Press, 2005).

129. McClung to Blackwelder, August 17 and September 11, 1957, and Blackwelder to McClung, August 24, 1957, McClung Papers. For information on Cristobal Carson and María Guadalupe Richards Carson, see McClung, comp., *Carson-Bent-Boggs Genealogy*, 79–81. There is no mention of the alleged murders or illegitimacy.

130. Blackwelder to McClung, September 18, [1957], and McClung to Blackwelder, October 9, 1957, McClung Papers. For information on Julián Carson and Pasqualita Tobin Carson, see McClung, comp., *Carson-Bent-Boggs Genealogy*, 75–76. There is no mention of the alleged murder.

131. Blackwelder to McClung, August 24, 1957, and McClung to Blackwelder, October 9, 1957, McClung Papers.

132. Several grandsons claimed the name "Kit Carson" in the third generation. See McClung, comp., *Carson-Bent-Boggs Genealogy*, 78, 80, 81.

133. McClung to Blackwelder, May 11, 1958, McClung Papers.

134. McClung, comp., *Carson-Bent-Boggs Genealogy*, 84, 89, 91–92, 102, 107, 176.

135. McClung to Blackwelder, May 11, 1958, McClung Papers.

136. McClung, comp., *Carson-Bent-Boggs Genealogy*, 91.

137. Ibid., 177–78 (italics in original).

138. Blackwelder to McClung, July 14, 1969, McClung Papers. I continue the story of Blackwelder and McClung's encounter with nonmarital intimacies in "A Traffic in Men."

139. For the dominant discourse, see Elaine Tyler May, *Homeward Bound: American Families in the Cold War Era,* rev. ed. (1988; New York: Basic Books, 1999), and for what that discourse obscured, see Joanne Meyerowitz, ed., *Not June Cleaver: Women and Gender in Postwar America, 1945–1960* (Philadelphia: Temple University Press, 1994); and Weiss, *To Have and to Hold.*

140. This was a deeply contested prescription in this era, linked as it was to even larger issues of national identity. See Miriam Reumann, *American Sexual Character: Sex, Gender, and National Identity in the Kinsey Reports* (Berkeley: University of California Press, 2005); and David Johnson, *The Lavender Scare: The Cold War Persecution of Gays and Lesbians in the Federal Government* (Chicago: University of Chicago Press, 2004).

141. Personal communication from Doris Lance, June 5, 2003 (emphasis added).

142. McClung to Stephanie Tally, October 29, 1972, and Tally to McClung, n.d. [Christmas 1973], McClung Papers.

143. On those prescriptions, see May, *Homeward Bound,* and Weiss, *To Have and to Hold,* who do not fully agree on their content. May sees more emphasis on the containment of women in the home, while Weiss sees a push toward greater gender egalitarianism in marriage. Both emphases, no doubt, coexisted—this was a time of change—but both also buttressed heteronormativity.

144. See Karen Manners Smith, "New Paths to Power: 1890–1920"; Sarah Deutsch, "From Ballots to Breadlines: 1920–1940," in *No Small Courage: A History of Women in the United States,* ed. Nancy Cott (New York: Oxford University Press, 2000); Nancy Cott, *The Grounding of Modern Feminism* (New Haven, CT: Yale University Press, 1987); Rosalind Rosenberg, *Beyond Separate Spheres: The Intellectual Roots of Modern Feminism* (New Haven, CT: Yale University Press, 1982); and Christine Stansell, *American Moderns: Bohemian New York and the Creation of a New Century* (New York: Henry Holt, 2000). It gives me pause to suggest that McClung and Blackwelder were middle-class women. They aspired to such a class status, and often benefited from appearing to occupy it, but the material conditions of their lives rarely matched their aspirations. I discuss this in "A Traffic in Men."

145. Blackwelder began to express racial animosity in the late 1960s, when she moved to Chicago. For this and McClung's relationships with women, see "A Traffic in Men."

146. Despite the different context, this line is inspired in part by Thomas Borstelmann, *The Cold War and the Color Line: American Race Relations in the Global Arena* (Cambridge, MA: Harvard University Press, 2001).

SELECTED BIBLIOGRAPHY

Acuña, Rodolfo. *Occupied America: A History of Chicanos*, 3rd ed. New York: Harper Collins, 1988.
Adams, David Wallace. *Education for Extinction: American Indians and the Boarding School Experience, 1875–1928*. Lawrence: University Press of Kansas, 1995.
Anderson, Gary C. *The Conquest of Texas: Ethnic Cleansing in the Promised Land, 1820–1875*. Norman: University of Oklahoma Press, 2005.
———. *The Indian Southwest, 1580–1830: Ethnogenesis and Reinvention*. Norman: University of Oklahoma Press, 1999.
Anzaldúa, Gloria. *Borderlands/La Frontera: The New Mestiza*. San Francisco: Spinsters/Aunt Lute Book Company, 1987.
Aquila, Richard, ed. *The American West in Popular Culture*. Urbana: University of Illinois Press, 1996.
Ariès, Philippe. *Centuries of Childhood: A Social History of Family Life*. New York: Vintage Books, 1962.
Barkan, Elliott Robert. *From All Points: America's Immigrant West, 1870s–1952*. Bloomington: Indiana University Press, 2007.
Barr, Juliana. *Peace Came in the Form of a Woman: Indians and Spaniards in the Texas Borderlands*. Chapel Hill: University of North Carolina Press, 2007.
Bean, Lowell John. *Mukat's People: The Cahuilla Indians of Southern California*. Berkeley: University of California Press, 1972.
Bean, Lowell John, and Thomas C. Blackburn, eds. *Native Californians: A Theoretical Retrospective*. Socorro: Ballena Press, 1976.
Bederman, Gail. *Manliness and Civilization: A Cultural History of Gender and Race in the United States, 1880–1917*. Chicago: University of Chicago Press, 1995.

Benton-Cohen, Katherine. *Borderline Americans: Racial Division and Labor War in the Arizona Borderlands*. Cambridge, MA: Harvard University Press, 2009.

Berebitsky, Julie. *Like Our Very Own: Adoption and the Changing Culture of Motherhood, 1851–1950*. Lawrence: University Press of Kansas, 2000.

Betty, Gerald-Louis. *Comanche Society: Before the Reservation*. College Station: Texas A&M University Press, 2002.

Blackhawk, Ned. *Violence Over the Land: Indians and Empires in the Early American West*. Cambridge, MA: Harvard University Press, 2006.

Blum, Ann S. *Domestic Economies: Family, Work, and Welfare in Mexico City, 1884–1943*. Lincoln: University of Nebraska Press, 2009.

Bouvier, Virginia M. *Women and the Conquest of California, 1542–1840: Codes of Silence* Tucson: The University of Arizona Press, 2001.

Briggs, Laura. *Reproducing Empire: Race, Sex, Science, and U.S. Imperialism in Puerto Rico*. Berkeley: University of California Press, 2002

Brooks, James. *Captives and Cousins: Slavery, Kinship, and Community in the Southwest Borderlands*. Chapel Hill: University of North Carolina Press, 2002.

Camarillo, Albert. *Chicanos in a Changing Society: From Mexican Pueblos to American Barrios in Santa Barbara and Southern California, 1848–1930*. Cambridge, MA: Harvard University Press, 1979.

Carter, Sarah. *The Importance of Being Monogamous: Marriage and Nation Building in Western Canada to 1915*. Edmonton: University of Alberta Press, 2008

Casas, María Raquél. *Married to a Daughter of the Land: Spanish-Mexican Women and Interethnic Marriage in California, 1820–1880*. Reno: University of Nevada Press, 2007.

Chávez, John. *The Lost Land: The Chicano Image of the Southwest*. Albuquerque: University of New Mexico Press, 1984.

Chávez-García, Miroslava. *Negotiating Conquest: Gender and Power in California, 1770s to 1880s*. Tucson: University of Arizona Press, 2004.

Child, Brenda J. *Boarding School Seasons: American Indian Families, 1900–1940*. Lincoln: University of Nebraska Press, 1998.

Clawson, Mary Ann. *Constructing Brotherhood: Class, Gender, and Fraternalism*. Princeton, NJ: Princeton University Press, 1989.

Cleland, Robert Glass. *The Cattle on a Thousand Hills: Southern California, 1850–1870*. 2nd ed. San Marino: CA: Huntington Library, 1962.

Coleman, Michael. *American Indian Children at School, 1850–1930*. Jackson: University Press of Mississippi, 1993.

Cook, Sherburne F. *The Conflict Between the California Indian and White Civilization*. Berkeley: University of California Press, 1976.

Corbett, Percy E. *The Roman Law of Marriage*. Oxford: Oxford University Press, 1930.

Costo, Rupert, and Jeanette Henry Costo. *The Missions of California: A Legacy of Genocide*. San Francisco: The Indian Historian Press, 1987.

Crosby, Harry W. *Antigua California: Mission and Colony on the Peninsular Frontier, 1697–1768*. Albuquerque: University of New Mexico Press, 1994.

Dejong, David H. *Promises of the Past: A History of Indian Education in the United States.* Golden, CO: Fulcrum Publishing, 1993.
Delay, Brian E. *War of a Thousand Deserts: Indian Raids and the U.S.-Mexican War.* New Haven, CT: Yale University Press, 2008.
Deloria, Philip. *Indians in Unexpected Places.* Lawrence: University Press of Kansas, 2004.
Deutsch, Sarah. *No Separate Refuge: Culture, Class, and Gender on an Anglo-Hispanic Frontier in the American Southwest, 1880–1940.* New York: Oxford University Press, 1987.
Devens, Carol. *Countering Civilization: Native American Women and Great Lake Missions, 1830–1900.* Berkeley: University of California Press, 2005.
Fanshel, David. *Far from the Reservation: The Transracial Adoption of American Indian Children.* Metuchen, NJ: Scarecrow Press, 1972.
Faragher, John Mack. *Women and Men on the Overland Trail.* New Haven, CT: Yale University Press, 1979.
Fear-Segal, Jacqueline. *The White Man's Club: Schools, Race, and the Struggle of Indian Acculturation.* Lincoln: University of Nebraska Press, 2007.
Fessler, Ann. *The Girls Who Went Away: The Hidden History of Women Who Surrendered Children for Adoption in the Decades before Roe v. Wade.* New York: Penguin Press, 2006.
Flandrin, Jean-Louis. *Families in Former Times: Kinship, Households, and Sexuality.* Cambridge: Cambridge University Press, 1979.
Foley, Neil. *The White Scourge: Mexicans, Blacks, and Poor Whites in Texas Cotton Culture.* Berkley: University of California Press, 1997.
Foster, Morris W. *Being Comanche: A Social History of an American Indian Community.* Tucson: University of Arizona Press, 1991.
French, William E. *A Peaceful and Working People: Manners, Morals, and Class Formation in Northern Mexico.* Albuquerque: University of New Mexico Press, 1996.
Garza-Falcón, Leticia. *Gente Decente: A Borderlands Response to the Rhetoric of Dominance.* Austin: University of Texas Press, 1998.
Gerstle, Gary. *Crucible: Race and Nation in the Twentieth Century.* Princeton, NJ: Princeton University Press, 2001.
Gilbert G. *Guest Workers or Colonized Labor: Mexican Labor Migration to the United States.* Boulder, CO: Paradigm Press, 2006.
Gómez, Laura E. *Manifest Destinies: The Making of the Mexican American Race.* New York: New York University Press, 2007.
Gómez-Quiñones, Juan. *Roots of Chicano Politics, 1600–1940.* Albuquerque: University of New Mexico Press, 1994.
González, Deena. *Refusing the Favor: The Spanish Mexican Women of Santa Fe, 1820–1880.* New York: Oxford University Press, 1999.
Gordon, Linda. *The Great Arizona Orphan Abduction.* Cambridge, MA: Harvard University Press, 1999.
———. *Pitied but Not Entitled: Single Mothers and the History of Welfare, 1890–1935.* Cambridge, MA: Harvard University Press, 1994.

———, ed. *Women, the State, and Welfare*. Madison: University of Wisconsin Press, 1990.

Griswold del Castillo, Richard. *La Familia: Chicano Families in the Urban Southwest, 1848 to the Present*. South Bend, IN: Notre Dame University Press, 1984.

———. *The Los Angeles Barrio, 1850–1890: A Social History*. Berkeley: University of California Press, 1979.

Gross, Ariela J. *What Blood Won't Tell: A History of Race on Trial in America*. Cambridge, MA: Harvard University Press, 2008.

Grossberg, Michael. *Governing the Hearth: Law and Family in Nineteenth-Century America*. Chapel Hill: University of North Carolina Press, 1985.

Guerin-Gonzales, Camille. *Mexican Workers and American Dreams: Immigration, Repatriation, and California Labor, 1900–1939*. New Brunswick, NJ: Rutgers University Press, 1996.

Gutiérrez, David. *Walls and Mirrors: Mexican Americans, Mexican Immigrants, and the Politics of Ethnicity*. Berkeley: University of California Press, 1995.

Gutiérrez, Elena. *Fertile Matters: The Politics of Mexican-Origin Women's Reproduction*. Austin: University of Texas Press, 2008.

Gutiérrez, Ramón. *When Jesus Came, the Corn Mothers Went Away: Marriage, Sexuality, and Power in New Mexico, 1500–1846*. Stanford, CA: Stanford University Press, 1991.

Hackel, Steven W. *Children of Coyote, Missionaries of Saint Francis: Indian-Spanish Relations in Colonial California, 1769–1850*. Chapel Hill: University of North Carolina Press, 2005.

Hafen, LeRoy R., ed. *Mountain Men and the Fur Trade of the Far West*. 10 vols. Glendale, CA: Arthur Clark, 1965–72.

Hagan, William T. *United States–Comanche Relations: The Reservation Years*. Norman: University of Oklahoma Press, 1990.

Hämäläinen, Pekka. *The Comanche Empire*. New Haven, CT: Yale University Press, 2008.

Hass, Lisbeth. *Conquests and Historical Identities in California, 1769–1936*. Berkeley: University of California Press, 1995.

Hodes, Martha, ed. *Sex, Love, Race: Crossing Boundaries in North American History*. New York: New York University Press, 1999.

Holt, Marilyn Irvin. *Indian Orphanages*. Lawrence: University Press of Kansas, 2001.

Horsman, Reginald. *Race and Manifest Destiny: The Origins of American Racial Anglo-Saxonism*. Cambridge, MA: Harvard University Press, 1981.

Hurtado, Albert L. *Intimate Frontiers: Sex, Gender, and Culture in Old California*. Albuquerque: University of New Mexico Press, 1999.

Hyde, Anne F. *Empires, Nations, and Families: A History of the North American West, 1800–1860*. Lincoln: University of Nebraska Press, 2011.

Jacobs, Margaret D. *Engendered Encounters: Feminism and Pueblo Cultures, 1879–1934*. Lincoln: University of Nebraska Press, 1999.

———. *White Mother to a Dark Race: Settler Colonialism, Maternalism, and the Removal of Indigenous Children in the American West and Australia, 1880–1940*. Lincoln: University of Nebraska Press, 2009.

Jacoby, Karl. *Shadows at Dawn: A Borderlands Massacre and the Violence of History.* New York: Penguin Books, 2008.
Jameson, Elizabeth, and Susan Armitage, eds. *Writing the Range: Race, Class, and Culture in the Women's West.* Norman: University of Oklahoma Press, 1997.
John, Elizabeth. *Storms Brewed in Other Men's Worlds: The Confrontation of the Indians, Spanish, and French in the Southwest, 1540–1795.* College Station: Texas A&M University Press, 1975.
Kessell, John. *Spain in the Southwest: A Narrative History of Colonial New Mexico, Arizona, Texas, and California.* Norman: University of Oklahoma Press, 2002.
Kramer, Paul A. *The Blood of Government: Race, Empire, the United States, and the Philippines.* Chapel Hill: University of North Carolina Press, 2006.
Kunzel, Regina. *Fallen Women, Problem Girls: Unmarried Mothers and the Professionalization of Social Work, 1890–1945.* New Haven, CT: Yale University Press, 1993.
Lasch, Christopher. *Haven in a Heartless World: The Family Besieged.* New York: Basic Books, 1977.
Lamar, Howard. *The Far Southwest, 1846–1912: A Territorial History.* Rev. ed. Albuquerque: University of New Mexico Press, 2000 [1966].
Leckie, Shirley, and Nancy Parezo, eds. *Their Own Frontier: Women Intellectuals Re-Envisioning the American West.* Lincoln: University of Nebraska Press, 2008.
Limerick, Patricia Nelson. *The Legacy of Conquest: The Unbroken Past of the American West.* New York: W. W. Norton and Co., 1987.
Lomawaima, K. Tsianina. *They Called It Prairie Light: The Story of Chilocco Indian School.* Lincoln: University of Nebraska Press, 1994.
Lopez, Ian Haney. *White by Law: The Legal Construction of Race.* New York: New York University Press, 2006.
Luibhéid, Eithne. *Entry Denied: Controlling Sexuality at the Border.* Minneapolis: University of Minnesota Press, 2002.
May, Elaine Tyler. *Homeward Bound: American Families in the Cold War Era.* Rev. ed. New York: Basic Books, 1999 [1988].
McCawley, William. *The First Angelinos: The Gabrielino Indians of Los Angeles.* Banning and Novato, CA: Malki Museum Press and Ballena Press, 1996.
Melosh, Barbara. *Strangers and Kin: The American Way of Adoption.* Cambridge, MA: Harvard University Press, 2002.
Mintz, Steven. *Huck's Raft: A History of American Childhood.* Cambridge, MA: Harvard University Press, 2004.
Mitchell, Pablo. *Coyote Nation: Sexuality, Race, and Conquest in Modernizing New Mexico, 1880–1920.* Chicago: University of Chicago Press, 2005.
Molina, Natalia. *Fit to Be Citizens? Public Health and Race in Los Angeles, 1879–1939.* Berkeley: University of California Press, 2006.
Monroy, Douglas. *Thrown Among Strangers: The Making of Mexican Culture in Frontier California.* Berkeley: University of California Press, 1990.
Montejano, David. *Anglos and Mexicans in the Making of Texas, 1836–1986.* Austin: University of Texas Press, 1987.

Montgomery, Charles. *The Spanish Redemption: Heritage, Power, and Loss on New Mexico's Upper Rio Grande*. Berkeley: University of California Press, 2002.

Montoya, María. *Translating Property: The Maxwell Land Grant and the Conflict Over Land in the American West, 1840–1900*. Berkeley: University of California Press, 2002.

Morgan, Jennifer. *Laboring Women: Reproduction and Gender in New World Slavery*. Philadelphia: University of Pennsylvania Press, 2004.

Nelson, Claudia. *Little Strangers: Portrayals of Adoption and Foster Care in America, 1850–1929*. Bloomington: Indiana University Press, 2003.

Ngai, Mae. *Impossible Subjects: Illegal Aliens and the Making of Modern America*. Princeton, NJ: Princeton University Press, 2004.

Odem, Mary E. *Delinquent Daughters: Protecting and Policing Adolescent Sexuality in the United States, 1885–1920*. Chapel Hill: University of North Carolina Press, 1995.

Pascoe, Peggy. *Relations of Rescue: The Search for Female Moral Authority in the American West, 1874–1939*. New York: Oxford University Press, 1990.

———. *What Comes Naturally: Miscegenation Law and the Making of Race in America*. New York: Oxford University Press, 2009.

Patton, Sandra. *Birthmarks: Transracial Adoption in Contemporary America*. New York: New York University Press, 2000.

Peterson, Jacqueline, and Jennifer S. H. Brown, eds. *The New Peoples: Being and Becoming Métis in North America*. Winnipeg: University of Manitoba Press, 1985.

Phillips, George Harwood. *Chiefs and Challengers: Indian Resistance and Cooperation in Southern California*. Berkeley: University of California Press, 1975.

Phillips, John Nieto. *The Language of Blood: The Making of Spanish-American Identity in New Mexico, 1880s–1930s*. Albuquerque: University of New Mexico Press, 2004.

Powers, Karen Vieira. *Women in the Crucible of Conquest: The Gendered Genesis of Spanish American Society, 1500–1600*. Albuquerque: University of New Mexico Press, 2005.

Prucha, Francis Paul. *The Great Father: The United States Government and the American Indians*. 2 vols. Lincoln: University of Nebraska Press, 1984.

Reyes, Bárbara O. *Private Women, Public Lives: Gender and the Missions of the Californias*. Austin: University of Texas Press, 2009.

Rich, Charlotte J. *Transcending the New Woman: Multiethnic Narratives in the Progressive Era*. Columbia: University of Missouri Press, 2009.

Richardson, Rupert N. *The Comanche Barrier to South Plains Settlement*. Austin: Eakin Press, 1996.

Ruíz, Vicki L. *From Out of the Shadows: Mexican Women in Twentieth-Century America*. New York: Oxford University Press, 1998.

Sánchez, George J. *Becoming Mexican American: Ethnicity, Culture and Identity in Chicano Los Angeles, 1900–1945*. New York: Oxford University Press, 1993.

Schackel, Sandra. *Social Housekeepers: Women Shaping Public Policy in New Mexico, 1920–1940*. 1st ed. Albuquerque: University of New Mexico, 1992.

Scholes, France. *Troublous Times in New Mexico, 1659–1670*. Albuquerque: University of New Mexico Press, 1942.

Schroeder, Susan, and Stafford Poole, eds. *Religion in New Spain*. Albuquerque: University of New Mexico Press, 2007.

Segura, Denise A., and Patricia Zavella, eds. *Women and Migration in the U.S.-Mexico Borderlands: A Reader.* Durham, NC: Duke University Press, 2007.
Shorter, Edward. *The Making of the Modern Family.* New York: Basic Books, 1975.
Simmons, Marc. *Kit Carson and His Three Wives: A Family History.* Albuquerque: University of New Mexico Press, 2003.
Simon, Rita J., and Howard Altstein. *Transracial Adoption.* New York: John Wiley and Sons, 1977.
Skocpol, Theda. *Protecting Soldiers and Mothers: The Political Origins of Social Policy in the United States.* Cambridge, MA: Harvard University Press, 1992.
Sleeper-Smith, Susan. *Indian Women and French Men: Rethinking Cultural Encounter in the Western Great Lakes.* Amherst: University of Massachusetts Press, 2001.
Slotkin, Richard. *Gunfighter Nation: The Myth of the Frontier in Twentieth-Century America.* New York: Atheneum, 1992.
Smith, Victoria. *Captive Arizona, 1851–1901.* Lincoln: University of Nebraska Press, 2009.
Spicer, Edward H. *Cycles of Conquest: The Impact of Spain, Mexico, and the United States on the Indians of the Southwest, 1533–1960.* Tucson: University of Arizona Press, 1962.
Stern, Alexandra M. *Eugenic Nation Faults and Frontiers of Better Breeding in Modern America.* Berkeley: University of California Press, 2005.
Stoler, Ann Laura. *Carnal Knowledge and Imperial Power: Race and the Intimate in Colonial Rule.* Berkeley: University of California Press, 2002.
———, ed., *Haunted by Empire: Geographies of Intimacy in North American History.* Durham, NC: Duke University Press, 2006.
Taylor, Quintard. *In Search of the Racial Frontier: African Americans in the American West, 1528–1990.* New York: W. W. Norton, 1998.
Trennert, Robert A., Jr. *The Phoenix Indian School: Forced Assimilation in Arizona, 1891–1935.* Norman: University of Oklahoma Press, 1988.
Van Kirk, Sylvia. *Many Tender Ties: Women in Fur-Trade Society, 1670–1870.* Norman: University of Oklahoma Press, 1980.
Van Nuys, Frank. *Americanizing the West: Race, Immigrants and Citizenship, 1890–1930.* Lawrence: University Press of Kansas, 2002.
Vučković, Myriam. *Voices from Haskell: Indian Students between Two Worlds, 1884–1928.* Lawrence: University Press of Kansas, 2008.
Wallace, Ernest, and E. Adamson Hoebel. *The Comanches: Lords of the South Plains.* Norman: University of Oklahoma Press, 1952.
Weber, David J. *The Mexican Frontier 1821–1846: The American Southwest Under Mexico.* Albuquerque: University of New Mexico Press, 1982.
———. *The Spanish Frontier in North America.* New Haven, CT: Yale University Press, 1992.
West, Elliott. *Growing Up with the Country: Childhood on the Far-Western Frontier.* Albuquerque: University of New Mexico Press, 1989.
———. *Contested Plains: Indians, Goldseekers, and the Rush to Colorado.* Lawrence: University Press of Kansas, 1998.
Zaretsky, Natasha. *No Direction Home: The American Family and the Fear of National Decline, 1968–1980.* Chapel Hill: University of North Carolina Press, 2007.

CONTRIBUTORS

DAVID WALLACE ADAMS is professor emeritus at Cleveland State University and author of *Education for Extinction: American Indians and the Boarding School Experience, 1875–1928* (1995), which won the Western History Association Caughey Prize for the best book in western history. He has also published articles in *Pacific Historical Review, Western Historical Quarterly, History of Education Quarterly, South Atlantic Quarterly,* and other scholarly journals. He is currently working on a history of childhood in the American Southwest.

TRACY BROWN is an associate professor of anthropology in the Department of Sociology, Anthropology, and Social Work at Central Michigan University, in Mt. Pleasant, Michigan. She has published work on a broad range of topics, including gender, stratification, and social change in the Pueblo communities of New Mexico during the seventeenth and eighteenth centuries.

CATHLEEN D. CAHILL is an assistant professor of history at the University of New Mexico. She is the author of *Federal Fathers and Mothers: A Social History of the United States Indian Service, 1869–1933* (2011). She also coedited a special issue on intermarriage in Native North America in *Frontiers: A Journal of Women Studies.*

CRISTA DELUZIO is an associate professor of history at Southern Methodist University. She is the author of *Female Adolescence in American Scientific Thought, 1830–1930* (2007) and the editor of *Women's Rights: People and Perspectives* (2009). Her current research focuses on the meanings and experiences of sibling relationships in American culture at the turn of the twentieth century.

RAMÓN A. GUTIÉRREZ is the Preston & Sterling Morton Distinguished Service Professor of American History and the College at the University of Chicago. He is currently working on a biography of Reies López Tijerina, one of the founders of the Mexican

American civil rights movement, as a resident scholar at the Huntington Library and Gardens.

ANNE F. HYDE is a professor of history at Colorado College. She is the author of *Empires, Nations, and Families: A History of the North American West* (2011), *The West in the History of the Nation* (2001), and *An American Vision: Far Western Landscape and National Culture* (1991).

MARGARET JACOBS is the Chancellor's Professor of History at the University of Nebraska–Lincoln. Her most recent book, *White Mother to a Dark Race: Settler Colonialism, Maternalism, and the Removal of Indigenous Children in the American West and Australia, 1880–1940* (2009), won the 2010 Bancroft Prize from Columbia University in New York.

KATRINA JAGODINSKY is a research fellow at the Clements Center for Southwest Studies at Southern Methodist University. She recently completed a Ph.D. in history at the University of Arizona, where she was a Louise Foucar Marshall Fellow. Her current project, "Legal Codes and Talking Trees: Indigenous Women in Imperial Courts, 1853–1912," is a comparative study of Native women's responses to new legal regimes in territorial Arizona and Washington.

SUSAN LEE JOHNSON is a professor of history at the University of Wisconsin–Madison and is also affiliated with the Chican@ and Latin@ Studies Program and the Department of Gender and Women's Studies. In 2001, her book *Roaring Camp: The Social World of the California Gold Rush* won the Bancroft Prize in American History and Diplomacy, as well as the W. Turrentine Jackson Prize for the Best First Book on the American West from the Western History Association. She is currently completing a book manuscript tentatively titled "A Traffic in Men: The Old Maid, the Housewife, and Their Great Westerner."

PABLO MITCHELL is an associate professor of history and comparative American studies at Oberlin College. He is the author of *Coyote Nation* (2005) and *West of Sex: Colonialism and the Making of Mexican America, 1900–1930* (2012).

MONICA PERALES is an associate professor of history at the University of Houston. She is the author of *Smeltertown: Making and Remembering a Southwest Border Community* (2010) and coeditor of *Recovering the Hispanic Heritage of Texas* (2010). Dr. Perales currently serves as a member of the board of directors of Humanities Texas, the state affiliate of the National Endowment for the Humanities.

ERIKA PÉREZ is a teaching fellow and visiting assistant professor in the American Cultures Studies Program at Loyola Marymount University, Los Angeles. She is the author of "'Saludos from Your Comadre': Compadrazgo as a Community Institution in Alta California, 1769–1860s," in *California History* (2011), and is working on a manuscript currently entitled "Colonial Intimacies: Interethnic Kinship, Sexuality, and Marriage in Southern California, 1769–1885."

JOAQUÍN RIVAYA-MARTÍNEZ is an assistant professor of history at Texas State University–San Marcos. He was a postdoctoral fellow at the SMU Clements Center for Southwest Studies in 2007–8. He is the author of "Incidencia de la viruela y otras enfermedades epidémicas en la trayectoria histórico-demográfica de los indios comanches,

1706–1875," published in *El impacto demográfico de la viruela. De la época colonial al siglo XX* (2010). He is currently working on a book manuscript provisionally entitled "Captivity, Slavery, and Adoption among the Comanche Indians."

DONNA C. SCHUELE is a member of the faculty in the Department of Criminology, Law & Society at the University of California, Irvine. She holds a J.D. and Ph.D. in Jurisprudence and Social Policy from Boalt Hall at the University of California, Berkeley. Her research focuses on the legal and constitutional history of California, and she has published in the *Yale Journal of Law & Feminism, Western Legal History,* and *California History,* among other publications.

INDEX

Note: Page numbers in italics indicate map, figures, or tables.

AAIA (Association on American Indian Affairs), 20
Act for the Promotion of the Welfare and Hygiene of Maternity and Infancy (Sheppard-Towner Act, 1921), 168–69, 182n28
Adams, David Wallace: introduction, 1–16
Adams, John Quincy, 5
adoption: of captive slaves (*criados*), 285; Comanche terminology for, 55; informal custody transfers, 25–28; statistics, 20. *See also* Comanche incorporation of captives; adoption and fostering of Indian children
adoption and fostering of Indian children: approach to, 11, 19–21; Arizona's prohibition against, 258–59; children's stories of, 23–24; defining success of, 39–42; Indian children–white mothers' relationships in, 29, 31, 32–37, 120–21; informal custody transfers in, 25–28; motivations for, 21–25; rescue rhetoric in, 30–31; by single white women, 25, 28–29; white women's initiation of, 28–30. *See also* Comanche incorporation of captives
The Adventures of Kit Carson (television program), 278, 298

affection and love: biological connections vs., 120–21; of Comanches and captured children, 54; complexities of, 19–20; exploitation intertwined with, 256, 258, 262, 263–67, 270–73; federal attempt to redirect children's, 71–73; in Indian children–white mothers' relationships, 29, 31, 32–37, 120–21; multiple forms of, 10–11; social and power dynamics underlying, 2, 11
African Americans, 119–20, 202–3. *See also* chattel slavery; civil rights movement
age of consent laws, 257, 274n7
Agustín (Pueblo): Catholic conversion and marriage of, 219–20, 224–25; failure to provide material support, 220–21; kinship system and home of, 215, 217–20. *See also* murder of Agustín; Tesuque Pueblo
Albuquerque Indian School, 80, *81*
Alfonso X (king of Castile), 122
Alianza Hispano-Americana, 140n51
All Saints School (S.Dak.), 34
Alpuente, Juan, 212
Alsop, John T., 261
Alta California: adaptation and assimilation of Indians, 248–49; Americanization of law and family, 143, 146–47, 148–53, 155–56; Baja Indians as cultural mediators in, 129, 132,

INDEX

Alta California *(continued)*
  232, 244–48, 253n67; Cota family's ties with Native peoples of, 231–32; godparenting patterns, 131–32, 232–33, 240–44 (*see also* godparentage); inheritance laws, 146–47; kinship and evangelization linked in, 232–33; land grants, *144*; marriage sponsorship in, 243–44; mission system and presidios along coast, 235–36; patriarchal culture of, 143–46, 147, 157–58n6, 158n7; precontact Native kinship relations in, 233–35, 239. *See also* Catholic kinship system; *and specific missions*
Altamirano, Juana Nepomucena, 159n15
amalgamation: use of term, 103
American Fur Company, 105–6
American GI Forum, 303
Americanization: hygiene emphasized in, 170, 171–72, 175–76; of law and family in Alta California, 143, 146–47, 148–53, 155–56; in progressive reform ideas, 163. *See also* assimilation
American Medical Association, 182n28
The American West (magazine), 296
Ammerman, John, 264, 276n38
Ancestry.com, 275n25, 308n11
Anglo/Anglo-American family and kinship relations: adoption practices, 21–32; captivity narratives, 48; ideal of, 165; Mexican criminal appeals cases involving, 187, 190; number captured by Comanches, 62–63, *63*; superiority assumed, 5; use of term, 48; western histories of, 7. *See also* colonialism; heteropatriarchy; patriarchy; Progressive era; whiteness
Anglo children: attitudes toward, 55–56; Indian schools and, 80, *81*, *82*, 83–85; recapitulation theory of development, 292, 311n58; scientific management ideas about motherhood and, 35–36, 40, 168–76. *See also* Comanche incorporation of captives
Anglo men: Native women's labor exploited by, 259–61, 274n18; school superintendents as, 74, 76, 90n40; in western history organizations, 294–96, 313n65. *See also* colonialism; heteropatriarchy; indenture system; Indian schools; law and family life; masculinity; patriarchy; patrilineal descent
Anglo women: assimilation policy implementation and, 20; double standard of, 26–27; idealized as mothers, 27–28; Indian children's relationships with, 29, 31, 32–37, 39, 120–21; racial etiquette in postwar period, 303, 317n120; as rescuers of Indian children, 30–31; social and cultural order and writing of, 299–301, 303–7. *See also* adoption and fostering of Indian children; Indian schools; Progressive era
Annual Report of the Commissioner of Indian Affairs (ARCIA), 71
Anthony, Susan B., 30
Anzaldúa, Gloria, 185–86, 203
Apache children: custody battles over, 261–62, 264; indentured, 255, 259–61, 276n38; in Indian schools, 25; raised as servants, 268–69, 271–73; recommended treatment of captured, 258–59; as wards, 263–68, 273
Apache people: attacks on, 255, 258, 262, 263–64; domestic arrangements of, 128–29; reservation, 63; as slavers, 257, 261
Aparicio, Frances, 202
Apuleius, 121
Arballa, Feliciana, 231
ARCIA (*Annual Report of the Commissioner of Indian Affairs*), 71
Arizona (including territorial period): history constructed for, 12, 270; Indian schools in, 77, 84, 86, 256, 271–72; political influences in, 268, 269–70; population (1864), 273n1; slave/Indian market in, 256–57; St. Joseph's orphanage in, 261; territorial claims of, 256–59; territorial fathers of, 255–56. *See also* Howell Code; indenture system; Phoenix
Arizona Historical Society, 270
Arizona Pioneers' Historical Society, 270
Arizona Supreme Court, *187*
Aron, Cindy, 75
Asenap, Herman (Grey Foot, Comanche captive), 61, 62
assimilation: adoption of Indian children in context of, 20, 27, 40–42; Indian employees' resistance to, 78–79, 80, 82; Indian land dispossession fostered by, 31, 88n3; intimate relationships and, 72–73; means of resistance, 240; outing system and, 88n8, 256, 272; unconverted Indians as discouraging, 238–39; white women's role in, 20, 30–31. *See also* Americanization; godparentage (compadrazgo); Indian schools
Association on American Indian Affairs (AAIA), 20

Australia: adoption of indigenous children in, 31; maternalism policies, 92n77
authority: family defined by, 121–23; of father over family, 124–25. *See also* law and family life; matrilineal societies; patriarchy
Ávila, Antonio Ygnacio: cattle gift to Juan, 148–49, 160n21; context of making will, 141, 143; decline and death, 143, 147–48; land ownership rights of, 157n2; patriarchal control of, 144–46; portrait, *142*, 159n17; rancho control and consolidation by, 145–47; testamentary capacity of, 149–50, 152–53
Ávila, Ascención (later, Sánchez), 145, 152, 157n3, 158n9, 161n32
Ávila, Concepción (later, Varelas), 147, 148, 154, 157n3
Ávila, Francisca (later, Sepúlveda), 145, 146, 158n9
Ávila, José Martín, 147, 158n13, 159n15
Ávila, Juan: later years of, 153, 162n37; lifetime gift of cattle to, 148–49, 160n21; marriage of, 145, 158n9; Marta's claims against, 149–53; reputation and status, 150, 151, 161n35
Ávila, Maria Ygnacia Feliz, 158n13
Ávila, Marta (later, Padilla): father's will contested by, 148–53; filial duties of, 147; household shifts of, 154; marriage of, 148, 150–51, 160–61n29; reflections on, 155–56; standing in judge's eyes, 161n35
Ávila, Pedro, 146, 147, 148, 159n15
Ávila, Pedro Antonio, 146, 147, 155, 159n16, 162nn42–43
Ávila, Rafaela (later, Vejar), 147
Ávila, Rosa Ruiz, 143, 148
Ávila, Soledad Yorba, 151, 158n9
Ávila estate in probate: context, 141, 143–48; debts of, 153, 154–55; demise and sale of rancho, 153–55, 162nn42–43; jury trial, 152–53; reflections on, 155–56; terms of will, 160n21; will contested by Marta, 148–53

Babb, Bianca, 47, 49, 51, 55
Babb, Dot, 54
Baca, Bernabe, 213–14
Baja Indians: Christianization of, 129, 132; as cultural mediators, 232, 244–48; number in Alta California, 253n67
Bajo el Sol (Under the Sun), 59–60
Bancroft, H. H., 100, 160n27

baptism: benefits of, 237; covert, 125; deathbed, 241–42; as family, 239–40; font for, *236*; Indians' need for, 126; of infants and children, 235; meaning of, 123, 124, 130, 131; mixed-race family and, 111; names after, 238; number of, 131, 226n18, 241, 243, 247; sponsors for, 129–31, 231, 240, 243–44, 246, 253n58. *See also* godparentage (compadrazgo)
Barclay, Alexander, 1–2, 11
Barstado, Pedro, 187
Bates, Albert R., 265, 267
Bear Flag Revolt (1846), 150, 151
Beasley, Delilah, 294
Benavides, Alonso de, 212, 214, 217, 226n18
Bennett, Kay, 28
Bent, Charles: captive trade of, 309n25; as Cheyenne Dog Soldier, 93, 111; death of, 290, 305; as governor of New Mexico, 283, 290; Kit Carson linked to, 283, 286, 288–89; mixed-race children of, 305–6, 308n18. *See also Carson-Bent-Boggs Genealogy* (McClung)
Bent, George, 110, 111
Bent, Ignacia, 288–89
Bent, Julia (later, Guerrier), 111
Bent, Juliana, 286, 309n27
Bent, Mary (later, Moore), 110–11
Bent, Robert, 110, 111
Bent, Teresina (later, Scheurich), 310n40
Bent, William (Little White Man): captive trade of, 309n25; death of, 110, 111; Kit Carson linked to, 283, 286; mixed-race marriages and family of, 1, 2, 109–11, 284. *See also Carson-Bent-Boggs Genealogy* (McClung)
Bent's Fort: demise of, 110; location, 1; mixed-race children raised at, 109–10, 288; as signpost of settler colonialism, 4–5
Berebitsky, Julie, 29
Berlandier, John Louis, 58–59
Betts, David U., 77
BIA. *See* Bureau of Indian Affairs (BIA)
biblical references: Ephesians, 124; John, 130
bilateral descent, 211, 215, 217–19, 221, 222, 227n35, 228n58
Billington, Ray Allen, 295, 299, 313n76
biographies: characteristics of, 287. *See also* Carson, Kit
biology, 119–21. *See also* blood
Black Kettle (Cheyenne), 111

Blackwelder, Bernice: background, 279, 280; Carson portrait written by, 12–13; civil rights movement and, 303–4; class status and, 318n144; Estergreen's rivalry with, 296–97; later direction of work, 284; living situation of, 300–1, 306, 315–16n107, 316n113; narrative grace of, 287; photograph, *300*; racial animosity of, 307, 318n145; reputation of, 299; social and cultural context of writing, 299–301, 303–7; upset by others' depictions of Carson, 278–79, 305–6; western history milieu of, 293–95, 296, 314n81. *See also* Great Westerner (Blackwelder)
Blackwelder, Harold, 280, *300*, 301, 303
Blish, William, 85
blood: family defined by, 121; purity of, 120, 127, 289
Bloom, John Porter, 314n81
Blum, Ann S., 166–67
Boggs, Lilburn, 286
Boggs, Rumalda, 286, 292–93, 305
Boggs, Thomas, 283, 286, 292, 305. *See also* Carson-Bent-Boggs Genealogy (McClung)
Bonanza (television program), 298, 315n102
Bonnin, Jerdine, 77–78
Bonnin, Leo, 77–78
Boone, Alfred, 110
Boone, Daniel, 286
Boone, Nathan, 110
Boone, Panthea, 286
Borderlands/La Frontera (Anzaldúa), 185–86, 203
borders: intercultural (mixed) marriage in, 211, 215–17, 223–25; medical inspection at, 182n30; multiple meanings of, 185–89; national concerns highlighted by, 166. *See also* Southwest borderlands
Borjino, José María, 247
Bosque Redondo, 291
Boston Times, 5
Boyd, Mrs. Oresmus, 26–27
Braithwaite, Minnie, 77
Bridger, Jim, 110
Brooks, James, 48, 54, 57
Brooks, Juanita, 312–13n64
brotherhoods. *See* confraternities (*cofradías*)
Brothers of Darkness (confraternity), 134
Brown, Domingo, 192–93
Brown, Estelle Aubrey, 84
Brown, Jennifer, 112–13n6
Brown, John (superintendent), 86
Brown, Tracy: essay by, 209–30; references to, 8–9, 10
Brown v. Board of Education (1954), 303
Bruno Garcia, Francisco, 231
Bucareli y Ursua, Antonio María de, 237, 245
Bureau of Indian Affairs (BIA), 20, 27–28. *See also Annual Report of the Commissioner of Indian Affairs* (*ARCIA*); Federal Indian Service
Burke, Charles, 86–87
Burnett, Robert, 154–55, 162nn42–43

Cabana, Tanis, 197–201, 202
Cahill, Cathleen D.: essay by, 71–92; references to, 8, 9, 27, 166
Cahuilla people: connections with other Native peoples, 246–47; dialects and language, 246; medicine women among, 242; precontact marriage and kinship practices, 234–35; puberty ritual, 238
California: Americanization of law and society in, 143, 146–47, 148–53, 155–56; estate administration process of, 148; legal code changes after statehood, 141, 143, 152–53; as model for legal code, 257. *See also* Alta California; Ávila estate in probate; Los Angeles; *and specific missions*
California Court of Appeals, *187*, 189–90, 191–92, 196–97
Californian: use of term, 196
California Supreme Court: Ávila estate issues, 153, 155; Mexican criminal appeals cases, *187*, 190, 191, 195–96
Californios. *See* Baja Indians
Campbell, Carmena, 271
Campbell, Edward, 35
Campbell, Robert, 96
Campbell, Walter S. (pseud. Stanley Vestal), 310n38
Camp Grant Massacre (1871), 255, 264
Canada: adoption of indigenous children in, 31; interracial marriages in, 100
Canuch, Francisco, 243
captive trade: adoption of Indian children based in, 21–22; Bent family's role in, *309n25. *See also* Comanche incorporation of captives; indentured Indian children
Cárdenas, Lázaro, 173
Carleton, James, 291
Carlisle Indian School, 36, 272

INDEX 335

Carrera, Oscar O., 174, 175
Carrillo, Alma, 189
Carrillo, Guillermo, 231
Carson, Adaline, 288, 290, 291
Carson, Andrew, 285
Carson, Cristobal (son), 305
Carson, Julián, 305
Carson, Kit: conversion and name, 284; death, 278, 286, 292–93; as family man, 12–13, 280–81, 286–88, 290–92, 306; genealogy of, 281–86; as "great Westerner," 292–93; inaccurate depictions of, 278–79, 305–6; intimate relationships and marriages of, 286, 288–89, 308n17, 310n38; Navajo view of, 307n2; occupations of, 290–92; photograph, 281; racial ascent by association, 288–90; social and cultural order underlying biographies of, 299–301, 303–7
Carson, Kit, III, 305
Carson, Lupe, 305
Carson, Samuel, 308n17
Carson, William, 282, 308n17
Carson-Bent-Boggs Genealogy (McClung): Carson made into family man, 280–81; *Great Westerner* compared with, 293; kinship made through women in, 283–86; publication of, 279; social context of writing, 303–4; "truly American pioneer family" idea, 283–85
casa as familial space, 123. *See also* household (*casa*)
Casas, Bartolomé de las, 127, 138n20
Cass, Lewis, 103
Castañeda, Celia, 192–93
Castillo, Juana, 269
Castillo, Prudencio, 269
Castro, Eulogio, 191
Catholic Church: *cofradías* (confraternities) in, 132–34; concerns about Mexican family in newsletter of, 163–64; incest prohibited, 124–25; indentured children in orphanage of, 261; marriage definition and rules of, 123–25, 127–28, 145; Pueblo marriage rates in, 222–25; Pueblo practices targeted by, 211, 212–14, 225; ritual objects of, 236, 238; role in Mexico, 173–75, 183n60; secularization and, 135–37; subordinated to state in Spanish America, 125–26. *See also* baptism; conversion; godparentage (compadrazgo); *and specific missions*

Catholic kinship system: approach to, 231–33; compadrazgo, power, and parallels of, 231, 235–40; marriage sponsorship in Alta California, 243–44; Native peoples and godparenting patterns of, 240–44. *See also* baptism; godparentage (compadrazgo); Hispanic family and kinship relations
cattle ranching: boon years of, 148–49; cattle vs. land wealth in, 149, 154; disaster in, 153. *See also* Ávila, Antonio Ygnacio; Rancho Sausal Redondo
Caxton Printers, 279, 296, 315n95
census records: inaccuracies of, 263, 271; Mexicans categorized and recorded in, 178, 186–87, 261, 275n28; no mixed-race category in, 100
Chamberlain School (S.Dak.), 34, 35
Chapman, Harriet, 78
Charles III (king of Spain), 126, 135–36
chattel slavery: Carson family in context of, 285; Comanche practice of, 50–51, 55, 58; connections broken by, 119–20; Indians in, 126–27, 130–31; miscegenation in context of, 97. *See also* Comanche incorporation of captives; slaves and slavery
Chávez-García, Miroslava, 151–52
Chayu, Lorenzo, 210
Chemawa School (Ore.), 34, 35, 80, 82
Chessire, Hertha, 174
Cheyenne people: bargaining for a wife from, 1–2; Bent's relationship with, 1, 109–11; Carson's relationship with woman of, 286, 288, 308n17, 310n38, 310n40; Dog Soldiers of, 93, 111. *See also* Owl Woman (Cheyenne)
Chica, María del Carmen, 248
Chicago Corral (chapter of The Westerners), 294
Chicago Tribune, 294
Chicanas, 166
Chigila, María Bernarda, 231–32
child removal policies, 5–6, 27, 71–72, 165–66. *See also* adoption and fostering of Indian children; Federal Indian Service; indenture system; Indian schools
children: age of majority and marriage, 145–46, 157–58n6; attitudes toward, 11–12, 55–56; baptism of, 235; custody battles over, 191–92, 261–62, 264, 276n38; Indians labeled as, 126–27; of married couples in the Federal Indian Service, 79–80, 81, 82, 82–85, 92n63; recapitulation theory of development, 292,

children *(continued)*
    311n58; scientific management ideas about motherhood and, 35–36, 40, 168–76; shortage of white adoptees, 29; state interests in, 165–67. *See also* Anglo children; Comanche incorporation of captives; Indian children; mixed-race children
Children's Bureau, 168–69
Chile: flag and symbolism, 270; labor systems of, 268
Chilocco Indian School (Okla.), 73, 84
Chinle School (Ariz.), 77
Chinook people, 98–99
Chouteau, Cyprian, 110
Christianity: Baja Indians as mediators and, 232, 244–48; Baja Indians' conversion, 129, 132; Church and colonizers' goals, 128–29; voluntary vs. forced conversion to, 240. *See also* baptism; Catholic Church; conversion; missionaries and mission system; spiritual kinship
Chumash people: Christianization, 242; connections with other Native peoples, 246–47; dialects and language, 246; female authority among, 243; naming ceremony, 238; precontact marriage and kinship practices, 234
Chumash Revolt (1824), 232
Chungichnish (deity), 238
citizenship: denied to Native peoples, 257; heteropatriarchy linked to, 201–3; Mexicans' claim to, 187, 188–89, 201; possibility for Native peoples, 259; women and motherhood in definitions of, 164–67
civilizing project, 226n15. *See also* adoption and fostering of Indian children; assimilation; Christianity; colonialism; godparentage (compadrazgo); Indian schools
civil rights movement, 280, 284–85, 300, 303–4
civil service regulations, 74–77, 79, 83. *See also* Federal Indian Service
class: adoption of Indian children in context of, 22; family and childhood categories linked to, 166–67; Mexican motherhood discourse and, 173–76; in *The Westerners* (group), 294, 313n70. *See also* gender; racial hierarchy
Clinton, Bill, 119
Cochimí. *See* Baja Indians
Cochiti Pueblo: daughter's forced move from, 217–20; mariticide at, 209–10, 214, 221–22; marriage order read at, 213; matrilineal system of, 215–17; raids on, 209, 226n4
Cody, Buffalo Bill, 22, 35
Coffin, Arthur, 200
Colby, Clara: adopted Indian infant as gift for, 22; suffrage work of, 32–33; suffragists' view of, 30–31; Zinkta's relationship with, 34, 40
Colby, Leonard: adopted Indian daughter institutionalized by, 35; adopted Indian daughter of, 22, 25, 28, 32–33, 40
Cold War: Carson as "family man" in, 12–13; family and frontier heroes in, 280, 293; social and cultural context of, 299–301, 303–7; Western's critique of, 298; white racial etiquette in, 303, 317n120
Collins, Mary, 30
colonialism: adoption of indigenous children in, 31–32, 40–42; "analogous," 202; denigration of Mexicans in, 186, 187–88, 290; evidence of, 188–89; extractive vs. settler types, 4–5; family scripts enforced in, 8; godparentage as tool of, 9, 236–37; imperialism distinguished from, 204n3; inclusion vs. exclusion in, 201–3; intimate spaces of, 8, 72, 76, 86–87; Mexican citizenship claims despite, 187, 188–89, 201; unique hiring policies of U.S., 75–76. *See also* federal government; imperialism and empire; Indian schools; law and family life; Spanish America
Colorado: Vigil and St. Vrain Grant in, 292. *See also* Denver
Colorado Genealogical Society, 296, 314n82
Colorado Historical Society, 301
Colville Reservation, 99
Comanche family and kinship relations: care for children, 49, 51, 53, 56; domestic arrangements, 48–49, 128; marriage practices, 53–54, 55, 56, 59; mixed ancestry and status in, 61–62; threats to adopted members in, 56–57. *See also* Comanche incorporation of captives
Comanche incorporation of captives: approach to, 11, 47–48; captives by ethnic background, 62, 63; captives by gender and age, 49–50, 52–53, 53, 57–58, 62–63; communication and cultural competence key to, 51–52, 55; corporal and psychological trials in, 50; documentation of, 48; hierarchy and terminology, 48, 50, 60–61; means of, 53–55; mixed ancestry due to, 61–62; return to

Anglo world, 63–65; treatment based on potential roles, 56–58; treatment of captured males, 50–51, 52–53, 58–61

Comanche language: adoption terminology, 55; brave warrior, 59; captives' learning of, 47, 51–52; full-bloods, descendants, and acculturated captives, 48, 58–59, 60–61; "true friendship" institution, 60

Comanche people: changing population of, 62–63; chattel slavery practices, 50–51; Cochiti Pueblo raided by, 209, 226n4; horse pastoralism and raiding practices, 49–50, 51–53, 57, 58–59; military campaign against, 291–92; population loss among, 47, 62, 63; revenge practices of, 50; social stratification, 49, 60–61. *See also* Comanche family and kinship relations; Comanche incorporation of captives

compadrazgo. *See* godparentage (compadrazgo)

confraternities (*cofradías*): definition, 132–33; shift into labor and political groups, 140n51; Spanish history of, 139n37; in spiritual family, 132–34; subversive power of, 136–37

Confraternity of Our Lord Jesus Nazarene, 134, 136

El Continental (newspaper), 174–75, 178–79

conversion: of Baja Indians, 129, 132; Baja Indians as cultural mediators in, 232, 244–48; community roles opened due to, 242; indigenous peoples targeted in, 235, 250n11; of Kit Carson, 284; voluntary vs. forced, 240. *See also* baptism; godparentage (compadrazgo)

Conzen, Kathleen Neils, 6–7, 310n31
Coontz, Stephanie, 12
Cooper, Gary, 298
Cornelius, Lavinia, 79
Cornell University, 176
Coronado, Francisco Vázquez de, 4
Costa, Lourdes, 163–64
Cota, Antonio, 231–32
Cota, María Antonia Marcela, 231
Cota, María Gregoria Matilde, 231
Cota, Nabor Antonio, 231
Cota, Pablo Antonio, 232
Cota, Valentín, 232
Council of Elvira, 124
Council of Rome, 124
Council of Trent, 125, 127
Covarrubias, Sebastián de, 122

Crawford, Joan, 298
Crazy Horse (Sandoz), 294
criada system, 122, 255, 256, 268–70, 272, 285
criminology: DNA testing, 119; sex crime trials, 190, 191, 192–93, 194, 195–201, 257–58; women as murderers, 209–11, 221–22. *See also* Howell Code; law and family life; mariticide; Mexican criminal appeals cases

Crow Creek Boarding School (S.Dak.), 84
Cruzat y Góngora, Gervasio, 213
Cuban Missile Crisis (1962), 280
Cuervo y Valdés, Francisco, 213
Cuinasum, Lucio, 239
Cupeño people, 234–35

Dawes Act (General Allotment Act, 1887), 5, 31, 259
Dean, James, 298
Death Valley Days (television program), 278
Debo, Angie, 312–13n64
DeKuhn, Richard, 271
DeLuzio, Crista: introduction, 1–16
Denver (Colo.): racial segregation, 301, 303, 316n116; social activists, 303; western history conference, 295–96
Denver Posse (chapter of The Westerners), 294
Denver Public Library, 279, 283, 301, 308n12
Devils Lake Sioux tribe, 20
Díaz, Mattina, 50–51, 52
Diccionario de la lengua española, 122–23
Diegueño people: connections with other Native peoples, 247; precontact marriage and kinship practices, 234–35; rituals, 238–39. *See also* Mission San Diego
Diné. *See* Navajo people
disease, 169–71, 182n30, 241–42
Dissette, Mary, 19, 32
Dix, Dorothy, 178–79
DNA testing, 119–20
Dog Soldiers, 93, 111
domestic servants: "family" etymology and, 121; mestizo or *criado*, 122, 255, 256, 268–70, 272, 285; outing system as providing, 88n8, 256, 272. *See also* indentured Indian children
Domínguez, Atanasio, 133, 134
Dominguez, Juan María, 248
Dozier, Edward, 227n35
Drips, Andrew, 110
Duggan, Cornelius, 25, 35–36, 39, 40

Duggan, Mary: adopted children's schooling and, 36–37; Indian children adopted by, 25, 26; scientific approach to childrearing, 35–36, 40; Wa Wa Chaw's sexuality and marriage overseen by, 39

Eastern Cherokee School, 80
Eastman, Elaine Goodale, 46n92
Eastman, Seth, 107
education: mixed-race families' concerns about, 98, 105, 106, 107–8, 110; in post-revolution Mexico, 172–73; vocational training for Mexican women, 163, 171–72, 177. *See also* Indian schools
Eggan, Fred, 216, 220, 227n35
elites: confraternities of, 134; cooperation of Anglo and Mexican men, 195; *encomiendas* of, 126–27; family size and, 143; mixed-race backgrounds of, 97. *See also* Ávila estate in probate; class; mixed-race families: specific stories
El Paso (Tex.): as crossroads of maternal discourse, 164; "good" Mexican mother defined in, 179; mother and infant health concerns in, 163, 169–72, 176–77; motherhood redefined in, 167; racial discrimination in, 177–78
Emancipation Proclamation (1863), 258–59
emotions vs. biological connections, 120–21. *See also* affection and love
empire. *See* imperialism and empire
Encarnación (Chumash), 242
encomiendas, 126–27
Engels, Friedrich, 129
Enríquez, Altagracia, 192
Esahaupt (Comanche), 57
Escalante, Trinidad (later, Swilling), 263, 265, 267, 272
Españoles: use of term, 289
Estep (superintendent), 77
Estergreen, Marion: Blackwelder's rivalry with, 296–97; Carson devotee, 278; death of, 315n95; on Making Out Road, 310n40; name used for publication, 297, 314n89; work: *Kit Carson*, 279, 296–97, 314n89, 315n95
Estraca, Fermín, 200
Estraca, Florentino, 199, 202
Estraca, Luisa (granddaughter), 197–200, 202
Estraca, Luisa (grandmother), 199–200, 202
ethnocultural groups: approaches to, 8–14; diversity of, 2–3. *See also* family (*familia*); racial hierarchy; Southwest borderlands; *and specific groups*
eugenics, 31, 167, 172
Euro-Americans, 48, 53–54. *See also* Anglo/Anglo-American family and kinship relations; colonialism; Hispanic family and kinship relations; imperialism and empire
Ewer, John, 295, 313n75
exogamy, 234–35

family (*familia*): approaches to, 8–14; confraternities (*cofradías*) in context of, 132–34; definitions and etymology, 6–7, 121–23, 233; hierarchy differences over time and place, 7; idealization of, 165, 300, 304–7; power of (and within), 124–25; problematics of term, 285–86; racialized references to Carson's, 292; secularization of, 135–37; as source of terror, 185. *See also* family and kinship relations; godparentage (compadrazgo); law and family life; power dynamics; Southwest borderlands; spiritual kinship
family and kinship relations: approach to, 121–25; arranged marriages to bolster, 145; bilateral descent in, 211, 215, 217–19, 221, 222, 227n35, 228n58; *casa* or household in, 123; cultural and economic impacts on (1840–70), 95–96; differences over time and place, 6–7; exogamy, 234–35; intrafamily power dynamics in, 9–10, 124–25; practices targeted in civilizing project, 226n15; precontact practices of Native peoples, 233–35, 239; real vs. fictive, 119–21; secular vs. religious theories of, 123–24. *See also* Anglo/Anglo-American family and kinship relations; Comanche family and kinship relations; family (*familia*); Hispanic family and kinship relations; matrilineal societies; Mexican family and kinship relations; mixed-race families; Native American family and kinship relations; patriarchy; Pueblo kinship, marriage, and intimate relations
Faragher, John Mack, 95, 97
Farnesaro, Mike, 189–90
fathers: in definitions of family, 121–23; power of, 124–25; unmarried daughter's duty toward, 148. *See also* heteropatriarchy; patriarchy
federal government: civil service regulations, 74–77, 79, 83; Indian land dispossession as

goal of, 31, 88n3; indigenous labor market in policy of, 272–73; marital status and number of female clerks in, 75–76; personnel key to power of, 72–73; power to disrupt families, 19–20. *See also* Bureau of Indian Affairs (BIA); Federal Indian Service; *and specific departments*
Federal Housing Administration, 301, 316n107
Federal Indian Service: appointment procedures in, 76–77; children of employees and, 79–80, 81, 82, 82–85, 92n63; employees key to mission of, 71–73; family model of, 74–76; internal divisions in, 77–78; Native Americans and former students hired by, 74–75, 77–80, 82–83, 87–88, 90n26, 91n42; number of women hired by, 75–76, 90n28; post-WWI policy changes of, 86–87; Schoolcraft's position with, 101, 103, 105; stagnant salaries of, 85–86; transfers of, 80, 82–83, 85. *See also* Bureau of Indian Affairs (BIA); Indian schools; married couples in the Federal Indian Service
Feliz, Maria Ygnacia (later, Ávila), 158n13
Fermín de Mendinueta, Pedro, 226n4
Fessler, Ann, 41
filial servitude (Comanche concept), 55–56
Fischer, Rudolph, 63–64
Fish, Suzanne, 229n63
Fitzpatrick, Thomas (Broken Hand), 110
Flood, Renee, 36
Flores Mogollón, Juan Ignacio, 213, 221
Fort Defiance Indian Boarding School, 71, 73
Fort Simcoe (Wash.), 80, 82
Fort Vancouver, 93, 98
Foster, Eugene, 119
fostering of Indian children. *See* adoption and fostering of Indian children
Fowler, Bernice. *See* Blackwelder, Bernice
Francisca (Comanche captive), 56
Franklin, H. Grace, 169–71
Freeman Clinic (El Paso), 170, 177
Frémont, John C., 290
French-Canadian people, 97, 100
frontier thesis, 298
fur and hide trade: captive women's value and, 57–58; mixed-race families in context of, 94–97, 109–11; studies of families in, 112–13n6. *See also* mixed-race children; mixed-race families

Gabrielino people: connections with other Native peoples, 246–47; disease among, 241–42; godparentage patterns, 241; precontact marriage and kinship practices, 233–34; puberty ritual, 238. *See also* Mission San Gabriel Arcangel (MSG)
Gallamore, Tom, 187
Galvan, Juan, 213
Garber (superintendent), 77
García, María Cristina, 190–91
García Jurado, Ramón, 213
Garza, Saturina, 187
Gates, Henry Louis, Jr., 120
Gelo, Daniel, 54
gender: author's name and, 297, 314n89; division of labor based on, 49, 128–29; generation linked to, in patriarchy, 143–44; godparentage patterns, 240–44; mixed-race families in context of race and, 97; whites' adoption of Indian children in context of, 29–30. *See also* class; heteropatriarchy; law and family; matrilineal societies; men; patriarchy; race and racial categories; women
genealogies, 282–83, 287, 308n11, 308n17. *See also* Carson, Kit; languages; McClung, Quantrille
General Allotment Act (Dawes Act, 1887), 5, 31, 259
genetics, 119–20
gente decente and *gente corriente*, 173
gente de razón: Baja Indians marginalized by, 247, 248; exemplar of, 150; *gente sin razón* distinguished from, 145; sex ratios among, 241–42, 252n39; Spanish Mexicans as, 231, 232, 237
Geronimo (chief), 259
Ghiselin, Hope, 25
Giant (film), 298
Gillmor, Frances, 24
Gilman, Charlotte Perkins, 29
GI loans, 301, 315–16n107
Ginsberg, Samuel, 190
Gladwin, Thomas, 59
godparentage (compadrazgo): Baja Indians as sponsors, 245; Catholic and Iberian traditions of, 232–33, 235–36; colonial desires vs. duties of, 131–32; Comanche "true friendship" compared with, 60; early example, 231–32; feminization of, 243–44; Hispanic and indigenous elements in,

godparentage (compadrazgo) *(continued)* 238–39; Indians' adaptation and assimilation of, 248–49; patterns of, 240–44; ritual aspects of, 237–38; social disparity in, 237; in spiritual family, 129–32; as tool of conquest, 9, 236–37. *See also* baptism; Catholic kinship system; spiritual kinship
gold rush, 108, 110, 148, 149
Goodwin, John Noble, 258
Gordon, Linda, 11, 87, 166
Gordon-Reed, Annette, 9
Government and Protection of Indians Act (1850), 21–22
Grant, Blanche Chloe, 310n40
Great Westerner (Blackwelder): Carson as family man, 280–81, 286–88, 290–92, 306; Carson as "great Westerner," 292–93; *Carson-Bent-Boggs Genealogy* compared with, 293; out of print, 297, 315n95; publication of, 279; racial ascent through association, 288–90; social context of writing, 303–4; "truly American pioneer family" idea, 283–85, 293
Green, Charlotte, 288
Grinnell, George Bird, 288, 310n42
Griswold del Castillo, Richard, 161n35
Grizzly, Annie, 100
Groover, Charles H., 76
Groover, Sarah H., 76
Gudeman, Stephen, 130, 131
Guerrero, Aniceto, 187
Guerrier, Ed, 111
Guerrier, Julia Bent, 111
Guerrier, William, 110
Guevara (priest), 223
Gunsmoke (television program), 298, 315n102
Gutiérrez, Ramón A.: essay by, 119–40; references to, 8, 216, 223, 228n58, 233
Gutiérrez, Tomás, 191–92

Haas, Lisbeth, 161n30, 162n43
Hafen, LeRoy, 95, 314n80
Hailmann (superintendent), 74
Hall, Dorothy, 187
Hall, Harwood, 272
Hämäläinen, Pekka, 48, 52, 54, 57
Hanke, Lewis, 138n20
Hare, William, 34
Hart, William S., 299
Harvey, Daniel, 100
Harvey, Eloisa McLoughlin, 100

Haskell Institute (Kans.), 34, 80, 84–85
Havasupi Agency (Ariz.), 84
Hawaii: missionaries in, 205n11
Hayes, Benjamin, 153, 161n35
Hebard, Grace, 312–13n64
Helmsley, Leona, 121
Hemings, Eston, 119
Hemings, Sally, 119
Heney, Ben, 270
Heney, Erminia Roca, 270
Heney, Lautaro, 270
Hereford, Margaret Sale (later, Wilson), 107–9
Herkeyah (Comanche captive), 56–57
Herland (Gilman), 29
Herlihy, David, 121
heteropatriarchy: approach to, 10; chaperonage practices in, 193–94; citizenship claims tied to commitment to, 201–3; concept, 186, 204n4; exemplified in Cabana case, 197–201; fraternal bonds of men in, 194–95, 200; reinforced in criminal appeals cases, 193–97; values of, 204n4
High Noon (film), 298, 315n101
Hilachap, María Serafina, 243
Hispanic family and kinship relations: Anglo denigration of, 186; approach to, 8, 10; domestic servants of, 255; extralegal slave trade and caste system of, 256–57; intermarriage and, 289–90; marital economic obligations in, 220–21; monogamy ideal, 248; postmarital residence in, 217–20. *See also* Catholic kinship system
Hispanicization, 128–29, 211, 224, 225, 232, 240
Hispanic people: as influential in early Tucson, 268, 269–70; number captured by Comanches, 62–63, 63, 64; purity of blood (*limpieza de sangre*) concept of, 120, 127, 289; in Taos uprising, 286; use of term, 48. *See also* Mexicans and Mexican Americans
Hispanic soldiers and settlers: Baja Indians marginalized by, 247, 248; changing conception of family among, 8; goals of, 128–29; as godparents, 231, 235–40; sex ratios among, 240, 241. *See also* Catholic Church; Catholic kinship system; Hispanic family and kinship relations; Spanish America
history of the family: Anglo-American families in, 7; cultural work of present volume in, 13–14; memory linked to, 12–13; nuclear unit focus of, 96; "sentiment debate" in, 10

history of the Southwest and West: Anglo-American families in, 7; changing landscape of, 279–80; competition in, 296–97; enthusiasts and amateurs in, 293–95; inaccurate depictions of, 278–79, 307nn2–3; objectivity claims in, 297–98; professionalization of, 295–96
History of Western America conferences, 295–96
Hodes, Martha, 113n13
Hoffman, Charles Fenno, 107
El Hogar (journal), 174
Hoja Parroquial de Smelter (Catholic newsletter), 163–64
Holt, Marilyn Irvin, 21
Hoopa Valley Reservation (Calif.), 82–83
Hopi people: childrearing and adoption practices, 21; spousal relations, 216, 220
Horn, Joseph, 61–62
Horn, Sarah Ann, 49, 54, 61–62
household (*casa*): advice on cleaning, 170, 171–72, 175–76; Church definition of, 128–29; as space of family, 123; terminology describing, in appeals cases, 189–93
Howard, Mary (later, Schoolcraft), 106–7
Howell, William T., 257–58. *See also* Howell Code
Howell Code (Arizona Territory, 1864): age of consent and witness exclusion provisions, 274n7; impetus for, 256; memory vs. reality of, 262; minor Indians and indenture provisions, 258–59, 264–65, 269, 270–71, 274n7; outing system in context of, 272; paradox of, 273; racial and gender hierarchies in, 257–58, 267–68, 271; sodomy law and rape statute, 275n20; women's reproductive and productive labor exploited, 259–61. *See also* indenture system
Hudson, Rock, 298
Hulbert, John, 105
human connections, 1–2, 96–97. *See also* affection and love; family (*familia*)
Hurtado, Juana, 213
Hyde, Anne F.: essay by, 93–115; references to, 9, 12

ICWA (Indian Child Welfare Act, 1978), 20. *See also* adoption and fostering of Indian children
Iliff, Flora Gregg, 84
Iliff, Joe, 84

immigrants: discrimination and deportation in El Paso, 177–78; hostile climate for, 187–88; Mexico's modernization and, 186–87; as progressive reform targets, 165; as public health threat, 169–71, 182n30. *See also* Mexican motherhood; *and specific groups*
Immigration and Naturalization Service, 177
imperialism and empire: characteristics summarized, 3–8; colonialism distinguished from, 204n3; mixed-race families in context of, 94–97. *See also* colonialism; law and family life
incest, 124–25
indentured Indian children: approach to, 11–12; children of, also indentured, 260–61; circumstances of capture of, 255; custody battles over, 261–62, 264; ignored in histories, 270, 271; origins of practice, 21–22; outing system and, 88n8, 256, 272; potential exploitation of boys, 275n20; renaming of, 269, 272–73
indenture system (Ariz., 1864–87): approach to, 255–56; contract terms in, 268–69; exploitation intertwined with affection in, 256, 258, 262, 263–67, 270–73; ignored in histories, 270–71; multiple meanings in, 263–67, 265, 266, 276n38; shift to institutional traffic of minor Indian children, 272–73; territorial claims strengthened via, 256–59. *See also* Howell Code
Indian children: as activists later, 39; forced removal from families, 5–6, 27, 71–72, 165–66; institutional traffic in labor of, 272–73; missionaries' targeting of, 235; recommended treatment of captured, 258–59; redirecting love and affection of, 71–73. *See also* adoption and fostering of Indian children; Apache children; children; godparentage (compadrazgo); indentured Indian children; Indian schools; mixed-race children
Indian Child Welfare Act (ICWA, 1978), 20. *See also* adoption and fostering of Indian children
Indianness: court's definition of, 29–30; elimination of, 42; tattooed onto white slaves, 256
"Indian problem," 5–6
Indians. *See* Indian children; Native peoples; *and specific peoples*

Indian schools: adopted Indian children and, 27–28, 34–35, 36–37; conditions, 23–25, 37, 73; employees key to mission, 71–73; function, 271; Native Americans and former students hired at, 74–75, 77–80, 82–83, 87–88, 90n26, 91n42; opposition to, 24–25, 40; outing system of, 88n8, 256, 272; priorities in hiring workforce for, 74–76; rescue rhetoric and, 30–31; shift from hiring married couples for, 85–87; staff portraits, 80, *81*, *82*; students' resistance to, 73; superintendents of, 74, 76, 77–78, 90n40, 91n42; teachers adopting children from, 24–25; types (day, on- and off-reservation boarding), 74; white children excluded then allowed, 83–85, 92n63. See also Federal Indian Service; married couples in the Federal Indian Service; *and specific schools*
The Indian's Friend (WNIA), 30
Inter-Posse Rendezvous (of The Westerners), 294
interracial couples. See mixed-race couples and marriage
intimacy: use of term, 249n9 *See also* family and kinship relations; marriage; sexuality
involuntary sterilization, 31, 42, 173
Ironquill (pseud. for Eugene Fitch Ware), 293, 312n60
irrigation plan, 263, 264

Jacinta Cota, María Ignacia, 231
Jacinto Cota, Roque, 231
Jackson, Andrew, 22
Jacobs, Margaret: essay by, 19–46; references to, 8, 11, 12, 51, 92n77, 165–66, 201
Jaeger, John Frederick, 271
Jagodinsky, Katrina: essay by, 255–77; references to, 11, 12, 51, 56
Jaramillo, Ignacia, 305–6, 310n40
Jaramillo, Josefa: Castilian (white) ancestors of, 288–90; children of, 284; death, 278, 286, 292–93; genealogy of, 281, 308n17; intercultural household of, 285; marriage, 286, 308n17; photograph, *282*; in story of Carson's racial ascent, 288–89; Taos home of, 278, 286, 290–91
Jaramillo, Pablo, 290
Jefferson, Thomas, 5, 119
Jobin, Lucy, 77
John (saint), 130
John, Elizabeth, 226n4

Johnny Guitar (film), 298
Johnson, Susan Lee: essay by, 278–318; references to, 12
Johnston, Anna Maria, 105
Johnston, George, 105–6
Johnston, Jane (later, Schoolcraft), 100–101, *102*, 103–5, 106
Johnston, John, Jr., 105–6
Johnston, John, Sr., 101, *102*, 103, 104–6
Johnston, Louisa Raymond, 106
Johnston, Susan (Oshahgushkodanaqua), 101, *102*, 106, 107
Johnston, William, 105–6
Juaneño people, 233–34, 247
Judaibit, Luís, 239
Jurado, Katy, 315n101

Kane, Selma, 78
Kanellos, Nicolás, 173
Kerno (Comanche), 47
Kessell, John L., 223, 228n52
Kicking Bear (Lakota), 40–41
kinship: use of term, 226n14. See also family and kinship relations
Kiowa-Comanche-Apache Reservation (Okla.), 63
Kiowa people, 291–92
Kit Carson (Estergreen), 279, 296–97, 314n89, 315n95
Kit Carson Home and Museum, 278
Kootenai people, 100
Kyselka, Frank, 86

LaForge, H., 198
Lakota people. *See* Sioux people
Lance, Doris, 315–16n107
Lange, Charles, 217
languages: Christianization in Native, 242; "family" definitions and, 121–23; of Pueblo communities, 227n36; Schoolcraft's recording of, 101, 103; white woman's learning of Navajo, 24, 28, 40, 44n41. *See also* Comanche language; Spanish language
Lasch, Christopher, 95
Lasuén, Fermín Francisco de, 239, 242, 247
law (Spanish), 218–19
law (U.S.): Anglo-dominated, 198, 206n33; individualistic, 143, 149, 152–53; male-dominated, 194–95; Mexican law vs., 143, 146–47, 148–53; social inequality vs. legal equality under, 202–3

law and family life: approaches to, 8–14; custody battles over children, 191–92, 261–62, 264, 276n38; informal custody transfers in adoption, 25–28. *See also* Ávila estate in probate; Catholic Church; Howell Code; mariticide; matrilineal societies; Mexican criminal appeals cases; Mexican motherhood; miscegenation laws; patriarchy
League of United Latin American Citizens, 303
Leal, Macario, 50, 59–60
Lecompte, Janet, 314n80
Left Handed (Navajo), 21
Leininger, Mrs. E. W., 189
lesbianism, 29
levirate practice, 53, 55, 234
Lewinsky, Monica, 119
Lezaún, Sanz de, 223
Limerick, Patricia Nelson, 3
limpieza de sangre (blood purity), 120, 127, 289
Locau, Thomas, 243
Lomawaima, K. Tsianina, 73
The Lone Ranger (radio and television program), 298, 307n3
Lopes, Francisco, 231
López de Mendizábal, Bernardo, 214
Los Angeles (Calif.): Americanization of law and family in, 143, 146–47, 148–53, 155–56; founding families, 145–46, 158n9; mixed-race family of, 93, 107–9. *See also* Ávila estate in probate
Los Angeles County Probate Court, 148
Los Angeles pueblo, 241
Lost Bird. *See* Nuni, Zintka (Lost Bird)
Luiseño people: connections with other Native peoples, 246–47; female shamans among, 242; precontact marriage and kinship practices, 233–35; puberty ritual, 238
Lujan, Juan, 195

maanet ceremony, 238
Magpie (Cheyenne), 111
Making Out Road (Southern Cheyenne), 286, 288, 308n17, 310n38, 310n40
mala vida: use of term, 147, 159n14
Malone, Sid, 199
mani ceremony, 238
manifest destiny, 5. *See also* colonialism; imperialism and empire
marginal man concept, 295, 313n75

María Francisca (Pueblo): Catholic conversion and marriage of, 219–20, 224–25; execution of, 222; husband murdered by, 209–11, 221–22; husband's failure to provide material support, 220–21; kinship system of, 215–17; move to Tesuque Pueblo, 217–20, 221
María Josefa (Pueblo): daughter aided by, 209–11; execution of, 222; on material support, 220; on motive for murder, 217–18
Maricopa people, 26, 260, 262
mariticide: intercultural (mixed) type of marriage and, 211, 215–17, 223–25; kinship and, 215–17; material support and, 220–21; postmarital residence and, 217–20. *See also* Pueblo kinship, marriage, and intimate relations
marriage: Church definition and rules, 124–25, 127–28; Comanche captives with other captives, 62; Comanche incorporation of captives via, 53–54, 56, 59; Crown's rules on, 135; expectation of material support in, 220–21; intercultural (mixed) type of, 211, 215–17, 223–25; levirate and soroate practices, 53, 55, 234; monogamy ideal, 248; murder as only way out of, 209–11, 221–22; *patria potestas* requirement, 145–46, 158n7; patriarchal vs. Church approaches, 145–46; polygamy practice, 127–28; precontact practices of Native peoples, 233–35, 239; Pueblo practices, 212–14, 222–25; secularization, 135–37; sponsorship in Alta California, 243–44; use of term, 226n14. *See also* mariticide; married couples in the Federal Indian Service; matrilineal societies; polygyny practices; Pueblo kinship, marriage, and intimate relations
married couples in the Federal Indian Service: appointment procedures for, 76–77; changing ideas about hiring, 85–87; children of, 79–80, 81, 82, 82–85, 92n63; federal motives for hiring, 71–73, 89n13; Indian Service troubles and, 77–78; as object lessons and models for students, 74–76; summary, 87–88. *See also* Native American family and kinship relations
Martínez, Jesse, 196–97
Martínez, Josefita, 195
Martínez, Lucía: custody suits of, 261–62, 276n38; escape and recapture of, 257; indentured children of, 255, 260–61; white man's exploitation of, 259–60

Martínez, Ramón, 195
Martínez Arellano, Diego, 223
masculinity: access to women's bodies as fundamental part of, 274n18; characteristics to overcome in, 287; Comanche notions of, 61; West as proving ground for, 12
masturbation, 197
Mata, José, 194
maternalism ideals, 28–30, 92n77
maternalist welfare state, 87
matrilineal societies: attempts to undermine, 212–14; development of, 227n35; father/husband's problematic place in, 216–17, 227–28n41; married couple's location in, 210–11. *See also* mariticide; Pueblo kinship, marriage, and intimate relations
matrilocal residency, 234
May, Elaine Tyler, 318n143
McClung, Quantrille: background, 279, 280; Carson portrait written by, 12–13; civil rights movement and, 303–4; class status and, 318n144; genealogical focus of, 296, 314n82; influences on, 308n11; living situation of, 301, 303, 306, 316n115; narrative eschewed by, 283, 308n17; photograph, *302*; reputation of, 299; social and cultural context of writing, 299–301, 303–7; upset by others' depictions of Carson, 278–79, 305–6; western history milieu of, 293–95. *See also Carson-Bent-Boggs Genealogy* (McClung)
McKay, Donald, 98–99, *99*
McKay, Thomas, 98–99, *99*
McKay, William Cameron, 98, *99*
McLoughlin, David, 100
McLoughlin, Eloisa (later, Harvey), 100
McLoughlin, John, Jr., 93, 99–100
McLoughlin, John, Sr., 93, 98–100, *99*
McLoughlin, Marguerite, 93, 98–100, *99*
Medina, Catharine, 196–97
Medina, Evaline, 196–97
memory. *See* politics of memory
men: fraternal bonds among, 194–95, 200–201; marriage sponsorship by, 243–44; number of fur trappers and traders, 94–95. *See also* Anglo men; heteropatriarchy; masculinity; patriarchy; patrilineal descent
Menchaca, Martha, 274n10
Méndez, Alvino, 189–90
Meritt, E. B., 86
Merry, Sally Engle, 205n11
Mesa, Juan, 195–96

mestizaje, 6, 172–73, 256–58. *See also* mixed-race children
Mexican-American War (1846–48), 5, 6, 107, 290
Mexican California. *See* Alta California
Mexican criminal appeals cases: context, 186–89; courts and numbers listed, *187*; critique of Mexican homes in, 189–91; defense of Mexican homes in, 191–93; as documents, 204–5n8; heteropatriarchy exemplified in, 197–201; heteropatriarchy reinforced in, 193–97; summary, 201–3
Mexican Department of Health, 174
Mexican family and kinship relations: Anglo denigration, 6, 186, 187–88, 290; chaperonage practices, 193–94; colonial rule over, 188–89; critiques of homes and, 189–91; defense of homes and support networks in, 191–93; fraternal bonds of males in, 194–95; heteropatriarchy in, 193–97; motives for interventions in, 165–67. *See also* Mexican motherhood
Mexican motherhood: approach to, 9, 164; dilemmas of, 178–79; meanings of, 166–67, 175; in Mexican nation building, 167, 172–73; as problem, 163–64, 170–72; racial discrimination and, 177–78; Spanish-language press view of, 173–76; state in borderlands and, 165–67; summary of, 179; wage labor linked to, 164, 171–72, 179; women's responses to prescriptions, 176–77
Mexicans and Mexican Americans: Anglo's marriage to elite Mexican woman, 93, 107–9; Anglo's view of otherness of, 198; citizenship rights claimed, 187, 188–89, 201; colonialism encountered by, 204n3; discrimination and deportation in El Paso, 177–78; heteropatriarchal values of, 186, 204n4; as largest single minority in Southwest, 3; motherhood ideals in press of, 173–76; number captured by Comanches, 62–63, *63*, *64*; racial stigmatization and stereotypes of, 6; relative privileges in racial hierarchy, 186–87, 202. *See also* Hispanic family and kinship relations
Mexican women: chaperonage practices for, 193–94; as domestic laborers, 164; forced sterilization of, 173; miscegenation laws' impact on, 274n10; others' perceptions of, 166–67. *See also* Mexican motherhood

Mexico: Ávila's ownership rights confirmed by, 143; Catholic Church's role in, 173–74, 183n60; citizenship definitions, 164; class boundaries and family in, 166–67; dispute resolution system, 145, 161n33; independence of (1821), 5; mestizos in, 263; motherhood ideals in press of, 173–76; motherhood redefined after revolution, 167, 172–73; public health concerns in (Ciudad Juárez), 174; slaves and godparentage in, 237
Mihesuah, Devon, 75
Milanich, Nara, 7
Milford Industrial Home (earlier, Nebraska Maternity Home), 35
military leaders: Indian children adopted by, 22, 44n33. *See also* Colby, Leonard
Miller, Dean, 200
Miller, Maud, 33
Minadbam, Luisa, 239
"Minor Indian" law (Ariz.), 258–59. *See also* Howell Code
miscegenation laws: class context of, 97; Mexican women impacted by, 274n10; passage of, 258; romanticization of Woolsey and, 262; tension of interracial intimacy with, 263–66, 265, 266
missionaries and mission system: Benavides's report on, 226n18; household arrangements targeted by, 128–29; Indians' adaptation and Christianization in, 248–49; Indian service employees compared with, 72–73; land grants to women and, 152, 161n32; paradox and demise of, 239–40; public health efforts in El Paso barrios, 170; Pueblo Indians, residence restrictions, and, 228n54; secularization of, 135–37, 141, 143, 146; transformation expected by, 205n11. *See also specific missions*
Mission La Purísima Concepción, 232, 248
Mission San Borja, 247
Mission San Buenaventura, 232, 241, 243
Mission San Diego: Baja Indians at, 246; establishment, 235; expedition to, 244–45; godparenting and marriage sponsorship patterns of, 243, 244, 253n58; marriages and baptisms at, 231–32. *See also* Diegueño people
Mission San Fernando de Velicatá, 244, 247
Mission San Francisco de Borja Adac, 245
Mission San Gabriel Arcangel (MSG): Baja Indians at, 253n67; baptisms and godparentage patterns at, 240–42, 247; disease epidemic at, 241; revered godmother of, 243. *See also* Gabrielino people
Mission San Joseph, 247
Mission San Juan Capistrano: Baja Indians at, 253n67; disease epidemic at, 241; godparentage patterns of, 241, 247; grazing permits for land of, 146; Juan Ávila's move to rancho, 148, 150, 153, 156; marriages at, 231–32; marriage sponsorship at, 243–44; Native language for instruction at, 242
Mission San Luís Obispo, 236, 241
Mission San Miguel Arcangel, 247–48
Mission Santa Gertrudis de Cadacamán, 245
Mission Santa Rosalia de Mulegé, 245
Mississippi Valley Historical Association (now, Organization of American Historians), 295–96
Mitchell, Pablo: essay by, 185–206; references to, 10, 166
mixed marriage: godparenting of children from, 231–32; implications among Pueblos, 211, 225; as one factor in murder, 215–17 (*see also* murder of Agustín)
mixed-race children: approach to, 9; custody battles over, 261–62; females as having more options than males, 94, 100, 108–9, 110–11; godparenting of, 231–32; parental hopes for, 96–97; stigmatization of, 11; troubled behaviors and death of, 93; unacknowledged, 12
mixed-race couples and marriage: banned in Arizona, 258; Canada, Mexico, and U.S., compared, 97, 100; common in West, 93–94, 97, 289–90; encouraged in early Spanish conquest, 127; McLoughlins as, 93, 98–100; stability of, 95. *See also* miscegenation laws
mixed-race families: approach to, 93–94, 96–97; Carson, Bent, and Boggs families as, 283–85; educational concerns of, 98, 105, 106, 107–8, 110; imperialism and trade as context, 94–97; reflections on, 111–12; specific stories: Bent family, 109–11; McLoughlin family, 98–100, 99; Schoolcraft family, 100–107; Wilson family, 107–9. *See also* Carson, Kit; mixed-race children; mixed-race couples and marriage
modernization, 167, 172–73, 186–87
Modesto, Ruby, 238
Modoc War (1860), 98–99
Mole, Flor, 239

Montour, Isabel, 98
Moore, Mary Bent, 110–11
Moore, Yndia Smalley, 270
Morago, Jessie, 78, 80
Moreno, Reyno, 269
Mormons, 21, 312n64
Morrison, Dorothy Nafus, 113n14
Morrison, Toni, 307n3
mortality rates: disease epidemic at missions, 241–42, 243; early Alta California, 235–36; mothers and infants, 167, 169, 170, 176, 178
Mortsolf (superintendent), 82–83
mothers and motherhood: blaming of, 163; Comanches' high regard for, 53, 56–57; dilemmas of, 178–79; scientific management ideas about, 35–36, 40, 168–76; state interests in, 165–67. *See also* Mexican motherhood
movies. *See* Westerns
MSG. *See* Mission San Gabriel Arcangel (MSG)
murder of Agustín: events of, 209–11, 221–22; executions for, 222; marriage practices in context of, 222–25; material support at issue in, 220–21; mixed marriage as one factor in, 215–17; postmarital residence at issue, 217–20; significance of case, 210–11
mutual aid societies. *See* confraternities (*cofradías*)
mythmaking, 12–13

naming rituals, 238
National Origins Act (1924), 187
National Park Service, 295, 313n70
nation building: "civilizing project" in, 226n15; meanings of motherhood in, 165–67; modernization and, 167, 172–73, 186–87; mothers and family co-opted into, 167, 172–73. *See also* citizenship
Native American family and kinship relations: attempts to change, 5–6; childrearing and adoption practices, 21; connections among, 246–48; Indian schools' hiring of individuals, 74–75, 90n26, 91n42; Indian Service employment and obligations to, 78–79, 80, 82–83; married couples hired by Federal Indian Service, 72–73, 78–79; mourning for children taken from, 40–42; pathologization of, 20; whites' assessments of, 8, 30; white women's relation to, 28. *See also* Indian children; Native peoples; Native women; *and specific peoples*

Native peoples: Church definition of marriage and, 127–28; citizenship and, 257, 259; confraternities of, 134; cultural mediators among other groups, 232, 244–48; distinctions and differences among, 2–3; domestic arrangements before conquest, 128–29; enslaved, 126–27, 130–31, 285, 309n21; extermination campaign against, 259; godparenting patterns in Alta California and, 240–44; Hispanicization of, 4–5, 128, 232, 240; juridical status defined, 123–24, 126–27; population loss among, 31, 47, 62, 63; precontact marriage and kinship in Alta California, 233–35, 239; puberty rituals of, 232, 237–38, 240; reinforcing communities of, 246–48; unconverted as discouraging missioned Indians from assimilating, 238–39. *See also* Native American family and kinship relations; *and specific peoples*
Native women: death in childbirth, 28; forced sterilization of, 31, 42; marginalization of, 11; white men's exploitation of, 259–61, 274n18. *See also* matrilineal societies
Navajo language, 24, 28, 40, 44n41
Navajo people (Diné): attacks on, 226n4, 291; attitudes toward Carson, 307n2; meaning of "Mother" among, 21; whites' adoption of children of, 23–24; women's death in childbirth, 28
The Negro Trail Blazers of California (Beasley), 294
Nelson, Claudia, 28
Nelson, Jesse, 310n41
Nemainit, Luís, 239
Nequatewa, Edmund, 21
Newark Methodist Maternity Hospital (El Paso), 177
New Mexico: Albuquerque Indian School of, 80, *81*; Benavides's report on missionary activities in, 226n18; Charles Bent as governor, 283, 290; Jaramillo and Vigil families of, 289–90; pilgrimage site in, 136; Spanish reconquest of, 212, 223–24. *See also* Santa Fe; Taos
New Mexico Supreme Court, *187*, 195
New Spain. *See* Spanish America
New York Evening Post, 76
New York Posse (chapter of The Westerners), 294
Norton, Ella, 83
Norton, Sherman, 82–83

Nuestro Señor de Esquipulas (statue), 136
Nuñez, Manuel, 38, 39
Nuni, Zintka (Lost Bird): adoptive white family of, 32–34; death, 35; fictionalized account about, 46n92; general's motive in adopting, 22; identity and longing for Indians, 34–35, 40–41; as Indian in suffrage pageant, 36; informal custody transfer of, 25; photograph, 23; suffragists' view of adoption of, 30–31

oaters: use of term, 298, 315n97
Office of Indian Affairs (OIA), 84, 85
Ojibwe people, 101–7
Oklahoma: Indian school, 73, 84; reservation, 63
Ompsil, Pedro, 231, 243–44
Oñate, Juan de, 4, 217
O'odham people, 255, 260, 262, 263, 264
Oregon: Indian school, 34, 35, 80, 82; McLoughlins as mixed-race family in, 93, 98–100
Oregon Historical Society, 100
Oregon Indian Wars, 98
Organic Act (1863), 257
Organization of American Historians (earlier, Mississippi Valley Historical Association), 295–96
The Origin of the Family, Private Property and the State (Engels), 129
orphans, 29, 30, 259, 261. *See also* Comanche incorporation of captives; indentured Indian children
Ortiz, Alfonso, 227n35
Oscan (language), 121–22
Oshahgushkodanaqua (Susan Johnston), 101, 102, 106, 107
Owl Woman (Cheyenne), 1, 109, 284, 308n18. *See also* Making Out Road; Yellow Woman (Owl Woman's sisters)

Paat, Guillermo, 247
Pacheco, Naomi Dawson, 79, 83
Padilla, Juan Nepomuceno, 150–51, 160n27, 160–61n29
Padilla, Marta. *See* Ávila, Marta (later, Padilla)
Pangua, Francisco, 237, 247
Park, Robert, 313n75
Parker, Cynthia Ann (Narua), 55, 61
Parker, Quanah, 61
Pascoe, Peggy, 3, 113n13, 274n10

paterfamilias: definition, 121–22
patria potestas concept, 121, 144–46, 147, 157–58n6, 158n7
patriarchy: contested will and breakdown of, 150–53; Crown's secularization as reinforcing, 135–37; expectation of material support for women in, 220–21; generation and gender in, 143–44; heteronormativity linked to, 10, 186; honor/shame complex of, 143; inheritance law changes and, 146–47; murder as only way out of marriage under, 209–11, 221–22; *patria potestas* concept of, 121, 144–46, 147, 157–58n6, 158n7; reciprocity of obligations in, 151–52. *See also* heteropatriarchy; Howell Code; law and family life; patrilineal descent
patrilineal descent: matrilineality transformed into, 129; practice of, 216, 218–19, 228n58, 229n63; precontact Native people in Alta California, 234–35. *See also* heteropatriarchy; patriarchy
Pattee, Lottie Smith, 80, 82
Paul (saint), 124–25
Paul III (pope), 127–28
Peacore, Maude, 78
pediatrics, 168
Pedro, Blazeo, 187
pem-pa-wvan kiksawal ceremony, 238
Peña, José de la, 136
Peña, Joseph Antonio, 231
Penelon, Henri, 142, 159n17
Perales, Monica: essay by, 163–84; references to, 8, 9
Pérez, Erika: essay by, 231–54; references to, 9, 131–32
personal genetic histories (PGH), 120
personhood, 130–31, 226n15
Peta Nokona (Comanche chief), 61
Peterson, Jacqueline, 112–13n6
Phoenix (Ariz.): "father" of, 263, 266–67; irrigation plan and, 263, 264. *See also* Swilling, Jack
Phoenix Indian School (PIS, Ariz.), 86, 256, 271–72
Pilar Villa, Maria del, 159n15
Pima people, 26, 263
politics of memory: approaches to, 12–13; indentured Indian children and, 262; narrators who are ignored, 288. *See also* Carson, Kit; history of the Southwest and West

Pollero, Gavílan (Guillermo Swilling), 264–67, 265, 271, 272–73
polygamy, 127–28
polygyny practices, 53, 57–58, 234, 250n17
Pomposa (Chumash chief), 242
Porfirio Díaz, José de la Cruz, 186
Portolá, Gaspar de, 244
Potomac Corral (Washington, D.C., chapter of The Westerners), 296, 313n70, 314n81
power dynamics: approach to, 2, 11; compadrazgo and Catholic kinship system, 231, 235–40; confraternities (*cofradías*), 136–37; exploitation and affection intertwined in, 256, 258, 262, 263–67, 270–73; of and within family, 9–10, 124–25. *See also* colonialism; federal government; law and family; matrilineal societies; patriarchy
Pratt, Richard, 36, 272
The Problem of Indian Administration (study), 85
professionalization: maternity practices, 168–69, 172–73, 174–75; western history, 295–96; women's wariness of, 177. *See also* scientific management
Progressive era: Mexican homes targeted in, 190–91; mother and infant care concerns in, 167–72; motherhood targeted in, 163; overall concerns of, 165; settlement-house programs, 170, 171, 177, 190–91. *See also* adoption and fostering of Indian children; scientific management
Project Innocence, 119
prostitution case, 187
Prowers, John, 111
public attitudes: children, 11–12, 26–27, 55–56; Kit Carson, 307n2
public health: immigrants as threat to health of, 169–71, 182n30; Mexican discourse on mothers and infants, 173–76; mother and infant concerns in, 168–70; women's wariness of clinics, 177
Pubols, Louise, 143, 145, 146
Pueblo Indians: animals revered by, 121; approach to, 8–9, 10; attacks on, 290; defeat of, 133; languages of, 227n36; Navajo disputes with, 291; residence restrictions on, 228n54. *See also* Cochiti Pueblo; Pueblo kinship, marriage, and intimate relations; Tesuque Pueblo; Zuni Pueblo
Pueblo kinship, marriage, and intimate relations: approach to, 210–11; attempts to regulate, 212–14; changes in, 214–15; domestic arrangements of, 128; implications of mixed marriages among, 211, 225; mariticide and, 209–10, 214–22; marriage rates in (eighteenth century), 222–25; material support and, 220–21; matrilineal and bilateral/bilocal kinship systems of, 215–17; matrilineality's development in, 227n35; murder in, 209–11, 221–22; postmarital residence in, 217–20; summary, 225; terminology for, 226n14
Pueblo Revolt (1680), 4, 212, 289
Puerto Rico: "analogous" colonialism in, 202
Puki (Comanche), 56

Quapaw Agency (Okla.), 83
Quintana, Manuela, 191

race and racial categories: colonialism sustained by, 189; development of, 111–12; mixed-race families in context of gender and, 97; whites' adoption of Indian children in context, 29–30. *See also* class; gender
racial hierarchy and discrimination: adopted children's encounter with, 34, 36, 37, 39; betrayals and state-inspired violence, 185–86; distinct aspects in western history, 2–3; housing segregation and, 301, 303; Mexicans' relative privileges in, 186–87, 202; Mexicans targeted in, 6, 186, 187–88, 290; Native Americans' place in, 5–6; rejected in 1960s social movements, 284–85; in settler colonialism, 4–5; Tonto figures in, 307n3; white women's racial etiquette and, 303, 317n120; women's health concerns and, 177–78. *See also* adoption and fostering of Indian children; class; Comanche incorporation of captives; gender; indentured Indian children; mixed-race families; *and specific groups*
Ramírez, Fíustino, 199
Ramírez, Frank, 190
Rancho Boca de la Playa, 147
Rancho Niguel, 146, 149, 152, 161n32
Rancho San Francisco, 148
Rancho San Joaquin, 146
Rancho Sausal Redondo: control and consolidation, 145–48; demise and sale, 153–55, 162nn42–43; family attempt to regain, 155–56; Juan Ávila's sale of interest in, 153, 162n37; legal codes at issue in

INDEX

probate, 141, 143; location, 143. *See also* Ávila estate in probate
Raymond, Louisa (later, Johnston), 106
Real Patronato (royal patronage), 126
recapitulation theory, 292, 311n58
Reel, Estelle, 25, 80
Rich, E. E., 113n14
Rivaya-Martínez, Joaquín: essay by, 47–70; references to, 11, 12, 128, 256, 260
Rivera y Moncada, Ferdando de, 244
Roca, Erminía (later, Heney), 270
Roca, Josefína, 255, 259, 267, 268–70, 272
Roca, (José) Miguel Gonzales (*el Chileño orgulloso*), 255, 259, 267–71
Roca, Tontíllar (originally Teutílla), 255, 259, 268–69, 270, 271, 272–73
Rocky Mountain trade fair, fight at, 288, 310n36
Rodgers, Betty Wetherill: adoption of, 23–25, 27; on informal custody transfer, 26; on Navajo birth mother, 41; photograph, *33*; success of adoption, 39–40; on white family, 32
Rodríguez, Natalia, 194
Rodríguez, Rudolfo, 194
Roman juridical thought: *consensus facit nuptias*, 125; *familia*, 121–22
Romero, Mary, 183n49
Rosebud Reservation Agency (S.Dak.), 84
Rose Gregory Houchen Settlement House (El Paso), 170, 171, 177
Ruiz, Rosa (later, Ávila), 143, 148
Ruíz, Vicki L., 193, 205n9
Rules of the Indian School Service, 79–80. *See also* Federal Indian Service
Rusk Settlement House (Houston), 190–91

Safford, Anson P. K., 268
Salazar, Carmelita, 190
Salazar, Elvira, 191
Salman, Michael, 317n122
Salpointe, Jean Baptiste, 136–37
San Antonio (Tex.): confraternities, 133
Sánchez, Ascención Ávila, 145, 152, 157n3, 158n9, 161n32
Sánchez, Guadalupe, 152
Sánchez, Juana, 152
Sánchez, Pedro, 157n3, 158n9
Sánchez, Tomás, 155–56
Sánchez, Vicente, 158n9
Sand Creek Massacre (1864), 93, 110, 111
Sandoval, María Teresa, 2

Sandoz, Mari, 294
San José del Rio Catholic Church, 163–64
Santa Fe (N.Mex.): confraternities in and near, 133–34, 136; executions for murder, 222; first western history conference, 295–96
Sault Ste. Marie (Mich.): interracial couple and mixed-race family of, 100–107, *102*
Save the Babies campaign, 169–70
Scheurich, Teresina Bent, 310n40
Schoolcraft, Henry, 100–101, *102*, 103–7
Schoolcraft, James, 105
Schoolcraft, Janee, 104, 105, 106, 107
Schoolcraft, Jane Johnston, 100–101, *102*, 103–5, 106
Schoolcraft, Johnston (Johnny), 104, 105, 106, 107
Schoolcraft, Mary Howard, 106–7
Schoolcraft, William Henry (Willy), 103, 104
School for Mothers, 170
Schuele, Donna C.: essay by, 141–62; references to, 10
Schwartz, Stuart B., 131
Schwinn, Paul, 311n58
scientific management: borderland women's responses to prescriptions, 176–77; in mother and infant care, 35–36, 40, 168–76
Scott, Jonathan, 161n33, 161n35
secularization: compadrazgo permutations due to, 132; family definitions and, 123–24; impetus for, 126; of marriage and family, 135–37; of mission lands, 141, 143, 146
Segar, Grace, 30
Semeno (Comanche captive), *64*
Seneca School (Okla.), 78
Sepúlveda, Francisca Ávila, 145, 146, 158n9
Sepúlveda, Francisco, 146
Sepúlveda, José, 146, 158n9
Sepúlveda, Juan Ginés de, 138n20
Serra, Junípero, 131, 237, 239, 244–46
Serrano people, 233–35, 246–47
settlement-house programs, 170, 171, 177, 190–91
sexuality: changing ideas about, 306; colonial judgments about, 201–3; criminal trials concerning, 190, 191, 192–93, 194, 195–201; females' age of sexual consent, 257, 274n7; lesbianism stigmatized, 29; masturbation and, 197; normativity forces and, 203. *See also* heteropatriarchy
Sheppard-Towner Act (Act for the Promotion of the Welfare and Hygiene of Maternity and Infancy, 1921), 168–69, 182n28

Sheridan, Clare, 206n33
Sherman, William Tecumseh, 287, 292, 311n53
Shorb, James DeBarth, 108–9
Shorb, Sue Wilson (María de Jesus), 107–9
Shumaker, Henry, 267
Sibley, Henry Hopkins, 107
Siete Partidas (legal code), 122
Simmons, Ruby Jane, 163–64
Singing Grass (Northern Arapaho), 286, 288, 290, 308n17
Sioux people (Lakota and Dakota), 20, 30, 40–41. *See also* Nuni, Zintka (Lost Bird)
Sitting in the Lodge (Cheyenne), 288
Skocpol, Theda, 87
slaves and slavery: Arizona market, 256–57; Carson family story in context of, 285; identification of, 256; Indians as, 126–27, 130–31, 285, 309n21; kinship terms for, 55, 68n62, 121. *See also* chattel slavery; Comanche incorporation of captives
Sleeper-Smith, Susan, 112–13n6
Smalley, George, 270
Smeltertown (Mexican barrio), 163–64
Smelter Vocational School, 163, 171–72, 177
Smith, Bonnie, 313n65
Smith, Clinton, 51, 58
Smith, Sherry, 22, 44n33
Smith, Victoria, 259, 260
soroate practices, 53, 55, 234
South Dakota: Indian schools, 34, 35, 84
Southwest and West: Cold War idealization of, 300; colonialism and expansionism, 3–6; ethnoracial diversity, 2–3; frontier thesis about, 298; as "geography of hope," 3; interracial couples common in, 93–94, 97, 110; mythologies of, 12; questions about cultural mingling in, 95–96. *See also* colonialism; history of the Southwest and West; Southwest borderlands
Southwest borderlands: approach to, 8; booming economy in early 20th century, 186–87; indenture system used to strengthen territorial claims in, 256–59; intercultural marriage in, 211, 215–17, 223–25; intersecting forms of oppression along, 185–86, 203; Mexican vs. U.S. law in, 141, 143; motherhood and state in, 165–67; social and physical landscape shaped by, 3. *See also* borders; Carson, Kit; Catholic kinship system; godparentage (compadrazgo); indenture system; mariticide; Mexican motherhood; Pueblo kinship, marriage, and intimate relations; Spanish America
Spain: family defined in, 121–23; kinship theories in, 123–24; marriage and family reforms in, 126, 135–37; reconquest of peninsula, 126. *See also* Hispanic family and kinship relations
Spanish America: Church subordinated to state in, 125–26; "civilizing project" in, 226n15; *cofradías* (confraternities) in, 132–34; compadrazgo (godparentage) in, 129–32, 232–33, 235–36; Indian domestic arrangements before conquest, 128–29; Indians "entrusted" to *encomenderos* in, 126–27; Indian unions before conversion and, 127–28; indigenous peoples targeted for conversion in, 250n11; pilgrimage site in, 136; Pueblo practices targeted in, 211, 212–14, 225; secularization of marriage and family in, 135–37. *See also* Alta California; Southwest borderlands
Spanish Americans: use of term, 290
Spanish conquest, 4–5
Spanish language: Catholic newsletter, 163–64; *familia* in, 122–23; Mexican motherhood discussed, 172–76
Spanish Royal Academy, 122–23
spiritual kinship: *cofradías* (confraternities) in, 132–34; ideal of, 240; motivations underlying idea, 124–25; theory of, 123–24. *See also* godparentage (compadrazgo)
Stacey, Judith, 13
Standing Rock Reservation, 35
Starr, Frederick, 217
Stasiulis, Daiva, 4
sterilization, involuntary, 31, 42, 173
Stern, Alexandra M., 164
Stewart, Irene, 71, 73
Stoler, Ann Laura, 7, 19, 72, 113n10, 201
Stone, Linda, 227–28n41, 228n58
Stonequist, Everett, 313n75
Sturm, Jacob, 47
St. Vrain, Ceran, 110
suffragists, 30–31, 33, 36
Summa Theologica (Thomas Aquinas), 123
Sunabam, Lucia, 239
Swagerty, William, 95
Swilling, Guillermo (Gavílan Pollero), 264–67, 265, 271, 272–73
Swilling, Jack: Apache wards indentured by, 255; background, 262–63; death, 267;

decline and addiction, 264; on his orphans, 259; intercultural ties and household, 263–64; photograph, 264–67, 265, 266; reflections on attitudes of, 270–71
Swilling, Trinidad Escalante, 263, 265, 267, 272

Tac, Pablo, 239
Taos (N.Mex.): Kit Carson's home, 278, 286, 290–91
Taos Pueblo, 290
Taos uprising (1847), 286, 290
Tate, Michael, 54
Taylor, Mary H. (later, Woolsey), 260–62
Tekwashana (Comanche), 47
television programs, 278, 298–99, 307n3, 315n100. *See also* Westerns
Tesbah (Navajo woman), 28
Tesoro de la lengua castellana o española (Covarrubias), 122
Tesuque Pueblo: bilateral/bilocal kinship system, 215–17, 219; language group, 227n35; murdered husband from, 210, 211, 226n7; woman's forced move to, 217–20, 221
Tewa people, 227n35
Texas: confraternities, 133; film's critique of wealth in, 298; independence from Mexico, 5; Mexicans barred from juries in, 206n33; women's organizations, 169–70. *See also* El Paso
Texas Congress of Mothers and Parent-Teacher Associations, 169
Texas Court of Criminal Appeals, 187, *187*, 192–93, 194, 197–201
Texas League of Women Voters, 169
Texas v. Tanis Cabana (1927), 197–201, 202
Texas Woman's Christian Temperance Union, 169
Thomas Aquinas (saint), 123
Thompson, Lanny, 204n3
Thorne, Tanis, 112–13n6
Timmee (Chinook), 98
Tissypahqueschy (Comanche), 57
toloache ceremony, 238
Tomah School (Wisc.), 78
Torres, Marina, 187
Toyabam, Flora, 239
Toyop (Neck, Comanche captive), 56–57
trade, 94–97, 256–57. *See also* captive trade; fur and hide trade
Treaty of Guadalupe Hidalgo (1848), 263
Trizio, Miguel de, 212

"true womanhood" concept, 165
Tuba City Indian Boarding School, 24–25, 40
Tucson (Ariz.): political influences, 268, 269–70. *See also* Roca, (José) Miguel Gonzales
Turner, Frederick Jackson, 298
Tyson, Timothy, 317n120

Ulpian, 121
Umatilla Reservation, 98–99
United Indian Traders Association Oral History, 32
United States. *See* federal government; *and specific states and agencies*
United States Philippine Service, 76, 87
University of Oklahoma Press, 297, 314n89
Uribarrí, Antonio de, 213
Uribes, José María, 231
Uribes, María Clara, 231
U.S. Congress, 85
U.S.-Mexico border. *See* borders; Southwest borderlands
Ute people, 24, 292
Utley, Robert, 295

Valentine, Robert G., 75
Valenzuela, Dolores de, 196
Valle, Francisco Marín del, 134
Valle, Ygnacio del, 148, 154
Valle, Ysabel Varelas del, 148
Van Kirk, Sylvia, 97, 100, 112–13n6
Varelas, Concepción Ávila, 147, 148, 154, 157n3
Varelas, Servulo, 147, 157n3, 158n14
Vejar, Emidgio, 147
Vejar, Rafaela Ávila, 147
Verdugo, Juana María, 231
Vestal, Stanley (pseud. for Walter S. Campbell), 310n38
Veteran's Administration, 301
Victoria, Francisco de, 127
Vicuña, Cruz, 190

Wade, Lousia. *See* Wetherill, Louisa Wade
Wahaomo (Two Legs, Comanche), 56
Ward, Seth, 110
Ward, W. G., 195
Ware, Eugene Fitch (pseud. Ironquill), 293, 312n60
Warm Springs Reservation, 99
Wa Wa Calachaw, Bonita: art, 45–46n90; identity and longing for Indians, 36, 37, 39, 40; Indian activist work, 39; on Indian

Wa Wa Calachaw, Bonita *(continued)* adoption, 25; informal custody transfer of, 26; marriage, 38, 39; scientific approach to childrearing and, 35–36
Weiss, Jessica, 318n143
West, Elliott, 6, 7
The Westerners (group), 294–96, 299
western history. *See* history of the Southwest and West
Western History Association (WHA): establishment of, 280, 295–96, 299; open membership policy of, 296; white male privilege persisting in, 296, 313–14n78, 314n80
Westerns: changing landscape of, 279–80, 298; objective history vs., 297–98; television programs as, 278, 298–99, 307n3, 315n100, 315n102; tenuous ties to reality, 278–79, 298–99, 307nn2–3
Westfall, Alice, 195–96
Wetherill, Ben, 25
Wetherill, Betty. *See* Rodgers, Betty Wetherill
Wetherill, Esther, 24
Wetherill, Frances (Fanny), 23–25, 32, 33
Wetherill, Georgia Ida, 24, 25
Wetherill, John, 23–25
Wetherill, Louisa Wade: adopted Indian daughter on, 32; friendship with Wolfkiller (Navajo), 44n41; informal custody transfers of children to, 26; Navajo children adopted by, 23–25; Navajo relationships of, 28, 39–40
WHA. *See* Western History Association (WHA)
whiteness: Carson's marriages and, 304, 307; Mexicans' relative privileges based on, 202; nonwhite household labor as emphasizing owner's, 267–68, 269–70; woman's denial of, 264; women historians and, 295, 317n120. *See also* racial hierarchy and discrimination
whites. *See* Anglo/Anglo-American family and kinship relations
White Wolf, Howard, 61
Wilson, Benjamin Davis, 93, 107–9, *108*
Wilson, John Bernardo (Juanito or Johnny), 93, *108*, 109
Wilson, Margaret Sale Hereford, 93, 107–9
Wilson, Michael R., 267
Wilson, Ramona Yorba, 107, *108*
Wilson, Sue (later, Shorb; María de Jesus), 107–9
Wind River Reservation (Wyo.), 37

Wissische (Curly, Comanche captive), 62
WNIA (Women's National Indian Association), 19, 30
Wolfkiller (Navajo), 44n41
Woman's Charity Association (El Paso), 169–70
Woman's Christian Temperance Union, Texas chapter, 169
The Woman's Tribune (newspaper), 33
women: age of sexual consent, 257, 274n7; barred from jury duty until 1950s, 206n33; defending rights to inheritance, 148–53, 161n30; language as circumscribing life chances, 297; marginalization of, 194–97, 243–44; mission land grants to, 152, 161n32; "nationalization" of, 164; as western history writers, 293–94, 312–13n64. *See also* Anglo women; matrilineal societies; Mexican women; Native women
Women's Legislative Council (Tex.), 169
Women's National Indian Association (WNIA), 19, 30
Woolsey, Bonifácio, 264, 267, 276n38
Woolsey, Clara, 261–62, 270, 272–73, 276n38
Woolsey, Guadalupa, 264, 267, 276n38
Woolsey, Johanna, 261, 262, 270, 276n38
Woolsey, King. S.: Ammerman's relationship with, 276n38; background, 263; death, 261–62; indentured children, 260–61; legislative activities, 257–58, 260; Lucía captured and exploited by, 255, 257, 259–60, 272; reflections on attitudes of, 270–71; Swilling compared with, 262–63
Woolsey, Mary H. Taylor, 260–62
workforce: Chilean traditions and, 268; dependence on nonwhite and Indian labor, 255, 256, 258; family model for schools (*see* married couples in the Federal Indian Service); Indian schools' outing system and, 88n8, 256, 272; Native Americans and former students hired at schools, 74–75, 77–80, 82–83, 87–88, 90n26, 91n42; nonwhite household labor, implications of, 267–68, 269–70; shift from indenture to institutional traffic of minor Indian children, 272–73. *See also* domestic servants; indenture system; slaves and slavery
Wounded Knee massacre (1890), 22. *See also* Nuni, Zintka (Lost Bird)
Wright, W. V., 200
Wyman, Sarah, 79

Yakima employees and schoolchildren, 82
Yellow Star (Eastman), 46n92
Yellow Woman (Cheyenne), 109, 110, 308n18
Yndios Californios. *See* Baja Indians
Yorba, José Antonio, 158n9
Yorba, Soledad (later, Ávila), 151, 158n9
Yorba family, 107–9, *108*, 145, 158n9

Yuma (Ariz.), St. Joseph's orphanage, 261
Yuma *Arizona Sentinel*, 262
Yuval-Davis, Nira, 4

Zapata, Eusebio, 199, 202
Zesch, Scott, 54
Zia Pueblo, 213
Zuni Pueblo, 19, 215